Romania's Tortured Road Toward Modernity

Thomas J. Keil

EAST EUROPEAN MONOGRAPHS, BOULDER
DISTRIBUTED BY COLUMBIA UNIVERSITY PRESS, NEW YORK
2006

EAST EUROPEAN MONOGRAPHS, NO. DCLXXXVI

Copyright 2006 by Thomas J. Keil
ISBN: 0-88033-584-x
978-0-88033-584-3
Library of Congress of Control Number: 2006923387

Printed in the United States of America

To Lorraine Keil
and to the memory of my parents,
Thomas L. and Mary H. Keil

Contents

Acknowledgements   vii

Introduction   ix

1   From Ottoman Rule to World War I   1

2   The Return of Romanian Princes Within   22
     the Context of Russian-Ottoman
     Contention for Balkan Hegemony

3   Political Mobilization for a   44
     Unified and Independent Romania

4   World War I Through World War II: From   98
     Building A Greater Romania to the
     Collapse of the Old Order, 1914-1945

5   Romanian Communism: 183
     The Dej Years (1945-1965)

6   Romanian Communism: 271
     The Ceausescu Years (1965-1989)

7   The Post-Communist Era   347

8   Discussion and Conclusions   533

References   558

Acknowledgements

I give special thanks to the following Romanian friends and colleagues: Dorel Abraham, Viviana Andreescu, Ilie Badescu, Septimu Chelcea, Ambassador Malitia, formerly of the Black Sea University, Dumitru Sandu, Dorin Stefanescu, Elena Zamfir, and Catalin Zamfir, all of whom helped give me a deeper insight into Romania than I otherwise would have achieved on my own. I also thank my American friends and colleagues Mark Asquino, Don Noble, Larry Bush, Jim Moldovan, Art Hellweg, Larry Watts and, especially, Tim Kenny, all of whom were willing to spend long hours with me reflecting on our experiences in Romania and tolerating my personal idiosyncrasies in the process. I thank Deborah Guenther for proofreading the initial manuscript and Jacqueline Keil for her critical insights into Romania's post-revolutionary labor movement. I also thank the American Fulbright Commission, USIA, IREX, and the University of Louisville and Arizona State University West for the time and financial support for data collection and for writing this monograph.

Introduction

This monograph is a study of the form and nature of the transition Romania has been undergoing since the fall of the Ceausescu regime in 1989. I argue that the post-1989 reconstruction of Romania has had to take place not only within the context of the legacy of state socialism, but within a context of even greater and more general historical, political, and economic legacies, and specific geopolitical conditions, many of which stretch back across several centuries.

I argue that these legacies can be discussed in terms of several central, inter-related problems that have faced Romania over the course of its development into an integrated nation state and the ways in which various Romanian elites and other collective actors within the society have tried to manage these problems. The key problematics on which I focus are:

1) Romanian development has been strongly affected by the fact that the Romanian lands are located in a very chaotic and, for Romanians, a very dangerous neighborhood. Situated in a region where the interests of powerful empires, nation states, and international power blocks have overlapped and coincided for centuries has had significant effects on Romania. I examine, in the various sections of the book, how Romania has responded to its external geopolitical environment, in some cases building strategic international alliances that have benefited the nation. Such international strategic alliances, for example, provided a basis for Romania to gradually gain emancipation from Ottoman dominance and hegemony and to begin the process of building a modern nation state. I also look at the "failures" in Romania's ability to deal with threats it perceived from its neighbors, especially the large multinational empires of Austro-Hungary, Imperial Russia, and the Ottoman Empire and, perhaps, most critically, its disastrous military alliance with Nazi Germany against the Soviet Union and its Western allies in the years leading up to and through World War II. Romania had joined Nazi Germany in invading the Soviet Union in June 1941. One of the most serious consequences of this alliance with Germany was that Romania fell under Soviet hegemony from the end of the Second World War until 1989. Within the current period, I focus on Romania's attempts to

anchor itself as a part of the European Union (EU) and NATO, with a strong tilt toward an alignment with the United States and its foreign policy. I point to the problems this has generated for Romania, at least in terms of its traditional pre-state socialist allies in Eastern Europe, especially France. At the same time that Romania is dealing with issues surrounding integration into European and transatlantic institutions, it also has had to manage relations with immediate neighbors. I also focus on the internal impact of Romania's contemporary foreign policy objectives in this area have had. For example, in its drive to become part of the EU, Romania has had to adopt social legislation that has run counter to popular opinion and social customs and no better example of this is found in the area of gay rights. Romania has been forced to liberalize its laws on homosexuality as one of the costs of eventual acceptance into the EU. In the same vein, it has had to make accommodations to national minorities, especially Magyars and Roma, to bring its policies into greater alignment with the demands of the EU.

2) A continuing conflict within Romanian history has been the struggle over the form and nature of economic and social inequality. I trace the historical development of patterns and levels of inequality from the 17th century onward, paying special attention to the repeated failure of Romanian elites to develop and implement an effective program for reducing the huge disparities in wealth and income in their society, especially the inequality between the peasantry and the rest of the society – an inequality that continually has dominated Romanian history. I examine peasant reactions to their extreme impoverishment and the counter-reaction of landlords and the state to peasant actions. Our analyses also focuses on the emergence of a nascent, state sponsored, state financed capitalism in Romania and its failure to achieve a high degree of institutionalization and mass acceptance in the late 19th and early 20th centuries. I look at how state socialism offered itself as an alternative to capitalism and the steps that the state socialist regime took to address the issue of inequality and to deal with uneven levels of economic and social development across the country. For the post-1989 period, I analyze how the economic policies of the post-state socialist regime, grounded as they are in the neo-liberal economic philosophy of the International Monetary Fund and the World Bank, have led to the rapid re-emergence of economic and social inequality in Romania. I further note that the social problems and the economic and political inequality

these changes have produced are likely to continue as long as these policies are in place. I also discuss how Romanian economic policies have led to the creation of a new and different type of bourgeoisie than previously had existed in the country. I show that the Romanian bourgeoisie that began forming in the 19th century largely had its origins in a "synthesis, of sorts." This synthesis entailed urban and rural class fractions of the boyars and certain strata of traditional, semi-feudal large landholders. I also show how this Romanian bourgeoisie successfully transformed itself into a *Bildungsburgertum* and, how, in the process of its self creation contributed to the creation of the first modern Romanian state. This class was virtually, but not entirely, destroyed by the communists in the years following World War II. Following the end of World War II, the communists, among other things, reengineered the Romanian social structure. Eliminating the remnants of the "classic" boyars and landed aristocracy and waging open class warfare against the bourgeoisie, the communists began to build their own dominant social strata. These strata, while initially based in the small proletariat and in segments of the peasantry, eventually expanded to include individual members of formerly dominant classes, class fractions, and strata. These various elements of the old society were fused with the rising leadership from the peasantry and the proletariat to form a dominant social group unique to state socialism – the nomenklatura. I argue that the nomenklatura was constructed as a synthesis of elements of the bourgeois class system and the older boyar estate system, and with principles of communist organizational theory. The nomenklatura oversaw and, in many cases, directly managed the Romanian economy, occupying most critical economic and political roles in the country during the state socialist period.

3) Following the collapse of the state socialist regime, Romania was faced with building a bourgeois capitalist society without the presence of an indigenous capitalist class and without the presence of basic institutions needed for the workings of a capitalist economy. I examine the formation of a new Romanian bourgeoisie in the post-1989 period, showing that the class origin of the new Romanian bourgeoisie is much different from the bourgeoisie that began forming in the 18th century and that had gained political control of the Romanian state until the monarchical seizure of power in the 1930s. Many, if not most of the new bourgeoisie, are drawn from the ranks of the old state socialist nomenklatura and have a much different conception of their economic and

social role than did the previous bourgeoisie, with its aristocratic origins and pretensions. I argue that in many respects the new bourgeoisie is a creature of the state and is maintained by current state policies. The relation between the state and the new bourgeoisie has been one of mutual dependence and mutual aggrandizement. Acting together, the new bourgeoisie and the leadership of the state have functioned as, what I call, "structural speculators." They have engaged in speculative activity with respect to the structures and processes of the economic and political systems in order to find and develop those policies that will maximize their mutual personal and collective interests, often without taking into account the costs of these policies to other sectors of Romanian society. I spend some time discussing the implications of the national consolidation of the new Romanian bourgeoisie, as a class in its own right, and the integration of this new bourgeoisie with the Romanian political elites. I also focus on the reorganization and emergence of independent and, often, militant Romanian trade unions, the role they have played in shaping, blocking, or advancing certain economic goals and policies in the post-state socialist period, and the resistance they have shown against state policies that would even more dramatically increase inequality in Romanian society.

4) One major theme in any treatment of contemporary Romania must be the struggle to build an open, effective, democratic system. I try to show that except for a brief period between the two world wars, Romania never had successfully built a democratic state. At best, what it achieved has been described, generously, as a "guided democracy," wherein real power was held by a small political and economic elite that claimed to represent the broad interests of the nation. Active political participation by those outside of the elite was highly circumscribed and restricted to very limited areas of national life. I also examine the form and functioning of pre-state socialist Romanian political parties, paying special attention to their top-down organization and their structure as personalized political organizations grounded in highly personalized, patron-client alliances and relations among local political, social, and economic elite networks, Organizations with such structures did not function as mass political organizations offering broad opportunities for popular participation and popular interest representation. I examine the extent to which this historical pattern is being re-institutionalized in contemporary Romania. I also examine the role that emerging NGOs and

interest groups representing women, minorities, trade unions, business associations, and the like are playing in contemporary Romanian politics. I are particularly interested in the roles such organizations, especially the NGOs have played in importing and attempting to import Western European social, political, and economic values into Romania.

5) Throughout the book I show that state building and state maintenance has been an ongoing historical project for the Romanian political and economic elites, (e.g. emancipation from Ottoman suzerainty; extrication of Transylvania from the Austro-Hungarian empire, subjection to Hungarian rule in parts of Transylvania during World War II; defending against Russian/Soviet claims on large parts of Bessaraba and Moldova; "resolution" of territorial issues following the end of the World War II). Within the larger issue of state building, I also deal with the ongoing historical tension between decentralization and centralization of the state and the manner in which this was formally resolved in the modern Romanian state constructed after independence. I also deal with the ways in which national institutions, especially national political and economic institutions, are constructed in the years following independence and the ways in which these national institutions have changed over time. I am especially interested in explaining why in the modern, post-state socialist period Romania has been unable to construct a viable centrist political movement (as represented, for example, by the Democratic Convention) and why politics has polarized around strong leftist parties and strong parties of the political and social right.

6) For the years after 1989, I address the question of how Romanian national identity and Romanian nationalism are being rebuilt following the collapse of Ceausescu's highly nationalistic form of socialism. I am especially interested, for the contemporary period, in the development of the two "polar opposite" forms of nationalism that have emerged since 1989: one built out of a synthesis of red/brown (technically "Green," although the meaning of Green has shifted from representing fascism to representing environmentalism in contemporary Romanian politics, as it does elsewhere in modern Europe) and the other around emerging ideas of Romania as a European state and Romanians as a European people fully "deserving" of complete integration into the European Union. I identify the social forces and political groupings aligned around these two identity poles in contemporary Romania and trace out the historical and contemporary political, social, and economic bases of and for the

two positions, both of which have contended for dominance in Romania since the founding of the first modern Romanian state, if not longer. I argue that a version of the Europeanist orientation, with some notable qualifications, was the dominant ideology among Romanian political elites from the founding of the modern Romanian state in the mid-19th century and that it prevailed until the mid-1930s, when it was displaced among key elites by a religio-ethnic-nationalism that stressed Romanian "uniqueness" and rejected Europeanism and European institutions as "unnatural" transplants. The "rejection" of Europe in the 1930s is traced to its earlier philosophical foundations in the works of religio-ethnic nationalists such as Eminescu and his allies and disciples. I examine the role these nationalist ideas played in the rise of Romanian fascism in the 1920s and 1930s how these nationalist arguments have been resurrected in contemporary Romanian nationalist politics, why they have appealed to some sectors of contemporary Romanian society, and what their likely long-term success will be as compared to the emerging European integrationist orientation in Romania. In dealing with nationalism, the book also discusses the nature and form of Romanian fascism in the 1930s and 1940s. In discussing Romanian fascism, I argue that the Legion of St. Michael the Archangel was unique in that it was a movement grounded in a religious-based fascism somewhat on a par with Slovak fascism, but to a greater degree than either Spanish or Portuguese fascism. In this respect Romania fascism differed markedly from the far more secular fascist movements in Italy, Germany, and Hungary. I explore the implications of this close affinity with Romanian Orthodoxy for the form and content of fascist ideology and mass appeal in Romania during the 1930s and 1940s. For the post-1989 period, our consideration of Romanian nationalism also deals with the situations of key Romanian minority groups, especially the Magyars, the Roma, and, to a lesser extent for the post-1989 period, the Jews. The situation of the Jews in Romania is treated more extensively in earlier sections of the book. In our discussions of contemporary Romania, most of our treatment of the Jewish population focuses on anti-Semitism in Romanian history, including the ways in which the radical right used it and continues to use it as a mobilizing strategy with specific sectors of the population, and the ways in which the Romanian state has handled the issue of the Romanian Holocaust. One of the major points I make in our treatment of Romanian anti-Semitism is a demonstration of the way anti-Semitism was used by

Romanian political elites, as well as other political actors, to construct a sense of Romanian identity in earlier historical periods. I argue that one cannot understand the construction of Romanian national identity without understanding the role anti-Semitism played in building this identity. Jews are the radical "other" around which Romanian identity initially was built before, during, and after national unification in the 19th century. The Jews are defined as the "cosmic enemy" against which all Romanian Christians are obliged to struggle. To a degree, Jews continue to play this role for part, if not all, of the modern Romanian radical right. Our discussions of nationalism and of minorities in Romania are written against the backdrop of the larger questions as to how and why Romania has had such difficulties in creating a pluralistic state in which citizenship is not seen as inextricably linked to ethnicity.

7) A great deal of my discussion of the post-1989 period focuses on the struggle to build a modern market economy in Romania and the dislocations this struggle has produced in Romanian life. I also deal with the role of Western institutions such as the EU, the IMF, and the World Bank have played in trying to establish a particular form of capitalism in Romania. I discuss the reasons why Romania has lagged behind many other countries in Eastern and Central Europe in putting into place institutional structures and processes conducive to the development of market relations and the ways in which various political and social realities are likely to shape the nature of Romanian capitalism. I pay special attention to the effects of capitalism on certain sectors of the Romanian population, especially women, children, the elderly, minorities, workers, peasants, and the middle classes that arose under the communists. In discussing the effects that economic change has had on these groups, I analyze the patterns and effectiveness of resistance of various groups to the installation of capitalist economic relations, especially those built along classic neo-liberal lines. I also discuss the effects that the dismantling of a centrally planned economy has had on Romanian institutions, such as the educational system, the health care system, and the Romanian social safety net. I try to show how many of the problems in building a market economy that face current Romanian elites are the result of historical patterns of economic development in Romania, how these historical patterns have shaped current economic issues and problems in Romania, and the ways that post-1989 governments have tried to resolve these problems and issues.

* * *

All of the above are interrelated and can be discussed separately for any period in Romanian history only for analytical purposes. In fact it is the way these problems and issues have interacted over time that has provided the substance of Romanian history, culture, and society and the basis on which Romania has been compelled to try to reconstruct itself since 1989.

In many respects, what has been happening in Romania since 1989 is a part of Romania's long term struggle to bring structural modernization to the country. In a cultural sense Romania has been "modern" at least since the 19th century, when many of its artists, poets, novelists, philosophers, and scientists stood at the forefront of European cultural modernism. However, cultural modernism did not spread widely or take deep root in Romanian society, which is not altogether surprising when one notes that even during the contemporary post-war period in Romania only approximately 7% of the population had a university education. Romania also consistently has lagged behind the rest of Europe in the area of structural modernization of many of its key institutions, especially in the political and economic spheres, where archaic economic and political forms lasted longer than in most other parts of Europe, including most parts of Eastern and Central Europe.

Transcending these archaic forms of political and economic organization, many of which pre-dated, adapted, or survived intact during the communist period, is the biggest issue facing the post-state socialist political, economic, and civic activists, most of whom are drawn from Romania's thin strata of intellectuals, not all of whom are convinced of the value of the project of modernizing Romania. Bringing structural and cultural modernity to Romania, in many cases, means dismantling or substantially changing the very institutions on which the success of the modern Romanian intelligentsia, historically, has been predicated. To drastically change them and to open Romania to cultural products from the West is to directly threaten the social and economic position of a good part of Romania's intelligentsia, especially those parts that have had little contact with the West in the past and whose contact with the West continues to be minimal. Romania faces many constraints as it tries to modernize, some of these are internal and some are external. All of the post-1989 Romanian governments have lacked sufficient de-facto sovereignty to formulate and implement ambitious policy initiatives to reduce unemployment, to raise wages, to expand production in the industrial and agricultural sectors, and to maintain the social safety net that had been in place under the communists. Romania's sovereignty, like so many other Central and Eastern European states has been restricted by Western political and, especially, Western financial institutions, such as the EU, the World Bank, and the IMF. These institutions have compelled Romania to restructure its economy, its political system, and, in limited cases, its public cultural values, so as to bring them into line with Western institutional structures. The demands from the West for structural "reforms" have created serious dislocations in the lives of millions of Romanians and have generated continuing political difficulties for all post-Communist Romanian governments.

1
From Ottoman Rule to World War I

Phanariot Rule

Romania is part of what Palmer (1970) has called "the lands between." Romania, as with other Central and Eastern European states, was connected in various ways to the cultural, economic, and political tendencies in the West, East, and the South of Europe. Yet, Romania was not totally part with any of these regions. Romania sat astride the three major fault lines that cut through Europe: the divisions between Islam and Christianity, between Western and Eastern Christianity, and between different trajectories of economic development dividing East from West (Stokes 1998).

Much of Romania's history has been shaped by the fact that it is located precisely where the interests of great powers intersect and collide. In the Middle Ages, Romania was one of the boundaries between Christian Europe and the Islamic Ottoman Empire. In the modern era, until 1918, it was the boundary between the Austro-Hungarian Empire, Imperial Russia, and the Ottoman Empire. From 1918 to 1941, Romania was one of the boundary states between the Soviet Union and the rest of Europe. From 1941 to 1944, Romania opted to be an Axis power. Following its conquest by the Soviet Union in 1944, Romania became part of a Bolshevik inter-state system, locked in a conflict with the West that lasted until 1989. Since 1989, it has struggled to redefine itself as part of a new, integrated Europe.

Romania also stood on the boundary between Orthodoxy and Western Christianity. The religious divide cut through Transylvania, which had large proportions of Western and Eastern Christians. Hungarians, Germans, and a large number of Romanians embraced Western religious traditions, while most of the Romanians identified themselves with Orthodoxy.

The provinces that now make up modern Romania also straddled Europe's economic divide. During the late Middle Ages, Transylvania began developing an urban economy that resembled those emerging in German lands, France, and England. Moldova and Wallachia, on the

1

other hand, were dominated by a feudal, agrarian economy based in an estate system of production.

Until they achieved independence in the 19th century, Wallachia and Moldova were under Ottoman suzerainty, while Transylvania was under Ottoman and, later, Magyar control. The Ottoman Turks gained hegemony over Wallachia in 1415 and Moldova in 1456. Under the Ottomans, both principalities retained a good deal of internal autonomy. Under the terms of their vassalage, the Romanian princes had to pay various forms of tribute to the Ottoman throne. The Romanian princes were expected to send cash payments to Constantinople, as well as various in-kind payments in exports of key commodities. The princes also were expected to raise armies to defend the empire. In return for agreeing to pay tribute to the Sultan, the Romanian princes were granted considerable autonomy in managing the internal affairs of their provinces. During the Ottoman period, not only the Romanian princes, but Romanians generally were autonomous from direct Ottoman control under the terms of the *millet* system. Ottoman rulers believed that in an Islamic society, which their empire was, matters of family life, justice, culture, education, and the like were best left to the regulation of local communities, be they Muslim, Christian, or Jewish communities. From the Ottoman point of view it was entirely legitimate to grant society a certain degree of independence from the state and the state an independence from the society.

Under the *millet* system, however, non-Muslims, even though they were granted these limited rights of communal self-organization, regulation and control, were second class citizens in the empire. Non-Muslims were subjected to heavier taxation than were Muslims and they faced laws that discriminated against them in a variety of areas of everyday life. These laws reminded them on a continuing basis of the inferior status of non-Muslims in the Ottoman Empire.

The Ottomans regarded the Romanian principalities as *dar al-ahd* territories (territories that were tribute paying by virtue of treaties). As such, they were an intermediate zone of peace standing between the Islamic lands (*dar al-Islam*) and those lands that were enemies of the Ottomans (*dar al-harb*).

Before 1730, with the exception of a brief period in the 17th century, the princes of Moldova and Wallachia were selected from among the principalities' local landed aristocracies, the boyars. The prince had to be approved by the Ottoman rulers. An important part of the approval process was a large payment to the Sultan. Ottoman policy, for financial and political reasons, encouraged a high turnover among Romanian princes. Financially, a new prince meant new funds. Politically, high turnover of princes made for internal instability within the Romanian local aristocracy. The turnover in office intensified local rivalries among the boyars and it insured that no single prince would be in office long enough to mobilize resistance to Ottoman rule.

The selection of princes generally was a contentious affair. As often as not, the matter of who would be prince was settled by the force of arms. Various contenders for the title of prince would battle among themselves. The victor would gain the throne, but, once won, there was no guarantee that the throne could be held. To stay on the throne, princes had to maintain the loyalty of fractious boyars and the support of powerful external allies, such as the rulers of Hungary, or the Ottoman Empire, or the Russian Empire, depending on time and/or place.

In the 15th and 16th centuries, Romanian princes vacillated between supporting Ottoman expansion or resisting it. The great leaders of resistance, and at times compromise with the Ottomans, included such figures as Vlad II Dracul, Vlad III Dracula, Stephen Cel Mare (the Great), and Michael the Brave (Mihai Bravo). Despite their sometime ferocious resistance to Ottoman rule, Transylvania, Wallachia, and Moldova remained vassal states of the Ottoman rulers in Constantinople until Transylvania was emancipated in 1699 and Wallachia and Moldova gained independence in the 19th century.

Ottoman power in Europe expanded dramatically in the 16th century under the great Sultan, Suleiman the Magnificent. During his rule, the Ottomans conquered Belgrade in 1521, defeated Hungarian armies in 1526 at the battle of Mohacs, and conquered Hungary completely in 1541, turning it into a Turkish pashalik. In 1529, under Suleiman's lead, Ottoman armies began their first unsuccessful siege of Vienna.

In the late 16th century, Michael the Brave, Prince of Wallachia, joined the Princes of Transylvania and Moldova in a revolt against the Ottomans. Michael engaged in wholesale slaughter of Turks living in Wallachia and attacked Ottoman military encampments along the Danube River. As often happened in Romania, Michael and his allies turned against one another. In the ensuing conflicts, Michael seized the thrones of Transylvania and Moldova. He was the prince of all three realms for only a very brief time. His rule ended in 1601 when he was assassinated.

In 1606, the Habsburg Empire signed a treaty with the Ottomans, ending a thirteen-year war between the two powers. Under the terms of the treaty, the Ottomans recognized the Habsburg emperor and agreed that the Habsburgs no longer would be required pay tribute to the Ottomans. In return, the Habsburgs recognized Ottoman hegemony over Moldova, ending Polish claims that Moldova was its vassal, and Wallachia.

From 1658 to 1662, serious revolts against the Ottomans broke out in Transylvania, Wallachia, and Moldova. While the Turks were able to suppress the uprisings, after defeating the insurrections the Ottomans reduced the tributes it required of princes in the three regions.

The reduction in tribute was only a temporary phenomenon. For most of the 17th and 18th centuries, the Sublime Porte increased the financial obligations owed by the Wallachian and Moldovan boyars and princes. The increased tribute placed an increasing burden on an already impoverished peasantry.

The Ottomans, after having appeared to be a power in decline, regrouped their forces in the second half of the seventeenth century and their armies again advanced northward to Vienna, to which the Ottomans laid siege for a second time in 1682. Led by the Polish King, John Sobieski, Christian armies broke the siege of Vienna and began to drive the Ottoman forces southward into the Balkans.

Habsburg armies forced the Ottomans to sign the Treaty of Carlowitz in 1699. The Treaty recognized Habsburg rule of most of Transylvania and present-day Slovenia. Under Sobieski, the Poles also attempted, but failed, to drive the Ottomans out of Moldova and reestablish Moldova as a vassal to the Polish throne. Russia, also sensing Ottoman weakness, attempted to extend its boundaries southward, but the Russian forces, under the direction of Peter the Great, were seriously defeated by the Ottomans in 1711 and were forced to abandon, temporarily, their goal of forcing the Ottomans out of the Balkans.

The Ottomans vigorously contested challenges to their control over the Balkans. The Balkans' region was the real center of their empire, despite the fact that the Ottoman capital was in Anatolia (see Lieven 2000). The Balkans supplied the Ottoman Empire with the larger part of their revenues and their food, as well as a considerable number of their military forces. In addition, the Balkans region was strategically necessary to the survival of the imperial center. Whoever controlled the Balkans had relatively easy military access to routes leading directly into Constantinople. The Ottomans, recognizing that they needed stable allies on their border with the Habsburgs and fearing the encroachment of the Russians, appointed Greek princes to control Wallachia and Moldova. The immediate precipitating events that led to the appointment of Greek princes was the move of Prince Dimitrie Cantemir (1710-1711) of Moldova to establish an anti-Ottoman alliance with Tzar Peter the Great and the attempts of the Wallachian prince, Constantin Brancoveanu (1688-1714), to negotiate an anti-Ottoman alliance with the Austrians and with the Russians. Cantemir was forced to flee Moldova and live in exile in Russia with the defeat of Russian forces at Stanilesti in 1711 by the Ottomans. Bracoveanu was executed in Constantinople, along with his four sons and his son-in-law, in 1714.

The Sultan appointed Nicolae Mavrocordat, Prince of Moldova, in 1711. Mavrocordat was a Greek from the Phanar district of Constantinople. The Greeks in this area were rich merchants who specialized in long-distance international trade. They had been long time supporters of Ottoman rule. Many had served as grand dragomans (chief interpreters and advisors) to the Sultans. Mavrocordat was appointed Prince of Wallachia in 1714, thereby extending Phanariot rule to that principality. The Ottomans took this step because they saw the indigenous Romanian princes as untrustworthy and unreliable vassals who were located in territories that had too great a strategic value to be ruled by possible traitors.

Greeks, under Ottoman sponsorship, had begun migrating into the Romanian principalities in the 16th century. It is worth noting that Greek colonies had existed along the Black Sea coast prior to the Romans' arrival in the region. More modern Greek migrants bought land and operated large estates that put them in direct competition with the indigenous boyars. They also established themselves as merchants on the Black Sea coast and dominated commercial activities in a large number of Romanian towns and cities. The Romanian boyars began a series of pogroms against the Greeks in the early part of the 17th century. Between 1617 and 1619, Wallachian boyars attacked and murdered a large number of Greek estate owners and Greek merchants. In 1631, another outbreak of violence directed at the Greek community in Wallachia led the Prince of Wallachia to order an expulsion of all Greeks from his principality, including all Greek monks. The boyars, in 1668, again demanded that the Prince expel all Greeks from Wallachia. There also were outbursts of violence against the Greeks in Moldova, although they were not as extensive or as intensive as in Wallachia, nor did the Moldovan princes attempt to expel Greeks, as had been done in Wallachia. The Porte abolished the election of princes by the boyars in 1730. After this date, Romanian princes were appointed directly by the Sultan. Tenure was highly precarious. Between 1730 and 1768, Wallachia had eighteen princes and between 1733 and 1769 Moldova had seventeen princes. Constantin Mavrocordat, during this period, was Prince of Wallachia six different times and was Prince of Moldova four different times. The rapid and frequent turnover of princes in the Romanian principalities was a boon to the Ottoman treasury, as each prince had top make a cash payment to the throne. High turnover also meant that the Phanariot rulers could not build stable alliances with the local boyar elites to challenge Ottoman rule.

While the Phanariots held power, the Ottomans tightened their economic control over the Romanian principalities. For example, Sultan Ooman II issued a decree in 1755 that required the principalities to deliver large quantities of grain annually, at below market fixed princes, to Constantinople. The Sultan also demanded that the Empire's needs for supplies had to be met before the principalities could sell agricultural products on the open market. The Romanian principalities also were expected to supply materials and labor to maintain the Ottoman's string of fortresses along the Danube and the border with Russia, as well as to sustain other Ottoman projects.

The Romanian Property Owning Estate: The Boyars

At the beginning of the 19th century, it has been estimated that the boyars, as an estate, controlled more than half the land in both Moldova and Wallachia (Hitchins 1996). This acreage represented a dramatic increase in the amount of land the boyars had at their disposal. Throughout the 18th century, according to Hitchins (1996), the boyars waged a relentless campaign of land expropriation directed against the Romanian peasantry. This was coupled with attempts on the part of the boyars in both Wallachia and Moldova to increase the financial and labor obligations of the peasantry. The boyars also pressed to have their estates recognized as private property, which they could alienate as they chose. In the 18th century, the princes had ultimate authority over all land in the principalities. Regardless of the status of the landlord, the prince had a traditional right of eminent domain. There was some support for converting land to private property among the more affluent peasantry, who began challenging the idea that all land, not controlled by the boyars and the prince, belonged to the village community (Hitchins 1996). In the independent villages, peasant families typically had sole control over a small plot of land and had access to additional land that was worked in common. If, for some reason, the "private" plot was vacated, the village commune had the right to assign it to another household. The original holders did not have a right to sell the land that was "theirs."

Boyars had begun to penetrate the communal villages in the 18th century, buying the "private" land of householders. As a result, boyars became co-owners of many of the traditional villages. The boyars thus reduced the collective resources of the village community and transformed rural land into a commodity in the process.

Also during the 18th century the boyars and, to a lesser degree, the large landholding monasteries began the practice of leasing land to tenants and to farm managers. Tenants included other boyars, urban and rural merchants, monasteries, and peasants (Hitchins 1996). There also were cases where whole village communities leased land for fixed periods of time (Hitchins 1996).

Under the Phanariots, the princes held almost absolute power over the state. The princes had total control over the administrative structures of the central governments and the local areas. He held executive, legislative, and judicial power. The prince also wielded considerable economic power. He had the right to set prices for all goods sold in Romanian markets, decide the levels of taxation, establish regulations governing the rights and responsibilities of all economic actors, and establish the state budget. There were few formal checks on his power.

Representative institutions were poorly developed in 18th century Romania. The corporate bodies that had been created to represent the interests of the boyars were relatively powerless; they had been eclipsed by the princes and the top boyar families. The ancient *adunarea de stari* (assembly of estates) which had been the major institution representing the collective interests of the boyars had been destroyed by the princes

(Hitchins 1996). It was replaced by *sfatul de obste* (general council), whose members were appointed by the princes (Hitchins 1996). The role of the council was not defined in Romanian law. Traditionally, it had the right to express its views on any or all aspects of Romanian life. It was not a rubber stamp of the prince, despite its membership being appointed by him.

Often, the prince and *sfatul de obste* entered into direct conflict over specific policies as well as the general orientation of the princes to centralize rule in both principalities. *Sfatul de obste* consistently fought to maintain a decentralized state system where control over local affairs would remain in the hands of the boyars (Hitchins 1996).

Members of the great boyar households made their influence felt over and above the actions taken by *sfatul de obste* through their participation in *sfatul domnesc* (prince's council) and by staffing the highest offices in the state (Hitchins 1996). The prince's council was the strongest and most influential corporate body in the principalities. Members of the council were appointed by the prince from families in the top tiers of the boyar hierarchy. Together with the prince, the council served as the ruling elite within the feudal system. It served a wide number of functions, including a judicial role for certain cases. Informally, it was responsible for organizing the boyars' interests and actions to bring them into harmony with the interests and needs of the princes, which was not always an easy matter in realms where boyars jealously guarded their ancient powers and prerogatives.

The princes presided over elaborate bureaucracies whose top offices were filled by boyars functioning as non-paid service nobility. Wallachia was divided into three distinctive regions, each made up of a number of *judete* (a structure similar to English counties). *Oltenia* consisted of five judete that lay to the west of the Olt River. It was presided over by a *Ban* (governor) whose formal powers had been considerably diminished over the centuries by the actions of centralizing princes. The *Ban of Oltenia* had his seat of power in Bucharest, from which he wielded considerable informal influence. The remainder of Wallachia was divided into the *Tara de Sus* (upper land), which was on the left bank of the Olt River and, farther east, the *Tara de Jos* (lower land). Each of these regions was presided over by a grand minister of justice (*Mare Vornic*) and a grand chancellor, the *Mare Logofat* (Hitchins 1996).

Expansion of State Bureaucracies

During the Phanariot period, each *judet* was administered by two local prefects (*ispravnici*). One prefect was Greek and the other was Romanian. The prefects held executive, judicial, and legislative powers in the *judete*. Below the prefects were local administrators who, like the prefects exercised combined legislative, judicial, and executive powers and functions. Each of these levels of administration had its own staff of functionaries (see Hitchins 1996).

Offices were filled not on the basis of competency or on the basis of an interest in public service but, rather, on the basis of how much one would pay to hold a position and what one's family connections were. It was regular practice for princes and others in the administrative hierarchy to auction offices to the highest bidder with the best family connections. It was customary for a new prince, in order to help pay the costs he incurred in gaining office from the Sultan and to make a substantial profit, to sell the highest state positions to those who made the best financial offers, all other matters being equal. In turn, the new office holders would sell access to the positions over which they had control. This took place all the way down to the local level, with prices being set based on how much money could be earned from the office in question.

Once in office, incumbents collected a continuing stream of revenues from taxes, fines, fees, and gifts given in return for favors rendered. This was not regarded as inappropriate, because state office holders did not receive regular salaries. Holding office, thus, was seen as an investment from which one enriched one's self at the expense of people over whom one exercised authority and control. Given the high turnover in office by princes, it was important for office holders to recover their investments as quickly as possible before they were required to re-bid for their positions. The ultimate costs of this predatory system fell on the backs of the Romanian peasantry, whose labor produced the surpluses extracted by the boyars.

One of the reasons behind the expansion of the bureaucracies in the Romanian principalities during the 18th century was the pressure exerted on the state by the surplus of boyars who could not be absorbed by the traditional agrarian economy without subdividing the great estates controlled by their families. The authorities, ever anxious to expand their revenues, were more than willing to create new state offices that allowed the boyars to colonize the public bureaucracy, because this increased the prince's income. Once in office, the boyars created subaltern positions to recoup their own investments. Thus, the very logic of state organization accelerated the expansion of the bureaucracy at the level of the principality and at local levels, as well.

The boyars who staffed the expanding bureaucracy did not constitute themselves as a reforming administrative elite or as an elite civil service, along the lines that were beginning to take shape in England, France, and selected German principalities. Indeed, it was in the interests of the boyar office holders to resist any attempts at modernization of the Romanian bureaucracies. Modernization in almost any form threatened their monopolies on offices and thus threatened to deprive them of a significant source of their income.

The entry of the boyars' colonization of state service had a long-term cultural impact on Romania. It established a tradition that state service was the gentlemanly thing to do. As a result, state service was accorded far greater respectability than was involvement in the worlds of commerce, finance, or, later, manufacturing for members of the elite and, eventually, for members of the rising middle classes in the late 19th and early 20th centuries.

One of the major administrative projects of the Phanariot rulers was modernization of the Romanian principalities' fiscal systems. The Phanariots attempted to rationalize the tax systems in both principalities, with a view toward making their jobs as "tax farmers" easier. Fiscal reform was important to the Phanariots because they had continuing heavy financial obligations to the Ottoman rulers, which they could meet only if they established an efficient system of tax collection.

In addition, the Phanariot princes had to pay large amounts of tribute to the Porte for their appointment. Their investments in acquiring their titles only could be recovered through developing and administering an effective tax bureaucracy. Extracting money from the Romanian principalities meant that the Phanariot rulers had to subordinate the boyars to their will, which was not an easy matter.

The *bir* constituted the main tax that financed the central state administration. The *bir* was a tax on the head of each household. It was collected directly by the prince's tax officers. The tax was paid mainly by the lower orders of society, with the heaviest burden being placed on the peasantry. Boyars were exempted from the paying the *bir*.

The population paid a number of other taxes to the prince and to local officials. For the most part, collection of these monies was farmed out to boyars and merchants, who bid for the privilege of being tax collectors. In turn, the holders of tax collection privileges could sub-lease these rights to others for large profits. The tax farmers, in order to garner profits, often collected far more revenues than they were required to turn over to higher authorities. This difference in revenues collected and revenues turned over constituted the profit for the tax farmers' services.

The Romanian Orthodox Church and Phanariot Rule

Along side of the boyars, the higher-ranking clergy of the Romanian Orthodox Church constituted an essential element of the political and economic elite in Wallachia and Moldova. The highest ranking clergy, i.e. bishops, metropolitans, heads of monasteries, typically were drawn from the families of the great boyars. They thus shared with the boyars a common social, political, and economic ideology. In the 18th century, the Romanian Orthodox Church was subordinate to the Patriarch of Constantinople. The Greek Patriarch approved the election of the metropolitans of Wallachia and Transylvania and had the final say in all matters of church law, church ritual, and church doctrine. The prince and his council played a determining role in choosing the metropolitan and the local bishops, giving them a powerful voice in church affairs.

The higher clergy had considerable latitude in running the church's day-to-day affairs. The principle legislative body of the church was the *adunarea obsteasca* (Hitchins 1996). It consisted of the metropolitan, the bishops, abbots of the major monasteries, the prince, and the members of his council. Beneath this assembly was a metropolitan synod made up of leading church figures. It dealt with routine ecclesiastical affairs. Between the higher clergy and the parishes stood archpriests (a protopope) who collected church taxes and fees and provided general supervision of parish clergy. The archpriests functioned under the direct authority of the bishops to insure that local priests were conforming to church doctrine and performing rituals appropriately.

Church authorities could not always be certain that the local clergy understood doctrine correctly or that they knew how to conduct rituals properly. At this time there were no formal seminaries that trained local parish priests. They learned their religious craft principally through apprenticeships to already established priests. Many of the local clergy, themselves, were sons of priests, giving the occupation a relatively closed, inherited, corporate character. For others entering the clerical ranks from the outside, the priesthood was a major avenue of social mobility for talented sons in peasant families. Aside from the spiritual benefits to one's self and one's family, the priesthood gave a young man a position of respect and authority in local village life, not to mention an opportunity for a stable income. A successful priest could be an economic, social, and political asset for an entire extended family. For this reason, there was a tendency to overproduce priests in the villages (Hitchins 1996).

The income of local priests came directly from boyars and/or through their churches, which they ran as religious shops, charging fees for the performance of various rituals, such as baptisms, weddings, and funerals, for which priests were either paid in cash, in goods, or in services. So, a priest could only be as well off as the village or villagers he served. The income of priests also was limited by a large number of fees and taxes they were expected to provide to higher church authorities, especially the fees associated with their ordination, which they could recover only over a number of years of service. Priests also were expected to make annual contributions for the support of their archpriests and their bishops. It also was the custom for priests to send large gifts when a new metropolitan or bishop was appointed. Priests derived respect because of the special relationship they had to the sacred and because of the various roles they played in local village life. Priests often were the men villagers turned to in order to resolve disputes among neighbors in the village, they ran local "schools," and, among other things, they mediated many of the relations between the village and outside political and economic actors, including other villages. Bishops cooperated in the over-production of priests because ordinations generated additional income to them.

Serfdom Under the Phanariots

As part of their attempt to modernize the economies of the principalities and weaken the power of the boyars, in the middle of the 18th century, the Phanariot princes tried to abolish serfdom. In August 1746, the Phanariot Prince, Constantin Mavrocordat of Wallachia, demanded that the landlords voluntarily free their serfs or to allow their serfs to buy their freedom. He made the same request of the Moldovan boyars in

1749. In Wallachia in August 1746, the assembly of boyars decided to allow dependent peasants to buy their freedom but it allowed the boyars to retain control over estate lands (Hitchins 1996). In order to gain access to lands, the Wallachian peasants were required to perform various labor services for the landlord, which the prince set at twelve days. Moldova's boyar assembly passed a similar law in April, 1749 (Hitchins 1996). However, in Moldova peasants were required to spend a minimum of twenty four days of labor as the cost of gaining access to estate land. This subsequently was reduced to twelve days in 1766. As a result of these legal changes, serfdom, as a de facto status, was limited. However, it continued to have a de jure existence. Serfs were converted into *clacasi* (persons who paid a *claca* – a labor service – in exchange for access to estate lands). As the boyars moved against the independent villages, buying up the "private" lands of peasant householders, more and more peasants fell into a dependent status, becoming *clacasi,* a status little different in practical terms from that of a serf. During the Phanariot period, fewer and fewer peasants qualified as *chiaburi,* free peasants who owned land or leased land from the boyars and, when needed, hired other peasants to work for them.

The *clacasi* were obligated to pay an annual tithe to the boyars. In return, the boyar landlords were expected to give the peasant access to land for planting, grazing rights, and rights to use forests on the estates. How much land the peasant would be given and how much pasture he and his household could use were matters of continuing dispute between peasant households and the boyars. Conflict between peasants and boyars also centered on the amount of compulsory labor peasants owed the boyars.

Hitchins (1996) notes that in the last part of the 18th century the boyars, and the monasteries with large land holdings, continually fought to increase the amount of compulsory labor services peasants were to supply to landholders. In 1805, the Moldovan boyars were successful when Prince Alexander Moruzi raised the effective labor obligation to thirty-three days. In addition, Moruzi lowered the amounts of land that custom had required the boyars to make available to peasants for pasturage and planting (Hitchins 1996). This was the culmination of a long struggle between peasants and landlords. The landlords in Moldova and, eventually, in Wallachia won the right to restrict peasant pasture rights and to reduce the amount of estate land that could be used for cultivation by the peasantry.

Besides furnishing compulsory labor to the landlords, peasants on boyar and monastic estates were required to support landlords' monopolies over the production, distribution, and sale of certain commodities, such as wine, meat, and vegetables and to recognize the landlords' right to build and to operate mills and other enterprises (Hitchins 1996). Peasants also were forced to comply with the landholders attempts to limit the peasants' access to forests. In custom, peasants had been allowed almost unrestricted access to estate forests. Peasants had enjoyed the right to cut firewood and lumber to build their houses or to sell. Landlords, according to Hitchins (1996), had permitted this because it resulted in more land being cleared for agricultural purposes. By the middle of the 18th century, forests were being depleted and the market for wood for building purposes in the cities had increased dramatically. As a result, the landlords attempted to restrict peasant use of forest lands.

By the end of the 18th century, the peasants' customary rights had been substantially eroded and their dependence on the boyars and other landowners had increased significantly. More of the estate lands had come under the control of the boyars, thus increasing the limits on peasant economic opportunities. This de facto clearing of peasant households and villages from access helped lay the foundation for the eventual development and expansion of commercial agriculture in Wallachia and Moldova. Peasants did not always passively accept these changes. There were a number of local outbreaks of violent peasant resistance, but they were contained and suppressed in relatively short order.

Early Modern Urban Development in Moldova and Wallachia
In the later part of the 18th century, Wallachian and, to a lesser degree, Moldovan cities began to show signs of significant economic development. These cities developed along political lines that differed sharply from cities in Western and Central Europe, including cities in Hungary and Transylvania. In these regions, cities had a high degree of autonomy from the local feudal nobility. They stood as modernizing enclaves within feudal regions. This was not the case in Wallachia or Moldova. Cities did not have political or economic autonomy. They developed under the direct control of the princes and, to a lesser degree, the boyars. Cities in Wallachia and Moldova did not have the right to self-government. The weak representative assemblies that they had developed in their early histories had just about been wiped out by the end of

the 18th century. In Wallachian and Moldovan cities, the princes maintained tight political and economic control over their development and ongoing life. For example, the Romanian princes maintained the right to set prices for goods sold and services provided in urban markets and to set standards of production and distribution of virtually all commodities and services through their ultimate control over the guild systems. The power of the princes constituted an important obstacle to the development and maturation of an entrepreneurial bourgeoisie who were capable of creating relatively open and free markets. Moreover, the lack of political autonomy of cities impeded the political development of the Wallachian and Moldovan bourgeoisie and limited the possibility for the formation of the bourgeoisie as a political class in its own right. In sum: princely control retarded the development of a *Burger* class and a *Burger* culture that, once rooted in the cities, might have spread out and conquered the remainder of the Romanian principalities and that might have provided a basis for the development of a capitalist economy. In Romania, princely dominance of the cities meant that urban residents could not govern themselves, had no right to establish their own legal system, could not tax themselves independent of the crown, and, ultimately, could not develop modern ideas and roles of "citizenship."

The status of cities in Moldova and Wallachia contrasted sharply with the situation of urban settlements in Transylvania. Cities began forming in Transylvania early in the 13th century. These cities were developed by "Sachen" (Saxon) settlers who were invited into the region by the ruling prince, Geza II. In 1224, King Andrew II granted the Sachen a new privilege, which he laid out in the "Golden Diploma" (Nagler 1998). This act, which granted the cities formal autonomy in administering themselves and which bound them only to the king and not to the feudal nobility, was directed toward the Sachen settlements in the region of Sibiu known as the *Sapta Scaun* (Seven Seats in Romanian) or the *Siebenburgen* (Seven Towns in German). In 1486, King Matthias Corvinus united the *Sapta Scauna* into an administrative-judicial union of Transylvania Saxons, the *Universitas Saxonum* (Nagler 1998). Romanians were prohibited by law from living in these cities, whose populations were both Sachen and Magyar. The Romanians were forced to live in the countryside or in districts just outside of the city walls. Thus, the larger part of Transylvania's Romanian population were left outside the development of a *Burger* mode of existence.

The upper most levels of the urban populations in Wallachia and Moldova consisted of the service nobility who were drawn into the cities to serve in the princes' administrations. There also were significant numbers of boyars who had leased their estates and who had moved into urban areas in order to participate in the social life of the larger cities. Some among them had even begun to invest in urban commercial enterprises. During the Phanariot period, both Romanian principalities had seen the beginnings of an urban-based proto-bourgeoisie grounded in the ownership of private property. This class was composed both of Romanians and non-Romanians, the latter being made up of temporary foreign residents and immigrants to Romania. At the pinnacle of the proto-bourgeoisie stood large merchant traders and master craftsmen, whose workshops employed large numbers of journeymen and apprentices. The proto-bourgeoisie was set apart from the rest of the urban population by the amount and sources of its wealth, its levels of living, and the fact that it employed the labor of others. Members of the proto-bourgeoisie constituted a very small proportion of the population of Romanian cities and an even smaller proportion of the national population. They also were a small proportion of the Romanian economic and social elite, most of whom were boyars. These wealthy urban residents of the late 18th and early 19th century did not constitute a bourgeoisie, in the full sense of that term. While they may have exhibited objective characteristics that set them apart from other urban residents, there is little evidence that they formed a social community that was aware of its distinctive economic interests and that it was willing and able to politically organize itself in order to pursue these interests. Indeed, they seem to have aspired to become part of the landed aristocracy. Their individual goals, in large part, appear to have included acquiring rural properties and gaining recognition as part of the boyar estate (Hitchins 1996). If some of the urban bourgeoisie did manage to acquire substantial rural property holdings and, even, were successful in obtaining the title of a boyar, there still remained the issue of their social acceptance. This was not always an easy matter. In the landed aristocracy, one was judged on the basis of one's lineage and of one's mastery of an aristocratic style of life, not on the basis of one's economic achievements. Attempts by the bourgeoisie to gain social acceptance as a boyar were not well received by the boyars, themselves, who saw movement into their ranks of economically successful urban residents as resulting in a diminution of their own status.

Production for the growing urban markets in Wallachia and Moldova was dominated at the local level by guilds. Guilds were chartered by the princes and remained under their control. The prince defined the terms of guild charters and reserved the right to intervene in the internal affairs of the guilds whenever he felt such intervention was necessary. He also had the right to dissolve guilds when he felt it to be appropriate. Guilds also had ties to the Romanian Orthodox Church. Individual guilds were under the immediate control of the master craft workers in each trade. The guilds organized work in each trade. Guilds set the standards of production, established work norms for the craft, set standards for training of craft workers, secured the raw materials necessary for production, regulated product distribution and product prices, provided various forms of social insurance, regulated competition within and among various crafts, and protected the monopoly rights of the craft. Guild control over production and distribution, while certainly working to the benefit of the craft workers, themselves, and especially to the benefit of the master craft workers, constituted a further obstacle to the development of a competitive, open-market, urban economy in Romanian cities.

Wallachian and Moldavian cities also contained a small group of independent professionals, e.g. lawyers, physicians, and the like. Many, if not almost all, of these professionals were drawn from boyar ranks. Thus, while many may have made less money from their professional activity than did the merchants and master artisans, professionals with boyar origins, due to their aristocratic backgrounds, had higher social status than did the merchants and artisans.

Lower level clerical jobs also began to increase during the last years of the 18th century. They provided the "technical" staff for larger enterprises and for the state bureaucracies. In terms of social location, they were on a par with the journeymen craft workers who toiled in the shops of the master craftsmen.

The vast majority of urban residents in the last years of the 18th century and the beginning decades of the 19th century were casual day laborers and household servants. Their living conditions in some ways were worse, even, than the dependent peasantry. They were subject to disease and high levels of mortality, to exploitation and abuse by employers, and to chronic hunger. They constituted a large floating urban population, moving around the cities and in and out of urban areas. The greater part of this urban lumpen population was drawn directly from the surplus populations of the countryside. They came to the city because of a variety of push and pull factors. The principal push factor was lack of access to land in the countryside. The principal pull factor was the hope of earning wages that could be repatriated to their cash-starved families in the countryside. Increases in the urban "lumpen" population were correlated positively with the shift toward a market-oriented production system on the great estates.

In sum: Wallachian and Moldovan cities, by the end of the 18th century, were beginning to develop complex systems of social stratification whose main outlines would remain more or less in place until the advent of industrial modes of production in the 19th century. Much the same was taking place in the growing small towns in both principalities, although on a smaller scale and with somewhat different groupings. The stratification systems of small towns also were more flat than those of the larger cities. The differences between the top and bottom social and economic ranks were not nearly as great as they were in the cities.

The End of Phanariot Rule

Phanariot rule ended in 1821, following the Greek rebellion against Ottoman rule led by Alexandru Ypsilanti, a general in the Russian Tzar's army. The Phanariot Prince in Moldova gave Ypsilanti limited assistance when his forces entered the principality. Russia did not support the rebellion and informed the Porte it would not fight Ottoman resistance against the rebellion. In Wallachia, the death of the Phanariot prince, Alexandru Sutu, in 1821, led to the boyars setting up a ruling council of their own in Bucharest. The boyars approached Tudor Vladimirescu to raise a military force. Vladimirescu was from a family of free peasants and had been raised by a boyar family. He had been a military commander of an Oltenian (a sub-region of Wallachia) peasant militia in the Russian-Ottoman war of 1806-1812.

Vladimirescu agreed to raise a military force and ally it with Ypsilanti. Lacking Russian support, the alliance, however, between Vladimirescu and Ypsilanti never materialized. Ypsilanti, disappointed with Vladimirescu's unwillingness to provide sufficient military support and support and faced with the arrival of a large Ottoman army in

Romania, had him assassinated in May 1821. By June 1821, Ypsilanti's forces had retreated into Moldova, where they were liquidated by the Ottoman army. Having seen the Romanian boyars' willingness to support rebellion, the Porte agreed to end Phanariot rule in 1821. The Porte appointed Romanians as princes in Moldova and Wallachia for terms of seven years. Because of their relatively short tenure, the Romanian princes were not able to dominate their own boyars. The boyars moved to reassert rights that they had seen erode under the Phanariot rulers.

The removal of the Phanariot princes not only benefited the boyars. It also helped stimulate the development of an indigenous Romanian bourgeoisie. Once in power, the newly appointed Romanian princes purged their bureaucracies of Greek officials and sympathizers, appointing Romanians in their place. The opening of bureaucratic office to Romanians laid the foundation for the early development of a state based Romanian petty and haute bourgeoisie.

Boyar support for rebellion should not be considered to be an early example of elite nationalism. Its sources, rather, were boyar political and economic interests that had very little connection with the idea of national independence, as that concept would come to be understood later in the 19th century. Politically the boyars wanted to reduce the powers of the princes and to replace centralized princely rule with a boyar regime, i.e. a regime of nobles. The boyars also wanted to cleanse the state bureaucracy of Greeks and open it to their own participation.

Economically, the boyars wanted to reduce, if not eliminate, the taxes and other forms of tribute, such as grain quotas, that the princes collected from them and sent on to the Porte. Taxes, fees, and other forms of tribute that the Porte demanded from the Romanian principalities had increased dramatically throughout the 18th century. These increases took revenues out of the pockets of the boyars. The boyars responded by intensifying the exploitation of their own peasantry, sometimes resulting in peasant uprisings and other forms of resistance.

Increasing demands on the Romanian principalities resulted from deepening economic and fiscal crises experienced by the Ottoman Empire, especially following the failure of the second siege of Vienna in 1683. After the failure to capture Vienna, the empire began to contract, especially in Europe. This was a gradual process, until the onset of a series of wars with Russia in the 18th and 19th centuries, when the loss of territory accelerated (McCarthy 1997). Geographic contraction meant the loss of tax revenues and other tributes these former territories had been sending to Constantinople. This meant that those lands remaining within the empire were compelled to make up for the losses by increasing the revenues and other forms of tribute they sent to Constantinople. The continuing military pressures that the Ottoman Empire faced from the Europeans and the Persians, as well as the pressures resulting from internal rebellions (see McCarthy 1997 for a discussion of rebellion inside the empire), meant that the Porte had to maintain large and costly military establishments, which consumed an enormous amount of state resources.

The Ottoman Empire's ability to support its military forces and carry out its other state functions also was hampered by an inefficient system of tax collection (McCarthy 1997), which only compounded the financial problems created by territorial losses that decreased the Ottoman tax base. Ottoman taxes and tax collection were ramshackle affairs. Ottoman tax laws exempted many of the most wealthy Muslim citizens from paying any taxes whatsoever. For example, wealthy Muslims could escape taxation by establishing a *vakif* (a charitable religious foundation. The wealthy could create a *vakif* and donate all of their resources to it, thereby avoiding paying taxes on what they had given to the foundation and what was earned from the gift At the same time, they could name themselves and their family members as "trustees" of the foundation and receive high levels of pay for working for it; thus guaranteeing themselves and their family members a continuing stream of revenue (McCarthy 1997). There also was a high level of outright tax evasion in the Empire, which further limited revenue collection.

Tax collection was especially chaotic outside of Anatolia, where the Ottoman bureaucracy was at its weakest. For example, in the Romanian principalities tax collection was in the hands of the local princes, who, basically, functioned as tax farmers of the Sultan. The Porte informed the princes of how much they needed to send to Constantinople in the way of cash and commodities and left it up to the princes to collect these. The Romanian princes, more often than not, collected far more taxes and tribute than they needed to send to the Porte and than they needed for operating their governments. The Romanian princes did this in order to recover the costs they had incurred in "winning" the throne and to make a profit on their investment in bidding for office. Moreover, they needed to do this as quickly as they could, given that a prince's tenure in office was short. In turn, princes turned over tax collection to their bureaucracies and to private agents, as explained above, who also needed to recover what they had paid for the right to collect taxes and to make a profit. Like the princes, these tax agents also had to collect as much money as they could in a relatively short time, otherwise they would not recover their costs of office, let alone make a profit. The boyars deeply resented these taxes going to the prince and to the Porte. This was money the boyars felt could be theirs if the Romanian principalities functioned as boyar ruled states that were not vassals of the Porte.

2
The Return of Romanian Princes Within the Context of Russian-Ottoman Contention for Balkan Hegemony

In 1822, the Sultan appointed native princes to rule Wallachia and Moldova. Grigore Ghica became prince of Wallachia and Ioan Sandu Sturdza assumed the throne in Moldova. With their appointments, the Ottoman armies withdrew from the principalities. The appointment of native princes did nothing to dampen the conflicts between the boyars, who wanted to reassert their historical rights of autonomy and local control, and the ruling princes, who were interested in continuing the centralizing efforts that had been carried out by the Phanariot rulers.

The conflicts between the boyars and the princes were played out against a background of international conflict that included issues of control and dominance over the Romanian principalities. At the beginning of the 18th century, the Romanian principalities had become one of the centers of conflict between the Ottoman and Russian empires. Russian power was on the rise at just the moment when Ottoman power in Europe was on the wane. The two empires were clashing on a variety of territorial and economic fronts. Russia was bent on expanding her influence and control in the Balkans and the Caucasus and in gaining direct access to the Black Sea. The continuing warfare with Russia, as well as various internal pressures, was seriously weakening the Ottoman Empire.

During the reign of Catherine the Great of Russia (1762-1796), the Russians and the Ottomans waged a costly war (for the Ottomans) between 1768 and 1772. The war ended with the signing of the Treaty of Kuchuk Kainardji (1774). As a result of this treaty, Russia was given land along the Black Sea and the Crimea was declared to be an independent region. This was the first time that Ottoman military defeat had led to the withdrawal of the empire from predominantly Muslim territory (McCarthy 1997). Their previous defeats by European forces had led them to cede control only over "Christian" lands. The Crimea was later annexed by Russia in 1783. The treaty also recognized the right of the Russian government to intervene in the internal affairs of the Ottoman

Empire in support of the interests of Orthodox Christians. It also contained a provision that gave the Russian ambassador to Constantinople the right to express Russian interests in various developments in the Romanian principalities. It also permitted Russia and, later, other European nations, to establish consulates in Bucharest and Iasi. These consulates, among other functions, extended various protections to their nationals who were conducting business in the Romanian principalities. Following the treaty, the Sultan issued guarantees of autonomy for the Romanian principalities and agreed to Russian demands that princes would be removed only for cause. The Sultan's proclamation also prohibited the forming of permanent Muslim communities in the Romanian principalities.

Despite the Treaty of Kuchuk Kainardji, Russian and Ottoman interests continued to collide. The two empires fought another war between 1787 and 1792. Russian forces moved into and occupied Wallachia and Moldova. They withdrew from the principalities following the signing of the Treaty of Iasi in 1792. As a result of the war, the Ottoman Empire was forced to cede more territory on the Black Sea. In 1800, using the pretext that it was the protector of Orthodox Christians, Russia seized Georgia from the Ottomans (McCarthy 1997).

In 1806, the Ottomans and Russians went to war once again. Russian forces rapidly advanced into the Romanian principalities, entering Bucharest on December 25, 1806. As Russian forces advanced southward out of Bucharest, Ottoman resistance stiffened and the war ended in a stalemate on the battlefield in 1812. Russia and the Porte signed the Treaty of Bucharest in May 1812 and Russian forces withdrew from the Romanian principalities in October of the same year. As a result of this fighting, Russia gained territorial concessions in Moldova. The Ottomans ceded Bessarabia, composed of the lands between the Prut and Dniester River, to the Russians. Russian control over Bessarabia was to become a serious point of dispute between Romania and Russia and, later, the Soviet Union down to the present day.

By 1826, relations between the Russians and the Ottomans again moved toward war. Russia claimed that the Ottomans were ignoring the basic provisions of the various treaties the two sides had signed. Russia was especially upset by the Turks unwillingness to involve Russia in consultations about the future of the Romanian principalities and by various unspecified alleged violations of the Treaty of 1812. Tzar

Alexander I sent an ultimatum to Sultan Mahmud II demanding a meeting between the two sides. The request for a meeting stated that if the Sultan ignored the Tzar's request, Russia was prepared to go to war. The Sultan agreed to meet. The two sides got together in the port city of Akkerman on the Dniester River. The Russians and Ottomans signed an agreement, the so-called Convention of Akkerman, in October 1826. The Convention was intended to ease tensions between the two empires. Among other things, the Convention recognized Russia as a "protecting power" in Moldova and Wallachia and stipulated means of election and appointment, as well as the length of terms, for the Romanian princes. It also included provisions requiring that the Russian ambassador to Constantinople and the Russian consuls in Bucharest be consulted on all matters relating to Wallachia and Moldova. Both the Romanian princes and Ottoman officials were expected to consult with the Russians. In exchange for these concessions, the Russians reaffirmed their recognition of Ottoman suzerainty over the Romanian principalities and the obligation of the Romanian princes to pay tribute to the Porte.

In 1826, Russia was putting indirect pressure on the Ottomans through its war with the Persian Empire. After its seizure of Georgia in 1800, the Russians attacked the ethnically Turk *khanates* of northwestern Iran. Russian imperial forces continued pressing south until 1826 when it went to war with Persia, resulting in the defeat of Persian armies in 1828 (McCarthy 1997).

Despite having agreed to the terms of the Convention, the Sultan failed to abide by their terms. In November 1827, Sultan Mahmud II formally repudiated the Akkerman agreements, setting the state for another war with imperial Russia, which, at the time, was also fighting the Persian Empire.

In April 1828, Russia declared war on the Ottomans and its forces rapidly moved southward, reaching Bucharest in the middle of May 1828. Leaving a garrison force in Bucharest, the Russian military pressed its attack toward the Danube and crossed it into Bulgaria. Fighting stalled with the onset of winter and with the stiff resistance put up by the retreating Ottoman armies. In the meantime, the Russian Tzar removed the two princes and replaced them with a provisional governor, Count Pehlen. Pehlen was a close friend and advisor of the Tzar.

Russian forces managed to break the stalemate on the battlefield in June 1829. By mid-summer the Russians had pushed through the Balkans and, in August, they seized control of Adrianople. At this point, the Russian armies were within less than a week of attacking Constantinople. In order to save control of the capital and, ultimately, Ottoman control over Anatolia, itself, the Porte agreed to peace on Russian terms. A treaty was signed in September 1829 (The Treaty of Adrianople). The terms of the treaty gave Russia a relatively free hand in administering Wallachia and Moldova, even though, formally, the two principalities remained Ottoman vassal states.

The Period of Russian Hegemony in Moldova and Wallachia: "Regulamente Organice" (The Organic Regulations)

In November 1829, Count Pavel Kiselev arrived in Bucharest from Russia to serve as Plenipotentiary President of the Divan of Wallachia and Moldova. From this position, he served as the de facto direct ruler of both principalities. Kiselev introduced a number of political and social changes into Romanian life. Working with representatives of the great boyars, Kiselev, even before he had left Russia, had begun drafting a basic law for the two principalities, which came to be known as *Regulamente Organice* (Organic Regulations or Statutes). The Regulations were approved by Extraordinary Assemblies convened in Iasi and Bucharest, composed mostly of members of the top strata of the boyars. Wallachia approved the document in May 1831 and they went into effect on July 1, 1831. Moldova's assembly approved the document in October 1831 and they took effect on January 1, 1832. Contrary to the provisions of the Treaty of Adrianople, Kiselev had the Regulations approved before they were shown to the Porte. The Regulations went a long way toward harmonizing the political structures and process in the two principalities. In the future, this would facilitate their unification.

The Regulations, for the first time in the modern history of the principalities, separated executive and legislative power. Each principality was to have its own legislative assembly (called *Obisnuita Obsteasca Adunare)*. The assemblies' legislative functions were highly limited. They could not initiate legislation. However, no legislation could become law if an assembly did not approve it. The assemblies were elected based on a very restricted franchise. According to Hitchins (1996), in Wallachia the assembly, which sat for a five-year term, consisted both of ex-officio and elected members. The ex-officio members were the Metropolitan, who was to serve as the unelected president of the assembly, and three of his bishops. The elected members consisted of twenty boyars of the first rank and eighteen boyars from the lesser ranks. The thirty-eight boyars and four clergy made up the entire membership of the Assembly in Wallachia. Seventy great boyars elected the twenty representatives from their rank and three thousand boyars from the second and third ranks elected their eighteen representatives. Under the terms of the Regulations, the Romanian principalities' ongoing polity did not extend to estates other than the boyars. In effect, the Regulations created two prince-boyar states.

Under the terms of the Regulations, the prince was the most powerful actor in the Romanian principalities. Princes were to be elected by an *Adunarea Obsteasca Extraordinara* (Extraordinary General Assembly). Other things being equal, once elected, a prince was expected to serve in the office for life. Provision of elections to the Extraordinary General Assembly guaranteed representation from the craft and merchant guilds, but were structured to insure that the boyars would be the dominant force in them.

The prince had the power to appoint ministers and high officials. The ministers and the bureaucracies reported to the prince and not to the assemblies. This meant that the bureaucracy was responsible to the prince and not to the elected assembly. This gave the prince a central control not only of province-wide functions but also of judet, city, and village administrations. Under the Regulations, the bureaucracy continued to function as a private enterprise of the office-holders. The prince, alone, had the power to introduce legislation in the assemblies. The prince served as the commander of the militias that the principalities were allowed to create under the provisions of the Regulations. Princes were to be advised by formal councils, called *Sfat Administrativ Extraordinar* (Extraordinary Administrative Council), which consisted of the ministers of interior, finance, foreign affairs, justice, cults (religion), and the army (militia) (Hitchins 1996).

The Regulations also provided a foundation for rationalizing law and its administration in the two principalities. This was a project first begun under the Phanariot rulers in the middle of the 18th century. At that time, law in the two principalities was a patchwork of Byzantine legal codes, princely proclamations and decisions, and informal local traditions and customs. Prince Stefan Racovita of Wallachia, who served from 1764 to 1765, began the process of codification of Wallachian law. His efforts were continued in Wallachia by Prince Alexandru Ypsilanti, beginning in 1775, and, later still by Prince Ioan Caragea in 1812. Caragea's work included the introduction of selected Western legal principles adopted from the French Civil Code of 1804 (Hitchins 1996). In Moldova, Prince Alexandru Mavrocordat, in 1785, began a modernization of that principality's legal codes and administration of justice. In 1817, Prince Scarlat Callimahi, who, for the third time was serving as Prince of Moldova, promulgated a legal code that, while drawing on traditional sources, also turned to Western law, particularly the Austrian Civil Code of 1811 (Hitchins 1996). Prince *Mihai Su*tu initiated a revamping of Moldovan criminal law in 1820. The new code relied heavily on the Austrian Penal Code of 1803 (Hitchins 1996).

Increasing Governmental Rationalization under the Regulations

While cities remained under the direct control of the prince under the terms of the Regulations, the emerging middle classes were given the authority to manage cities' day-to-day affairs. The guilds were granted the right to elect five member city councils (*sfat orasenesc*). The *Obisnuita Obsteasca Adunare* appointed the presidents of the city councils and the prince appointed a commissioner to represent his interests in the cities (Hitchins 1996). The dependence of the cities on central authorities continued to retard urban political development and the development of an effective local government tradition within Romanian society.

The Regulations also rationalized the fiscal operations of the two principalities. The Regulations provided for the formal development of an annual budget and it rationalized the tax system by doing away with a large number of indirect taxes and fees. In their place, the Regulations provided for a per capita tax on heads of households, from which clergy and boyars were exempted (Hitchins 1996).

The Regulations formalized the subordination of the Orthodox Church to the secular authorities of the principalities. The boyars, as well as the prince, were given a role in the appointment of all bishops. The Regulations also set standards for the appointment of priests and the heads of monasteries. The Regulations also limited the economic power of the monasteries and diocese. Priests were put on the state payroll, making them directly dependent on the state for a large part of their income. Finally, churches were put under the direction of a Ministry of Cults (religion).

Despite consolidating the position of the princes, the Organic Regulations amounted to a restoration and expansion of boyar power backed by the Russian Tzar. The Regulations went a long way to validating the boyars view of themselves as the expression and embodiment of the essence of Romanian society and culture. Boyars were given control of the legislature, were insured a dominant role in the election of princes, were given senior appointments in the administration of the principalities and the judets, were exempted from taxation, and had their property rights over their estates confirmed (Hitchins 1996). The last was especially important to the boyars, who had struggled for almost a century to be recognized as owners of estates rather than, simply, as "masters" of the estate who lacked the right to alienate their properties in part or in total. Boyars were given ownership rights of one-third of the land on their estates and they remained "masters" of the land on the other two-thirds. The Regulations left it open to the individual boyars to decide what land they would allow peasants to use and what they would reserve for themselves. Invariably, the boyars kept the best land for themselves and gave peasants use rights to the poorer lands on the estate. Under terms of the Regulations, boyars also were given the freedom to establish the norms as to how much land would be given to households for planting and pasturage. Under the terms of the Regulations, the situation of peasants deteriorated markedly. Not only did increasing numbers of free peasants move into states of dependency, but dependent peasants experienced significant economic losses, making Romanian peasants one of the poorest peasant populations in Europe at the time (Mazower 2000). Peasants barely had enough land to engage even in subsistence agriculture and they were forced to pay increased tithes and supply more compulsory labor to the boyars.

In the years following the adoption of the Regulations, the boyars, especially those who were interested in transforming their estates into commercial farms, used provisions of the Regulations to try to reconfigure the ecology of agricultural production along more rational lines in order to maximize production efficiencies. The Regulations provided a basis for the landlords to do this in order to facilitate its tax collection efforts. Over the centuries, land use on the estates had become increasingly chaotic. Plots of land worked by peasants were not necessarily adjacent to one another, households were widely dispersed, and often the households in an area were far removed from local villages. In almost a precursor to Ceausescu's abortive program of rural systematization, landlords and state officials began pressuring peasants to move their households closer to villages and to exchange plots of land with one another in order to concentrate production points. The efforts of the state and the legislators were not successful. Peasants resisted the reorganization of the rural landscape, showing the limits of boyar and state power in this regard. Overall, the changes that took place after the passage of the Regulations destabilized social relations between landlords and peasants and produced intensified conflict between the two groups. The countryside was a site of continuing struggles, sometimes violent and most times not, between boyars and the larger part of the peasantry. Peasants were not behaving as a revolutionary force when they engaged in insurrections. Peasant uprisings largely were defensive in nature. They were attempts to preserve rural customs and traditions, rather than attempts to overturn the social order and replace it with some alternative.

Despite their conflicts, peasants and boyars, however, shared a common interest in gaining emancipation or, at least, some relief from the burden of paying tribute to the Ottoman overlords. Boyars were not without class allies in the countryside. Generally, they were supported by the church, cspccially the hiigher clergy, by the traditional intelligentsia in the small towns and villages, by the richer landowning peasants, and by large farmers who were not boyars.

In sum: under the terms of the Regulations, princes and boyars were given relatively wide freedom of action to manage their own affairs and the affairs of the principality. Their freedom, however, had to be exercised within the limits of Russian hegemony. They did not have the latitude to take actions that would damage Russia's imperial interests in maintaining and expanding its growing dominance of the Black Sea and the Balkan region and in containing the power of the Ottoman and Austrian Empires, as well as that of any other European state that developed interest in the Balkans.

The adoption of the *Regulamente Organice* was of critical importance to the future political and economic development of the Romanian principalities and, later, the unified Romanian state. The Regulations defined pathways for organizing Romanian political and economic structures that lasted well into the 20th century. For example, first, among other things, the Regulations established the pre-eminence of the throne in Romanian political life and the pre-eminence of the central government, as opposed to local governments. This weakened the role that cities would play as relatively autonomous political forces in Romania. Second, the Regulations helped establish the consolidation of boyar political preeminence in Romanian politics, at the same time that they excluded the middle classes from effective political roles in the Romanian state. The fact that the middle classes had no role in the polity retarded the political development of these strata. There was little reason for them to organize themselves politically when they largely were defined out of the state system. Third, the Regulations reaffirmed the dependent status of the peasantry and their place in the Romanian fiscal system as the primary source of tax revenue for the Romanian state. Fourth, the Regulations led to the absorption of the Romanian Orthodox Church into the state as an entity subordinate to secular authority, limiting the Church's ability to serve as an independent moral voice and moral force in Romanian society. Fifth, by standardizing the basic law of the two principalities it provided a common foundation for eventual unification of Moldova and Wallachia. The Russians withdrew from the Romanian principalities in 1834. Except for the revolutionary period of 1848-1849, the Regulations remained as the basic "constitutional" documents of both Wallachia and Moldova until the end of 1858.

Before the Russians left Wallachia and Moldova, they also introduced a number of other changes into the Romanian principalities. For example, Kiselev brought town planners to Bucharest. The planners gave the city a more modern shape and introduced a new lighting system and waste disposal system, improving sanitary conditions and the overall physical environment in the city. The Russians also helped improve the urban road systems in Bucharest, as well.

While the Regulations had provided for a temporary stabilization of boyar political and economic rights and boyar hegemony in the post-Regulations period, there were signs that countryside was beginning to undergo major economic changes. New economic actors started to appear in rural areas. In the middle of the 19th century, there was evidence that agricultural production was beginning to undergo transformation in Moldova and Wallachia. Agricultural capitalists from the cities, who often were not part of the hereditary aristocracy, were consolidating large farms, as had Greek settlers in the 17th and 18th centuries. Elements of the boyar class, themselves, also were beginning to move in the direction of agricultural capitalism, indicating the early beginnings of boyar decomposition as an economic class. Many of the non-boyar agricultural capitalists were drawn from rising urban bourgeois families (Jelavich 1983) and others came from families that initially had been part of the boyar class. While sometimes differing in social origins and status, the boyars and the rural capitalists shared some basic economic interests. Most importantly, they had a common interest in maintaining private property relations in the countryside. They also had a shared interest in maintaining large supplies of cheap and politically docile agricultural labor. Agricultural capitalists and boyars had a common interest in maintaining the Romanian principalities as agrarian states in which they were the dominant economic actors.

While sharing basic economic interests, boyars' and agrarian capitalists' interests diverged in certain key respects. The agrarian capitalists resented the competitive advantage enjoyed by the boyars because of their historically privileged positions. Boyars owned the most productive lands. The estate system over which the boyars presided kept large tracts of agricultural land off of the market, even if it was not being used productively. The estate system also tied up huge quantities of agricultural labor, thus "inflating" the price the agricultural capitalists had to pay peasants for working their farms. To expand and to effectively compete with the boyars, the rural capitalists understood that they needed access to the land tied up in estates and to the peasant labor controlled by the boyars. Agrarian capitalists also understood that if agriculture was to be modernized, the political, social, and economic dominance of the boyars in the countryside had to be broken. As long as the boyars maintained their dominant position, Romania's path toward becoming a modern capitalist economy would be blocked.

Economic Organization and Social Stratification
During the Period of the Regulations

Opportunities for commercializing agriculture increased considerably in the 19th century because of two interrelated phenomena: Romanian urbanization and the emergence of long distance trade networks for Romanian agricultural products. In the mid- to late-1800s, Romanian cities, especially Bucharest and Iasi, grew rapidly. This led to increasing demand for agricultural products. City growth proceeded along the pathways established prior to the Regulations. The two capitals, Iasi and Bucharest, continued to be dominated partially by the large merchant capitalists, many of whom were not ethnic Romanians, and by the masters of the guilds. The Regulations reinforced the guild system by giving them, the guilds, a limited monopoly over commodity production and distribution and the Regulations maintained the prince's control over the guilds and, indeed, over the economy. The princes continued to have the right to charter or abolish guilds, to set standards of guild membership and training, to define standards of production, and to set prices. The Regulations stipulated that all master craft workers had to be members of guilds. This meant they could not be completely independent producers. In these ways, as well as others, the Regulations perpetuated the structural outlines of a traditional, customary economy in Romanian cities. In effect, the Regulations impeded the ability of economic actors to move Romanian urban economies along more modern capitalist lines such as had developed in cities in Western Europe and were developing in cities in parts of Central Europe. The emergence of more fully modern capitalist urban economies also was blocked by the lack of an efficient and effective credit system. Neither principality had a "national" bank or other formalized ways to facilitate the accumulation and smooth circulation of capital. The economies of the cities and, indeed, of the principalities also had to contend with obstacles resulting from the fact that they did not have their own currencies. The Porte would not permit the Romanian principalities, for obvious reasons, to have their own monetary system. If they had their own currencies, this would give them more sovereignty that the Porte wanted them to have. Lacking monetary systems meant that, ultimately, the control over the economies of the principalities lay elsewhere, in Constantinople, Vienna, Paris, and London. The lack of a system of credit and national currencies also limited the development of large scale manufacturing enterprises in the mid- to late-1800s, compounding the problems resulting from the draining of capital to Constantinople through the tribute system in left in place by the Treaty of Adrianople.

The continuing development of the urban merchant guilds was stimulated not only by the growth of cities. Also important was the gradual opening of the economies of Wallachia and Moldova to trade with Western and Central Europe, which, in part, was a result of the Treaty of

Adrianople. The Romanian principalities entered the Western trade zones on unequal terms. They shipped raw materials and unprocessed agricultural goods to Western Europe, while importing manufactured goods and luxury items meant for the boyars and other persons of wealth. The unequal terms of exchange drained additional potential capital from the principalities. In the early to mid-19th century, there was little direct foreign investment in either principality, other than that related to the support of long-distance trade.

While the number of capitalist economic actors increased in number in the cities, they still showed no signs of organizing themselves into a coherent political and economic class. Indeed, they continued to aspire to boyar status. The capitalist producers, traders, and merchants consisted of a number of loosely defined class fragments and fractions. They were divided from each other not only by economic interests specific to their functional sectors but also by ethnicity and social origin. Parts of the bourgeoisie were drawn from national minorities – Jews, Armenians, Greeks, Germans, Italians, and the like. In the early eighteen hundreds, there were no institutional structures of corporate actors that had the capacity to pull the capitalist economic actors together into a coherent class that was politically organized and that acted, as a class, in terms of its general political, economic, and social interests.

As in the 18th century, Romanian cities, while becoming clearly more urban in an ecological sense, lacked the development of a specific urban culture. In part, this was the result of the inability of the urban bourgeoisie, either in its cultural form or in its economic form, to take control over urbanization and to impose its own culture on city life. The Romanian cities, as a result, were more pre-modern than modern settlements. Large parts of the city were made up of urban villages that retained many of the social characteristics of the countryside, as they were composed of shifting populations of migrants from rural areas who came into the city in search of jobs in the cash economies of the cities. With continuing, relatively large streams of rural migrants, the cities were as much "rural" in their social and cultural characteristics as they were "urban." Nonetheless, by the middle of the 19th century cities were different enough from the countryside that one could see the clear beginnings of a split between life in the cities and life in the countryside. Urban and rural areas were becoming two very different economic, social and political worlds, dominated by two distinctive elites.

Uneven development between regions and between the cities and the countryside characterized Romania until well into the 20th century. The Romanian State concentrated investment in the cities. Rural areas were left to fend for themselves. Because of this, the countryside fell farther and farther behind the cities on almost all indicators of economic development, modernization, and well-being. In addition, they were cut off, physically, from the large cities. Roads within the countryside and roads connecting the cities to the rural areas were little more than dirt lanes that were all but impassible in the rainy season and in the winter. Overall, large parts of the Romanian countryside were left outside of "world time." These areas, in a sense, were doubly damned. They were peripheral zones in a peripheral economy (see Braudel 1979). They were being formed as economic "black holes" that were cut off from the major zones of economic and social development in Romania and that were largely populated by miserably poor dependent peasants who barely managed to eke out a living for themselves and their families. The continuing presence of a largely immiserated peasantry "plagued" Romania throughout its history, proving to be an intractable problem for the bourgeoisie in the inter-war period, for the fascists, for the communists, and, thus far, for the post-communist state.

The Formation of a Romanian "Bildungsbergertum" under the Regulations

One of the most significant developments in Romanian urban life taking place in the early 18th century was the consolidation of the cultural bourgeoisie in the Romanian principalities larger cities. Many of these urban intellectuals were drawn from boyar families of the second and third rank and most, if not all, of them, had studied in Europe. The Wallachian intellectuals tended to study in Paris, while a good number of the Moldovan intellectuals took degrees in Austrian or German universities. Since many from both principalities studied law, differences in where they studied might reflect the different legal codes (see above) that had been adapted and adopted by the two provinces, with Wallachia relying on French codes and Moldova relying on Austrian codes. Urban intellectuals in this period, despite their boyar origins, were developing clear organic connections (Gramsci 1971) to the bourgeoisie. To Moldovan and Wallachian urban intellectuals, the bourgeoisie was the progressive class that they hoped would carry the future of Romania as a modern society and state that was capable of standing on equal terms with Western nation-states. Given all of this, it would appear that the Romanian urban intelligentsia was beginning to show signs of becoming organized into what Kocka (1988) calls a *Bildungsburgertum*, or "cultural bourgeoisie."

According to Eyal et al. (1998), Kocka, in analyzing the development of capitalism in Europe, drew a clear distinction between different paths that eventually led to the emergence and stabilization of capitalism in different parts of Europe. In Western Europe, according to Kocka (1998), capitalism developed under the general direction of the *Wirtschaftsburgertum,* the "economic" or "property-owning" bourgeoisie, while in Central Europe, capitalism developed because of an alliance between the cultural and the economic bourgeoisie. In this alliance, the cultural bourgeoisie played the leading role by virtue of its being "older, more numerous, and well positioned in the state apparatus and the universities" (Eyal et al. 1998: 52).

However, despite showing early signs that they were emerging as a cultural bourgeoisie that was capable of transforming Romania into a capitalist society, as would take place in Central Europe, events unfolded differently for Romania's intellectuals. They were unable to accomplish what intellectuals in other parts of Eastern Europe were able to achieve in leading their countries from feudalism to capitalism. There were a number of reasons why Romanian intellectuals eventually proved unable to achieve such a transformation. First of all, in Romania, the cultural bourgeoisie did not form itself into a highly autonomous grouping. Romania's cultural bourgeoisie's class origins were in the boyar estate and its members maintained a continuing high level of identification with their class of origin and they lived lives defined more by boyar standards than by bourgeois standards. The lack of a clear identification of Romania's intellectuals with the bourgeoisie and its ideals can be seen, in part, in the fact that Romanian intellectuals did not embrace a utilitarian approach to education. They regarded any form of technical education as inferior to a classical education or to education in one of the liberal professions. Second, the cultural bourgeoisie was seriously split as to what Romania ought to become. While some of Romania's leading intellectuals embraced the development of capitalism as a national goal, a good many others, including some of the country's most distinguished intellectuals, rejected capitalism and the development of bourgeois social practices culture. Third, the Romanian cultural bourgeoisie proved itself unable to develop as a political class, organized according to "modern" political principles, that was capable of conquering the state and using state power to produce a revolutionary social transformation.

Romania's "Bildungsburgertum" and the Revolution of 1848

The intellectuals who constituted the core of Romania's Bildungs-burgertum in the mid-19th century would come to be known as the "Generation of 1848." They became a model for many Romanians intellectuals in subsequent generations. In Paris Romanian students, organized into the *Societatea Studentilor Romani de la Paris* (Society of Romanian Students in Paris). Both Moldovan and Wallachian students were members of the society and of other organizations and political clubs that were proposing radical change for European states. The *Societatea Studentilor Romani* absorbed the revolutionary ideology that was especially strong in student circles in the Parisian universities of the early 1840s. Many of its members had become convinced that Romania was in need of massive social change, not merely reform, as some parts of the boyars were demanding. The radical students had come to believe that only revolution could bring Romania to an economic, political, and social level comparable to Western European states.

Following the widespread breakout of revolution in Western Europe in the spring of 1848, a revolutionary committee was set up in Bucharest on June 21, 1848. The Wallachian revolutionaries embraced what, for the time, was a radical democratic agenda. They demanded legal equality for all citizens, an expansion of the franchise, basic freedoms of speech, press, and assembly, and universal public education. They also made several economic demands: they advocated a more equitable tax system and, most critically, the abolition of peasant dependency. Politically, they advocated the abolition of all feudal ranks and titles, the election of princes for five year terms, and the opening of the office of prince to the bourgeoisie. The revolutionaries defined the Romanian nation in "universalistic" ethnic terms. All Romanians were seen to belong to the same nation and, as such, they all should share the same basic rights. The Revolutionaries clearly implied in their use of the term "Romanian" that they were using this not in a legal/political sense, but, rather, in an ethnic sense. The revolutionaries also demanded a return to what they believed was the original guarantees of autonomy from the Ottomans that they believed had been basic principles in the old treaties that gave the Porte suzerainty over Wallachia and Moldova (Hitchins 1996). All of these demands were put forward in a proclamation issued by the revolutionary committee ("The Proclamation of Islaz"). The Wallachian Prince, George Bibescu, who had held office since 1842, quickly signed the revolutionaries' proclamation and accepted a new cabinet under the control of the revolutionary leadership. One June 24, the Russian consul informed Bibescu that the Tzar's government regarded his signing of the proclamation to be a violation of the terms of the Organic Regulations and demanded that he leave the capital. The next day, June 25, 1848, Prince Bibescu left Wallachia for the city of Brasov in Transylvania. At the time, Brasov was under the control of the Habsburg Empire.

The rebels responded to Bibescu's flight by forming a provisional revolutionary government on June 26. On the "Field of Liberty," just outside of Bucharest, the Wallachian revolutionaries convened a large popular assembly on June 27, which approved the proclamation as a new constitution of Wallachia. The new government moved quickly to consolidate its rule. Organizers were sent into the countryside to gain support in the small towns and rural areas for the provisional government's political program. It also established a military force to defend the revolution.

One of the most critical issues the provisional government faced was what to do about the "rural question." The revolutionaries were seriously split as to the how best to deal with the social and economic problems in the countryside. The more radical elements had published a pamphlet entitled *"Ce sint meserasi?"* (What is professed?). In it they argued for the abolition of peasant feudal obligations, complete liberation of the peasants from all feudal ties to the boyars and the monasteries, adequate land grants to the peasants, with state compensation to the landlords. This, along with the proclamation, which had declared an end to *claca*, was greeted with enthusiasm by the peasantry, many of whom ceased performing their labor obligations to the landlords and leaseholders. More conservative factions in the revolutionary movement resisted peasant emancipation and land redistribution, believing that it would have disastrous effects on the economy and, further, that it would contribute to mobilizing the boyars against the revolution.

On June 28, the moderates on the agricultural question appeared to have the upper hand. The government issued a decree abolishing *claca*, declared that it would begin to redistribute land within three months, and asked the peasants to continue to meet their obligations in order to bring in the current year's harvest (Hitchins 1996). Peasants reacted negatively to the government proclamation and refused to comply with the revolutionaries' demands.

On July 8, 1848, the new government proclaimed the emancipation of Rroma slaves and set up a mechanism for compensating slaveholders for their financial losses. This decision seems to have had the support of both radicals and moderates in the revolutionary movement and does not seem to have met with much opposition from the boyars and the monasteries, who were the largest slaveholders in Wallachia and in Moldova.

Having threatened, to no avail, to force peasants to pay for economic losses to landlords should they refuse to meet their current obligations, the revolutionaries decided to establish a committee to deal with the issue of property and feudal obligations. The committee was to be made up of a peasant representative and a boyar representative in each judet. The committee was charged with developing laws to be submitted to a forthcoming national assembly. The committee held its first session on August 21, but it soon became apparent that the moderates and the radicals, who were supported by a large part of the peasantry, could not reach an agreement. The revolution was defeated before the committee brought any recommendations forward.

The revolutionaries, imbued with the political philosophy of the West, especially France, sought to create a more democratic polity in Wallachia. However, the ideas of democracy that they put forward were very limited. For example, the new government established rules for electing an assembly that was to be charged with drafting a new constitution that would express the principles of the revolution. The limited way in which the revolutionaries conceptualized democracy can be seen in the rules that the provisional government laid down for the composition of the assembly. First, as was common in the era, the franchise and membership in the assembly was restricted to men. Second, the representative system was weighted to favor the upper classes. The approximately 7000 boyars were to elect 100 delegates, 50,000 middle class men were to elect another 100, and the almost 2,000,000 male peasants would elect 100 delegates (Hitchins 1996). The constitutional assembly never convened. However, it is clear that the Wallachian revolutionaries did not see democracy in the broadest and most liberal terms. The revolutionaries could not move to a point where they saw each male as having an equal voice in electing delegates to the assembly. Instead, they remained prisoners of an ideology that saw the boyars as having more weight in political decisions than other social groups. Their liberalism was embodied in the rather limited idea that some (but not equal) political rights should be extended to the general population of males. While not really seeing themselves as bourgeoisie, the revolutionaries saw themselves as carrying out a revolution in which they, the revolutionaries, would play a mediating role between the two major contending forces in Wallachia, the boyars and the peasants. Their own class situation, which involved standing in contradictory class positions (see Eric Olin Wright 1978 for a discussion of the concept of "contradictory class location"), blocked them from developing a more comprehensive liberal conception of democracy. Being, in large part, drawn from the boyars and continuing to share many of their fundamental presumptions about the nature of Wallachian society, they could not free themselves from their prejudices about the preeminent role the boyars deserved to play in the Wallachian polity. Yet being part of the urban middle classes in terms of modes of living and sources of income, they were not willing to see the boyar monopoly established by the Regulations continue. They wanted the rising bourgeoisie to share in Wallachian political life, as well as the peasantry, although they saw the boyars as continuing to play the leading role in Wallachian political life. The political concepts of the Generation of 1848 would play a major role in shaping the nature of the state that would be created when Wallachia and Moldova unified.

In Moldova, the revolutionaries had almost no success. In March 1848, protests and demonstrations against Prince Mihail Sturdza broke out. At first, it appeared that Sturdza was willing to listen to popular opinions about the current regime and that he would entertain proposals for reform. However, in April, with the support of his military forces, Sturdza moved against the insurgents. He arrested and exiled the main leadership of the revolutionaries as well as several hundred of their supporters, effectively ending the rebellion before it had much of a chance to spread beyond Iasi. Many of those who were exiled fled to Bucovina, which, at the time, was under Austrian administration.

In early July 1848, Russian forces moved into Moldova and occupied Iasi. The revolutionary provisional government in Bucharest retreated from the city, but it returned in a few days when the Russian forces stayed in place in Moldova. In the meantime, the Wallachian rebels approached the Porte. They offered to continue Wallachia's relation with the Porte in exchange for recognition of the provisional government (Hitchins 1996). The Russians, however, were putting pressures on the Ottomans to take decisive action against the insurrection. The Ottomans sent an army of 20,000 men to the Danube River, part of which crossed the river on July 31, 1848. The Ottoman forces then began negotiation with the boyars and the revolutionaries. The Ottomans and the Wallachians reached a compromise in which the Ottomans would accept a government headed by a *Voivedal Lieutenancy* (a princely lieutenancy) and a ministerial council that they, the Ottomans, would appoint. Under the lieutenancy, all of the radicals were purged from the government.

A delegation of Wallachians went to Constantinople with proposals as to how they planned to implement liberal changes into Romania. Facing pressures from indigenous Wallachian boyars and from the Russians, the Sultan refused to meet with the delegates. Instead, the Porte prepared to invade Wallachia, which it did in September 1848. An Ottoman army of around 20,000 soldiers entered Bucharest on September 25, 1848. They encountered fierce resistance from the recently formed Wallachian military forces. After defeating the Wallachians, Ottoman forces looted and pillaged Bucharest (Hitchins 1996). The leader of the Ottomans dissolved the lieutenancy and the council of ministers was dissolved. The Ottomans appointed Constantine Cantacuzino as caimacam (temporary administrator of the principality). Cantacuzino was a member of an old and powerful family, whose members had sat on both the Wallachian and Moldovan thrones in the 17th and 18th centuries. The Russians, not wanting to see the Ottomans reduce Russian rights in Wallachia, sent its own army into Wallachia and took control of Bucharest on September 28. The Ottoman forces did not resist the Russian incursion. The Russians and Ottomans signed an agreement, the Convention of Balta Lima, on May 1, 1849, which ended direct Russian military administration of the principalities.

The Balta Lima Convention amounted to a restoration of joint Ottoman-Russian control over Wallachia. Under the terms of the convention, the autonomy of Wallachia was substantially reduced. The two empires appointed a joint commission to revise the Organic Regulations. A joint army of occupation remained in the province and Barbu Stirbei was appointed as Prince of Wallachia. Stirbei held office from 1849 to 1853 and, again, from 1853 to 1856. Stirbei was a strong opponent of the goals of 1848.

The Ottomans and Russians agreed to appoint Grigore Ghica as Prince of Moldova. He replaced Mihail Sturdza, who had managed to contain the Moldovan revolutionary forces. Ghica was Sturdza's nephew. Ghica was Prince of Moldova from 1849 to 1853 and from 1854 to 1856. Ghica attempted to introduce modern forms of administration into Moldova and invited former revolutionaries to return from exile. Ghica, however, did not surrender to revolutionary ideas. Throughout his reign, Ghica maintained an authoritarian state that dominated the boyars, while giving the boyars considerable latitude to "govern" the countryside.

Thus, by 1849 the insurrection in both principalities was in total defeat. Under the Ottomans and the Russians, the broad outlines of the prince-boyar regimes were restored. The middle classes and the peasantry again were excluded from political life. Moreover, the economic liberation of the peasants from their feudal obligations to the boyars and the monasteries never materialized. The peasants were no better off at the end of the revolution than they had been at its beginning, despite some modest attempts at rural reform by Stirbei.

The Crimean War and its Consequences for Romania

In 1853 war again erupted between the Russians and the Ottomans. The immediate cause of the conflict, known in Western historiography, as the Crimean War, was Russia's insistence that the Ottoman's grant the Orthodox Church a special role in overseeing Jerusalem's and Palestine's sacred Christian cites (McCarthy 1997). Had the Ottoman's agreed to Russian demands, the Porte would have faced problems with Great Britain, France, and Austria, whose Protestant and Catholic churches would have lost their roles in the "Holy Lands." But there was more to the Crimean War than just this issue. The Ottomans had been dealt a series of serious defeats by the Russians, as had the Muslim Persian Empire. Russian power was penetrating ever more deeply into the outlying provinces, threatening, in the not too distant future, the very center of the Ottoman Empire. France and Britain saw Russian advances into the

Caucus region and the Balkans, as a clear threat to the balance of power in these regions and in Europe, as well. Because of these perceptions, as well as pressures from their domestic churches, France and Britain sided with the Ottomans and declared war on the Tzar in 1854.

In July 1853, Russian armies moved into Wallachia and occupied Bucharest, setting up a military administration. The princes of Wallachia and Moldova fled Bucharest and Iasi and took refuge in Austria, under the protection of the Habsburg emperor. The Habsburgs saw Russian occupation of the Romanian principalities as a clear threat to Austria's own geo-political interests in the Balkans and sided with the Ottomans, France, and Britain against the Russians.

In June 1854, Austria and the Ottomans signed the Convention of Boyadji Koy and Russian forces began withdrawing from Wallachia in June and July 1854 and from Moldova in September. Among other things, the Convention allowed the Habsburgs to occupy the two principalities after the Russians completed their withdrawal (Hitchins 1996). However, before Austrian forces could move into Wallachia and Moldova, a large Ottoman army entered the two provinces and occupied Bucharest in early August 1854. Immediately on occupying Bucharest, the Ottomans began organizing a civil administration under imperial control.

In August 1854, in response to the Ottoman incursions and occupation, the Habsburgs sent armies into Wallachia. In September the Austrians moved military forces into Moldova. The Ottomans withdrew, leaving behind only a token military force, in December 1854. With Ottoman withdrawal, the Habsburgs replaced Russia as the "protective" power in the two principalities, which remained under ultimate Ottoman suzerainty. The Austrians allowed Stirbei to return to his throne in Bucharest in October 1854 and, a month later, Ghica was allowed to return to Iasi and create a new princely government.

Meeting in Vienna, the Great Powers began discussions on ending the Crimean War. The issue of what was to be done with the two Romanian principalities became part of these discussions. There was disagreement among the belligerents as to what should be the final disposition of Wallachia and Moldova, some of the delegates supported putting them under permanent Austrian control, while the Ottomans maintained that Wallachia and Moldova were integral parts of the empire and should remain under the Porte's control. Romanians, at this time, had begun to see the war as an opportunity to unify the two principalities and to advance the cause of independence. The interrelated issues of Romanian unification and independence were taken up by former activists in the 1848 Revolution in Romania and they received the support of both princes. The boyars were divided, with some seeking independence and unification and others supporting a return to the status quo ante.

The Conference of Vienna ended without a clear resolution of the so-called "Eastern Question," which included the future of the Romanian principalities. A peace conference, beginning in February 1856, opened in Paris. Before the conference had begun, Russia had been forced to agree to cede Bessarabia to Moldova. In March 1856, the Conference ended with the signing of The Treaty of Paris, formally ending the Crimean War, was signed in March 1856. The Conference was of tremendous significance to the future of Wallachia and Moldova in that it established a set of procedures to explore what was to be done with the two principalities. In addition, Conference participants formally ratified the two principalities' right to be administratively and legislatively independent of Ottoman, Russian, or Habsburg rule, to maintain their own armies, to open their economies to trade with any state they chose, and demanded the removal of the Austrian and Ottoman armies (Hitchins 1996).

The Great Powers established a committee to visit Bucharest and Iasi to explore what changed might be needed in the Regulations in order to accommodate what the Romanians perceived to be their national needs. Both principalities were asked to form advisory assemblies, adunare ad hoc, that would communicate public opinion to the committee. In turn, the committee would communicate its recommendations to the Great Powers, who would make the final decisions on Wallachia's and Moldova's future.

3

Political Mobilization for a
Unified and Independent Romania

In Moldova and Wallachia local forces in favor of unification and independence began mobilizing. These were broad based movements that included both boyars and the urban intellectuals. By June 1856 the Wallachian supporters of unification, with the backing of Prince Grigore Ghica, had organized themselves into Societatea Uniunii (the Union Society). However, the Sultan replaced Ghica by Theodore Bals, who served as caimacam in 1856 and 1857. Bals was strongly opposed to unification and took repressive measures against its supporters. Nonetheless, in February 1857, supporters of unification formed the "Electoral Committee on Union" which set about trying to organize mass public support for its agenda, which went far beyond merely joining the two principalities. The Committee set out a political agenda for the united principalities that included support for the formation of a popularly elected legislature, an independent judiciary, and "respect for property" (Hitchins 1996). The Electoral Committee was the base for the forming of the National Party, which came to be principal voice of Romanian nationalism in the second half of the 19th century.

In March 1857, Bals died and was replaced as caimacan of Moldova by Nicolae Vogoride. Vogoride increased the levels of repression directed at unionists. At the same time, Alexandru Ghica, who was serving as *caimacan* of Wallachia (1856 to 1858), gave supporters of unification largely unfettered rights to organize the population in support of their project, even though he, himself, did not support unification. As in Moldova, the Wallachian pro-unionists formed themselves into a National Party. The Wallachians coordinated their activities with the Moldovans and they agreed to support the Moldovans' larger political agenda of building a liberally oriented unified state. In both Moldova and Wallachia the leadership of the *National Party* was in the hands of members of the "Generation of 1848."

Elections to the Moldovan *adunare ad hoc* were held in July 1857, before those scheduled for Wallachia. The National Party decided to abstain from participating in the vote in protest over what they regarded as the blatant corruption of the election process by Vogoride and his backers. Because of the National Party's boycott of the Moldovan election, opponents of unification won the majority of seats in the Moldovan *adunare ad hoc.*

Charges that the election process had been corrupted by Vogoride set off an international crisis. Napoleon III, who supported unification, demanded that the results of the election be set aside by the Sultan. The Sultan, with the support of England and Austria, both of which were opposing unification, refused France's demands. In August, France, along with Russia, Prussia, and Sardinia, all of which supported unification, broke diplomatic relations with the Ottomans in August 1858. These events threatened the Treaty of Paris.

Meeting on the Isle of Wright in August 1857, Napoleon III and Queen Victoria reached a compromise that ended the crisis. The compromise was expressed in the so-called Pact of Osborne. According to the terms of their agreement, France agreed to not back full unification. Instead it would support an administrative unification of the two provinces. The British, on the other hand, agreed to use its influence with the Austrians and the Porte to annul the results of the vote in Moldova and to hold new elections. The Sultan and the Habsburg agreed to support the call for new elections in Moldova.

New elections were held in Moldova in September 1857. Wallachia held its elections in the same month. The National Party carried the day in both principalities. However, because of the rules specified by the Sultan for the election, the boyars, along with their class allies among the high clergy, held a majority of seats in both *adunare ad hoc.* The Sultan had counted on the boyars and the high clergy to block the nationalists.

However, despite boyar dominance, a consensus quickly emerged in both assemblies. Both recommended the unification of Moldova and Wallachia under one prince, preferably appointed from a foreign country. The unified state, in the view of the two *adunare ad hoc*, should have sufficient autonomy to control its own internal affairs free from Ottoman, Austrian, and Russian direct control. The two *adunare ad hoc* also recommended that the new state have a parliamentary system, based on a broad (but not universal) electorate, in which government ministers would be responsible to the legislature rather than to the prince. They also called for an independent judiciary and for legislation that would secure basic civil liberties in any new government.

The Moldovan *adunare ad hoc* also considered the issue of agricultural reform. It, however, was unable to arrive at a consensus on this issue. Urban intellectuals and peasant representatives favored the introduction of rural land reform, while the boyars and the high clergy opposed any program that sought to restructure the rural economy, especially a program that would "compromise" the landlords' private property rights.

The results of the two bodies' deliberations were sent forward to the Great Powers, who met in Paris in May 1858 to discuss the recommendations made by the two *adunare ad hoc*. The Great Powers agreed to an agenda for Romania that fell far short of Romanian nationalists' aspirations. While agreeing that the Romanian principalities would remain Ottoman vassals and would continue to pay tribute to the Porte, the principalities were granted considerable autonomy in administering themselves. In addition, much to the disappointment of the supporters of Romanian unification, the Paris Conventions did not permit total unification of Moldova and Wallachia. Though the two principalities were given the name of the "United Principalities of Moldova and Wallachia," the Conventions required that the principalities remain separate, with two capitals, two assemblies, and two governments, including separate bureaucracies. The ministers in both principalities were made responsible to the assemblies and not to the princes. The principalities' two armies were allowed to operate under a joint command and the principalities were allowed to establish a committee, to meet in Focsani, a town on the Wallachian–Moldovan border, to discuss common concerns and common legislation for the two principalities.

The governments of Wallachia and Moldova were put under the control of three regents in each principality, until such time as princes could be elected to office for lifetime terms. The regents also were charged with organizing and conducting elections to assemblies in each principality. The assemblies were to elect the princes for each principality. In Moldova, the assembly election was carried out in a relatively straightforward manner and the pro-unification forces, represented by the National Party, won a large majority. In Wallachia, on the other hand, the conservative regents engaged in massive repression in order to lessen the vote for candidates sympathetic to the National Party's agenda. As a result of the regents' repressive actions, the Wallachian assembly was dominated by opponents of unification. The Moldovan assembly convened first, opening on January 9, 1859. Delegates wanted to elect a prince who supported unification. There were 38 candidates who stood for election (Hitchins 1996). Neither the boyar delegates nor the National Party delegates could agree among themselves or with each other on a suitable candidate. Finally, however, the National Party backed Alexander *Cuza* and he won enough votes to secure the title of prince in Moldova.

At the end of January 1859, the Wallachian assembly met. Neither the National Party delegates nor the boyars could agree among themselves as to who should be prince. Finally, Dimitrie Ghica, the son of the *caimacam* Alexander Ghica, proposed that the assembly cast its vote for Alexander Cuza. The delegates opposed to unification were coming under increasing pressures from public demonstrations and marches organized by the National Party leaders and their supporters. As a result, they agreed to vote for Cuza and he was elected unanimously.

Alexander Cuza, Prince of Moldova and Wallachia

Cuza was from a Moldovan boyar family. He had a taste for rum, gambling, and women. He was educated in Iasi and Paris. In Paris, he was active in student revolutionary organizations, while obtaining a degree in letters from the Sorbonne. Cuza also studied law in Paris. He returned to Moldova in 1839 where he briefly served in the army and then began a career in the provincial judicial system. In the second half of the 1840s, Cuza became involved in nationalist politics and in social and economic "reform" movements. He was active in the insurrectionary assembly in Iasi in March of 1848. Cuza's revolutionary activities led Prince Mihail Sturdza of Moldova to order his arrest. Cuza was wounded in the attempt to arrest him. He escaped Moldova and went to Transylvania. In Transylvania Cuza took part in the Blaj Romanian National Assembly in May, 1848, where the Romanian "nation" proclaimed its existence. Also in May he signed the Moldovan revolutionaries' "Brasov" program. In June 1848 Cuza was in Bucovina, where he served as a member of the executive committee of the Moldovan Revolutionary Committee.

Following the defeat of the 1848 Moldovan uprising, Cuza went into exile in Paris and Constantinople. Prince Sturdza offered Cuza an amnesty, which he refused to accept. When Grigore Ghica became Prince of Moldova in 1849, Cuza returned home and reentered government service. Cuza remained active in nationalist politics, becoming active in the National Party. In 1858, he was appointed commander of the Moldovan army and the following year he was elected Prince of Moldova and, shortly thereafter, Prince of Wallachia.

Cuza received substantial support for becoming prince from Wallachia's urban intellectuals, men such as the brothers Dumitru C. and Ion C. Bratianu, and C.A. Rosetti, and from Moldovan intellectuals such as Mihail Kogalniceanu and his allies. These men would go on to dominate Romanian political life for most of the 19th century. A brief review of the biographies of the Bratianus and Rosetti gives an idea of the types of people who were supporting unification and Cuza.

The Bratianus and Rosetti had participated in the 1848 uprisings. The Bratianus were members of a provincial Wallachian boyar family. Dumitru Bratianu had gone to Paris in 1835 to study law. In Paris, he became a leader in the Romanian Students Society. He also developed contacts with other Eastern and Central European émigré intellectuals and political activists. Ion Bratianu was educated at home. In 1835, he joined the newly formed Wallachian national militia. Ion moved to Paris in 1841 to study military science at the General Staff College and, later, at the *College de France*. Ion, like his brother, became involved in various politically active lodges, where he developed extensive contacts with a broad range of Central and East European intellectuals and revolutionaries.

Both Bratianus were involved in the February 1848 revolt in Paris. In April 1848 Dumitru Bratianu was a member of Bucharest's Revolutionary Committee. He acted as a liaison between the Bucharest committee and their Transylvania counterparts. Dumitru helped organize the Bucharest revolution of June 1848 and he served the revolution as a diplomatic agent in Pest and in Constantinople.

Ion Bratianu returned to Bucharest in April 1848 and took a leading position among revolutionary activists. Along with his brother, he was one of the principal organizers of the June 1848 uprising. He assumed the position of secretary of the Provisional Government in Bucharest and later prefect of the capital's police and the organizer of the popular militia.

When Russian and Ottoman imperial troops defeated the Bucharest revolution, both Bratianus fled Romania. Dumitru went to London, where he represented Romania on the Central European Democratic Committee. Ion fled to Paris following his arrest and exile in September 1848. C. A. Rosetti, born in Bucharest, was a member of a Phanariot Greek family. Phanariot princes, appointed by the Porte, had ruled Wallachia and Moldova in 1711 and from 1716 to 1821. Rosetti's family was part of Bucharest's economic and social elite. In 1845 at age 29, Rosetti went to Paris to study and to write. He had already published a book of poetry, *Ceasuri de multumire*, in 1843. As a poet, he was particularly attracted to the work of Byron. He produced the first Romanian translation of Byron's *Manfred*. In Paris, Rosetti became actively involved with revolutionary Romanian students and participated in the meetings of a number of Parisian political lodges.

Upon returning to Romania, Rosetti took up revolutionary politics with a vengeance. Prince Gheorghe Bibescu of Wallachia arrested him on charges of plotting to assassinate the prince. When the revolutionary provisional government was in power, Rosetti served as Bucharest's chief of police, as a secretary of the provisional government, and as its Minister of Interior. In the last post, he was in charge of all security forces.

With the revolution's defeat in September 1848, at the hands of Romanian, Russian, and Ottoman forces, Rosetti was placed under arrest. He later was released and went into exile in Paris. Rosetti returned to Romania in 1857, one of the last exiles of 1848 to do so. He bought the newspaper *Romanul*, which had been a strong advocate for the ideas of 1848. Rosetti continued this tradition and used the paper to support Romanian unification.

Men with personal profiles and class origins similar to the Bratianu brothers and Rosetti provided the bulk of the leadership behind the movement to unify Wallachia and Moldova. They also provided the backbone of Cuza's support for prince. To men such as these, Cuza had all the necessary credentials for election as prince in the view of nationalists and reformers. He was a member of a boyar family, he had been active in the uprisings of 1848, he had military credentials, he supported moderate reform of administrative practices, and he was an ardent nationalist. Some of these very same credentials, such as his boyar background, his military experience, and his experience as a seasoned administrator, also made him attractive to the more conservative elements in Romanian political life.

Between 1859 and 1861 Cuza oversaw two different principalities' governments, two parliamentary assemblies, and two different administrative and legal systems. Between 1859 and 1861, there was a high level of governmental instability. In Wallachia and Moldova, there were eleven and nine different governments. Government turnover reflected the inability of any one fraction within either principality to develop a stable political hegemony, let alone a direct domination of the state.

The European powers, at first, were unwilling to allow Moldova and Wallachia to form a unified state, even if they had the same prince. Only after Cuza managed to gain the support of Napoleon III for unification in 1861 did the European powers give Cuza the authorization to begin unifying Wallachia and Moldova into the United Romanian Principalities at the Conference of Constantinople. The Ottomans had withdrawn their objections to unification with the understanding that the unified principalities would still be part of their empire.

In 1862, the first unified Romanian parliament was created. Using the terms of the Paris Conventions, which imposed a Prussian style Electoral College voting system on Romania, a very small proportion of the population elected the parliament. Only large landholders and the very wealthy were given the right to vote, which resulted in boyar control of the parliament. According to the terms of the Paris Convention, the Romanian parliamentary system was modeled after the French constitution of 1852, which featured a strong executive and a relatively weaker parliament. According to the Convention, the Romanian parliament would have a single house that had the power to initiate, debate, amend, and ratify or reject legislation, giving it a good deal of independence vis-à-vis the prince. The Conventions gave the prince the right to initiate, approve, or veto legislation coming from the parliament. The prince was allowed to form governments by appointing ministers who were responsible to him and who need not be members of parliament. This limited the parliament's ability to exercise democratic control over the government. The prince also was given the right to call the parliament into session and to dismiss it as he saw fit. When the parliament was not in session, the prince could issue decree laws, as long as he had a minister co-sign the legislation, which never was a problem, given that ministers served at the prince's pleasure. The definition of powers gave the prince the upper hand in the united principalities, setting a precedent for a strong executive that stayed a part of Romanian political structure and culture into the present era.

One of Cuza's earliest reforms dealt with the church. Cuza, who was a Mason, confiscated the land held by the so-called "dedicated" monasteries that were under the control of the Patriarch of Constantinople. The monasteries dedicated monasteries owned somewhere between twenty-five to thirty per cent of Romanian agricultural land and pasturage. Revenues produced by these monasteries were used to support Orthodox monasteries and monks on Mount Athos, in Jerusalem, and elsewhere. The confiscation of these estates was a popular move in Romania. Even the Romanian Orthodox Church supported it, as it helped the Church's claims of independence vis-à-vis the Greek Patriarch. *Cuza* offered to compensate the Patriarch of Constantinople for confiscating the monastic estates. The Patriarch refused to negotiate with Cuza. Consequently, the Romanians never paid the Patriarch for the land it acquired. The acquisitions of these estates gave the crown a huge asset that it could use to enhance its own position.

Cuza put all of the clergy in the two provinces on the state payroll. He also took control over appointment of Metropolitans, a practice continued by the later Hohenzollern-Sigmaringan dynasty. Thus, the Romanian Orthodox Church became highly dependent on the state, in general, and the crown, in particular. Cuza's moves against the Romanian Orthodox Church established the principle that the crown was superior to the cross in Romania. This followed a pattern long practiced in other Orthodox states.

In October 1863, Cuza appointed Mihail Kogalniceanu, as Prime Minister. At this time, Cuza was interested in revamping the Romanian government, with a view toward enhancing the power of the prince at the further expense of the legislature. Kogalniceanu had been active in the Moldovan revolution of 1848 and, later, was a leader of the national movement in Moldova. He was from a wealthy boyar family. He had considerable landholdings of his own, as well as investments in various manufacturing and commercial enterprises. Kogalniceanu continued as Prime Minister until February 1865. During his tenure in office, relations between the government and the assembly were marked by strife over a large number of issues.

One of the first points of conflict was a battle over electoral reform. Kogalniceanu introduced legislation on behalf of Prince Cuza that would have reduced the tax requirements for voting. This would have expanded the electorate significantly beyond the numbers allowed by the Electoral College system that had been used to elect the Romanian assembly. Prince Cuza and Kogalniceanu believed that if the electoral base were expanded it would result in an assembly less likely to be dominated by the most conservative class fraction of the boyars. The boyars, along with the urban intellectuals, refused to support Kogalniceanu's proposed legislation, albeit for different reasons. The conservative boyars understood that the legislation was intended to reduce their role in the assembly. The urban intellectuals were reluctant to support the legislation because they believed that the general citizenry, especially the peasantry, were not intellectually or socially prepared to participate in politics or to cast votes. There was a great deal of irony in the intellectuals' position in that they did not hesitate to mobilize this "ignorant" citizenry in mass actions, such as protests, demonstrations, and marches, when it suited their needs. So, while the intellectuals trusted the citizens to become involved in street politics on behalf of the intelligentsia's causes, it did not trust them to make independent decisions in the political process.

Conflict between Cuza and his parliament over voting issues was nothing compared to the conflict and animosity generated by the issue of agrarian land reform. In March 1864, Cuza's government proposed a major land reform. The landlords had proposed a bill on land reform in 1862, which Cuza had rejected. The boyars' proposed legislation offered peasant households a very small amount of land, about one and a half hectares, for each household, which was far too small for a peasant household to support its self. Cuza's proposed land reform legislation went far beyond what the boyars had proposed and far beyond anything they were willing to accept. He not only wanted to give the peasants more land per household than had the boyars proposed, but he also wanted to end what remained of peasant feudal obligations to the boyars. Under the terms of Cuza's plan, the peasants would buy their lands from the boyars over a twenty-five year period. Those who were not eligible to buy boyar estate lands would be allowed to purchase land owned by the state.

By May 1864, relations between the assembly and the prince and his government had reached a point where the prince called a special session of the legislature. At the special session Kogalniceanu announced that the prince was dissolving the assembly. Military force was used to remove assembly members who refused to vacate the assembly hall (Hitchins 1996). On dismissing the parliament, Cuza announced to the public that he would submit a proposed new electoral law and a new constitution to a general "plebiscite."

The new constitution that Cuza and Kogalniceanu put forward was designed to give the prince near dictatorial powers, much like those of France's Napoleon III. Cuza's proposals won an overwhelming majority. The new election system increased the number of persons eligible to vote from about 4000 to over half a million. However, the election code retained the Electoral College system. Under the proposed constitution's provisions, greater weight was given to higher ranks' votes than to voters of lower social rank, especially the peasantry.

The plebiscite victory gave Cuza a constitution that allowed him to rule by decree, rather than having to rely on parliament for legislation. In August of 1864, Cuza initiated a decree law that put the land reform into place. In addition to redistributing land to the peasantry, Cuza's decree law abolished all feudal restraints on the peasantry, turning them into free agricultural labor. Cuza's law not only abolished the peasants' feudal obligation to the boyars, but it gave the peasants title to the land they worked, and expropriated two-thirds of all the large estates, with large amounts of the expropriated lands being redistributed to landless peasants. Despite the passage of this legislation and its implementation, the landlords continued to hold a bit more than 70% of the principalities agricultural and pasture land, while the peasants held a little less than 30%.

In order to meet the demands for land, Cuza also redistributed part of the property he had taken from the dedicated monasteries. The boyars were compensated for the lands taken from them. The boyars were able to use the money they received to modernize their agricultural operations so that they could become commercial farmers and/or to invest in other forms of capitalist activity in the countryside and/or the cities. Cuza's land reforms had the support of the Wallachian and Moldovan urban political elites who had backed his election as prince.

There were a number of problems with Cuza's land reform program. First, the boyars were able to retain the best and most productive land. Second, land redistribution did not give the peasants enough land to develop viable farms. The farms barely were large enough for peasant families to subsist. Peasants also were not given agricultural credits, so there was little that they could do to begin modernizing their farms. During his tenure as prince of the United Principalities of Romania, Cuza was successful in introducing a number of significant reforms, beyond those dealing with the church. For example, drawing on his own military experiences in Moldova, Cuza began modernizing the Principalities' military forces. He also revised the state's fiscal system, introducing more modern accounting and budgeting systems, established Romania's first real universities, and initiated reforms in the legal system and the system of justice administration in an attempt to make the legal systems in Wallachia and Moldova compatible. In general, he received broad support in the assembly for these projects.

In 1864, Cuza, responding to his political base among Romania's urban intellectuals, introduced legislation that significantly revamped Romania's educational system. His educational reform included establishing a state university in Bucharest. The University of Bucharest, along with the university in Iasi, helped provide a foundation for the creation, employment, and organization of Romanian intellectuals, all under the auspices and control of the state. The creation of modern universities in Iasi and Bucharest returned these two cities to the preeminent intellectual position they once had held as centers of theology and philosophy within the Greek "commonwealth" (Mazower 2000).

Cuza introduced other significant changes into the Romanian principalities. Among the more important was adopting a new legal framework based on the Napoleonic Code. He introduced the metric system as the standard for weights and measures, he restructured the Romanian judicial system, including the courts, and reorganized administrative practices in the United Romanian Principalities.

In 1864, Cuza was able to successfully negotiate with the Porte the right of Romania to manage its own internal affairs. While this fell short of the nationalists' demands for complete independence, it did give the united principalities almost complete internal autonomy within the constraints still in place by virtue of Romania being as a part of the Ottoman Empire.

Cuza also completed the emancipation of Rroma slaves. As early as the 13th century, Rroma were enslaved in Romania and the Balkans. The largest slaveholders were the princes, the boyars, and the monastic estates. In 1818, according to Hancock (1991) the Wallachian penal code strengthened control over the Rroma slaves. Among other things, the new laws stated that "Gypsies (Tigani) are born slaves," "Anyone born of a mother who is a slave is also a slave," "Any owner has the right to sell or give away his slaves," and "Any Gypsy without an owner is the property of the Prince." In 1833, Prince Paul Kisseleff, during the Russian occupation, also had introduced stricter legal controls over the Rroma in the Principality of Moldova.

An abolitionist movement of sorts began to appear in Wallachia and Moldova in the mid-19th century. According to Hancock (1991), technical modernization of production on the largest estates made the slaves economically redundant and expensive to maintain in that context so the great boyars had no economic interest in maintaining slavery as an institution. However, on smaller estates, where technology was less important in agricultural production, slaves remained a vital component of the production process. Therefore, the lesser boyars resisted emancipation.

In 1847, the Orthodox Church in Wallachia had freed all of its slaves. Demands for emancipation of Rroma slaves figured in the uprisings of 1848. The revolutionaries saw slavery as incompatible with the ideals of the revolutionary movement. Tentative steps toward emancipation took place in Moldova in 1855 and in Wallachia in 1856 (Hancock 1991). It, however, was not until 1864 that complete emancipation was achieved. Hancock (1991) estimates that Cuza freed roughly 600,000 Rroma slaves in 1864.

Despite the liberally oriented changes he introduced, Cuza eventually lost his base of support among Romania's nationalist intellectuals in Parliament, many of whom identified themselves with the goals of the 1848 revolutionaries. The nationalists had become increasingly alienated from Cuza after he had dissolved the parliament, partly over the issues of national unity and national independence and partly because of his increasingly personalized, autocratic rule, which had completely subordinated parliament to his will, depriving them of a voice in the running of the state.

The nationalist intellectuals had expected, or, at least, hoped, that Cuza would not be satisfied merely with unifying Wallachia and Moldova as self-administered parts of the Ottoman Empire. They had expected he would press Romanian claims for complete independence and for territorial expansion. The nationalistic political elites wanted Romania to gain control of Transylvania, Bucovina and the Banat, that were controlled by the Habsburgs, to the Romanian portion of Dobrodgea still in the hands of the Ottomans, and to those parts of Moldova that had been annexed by Russia. Cuza was reluctant to pursue such policies. He realized that there was little international support for either Romanian independence or Romanian territorial expansion. He feared that without international support, Romania was likely to lose what it had just gained if it began making additional demands for freedom and expansion.

An alliance of the liberal intellectuals, the boyars, and elements of the army mounted a coup against Cuza. On February 26, 1866 Cuza was arrested by the military. Cuza agreed to abdicate the throne and went into exile in Austria. After his overthrow, he never returned to Romania. He died in exile in Austria in 1873.

What were the results of Cuza's reign? The years 1859-1866 marked a significant turning point in the two Romanian principalities. Not only did they achieve de-facto unification in a state that had considerable autonomy in administering itself, but between these years a number of political practices were established which would effect the long-term processes of state building in the Unified Principalities. Cuza's behavior during his tenure in office established that the United Principalities would be led by a strong executive, who presided over an increasingly centralized state administered from Bucharest. Cuza, from the time he dismissed the legislature forward, ruled as a paternalistic authoritarian monarch. Cuza's actions also established the principle that the rule of law was secondary to the will of the prince and that the use of force was an acceptable means for the prince to realize his will.

During Cuza's reign, the bourgeoisie, weak and disorganized as it was, achieved rights of participation in the new state. The constitution that followed Cuza's royal coup extended voting rights to a larger part of the population than heretofore had been the case. The bourgeoisie were specially benefited by the expansion of the electorate. The politicians that emerged as functional representatives of the Romanian bourgeoisie in the unified state, for the most part, were themselves of boyar origin and had both subjective and objective interests that continued to bind them to the landowning class. The new system of voting guaranteed that peasants and the very small working classes would play a subordinate role to the boyars and the bourgeoisie in Romania's formal political life. Organized political parties during Cuza's tenure in office represented neither the boyars nor the bourgeoisie in the legislature. Instead, politics was organized along feudal lines, in which personalities and extended kinship networks and other forms of patron-client relations were the principles of political organization. This had serious consequences for the future development of the Romanian state and for the development of the Romanian class structure. Among other things, the absence of a party system meant that politics were volatile and political alliances were fragile. As a result, the legislature was highly disorganized politically, making it easy for the prince to dominate it. The lack of formal parties also limited the processes of class development in Romania, insofar as parties organize their class base as much as they emerge from them.

Under Cuza the principle of the boyar's rights over their estates was expanded considerably. However, Cuza did not give the boyars legally defined property rights to estate lands. It was during the time of the Organic Regulations that the boyars won private property rights, albeit to no more than one-third of their estates. The extension of bourgeois property rights to the countryside was not a victory of the urban bourgeoisie over feudalism, nor, even, was it a victory won by those segments of the landed aristocracy who were undergoing an economic embourgoisment. Neither of the urban bourgeoisie nor the "modernizing" boyars had the political capacity to bring about these changes; rather, this change was imposed from above by the Russian occupiers. Ironically, given later historical developments, it was the Russians who introduced the legal reforms that made widespread agrarian capitalism possible on Romania's feudal estates. The private property relations the Russians introduced in rural areas, however, were not "completely" capitalist. The Regulations recognized the peasants' rights to use the remainder of the land, albeit on terms set by the boyars. The awarding of use rights to the peasants, however, limited the degree to which capitalist social relations of production could be fully institutionalized in the countryside. Nonetheless, the changes the Regulations introduced were a significant step forward in abolishing custom as a regulating economic principle in the countryside and establishing market relations in land use as the overarching principle. From this point forward, economic relations between peasants and boyars no longer would be embedded in customary, normative principles, but would be defined by market relations that gained increasing autonomy from social and political forces.

The Hohenzollern-Sigmaringen Dynasty in Romania (1866–1947)

Following the coup that overthrew Cuza, Romania offered the title of prince to Karol Hohenzollern-Sigmaringen. Karol was from the Southern German and Catholic branch of the dynasty that ruled Prussia. He took the name Karol I when he accepted the crown and he converted to the Orthodox religion. Karol had the support of Napoleon III and Prince Otto von Bismarck, Prussia's Chancellor, for becoming Prince of the United Principalities. The appointment of a Hohenzollern to the Romanian throne fit nicely with the interests of each of these Great Powers, both of whom were opposed to long term Austrian, Russian, or Ottoman control over the Balkans.

Karol's appointment, in part, was an attempt by the Romanian political elites to find a way to overcome the country's intra- and inter-class conflicts. The political elites hoped that Karol's status as an outsider would put him in a position to mediate and to reconcile conflicts among and within the dominant classes. Internal politics was not the only reason why the Romanian elites chose Karol as prince. As a member of one of Western Europe's more powerful dynastic families (the Hohenzollerns), the Romanian elites believed that Karol would be an asset for Romania in international affairs. The elites had hoped that Karol would help Romania achieve its goal of complete independence from Ottoman rule, while also protecting it from the intervention of the other Great Powers, especially Russia and Austria.

The Reign of Karol I: 1866 to 1914

Following Karol's appointment, a new constitution was put in place. The Constitution of 1866 reflected the divisions among the various interests contending for power in Romania. The boyars managed to incorporate into the constitution provisions that restricted peasant rights, in effect undoing the practical reforms proposed by Cuza. In addition, with Karol's support, the boyars succeeded in proposing that there be a bicameral legislature. Rules covering election to the upper house guaranteed it would be controlled by the boyars. The constitution also restricted the right to vote for members of parliament's lower-house to men who met a stringent income requirement. This meant that almost the entire peasantry and the relatively small working class were excluded from direct political participation in the Romanian State. Control of the legislature was entirely in the hands of a small oligarchy that was split, mainly, along class lines between the boyars and the bourgeoisie.

Under the terms of the 1866 Constitution, Jews were denied Romanian citizenship, even if they were born in the country. An earlier draft of the 1866 Constitution had granted citizenship to Jews and other non-Christians. This, however, had set off a round of protests and riots among those who wanted to restrict Jewish political rights. In the face of the protests, the constitution was changed to deny citizenship to non-Christians.

In 1859 there were about 127,000 Jews living in Romania. The vast majority, approximately 118,000 lived in Moldova (Jelavich 1983). The Jewish population, which had begun arriving in Romanian lands early in the 16th century, was increasing rapidly by the middle of the 19th century. By 1899 the Jewish population increased to over a quarter of a million, with the larger concentration in Moldova (Jelavich 1983).

Jews have had a long, troubled history in Romania. Petru Schiopul, Prince of Moldova, expelled Jews from his province in 1589, claiming that they were unfairly competing with native merchants. Along the Black Sea, Greek, and Bulgarian merchants often incited Easter riots directed at Jews in the 16th and 17th centuries. As elsewhere in Europe, the Easter Season was an especially hard time for Jews. Christian liturgies during the Paschal Season reinforced the idea that Jews were guilty of deicide. Acting on such beliefs, the Orthodox Churches of Moldova and Wallachia, in 1640, proclaimed new church law defining Jews as infidels and forbidding Christians from interacting with them. Two of the earliest accounts of mass slaughter of Jews in Romania are recorded in Moldova in 1652 and 1654. Marauding Cossack bands crossed into Moldova and killed a large number of Jews in Iasi. During the period of the Organic Regulations when Moldova and Wallachia were protectorates of Russia (1835 to 1856), Russian anti-Semitic legislation was introduced into the two Romanian principalities. Jews were forbidden to own or lease land, they were forbidden to open factories in towns and cities, and they were denied citizenship.

Popular anti-Semitism during this period was strengthened by clerical anti-Semitism in the Protestant and Catholic congregations of Transylvania, where Jesuits had a strong presence (for an extended discussion of the Jesuits and anti-Semitism in the 19th century Roman Catholic Church, see Kertzer 2001, among others) and in the Orthodox Church. In 1803, a Moldovan monk, who claimed he had once been a rabbi, wrote a book that claimed to authenticate and to describe the alleged practice of Jewish "ritual murder" of Christians. The book was translated into Greek in 1834 and was published in Wallachia (Kertzer 2001: 92). It was widely circulated among Romanian Orthodox clergy and, later, among Roman Catholic clergy and church leaders. From the Orthodox and Catholic clergy, the scurrilous charges of Jewish ritual murder quickly were circulated to the Christian masses.

As the Jewish population grew in the Regat, its composition changed. Early Jewish immigrants to Romania had been Ashkenazi Jews from Germany and Austria. This gradually changed as Jews from the Russian Pale of Settlement and the Ukraine moved southward to escape pogroms and other forms of discrimination and repression. Jews were concentrated in Romanian cities and towns, where they were active in commercial activities and small-scale craft production. Jews also made up a significant proportion of the urban working class in Iasi and Bucharest, as well as in the larger provincial cities.

Under Ioan Cuza, conditions for Jews improved modestly. Cuza granted Romanian born Jews the right to vote in local elections and Romanian Jews were allowed to buy land. Jews born outside of Romania, however, were not given the vote nor were they allowed to purchase property. However, during Cuza's rule, the Romanian parliament passed legislation that prohibited Jews from working as peddlers. Scores of thousands of Jews lost their jobs as a result of this legislation. In December 1864, Jews were prohibited from serving as lawyers (Levy 2001).

Jews faced continuing economic discrimination throughout the 19th century. In 1868, Jews were barred from employment in Romania's medical profession. In 1869, they were prohibited from being tax-farmers in for the Romanian state in rural communes and Jews were banned from employment as apothecaries, except where no Romanians were available. They were forbidden to become tobacco dealers in 1872. In 1873, Jews were prohibited from dealing in alcoholic beverages in

Romania's rural areas and Jews were banned from being chief physicians of Romania's sanitary districts. In 1874, Jewish physicians were blocked from being directors of medical services at Romanian hospitals. Romanian Jews, as of 1878, were not allowed to become directors of pharmacies. As of 1880, Romanian Jews were not allowed to serve as directors or auditors for the Romanian National Bank. Jews could not be state employees in Romania after February 1887 and, in May 1887, Romanian businesses were informed that the majority of their managers had to be ethnic Romanians (Levy 2001).

The prohibitions outlined above were designed to eliminate Jewish competition for employment and for control over selected economic markets with Romanians. It also was motivated by a desire to create pressures on Romanian Jews to migrate. Members of the Jewish working classes faced similar legal restrictions in the late 19th and early 20th centuries (Levy 2001). The Romanian State, in May 1887, declared that within five years of their founding all Romanian factories were required to have ethnic Romanians make up two thirds of their employees. The so-called Artisan Bill (1902), which was designed to eliminate Jews from all skilled crafts and trades, directly affected 30,000 Jewish workers, along with an estimated 100,000 of their dependents (Levy 2001).

In the riots that took place in 1866 in opposition to granting Jews citizenship and voting rights, the Choir Temple in Bucharest was ransacked and destroyed and the large Jewish quarter was attacked. Many Jewish shops and businesses were looted during the course of the riots. In response to the rioting, which Jews claimed, was organized by the police, parliament passed added Article 7 to the Constitution. This article denied citizenship to all non-Christians. Turks, Jews, Tatars, and Rroma who followed their traditional religion, all were excluded from Romanian citizenship because of the provisions of Article 7.

In early 1867, Ion Bratianu, who was serving as Minister of Interior, began expelling Jews from their villages and towns. Bratianu wanted to expel all non-citizens from Romania, creating a more ethnically homogeneous state in the process (Bar-Avi 1996). Expulsions of Jews often followed peasant rebellions or uprisings (Levy 2001). Great Britain, France, Germany, and Holland protested Bratianu's actions to the Romanian government. The government, however, did not try to block Bratianu's actions. Such expulsions continued until World War I and, in some cases, expulsion resulted in the loss of Jewish lives, such as took place in the Moldovan city of Galati, where a number of Jews drowned as they were being forced to cross the Danube River. The Constitution of 1866 gave the prince considerable power. The prince's most important power was the right to appoint and to dismiss ministers and governments. All ministers and governments served at the prince's pleasure. Government ministers, including the prime minister, did not need to be members of parliament to be appointed to office. They were not under parliamentary control. Ministers served the king, not the parliament. The prince and his cabinet held all executive powers. This had been the common organizational principle of European constitutional monarchies throughout the 18th and 19th centuries. In the 1830s, however, Britain had adopted a different system, one in which ministers were responsible to parliament and not directly to the throne. The Romanian prince also had the right to propose and to veto legislation.

The Romanian constitution introduced a French style administrative system into the country. The prince's government had the right to appoint all prefects and sub-prefects, who constituted the presence of the central authority in the provinces. In this way, the central authorities attempted to subsume local elites under their direct control. The centralized administrative structure resulted in a rapid expansion of a state bureaucracy that was entirely under the direct control of the prince, strengthening the centralizing tendencies that had been recognized by the Organic Regulations. The prince approved all appointments to and dismissals from state offices of any importance. The parliament had little say in the operation of the state bureaucracy or the appointment of its officials.

Over time, the state bureaucracy played an increasingly important role in directing the development of and management of the national economy. The bureaucracy grew rapidly during Karol's reign. In the late 18th century, there were more persons employed in the Romanian bureaucracy than there were in industry. The bureaucracy was the main source of employment for surplus intellectuals and surplus boyars. The state bureaucracy, which earlier had been colonized by the boyars, eventually came to be dominated by the urban bourgeoisie, who used it to enhance their own personal interests, much as the boyars had done when state offices were under their control. The Romanian bureaucracy never became an instrument for national development either alone or in alliance with other classes. The bloated bureaucracy constituted a continuing drain on the Romanian treasury. The Romanian bureaucracy was not known for its efficiency. Its expansion did little to make government run more smoothly, in fact, its effects often impeded the smooth operation of the state.

The state bureaucracy worked in ways that Westerners increasingly came to define as corrupt, although, whether it would have been viewed that way in the West in the middle 19th century is an open question. Romanian intellectuals sought state office as a way to generate a steady income stream, just as bureaucrats did in the West (Ferguson 2001). In Romania, as in many other areas of Europe at the time, holding a position in a state bureaucracy provided numerous opportunities for supplementing one's "normal" salary.

The Romanian bureaucracy institutionalized the ancient practice known in Italian as *raccomadazione,* in which people desiring or in need of state services are expected to pay appropriate state officials a gratuity. In return, the official sees to it that the person's needs are met, either through direct action or by bringing the issue to the attention of an appropriate bureaucrat. In such an exchange relationship, state officials see it to be their right of office to expect a gratuity for any special attention they give to a person requesting services from them. Gratuities were expected to be proportional to the requests being made. In return for the gratuity, the person paying expected his/her needs to be met. The *raccomadazione* system was normative in 19th century Romania. It was what made the highly centralized, bloated bureaucracy work with some degree of efficiency. Of course, those who were hurt most by the system were people who had nothing to offer an official in exchange for his services.

The Constitution of 1866 provided opportunities for the bourgeoisie to gain greater participation rights in the state, giving them a base for challenging boyar hegemonic control over the state and the government and for consolidating their class rule in Romania. The history of Romanian politics between 1866 and 1914 largely can be understood in terms of the contest between the boyars and a rising, more politically conscious and active bourgeoisie for control of the state and its economy. The stakes in this contest were high. The bourgeoisie needed to take control of the state in order to dismantle the boyars, as a class, and establish the conditions for their own economic and political domination.

The boyars, on the other hand, clearly recognized that if they lost control over the state, they would lose their key economic resource, the landed estate.

Under the terms of the electoral system in place between 1866 and 1914, neither of these two forces was able to win decisive control of the state. This worked to the advantage of the prince (later the king), who was able to use his power to appoint and dismiss governments to keep either class from becoming permanently ascendant. The throne thus was able to protect and enhance its own position within the state.

The Romanian parliament was dominated by political oligarchies representing boyar and bourgeois interests. Within each general group, control of the parliament was fought over by myriad political groupings organized along highly particularistic lines. Formal party development did not emerge until relatively late in Karol's regime. These groupings were formed as the political instruments of alliances among powerful individuals and powerful families and their clients who dominated politics in various regions of the Regat. Political groupings, even when they eventually came to be organized into parties, did not have the character of modern, rational-legal political organizations. Instead, even formed into parties, the political groupings remained feudal in all of their essentials. Leadership within the parties was organized around personal charisma, often in combination with patron-client relations.

The political coalitions could, and did, carry on their activities independent of broad, society wide interests. This was made possible by the restrictions placed on the right to vote. Without universal suffrage, there was no need to attend to the political interests and demands of the general population. The political groupings only needed to cater to their general class interests and, within this context, to the particular interests of their narrowly defined constituencies, which they did, with more or less effectiveness depending on circumstances. The interests of the remainder of the society were organized out of the state, rendering silent the largest part of the Romanian population.

The Romanian political process was marked by seemingly high levels of "corruption," which was tolerated by Karol I when it suited his purposes. During elections, the political party controlling the parliament used various means of subterfuge, bribery, force, coercion, and repression to maintain their parliamentary majorities. With so many political weapons at its disposal, it was rare that a party in power lost an election.

Turnovers in government were the result of decisions of the prince rather than of an electorate. Once he dismissed a government and appointed a new one, based in a different, party elections would be called. New governments then used the powers of the state to engineer the vote so that they had a parliamentary majority.

The Constitution of 1866 marked the first major attempt to introduce Western political forms into Romanian life. Not all Romanians were prepared to see their country embrace Western political structures and ideals. While veterans of the revolutions of 1848 saw the ideals of the French Revolution of 1789 and the Revolution of 1848 as guideposts for Romania's development, other intellectuals were not so sure that this was the best path for Romania to follow. The best example of this suspicion of Western European political structures, values, and culture can be found in the writings of Mihai Eminescu, Romania's greatest poet, and his associates in the Junimea Literary Society. Eminescu and the Junimea group strongly resisted the embourgeoisment of Romanian society. They saw the bourgeois order, in part, as shallow, materialistic, and fundamentally alien to Romania and its spiritual essence.

As a young man, Eminescu had studied in the Moldovan city of Cernauti. He then studied in Vienna, and Berlin. Returning to Romania, he became active in the Junimea Literary Society in Iasi, the capital of Moldova. The Junimea group founded a literary journal called *Convorbiri literare* in 1867. It quickly established itself as one of Romania's premier intellectual publications. One of the main themes of the Junimea group was criticism of "forms without foundation" (*forme fara fond*), which they applied to Romania's attempt to import Western institutions and to impose them on a society that they believed was not yet suitably developed to make them work. This was the intellectual stance Eminescu took after he moved to Bucharest in 1877 and assumed editorship of the newspaper *Timpul*. Eminescu was deeply suspicious of and ambivalent toward those intellectuals who felt that only by instituting Western political, social, and economic forms would Romania become modern. Eminescu was committed to examining Romania's history and culture to see what from it could be recovered to make Romania a modern nation on its own terms, rather than in purely Western terms. Eminescu was deeply suspicious of the newly emerging world of bourgeois Europe. This was reflected in his poetry, which was profoundly Romantic. It stressed the importance of pre-capitalist and pre-urban values in forming the Romanian character and Romanian culture. In Eminescu's view, as well in the view of most of the Junimists, Western industrial capitalism and its associated social, political, and economic values were a profound threat to Romanian character, culture, and civilization. In formulating this position, they drew heavily on the social thought of Mihail Kogalniceanu and others who were developing ideas that a society was more than a sum of its parts, but, rather, had to be seen an organic whole built around its unique historical experiences.

Eminescu and his colleagues in the Junimea group articulated a tradition that has had a continuing impact on Romanian intellectuals and Romanian popular culture. This tradition lays stress on the "uniqueness" and "nobility" of the Romanian soul and the need for Romanian institutions to capture and express the essential character of the Romanian people and their culture. They strongly opposed those who wanted to ape social, political, and economic institutions imported from the West, especially institutions that have little, if any, fundamental connections to what it means to be a Romanian. The Junimea intellectuals also rejected the idea that Romania could be changed radically and abruptly. From the Junimea perspective, only gradual change that built on existing culture, traditions, and social practices would be effective in reshaping Romania. The Junimea group constituted the organic intelligentsia of the boyars and the Conservative Party. As such, their work provided a general theoretical justification for trying to maintain Romania as an agrarian society.

Between 1866 and 1871, Romania had eleven governments, some of which only lasted a few months. This political instability reflected the structural weakness of the economic forces in Romania, none of which could gain control of the state and consolidate its hold. In that year, a small group of insurrectionists in Ploesti declared the formation of a republic. They were quickly arrested and tried, but were acquitted on all charges.

In 1871, there were major riots in Bucharest directed against Karol I, who was facing a major political crisis. The crisis was generated by a fraction of the Wallachian urban bourgeoisie who were demanding an extension of suffrage, the protection of civil liberties, and the modernization of key state institutions, such as those dealing with finance and commerce. The demand for modernization of these sectors indicated the class orientation of the dissidents. They wanted to develop institutions that would increase the possibilities for the development of urban capitalism. The dissidents, organized around Ion C. Bratianu and C.A. Rosetti, also pressed for the unification of Transylvania and Bucovina with Romania. For a brief moment, it appeared as if support for Karol I among the dominant classes in Romania had dissolved.

In response to growing dissent, Karol submitted a letter of resignation to the regents who, in 1866, had extended the invitation to him to become prince. The regents refused to accept his abdication. The regents assisted Karol in putting together an extremely conservative parliamentary coalition that represented the interests of the large rural landowners. In collaboration with Karol, the conservative parliamentarians moved against Bratianu, Rosetti, and their allies. The new government appointed by Karol, stressing the need to return to order and stability, instituted a program that rolled back the gains of the peasantry, strengthened the prince, and supported an economic agenda that favored the interests of the boyars.

Among other things, this governing coalition expanded Romania's rail system into rural areas and developed the Rural Credit Bureau to funnel state revenues to the boyars and the large landlords. In 1872 and 1873 it passed legislation that made it even more difficult for peasants to succeed as independent farmers. The conservative coalition held together until 1876, when Karol I made use of an international financial crisis, that had started in 1875, to build an alliance with the urban bourgeoisie. He dismissed his boyar- dominated government and appointed a liberal government with Ion Bratianu serving as prime minister. The international crisis provided an opportunity to meet one of the nationalists' continuing objectives, complete Romanian independence from Ottoman rule.

In 1875 rebellions against Ottoman rule had erupted in Bosnia-Herzegovina. In 1876, in response to Ottoman repression in Bosnia-Herzegovina, Montenegro and Serbia declared war on the Ottoman Empire and, in the same year, a revolt against the Ottomans broke out in Bulgaria, where an independence movement had achieved considerable strength among the Slavs living there. To further complicate matters for the United Principalities, the Ottomans adopted a new constitution in 1876 that clearly identified Romania as an imperial province, which challenged the Romanians' understandings of their situation in the empire.

Reacting to a perceived abrogation of its rights and its traditional status in the Ottoman Empire, in April 1877 Karol's government signed the Russian-Romanian Military Convention. In return for a promise to defend Romania from an Ottoman invasion, the Romanians granted Russia the right to move military forces through the principalities to the Danube, where they could engage Ottoman garrisons. Immediately after the convention's signing, Russians forces crossed the border and moved toward the Danube and an invasion of Bulgaria. From Bulgaria, Ottoman forces shelled several Romanian villages on the other side of the Danube. Karol ordered the Romanian army to use its own artillery to shell Ottoman strongholds along the Danube and he mobilized the Romanian army. Events were unfolding rapidly. On May 21, 1877, Mihail Kogalniceanu, who was serving as Bratianu's foreign minister, appeared in parliament and asked its members to pass legislation authorizing the United Principalities to declare their independence.

After months of bitter fighting, Russian and Romanian forces began advancing on Constantinople and the Ottoman Empire agreed to negotiate a peace agreement. In 1878, Russia and the Ottomans signed the Treaty of San Stefano. The treaty ignored the Romanian Principalities' claim of independence. Shortly after the treaty was signed, the Tzar informed Prince Karol that Russia intended to reclaim southern Bessarabia from Romania. Romania could not raise too great an objection to Russian claims, given that Russian military forces had surrounded Bucharest and were poised to attack if Russian demands for a return of southern Bessarabia were not accepted.

Russia's victory over the Ottomans raised concerns among the Great Powers as to what Russia's long term ambitions might be. Russia's victory directly threatened the interests of the French and the Austro-Hungarian Empire. Meeting in the Congress of Berlin (1878) the European Powers tried to reestablish a balance of interests and power in the Balkans. Because of the Congress, Romania was given a large part of the Dobrodgea region and the Danube Delta. These territorial awards were given by the Great Powers in the hope that an enlarged Romania would help limit Russian dominance of the Black Sea and the Balkans. By 1878, as a result of successive military defeat of the Ottomans by the Romanovs, the Black Sea had turned into a virtual Russian lake. Austria was awarded control of Bosnia-Herzegovina.

The territorial acquisitions resulting from the Congress of Berlin strengthened Romania's geopolitical position in the Black Sea region. However, the Great Powers refused to recognize Romania's independence. They were unsure of the strategic value of such a decision, given likely opposition from Russia and the Ottomans. The Great Powers bought themselves some time on making this decision by telling Romania they would not support independence unless it changed its constitution so as to give Romanian-born Jews citizenship in the proposed state.

In 1879, Romania partially acceded to European demands and made limited changes in its constitution. Jews were allowed to become Romanian citizens with special petition to the government, which would grant or deny citizenship on a case-by-case basis. Only a very small number of Jews actually petitioned for citizenship, once they were allowed to do so. The situation of Romanian Jewry did not improve with the modification of Romania's citizenship laws. Indeed, in many respects, the circumstances of Jews worsened. For example, Jews were not allowed to enter many occupations. They could not be lawyers, teachers in state schools, or stockbrokers. They also were prohibited from holding a large number of offices in the state bureaucracy and in 1893, Jewish students were expelled from Romania's public schools.

Following the change of its constitution, Great Britain, Germany, and France recognized Romanian independence in 1880. All three of these countries came to believe that an independent Romania would help stabilize the political situation in the Near East. All three of the Great Powers were concerned with Russia's ability to take advantage of a decaying Ottoman Empire and the threat this would pose to their own interests in the Balkans and beyond.

It is difficult to sum up what the long-term effects Ottoman hegemony were on the Romanian principalities. It is clear that during the centuries the Ottoman Empire was the hegemon in Wallachia and Moldova the Porte drained substantial amounts of wealth from the two principalities and limited and deformed their economic development. Whether the limitations that resulted from the Ottomans' control were of greater or lesser significance than the behavior of the boyars and the princes, themselves, is a continuing open question. There, however, is a tendency among Romanian historians to see Ottoman hegemony as one of the decisive factors that led to Romanian economic backwardness in the 17th through the 20th centuries.

Romanian historians also see Ottoman rule as having had serious negative cultural characteristics in the two principalities. The generally prevailing view among Romanian historians is nicely summed up in the falling quote taken from Mihai Maxim (1998):

> What the Romanians also inherited from the Turks are some habits and attitudes, in which the 'stamp of Istanbul' is perhaps stronger than in language and foods. As Wayne S. Vucinich (1965 – reference date added to text), who studied this matter says: ' The Ottoman social system fostered many undesirable habits (e.g. the bribe or bakshish, distrust of the government, and so forth) that lived on after the Empire's demise. Centuries of feudal bondage contributed to the prevalence of vavashlik, a state of being characterized by lethargy, indifference, and a tendency toward submissiveness, which grew out of the necessity for survival. This can be easily detected in the attitudes toward authority – apprehension but at the same time humility and acquiescence. Coupled with submissiveness is cleverness, expressed in attempts to get around obstacles, including those erected by authority, by using none-too-ethical (from the point of view of government) or even illegal means. The notion persists that it is perfectly permissible to cheat and steal from the government, the police agent, and the tax collector has its origin, at least partially, in his experience under Ottoman rule.
>
> The future being uncertain, the subjects of the Ottoman Empire developed a rather hedonistic attitude toward life and a great appreciation of leisure.

Maxim goes on to state, in support of Vucinich's argument:

> True enough, the Romanians were not part of the Ottoman Empire the way the peoples south of the Danube were. Nevertheless, Ottoman practices were widespread in the Romanian countries, especially during the Phanariot rule, when 'dissimulation, evasive tactics, and white lies became part of daily life' (Sugar 1977 – reference added to the text) north of the Danube as well. Perhaps even more so, as the past Byzantine influence provided a fertile ground for such practices. Afterwards, the communist regime, having

much in common with 'Ottoman socialism' (first of all a dominant state property, a powerful central authority, with the individual counting for naught) has revived the old habits and attitudes from the Ottoman times. That would explain why that inheritance has lasted for such a long time north of the Danube both on the planes of reality and of mentality. Hopefully, as the factual and political reality is changing, the old Oriental, Balkan habits are expected to wane away.

Despite this generally negative view of the Ottoman influence on Romania, Maxim finds some value in Ottoman suzerainty. He states:

By and large, one ought to remember that the Ottoman factor had represented a powerful political and military counterbalance to the Austrian and moreover, the Russian expansionistic tendencies, a fact that enabled the Romanian Countries to survive as distinct state entities and distinct spiritual entities, and the huge advantages this entailed, which is no small matter.

Maxim's quotations and statements are interesting in several important respects. First, his views are not unique among Romanian historians, who, on the whole, tend to identify certain historical "failures" or "deficiencies" of Romanian culture and behavior and attribute these alleged deficiencies to the influence of the Ottoman Empire. In doing this, they adopt a view of the Ottomans that reflects what Said (1979) has described as "Orientalism." One gets a clear indication in Maxim's statement, as well as the quotations he uses, that the Ottomans' introduced into Romania and perpetuated economic and social backwardness, a lack of industriousness, a tendency toward deceptiveness and general untruthfulness, a general tendency toward criminal behavior when dealing with state authorities, institutionalization of despotic rule, and a generally hedonistic approach to life. The implicit contrast is with the West, where these traits, as well as others, are thought to be absent or, at least, less prevalent than they are in the Orient, as embodied in the Ottoman Empire. The Ottoman Empire, in Maxim's view, has come to symbolize to Romanian historians and social analysts an old terror. It, the Ottoman Empire, is seen as a demonic presence introduced into the Romanian (European) society that distorted its development and locked it into an aberrant development. Moreover, Ottoman rule is seen as having isolated Romania from progress in the arts, the sciences, and economic development. This view overlooks the fact that during much of the period of Ottoman dominance, Romania, through the Porte, was connected to a "world economy" that was far wealthier and far more dynamic than that which existed in Western Europe and in Russia (for a discussion of such differences, see, among others, Goldstone 2000: 175-194).

Also of interest in Maxim's position is the implicit idea that Romania got back on the track to becoming a "normal" society during its period of independence, up until the time of communist rule. Communism, in this view, is seen as a return to Orientalism. Indeed, Maxim, contrary to what virtually all other analysts of the Ottoman Empire would argue, sees the Ottoman regime as having been a "socialism" of a certain type and Bolshevism, in some ways, as a reversion to "Orientalism."

In Maxim's view, almost all of Romania's problems can be traced back to its having been under Ottoman and, later, communist (Russian) hegemony. Had these forces not been dominant, Romania would have been a more fully European country. Therefore, Romania and its inhabitants, especially its leading classes, are absolved of all of the negative characteristics that might have emerged in its history.

Unfortunately, the implication that independent Romania was a "golden-age," of sorts, in which Romania was moving in the direction of developing into a "normal" European country is not supported by the facts of Romania's history between 1866 and 1914. Romania did not develop as a modern, liberal, parliamentary democracy, let alone as a capitalist state, during these years. Its liberal institutions, as will shown below, were more liberal in form than in substance. Democracy, as it was understood in Western Europe, did not take root in Romania. The Romanian political elites constituted themselves as an oligarchy, organized according to feudal principles, that ruled in their own personal and class interests, rather than in the national interest. This gave rise to a number of dissident movements, some on the radical right and others on the radical left, which, in turn, produced a monarchical dictatorship under Karol II, followed by the fascist National Legionary State, the fascist dictatorship of Ion Antonescu, and, following World War II, the communist dictatorships led by Dej and Ceausescu.

The Romanian Kingdom: 1866–1914

With the support of his bourgeois allies, in 1881 Karol proclaimed Romania a kingdom and had himself named king. The bourgeois were more than willing to go along with the establishment of a monarchy. By agreeing to support Karol on this issue, the bourgeois politicians hoped to cement their relationship with the new king and make it more difficult for him to act in support of the political agenda of the boyars and their conservative intellectual allies. Given their nationalist tendencies, it was important for the intellectuals to have Romania ruled by a king because it gave Karol symbolic parity with other European rulers, something he lacked by holding the title of Prince.

During this period, Prime Minister Bratianu, who was one of the founders of the National Liberal Party and remained its president until his death in 1891, strengthened The Liberals alliance with the throne. The National Liberal Party government, with Karol's support, pressed ahead with the economic modernization of Romania, laying the foundation for rapid capitalist expansion, including the foundation for growth of capitalist agricultural production. In 1886, Bratianu passed new tariff legislation that the bourgeoisie was demanding. This legislation was meant to protect Romania's nascent industrial sector from foreign competition. In 1877, Bratianu had parliament pass legislation that fostered the further development of industry in Romania. The Liberal Party, in taking these stands, was acting to accelerate the development of their own bourgeois class base, at the expense of the boyars. Romania's trading partners at the time responded to the new tariffs by restricting imports from Romania, most of which were agricultural products.

Serious splits began to appear within the National Liberal Party in 1882. Rosetti and his allies began to press for electoral reform. They wanted Bratianu and the king to eliminate the voting system based on electoral colleges, which were modeled after the Electoral College system in place in Prussia, and replace it with a single electoral organization. The parliamentary debates over this issue led to the Conservatives' mass resignation from the parliament in 1883. The boyars knew that voting reform would substantially weaken them politically. Bratianu was willing to modify the electoral system, but he was not willing to abandon it and adopt Rosetti's proposals. Instead, Bratianu proposed that the number of electoral colleges be reduced and that the rights of the press to criticize the monarch be sharply curtailed. Rosetti and his allies walked out of the parliament, leaving Bratianu with the votes to pass his bill, which expanded the size of the electorate to around 50,000 voters. This expansion of the electorate was enough to seriously compromise the boyars' ability, and the ability of their main party, i.e. the National Conservative Party, to successfully contest elections in an open manner. The only way the National Conservatives could hope to win office was to engage in fraud and intimidation of the small electorate and to count on the prince being willing to appoint National Conservatives to run the government, despite their minority status among voters.

At the same time, the election law assured the political oligarchy never would be able to be successfully challenged from below. The right to vote was extended in such a way that peasants and workers were not given voting rights. Thus, lower orders continued to be excluded from effective participation in the Romanian political process.

In 1884, Bratianu directed parliament to pass legislation granting the crown huge estates. This was Bratianu's reward to the king for having supported him personally and for having supported the National Liberal Party. The granting of domains to the throne substantially increased the monarchy's independence from parliament. The king no longer needed to turn to parliament for his personal expenses, he now could finance his own household from the revenues of his estates.

Bratianu's policies, during his tenure as Prime Minister, tended to focus on consolidating the position of the National Liberal Party as the leading force for economic and social modernization of the kingdom. The largest number of reforms he introduced had to do with developing the conditions for the expansion and stabilization of capitalist economic activities in Wallachian and Moldovan cities, which had begun to experience considerable growth and prosperity. Bucharest, having been the Wallachian capital, already was a large city when the Regat was formed. It grew even larger and more prosperous when it became the capital of the United Principalities. Romanian architects, many of whom had been educated in France, modeled the development of Bucharest after Paris. Bucharest was transformed into a city with beautiful parks, broad tree lined boulevards complete with flaneurs, and public and private buildings patterned after French designs. Bucharest also had its own Arcade, modeled after those in Paris. Given all this, Bucharest well deserved its reputation as the "Paris of the East."

Bratianu and his party largely ignored the situation of the peasants in the countryside, whose economic position continued to deteriorate. In early 1888, peasant unrest turned to violence. The king, after having put down the peasants with the loss of as many as a thousand peasants' lives, called elections, which the Conservatives won, using the same strategies of intimidation, bribery, and coercion that the Liberals had used for so many years to stay in power.

The Conservatives controlled the government until 1895, when the Liberals replaced them. During their tenure in office, the Conservatives followed an agenda grounded in the interests of the boyars. In response to the rebellion, they introduced minor agricultural reforms in order to reduce the worst abuses and economic burdens the peasants were experiencing. For example, they passed legislation to sell state land to peasants, but they made no provision for the peasantry to receive cheap credit to support the purchases. These reforms did nothing to alter the fundamental nature of class relations in the countryside. Economic power in rural areas remained in the hands of the boyars and the large agricultural capitalists. They also passed legislation that opened Romania's mining industry to foreign investment. In 1889, the Conservatives anchored the Hohenzollern-Sigmaringen dynasty by recognizing Karol's nephew Ferdinand as his successor. Karol's only child, a daughter, had died in 1874, so he had no direct heirs.

Between 1895 and 1914, the Liberals and the Conservatives were shuttled in and out of office by the crown. Control of the government was rotated on a regular basis. Because neither party had a mass base that could be mobilized in general elections, they were not able to resist the king whenever he decided he wanted a new government. Once in office, the new government would use the power at its disposal to engineer the elections to produce a majority for its party. The practice of regularly changing parties in power worked to the benefit of the king. It made the monarchy the principle political power in the realm. Parties were totally dependent on his good will to stay in office. At the same time, by circulating control of government to the two major parties, the king insured that both parties would stay loyal to the monarchy and would not move in the direction of republicanism.

The king's policy vis-à-vis the Conservatives and Liberals meant that whichever party controlled the government no major changes in society or the economy would be attempted. The king would not allow parties to upset the delicate equilibrium of political and economic forces that he had constructed and over which he presided. The balancing policy meant that the state did not have the ability to respond effectively to an increasing deterioration of the economic condition of the peasantry. The peasants' lot had worsened as a result of a trade war between Romania and the Austro-Hungarian Empire. The trade war started in 1886 and lasted until 1883. Because of the trade war, Romanian agriculture lost access to its Austro-Hungarian markets (Jelavich 1983). Agricultural trade also was negatively affected when Romania passed steep import tariffs in 1904. This led to Romania's trading partners responding in kind.

In 1907, the continuing deterioration of the peasants' economic conditions produced a serious political crisis for the king and the Conservative government he had appointed. Early in 1907, peasants began peaceful protests in northern Moldova. Peasant protests were directed against the boyars and their land agents, many of whom were Jews. Peasants received support for their protests from some sectors of the rural petty bourgeoisie who were part of the "traditional" intelligentsia (Gramsci 1971), such as teachers in village schools, professionals in subaltern occupations, and village priests. Protests quickly spread throughout Moldova and into Wallachia. As they spread, the protests turned violent. The peasants attacked government offices, burned the estates of boyars, and seized crops that were in storage. They also attacked the boyars' leaseholders, many of whom were Jewish. The local police and militia units could not contain the violence.

In the heat of the crisis, Karol replaced the Conservative government with a Liberal cabinet presided over by Dimitrie Sturdza. Sturdza, with the king's support, ordered the new minister of war, General Alexander Averescu, to put down the rebellion. Using massed infantry tactics and heavy artillery, Averescu advanced on the peasants with a force of 120,000 men and crushed the insurrection. Thousands of peasants and their supporters were arrested. It has been estimated that over 11,000 peasants were killed and countless peasant villages were destroyed before calm finally was restored (Mazower, 2000). Romania at this time had one of the highest levels of land concentration in the Balkans, if not in Europe as a whole. According to Mazower (2000), one per cent of the population in Romania held almost fifty per cent of the land available for agriculture and grazing and roughly eighty five per cent of Romania's peasants were producing at or below bare subsistence levels. The Liberals' ruthlessness in suppressing the peasant rebellion showed that they were no more no more tolerant of peasant dissent than had been the Conservatives.

Following the rebellion's suppression, the government immediately passed legislation that ordered the expulsion of all "foreigners" (read Jews) from Romania's villages. The new law was enforced immediately and all Jews were expelled from rural areas in Iasi and Dorohoi judets. Many were given only forty eight hours to gather up their things before they were expelled (Bar-Avi 1996).

The peasant uprising of 1907 was a pre-political insurrection (Hobsbawm 1959), just as had been the major uprising of 1888 and countless other, but often more localized, peasant rebellions in the modern era in Romania. During the 1907 rebellion, the peasants lacked an explicitly articulated program of demands or reforms and they lacked effective organization. Lacking organization and a political agenda, once their rebellion was crushed, the peasantry retreated to the countryside, where they could do nothing but wait to see how the state would respond to their needs.

With the rebellion defeated, the Liberal government introduced legislation meant to show they were interested in improving the life of the peasantry. As in the past, this legislation offered a palliative rather than fundamental transformation of the structures of accumulation and repression in the countryside. The Liberals passed laws meant to stimulate the formation of cooperatives, as they had in the past, to extend credit to peasants, to reduce peasant dependency, and to make government land available for purchase. Liberals were unable to do anything to dismantle the large agricultural estates nor did they pass legislation to extend the vote to the peasantry. To attempt such changes would have threatened the continued existence of the ruling bloc of boyars, bourgeoisie, and the crown.

In some Romanian circles, Jews were blamed for having precipitated the 1907 peasant rebellion, given that it had broken out on a Moldovan estate managed by a Jewish lease holder, Mochi Fischer. The Fischer brothers, of Austrian Jewish background, controlled 75% of the agricultural land in the Suceava, Dorohoi, and Botosani judets (Levy 2001). The Fischer brothers were part of a general class of farm leaseholders that were called *arendasi*. The term embraced a number of different types of leaseholders. Some were peasants who leased lands from the great estates, others were independent farmers who were using leases to expand their holdings, and still others were persons who took leases and ran the farms as entrepreneurs.

The *arendasi* emerged as a significant factor in organizing agricultural production in the middle of the 18th century. Romanian boyars in large numbers began moving to the cities, especially Bucharest, which had become the capital of the United Principalities and, hence, the center of court activity. They also moved to avoid the periodic outbursts of peasant rage that sometimes threatened them and their families. Many of the boyars who moved to the cities turned over operation of their estates to leaseholders, the *arendasi*. According to Roberts (1951), by 1900, 56% of the properties over 50 hectares were leased to tenants and 72% of the large estates over 5000 hectares were being managed by the *arendasi*.

Romanian popular opinion held that Jews made up the largest part of the *arendasi* and that they, the Jews, were responsible for retarding, if not setting back, the development of Romanian agriculture and for impoverishing the peasants, resulting in widespread discontent and rebellion in the countryside. With respect to the first charge, Levy (2001) has argued that Jewish leaseholders, especially in the early years of the system, were agricultural modernizers. They acted as profit maximizing agricultural entrepreneurs, investing in machinery, rationalizing planting and harvesting practices, and remodeling millworks, granaries, and the like. Levy (2001: 261) also cites data showing that Jews, in fact, did not predominate in the *arendasi* system. He notes that in Moldova, where the system was most widespread, that in 1902 there were 1102 *arendasi.* Romanians counted for 556 leaseholders, 440 were Jews (an overrepresentation, but not a majority), and 106 were Greeks or Armenians.

In 1875, Romanian agriculture went into a deep crisis, as agricultural prices dropped substantially across Europe. Romanian agriculture also was affected by the increasing penetration of American grains, especially wheat, into the European markets that normally had been supplied by Romania. During this crisis, agricultural modernization ground to a halt in Romania. Landlords and their leaseholders responded to the crisis by cutting costs wherever they could and by intensifying the exploitation of the peasantry. With falling profits, the boyars raised land rents considerably, which intensified leaseholders' economic problems.

Jews were especially affected. Jews were prohibited from owning agricultural land and they were restricted from holding leases for more than five consecutive years. Because of time restrictions, Jewish leaseholders had to extract their profits in a relatively short period. Jews could not take a gradualist approach to sharp increases in land rents, recovering their increased costs over a long period. When rents increased, Jews had to extract more value, more quickly, from peasant workers and from holders of sub-leases. This is not to say that a large number of Gentile leaseholders may not have behaved in exactly the same way Jews were accused of behaving or that all Jewish leaseholders behaved in a profit maximizing manner. But this did not matter, Jews were stereotyped as the exploiter of the peasantry – a charge on which the Iron Guard would be able to capitalize in the 20th century.

In 1912, the First Balkan War started. The war followed a breakdown of the Great Power agreements and understandings about the Balkans that had helped keep the peace in the region. These agreements began to unravel when the Austro-Hungarian Empire decided to annex Bosnia-Herzegovina in 1908, making "permanent" the administrative rights they had gained in 1878. The Russians saw this as a threat to the prevailing balance of power in the Balkans. The Serbs saw the annexation as a naked act of aggression against the Serbian people and their territory. The annexation set off a series of treaty negotiations among the Balkan states. These treaties were encouraged by Russia in order to build a bulwark against further expansion of the Austro-Hungarian Empire into the Balkans. Serbia, Bulgaria, Montenegro, and Greece eventually came to be integrated into a general Balkan alliance.

By the middle of 1912, it became apparent to Russia and the Austro-Hungarian Empire that the Balkan nations were on a war footing and that the likely target of the war was the apparently decaying Ottoman Empire. The Tzar and the Austrian Emperor tried to dissuade the allied Balkan countries from attacking the Ottomans. The two emperors acted too late. In October 1912, Macedonian forces attacked Ottoman troops. The other Balkan powers immediately joined in the war, with the exception of Romania, which had not been included in any of the Balkan bilateral or multilateral military treaties. The war ended in 1913 with the signing of The Treaty of London. The Treaty led to major losses of territory for the Ottomans and significant territorial gains for most of the participants. But the treaty left several major territorial issues unresolved. Because it had stayed out of the war, Romania did not share in the carving up of Ottoman land.

After the war, Bulgaria felt that it had not been justly compensated for the role in had played in pushing the Ottomans out of the region. It was particularly upset that Greece and Serbia wanted Macedonian lands that Bulgaria believed it should receive (Jelavich 1983). In June 1913, Bulgaria declared war on Greece and Serbia. Greece and Serbia had signed a secret mutual defense treaty that required them to assist each other in the event of a Bulgarian attack on either. Thus, both went to war against Bulgaria. Military forces from Montenegro, Romania, and the Ottoman Empire joined Greece and Serbia. Bulgaria was defeated in little more than a month of fighting. The war ended with the signing of the Treaty of Bucharest in August 1913. The terms of the treaty resulted in Serbia almost doubling in size, as it acquired a large part of Macedonia. Greece also gained territory and Romania was awarded southern Dobrodgea. The Treaty of Bucharest, at the urging of Italy and the Austro-Hungarian Empire, established an independent Albania. Both Italy and the Austro-Hungarian Empire had hoped that an independent Albania would be able to limit Serbian access to the Adriatic, as well as access to Serbian ports by the Russian fleet. The new Albanian state was truncated geographically. It did not include all of the land that had a significant, if not a majority, Albanian presence. Albanian nationalists were disappointed with the new state's boundary. The nationalists never gave up on the idea of a "Greater Albania," which they saw as including all lands where Albanians lived, not just the lands assigned to the newly formed rump state. This idea of a "Greater Albania" has reemerged, leading to warfare in Kosovo and Macedonia.

The Conservative Party held power during the second Balkan War. At the war's end, Karol replaced them with the Liberal Party. Ioan I. C. Bratianu became Prime Minister. Ioan I. C. Bratianu was the son of Ion C. Bratianu. Ioan I. C. Bratianu had studied in Bucharest and, then, like his father had gone to Paris for further education. In 1895, at the age of 31, Ioan I. C. Bratianu was elected to parliament. In 1908, at the age of 44, he was appointed Prime Minister for the first time. He was Prime Minister in 1908, 1909 to 1910, 1911, 1914 to1918, 1918 to 1919, 1922 to 1926, and from June 1927 to November 1927.

Gavrilo Princip, a young Serb nationalist, shot and killed Archduke Franz Ferdinand of Austria and his wife on June 28, 1914 in the Bosnian city of Sarajevo. The Archduke was heir to the Habsburg throne. Few Europeans of the time could have expected what would follow from this act of political terrorism.

Franz Ferdinand's assassination gave Austro-Hungarian "hawks" the opportunity for which they had been waiting. The Austro-Hungarian pro-war faction already had secured Germany's support for any action that it decided to take against Serbia. It, however, did not inform King Emmanuel of Italy's government of its intentions. This proved to be a serious error, because it allowed Italy to renounce its obligations of mutual defense under the provisions of the Triple Alliance Treaty of 1883. Under the provisions of the Treaty's renewal in 1883, Italy and Austria-Hungary agreed that either state needed to consult the other and work out terms of compensation with its partner if either of them intended to change the status quo in the Balkans (Jelavich 1983).

In July 1914, Austria-Hungary delivered a diplomatic note to the Serbs. Among other things, the Austro-Hungarian Empire demanded that it be allowed to conduct its own independent investigation in Serbia and Bosnia of the circumstances surrounding the assassination. The Serbs rejected the Austro-Hungarian ultimatum. Austria-Hungary responded by declaring war on Serbia on July 28.

On July 29, Nicholas II of Russia mobilized his forces. Russia could not accept a Serbian defeat. Russia had allowed the Habsburgs to annex Bosnia-Herzegovina. To now allow its Serbian ally to be defeated by the Dual Monarchy would be to surrender its status as a Great Power with critical interests in the Balkans. Moreover, its claims to be the protector of Orthodox Christians would prove to have been merely bombastic rhetoric. Germany responded to Russian mobilization by declaring war of Russia and its ally, France. Germany, at the time, felt that they could defeat the French, as they had done in 1870, before Russia's mobilization was complete. On August 4, 1914, Britain responded to Germany's declaration of war with France and Russia by declaring war on Germany.

As the Central Powers and the Triple Entente maneuvered to prepare for war, Romania was divided as to whom it should support. Karol and the Conservative Party leaned toward the Central Powers. Karol, after all, was a former Catholic and a southern German who had cultural affinities with the Austrian Habsburgs. Moreover, he was a Hohenzollern and a cousin to Germany's Kaiser Wilhelm II. In addition,

Romania had signed a secret treaty, and periodically renewed it, with Italy, Germany, and the Austro-Hungarian Empire.

Ioan I. C. Bratianu and the Liberal Party supported the Triple Entente. Many of the original founders of the Liberal Party had studied in France and remained Francophones all of their lives. The major leaders of first generation of the Liberal Party also had been an active part of the "Generation of 1848." They had fought in the uprisings in Paris and in Romania and remained more or less committed to the cause of the "48ers." In addition, the Liberal Party's second generation of leaders, such as the Romanian Prime Minister Ioan I. C. Bratianu, had studied in Paris, like the earlier leaders.

The Liberal Party, long identified with the cause of Romanian integration and independence, also had difficulty entering into an alliance that included the Ottomans, who had agreed to go to war as Germany's ally. They also did not want to ally themselves in a war on behalf of the Austro-Hungarian Empire, which they saw as the illegitimate occupier of Romanian territories in Transylvania, Bukovina, and the Banat.

The issue of Transylvania continued to spoil relations between the Dual Monarchy and Romania. The issue of Transylvania had long complicated relations between Romania and Hungary, both of which claimed the area and saw control over it as essential to their national identity and realization of their national "destiny." Late in the 17th century, the Habsburgs wrenched control of Hungary and Transylvania from the Ottoman Empire. Transylvania was incorporated into the Habsburg Empire as a principality and the Emperor assumed the title "Prince of Transylvania" along with that of "King of Hungary."

Under imperial rule, three nationality groups were given extensive political rights. These were the Magyars (Hungarians), the Germans, who had moved into the region in the 12th century and were referred to as Saxons, and the Szecklers. The Szecklers were a Magyarized population that had been sent into Transylvania and other border areas of the Magyar kingdom to build defensive militarized village outposts. The Saxons had developed a string of semi-autonomous cities across Transylvania. These cities were economically powerful settlements. They became the foundation on which Transylvania developed an advanced economy in the 18th and 19th centuries. Swabian Germans also had moved into the region in the Middle Ages. They were concentrated in the Banat, especially in and around the city of Timisoara.

The Romanians, who made up a majority of Transylvania's population, were not recognized as a national minority with their own political rights. Under the Habsburgs, the Lutheran, Catholic, Calvinist, and Unitarian churches were accorded state recognition. The Romanian Orthodox Church was not recognized by the imperial regime. In the 1700s, recognition was given to a Romanian Uniate Church. Tied to Rome, this church used an Orthodox liturgy. It attracted a large number of converts from the Romanian Orthodox Church, especially from among those Romanians who aspired to upward mobility within the imperial system. The creation of the Uniate church was partly the result of the Roman Catholic Church's attempt to offset losses in its membership because of the Reformation. The formation of the Uniate tradition was also supported inside the Roman Catholic Church by a small number of theologians and clergy who saw the Easter rite liturgies as more moving spiritual experiences than was the case with their own Latin liturgy. The Eastern liturgies, to these Roman Catholic "Orientalists," provided a deeper a and more significant experience of the mystery and awe of the Sacred than did the Roman Catholic liturgy standardized at the Council of Trento.

The Uniate tradition was useful to the Habsburgs for the simple reason that it was useful a means for tying populations in border regions to the empire. The Uniate branch of Roman Catholicism was a religion of the borderlands between the Latin Christianity of western European kingdoms and the Orthodox Christianity of eastern European kingdoms. The Habsburgs supported the Uniates in Transylvania and in Galicia. By supporting Uniates, the Habsburgs enhanced their "standing" as the major defender and promoter of Catholicism in Europe. Catholicism helped give the empire an identity and a symbolic unity that it otherwise lacked (Taylor 1948; Lieven 2000).

By the end of the 16th century, a large part of the aristocracy and peasantry in most of the crown lands of the Austrian Empire were Protestant. In alliance with the Roman Catholic Church, the Habsburgs, relying heavily on the Jesuit order, mounted a highly successful counter-reformation in the territories under their control. The counter-reformation brought large numbers of the great landowners back to Catholicism and with them came their peasants. However, despite the success of the Habsburg's counter-reformation efforts, pockets of resistance to Catholicism remained. Resistance was especially strong among the minor gentry in Bohemia and Transylvania and in the Eastern parts of Transylvania, again among the minor gentry and the Saxon populations in Transylvania's German towns. With reconversion to Catholicism beginning to meet violent resistance in parts of the Habsburg crownlands, the empire became more tolerant toward the Protestants and turned its attention to the conversion of the Orthodox believers in Galacia and Transylvania; hence, the formation of the Uniate tradition in Transylvania in 1699. The Eastern Orthodox Church had a long standing history of opposing the Uniates, wherever they appeared. In 1839 the Orthodox Church in Russia lobbied the Tzar to ban the Uniate Church throughout his territories, which he did. Uniate property was confiscated and turned over to the Russian Orthodox Church and Uniate believers were strongly "encouraged," if not coerced, into joining Russian Orthodox congregations. Stalin would repeat this ban in the 20th century and the Romanian communists would do the same thing after World War II.

The Split between Eastern and Western Christianity

The split between Eastern and Western forms of Christianity has a long history and it involved differences in canon law, liturgy, theology, and secular politics. Accumulating differences in all three areas, in Christianity's early centuries easily could be seen as examples of differences within a larger unity. However, as these differences emerged and coalesced, unity between Christianity in the East and West became harder to maintain. One of the earliest significant rifts between church authorities in Rome and Constantinople had emerged around the *iconoclastic* policies of the Byzantine emperors between 762 and 843 (see Fletcher 1997). Under these policies, all "graven" religious images were to be destroyed, regardless of the medium in which they were presented. The *iconoclasts* and their supporters had come to believe that religious representations were being venerated, in and of themselves, rather than what the representations supposedly signified. Western church authorities were strongly critical of Eastern *iconoclasm* and publicly attacked it. This is the first time such a major public denunciation of the Eastern Christians had come from the Roman Christians (Fletcher 1997).

Tensions between Rome and Constantinople coincided with a major political challenge of the latter's secular preeminence by the former. On Christmas Day in 800, Pope Leo III crowned the Frankish king, Charles (who we have come to know as *Charlemagne*), as the Holy

Roman Emperor. This was a direct challenge to the authority not only of the Byzantine throne, but also to the Eastern church. Eastern churches had come to see the emperor, whose seat only could be in Constantinople (after all it was the emperor Constantine who had made Christianity the state religion of the Roman empire), as a direct representative of God on earth. The emperor's power and authority were seen to be one and indivisible. There could not be two emperors. To Eastern church authorities and theologians, the Western church's coronation of another emperor was tantamount to heresy. It also was seen as a direct challenge to the political legitimacy, and all that entailed, of the "Second Rome" in Constantinople. To use modern political terminology, having a second emperor was tantamount to a secession from the then existing Christian empire.

Another significant conflict erupted between the two churches in 858 over who was the legitimate patriarch in Constantinople. In 858 the Eastern emperor had attempted to remove the then patriarch of Constantinople, Ignatius, and replace him with a man named Photius. At a church Council in Rome in 863, Pope Nicholas I declared that Ignatius was the legitimate patriarch. The fact that Rome had decided to formally intervene in this internal conflict in Constantinople infuriated a large part of the Eastern hierarchy. The Council's actions implied that the Church in Rome and its patriarch had a superior position of authority to other churches and other patriarchs. This was something that the Eastern churches and patriarchs could not accept. It violated long standing traditions of local patriarchal autonomy in matters of church organization and governance.

In 867 Photius declared that the Latin church was guilty of heresy and excommunicated the pope. The doctrinal issue that precipitated Photius' accusation was the Latin insertion of the word *filique* into the section of the church's creed dealing with the nature of the Holy Spirit (the "third person" in the Trinitarian conception of God). The use of the word *filique* changed the nature of Christian theology, according to Photius and like minded theologians. Its use declared that the Holy Spirit proceeded from the Father and from the Son, rather than just from the Father, as the Eastern Christians believed. This distinction became, and continues to be, the main theological conflict between what became the Roman and the various Orthodox Churches.

Late in 867 a new emperor took the throne in Constantinople. He removed Photius and restored Ignatius as patriarch. Ignatius repealed the excommunication of the pope, which the Western church had not recognized. Tensions between Rome and Constantinople, at least on the immediate issues of the day, were reduced and a formal split between the two traditions was avoided.

However, the two churches continued to view each other with suspicion and distrust. Rome continued to pursue policies designed to give it the preeminent position in the Christian world, while Constantinople continued to defend church traditions which recognized its autonomy and its primacy as the first church among equal churches. Over the next two centuries the two traditions entered into direct conflicts over missionary activities. Both the Western and Eastern emperors used their churches as instruments of conquest in the Balkans and in Eastern and Central Europe (see Fletcher 1997 for an excellent discussion of the conflicts between Eastern and Western missionaries).

In 1054, matters came to a head. A long-term accumulation of differences, grievances, and conflicts led to a formal split between the Latin church and the Orthodox churches. The Roman Pope, now the overwhelming power in Latin Christianity, and the Patriarch of Constantinople exchanged mutual recriminations and mutual ex-communications, leading to a formal division of the European Christian world. There might have been possibilities for overcoming this conflict after 1054. But these possibilities disappeared when the Western Christian armies that formed the Fourth Crusade attacked and plundered Constantinople in 1204, rendering the Eastern empire more vulnerable to defeat by the encroaching Islamic armies.

In the division between the two forms of Christianity, Romania's church sided with the Eastern patriarchs and Romania's elite defined itself as part of the Near East. As a result, Romania came to be recognized as part of the Orient. It was seen to be part of Europe, geographically, but not in Europe, culturally. Rather, it was defined as part of the Greek "commonwealth" of peoples, which, after the fall of Constantinople to Islamic armies, was seen as a broad swath of people who shared certain general cultural characteristics, chief among them, a commitment to what came to be called the "Orthodox" tradition. It was this religious tradition and all that it implied that the Uniates were seen as undermining in Transylvania. The Uniates were perceived, despite their Romanian nationalism, as agents of the Catholic Church and, hence, of the West. They were defined as a "fifth" column, so to speak, whose goal was to detach Romania from its historical inclinations and move into the orbit of the Vatican and the Western powers, principally the Habsburgs.

The Revolution of 1848 in Transylvania

In Transylvania, Romanian intellectuals carried on a long struggle for recognition of their political and social rights, which moved from demands for equality with other groups to demands for independence and integration with the Regat. Growing Romanian nationalism came into direct conflict with growing nationalism among the Magyars. Matters came to a head in 1848. Revolutions had erupted in Vienna and then in Hungary in March. The Hungarian uprising was lead by the liberal, revolutionary nationalist Lajos Kossuth. At Kossuth's urging, the Hungarian revolutionaries advanced a radical nationalist agenda, coupled with more modest social and economic agendas, except as these bore on the issue of the Magyar nation. Kossuth proposed and had passed at a Diet (a representative assembly that was more feudal in nature than it was parliamentary) held in Bratislava in March 1848, a set of proposals that came to be known as the "March Laws" (Taylor 1948). These laws were meant to redefine the nature of the Magyars' relationship with Vienna and, hence, the very nature of the Habsburg Empire, itself. The proposed laws, which would be realized partially in the *Ausgleich of 1867,* that created the Austro-Hungarian dual monarchy, demanded that the ties between Hungary and the emperor be defined as a personal union; that the Hungarian Chancellery in Vienna be eliminated; that there be created an autonomous Viceroy in Budapest, who would govern Hungary independent of the emperor; that a Hungarian emissary be attached to the imperial court; that Hungary would be given its own army and budget; and that Hungary be given the right to form its own foreign policy. The proposed laws also demanded that Hungary be allowed to create its own representative parliament and its own cabinet, responsible to the parliament. The parliament would be based on a restricted franchise but would be designed to represent the interests of the Hungarian magnates, the lesser nobility, the bourgeoisie, and the towns. According to what Kossuth proposed, Magyar was to be the official language of Hungary. No one who did not speak the language would be able to stand for election to parliament or serve as a minister. Kossuth also proposed that the peasant *Robot* (feudal work requirements) be abolished and that feudal landlords be compensated for their loss of peasant labor, and the landlords would retain their control over the administration of local areas (Taylor 1948). If these had been adopted, the Kingdom of St. Stephen, which would include all of the "historical" Magyar territories, would have become a mere dominion of Austria, rather than an integral part of it. The laws also would have resulted in a substantial diminution of the political rights of national minorities inside of greater Hungary, a territory where ethnic Magyars actually would be a minority, themselves.

The Hungarian revolutionaries convened a Diet that met in the Transylvania city of Napoca, now called Cluj-Napoca. The Diet, in May 1848, passed a proposal that demanded the unification of Transylvania and Hungary. Emperor Ferdinand I, confronting revolutionary forces in Vienna, approved the union.

The events of 1848 radicalized Romanian nationalists. In April 1848, Romanian nationalists convened a gathering in Blaj. The first Blaj meeting set out an agenda for Romanian emancipation within Transylvania. Among other things, it called for the abolition of serfdom. This meeting served as the basis for a second and larger gathering in Blaj in May 1848. The second Blaj meeting rejected the merger of Transylvania with Hungary under the terms demanded by the Magyar nationalists. The Romanians adopted a set of demands that included establishing a proportionally elected popular assembly that would negotiate the terms of a union of Hungry and Transylvania. The Romanians demanded religious, political, social, and economic freedom and recognition of their language rights in Transylvania. They also pushed for the abolition of serfdom. The Romanians established a Romanian National Committee that was to serve as a provisional government sitting in Sibiu.

The split between Eastern and Western forms of Christianity has a long history and it involved differences in canon law, liturgy, theology, and secular politics. Accumulating differences in all three areas, in Christianity's early centuries easily could be seen as examples of differences within a larger unity. However, as these differences emerged and coalesced, unity between Christianity in the East and West became harder to maintain. One of the earliest significant rifts between church authorities in Rome and Constantinople had emerged around the iconoclastic policies of the Byzantine emperors between 762 and 843 (see Fletcher 1997). Under these policies, all "graven" religious images were to be destroyed, regardless of the medium in which they were presented. The *iconoclasts* and their supporters had come to believe that religious representations were being venerated, in and of themselves, rather than what the representations supposedly signified. Western church authorities were strongly critical of Eastern *iconoclasm* and publicly attacked it. This is the first time such a major public denunciation of the Eastern Christians had come from the Roman Christians (Fletcher 1997).

Tensions between Rome and Constantinople coincided with a major political challenge of the latter's secular preeminence by the former. On Christmas Day in 800, Pope Leo III crowned the Frankish king, Charles (who we have come to know as *Charlemagne*), as the Holy Roman Emperor. This was a direct challenge to the authority not only of the Byzantine throne, but also to the Eastern church. Eastern churches had come to see the emperor, whose seat only could be in Constantinople (after all it was the emperor Constantine who had made Christianity the state religion of the Roman empire), as a direct representative of God on earth. The emperor's power and authority were seen to be one and indivisible. There could not be two emperors. To Eastern church authorities and theologians, the Western church's coronation of another emperor was tantamount to heresy. It also was seen as a direct challenge to the political legitimacy, and all that entailed, of the "Second Rome" in Constantinople. To use modern political terminology, having a second emperor was tantamount to a secession from the then existing Christian empire.

Another significant conflict erupted between the two churches in 858 over who was the legitimate patriarch in Constantinople. In 858 the Eastern emperor had attempted to remove the then patriarch of Constantinople, Ignatius, and replace him with a man named Photius. At a church Council in Rome in 863, Pope Nicholas I declared that Ignatius was the legitimate patriarch. The fact that Rome had decided to formally intervene in this internal conflict in Constantinople infuriated a large part of the Eastern hierarchy. The Council's actions implied that the Church in Rome and its patriarch had a superior position of authority to other churches and other patriarchs. This was something that the Eastern churches and patriarchs could not accept. It violated long standing traditions of local patriarchal autonomy in matters of church organization and governance.

In 867 Photius declared that the Latin church was guilty of heresy and excommunicated the pope. The doctrinal issue that precipitated Photius' accusation was the Latin insertion of the word *filique* into the section of the church's creed dealing with the nature of the Holy Spirit (the "third person" in the Trinitarian conception of God). The use of the word *filique* changed the nature of Christian theology, according to Photius and like minded theologians. Its use declared that the Holy Spirit proceeded from the Father and from the Son, rather than just from the Father, as the Eastern Christians believed. This distinction became, and continues to be, the main theological conflict between what became the Roman and the various Orthodox Churches.

Late in 867 a new emperor took the throne in Constantinople. He removed Photius and restored Ignatius as patriarch. Ignatius repealed the excommunication of the pope, which the Western church had not recognized. Tensions between Rome and Constantinople, at least on the immediate issues of the day, were reduced and a formal split between the two traditions was avoided.

However, the two churches continued to view each other with suspicion and distrust. Rome continued to pursue policies designed to give it the preeminent position in the Christian world, while Constantinople continued to defend church traditions which recognized its autonomy and its primacy as the first church among equal churches. Over the next two centuries the two traditions entered into direct conflicts over missionary activities. Both the Western and Eastern emperors used their churches as instruments of conquest in the Balkans and in Eastern and Central Europe (see Fletcher 1997 for an excellent discussion of the conflicts between Eastern and Western missionaries).

In 1054, matters came to a head. A long-term accumulation of differences, grievances, and conflicts led to a formal split between the Latin church and the Orthodox churches. The Roman Pope, now the overwhelming power in Latin Christianity, and the Patriarch of Constantinople exchanged mutual recriminations and mutual ex-communications, leading to a formal division of the European Christian world. There might have been possibilities for overcoming this conflict after 1054. But these possibilities disappeared when the Western Christian armies that formed the Fourth Crusade attacked and plundered Constantinople in 1204, rendering the Eastern empire more vulnerable to defeat by the encroaching Islamic armies.

In the division between the two forms of Christianity, Romania's church sided with the Eastern patriarchs and Romania's elite defined itself as part of the Near East. As a result, Romania came to be recognized as part of the Orient. It was seen to be part of Europe, geographically, but not in Europe, culturally. Rather, it was defined as part of the Greek "commonwealth" of peoples, which, after the fall of Constantinople to Islamic armies, was seen as a broad swath of people who shared certain general cultural characteristics, chief among them, a commitment to what came to be called the "Orthodox" tradition. It was this religious tradition and all that it implied that the Uniates were seen as undermining in Transylvania. The Uniates were perceived, despite their Romanian nationalism, as agents of the Catholic Church and, hence, of the West. They were defined as a "fifth" column, so to speak, whose goal was to detach Romania from its historical inclinations and move into the orbit of the Vatican and the Western powers, principally the Habsburgs.

The Revolution of 1848 in Transylvania

In Transylvania, Romanian intellectuals carried on a long struggle for recognition of their political and social rights, which moved from demands for equality with other groups to demands for independence and integration with the Regat. Growing Romanian nationalism came into direct conflict with growing nationalism among the Magyars. Matters came to a head in 1848. Revolutions had erupted in Vienna and then in Hungary in March. The Hungarian uprising was lead by the liberal, revolutionary nationalist Lajos Kossuth. At Kossuth's urging, the Hungarian revolutionaries advanced a radical nationalist agenda, coupled with more modest social and economic agendas, except as these bore on the issue of the Magyar nation. Kossuth proposed and had passed at a Diet (a representative assembly that was more feudal in nature than it was parliamentary) held in Bratislava in March 1848, a set of proposals that came to be known as the "March Laws" (Taylor 1948). These laws were meant to redefine the nature of the Magyars' relationship with Vienna and, hence, the very nature of the Habsburg Empire, itself. The proposed laws, which would be realized partially in the *Ausgleich of 1867,* that created the Austro-Hungarian dual monarchy, demanded that the ties between Hungary and the emperor be defined as a personal union; that the Hungarian Chancellery in Vienna be eliminated; that there be created an autonomous Viceroy in Budapest, who would govern

Hungary independent of the emperor; that a Hungarian emissary be attached to the imperial court; that Hungary would be given its own army and budget; and that Hungary be given the right to form its own foreign policy. The proposed laws also demanded that Hungary be allowed to create its own representative parliament and its own cabinet, responsible to the parliament. The parliament would be based on a restricted franchise but would be designed to represent the interests of the Hungarian magnates, the lesser nobility, the bourgeoisie, and the towns. According to what Kossuth proposed, Magyar was to be the official language of Hungary. No one who did not speak the language would be able to stand for election to parliament or serve as a minister. Kossuth also proposed that the peasant *Robot* (feudal work requirements) be abolished and that feudal landlords be compensated for their loss of peasant labor, and the landlords would retain their control over the administration of local areas (Taylor 1948). If these had been adopted, the Kingdom of St. Stephen, which would include all of the "historical" Magyar territories, would have become a mere dominion of Austria, rather than an integral part of it. The laws also would have resulted in a substantial diminution of the political rights of national minorities inside of greater Hungary, a territory where ethnic Magyars actually would be a minority, themselves.

The Hungarian revolutionaries convened a Diet that met in the Transylvania city of Napoca, now called Cluj-Napoca. The Diet, in May 1848, passed a proposal that demanded the unification of Transylvania and Hungary. Emperor Ferdinand I, confronting revolutionary forces in Vienna, approved the union.

The events of 1848 radicalized Romanian nationalists. In April 1848, Romanian nationalists convened a gathering in Blaj. The first Blaj meeting set out an agenda for Romanian emancipation within Transylvania. Among other things, it called for the abolition of serfdom. This meeting served as the basis for a second and larger gathering in Blaj in May 1848. The second Blaj meeting rejected the merger of Transylvania with Hungary under the terms demanded by the Magyar nationalists. The Romanians adopted a set of demands that included establishing a proportionally elected popular assembly that would negotiate the terms of a union of Hungry and Transylvania. The Romanians demanded religious, political, social, and economic freedom and recognition of their language rights in Transylvania. They also pushed for the abolition of serfdom.

The Romanians established a Romanian National Committee that was to serve as a provisional government sitting in Sibiu. When the Hungarian Diet refused to abolish serfdom, there was widespread violence among the Romanian peasantry. Peasants rioted, attacking and burning estates of the Hungarian nobility. The Hungarian revolutionary forces responded with violence, repressing the peasants through arrests and killings. When the Habsburg armies attacked the Romanian National Committee and arrested several of its members in Sibiu, a combined force of armed peasants and Romanian soldiers from the imperial army forced the Habsburgs to release their prisoners.

Romanian nationalists also organized in the Banat, which also was under the control of the Habsburg Empire. Banat Romanians met for a second time in Logoj in June 1848 and created a popular militia. Among their demands was that that the Serbian Orthodox Church end its control over the Romanian Orthodox Church in the Banat.

Transylvania Romanians met for a third time in Blaj in mid-September 1848. The meeting restated the demands made in May. The assembly demanded that a truly representative parliament be convened in Transylvania, that Transylvania not be united with Hungary, and that serfdom be abolished. The third Blaj assembly elected another provisional government and created a popular militia.

In October 1848, the Habsburg military commander in Transylvania moved against the Hungarian revolutionaries. The Romanian revolutionaries, having been promised that the emperor would recognize their national rights, sided with the Austrian forces and fought against the Hungarian revolutionaries. In the meantime, revolutionaries from Wallachia tried to end the fighting between the Hungarians and the Romanians. A compromise of sorts was reached when the Transylvania Diet adopted a law dealing with nationalities that was more acceptable to the Romanians. However, the Diet, while compromising on the law pertaining to nationalities, still demanded unification of the province with Hungary. In August, before any unification could take place, Kossuth's forces were defeated in Transylvania and the empire reasserted its control over the province.

Transylvanian Autonomy under Magyar Rule

In 1861, the empire, in two decrees, granted more autonomy to its provinces. Transylvania reopened its Diet. The Diet met in Sibiu in 1863 and 1864. The elections for representatives to the Diet had been conducted under the terms of laws that broadly extended the voting franchise. Because of the larger pool of eligible voters, Romanian delegates held the greatest number of seats in the Diet, followed by Hungarians, then by Germans. The Diet granted Romanians a number of important political and cultural rights, including the identification of Romanian as an official language in Transylvania. The emperor also recognized Andrei Saguna as Romanian Orthodox Metropolitan of Transylvania, with his seat being in Sibiu in 1864. This emancipated the Romanian Orthodox Church from Serbian control. In 1855, the Romanian Uniates (Greek Catholics) had been allowed to seat Alexandru Streca Sulutiu as a Metropolitan in Alba Iulia. With the calling of the Diet, Transylvania's Romanians had reason to hope that their situation in the principality had finally showed promise of improvement. This, however, was not to be. A large number of influential Hungarian nationalists rejected what the Diet had tried to accomplish and sought to overturn the gains in had granted the Romanians.

From the middle 1860s on, the Habsburg Empire was facing several major crises. Prussia had achieved hegemony in Germany and was creating a unified state under Hohenzollern control. It was clear to Austria that it would be excluded from the newly forming German Reich. The expansion of Prussian power reduced Habsburg influence in the German lands. The Habsburgs also lost control of Venice. With the loss of Venice, the Habsburgs no longer had a presence on the Italian peninsula and their position as a naval power in the western Adriatic was weakened. Through its control of Slovenia and Dalmatia, however, the empire retained a powerful presence in the eastern Adriatic.

The empire's problems further were complicated by continuing Hungarian demands for greater autonomy. In 1865, bowing to Hungarian pressures, the emperor dismissed the Diet and convened another in Cluj. Using the electoral law of 1791, the Cluj Diet was dominated by Magyar nobility. Romanians only had a small representation. The Cluj Diet voted to unify Transylvania and Hungary. The Diet also annulled the laws adopted in Sibiu that extended equal civil status to Romanians and that recognized Romanian as an official language of Transylvania.

In 1867, Austria and Hungary agreed to a compromise on the nature of the imperial state (the so-called *Ausgleich of 1867*). Franz Joseph was recognized as Emperor of Austria and King of Hungary.

Vienna was given control over foreign and military affairs for the two regions, as well as control over Austria's internal affairs. Budapest was given the right to develop its own institutions to govern its internal affairs. The *Ausgleich* also resulted in a division of colonial authority, with Dalmatia, Slovenia, and Bukovina falling under Austrian control and Croatia, Slovenia, the Vojvodina, and Transylvania being assigned to Hungary (Jelavich 1983). Retaining Slovenia and Dalmatia, was crucial to Austria. Without these lands, Austria would not have access to the sea, except through territories where Hungary had primary responsibility for administration.

Hungary used the terms of the *Ausgleich* to incorporate Transylvania into the Hungarian kingdom. One dimension of incorporation was the development and implementation of a comprehensive process of Magyarization of the various nationalities. As Transylvania's largest population group, Romanians were especially targeted for Magyarization. The education laws passed in 1879, 1883, 1891, and 1907 all worked to Magyarize Transylvania's schools (Seton-Watson 1934). Education laws passed by Hungary also made it more difficult for Romanian schools to meet state requirements and many of them had to close.

Romanians who did not have the opportunity to undergo Magyarization or who rejected the process faced highly restricted mobility opportunities in Transylvania. They were cut off from access to universities, to the professions, and to employment or office holding in the state sector.

Before 1918, the vast proportion of Romanians in Transylvania lived in rural areas or small towns. Only twenty per cent of Romanians lived in urban areas in Transylvania as late as 1910 (Livezeanu 1995), this was a legacy of the period when Romanians, by law, had been prevented from living in Romanian cities. The vast majority of the urban Romanians were in small towns, rather than large cities. Within the cities, as Livezeanu (1995) notes, the Romanians were highly ghettoized. Because they were ghettoized, the Romanians had very limited economic opportunities. Hungarians, Germans, and Jews, many of whom had assimilated into Hungarian culture, dominated the economic life of Transylvania's cities at the expense of the Romanians.

Most of the Romanians living in Transylvania before World War I were peasants who had small farms or worked on the large estates of the

Magyar nobility. The larger part of the peasantry had an economically marginal existence and could neither read nor write. Under the electoral law adopted by Hungary in 1874, the bulk of the Romanian peasantry, because of their poverty and/or their illiteracy, was denied voting rights. This also was the case for impoverished Romanians who lived and worked in Transylvania's cities.

As early as 1868, Romanians agitated against the repeal of the laws passed by the Sibiu Diet. At this time, the Romanian elites in Transylvania were divided as to how to respond to the new order the Magyars were putting in place in the formerly autonomous principality. One group stressed the need for Romanians to withdraw from public life and organize their own community institutions in those areas where they were a majority. Another group stressed the need for Romanian political engagement.

In 1869, Romanians organized a National Party. The party demanded provincial autonomy and the creation of a democratically elected provincial parliament. Romanians in the Banat also organized themselves into a National Party. Both of the National Parties, which would unify in 1881, wanted recognition of Romanian national rights in an autonomous Transylvania. Especially important to the Romanians was the protection of their language rights, including the right to be educated in their national language. Education in Romanian became especially important after 1875. Kalman Tiza, a militant Hungarian nationalist, was elected Prime Minister of Hungary in 1875. Tiza pursued a policy of aggressive Magyarization, directed largely at Romanians.

The tension between Romanians and Hungarians in Transylvania intensified. Both Romanians and Magyars had come to see control of Transylvania as essential to their national identity. Magyars and Romanians each constructed their own "histories" of Transylvania to establish the justice of their claims over Transylvania and undermine the claims of the other. In some cases Romanians and Magyars even identified same heroes under different names and used their legacies to buttress their claims that they were the rightful rulers of Transylvania. For example, the Hungarians count John Hunyadi as one of their nation's leading heroes because of his wars against the Ottomans. The Romanians call him Iancu Hunedoara and recognize him as one of Romania's great proto-nationalists.

In 1892, leaders of the unified Romanian National Party wrote a petition to the Austro-Hungarian Emperor complaining of Romanians' situation in Transylvania and asking that he redress their grievances. Franz Joseph rejected their petition. Magyar authorities arrested the leaders of the National Party in 1893 and tried them in 1894 on charges of fomenting opposition to the Hungarian state. Of the twenty-nine leaders tried, fifteen were convicted and sentenced to prison.

Between 1894 and 1914, Romanians in Transylvania defined themselves as an oppressed minority in a state that was bent on liquidating their culture. Given Vienna's inability and/or unwillingness to force Hungary to change its policies toward Romanian Transylvanians, Romanian nationalists in the Regat came to see not only Hungary, but also the Habsburg Empire as a whole, as its enemy. This made Romanian nationalists reluctant to enter the war on the side of the Central Powers, although this was what Karol I wanted. The nationalists wanted nothing to do with an alliance they believed would contribute to the consolidation of Magyar rule over Romanians in Transylvania.

The Romanian political elite also resisted siding with the Central Powers for cultural reasons. Many in Romania's political elite were Francophones. Educated in Paris, they strongly identified with French culture. When the war started, Romania, like Italy, which also had treaty obligations to the Central Powers, refused to fight against the Triple Entente of Great Britain, France, and the Russian Empire.

4

World War I Through World War II: From Building A Greater Romania to the Collapse of the Old Order, 1914-1945

Karol I died in October 1914. His nephew Ferdinand I succeeded him. Karol's reign lasted forty-eight years. For most of the period of his rule, the monarchy was the preeminent power in Romania's internal affairs. Karol I made use of his considerable political skills to balance the political demands of the urban bourgeoisie, largely represented by the National Liberal Party, and the boyars, represented by the National Conservative Party. He was able to create this political equilibrium because of the overall weakness of the classes in which these two parties were based. Neither class had the capacity to take control of the Romanian State. While the boyars were the economically stronger of the two, electoral laws made it difficult for them to take control of the state. Moreover, the boyars had significant internal divisions of wealth, rank, and size of property holdings that limited its political effectiveness. The boyars also were locked in a growing struggle with agrarian capitalists for dominance over accumulation in the countryside. Despite their precarious position, however, the boyars saw themselves as *the* embodiment and conservators of Romanian culture.

To the boyars, Romania was and always should be an agrarian society based on estate production. The boyars saw their class as having defended Romanian territorial integrity from the threats posed by the Russian and Ottoman Empires in the east and the threats from Austria-Hungary and the Catholic Church in the west. The boyars and the conservative intellectuals who identified with them saw Romania's urban bourgeoisie and urban intelligentsia as threats to the old order over which the boyars presided. From the perspective of the boyars and the conservative intellectuals, the bourgeoisie and the urban intellectuals intended to destroy the old Romania in the name of modernization and progress.

The boyars looked to the throne to insure that their economic position was not undermined by policies supported by the National Liberal

Party. The boyars, the conservative intellectuals, and the National Conservative Party did not have any coherent political agenda for Romania other than defending boyar economic interests, protecting traditional values and culture, and maintaining a political system that insured the boyars' interests would be represented in the state.

Like the boyars, the bourgeoisie was internally divided. It was split between the petty bourgeoisie and the large bourgeoisie. It also was divided between those grounded in the private sector and those grounded in the state. Divisions also existed among private sector bourgeoisie based on the sector or sectors of activity in which they were involved. The bourgeoisie also was fragmented along ethnic lines. The principle ethnic cleavage was between the Jews and Romanians. The Romanian bourgeoisie does not appear to have held the same degree of animosity toward Greek, Armenian, German, or Turkish entrepreneurs or professionals as it did to Jews. Members of these nationality groups never faced the discrimination and exclusionary practices that Jews encountered. For example, they were not restricted from entering universities, the professions, or, even, the state bureaucracy.

What gave the Romanian bourgeoisie's various fractions their overall unity, other than a common commitment to maintaining private property, was a desire to reconstruct Romania along the lines of a modernizing Western European nation-state, taking into account the "unique" characteristics of the Romanian nation. The Romanian bourgeoisie, led by its cultural fraction, had come to see itself as the only group who could bring national unity and who could move Romania toward becoming a "modern" European society. At the same time, the Romanian bourgeoisie came to view the boyars, their political allies, and their intellectuals as agents of stagnation, if not reaction.

Karol's political genius lay in the fact that he gave partial support to both classes, without allowing one to gain ascendance over the other. When required, usually because of pending or actual crises, Karol supported Liberal proposals for modest social reform, most of which was directed at relieving immediate economic pressures on the peasantry in order to prevent or quell disorder. None of the reforms introduced ever attempted to fundamentally alter the nature of property relations and accumulation in the countryside. Karol also supported part of the Liberal and bourgeois agenda by supporting legislation that fostered urban capitalist development, under the control of the Romanian bourgeoisie.

Karol I supported the boyars by defending their accumulation rights. He never allowed land reform or political reform that would have undermined the boyars' class position. Karol repeatedly blocked reforms that would have expanded the franchise and thus would have reduced the likelihood that the boyars would be able to achieve electoral success. Karol, by rotating governments, also insured that the boyars would have an opportunity to govern the country and share in the spoils that came from controlling the government. By developing working accommodations with the National Liberal and National Conservative Parties, Karol Insured that control of the government would remain in the hands of a small oligarchy drawn from the boyars and the bourgeoisie. Neither of these parties had an interest in challenging the role of the monarchy as the dominant political force in Romania.

The king was able to achieve a grand synthesis of the interests of the boyars and the bourgeoisie. Through the throne, the bourgeoisie and the boyars were united as the governing classes of the Romanian State. Because Karol did not have the power to become an absolute monarch and because neither the bourgeoisie nor the boyars were able to defeat each other and take control, the Romanian State was a fusion of medieval and modern structures. Its modern elements deformed its medieval elements and the medieval elements deformed its modern components. The Romanian State, as a result, was neither archaic nor modern. It was both, at the same time, making it an example of what Trotsky (1932) calls *mixed development*. Mixed development occurs when modern social forms are grafted on to and fused with pre-modern structures. The result often yields a deformed modernization.

The Romanian Constitution of 1866, as already noted, was modeled after the Prussian Constitution. It provided for three electoral "colleges" defined in terms of the levels of taxes paid. This type of electoral system was essentially "feudal," in that it was an estate-based system that rejected one of the core ideas of a liberal, constitutional system – individual equality. Those paying the top one-third of national taxes constituted one college, those paying the middle third were a second, and those paying the lowest third of taxes were the last electoral grouping. Each college elected an equal number of delegates to a convention, which then elected the parliament. This voting system guaranteed that the boyars and the bourgeoisie dominated the parliament and used it to serve their corporate interests. In addition, the constitution concentrated a high level of power in the throne. Among the more important powers given to the royal prince was the right to appoint and dismiss governments at will. This put the prince in a position of superiority to parliament. Karol also built the state bureaucracy. He designed it and extended it into all parts of the country. His hope had been that the bureaucracy would be an instrument to unify the principalities under the throne's control. He was only partly successful. The national bureaucracy never became established as completely autonomous from local forces. As often as not, the national bureaucracy was absorbed into local systems of power, becoming an instrument of local elites, rather than serving exclusively as an instrument of the national center. Officials of the national bureaucracies became incorporated into the networks of power of local rural, town, and urban elites. Often this resulted in distortions, on the local level, of national policies.

The bureaucracy Karol built eventually became one of Romania's dominant institutions. The Romanian bureaucracy was larger than either England's or France's (Longworth 1997). It absorbed large quantities of literate labor. Romanians called lower level state functionaries *"Cinces"* (Fivers), in reference to their low pay (Longworth 1997). Given their low pay, it was almost inevitable that bureaucrats would use the prerogatives of their office to increase their incomes. In Romania, holding a state office, no matter how petty, was viewed as far superior to employment in the private sector. Employment in the business sector was, and continues to be, stigmatized. Business was not something one did, if one aspired to be recognized as a "gentleman." In its upper reaches, the gentry and the urban bourgeoisie dominated the state bureaucracy.

One of the most important functions of any state bureaucracy is to develop an effective system for procuring revenue. The Romanian State was not successful in developing an efficient tax system and an efficient means for collecting taxes, partly as a result, financial difficulties continually plagued Romania. Throughout Karol's tenure, the state had financial problems, which were exacerbated by the perceived need to maintain a large military force. The ineffective and inefficient domestic tax system made it difficult for Romanian State to raise money on international credit markets, further complicating the state's financial population.

Under Karol's rule, the Romanian State had been built from above by the urban bourgeoisie and the boyars, in collaboration with the throne. Schopflin (1990) recognizes that there is an inherent contradiction in trying to create a state and society from above when this process is controlled by a political elite that really had no interest in reform and that sees itself as the carrier of modernization in a society they regard as backward. Under these conditions of state formation, it is difficult to develop a political system that represents the broad interests of the population.

The state lacked a mass base both in the peasantry and the emerging working classes. The rules of the political game were organized to exclude workers and peasants from participation in the political system under Karol, as it had been under Cuza. When the state confronted these groups in situations of conflict, it seldom hesitated in using repression to keep them under control. For example, Karol was willing to use military force against the peasantry when they rebelled. Such dramatic instances of repression, however, don't tell the whole story. The state used censorship, police spying, and various forms of intimidation to keep any potential opposition to the oligarchy from becoming a center of organized opposition to, or organized opposition within, the existing political framework. The state also allowed the two political parties to use the its coercive powers to engineer elections to produce the outcomes they wanted.

The Romanian State, like other states in Eastern and Central Europe was not based on the "rule of law." A state based in the rule of law recognizes the autonomy of private people from the state and recognizes the autonomy of the state from various corporate groups (Seligman 1992). This was not the case in Romania. Nor was it the case in Romania that individual rights were seen to be prior to collective rights. In Romania and elsewhere in Eastern and Central Europe, individual rights always were seen as contingent. They were concessions granted by the state and were recognized as long as they did not conflict with the perceived interests of the organic whole, as defined by the state.

In addition, in Romania, as well as in other parts of Eastern and Central Europe, the state was conceived in organic terms and did not recognize the idea, essential to the rule of law, that all persons were equal on the basis of shared citizenship in the state. We already have seen how the Romanian State attempted to limit the rights of citizenship of Jews. Jews were seen to be excludable from the state by virtue of the fact that they, in essence, were not part of the Romanian "community." Jews were seen to occupy a different "metaphysical universe," to use a concept of Vincent Wright (1978), from Romanians and, thus, undeserving of full membership in the Romanian State. Jews and others, especially Rroma, were not seen to possess the intrinsic human dignity that gave them the right to full participation in the Romanian polity.

According to Habermas (1989), the idea of the rule of law requires a specific philosophical base. First, the rule of law presumes that the basic unit of society is the private, autonomous individual. Each individual is a repository of intrinsic moral value that exists prior to the state. Individuals are not seen as being derived from the state; rather the state is seen to be constructed from the consent and assent of autonomous individuals who possess intrinsic rights that the state may not abridge. One of the most important of these is the right of the individual to effectively participate in the state, either directly or through elected representatives. Second, a state organized under the rule of law presumes law to be universal and binding on everyone, including the executive and judiciary. The state also is expected to acknowledge that there are to be no exemptions or special privileges written into the law for individuals or for corporate groups.

Third, the rule of law recognizes the division of society into public and private spheres. According to Habermas (1989: 83), where the rule of law prevails, basic rights are clearly identified. He states:

A set of basic rights concerned the sphere of the public engaged in rational-critical debate (freedom of opinion and speech, freedom of press, freedom of assembly and association, etc.) and the political function of private people in this public sphere (right of petition, equality of law, etc.). A second set of basic rights concerned the individual's status as a free human being, grounded in the intimate sphere of the patriarchal conjugal family (personal freedom, inviolability of the home, etc.). The third set of basic rights concerned the transactions of the private owners of property in the sphere of civil society (equality before the law, protection of private property, etc.). The basic rights guaranteed: the *spheres* of the public realm and of the private (with the intimate sphere at its core); the *institutions* and *instruments* of the public sphere on the hand (press, parties) and the foundation of private autonomy (family and property), on the other; finally, the *functions* of the private people, both their political ones as citizens and their economic ones as owners of commodities (and, as "human beings," those of individual communication, e.g. through inviolability of letters).

From 1866 on, none of Romania's regimes recognized the inviolability of such rights, making it difficult for the Romanian State to resist anti-democratic forces when they arose in the 1930s. Romania lacked the structural prerequisites that Habermas (1989) and Seligman (1992), among others, have identified as essential to the development of a state grounded in the rule of law. In this regard, Romania had not developed an autonomous national bourgeoisie. Rather, the bourgeoisie that formed in Romania largely was built by the state and depended on the state for its continued existence and expansion. A significant portion of the bourgeoisie was made up of national minorities, which, according to the prevailing Romanian political theory, never could be regarded as full members of the national community.

Romania also did not participate in the cultural transformations that, in the West, provided the philosophical underpinnings for the rule of law (Habermas 1989; Seligman 1992). Romania was outside of the European areas that were significantly influenced by the Enlightenment. Also, Romania, except among parts of the Hungarian and the German minority communities, had not undergone anything equivalent to the Protestant Reformation, which Seligman (1992) saw as essential to the development of a bourgeois state committed to the rule of law.

World War I Begins

In October 1914, Romania's Prime Minister, Ioan I. C. Bratianu, signed a secret agreement with the Tzar. Romania agreed to maintain a position of neutrality that generally favored the interests of the Triple Entente. In return, Russia agreed to support Romania's territorial claims against the Austro-Hungarian Empire and to award these territories to Romania if it occupied them before the end of the war. Bratianu also reached an agreement with Italy in which both states agreed to inform each other if they decided to enter the war and they agreed to assist one another if either was attacked by Austro-Hungarian forces.

Popular support for entering the war on the side of the Triple Entente rapidly grew between 1914 and 1916. Ferdinand I provided no resistance to entering the war on the side of the Triple Entente. Unlike his uncle, he did not share a sense of identification with the Hohenzollerns or the Habsburgs. The only opposition to abandoning neutrality came from the organized left. Romania's working class parties did not want to enter the war. They argued that this was a capitalist war and that participation in it was against the interests of the proletariat. For taking this stand, the working class parties were accused of acting in the interests of Germany and of the Jews, who, it was claimed, controlled the international socialist movement.

In 1915, the Central Powers informed Romania that if it entered the war on their side they would award Romania Bessarabia and Bucovina and, furthermore, they would guarantee to protect the rights of Transylvania's Romanians. In the meantime, Italy had entered the war on the side of the Entente, opening another front on which the Austro-Hungarians had to deploy troops. If the tide of war turned against the Central Powers and if they sued for peace before Romania entered the war, Romania would lose Transylvania and the other territories the Entente had promised to award to Romania for participating in the war as their ally.

With growing domestic pressure and the threat of an early victory by the Entente, Romania agreed to declare war on the Central Powers in August 1916. In return the Entente promised Romania Bucovina, the Banat, and Transylvania and said that they would support these territories being merged with Romania at the war's end. The king's council announced the declaration of war on August 27, 1916. On the same day, the Romanian army invaded Transylvania. Two days later they seized Cluj and began advancing on other Transylvania cities.

Bulgarian and German forces attacked Romania in the south and inflicted heavy casualties. The Germans and Austro-Hungarians launched a counter-attack in Transylvania and Moldova. Fighting on their own, the Romanian military was no match for the better equipped and more battle experienced armies of the Central Powers. In late November 1916, German and Bulgarian forces, pushing northward, entered Bucharest. The capital was not defended. The king and the government had evacuated to Iasi in Moldova, where it was protected by what was left of the Romanian army.

From its bases in Moldova, the remnants of the Romanian army regrouped. Assisted by a French military mission, the Romanians built a military force that fought the armies of the Central Powers to a stalemate in Moldova. Romania's military situation became untenable after the Russian Revolution. The new Russian government signed an armistice with the Central Powers on December 1917 and in March 1918 the Russians signed the Treaty of Brest-Litovsk which meant that Romania was the only Entente army left fighting on the Eastern front.

On December 9, 1917, Romania, over the strenuous objections of its allies in the Entente, signed an armistice with the Central Powers. Romania sent its military forces into Bessarabia to seize control of the province. The Russian government had no effective control over Bessarabia at this time. Its army had dissolved and the Russian civil administration had abandoned the region. The Russian regime broke diplomatic relations with Romania following the occupation of Bessarabia.

In late February 1918, the Germans sent Romania an ultimatum demanding that it sign a peace treaty with the Central Powers. The Germans set a high price for Romania's surrender, including significant territorial concessions. The Central Powers made it clear to Romania that it would be liquidated as an autonomous state if it failed to agree to the treaty's terms. General Averescu, who had been in command of the army that defeated the peasant uprising in 1907, was the Prime Minister. He signed a preliminary treaty in March 1918. After he signed the preliminary agreements, the king formed a new government that signed a final treaty in Bucharest in May 1918. However, before the Treaty of Bucharest was signed, the new Romanian government obtained recognition of Romania's conquest of Bessarabia, which served as an inducement for Romania to sign the separate peace treaty. Once Romania signed The Treaty of Bucharest, The Central Powers treated Romania as an occupied state.

The king did not return to Bucharest. He remained in Iasi. When it became apparent late in the summer of 1918 that the Central Powers were on the verge of defeat, Romania began preparing to reenter the war on the side of the Entente. On November 4, the Romanian army moved into and occupied Bucovina. The Austro-Hungarian Empire's forces had effectively dissolved in this region by the time Romania invaded. On November 10, 1918, Romania formally reentered the war on the side of the Entente. The next day, Germany surrendered to the Entente. Romania formally annexed Bucovina at the end of November 1918.

In early December 1918, the Romanians in Transylvania declared their intention to merge with the Regat. In the same month, the Transylvania Germans endorsed the Romanians' declaration for unification with the Regat. The Regat responded on December 28. The king declared the unification of Transylvania with the Regat. The Transylvania Romanians had "conditioned" their desire to merge with the Regat on the meeting of several key demands. The Transylvanians wanted the former principality's traditional autonomy to be respected, they wanted universal male suffrage and the formation of a democratic national assembly that recognized civil rights and the rights of national minorities, and they wanted national legislation that improved the legal positions of workers and peasants (Jelavich 1983).

At the end of the war, Hungary was in desperate straits. Following the collapse of the Habsburg Empire, a republican government took power. It was short lived, being replaced by a governing coalition of Social Democrats and Communists. Bela Kun, in March 1919, proclaimed a Hungarian Soviet government. A month later, Romanian troops crossed the Hungarian border and seized Budapest, forcing the Kun government to resign.

The Trianon Treaty of 1920 recognized Romania's merger with Transylvania. According to the terms of the Trianon Treaty, Romania was awarded not only Transylvania, but also large sections of Eastern Hungary, where significant numbers of Romanians lived. This included Crisana, Satu-Mare, Maramures, and part of the Banat. The last was divided between Romania and Serbia, with Romania getting control of Timisoara and the areas around it. In addition, Romania was allowed to retain control over Bukovina, Bessarabia, and Dobrodgea.

The annexation of Bessarabia presented several problems for Romania. It was a fairly large territory with over three million people, about sixty per cent of whom were Romanian (Jelavich 1983). The major minorities were Ukrainians, Russians, Bulgarians, and Tatars. The Romanians were concentrated in the central areas of the region, while the Ukrainians and Russians were in the north and the Bulgarians and Tatars were in the south.

Bessarabia had been under Russian control since 1812. During its dominion over Bessarabia, the Tzar had implemented policies of forced

Russification. Romanian language schools, cultural institutions, and publications were not permitted. Without these key institutions, the Bessarabia Romanians had not formed national movements as they had done in the Banat and Transylvania.

Bessarabia's economy was much like that of Moldova. It was based on an estate system of agricultural production. Most of the great estates had been owned by Russian boyars and worked by peasant labor. The Tzar had freed the peasants from serfdom in the 1860s. Even after emancipation, Bessarabia peasants, like their counterparts in Romania, had suffered from intense exploitation by the boyars.

When the Romanian army entered Bessarabia in December 1917, it found a territory in the midst of revolution. The peasants, the workers, and remnants of the old imperial army had established a system of self-governing soviets, following the model of what had been happening in Russia in general. The peasants had risen up against the boyars, seized their large estates, and had begun redistributing the land. According to Jelavich (1983), by July 1917 peasants had taken control of more than two-thirds of the boyar estates.

The revolutionaries had formed a provisional government in November 1917. The provisional government petitioned the U.S.S.R. to allow it to join the Soviet Union as a federated republic (Jelavich 1983). When the Soviet Union did not act on the petition, the Bessarabia government declared itself an independent state in January 1918. By this time Romanian forces were moving on the capital, Kishinev (in Romanian it was called *Chisinau*). Before it was dissolved, the provisional government petitioned to join Romania. It stipulated conditions for unification similar to those that had been advanced by the Transylvania Romanians. These stipulations were withdrawn following Romania's complete conquest of the province and Bessarabia was incorporated into Romania without any special conditions being attached to the annexation. The reconquest of Bessarabia spoiled Russian-Romanian relations for the rest of the century. It was one of the leading causes for Romania invading Russia, along with Nazi Germany, in June 1941.

The Inter-War Years: The Collapse of Democracy and the Turn to Fascism and Dictatorship

With the end of World War I, Romania encountered a new geopolitical context. Romania faced a militant communist state to its north and east that was anxious to export its revolution once the new regime was consolidated. Romania also bordered a considerably reduced Hungary which, for a brief period, established its own Bolshevik regime and in which irredentism was strong. On its southern border, Romania had to deal with a Bulgaria that resented the loss of Dobrodgea. However, on the positive side, the new Soviet Union was too preoccupied with internal affairs and too weak to provide an immediate threat to Romania. The Austro-Hungarian Empire was dead and neither of its main successor states had a military force that could challenge Romania. Turkey and Bulgaria, to the south, also had been seriously weakened and neither appeared to be able to mount attacks on Romania.

The breakup of the old empires in Europe established a new economic context for the Balkan countries, including Romania. Longworth (1997) notes that because of the war agricultural production in the region was seriously disrupted and the United States and Canada displaced the Balkans and the Ukraine as Europe's principal grain suppliers. In addition, government budgets were under heavy stress, governments had borrowed heavily to pay for the war. States also increased their money supplies, causing high rates of inflation. Longworth (1997) also notes that the new national boundaries carved out of the Austro-Hungarian Empire disrupted old patterns of trade, economic exchange, and communication throughout the Balkans.

Romania also faced a significant challenge in absorbing the new and heterogeneous populations that it acquired at the end of the war. The Romanian political elites were forced to struggle with how they would deal with the presence of increased numbers of national minorities – Jews, Germans (both Saxons and Swabs), Magyars, Szeklers, and some Slavs – in the expanded state. As Fischer-Galati (1998a) notes, many of these new minorities, in effect, constituted elements of the political, social, and economic elites in the newly acquired Romanian territory, even if they had been numerical minorities. The drive to Romanize the new territories put the Romanian state in direct conflict with these former elites. For example, shortly upon acquiring Transylvania, the politicians in the Regat launched a drive to remove all "foreigners" from government positions. In addition, the Romanian state expropriated the property held by the so-called "foreign" landlords in the newly acquired territories.

In September 1919, a coalition between the National Party of Transylvania and the Peasant Party of Wallachia defeated the National Liberal Party in the newly expanded state's first post-war national elections. The two parties, led by Ion Mihalache and Vaida Voevod, had immediately begun to craft legislation that would have produced meaningful agrarian reform.

Before they could introduce their legislation into parliament, the king dismissed the government and turned power over to General Alexandru Averescu and his People's Party in March 1920. General Alexandru Averescu was the military commander who had "distinguished" himself in suppressing the peasant rebellion in 1907 and he had been among the more successful Romanian generals in World War I. Averescu was a man from the traditional right, as were most of his political allies. He was a monarchist, was strongly suspicious of democracy, was strongly opposed to communism and to the Soviet Union, and was hostile toward minorities, especially Jews, Magyars, and Szecklers. He also saw no need to introduce major social or economic reform in Romania. His party, the People's Party was a jerry-rigged political organization put together by members of the pre-war traditional conservative political and economic elite who saw themselves threatened by the potential rise to power of peasant advocates, by the emergence of radical socialist, pro-Soviet political activists attempting to organize the Romanian peasantry and working classes, and, even, by the modest reforms that the National Liberal Party had supported in the past. Averescu's government called for elections in May 1920. Using all of the legal and, more importantly, illegal means at its disposal, the People's Party, not surprisingly, won the election.

Its tenure in office, however, was short-lived. The king dismissed Averescu's government and the Liberal Party came back into power and formed a new government in January 1920. The Liberals introduced a number of changes into the 1921 land reform legislation, which limited the overall effects of the new legislation. Using their land reform legislation as a weapon, the Liberals cast themselves as leaders and protectors of the Romanian peasantry. The new land reforms involved breaking up estates over 100 hectares. Over two-thirds of the land from these estates (roughly six million hectares) was expropriated with compensation to the owners. The boyars were allowed to retain ownership of the one-third of their estates that had been recognized by the Organic Regulations. A large part of the expropriated land, but not all of it, was redistributed to the peasants. The state retained ownership of a little more than half of the expropriated property.

The state also expropriated and redistributed communal lands to the peasantry. All totaled, roughly six and a half million hectares of land were given to almost a million and a half peasant families. Over 500,000 peasant families remained landless, even with this reform (Longworth 1997). The average peasant plot that resulted from land reform was a little less than four hectares. However, it was estimated that peasants needed at least five hectares to produce enough for their families to meet their basic subsistence needs. Peasants, therefore, on small plots found that land ownership did not end their economic misery. By increasing small plot production, the land reform reduced overall agricultural efficiency in Romania. Peasant families on small plots barely could produce enough for their own survival, let alone a large enough surplus for international export or for feeding large urban populations.

The land reforms introduced by the liberals, thus, did little to improve the economic situation of the peasantry. However, that never was the intention of the legislation that finally had been passed. Rather, the purpose was to create a base of support among the peasantry for the new Romanian state and for the throne among the formerly landless peasantry (Fischer-Galati 1998a). Another factor that motivated land redistribution was the desire to reduce the likelihood of peasant insurrection. The war had brought tens of thousands of peasants into the military. Politicians and the king did not want to see a disenchanted peasantry that had received military training mobilized by radicals, especially by socialist and, later, communist organizers.

Under the National Liberals, Romania drafted and adopted a new constitution, the Constitution of 1923, which served as the country's basic law, until the communists came to power after World War II. The 1923 Constitution, on the surface at least, was an attempt to introduce liberal principles into the operation of the state. However, as things turned out, the guarantees of civil and political rights meant little to those running the state. In the period between 1923 and the end of World War II, civil rights, especially for minorities, were regularly ignored, disregarded, or suspended by government actions.

The introduction of "universal" suffrage at the end of World War I and the limited land reforms of 1921 did have one major positive effect on Romania's internal political life. Land reform and universal suffrage significantly weakened the boyars' ability to play a direct dominant role in the Romanian state, as they had done in the years prior to World War I. Universal suffrage consigned the National Conservative Party, which had been the main voice expressing the political interests of the boyars, to the position of a permanent electoral minority. As a result, it disappeared from Romania's political scene. With the demise of the National Conservative Party, the National Liberal Party had a relatively free hand in reorganizing the state and the Romanian economy in the interests of the Romanian bourgeoisie, its allies in the state bureaucracy, and the Liberal Party's supporters in the professions and among the mainly urban intelligentsia.

However, even though their direct participation in the state had become more limited and some of their estate land had been confiscated, the boyars still were the dominant economic force in Romania. Despite land reform, the boyars continued to have significant land holdings in the Romanian countryside. In addition, the boyars had continued to transform themselves into capitalists, investing large amounts of money not only in turning their estates into commercial enterprises but also in other economic activities.

The boyars, despite losing their position as one of the two dominant classes competing for direct control of the Romanian state, continued to play an important role in state affairs. They still held top positions in the bureaucracy, the army, and the court. If they lived in the countryside, they continued to dominate rural political, economic, and social life, including in the towns and smaller cities. Moreover, they continued to be the exemplar of what it meant to have high social status in Romanian society. They were the class that the highest levels of the bourgeoisie emulated in trying to win social recognition in Romania.

The National Conservative Party, as already noted, was the political home for a large number of Romanian intellectuals who supported Romania's old agrarian order and its associated political, economic, the cultural values. The diminished economic position of the boyars and the disappearance of the National Conservative Party left these conservative intellectuals without a political base. Consequently, many of the intellectuals who had been tied to the interests of the boyars and to the National Conservative Party became detached from parties of the traditional right. They became a group of "free-floating" intellectuals of the right. These free-floating intellectuals became ever more suspicious of the direction of change that was being introduced into Romania by the now dominant National Liberal Party and the king. The right wing intellectuals saw no good coming from the development of market capitalism, in which over two-thirds of capital in the industrial sector was held by foreign investors as late as 1916, and an expansion of parliamentary democracy. They also tried to resist the penetration of the general values of Western culture into Romanian society.

Having emerged as the preeminent political force in Romania, following the war, and without the presence of an organized class of boyars contending with them for state domination, the National Liberal Party was free to aggressively pursue an agenda of rapid economic modernization, designed, in no small part, to advance the corporate interest of the bourgeoisie. The National Liberal Party, recognizing that the Romanian economic bourgeoisie, in and of itself, was too weak to carry on a project of economic and social modernization with its own resources, used the state as the main engine for national transformation. In essence, the National Liberal Party, at this time, was trying to consolidate bourgeois class rule in the absence of a politically effective and economically powerful bourgeoisie. This entailed the National Liberal Party building an alliance between the state bourgeoisie and private sectors of the bourgeoisie to turn Romania into a more economically modern state.

The National Liberal Party looked toward building a state stimulated, state organized, and state protected capitalism under the leadership of a Romanian national bourgeoisie to carry out its economic modernization agenda. The National Liberal Party realized that its own political success depended on it being actively engaged in building a larger bourgeoisie in Romania. Despite the economic growth of the late 19th and early 20th century, the Romanian bourgeoisie remained small, especially that portion of the bourgeoisie who were "Romanian" by ethnicity. Many key market oriented enterprises, especially in the larger towns and cities, were in the hands of ethnic minorities such as Greeks, Armenians, Germans, and Jews.

One of the agenda items in the drive to develop a modern capitalist Romania involved wresting control over industrial development from foreign investors. Foreign capital had controlled over three-fourths of industrial production in Romania before World War I. In order to foster the development of Romanian industrial capitalism, the National Liberal

Party advocated a system of high tariffs on industrial imports, as well as other protectionist measures. The Romania State began constructing a modern transportation and communication infrastructure, it developed a system of credits for industrial loans, extended its control over foreign trade, and heavily subsidized key industries, such as mining, petroleum drilling and refining, and metallurgy.

The National Liberal Party's modernization project was opposed by a new configuration of forces in the countryside. Peasants, agrarian capitalists, traditional rural intellectuals, and conservative intellectuals, especially, but not exclusively, from Moldova, who had been part of the organic intelligentsia of the boyars, came together behind a "peasantist" political agenda. Similar movements had emerged in Croatia and other parts of the Balkans around the same time (Jelavich 1983). The peasantist movement in Romania found its organizational embodiment in the National Peasant Party, which was created from a fusion of the National Party of Transylvania and the Peasant Party in 1926. The National Peasant Party offered a different path to economic modernization than that put forward by the National Liberal Party. The National Peasant Party saw agriculture as the only real basis on which Romania could pin its hopes for development. The peasantists did not believe that it was economically senseless for Romania to involve itself in a major industrialization and urbanization effort. Like the intellectuals who supported the old National Conservative Party, the peasantist intellectuals and political leadership contended that industrialization and urbanization would deform Romanian society and culture.

In the view of peasantist and other rightist and nationalist intellectuals, industrialization and urbanization were Western creations. They were seen to be alien forms that could not easily be introduced and adapted to the realities of Romanian history, civilization, and culture. Western civilization was seen to introduce artificiality into interpersonal relations and eroded the naturalness of the human order. From the perspective of the peasantists, Romania could thrive only when it developed institutions appropriate to its civilization and these institutions had to reflect the "facts" that Romania was and always would be an agrarian state and society. The National Peasant Party offered a political agenda that stressed free trade. It saw Romania's growth as being tied to the export of foods and the import of industrial products.

Both the National Liberal and the National Peasant Party stood in defense of private property. They both advanced agendas of the urban and agricultural bourgeoisie, respectively. Neither party, in a real sense, represented the interests of Romania's impoverished peasantry or of Romania's emerging working class. The peasantists stood for the defense of property-owning capitalist agriculturalists. The first Romanian political party that represented the interests of the working class was the Social Democratic Party. The Romanian Social Democratic Workers Party appeared in 1893. By the beginning of the 20th century the party had split, with a good number of its key leaders moving to the Liberal Party, believing that developing a working class party was futile given the small size of the pre-war working class. It was revived in 1910 and, in 1914 the SDP was wracked by internal conflict over whether the party should support Romania participating in World War I. A second, and more important division, came about because of the Russian revolution. The Romanian Social Democrats split over the stance their party should take toward the new Bolshevik regime. Moderates in the party felt that the Romanian Social Democrats should avoid any contact with the Bolsheviks. More radical Social Democrats, believing that the Bolsheviks were the future of international socialism, split from the moderates in 1921 and created the Communist Party of Romania.

The Romanian government, under Prime Minister General Alexandru Averescu, had immediately moved to repress the communists, arresting delegates to the party's first national meeting. In 1924, the Romanian government of the time declared the communist party to be an illegal political organization, forcing the communists to go underground. From 1924 to 1944, the party was forced to act as an illegal, clandestine organization. This fact shaped an entire generation of party leaders and members, who never had been given the opportunity to participate openly in the Romanian political process.

While not large in numbers during the inter-war period, the Romanian communists had an effective presence within the working classes. They developed strong links to the emerging working classes and contributed to the overall organization of workers in Romania, especially at the grass roots level. For example, the communists were successful in organizing a mass strike in the oil and transportation industries in 1933. The state used force to break this strike. Communists also were active in organizing several other strikes of substantial size before World War II (Deletant 1999b).

It has been estimated that when World War II began there were no more than a few thousand members in the communist party (Deletant 1999a; 1999b). Party leaders were not discouraged unduly by the small party membership. After all, the Bolsheviks had been comparatively few in number when they had conquered power in Russia. Lenin had "shown" that a small, disciplined revolutionary force, if it followed the right tactics, could conquer power under the right circumstances. Romania's communist leaders also knew that there were serious dangers in trying to become a mass party under the political conditions prevailing in Romania in the 1920s. Opening membership roles would leave the party susceptible to penetration by the state's security forces and by opportunists who were not committed to revolution.

Party membership in the pre-war period had a high proportion of minorities, especially Hungarians from Transylvania and Jews from Bessarabia. It should be noted that while Hungarians and Jews were over represented in the party by no means should this be taken to mean that the majority of these populations were party members. In fact, the opposite is true.

Despite its illegal status, the party remained active within the general workers' movement. For example, it played a significant role in organizing major strikes, the largest of which involved oil and railroad workers in 1933, and it was politically active within the working class and among selected ethnic minorities and intellectuals. It also played a major role in organizing the Peasants' and Workers' Bloc, a political organization that, in 1931, won five parliamentary seats. However, the government would not let these representatives take their seats. From its founding until after the war, the party faced continuous harassment by the government and by the growing far right. Many of its key leaders who had remained in the country, rather than going to Moscow, served long prison terms. This included two men who would define the nature of post-war communism in Romania – Gheorge Gheorghiu-Dej, a Moldovan worker, and Nicolae Ceausescu, a young shoemaker by trade.

The Romanian Social Democrats did not have as good ties to workers as did the communists. The Social Democrats were more of a parliamentary party than a class movement. The larger part of the Social Democrat party leadership believed that Romania's economy was too immature to support a broad based socialist revolution. They believed that Romania first had to form a bourgeois social order before it could move on to developing a socialist society. The Social Democrats also rejected the idea that only violent revolution could bring about a transition to socialism. For these reasons, the Social Democrats allied themselves with various bourgeois parties, such as the Liberals and, later, the National Peasant Party, in order to complete a bourgeois revolution in Romania, and, thereby, establish the conditions necessary for the movement to socialism.

The communists, however, after 1931, facing severe repression and being blocked from open political participation, abandoned electoral politics and turned to a politics of conspiracy and direct, sometimes, violent revolutionary action. This was forced upon them as much as it was a matter of their own choice. The state had outlawed the party in 1924 and had continually harassed and imprisoned its members. The state also had refused to seat communists who had won election to parliament. All of this convinced the communist leadership that the road to power could not be found by participating in normal politics, even if they had wanted to follow this strategy.

After World War I, radical right wing parties began forming in Romania. The more important of these emerged in the Moldovan city of Iasi. Iasi, in the immediate post-war years, appears to have been a center of left wing political activity. Various leftist groups, representing a variety of political tendencies, were engaged in organizing university students and faculty, ethnic minorities, and workers. Rapid leftist mobilization contributed to radical right wing counter-mobilization. The right feared the growing influence of the left in the university in Iasi and in the Moldovan workers' movement. In no small part, the growth of right wing movements in Moldova was helped along by the pressures the Soviet Union placed on Moldova following World War I. Repeated negotiations to settle Soviet land claims had failed to resolve the conflict between the Soviet Union and Romania over Romania's annexation of Bessarabia. Between 1918 and 1925, the Soviet Union sponsored numerous incursions across its boarder with Romania and a large number of what Romanian authorities dubbed "terrorist" incidents (King 2000). In addition, the Soviet Union waged a continuing propaganda war against the Romanians and created a new Moldovan Autonomous Socialist Republic on October 12, 1924. The Republic was designed to serve as an alternative state for Bessarabians disenchanted with life in the "aristocratic-led" Romania and its "landlord-capitalist" economic system, as the Soviets described the Romanian kingdom in their propaganda (King 2000).

This Soviet threat, in the eyes of Romanian nationalists, was made more real by the negative reaction of many Bessarabians to integration into the Romanian kingdom (King 2000). Union with the kingdom put the region under the control of the often corrupt and incompetent officials Romania sent into the region. Romania also did not follow through on its promises that it would acknowledge and respect regional autonomy for Bessarabia. Romania also purged a host of former officials who had risen to power under the Russians and who were suspected of seeing themselves more as citizens of Russia or the new Soviet Union than as citizens of the Romanian kingdom. Finally, the peasantry, the largest number of who were Romanian speakers, had only a weak national identity as Romanians. As King (2000) notes, under Russian rule since 1812, the peasantry largely had been unaffected by the nationalist movements in the Regat and in Transylvania, they, thus, had a limited national consciousness. This fact helped lead to Romanian nationalists believing that the kingdom was in need of a national, moral refurbishing.

One of the leading Iasi activists on the radical right was A. C. Cuza. In 1910, Cuza and the philosopher Nicolae Iorga had founded a nationalist and anti-Semitic party called the Democratic Nationalist Party. This party seems to have been culturally, but not racially, anti-Semitic. The party proved attractive to Moldova's petty bourgeoisie and its traditionalist intellectuals. It also drew support from elements of the working classes. The main political agenda of the Democratic Nationalists was the creation of a unified Romanian nation "purified" of the influence of national minorities, especially the Jews. The Democratic Nationalist Party was but one radical right, anti-Semitic movement in Romania before World War I (see Oldson 1973; 1991). As has been noted already, Romanian anti-Semitism had been strong enough in the mid-1860s to force writers of the Constitution of 1866 to exclude Jews from citizenship and, hence, from the right to vote. Jews only had been allowed to become citizens in Romania because of pressure from the Western Great Powers, as we have seen above. Romania, at this time, was not the only European state that resisted the emancipation of Jews, so did the Vatican

(Goldhagen 2002). Romanian Orthodox Christians shared many of the same prejudices toward and fears about Jews as did Western Christians. In 1922, Cuza and a professor in the medical school at the University of Bucharest, Nicolae Paulescu, founded an organization called *Uniunea National Crestina* (National Christian Union). Paulescu's was a physiologist whose intellectual reputation, in part, was gained from his efforts to demonstrate "empirically" the importance of the human soul in animating the body. Paulescu's intellectual efforts were directed against work he thought was excessively materialistic and, hence, atheistic. When the National Christian Union was established, the Romanian parliament was debating the terms of a new constitution. The constitution largely was written by members of the National Liberal Party, whose political program and political ideology was anathema to the radical right, in general, and to Cuza, in particular. The proposed constitution, based in the liberal ideology of the time, was designed to foster conditions of capitalist development and to provide basic rights of citizenship to a broad range of Romanian residents, including Jews.

The Western Allies had forced Romania to sign the Treaty of St. Germain in 1919. The provisions of this treaty, among other things, required Romania to naturalize all of its Jewish citizens and extend to them the full liberties enjoyed by other nationality groups, including Romanians. If Romania had refused to sign the Treaty of St. Germain; it was unlikely that it would have been awarded as much territory as finally was assigned to it under the terms of the Treaty of Trianon (1920). The Treaty of St. Germain had been deemed necessary by the allies because of the fact that Jews in Bukovina, Bessarabia, and Transylvania all had held citizenship rights in the Austro-Hungarian Empire and the Western allies did not want to see Jews lose citizenship rights when these territories were transferred to Romania. The Western powers remembered what had happened after the signing of the Treaty of Berlin in 1878. The Romanians had tried to make use of the treaty negotiations in order to gain full sovereignty, as previously noted. The allies demanded that Romania guarantee equal rights to its Jews in return for such recognition. Romania agreed to these terms, but managed to evade the consequences. From 1878 to 1914, out of several thousand applications for citizenship by Romanian Jews, only 361 were approved, an action which required the approval of both houses of the Romanian parliament (Sacher 2002). The Allies were determined that Romania would not repeat the evasions in which they had engaged following World War I.

Cuza, while objecting to the basic liberal principles behind the proposed constitution, was especially incensed that, under the terms of the new constitution, Jews would be given rights equivalent to ethnic Romanians. Instead of extending rights to Jews, the National Christian Union advocated a new constitution that would institutionalize a broad anti-Semitic agenda (Livezeanu 1995). Among other things, the National Christian Union demanded that the new constitution provide for the expulsion from Romania of all Jews who had arrived in the country after the start of World War I. It also wanted the constitution to allow the state to set quotas on the number of Jews admitted to schools and universities and to permit the state to set limits on the number of Jews who would be allowed to practice medicine and law and, on the number of Jews who would be allowed to enter certain trades, crafts, and industries. It also wanted to prohibit Jews from teaching in public universities, from serving in the army, and from running for political office. Cuza's opposition to the extension of rights to Jews continued a long tradition among Romanian intellectuals of nationalistic chauvinism toward minorities, especially Jews. Nationalist chauvinism and its compliment, anti-Semitism, however, were not confined merely to intellectuals. These were Ideologies that spilled over class boundaries, uniting Intellectuals, remnants of the boyars, the clergy, peasants, parts of the working class, the petty bourgeoisie, and the grand bourgeoisie (Sachar 2002: 82).

The National Christian Union was successful in organizing students in support of its radical right wing anti-Semitic agenda in a number of Romanian universities. In 1922, students launched demonstrations in support of the UNC's exclusionary agenda. Meeting in December 1922 in Bucharest, student representatives from Romania's four state universities drew up a list of demands that paralleled those of the National Christian Union (Livezeanu 1995). The students threatened a general strike against the universities unless their anti-Semitic demands were met. Right wing students engaged in militant protest throughout the Easter (Spring) Term, forcing the universities to suspend operations. The university rectors did not cave in to student demands. Nicolae Iorga, who earlier had been allied with Cuza and who was an ardent nationalist, resigned his position at the University of Bucharest in opposition to the students' demands that quotas for Jewish enrollment to universities be established. This earned Iorga the eternal wrath of the student right and eventually it led to his assassination while in prison on the orders of the Iron Guard.

When the constitution was adopted in 1923, without restrictive provisions directed against Jews, the student strikes petered out. However, in response to the student protests, within two months following the adoption of the constitution, the state published administrative regulations that excluded Jews from appointments to the state bureaucracy, to the judiciary, to professorships in public universities, and to officer rank in the military.

The student protests of 1922-1923 were reminiscent of the agitation that had surrounded the drafting of the Constitution of 1866. Then, however, protests, demonstrations, and riots had forced the parliament to remove proposed constitutional protections for Jews. In 1922-23, however, while protests did not result in constitutional restrictions on Jews, they eventually did succeeded in having restrictive regulations adopted that limited Jews' access to key professional positions.

In 1923, Cuza founded the League of National Christian Defense (LNCD) in Iasi. The LNCD was a nationalist organization that was rabidly anti-Semitic and rabidly anti-communist. Indeed, anti-Semitism and anti-communism constituted almost the whole of its political ideology. The LNCD attracted a large number of radical right Romanian intellectuals and students from the University of Iasi and it spread to other university centers in Romania. In 1935, the LNCD merged with the National Agrarian Party, another right wing party. At the time, Octavian Goga led the National Agrarian Party.

The League of National Christian Defense marked a turning point of sorts in Romanian politics. Before the League's formation, Romania had long been marked by popular anti-Semitism which, from time to time, would erupt in attacks on Jews. These "pogroms," more often than not, grew out of local conflicts between Romanian Jews and Gentiles. This popular anti-Semitism was embedded in a number of cultural institutions, not the least of which were the Christian churches. The emergence of the League, however, helped to crystallize anti-Semitism into a nation-wide social movement and, eventually, a political program on the Romanian radical right.

At the time the League was being organized, the left was unable to do much to oppose popular anti-Semitism. The left had split into social democratic and communist factions and it faced continual police harassment, including the arrest and imprisonment of some of its leading activists. Moreover, the leftist parties were not strong in the countryside, except perhaps in those parts of Moldova bordering on the Soviet Union. Romania's rural areas, especially in Moldova and in Bukovina would prove to be especially susceptible to mobilization around anti-Semitic ideologies.

The National Agrarian Party, which was formed in 1932, was a splinter group from General Averescu's People's Party. The National Agrarian Party had been formed in 1932. The party's founders had split from Averescu's group because of personality conflicts and political differences. The People's Party was a party of the more traditional right, supporting the agenda of intellectual conservatives. It stood for a strong monarchy, authoritarian rule, maintaining the traditional privileges of the elite, limited social change, anti-Communism, and traditional anti-Semitism The National Agrarian Party, on the other hand, was more of a party of the radical right. It was semi-fascist and favored Romania building strong alliances with Italy and Nazi Germany and other radical right states.

The most important radical right movement in the inter-war period in Romania was The Legion of the Archangel Michael. The Legion, founded in 1927 in Iaşi, was organized as a student movement. It was founded by the charismatic student leader Corneliu Zeal Codreanu, *Cuza*'s protégé and a militant activist in the UNC. Codreanu had organized, orchestrated, and led much of the anti-Jewish student protest in 1922-23. The Legion rejected democracy, was highly nationalistic, was anti-communist and anti-Semitic, and embraced a mystical, apocalyptic world view. To the Legion, both Jews and Communists, which, in their view, amounted to the same thing, were defined as inherently "evil," in a social, political, economic, and theological sense. Communists and Jews were defined as beings whose mere presence in Romania threatened the national "essence." Jews and Bolsheviks were defined as part of a long list of forces that had victimized Romania and had kept it from realizing its national "destiny." In this way, in part, both Jews and Bolsheviks were pathologized and defined as "legitimate" targets for purge and, ultimately, for destruction in Romania.

The Legion, initially, defined itself as a movement and not a political party. The Legion, like an increasing number of organizations and political movements on the right, had lost faith in parliamentary democracy, in general, and parties and party politics, in particular. Legionnaires saw parliamentary democracy and political parties as alien political forms imported from the West that only led to the fragmentation of the Romanian nation and to political paralysis.

There was a grain of truth in the Legionnaires' diagnosis of the Romanian political system, but it was not because of parties or parliamentary government, per se, that Romanian political parties were chaotic and its parliamentary government was ineffective during the inter-war period. Romanian political parties and the parliamentary system, in part, were failing because of the peculiar nature of Romanian political parties.

As noted above, Romanian political parties had not developed along the same lines as they had elsewhere in Europe. Romanian parties were composed of oligarchies representing various fractions of the political elite grounded in loyalty to large political clans or strong political leaders. The parties made no attempt to organize themselves as representatives of more general social interests or to incorporate within themselves various interest groups within Romanian society. As a result, the larger part of the Romanian population, especially the peasantry, had few opportunities for effective participation in the life of the mainstream parties. Indeed, one could argue that Romanian parties existed as much to organize the elites into politics as to organize the masses out of politics. Romanian political parties also were unstable organizations. Parties were continually splitting and reforming based on a variety of conflicts within the leading circles of the political oligarchy. Because of the nature of Romanian parties, the radical right had a large social space within which they could begin organizing those who were excluded from the political process and who, as a result, believed that their interests were being ignored by the Romanian state. This especially, but not exclusively, was the case with the peasantry.

Codreanu had been active in various radical right wing movements and activities as a teenager. For a brief period in 1919/1920, he was a member of the *Garda Constiintei Nationale*, which can be translated as the "Guard of National Consciousness" or the "Guard of National Conscience." This organization was founded in Iasi in 1919. It was a right wing, highly nationalistic workers' movement, the main function of which was attacking leftist working class organizations and breaking strikes led by socialist workers. The movement also was anti-Semitic.

As a young university student in Iasi, Codreanu had engaged in a number of violent actions against Jews and Jewish organizations (Livezeanu 1995). Because of his violent and disruptive behavior, the University of Iasi expelled him in 1921. The Faculty of Law, whose dean was A. C. Cuza, refused to recognize the expulsion and allowed Codreanu to finish his degree (Livezeanu 1995). During his last year of study, with the support of *Cuza* and other faculty, Codreanu actively engaged in organizing radical right students. Codreanu created a student group called *Associatia Stundentilor Crestini* (Christian Student Association). The Association, as its name indicates, excluded Jews. It also excluded socialists and communists. The Association was the major force behind the 1922-1923 students' strikes and demonstrations. Between 1923 and 1927, when he founded the Legion, Codreanu and the Association continued to engage in anti-Semitic violence, including several murders of Jews. Romanian courts invariably acquitted the overwhelming majority of the Association's members who were tried for various property and violent crimes, including murder.

In 1923, Romanian authorities uncovered a plot to assassinate key Jewish leaders and those Romanian politicians who had supported Jewish emancipation (Livezeanu 1995). The plot was discovered when one of its participants informed the police about its existence. The conspiracy had originated with Ion Mota, a member of the Association and a friend and political ally of Codreanu. The conspirators, including Codreanu, were arrested. Reportedly, the conspirators did not deny the police charges against them. On the night before their trial was to start, Mota killed the police informer. On the next day, March 29, 1924, all of the conspirators were acquitted, including Mota. Mota, however, was kept in prison on new charges stemming from the murder of the informer. Mota was tried for murder of the informant in the fall of 1924. He was acquitted based on his argument that the informer had deserved to be killed because he had deliberately and willingly betrayed his Romanian colleagues (Livezeanu 1995).

In 1925, Codreanu shot and killed the prefect of police in Iasi. The prefect long had been an outspoken and aggressive enemy of the Association. He regularly ordered the arrest and torture of Association activists (Livezeanu 1995). In carrying out the assassination, Codreanu shot two other police officers, neither of whom was killed.

The authorities, fearing violence from Codreanu's supporters, decided to hold his trial in Focsani, a town on the border of Moldova and Wallachia (Livezeanu 1995). Before the trial, anti-Jewish rioting broke out. Rioters targeted Jewish businesses and property. The government sent military forces from Bucharest to suppress the violence. Shortly after the trial began, it was decided to move the case to another jurisdiction, given the tensions still building in Focsani. Violence again broke out. The police could not contain the rioters.

The new site of the trial was Turnu Severin, a small community with no history of anti-Semitic or nationalist violence. Throughout the trial, thousands of Codreanu's supporters had come to the city to demonstrate their commitment to their leader. Codreanu also received considerable support in the nation's radical right wing press. After a six-week trial, Codreanu was acquitted on all charges. According to Livezeanu (1995), on the day they announced their verdict all of the jurors where wearing swastika pins in their coat lapels.

In the face of an increasingly violent anti-Semitism, Romanian Jews began to organize into "autonomous" political organizations. Sachar (2002:81) notes that following the end of World War I Jews in Romania's newly acquired territories followed the traditions of the Jewish communities in the Regat by working with the traditional Romanian political parties. However, in the face of rising popular and political anti-Semitism, the Jews in the new territories began organizing themselves into formal political groupings.

In 1926, for the first time, the Jewish community was able to elect representatives to parliament from Bukovina, Transylvania, and Bessarabia. These electoral successes stimulated the formation of the National Jewish Club, in which representatives of Zionist parties also participated. The first Club was formed in Bucharest. They, however, quickly spread to all of Romania's major cities. In the 1928 elections, four Jews were sent to parliament. Two were from Transylvania, one was from Bessarabia, and one was from Bukovina. When parliament convened, they formed themselves into a parliamentary caucus group. These limited successes prompted Jews to form their own political party, *Partidul Everesc* (the Jewish Party), in 1930 (Sacher 2002: 81). The party was established in the former Regat, where Jews had been less successful in contesting elections than they had been in the provinces Romania acquired after World War I. The new *Partidul Everesc* was self-consciously Zionist, as that was understood in the 1920s and early 1930s.

The Jewish Party held its first congress in May 1931. In the June 1931 election, it won five seats. It also won five seats in 1932. This was the last electoral success Jews would have until the communists took power. After 1933, the only Jew in the Romanian parliament was Chief Rabbi J. Niemirover, who sat in the Senate by virtue of his religious position. In 1928, the Romanian parliament had passed a Law on Cults that had recognized Judaism as one of eight historical religions in Romania. Because of this newly recognized status, the leader of the Jewish community was entitled to hold an appointment to the Senate.

By the end of the 1920s, it was apparent that anti-Semitism was a generalized and diffuse discourse in Romania that had been assimilated into the national agenda. Its influence extended far beyond just the radical right. Nationalism and anti-Semitism reinforced each other so that anti-Semitism came to be a significant part of the Romanian political agenda. It was expressed by all levels of the society, from high- ranking officials and intellectuals to the peasantry. Anti-Semitism was a feature not only of parties on the right. It also was part of the ideology and ruling practices of the Liberal Party from its earliest days. The Liberals had advocated expelling Jews from Romania in the 1860s and 1870s. Jewish emancipation, we should recall, had to be imposed on Romania from without by the Great Powers. The only part of the political spectrum where anti-Semitism was not a powerful force was on the political left. Neither the communists nor the socialists embraced anti-Semitism, but both of these political tendencies were marginal in Romanian political life.

Anti-Semitism was something more than an abstract ideology. By the 1920s, anti-Semitic beliefs and attitudes were widely accepted, even in regions where there were few or no Jews. In these regions, the Jew was an abstract symbol of an alien and threatening world. It was "common" knowledge among peasants and village clergy that Jews kidnapped gentile children (and used their blood in Jewish Passover rituals and that Jews were part of international conspiracies, either communist or capitalist. As Carroll (2001) notes, this idea of the Jews as a conspiratorial people can be traced back to the 14th century, when Jews in Toledo were held responsible for poisoning Christian wells and bringing on the Black Death. Rroma, for different reasons, also were seen as a kidnapping people in Romania, as well as in other parts of Europe. Romanian nationalists, following in a long line of Christian belief that can be traced back to the 1547 Statute of Toledo (Carroll 2001), if not earlier, defined Jews as a separate race, not merely believers in a different creed. Moreover, Jews were seen as a separate race bent on destroying the Romanian nation.

Anti-Semitism was not a creation of nationalism. Rather, it was assimilated into Romanian nationalism as one of its key elements. The modern Romanian nationalist project struggled with the "origins" of and the identity appropriate to the Romanian people. One thread of the nationalist tradition traced the origins of the Romanian people back to the Dacians, a pre-Roman, pre-Christian population in the Black Sea region. In this theoretical position, contemporary Romanians were identified as being direct, lineal descendants of this "original" population of Dacians (Verdery 1991). The Dacians were seen to have remained ethnically "pure," despite the numerous invasions and conquests of the territory making up the Romanian lands. According to this theory of origins, the Dacian people were relatively advanced, in that it was argued that the Dacians had developed an elaborate political structure even before the Romans had entered the region. One problem with assuming that modern Romanians were descendents of the Dacians (aside from the scientific validity of the position) was that this removed Romanians from being seen as part of the common roots of Western Europe.

A second theory of origins saw Romanians as descendants of Roman colonists who had entered into the area after it was conquered by Emperor Trajan in 106-105 BC (Verdery 1991). The Transylvanian writer Ioan Inochentie Clain claimed that the Romanians were the descendants of the Roman colonists who had stayed in the region after the withdrawal of the Romanian legions (Giurescu 1998). The writers George Sincai and Petru Maior held the same opinions. This view of Romanian origins emerged in Transylvania as a means for Romanian nationalists to claim a more ancient and "noble" ancestry than that of the other populations living in the region.

A third theory of origins saw contemporary Romanians as a synthesis of Dacians and Roman colonists (Verdery 1991). According to this view, the Romans had subdued the Dacians and, over the course of time, had Latinized them, linguistically and culturally. The Latinized Dacians were claimed to have had an unbroken continuity of existence on the territory of what would become the modern state of Romania. Nationalist historians never adequately explained what had happened to the other indigenous populations in the region and to the various populations who had migrated into it (Ascherson 1995) and how the Latinized Dacians had been able to maintain their ethnic "purity" over 2000 years. It was culturally and politically important for Romanian nationalists, then and now (for a contemporary statement of this intellectual position see Giurescu 1998) to claim descent from the Dacians. Dacian descent made the Romanians a Balkan people at least as old as the Greeks and the Albanians. That the Dacians had developed a rudimentary state and that evidence of this state could be traced back to antiquity, buttressed Romanian territorial claims. This was especially useful for arguing against Hungarian territorial claims in Transylvania, where the legendary Dacian chieftain Dachibal had raised a band of fighters to resist Roman encroachment.

In addition to developing claims to a common ancestral people, Romanian nationalists, drawing on Herder, argued that the Romanian people were one in their origins, because of a common language whose roots were the vulgar (popular) Latin used by soldiers in the Roman armies and by Roman colonists. Nationalist historians maintained that this language had retained its "purity" of grammar and syntax since the days of the Roman conquest, even though it might have absorbed some words from Slavic and Turkic languages. To the Romantic nationalists, the use of a Latin language meant that Romanians thought differently than populations that surrounded them, mostly Hungarians and Slavs. It was believed that Romanians, by virtue of their presumed ancestry and their Latin language, constituted a unique "metaphysical universe" (see Wright 1978 for a discussion of this concept) in their region. Because they had a Latin language, some elements of Romanian nationalism came to believe that Romanians were more Western than other populations in the Balkans and Central Europe. From the 1860s on, Romania westernized its language. In 1863, Romanians abandoned the Cyrillic alphabet and replaced it with a largely Latin alphabet, using diacritical markings to produce pronunciations expressible in the Cyrillic alphabet. Romanian universities and schools led the movement for linguistic standardization, at least in written form. Popular spoken forms of Romanian that did not conform to the emerging literary forms of Romanian, were stigmatized, suppressed, or reduced to the status of non-standard dialects. As such, they might be appropriate to use in private life, but not in public spheres.

In addition to debates about the theories of origin of the Romanian people and their language, beginning in the late 19th century and continuing well into the 20th century, Romanian intellectuals debated the "essence" of Romanian identity. This debate continued under communism and has continued into the post-communist period. Verdery (1991: pp. 47ff) has identified three distinct positions that emerged around this question: "westernizers," "indigenists," and "pro-Orientals" or "Orthodoxists," with the larger part of the debate being between the first and the second. One of the major "Orthodoxists" was Nichifor Craniac, a theology professor at the University of Bucharest. Verdery (1991, 48-49) presents two quotes from Craniac that illustrate the "Orthodoxist" position:

> If the mission of the Romanian people is to create a culture after its image and likeliness, this implies as well how its orientation must be resolved. Whoever recommends an orientation toward the West speaks nonsense. 'Orientation' contains within itself the notion of 'Orient" and means directing ourselves toward the Orient, in accord with the Orient. Altars face toward the Orient, the icons of the hearth face us from the Orient; the peasant who kneels in the field faces the Orient. Everywhere it is said light comes from the East. And for us, who find ourselves geographically in the Orient and who, through our Orthodox religion, hold to the truths of the eastern world, there can be no other orientation than toward the Orient, that is toward ourselves.... Westernization means the negation of our orientalness; Europeanizing nihilism means the negation of our creative potential. Which means to negate in principle, a Romanian culture, to negate a destiny proper to Romanians, and to accept the destiny of a people born dead (Craniac 1929: 3).

The second quote from Craniac is as follows:

> A great river of orientalness, then, flowed in the riverbed of our people's soul. Byzantine and Kiev took their toll of as it passed by, flowing underneath Orthodoxy – that import, which in time dissolved into the reservoir of our primitive forces. [Orthodoxy] thus forms part of our people's wealth and constitutes yet another part power by which our patriarchal mentality, our native genius,

differentiates itself from and resists the currents of European civilization, so fresh in their historical origin (Craniac 1936: 90).

The "Orthodoxists" saw Romanian identity as being firmly a part of the old Greek "commonwealth" of peoples whose religion was Orthodox and whose traditions, laws, politics, and general social practices were Byzantine in origin and in character. As such, Romania and the Romanians were taken to be part of the "Near East" (the Orient) and, as such, were not really part of "Europe," as they understood it. To the "Orthodoxists," Europe was grounded in a Roman Catholicism and/or Protestantism that was slowly giving way to a base materialism (embodied in industrial capitalism, Marxist socialism, and communism) that was stripping it of its former spiritual heritage. To which it must be added the idea that Western spirituality was based on Christian heresy, to begin with, so that one might not expect it to be as resilient as non-heretical Eastern spirituality or even as worthy of preservation as is Eastern Christian spirituality. The emphasis on Orthodoxy and, to a lesser degree, Christianity became a lasting contribution to Romanian nationalists' conception of the nation's identity. This was strengthened by the emphasis some nationalists placed on the role Romania had played in defending the "boundary" of Christendom against Muslim encroachment, overlooking the fact that Romanian princes often fought as an ally of the Ottoman Empires, as their personal circumstances demanded.

Many nationalists came to believe that one could not be a "true" Romanian without being Orthodox or, at least, without being a Christian. Thus, Muslims, Jews, and other non-Christians were excluded from consideration as members of the Romanian nation and, by more extreme nationalists, were seen to be ineligible for citizenship in the Romanian state. This idea eventually became further refined and restrictive so as to exclude anyone who was not an Orthodox Christian. The particularization of the form of Christian one had to be in order to be accepted as a Romanian created problems for Romanian Protestants, Catholics, and Uniates. From the Orthodox point of view, the Uniates were apostates who had rejected the true faith by aligning themselves with the papacy for personal gain. By linking Romanian identity with Orthodoxy, nationalist intellectuals reaffirmed Romania's links to the world of Byzantium.

The "Orientalists" played a leading role in valorizing the peasantry as a continuing reservoir of Romanian identity. The Romanian peasantry was seen to have been "uncorrupted" by history and, as such, in the future would serve as "... the sure foundation of an authentically Romanian history (Blaga 1980 [1937]: 258)." Romanian nationalist intellectuals, like Romantic nationalists elsewhere in Europe (see Hobsbawm (1990), saw the peasantry as the purist, least adulterated embodiment of national culture. Peasants, alone, were seen to express authentic national values and cultures. This idea generated a good deal of interest in the study of peasant customs and folkways, social organization, and folklore and myth in order to "recover" and "restore" what had been overlooked or lost in Romanian culture as a result of foreign domination and Western modernization.

The "indigenists" resembled the "Orientalists" in some respects, yet the "indigenists" rejected the basic premises of the "Orientalists." The "indigenists" were looking for Romanian identity in what they took to be unique characteristics of the Romanian people and their history, which was something more than just being an Orthodox people. The "indigenists" sough to identify what was unique to the Romanian soul and to Romanian culture that marked them off, as a people, and as a civilization. Discovering Romanian identity, however, was not an end in itself. What was important was to use the idea of Romanian identity as a benchmark for evaluating institutions and for designing institutions that would be compatible with the national essence. The "indigenists" saw modern educational systems, Western legal systems, and the bourgeois system of industrial production as all being worthless models that Romania should not seek to emulate (Verdery 1991). As "indigenists'" ideas were picked up by various nationalist political movements and woven into their ideologies, this came to mean that Romanian institutions should reflect the fact that the "nation" was Christian, was overwhelmingly peasant, and was a Latin people surrounded by Magyars and Slavs that possessed a unique spiritual and cultural sensibility that made them different from any other people in Europe.

In addition to the ideas of the "indigenists" and the "Orientalists," Romanian nationalist movements saw an inextricable bond between the people and their land. The Romanian people and "their" land were defined as one and indivisible. To the Romanian nationalists, the Romanian state had the right and the moral obligation to extend its dominion over all lands where Romanians lived. The Romanian State was morally obligated to organize its land in ways that would eliminate sources of "impurity." The Romanian State was seen to have the right to remove all foreign elements from the soil of the Romanian people. Non-Romanians lived on Romanian lands only on the sufferance of the state. They had no rights to remain within Romanian boundaries other than those the state granted them. Non-Romanians' rights to live within the lands of the Romanian community were defined as contingent rights. They only existed insofar as the state granted them and continued to recognize them.

Standing somewhat over and against the "Orientalists" and the "indigenists" the "westernizers," as the designation implies, saw that it was in Romania's national interest to reach out to Europe and find things of value that Romania needed in order to develop socially, culturally, and economically. As such, they stood somewhat apart from and against various nationalist movements. The "westernizers" believed that without adopting and adapting Western institutions to the Romanian situation, Romania would remain a "semi-Asiatic, oriental country" (Ibraileanu 1906: 261). Some of the "westernizers" were extremely hostile to the visions of the "Orientalists" and the "indigenists." Verdery (1991) presents a quote from Filotti (1924) that illustrates the attitudes of some of the "westernizers." According to Filotti (1924: 2-4):

> Under the banner of Orthodoxy and tradition some persons flourish the ideal — static and immobilized in hieratic byzantine-muscovite forms — of a primitive [Romanian] culture without development or prospects. **Our** cultural ideal [in contrast] is dynamic, eager for growth, renewal and fructification.... We mean to propagate a sense of culture that is European. Our light comes from the West. We see our deliverance in the occidentalization of this country, many of whose vital organs are putrefying even before it has reached maturity. Balkanism, our cherished and idealized orientalness...now shelters all the brigands who have impeded political purification and opposed uplifting the people from the cultural cesspool in which they flounder.... [We seek] the affirmation of our genius and specific character in the forms of European culture , in the harmonious and shining framework of the culture of the West.... We have faith that soap, comfort and urbanism, the telegraph and civil law in no way threaten the purity of our race....

Nationalist ideology gave Romanians a theoretical basis for constructing a set of binary oppositions between themselves and other populations. Not all of these distinctions were antagonistic, although some were. For example, the form nationalism took in Romania vis-à-vis Jews was based on perceptions and definitions not only of otherness, but also of antagonistic otherness. Romanian nationalism totalized and absolutized Romanian social structures and Romanian culture. In the process, it devalued and negated everything that differed from itself in varying degrees. Jews were seen as being at the far end of otherness. Nationalist ideology made it impossible for Jews to become Romanians in any sense of the word.

When we look at these elements of modern Romanian nationalism, it is easy to understand why Jews, along with Rroma, would be seen as the ultimate and eternal outsiders. Jews could not trace a lineage from the Dacia-Romans, nor did they have an "organic" connection to the Romanian language, religion, land, and peasantry.

In addition, the Christian churches defined the Jews as an untouchable, polluting population. Christians were seen to have a moral obligation to have as little to do with Jews as possible and a moral obligation from keeping Jews from owning land in a Christian state. Jews, as Christian scripture then was interpreted, had killed Christ and they bore a collective guilt for this. As elsewhere in Eastern Europe, Romanian peasants believed that Jews captured and sacrificed Christian children for their Passover rituals.

The idea that Jews had inherited a collective guilt for deicide (see Carroll 2001 for an extended discussion of the role that charges of Jewish "deicide" played in the formation of anti-Semitism) was easy to assimilate into popular culture given the Christian doctrine of intergenerational inheritance of "original sin." It made sense to Christian believers that if Christians inherited the stain of Adam and Eve's transgression then Jew's could (and did) inherit the collective moral guilt of their ancestors' "deicide." The Jews, thus, were seen as an alien presence that constituted the ultimate contradiction of the Christian moral order in Romania.

Because Jews were not connected to the folk culture of the peasantry, it also was believed that they never could fully appreciate, understand, or creatively participate in Romanian culture, according to nationalist ideology. Instead, Jews were seen as a threat to authentic Romanian values. Nationalists came to define Jews as carriers of a debased Western capitalist culture and, at the same time, as carriers of

Bolshevism, both of which were seen to be alien to authentic Romanian culture. To the nationalists, the Jews wanted to impose foreign and destructive forms of life on the Romanian nation. Finally, from the perspective of nationalist ideology, the Jews, being immigrants to the region did not have an organic connection with the Romanian land. The Jews, like the Rroma, were seen as a wandering, cursed people. Neither people had a homeland and both were seen as incapable of forming permanent attachments anywhere. This made Jews and Rroma pariah peoples in a country where land ownership defined one's status.

Anti-Semitism shaped and reshaped the nature of all transactions Romanians had with Jews. Because of anti-Semitism, all Romanian-Jewish interactions were spoiled relations (Goffman 1963). In all inter-actions with Romanians, Jews were expected to show "appropriate" forms of deference to the dominant group. With Jews being a stigma-tized population to the vast majority of Romanians, even normal economic activity came to be defined as an example of the perfidious character of Jews. The Romanian bourgeoisie persisted in demanding that the state limit Jewish economic activity and confine it to certain sectors. The modern Romanian state, as already noted, responded by passing a number of laws and promulgated numerous administrative regulations limiting what economic roles Jews could fill.

Romanian intellectuals, like Romanian businessmen, wanted to restrict competition from Jews. The intellectuals wanted Jews removed from Romanian universities, certain professions, and state offices of various kinds. Intellectuals believed that Jews, if not restrained by law, would monopolize white collar, intellectual, and professional occupa-tions. That is why, in part, they sought to establish quotas for Jews in university admissions and in professional licensure.

Peasants saw Jews as exploiters, driven by a hatred of Christians. In Moldova Jews often were employed by the boyars to manage estates. Jews were responsible, in the peasants' eyes, for establishing punishing land rents and for evictions of families who could not meet the costs of tenancy. Jews, throughout Romania, also were heavily involved in money lending and peasants blamed the Jews for their heavy debts. Also, Jews often dominated commercial activity in many parts of Romania. To the Romanian peasantry, Jews, by being involved in local trade, were economic parasites. Jews were seen to be were making money without producing anything of value, which the peasantry saw as fundamentally immoral. Peasants also were highly susceptible to religiously based anti-Semitism. In sum, because of the synthesis of anti-Semitism with nationalist ideology, Romanian Jews came to be defined as radically *Other*. The Jew was seen as not simply different, but was defined as an embodiment of a total and fundamentally threatening, exploiting, and corrupting evil. The Jew was an object of disgust and rejection. They were not fully human and, hence, did not deserve to be accorded civil rights in Romania. From the perspective of the Romanian anti-Semite, it was perfectly moral to limit Jewish rights and to want them expelled from the country, as Bratianu had wanted to do in 1867. In 1937, Jews lost their Romanian citizenship and most of their civil and political rights and liberties.

The Legion of the Archangel St. Michael

Codreanu, unlike other radical right political activists, was able to build a political movement grounded in the synthesis of nationalism and anti-Semitism and develop it into a major force in Romanian society. Codreanu broke with his mentor Cuza in 1927, when he, Codreanu, founded the Legionnaire movement. Codreanu had come to believe that Cuza's political program was far too limited and was likely to remain only a marginal political force in Romania. Codreanu had come to believe that Romania was in need of a major social, cultural, and moral transformation. This transformation needed to be firmly grounded in the ancient principles and practices of Romanian folk-culture and in the theological principles of the Romanian Orthodox Church and he fully expected that only he could lead such a total revolution. Codreanu's movement stood for developing an Orthodox Christian nation. The movement was rabidly nationalistic, militaristic, anti-communist, anti-Western, anti-Semitic, and anti-democratic.

Codreanu, who became known to his followers as *Capitan*, set about building a strong national network that reached into all parts of Romanian society. The Legionnaire movement, while initiated by intellectuals, focused itself on attracting peasants, workers, shopkeepers, artisans, and merchants, clergy, state officials, military officers, capitalists, and university professors, among others. The Guards' anti-Semitic message to these groups fell on ears that had been well prepared for receiving this message.

The basic organizational unit of the Legion was the "nest" (*cuib*). Each nest was a small operational unit seldom consisting of more than about a dozen men. The members of each nest usually selected their own leader from among their own number. The nests were grouped together by villages, judet, and province into a nationwide organization. There were parallel organizations for women and for youths.

In 1930, Codreanu formed the Iron Guard. The Iron Guard was the military wing of the Legion. The Iron Guard emulated, in many respects, the uniform and rituals of the paramilitary units of the Spanish, Portuguese, German, and Italian fascist parties. Dressed in uniforms with green shirts and high boots, each Guardist wore a necklace, from which hung a small bag containing Romanian dirt.

The Legion advocated the building of an organic political order. As such, its theory of the ideal society was similar to Spanish, Italian, and Portuguese corporatism. Codreanu's image of a properly ordered society was one in which corporate bodies would be functionally integrated into an organic whole. Through participation in the whole, corporate groups would be able to transcend and annihilate all particularisms of class, region, and the like and create an organically integrated Romanian society. Codreanu's views of democracy were laid out in his *A Few Remarks on Democracy* (1937). Codreanu stated that:

> 1. Democracy destroys the unity of the Romanian nation, dividing it among political parties, making Romanians hate one another, and thus exposing a divided people to the united congregation of Jewish power at a difficult time in the nation's history. This argument alone is so pervasive as to warrant the discarding of democracy in favor of anything that would ensure out unity – or life itself. For disunity means death.
>
> 2. Democracy makes Romanian citizens out of millions of Jews by making them the Rumanians' equals. By giving them the same legal rights. Equality? What for? We have been here for thousands of years. Plow and weapon in hand. With our labors and blood. Why equality with those who have been here for only one hundred, ten, or even five years? Let's look at the past: We created this state. Let's look at the future: We Romanians are fully responsible for Greater Romania. They have nothing to do with it. What could be the responsibility for Jews, in the history books, for the disappearance of the Romanian state? Thus: no equality in labor, sacrifice,

and struggle for the creation of the state and no equal responsibility for its future. Equality? According to an old maxim: Equality is to treat unequally the unequal. What are the reasons for the Jews' demanding equal treatment, equal political rights with the Romanians?

3. Democracy is incapable of perseverance. Since it is shared by political parties that rule for one, two, or three years, it is unable to conceive and carry out plans of longer duration. One party annuls the plans and efforts of the other. What is conceived and built by one party today is destroyed by another tomorrow. In a country in which much has to be built, in which building is indeed the primary historical requirement, this disadvantage of democracy constitutes a true danger. It is a situation similar to that which prevails in an establishment where masters are changed every year, each new master bringing in his own plans, ruining what was done by some, and starting new things, which will in turn be destroyed by tomorrow's masters.

4. Democracy prevents the politician's fulfillment of his obligations to the nation. Even the most well-meaning politician becomes, in a democracy, the slave of his supporters, because either he satisfies their personal interests or they destroy his organization. The politician lives under the tyranny and permanent threat of the electoral bosses. He is placed in a position in which he must choose between the termination of his lifetime work and the satisfaction of the demands of party members. And the politician, given such a choice, opts for the latter. He does so not out of his own pocket, but from that of the country. He creates jobs, sets up missions, commissions, sinecures – all rostered in the nation's budget – which put increasingly heavy pressures on a tired people.

5. Democracy cannot wield authority, because it cannot enforce its decisions. A party cannot move against itself, against its members who engage in scandalous malfeasance, who rob and steal, because it is afraid of losing its members. Nor can it move against its adversaries, because in so doing it would risk exposure of its own wrongdoings and shady business.

6. Democracy serves big business. Because of the expensive, competitive character of the multiparty system, democracy requires ample funds. It therefore naturally becomes the servant of the big international Jewish financiers, who enslave her by paying her. In this manner, a nation's fate is placed in the hands of a clique of bankers.

We can see in this quote, a number of themes of the Legionnaire movement. Like other radical right movements in Europe at this time, Codreanu and his followers saw Western parliamentary democracy as a force that divided Romanians, leaving them open to manipulation and domination by Jews and foreigners. Codreanu was looking to find a way to create a state that was built around an organic solidarity and that was based on methods of decision-making grounded in an authoritarian hierarchy. Codreanu saw Jews as an evil presence in Romania who did not deserve equality with those he regarded as true Romanians. Jews were seen to be agents of a large, international conspiracy of Jewish financial capitalists. The quote also illustrates the Legionnaires' belief that democracy was inherently corrupt, that politicians served only their interests and the interests of Jewish financial capital, not the interests of the Romanian people and its nation.

Codreanu went on to outline his conception of the Romanian nation. He wrote:

> When we speak of the Romanian nation, we refer not only to the Rumanians currently living on the same territory, with the same past and the future, the same habits, the same language, the same interests. When we speak of the Romanian nation we refer to all Romanians, dead or alive, who have lived on this land of ours from the beginnings of history and will live on it also in the future.
> The nation includes:
> 1. All Romanians currently alive.
> 2. The souls and tombs of the dead and of our ancestors.
> 3. All souls who will be born Romanian.
>
> A people becomes aware of its existence when it becomes aware of its entirety, not only of its component parts and their individual interests.
> The nation possesses:
> 1. A physical, biological patrimony: the flesh and the blood.
> 2. A material patrimony: the country's soil and its wealth.
> 3. A spiritual patrimony, which includes:
>   A. Its concept of God, people, and life. This concept constitutes a possession, a spiritual patrimony. The limits of this domain are set by the limits of the brilliance of the concept. There is a country housing the national spirit,

the expectations of that spirit, a spirit resulting from revelation, and the nation's own efforts.

B. Its honor, which shines in proportion to the acceptance by the nation, during its historical existence of the norms derived from its concept of God, people, and life.

C. Its culture: the fruit of its life, the product of its own efforts in thought and art. This culture is not international. It is the expression of the national genius, of the blood. The culture is international in its brilliance but national in origin. Someone made a fine comparison: bread and wheat may be internationally consumed, but they always bear the imprint of the soil from which they come.

Each of these three patrimonies has its own importance. All three must be defended by the nation. But the most important of all is the spiritual patrimony, because it alone bears the seal of eternity, it alone transcends all times. The ancient Greeks are with us today not because of their physiques, no matter how athletic – these are only ashes now – nor because of their material wealth, if they had such, but because of their culture.

A nation lives forever through its concepts, honor, and culture. It is for these reasons that the rulers of nations must judge and act not only on the basis of physical and material interests of the nation but on the basis of the nation's historical honor, of the nation's external interests. Thus: not bread at all costs, but honor at all costs.

Codreanu continues with a discussion of "The Nation's Ultimate Goal:"

Is it life?

If it be life, then the means whereby nations seek to ensure it become irrelevant. All are valid, even the worst.

The question may thus be asked: What are the norms for international behavior? The nations' animal instincts? The tiger in them? Do the laws of the fishes in the sea or of the beasts in the forest apply?

The ultimate goal is not life? It is resurrection. The resurrection in the name of Jesus Christ the Savior. Creation and culture are only means – not the purpose – of resurrection. Culture is the fruit of talent, which God implanted in our nation and for which we are responsible. A time will come when all the world's nations will arise from the dead, with all their dead, with all their kings and emperors. Every nation has its place before God's throne, The final moment, "resurrection from the dead," is the highest and most sublime goal for which a nation can strive. The nation is thus an entity that lives beyond this earth. Nations are realities also in the other world, not only on this one. To us Romanians, to our nation, as to every nation in the world, God assigned a specific mission: God has given us a historical destiny.

The first law that every nation must abide by is that of attaining that destiny, of fulfilling the mission entrusted to it.

Our nation has not abandoned that goal no matter how long and difficult has been its own Golgotha.

And now we are faced with mountain- high obstacles.

Are we going to be the weak and cowardly generation that will relinquish, under threats, the Romanian destiny and renounce our national mission?

The discussion of the nation and its mission shows the mystical Christian messianic tenor that marked Codreanu's ideology and the ideology of the League. In Codreanu's ideological vision, the Romanian nation had to realize its historically given spiritual and material missions. The spiritual mission was one of national resurrection. Resurrection entailed a nation coming to a consciousness of itself, uniting itself, and purifying itself. To Codreanu, God demanded ridding the Romanian nation of corrupting Western influences, communists, and Jews. By ridding Romania of these groups, the nation would be freed from the "forces of evil," and it would be possible to organize the nation according to the principles of "the good."

In using the idea of "national resurrection," Codreanu was developing and applying an idea that also had been articulated by Adam Mickiewicz, a 19th century Polish Romantic nationalist poet, and applying it to Romania. Mickiewicz defined Poland as a Messianic nation because of its suffering. Mickiewicz compared Poland's suffering to Christ's crucifixion, while Codreanu identified Romania as a messianic nation through equating its resurrection and consequent national salvation with Christ's resurrection as the saving event for humanity. The difference between Codreanu and Mickiewicz as to what symbol was used to indicate the messianic event reflected differences in the theology of Orthodoxy and Latin Christianity. In the former, the key event in human salvation is the resurrection, while in the latter it is the crucifixion (Carroll 2001). It is worth noting that Mickiewicz had a pronounced influence on Romanian nationalism by virtue of his association in Paris with many of the leading figures of the 1848 generation from Romania. Romanian fascism, in its Legionnaire variant, was not an imported ideology. Romanian fascism was a synthesis of a long standing tradition of fundamentalist nationalism and of deep-seated anti-Semitism, between which there is a strong elective affinity (Mosse 1999: 61). In Romania, nationalism grew within an anti-Semitic context and anti-Semitism grew within a fundamentalist nationalist context, making possible an interchange of ideas between the two ideological systems. Romanian intellectuals' quest to identify the nation's unique and, for the most part, believed to unsullied biological roots, and their quest to use these purported roots to give Romania a unique identity and Romanians a unique national character and national culture opened nationalism to the racialist ideas being promulgated by the anti-Semitic right. All of the ideological components of Romanian fascism were drawn from intellectual traditions, movements, and currents "native" to Romania. The Legionnaires' anti-Semitism, as we have shown, had deep roots in Romania and was part of the political program of several mainstream parties. Codreanu's mysticism and the Legion's ritual practices were drawn from and based on Romanian Orthodox theology, as was a good part of his anti-Semitism. Codreanu was highly successful in drawing on Romania traditions of popular piety in order to build a multi-class fascist movement. In rural communities, this use of rhetoric of popular piety was a major factor in drawing peasants to the Legion's cause. Such rhetoric helped mask class conflict by offering an ideology that seemingly had the potential to transcend class divisions. In addition, by drawing on such ideological traditions, the Legion offered an opportunity for many Romanians to "overcome" the estrangement that people felt from what they perceived to be the growing influences of modernism and Westernism, which many believed were undermining Romanian culture, values, and social practices.

Codreanu's stress on personal piety, Orthodox theology and liturgy, and on a morality of respectability drew thousands upon thousands of Romanians to his cause. Through such ideological themes, Codreanu was able to create a promise of a new Romanian moral universe in which the effects of the social, moral, and cultural ambiguities and contradictions of the modern world would be rendered less threatening to the average Romanian. To Codreanu and his followers this new moral universe would be built on older and "purer" Romanian Orthodox traditions and values and would lead Romania to a re-wakening both to its past and to its national destiny. The emphasis on, or at least use of, traditional Romanian Orthodox rhetoric by the Legion and its placing of the Romanian Orthodox Church as one of the cornerstones of Romanian national identity solidified the support of a large number of Romanian clergy, especially in rural areas, for the fascist movement. In using traditional Christian values as one of the sources for its ideology, the Legion was similar to the Belgian fascist Rexist movement (Mosse 1999:20).

However important these ideological/value issues and orientations may have been in attracting individuals across the class spectrum to the Legion and its general "program" for reconstructing Romania and leading it to the "grandeur" it was believed it deserved in the community of nations, we can not ignore the fact that the Legion's goals offered significant economic opportunities to a number of Romanian social strata and social classes. For example, to the bourgeoisie the Legion held out the promise not only of valorizing their life-style, with its emphasis on rationality, self-denial, self-discipline, and social respectability, it also promised them, implicitly, at least, a disciplined work-force that would be insulated from socialist and communist influence, as one of the Legion's major goals was the total liquidation of the left. The Legion also, again at least implicitly, offered to the bourgeoisie an opportunity to profit from the elimination of Jewish entrepreneurs. By driving Jews out of major economic sectors, investment opportunities would be opened for native Romanian entrepreneurs and investors. In addition, the bourgeoisie were given the chance to profit from the plunder and forced sale of Jewish property to the state. The Romanian National Bank, for example, acquired super profits from financing the re-sale of Jewish property the state had forced to be sold at prices far below their fair market-value.

To Romania's working class and peasants, the fascists promised them the opportunity to participate in their own self-rule through their institutions of "direct democracy." Also, they pledged to workers and peasants that they no longer would be economically "subject" to Jewish capitalists and Jewish estate managers.

The Legion complimented their rhetoric of "concern" for the plight of workers, peasants, and the middle classes by engaging in public works projects across Romania. Legionnaires sent work teams into small towns and villages to repair and build roads, bridges, churches, schools, and public health clinics. All of which was a part of the Legion's efforts to build a grass-roots state-within-a-state as a means for taking power in Romania.

Under fascism, professionals were promised that they would benefit economically from the removal of Jewish competitors. Lawyers, physicians, professors, teachers, accountants, managers, etc. all would face better occupational opportunities if the fascists took power and followed through on their threats to remove Jews from these occupations or only allowed Jewish professionals to serve a Jewish clientele.

To the military, the fascists offered a chance for them to redeem their failures during World War I. Under the fascists, allied with a powerful Nazi Germany and Fascist Italy, the Romanian military would have the opportunity to bring glory to the nation and to recover territories "lost" to the Soviet Union as a result of the Nazi-Soviet Non-Aggression Pact.

The idea of the nation as forming an organic whole was a conception popular with Romanian intellectuals. For example, it had been a major theme in Kogalniceanu's work, as well as in the writings of the Junimea movement. Codreanu's distrust of Western ideas and institutions, including capitalism and parliamentary democracy, was widely shared by Romanian intellectuals, be they "Orientalists" or "indigenists." Many Romanian intellectuals saw the penetration of Western values and institutions as having had the effect of corrupting Romanian culture and society. As opposed to the ideas of Western individualism, many of Romania's leading intellectuals during the post-war period saw individualism in entirely different terms – one could be truly an individual only within the setting of the national community. The highest form of such an individualism only could be realized when the person was able and willing to subordinate personal needs and interests to needs and interests of the collective.

Conservative and radical right Romanian intellectuals shared with the radical right political movements a belief in the value of creating a state that expressed the organic unity of the Romanian "nation," an idea that, in Romania, can be traced back to Kogalniceanu's writings about the nature of society. The conception of organicism that they held had less to do with biological models than it did with the French sociologist Emile Durkheim's ideo-organicism. In this conceptualization, the Romanian nation was seen as one and indivisible. In the view of the conservative and radical right intellectuals, the organic national community demanded a state that expressed this fundamental unity of the Romanian people. This organicism created an archetype of the true Romanian and his/her relation to the national community. At the same time, it created a counter-type of the outsider (Mosse 1999: 50) who never could be fully a part of the nation, as the fascists' organic model conceived the idea of the nation.

To traditional conservatives and radical right intellectuals, the state was legitimate only insofar as it had a higher moral purpose. The traditional and the radical right demanded a state that, as Perez-Diaz (1993) puts it, was "the bearer of a moral project." Codreanu and his men with dirt bags continually challenged the Romanian State for lacking a higher moral purpose that they, alone, believed that they were able to supply. Only the Legion, in Codreanu's view, could lead the nation to its true destiny – national resurrection. It could do so, in Codreanu's opinion, because only the Legion was capable of understanding, expressing, and realizing the "general will" of the Romanian nation.

The radical right and key members of the traditional, conservative intelligentsia, such as Eliade, believed that the Romanian State, as it currently existed, was too divisive and fractured to lead a united nation. Only a single, unitary movement that transcended all forms of particularisms, such as class, political party, and region, was needed to insure the nation's unity. Political parties and parliamentary democracy were incapable, in fact, of allowing the national community to realize its completeness. Instead, parliamentary democracy was seen as a system that fragmented and weakened the national community. Only a unifying movement, such as the Legion, would reconcile all of the national contradictions into a more general synthesis.

It was irrelevant to the radical right and to parts of the traditional, conservative intelligentsia if the take over of the state by the national movement led to authoritarian rule by a great leader or by a "new aristocracy" that would rule through a system of direct democracy, rather than through a parliamentary system. This new aristocracy would be constituted not by ownership of property, or by academic achievement, or by birth. Rather it would be formed from all of those men who were willing to give over their Western concepts of individualism in order to achieve the true individualism that only could be realized within the context of movement that expressed and embodied the organic life of the nation. It would be a "new aristocracy" built around a willingness to act on behalf of the national interest, to spill its own blood and the blood of its enemies, and which would transcend the narrow materialist ethics and culture of the bourgeoisie. The new aristocrats would be men who would, according to Hora Sima (n.d.), one of the Iron Guard's major leaders, integrate the spiritual and the political to forge a new national history.

Both the traditional conservative right and the radical right in Romania came to believe that their organic society was meant only for those Romanians who completely shared the same essential biological heritage derived from the Dacia-Romans, the same "complete" cultural heritage, and, what Wright (1978) calls, the same "metaphysical universe." This meant that Romanians who were not Orthodox or who rejected their "true" national identity by, among other things, supporting communism were not part of the national community. It also excluded minorities from the national, organic community. The state had no obligation to protect or defend those who fell outside of the community's moral boundaries. Indeed, if anything, the state ought to seek ways to expel them from its territory because they disrupted the fundamental harmony and integration of the nation and they threatened to pollute the nation and sap its will and its strength.

We can look at the work of the prominent Romanian, and later American, writer, Mircea Eliade, to see a clear example of the way in which large numbers of traditional, conservative intellectuals provided ideological support for fascism. Intellectually, Eliade moved from being an example of a traditional, conservative intellectual to being a supporter of the radical right. Eliade's mentor was Ion Antonescu, a prominent Romanian philosopher at the University of Bucharest. Eliade, after completing his undergraduate degree at the University of Bucharest, had gone to India to conduct research. He returned to the University and completed a Ph.D. with a thesis on Yoga. He was appointed to the faculty as an assistant to Ion Antonescu. Antonescu went on to become a strong supporter of and propagandist for Italian fascism and German national socialism and a supporter of the Iron Guard (Manea 1992).

Eliade's conservative orientation had links with Orthodox Christian theology. In 1934, he wrote:

> There are a great many revolutionary impulses that have been waiting for thousands of years to be put into practice. That is why the Son of Man descended to teach us permanent revolution.

Eliade, like Antonescu and many of Romania's conservative philosophers, rejected democracy. To Eliade:

> Democracy has been unable to inspire in the people a spirit of fervent nationalism – to make of them a strong, virile, optimistic nation, imbued with a sense of mission and destiny. Being a foreign import, democracy is concerned with matters that are not specifically Romanian concerns: with 'abstractions' such as individual rights, rights of minorities and freedom of political consciousness and these do not strike at the heart of Romania's problems. (Ricketts 1988).

Eliade (1937) looked to a strong leader to "solve" Romania's problems. He wrote: "We know of several tyrants who have transformed stupefied countries into powerful states: Caesar Augustus, and Mussolini,..." He continued:

> To me, then, it is a matter of complete indifference whether or not Mussolini is a or is not a tyrant.... It is immaterial what will happen to Romania after the liquidation of democracy behind, Romania becomes a strong state, armed, conscious of its power and destiny – history will take account of this deed.

In the same article, Eliade stated that:

> In the name of this Romania that began many thousands of years ago and will not end until the apocalypse, social reforms will be enacted with considerable brutality, every corner of the provinces now overrun with foreigners will be recolonized, all traitors will be punished, the myth of our State will extend all across the country, and the news of our strength will stretch beyond it borders.

In 1938 Eliade observed:

From those who have suffered so much and been humbled for centuries...by the Hungarians – after the Bulgarians the most imbecilic people ever to have existed – from these political leaders of heroic martyred Transylvania, we await a nationalist Romania, frenzied and chauvinistic, armed and vigorous, ruthless and vengeful.

Eliade was a strong supporter of Codreanu and the Iron Guard. He believed that the members of the Guard constituted a new national aristocracy (*noua aristocratie*) that was destined to lead the country to national fulfillment. In 1938, he also wrote:

The Legion member is a new man, who has discovered his own will, his own destiny. Discipline and obedience have given him a new dignity and unlimited confidence in himself, the Chief, and the greater destiny of the nation.

Eliade ran into political difficulties in 1940 for his support of the Guard. Nonetheless, Antonescu appointed him cultural attaché to the Romanian embassy in London. In 1941, he was given the same post in Lisbon. After the war, he received an academic appointment at the University of Chicago, where he finished his career. Eliade never repudiated his early writings in support of fascism and his rejection of democracy.

What made Codreanu unique in Romanian history was his ability to synthesize conservative Romanian cultural themes and values into an ideology and a social movement that gained widespread acceptance in the Romanian population. Codreanu was able to use his considerable skills as a political organizer to give his political program a mass base. Codreanu sent organizers into rural areas, where Legionnaires built close ties with the Romanian peasantry. Legionnaires worked side by side with peasants on various community and village projects. At the same time, the Legion's activists engaged in political education and recruitment. In the area of political education, Legionnaires used popular religious beliefs to mobilize peasant anti-Semitism, strengthened nationalist sentiments, and spread a gospel of anti-communism. Legionnaires also provided peasants with a critique of Western economic and political forms that they could understand and appreciate. Organizationally, the Legion's goal was to leave behind at least one and, preferably, more than one nest. Because of its work in the countryside, the Legion was able to position itself as a defender and advocate of peasantism and under this guise, it attracted a large number of peasant recruits to the movement. The Legion's political program included the socialization of industry and the breaking up of the remaining large estates, with the land being redistributed to the peasantry (Longworth 1997).

The Legion's mobilization efforts were helped by the onset of the Great Depression and because of the nature of the Romanian political party system. Between 1923 and 1928, the Romanian economy had experienced a general prosperity that communist historians described as a "relative stabilization of capitalism" (Fischer-Galati 1998a). In part, Romanian prosperity was the result of the more global prosperity experienced by North America and Europe, except for the defeated powers, especially Germany and Austria, and the new Soviet Union, which was fighting a bitter civil war with the reactionary White armies, in the years immediately following World War I. However, prosperity in Romania was not merely an overflow from more general European economic growth, it also partly resulted from the economic policies pursued by the National Liberal Party. The National Liberal party stimulated Romanian industrial growth by imposing high import tariffs, restricting foreign investment, and by providing a wide variety of direct and indirect financial incentives to local investors in Romanian industry (Fischer-Galati 1998a). However, it paid less attention to agriculture. Little in the way of state support was given to modernizing Romania's rural economy (Fischer-Galati 1998a). Despite fairly good prices on world markets and relatively high demand for Romanian grains and other agricultural exports, in the absence of significant state investment the rural economy remained underdeveloped, functioning almost as a pre-modern economic sector.

The dramatic loss of value on the New York Stock Exchange in September 1929 led to a collapse of world grain prices, setting in motion a process that resulted in a global financial crisis. Romania was affected by the subsequent European financial crisis of 1931, although, Romania's mass production industry appears to have recovered fairly quickly and to have experienced net increases of industrial production between 1931 and 1938. Grain was one of Romania's principal exports during the period between World War I and World War II. With declining prices, Romanian peasants were pushed into a major debt crisis, the government responded by adopting a system of price supports and placed a moratorium on peasant loan repayments. But this did little to salvage the economic situation of the peasantry, which declined dramatically as a result of the global economic downturn. The crisis in the countryside had negative effects far beyond the peasantry. The commercial sector in rural areas as well as petty craft production for rural markets also experienced severe adverse effects. The state, constrained by its ideology and by the economic downturn, was unable to respond effectively to the crisis in the countryside, where larger and larger parts of the population were being immiserated.

The virtual collapse of the rural economy made it possible for the Guard to organize peasants and others in the countryside. Codreanu and the Guard developed an economic "program" that was directed against specific forms of capitalism, especially finance capitalism, which it blamed for the ruination of the Romanian economy, especially its agricultural economy. In the Legion's view, the forms of capitalism which were "dominated" by the Jews and, to a lesser degree, other foreigners were responsible for Romanian's economic problems. This was a shrewd organizational tactic in that it allowed the Guard to benefit from traditional peasant anti-Semitism fed by religious beliefs and by the recurring economic exchanges between peasants and Jewish shop-keepers, rent collectors on the estates, and Jewish holders of estate leases.

The Guard's organizational efforts in the towns and cities also were helped by the global depression. The onset of the Great Depression and the seeming inability of the Romanian political class to manage the economic crisis seriously compromised the legitimacy of the ruling elites. The lower middle classes and the upper reaches of the urban working classes, as well as professional workers, were especially susceptible to fascist mobilization in Romania, even before the Great Depression. The Depression merely enhanced the appeal of fascism among these populations. It was these groups who were threatened from above by the rise of big businesses and from below by the emergence of an increasingly organized working class movement. It is small wonder that *Cuza*'s National League and, later, the Legionnaires first developed in Moldova, which was on the frontier of the Soviet Union and where there was a relatively strong, although not clearly communists, workers' movement. It also was among these strata where Jews were perceived as an economic threat.

Romanian fascism's mass appeal also, in part, stemmed from its glorification of and its willingness to use violence against its enemies in order to "cleanse" and to "purify" the nation and move it toward national resurrection. Violence was one of the means a man could use to become part of the "new aristocracy" the fascists saw as destined to vindicate Romania's history. Tens of thousands of Romanian men had gone through the brutalizing experiences of World War I and many had come away from these experiences humiliated at the defeats the Romanian army had suffered in most of its major battles. But, at the same time, they had come away from the war inured to violence as a means for resolving political conflict. Fascist violence offered these men a way to redeem the humiliation of military defeat and to punish those internal "enemies" of the Romanian nation, such as Jews, socialists, communists, monopoly capitalists, financiers, and the rest, who were believed to have contributed to the military disasters and who it was believed had profited from them and who continued to profit from them. Violence was a means for the national to achieve its redemption. It was a tool for helping to forge the bonds within the "new aristocracy," which was marked by destiny to lead the nation out of its wilderness and toward its deserved place of grandeur among nations. Under the rule of the Guard, a Romanian nation would emerge in which its people would be one. Unified with a common vision, a common sense of patriotism, and a common purpose, the Romanian nation, would be purged of impurities, including undesirable ethnic and religious minorities, would transcend the divisions of region and class, and create a state that embodied and expressed the national essence.

Peasants, especially, readily embraced the Guard's message, even if they did not vote in over-whelming numbers for the Guards' parliamentary candidates. The Guard was a master of political theater. In a country where few workers or peasants were literate, it used theatrical techniques, heavily influenced by popular Romanian Orthodox liturgy, to get across its message. When Guard organizers came into villages, dressed in their uniforms, with a feather in their caps, and a bag of Romanian dirt hanging from around their neck, they were enthusiastically welcomed by the peasants, the local priests, and local dignitaries. The Guards' message put the peasants at the center of their ideology and their economic and political program. It was they, who the Guard promised, would benefit from the Legion's capture of the state, while all of the historical "enemies" of the peasants – industrial capitalists, financiers, Jews, and communists – would get their just reward at the hands of the Guard. The Romanian peasantry at this time was politically disorganized, economically devastated, and socially disoriented. It had no popular political party of its own to represent its interests, unless one were to count the National Peasant Party whose leadership was not drawn from the peasantry and whose agenda was more a program of palliative reform than a fundamental restructuring of economic and political relations in the countryside. It was trying to make sense of a world in which economic relations had lost their embeddedness in traditional social practices, customs, and norms and had come to be dominated by market relations that stood autonomous from social and customary considerations. The peasants, in effect, were strangers living in a strange world in a countryside that was not of their own making and over which they felt they had little control.

Livezeanu (1995) provides a number of examples of the violence the Guard inflicted on Jews. Guard organizing activities led to violent anti-Semitic outbursts in Maramures, Bukovina, and Bessarabia in 1930. One of the more dramatic acts of anti-Jewish violence took place in Borsa, a commune in Maramures. Peasant mobs attacked Jews and burned their houses. The town's Jews were forced to flee into the forests and hide. Codreanu, in defending those accused of having engaged in the violence, claimed that it had been precipitated by the town's Jews. The anti-Semitic message of the Legion and the Guard fell on ears well prepared for it. Generation after generation of Christians had heard the story of how Jews allegedly had rejected the Christ, betrayed him, killed him, and called down on themselves and their descendants an everlasting curse for these acts.

As support for the Legion and the Guard increased, the state acted against the movement. The Ministry of Interior, in 1931 and, again, in 1932, ordered the Guard disbanded, but the Legion ignored the orders. In 1933 the Romanian government formally declared the Guard an illegal organization and directed the Romanian police to repress it. In ensuing actions against the Guard, the police shut down the Legion's newspaper and arrested key leaders in the movement. Police action resulted in the deaths of several Legionnaires. The Guard responded by assassinating Prime Minister Ion Gheorghe Duca at a train station in Sinai on New Year's Eve 1933. Upon becoming Prime Minister, Duca had ordered the arrest of a number of Guard Leaders on charges of "terrorism." This was something the Guard would not tolerate.

Duca's assassination led to the arrest of a large part of the Guard's leadership, as well as the three men directly responsible for the killings. In a subsequent trial, the three assassins were given life terms for murder, but the leaders, who had been charged with ordering and planning the killing were acquitted.

In 1936, ten Guardist assassins killed Mihail Stelescu. Stelescu was a member of parliament who the Legion saw as a traitor to its cause. He once had belonged to the Guard. He had left the Legion and Guard and formed his own ultra-right movement, which only had limited success. The ten assassins received life sentences.

The League won five parliamentary seats in 1932. Codreanu, in 1934, along with General Gheorghe Cantacuzino-Granicerul, an authoritarian anti-Semite who was a hero of World War I, started a new political party called "All for the Country" (*Totul pentru Tara*). This was a radical right wing, anti-Semitic, anti-communist, and anti-democratic party. The Legion was the party's main base.

The new party developed close ties to the National Peasant Party, especially with its leader Iuliu Maniu. Both parties shared a peasantist and nationalist orientation and, at their base, their members shared anti-Semitic and anti-Bolshevik values. They also both opposed state policies directed at transforming Romania into an industrial state, modeled on Western European countries. The two parties formed an electoral alliance for the 1937 elections. The goal was to block the National Liberal Party from winning a majority in parliament. The National Peasant Party hoped that if the National Liberals lost the election that the king would turn to them to form a government. If this were to occur, the Legion expected that they would gain representation in the government in exchange for the support the Legion had given to the National Peasant Party. In addition to its alliance with the National Peasant Party, Codreanu formed an electoral alliance with the National Liberal Party-Gheorghe I. Bratianu. The latter was a splinter group from the National Liberal Party and it was led by Gheorghe Bratianu, the son of Ioan I. C. Bratianu. In the 1930s he was a professor of history at the University of Iasi. These electoral alliances gave Codreanu's new party new legitimacy among Romanian voters.

In the 1937 elections, All for the Country came in third among the parties contesting for parliamentary representation, winning over fifteen per cent of the total vote, which translated into thirty-six seats, a substantial increase over the five seats they had won in 1934. It is likely that the All for the Country Party had won even more votes that went unrecorded and unreported (Fischer-Galati 1998a). A good part of the Romanian electorate had responded positively to the Guards' economic message, its anti-Semitic propaganda, and its claims that it, alone, could give the Romanian state and nation a renewed moral purpose that would lead to "resurrection" of the Romanian people.

The electoral alliance led to the parliamentary defeat of the National Liberal Party and its leader Gheorghe Tatarascu. The National Liberal Party failed to get the minimum of forty per cent of the votes which, under the terms of the Constitution of 1923, would have given it control of parliament. The 1937 election was the inexorable outcome of the decay of the parliamentary system in Romania following World War II.

Throughout the 1920s and the 1930s, Romania's parliament was highly fractured. No single party could dominate the parliament on a regular basis. Between World War I and World War II, only two governments managed to serve out the four-year terms to which they were entitled under the terms of the Constitution of 1923. Both of these were governments controlled by the National Liberal Party. Between 1918 and 1938, Romania had twenty-four governments, meaning that the average government held power for less than twelve months. The fragmented political party system led to a loss of confidence in parliamentary government among Romanians, in general, and among the political elites, in particular. The parliamentary system was proving it was incapable of dealing with Romania's multiple internal contradictions and the effects that the international economic crisis was having on the country, especially in rural areas.

By the 1930s, it was evident that the forms of the liberal state that Romania had built, beginning in 1866, were empty structures. Romanian political institutions lacked democratic content. Romania never had institutionalized democracy. Political power was in the hands of a small, oligarchic elite that manipulated elections and engaged in a variety of repressive actions in order to eliminate any opposition to elite hegemony. Political parties, when in power, manipulated elections, falsified vote counts, and engaged in other practices to insure the outcomes they wanted. Laws governing elections were ignored and violated with impunity, indicating that the parties and the state had no respect of the rule of law. The upshot of the "engineered democracy" that characterized Romania during the inter-war period and before was that peasants and workers were excluded from opportunities for effective political participation in the Romanian State. This exclusion was reinforced through the top down organization of Romanian political parties. The traditional parties had shallow roots in the general society. This opened the peasants and workers to appeals from the fascist right and made their mobilization by the Legion much easier than it might otherwise have been had the peasants and the workers been able to develop autonomous democratic organizations of their own. Peasants and workers did not need much convincing as to the validity of the charges of corruption and ineffectiveness of parliamentary government raised by the radical right.

The state also violated basic civil rights with impunity, using a powerful secret police, among other weapons, to intimidate and to liquidate opponents of the regime and of the governments in power. The main targets of the secret police (the *Directia Politiei de Siguranta* or the DPS) were parties and political movements that stood outside of the governing oligarchy, especially the communists. The state declared leftist parties to be illegal organizations, arrested and imprisoned their members, broke up their meetings and political rallies, and censored their publications, among other things.

Just as the parliamentary system showed signs of increasing paralysis and increasing political decay, so, too, did the monarchy. Ferdinand had followed Karol I as king in 1914. He held office until 1927. During his tenure as king, Ferdinand allied himself with the National Liberal Party. Under Ferdinand, the National Liberal Party exercised hegemony over the state and went a long way to realizing its agenda of developing Romania as a modern industrial capitalist state organized and controlled by the political "directorate" of the national urban bourgeoisie. Ferdinand and, later, Karol II contributed to parliamentary political instability. Between them, they dissolved eight of the ten parliaments elected between 1918 and 1938.

When Ferdinand died in late 1927, his grandson Michael, who was six years old at the time, succeeded him. Ferdinand's oldest son, Prince Karol had renounced his rights to the throne and was living in exile. As heir-apparent Prince Karol had acquired a reputation as a playboy and a philanderer, which probably would not have caused him much trouble if he had not taken up with Elena Wolff, more commonly known in Romania as Magda Lupescu ("Lupus" is Romanian for "wolf"). Doamna Lupescu was the product of an ethnically mixed marriage. Her father was a Jew who had been baptized as a Christian; her mother was not Jewish (Sachar: 2002: 90). In 1923, Karol divorced his wife, Princess Helen of Greece, and began openly living with Doamna Lupescu. This was too much for the Romanian Orthodox Church and for Romania's political elites. Prince Karol was forced to give up his right of succession and he left Romania to live in exile.

Between 1928 and 1930, the power of the throne was held by a Regency Council. Being in a weakened state, the throne came under attack by a number of political parties, who sought to reduce its considerable powers. In 1930, Karol, at the urging of the National Liberal Party, returned to Romania and claimed the throne as Karol II. In exchange for the throne, Karol had promised that he would abandon Doamna Lupescu. However, no sooner had he returned to Romania and been crowned king than Doamna Lupescu returned to Romania and took up residence not far from the Royal Palace (Sachar: 2002: 91). Karol repaid the support he had gotten from the National Peasant Party Leader and Prime Minister, Iuiu Maniu, to return as king by forcing Maniu to resign as Prime Minister in 1930.

Maniu was followed by a number of weak and ineffective Prime Ministers appointed by the king, who used their ineffectiveness to build his own power base. In 1934, the National Liberal Party won control of the parliament and formed the national government. Using its parliamentary power, the National Liberal Party voted to allow its leader, Prime Minister Gheorghe Tatarascu, to govern by decree. In effect, this removed parliament from the governing process in Romania. Government was left in the hands of the king and the prime minister. This action by the National Liberals seriously undermined the party's claim to be a defender of democracy.

With no party acquiring enough votes to form a government in 1937, Karol II asked Octavian Goga and A. C. Cuza to organize an administration. Their party, The National Christian Party, had received slightly more than nine per cent of the vote. The National Christian Party had been formed in 1935 by a merger of Cuza's League of National

Christian Defense and Octavian Goga's National Agrarian Party. Both of these parties were on the radical right and both were virulently anti-Semitic. We have already seen how Cuza had long been associated with anti-Semitism, having first organized an anti-Semitic party in 1910, and having played a role in organizing student anti-Semitic movements in the early 1920s. Octavian Goga was Romania's pre-eminent poet in the first third of the 20th century. He also was an able politician, having served as Minister of Interior in 1920-21 and, again, in 1926-27 in governments under the control of the National People's Party, led by General Averescu. As shown by Livezeanu (1995), Goga strongly supported the anti-Semitic student movement of 1921-22. Livezeanu (1995) shows that Goga, like the students, saw Jews as a clear threat to the integrity of Romanian culture and the Romanian nation. Goga was a strong advocate of deporting all Jews who were not citizens under Romanian law.

The Goga government lasted forty-four days. During its short tenure, however, the Goga and Cuza government passed a number of anti-Semitic laws, many of which were directly modeled after the Nazi racial laws. These laws, in effect, stripped Romania's Jews of their citizenship rights and civil liberties. The government also launched an attack on the Romanian press, forcing a number of newspapers to shut down.

As Romania's parliamentary government came under increasing pressure in the 1930s, neither the National Peasant Party nor the National Liberal Party was in a position to defend even the pretense of democracy. Their ideological differences and their continuing battles for control of the state and the prerogatives that came with such control immeasurably contributed to the radical right's eventual accession to power.

Perceiving the radical right to be a clear threat to his position, Karol II ordered the arrest of Codreanu and several of his colleagues in the Iron Guard. On the night of November 29-30, 1937 (which came to be known as the "Night of the Vampires"), Codreanu and thirteen other Guardists were killed while allegedly trying to escape (Longworth 1997). The Guard claimed that Codreanu had been strangled in his cell and retaliated by assassinating its long-time enemy Prime Minister Duca.

The king reacted almost immediately. He ordered the arrest and summary execution of the Guards' key leadership cadres. Over two hundred and fifty members of the Guard were killed and their bodies were displayed in town centers across Romania. The leaders who avoided capture fled to Germany. Karol II seized power in 1938, establishing a royal fascist dictatorship. When the Goga government fell, Karol II declared Romania to be in a state of siege and took power himself. At his direction a new constitution was drafted in February 1938 and was overwhelmingly approved in a national referendum conducted on February 24, 1938. Voters went to the polls and were asked if they approved or disapproved of the proposed constitution. They were required to give a verbal vote. Not surprisingly, of more the four million votes cast, the proposed constitution was endorsed by almost 99.9% of the voters.

Under the terms of the 1938 Constitution, all power resided in the king. He had the right to appoint and dismiss the government, completely independent of parliament, and he held the right to appoint all ministers. The king also had the right to veto any piece of parliamentary legislation with which he disagreed. In addition, the king served as the chief executive officer of the state, overseeing the state bureaucracy, including the military. The king was intent on using his newly consolidated position of power in order to reconstruct Romania as a corporate society, using the economic and social theory of the Romanian economist Virgil Madgearu. The 1938 constitution contained provisions that defined membership in the Romanian nation in terms of "blood," drawing a distinction between Romanians "by race" and Romanians "by residence" (Ioanid 2000), which was an ominous portent of things that were to come for Romanian's Jews and, to a lesser degree, Romania's Rroma.

A month after the new constitution was adopted the king abolished all political parties and created his own national party. It was called the National Renaissance Front. All members of parliament were required to join the king's party. By April 1938, the National Renaissance Front had over three million members. The party's growth was an example of the throne's capacities for mass political mobilization and the Romanian electorate's opportunism and its acquiescence to dictatorship.

The king appointed Romanian Orthodox Patriarch, Miron Cristea, as Prime Minister. Patriarch Cristea was both anti-Semitic and anti-democratic. Cristea believed in an organic connection between the Orthodox religion and the Romanian State. They were seen as two sides of the same coin. The idea of separation of Church and state was regarded by a good part of the Church, and by conservative Romanian intellectuals, as but one more perverted Western value that was of little use to Romania. Cristea supported a large part of the Legion's agenda. Cristea was just one of many clerical fascists in Romania. In his inaugural address as Prime Minister, Patriarch Cristea denounced the Romanian parliament and its 29 political parties. He said:

> Today the monster with 29 electoral heads was destroyed, which turned everyone against everyone to the ruin of the whole country. Today everyone's vision became clear, and we all understand that our salvation comes from his Majesty. (Mungiu-Pippidi 1998).

It would appear that, during the 1930s, the Romanian Orthodox Church, drawing on its own spiritual history, was developing an indigenous version of the German *Reichstheologie* (Carroll 2001).

The leadership of The National Peasant and National Liberal Parties, like the Orthodox Church, acquiesced in the dismantling of democracy. The parties mounted no systematic opposition to their own destruction or to the liquidation of parliamentary powers. Indeed both parties provided substantial support for the royal fascist dictatorship and, later, for General Antonescu's fascist oriented military dictatorship and a former National Liberal Party prime minister served in the same role in 1939-40 during Karol II's monarchical fascist regime.

During his dictatorship, Karol II moved Romania ever closer to a formal alliance with Italy and Nazi Germany. Karol II long had admired Mussolini and saw him as a role model for modern state leaders (Sachar 2002: 91). In large part, the historical anti-Semitism of Romania and the use of this ideology by the Legionnaires and the Iron Guard laid one of the foundations for Romania's alliance with the Italian fascists and Germany's Nazis. Anti-Semitism was respectable in Romania, so there was no reason to see Germany, in a negative light because of its racial policies toward Jews. Furthermore, in the view of Karol II and the Romania political elite, it was better to be part of a European international order dominated by Germany than to stand isolated against the Soviet Union.

In 1935, Karol II directed the signing of the first of several trade agreements with Germany. These agreements gave the Germans access to a variety of Romanian raw materials, the most important of which was oil (Longworth 1997). Romania was one of the world's largest oil producers, with fields located in and around Ploesti. Germany saw access to Romanian oil as essential to its war machine and believed it would remain so until German forces could capture the Soviet oil fields around the Caspian Sea. Germany never was able to capture the Caspian fields, so it remained highly dependent on Romania's oil throughout the war.

In 1938, Karol II introduced a package of anti-Semitic laws. This was the same year that Italy introduced its racial laws directed against Jews. In both cases, the anti-Semitic legislation owed a heavy debt to earlier German laws directed against the Jews. In Romania, there was no significant internal protest against the introduction of the anti-Semitic legislation. In fact, the legislation was supported by the Orthodox Church hierarchy. The leadership of Romania's other churches did nothing of significance to protest Karol II's anti-Semitic laws. For example, the Catholic Church in Transylvania, a good part of which was made up of Magyars, apparently saw nothing inherently wrong with the anti-Semitic legislation. It had its own anti-Semitic tradition which, in many ways, was stronger than that of the Romanian Orthodox Church (see, among others, Kertzer 2001 for an extended discussion of the role of the Catholic Church, in general, and the Vatican, in particular) in the development of modern anti-Semitism). Romania's major religious organizations long had used anti-Semitism to bind the faithful to their churches and anti-Semitism bound the religious organizations and their congregations to the forces of reaction. The Hungarian Catholic Church, which had a strong presence in Transylvania, had its own long history of religious anti-Semitism.

While the king's attacks had weakened the Guard, they had not eliminated it. In 1939 Guardists had assassinated Prime Minister Armand Calinescu. In 1940 the king moved toward a rapprochement with the Guard. He declared a general amnesty for Guardists who were in prison and appointed Hora Sima, who then was commanding the Guard, to a position in the government, along with two other members of the Iron Guard. A large number of Guardists returned from their German exile and began reorganizing their movement, especially in the Romanian countryside, where the Guard always had its strongest support.

Karol II, having failed to suppress the Guard, apparently came to believe that the traditional right and the radical right could form an effective alliance, over which he would preside, much as his predecessors had presided over the alliance between the boyars and the bourgeoisie. After all, both the traditional and the radical right shared a tradition of opposition to democracy, anti-Semitic beliefs, suspicions about bourgeois capitalism, and both feared trade unionism and, even more, socialism and communism. In addition, the right shared in rejecting cultural modernism as an alien import from the West that was degrading and deforming Romanian culture. For both the traditional and radical right, the Jew provided the explanation for and the symbol of all that had gone wrong with Romania. The Jews were seen as responsible for Romania's "suffering, just as they were responsible for the suffering of Christ. And, just as Christ was resurrected, so, too, would Romania. Each embraced a nationalism wherein the Jew never could be a complete Romanian citizen. To the radical and traditional right, whatever "rights" Jews enjoyed within Romania were *privileges* accorded them by the state, they were not seen as intrinsic rights that had the same ontological status as the rights of "true" Romanians.

Karol II suffered two major foreign policy losses in 1940. In the first, Hitler and Mussolini forced Romania to accede to a transfer of Northern Transylvania to Hungarian rule under the terms of the Second Vienna Accord. Hungary was given this territorial reward in return for having supported Hitler's seizure of the Sudetenland from Czechoslovakia. The transfer of Northern Transylvania to Hungary produced a mass migration of almost a million Romanians across the new border (Longworth 1997). These refugees feared the reestablishment of Hungarian rule. Hungary was under the control of Admiral Horthy's authoritarian government that the Romanians expected would exercise retribution on them. In the second, the Soviet Union moved troops into Northern Bessarabia, forcing Romania to cede control over this area, which Romania had occupied toward the end of World War I. The Russian seizure of Romania's territory was carried out with the acceptance of Nazi Germany (Longworth 1997), which had agreed to the land transfers in the Soviet-Nazi non-aggression pact.

In October 1940 German military forces moved into Romania. They did not enter as occupiers, but as Romanian allies. A large part of the German forces were deployed around Ploesti to protect the oil fields. Others were used to train the Romanian military for the role they were to play in any upcoming offensive on the Eastern Front.

In August 1940, Karol II introduced additional anti-Semitic legislation. The legislation excluded Jews from a number of public and private offices and occupations and forbade Jewish-Romanian marriages, just as had Nazi Germany's infamous Nuremburg Laws. This type of legislation had ancient origins. It can be traced back to the Papal Bull *Cum Nimis Absurdum* (1555), which, among other things, stated, according to Carroll (2001: 375), that

> Jews are to own no real estate. Jews are to attend no Christian university. Jews are to hire no Christian servants. Jews' mercantile roles are to be strictly regulated. Jews taxes are to be increased. Jews are no longer to ignore the ancient requirement to wear distinctive clothes and badges...

The Bull was promulgated by Pope Paul IV. Paul IV, before becoming pope, was the Grand Inquisitor Gian Pietro Caroffa (Carroll 2001). The Bull also commanded that Jews were to be segregated into ghettoes.

In early September 1940, Karol II named General Antonescu Romania's *Conducator*, or Chief of State. Karol II abdicated and his son Michael was given the throne for the second time. Michael was nineteen years old. Antonescu turned to the Iron Guard and, together, he and the Guard formed the National Legionary State. This was an attempt to fuse the forces of the traditional right, especially in the military and in state offices, with the radical right. The National Legionary State was unquestionably fascist in structure, ideology, and in its political program. The Guard had control of five ministries and was put in charge of exercising control over Romania's newspapers. Especially important was the fact the Guard controlled the Ministry of Interior. This gave the Guard authority over all Romanian police forces. The Guard also was given the power to appoint and monitor Romania's local prefects, which meant that it supervised a large part of Romania's judicial system on the local level.

In August 1940, just before the end of Karol II's monarcho-fascist regime, the Ministry of National Education, Religion, and the Arts took steps against Jews enrolled in schools in Romania. All Jewish schools were required to teach Romanian history, geography, and language. These classes were to be taught by persons appointed directly by the ministry and not by persons hired by the school. A *numerus clauses* was introduced that required that Jews make up no more than 6% of any *gymnasium* class – a *gymnasium* being an academic high school that awarded baccalaureates to its graduates. Jews were allowed in state schools only if there were vacancies and only if they were willing to pay a special tax (Ioanid 2000). The same 6% standard was applied to admission of Jews to universities, technical schools, and professional schools.

In October 1940, the *numerus clauses* was eliminated and Jews were denied admission to any institutions of higher education in Romania and Jews were prohibited from teaching Christian students in any schools or from enrolling in schools that also served Christian students.

Throughout the fall of 1940, Jews were purged from a variety of professional associations. They were no longer allowed to be members of the Romanian bar association, the association for professional architects, and the unions of writers and journalists. As Ioanid (2000: 29) notes, this "Professional and social discrimination went hand in hand with ministerial orders that essentially outlawed the recognition of Jews as human beings."

In September 1940, Romania adopted a policy of *Romanization* of Jewish property. In its early stages the policy was a form of what one might call "primitive fascist accumulation." The Legionnaires, who had been given charge of the program by General Antonescu, simply confiscated Jewish property or compelled Jews to sell their property at prices far below market value. Few prominent Romanians spoke out against this clear violation of private property rights, indeed prominent Romanians benefited from these seizures. In October 1940, the state adopted Law 3347, which provided for the nationalization of Jewish property. The law was very broad in terms of its definition of who was a Jew. Anyone who had at least one parent who was Jewish was considered to be a Jew, whether they were a Romanian citizen or not and whether they practiced Judaism or not (Ioanid 2000). In November 1940, a decree was issued to supplement Law 3347. This nationalized Jewish owned forest land, non-arable land, distilleries, mills, granaries, and lumberyards (Ioanid 2000). Law 3347 and the November supplement virtually completed "Romanization" in the countryside. Few assets were left in Jewish hands in rural areas of Romania. In December 1940, a further decree nationalized barges and ships owned by Jews.

Also in December 1940, the state adopted legislation that forced Jews to provide uncompensated, compulsory labor to the state, under the supervision of the Minister of National Defense or the Minister of Labor. During the time Jews were performing this work, the Jews' behavior was governed by military law. This legislation was passed shortly after a purge of Jewish workers from state jobs had begun. In November 1940, Law 825 required that all Jews be dismissed from what we would consider white collar jobs in all private enterprises (Ioanid 2000). In the same month, Jewish physicians and other health care workers were forced out of the National Association of Physicians and were required to join their own ethnic association. Jewish physicians and health care workers also were prohibited from treating non-Jewish patients, from joining scientific societies of any type, and from publishing in professional and scientific journals (Ioanid 2000).

Nationalization of Jewish property did not end when the Legionnaires were driven from the government, indicating that this was not just a policy of the most radical elements of the extreme right in Romania. For example, Decree Law 842, published in March 1941, after the collapse of the National Legionary State, provided for the "transfer of Jewish buildings to state-owned assets" (Ioanid 2000). In August 1941, the National Bank of Romania was given the authority to grant credits to borrowers who wanted to acquire Jewish properties. The Ministry of Finance guaranteed these loans.

The government often went to absurd lengths to humiliate and degrade Romania's Jews. For example, in early May 1941 a decree law was issued that required all Romanian Jews to turn in their radios to the police. The pretext was that Jews were receiving and disseminating propaganda over the air waves and was using this information to undermine the morale of the rest of the society.

The Guard launched a reign of terror against Romanian socialists, communists, and Jews. Jews were especially singled out as targets for violent repression and state terror (see Butmaru 1992; Heinen 1986; and Veiga 1989). The Guard plundered and confiscated Jewish property. Jews were attacked, beaten, and killed with impunity. Jews were subject to arrest and interrogation (torture) at any time and in any place. The Guard subjected Jews to continuing rituals of public humiliation, whenever and wherever they encountered them. This was meant to continually remind Jews of their degraded status in the National Legionary State.

According to Mazower (2000), thousands of Jews were killed in the rampages orchestrated and led by the Iron Guard. The Guard built on and extended the brutalization of interpersonal relations between Romanians and Jews. Their behavior helped legitimate a general attitude that violence toward Jews was perfectly acceptable.

On November 26 and 27 1940, Guard units slaughtered sixty-five political prisoners, including politicians, police officers, and several senior military officers, being held in the Jilava prison. Included among those killed was the Romanian philosopher Nicolae Iorga who, in 1910, had been a political ally of A. C. Cuza. Iorga had broken with Cuza in 1922 over the issue of violence in the anti-Semitic university student protests and riots of 1921-1922 (see above). The communists housed in Jilava prison avoided being murdered. The prison guards protected the communists from the violence of the Iron Guard rampage.

For a time, Antonescu stood by as the Guard went on its murderous rampages. His seeming disinterest in the Guards' violence continued until late January 1941, when the Guard launched a violent attack against its enemies and attempted to seize power from Antonescu. The Guard went on a broad offensive. It attacked and looted Jewish shops and properties, physically assaulted Jews in their homes and on the streets, and sacked and desecrated Jewish holy places. In one of its most gruesome acts, it slaughtered over 100 Jews and hung their bodies from hooks in a meat processing plant in Bucharest.

Following this rampage, Antonescu, whose forces did not intervene to put an end to the Guards' two-day reign of terror, moved against the Guard. Eventually almost 10,000 Guardists were arrested and tried on various charges relating to the prison murders and the slaughter of Jews. Again, a large number of Guards took refuge in Germany, including Hora Sima, its commander. The Guards who were imprisoned in Romania were confined until June 1941, when they were sent to the front to fight with the Romanian army and the Germans against the Soviet Union.

The end of the Nationally Legionary State did not end anti-Semitic policies and practices in Romania. Antonescu continued to enforce the anti-Semitic laws passed by Karol II's royal dictatorship and, indeed, extended them.

Antonescu abolished the Guard's office for confiscation of Jewish property and replaced it with one of his own design, over which he assumed direct control. In March 1941, Antonescu issued a decree law to confiscate all property of Jews in Romanian cities. None of the leaders of Romania's former political parties protested these laws which were a clear violation of Romanians' rights to property ownership. There is no evidence to suggest that if they had protested they would have faced arrest, imprisonment, or any other form of punishment.

Post-Legionnaire Anti-Semitism and Anti-Rroma Actions

Under Antonescu, the Guard was not the only perpetrator of organized, homicidal violence directed at Jews. Between June 29 and July 2, 1941, Romanians carried out a pogrom against Jews in Iasi. Jewish property, including synagogues, was destroyed and there were widespread assaults on and killing of Jews. The Romanian military and local police were actively involved in the violence against Iasi's Jews, as they would be in the mass slaughter of Jews in the Romanian town of Tighina in September 1941. Moreover, there was significant involvement of civilians in the pogroms, as was the case in other countries under Nazi control or allied with the Nazis (see Gross 2001 for a discussion of civilian communal violence directed against Jews in Poland). In the Iasi pogrom some 13,000 Jews were killed. A month later, July 1941, another 11,000 Jews were murdered in Bukovina.

In October 1941, the Soviet resistance movement in Odessa blew up the Romanian military headquarters. One hundred and twenty eight people were killed, included among the Romanian casualties was a commanding general (Deletant 1999b). Antonescu ordered the Romanian military to carry out reprisals. For every German or Romanian officer who had died, the military was ordered to kill two hundred communists and for every Romanian and German enlisted man killed there were to be one hundred communists executed. The order did not specify that only combatants or resistance activists should be selected for retaliation. On October 22, 1941, the military authority in Odessa hanged 450 Jews, whose bodies were left hanging on display in the city's central town square (Deletant 1999b). Jews, in part, were selected for destruction because Romanian nationalist ideology equated Jews with communists. Approximately 50,000 additional Jews were arrested and were marched to a location about eight kilometers from the city, where they were to be executed. Before they reached their destination, the column of Jews was turned back. Marching back to Odessa, thousands of Jews were put in sheds, where they were shot and their bodies were burned. It is estimated that over 20,000 Jews were killed in these reprisals.

It is important to recognize that "ordinary" Romanian military forces carried out these killings, as had happened with other attacks on and killings of Jews. The murders were not the work of special units or of fanatical Guardists, nor where they carried out under German compulsion. This is further evidence that murderous anti-Semitism was a highly generalized attitude set in Romania, much as it was in Germany (Goldhagen 1997) and in parts of Eastern and Central Europe (see Gross 2001 for an extended analysis and discussion of popular, murderous anti-Semitism in a Polish village during World War II). In making this point that murderous anti-Semitism was a highly generalized attitude within Romania is not to adopt the highly dubious assumptions that Romanian culture, per se, or that the Romanian population, per se, was "essentially, intrinsically, or inherently" anti-Semitic. It merely is to say that by the late 1930s the forces of the anti-Semitic right were the dominant political forces in Romania. The radical right's ideology of anti-Semitism had penetrated deeply into a population that was in the midst of a deep economic and political crisis.

The Great Depression had devastating effects on Romania, especially in rural areas, and the major political parties were totally ineffective in governing the country in ways that would have contributed to some solution to these economic problems. Moreover, the major political parties' behavior had begun to discredit the very idea of democracy among key sectors of the Romanian population. To this, we must add that anti-Semitism long had been a matter of state policy, especially under Karol II's dictatorship and Antonescu's various governments. The Romanian state, even before the advent of dictatorship, never attempted to counter popular anti-Semitism. Indeed, the state fostered these ideas and exploited them for its own purposes. Most of Romania's elite and the key institutions they dominated, e.g. the professions, the universities, the churches, also advanced anti-Semitic ideology and anti-Semitic policies. With the organization, promulgation, and institutionalization of anti-Semitism from above, there were few parts of Romanian society that had the capacity to resist being conquered by anti-Semitic ideology and policies.

Romanian forces, which fought primarily on the German Eastern Front, joined the SS and the Wehrmacht in committing atrocities against

Jewish populations in areas that came under their control (Ioanid 2000). The fact that ordinary Romanian soldiers, with the open support of their officers, engaged in war crimes against the Jews is consistent with what Goldhagen (1997) found about the willingness of "ordinary Germans" to participate in the routine killing of Jews. The fact that ordinary Romanian soldiers willingly engaged in the murder of Jews, as well as Rroma, is indicative of the degree to which an "eliminationist" anti-Semitism (see Goldhagen 1997 and Carroll 2001 for a discussion of similar ideas) permeated Romania's military. From its aristocratic officer corps to its rank-and-file peasant and working class soldiers, eliminationist anti-Semitism was a commonly accepted attitude in the Romanian military forces.

In addition, ordinary Romanian citizens openly engaged in lethal assaults on Jews. Ionanid's (2000) work shows how average Romanians engaged in violent pogroms against the Jews and victimized Jews who were being transported to the camps in the Transnistria region, physically attacking some and price gouging and robbing others. It was common practice for Jews being transported to the camps to be beaten, robbed, raped, and killed while in transit. There also were cases were guards killed Jews and sold the corpses to peasants, who harvested their clothes and any other goods they could take from the bodies of dead Jews (Ioanid 2000). Jews were sequentially plundered as they moved from their homes to the camps, so that those who managed to survive the trips arrived destitute in the camps. As with the case of the military, the fact that ordinary Romanians engaged in such behavior should not be taken to build an essentialist argument that Romania was intrinsically anti-Semitic. It was not. Had not anti-Semitism become the ideology of key elites and the institutions they controlled – the churches, the schools, the professions, and the historical political parties – and had not the state chosen to make anti-Semitism explicit state policy, it is highly unlikely that anti-Semitism would have been raised to murderous levels in the general Romanian population.

Jews from outside of the Regat (Wallachia and Moldova) died in large numbers while in route to and while in residence in the camps in the Transnistria. These deaths resulted from direct physical attacks on Jews, from starvation, from brutal work assignments, and from disease. Ioanid (2000) estimates that Romania's anti-Jewish policies, including internment in the camps, resulted in the deaths of over a quarter-million

Jews and that this figure would have been substantially larger but for the defeat of German and Romanian forces at the battle of Stalingrad. With the war turning against Germany and its allies, the Romanian state scrapped plans to extend its policy of transporting Jews to camps to those Jews living in the Regat and in Transylvania.

As it was, somewhere between 125,000 to 145,000 Jews were transported to the camps in the Transnistria. Of this number, only some 50,000 managed to survive until the end of 1943, when they were released by the Romanian authorities. Totaling the deaths in the camps and those killings that took place in various pogroms, Ioanid (2000) estimates that the Romanian Holocaust took over a quarter of a million lives, the vast majority of whom were Jews, with the rest being largely Rroma. Romanian Jews living abroad in countries that were under the control of Germany also were subject to deportation to the death camps run by the Nazi death machinery. Romanian Jews living in Germany, itself, Austria, Poland, Bohemia, Moravia, Prague, Holland, and France were rounded up and sent to extermination centers. It was not until 1943 that Romania extended diplomatic protection to its Jewish citizens living outside of the country (Ioanid 2000).

Eliminationist racism was not directed only at Jews in Romania. Rroma also were targeted for elimination in what Rroma call the "Great Devouring" (the *Porrjamos* in the Romany language) just as they were in Germany and its conquered territories (see Hancock 1996 and Lewy 2000 for a general discussion and two different views of the Rroma and the Holocaust and Ioanid 2000 for a discussion of the Holocaust and the Rroma in Romania). Like Jews, Rroma were defined as sub-humans that polluted Romanian soil and Romanian culture in militant nationalist and fascist circles.

There is a debate, often vitriolic, in the literature on German crimes against humanity during World War II centering on the question of whether the slaughter of Rroma amounted to a holocaust in the same way that term had been applied to the murder of Jews. Tyranauer (1986), Hancock (1996) and Ioanid (2000) see the murder of Jews as part of the Holocaust, while Lewy (2000) rejects this idea.

Lewy (2000) notes that estimates of the number of Rroma killed by the Germans range from 196,000 out of a population of 831,000 to 219,000 out of almost a million (Kenrick and Puxon 1972; Kenrick 1989). While these numbers are horrifying in and of themselves, they indicate that proportional losses among Rroma were less than those among Jews, reflecting the ideological priority the Nazis gave to exterminating Jews.

In addition to this difference in the relative loss in the two populations, Lewy (2000) argues that there was a fundamental difference between how the Germans dealt with the Jews and how they dealt with the Rroma. First, he notes that Jews were targeted for mass extermination as Jews, not because of any other characteristics. Rroma, on the other hand, were executed only if they were migratory, "asocial," and/or were *Mischingle* (mixed "race," given the bizarre concept of race used by the Nazis). Second, Lewy (2000) points out that while one can build a chain of evidence showing that the policies dealing with the liquidation of Jews came from the center of Nazi leadership, this can not be done for the Rroma. The drive against the Rroma, rather, appears to have been "opportunistic" and to have emerged from pressures from local populations and officials who wanted the state to deal with Rroma "threats" to local health and safety. To Germans who called for the liquidation of Rroma, the Rroma were seen as a nuisance and a "plague," which is much different from the way Jews were defined in Germany. Third, the fact that the Germans did not develop policies to liquidate "racially pure" Rroma, while they did target *Mischingle* indicates a fundamental difference between Rroma and Jews in the Nazis' eyes. The Nazis' main interest was liquidating "ethnically pure" Jews while, under special circumstances and conditions, Jews who were of mixed background were not subject to extermination. For these reasons, Lewy (2000) believes it is appropriate to argue that the Nazi treatment of Rroma does not amount to genocide nor should it be equated with the *Shoa* (the Holocaust).

In contrast to Lewy's (2000) position, Hancock (1996) has argued strongly that the liquidation of the Rroma in the "Devouring" was a parallel to the *Shoa* and, in their recent book, Kenrick and Puxon (1995) make the same point, stating that the "ultimate aim of the Nazis was the elimination of all Gypsies" and that "the Holocaust ... encompassed Jews and many other people." While not directly engaging in the debate as to whether or not is appropriate to see Rroma as victims of the Holocaust, Ioanid's (2000) research shows that the Romanian state's attacks on Rroma were identical, in most respects, to those of the Germans. In Romania, 25,000 Rroma (approximately 2.5% of the Rroma population in Romania) were transported to camps in the Transnistria. Only about

6000, less than a quarter of those sent, returned from the camps. Having looked at the evidence of Romania's treatment of Rroma, Ioanid (2000) does not seem to hesitate about identifying Rroma as victims of the Holocaust in Romania.

Recognizing the Rroma as victims of the Holocaust does nothing to enhance the nature of the suffering they endured nor does it diminish the suffering of the Jews. Without taking sides in this debate, there are a number of points that need to be made about Lewy's (2000) conclusions. First, not all Jews in Romania were transported to Transnistria, the Romanians concentrated their ultimately lethal attacks (except for the slaughter of Jews in Bucharest by the Iron Guard during the National Legionary State's existence). Jews in the Regat, generally, were not rounded up and transported to camps. This fact should not lead one to conclude that Romanian Jews were not victims of the Holocaust. It is very likely that if the war had gone better for the Nazi and Romanian armies, Jews of the Regat would have been subjected to the same treatment. Second, Lewy's (2000) conclusions presume that the level of prejudice against and hostility toward the Rroma was not of the same type and degree as it was toward the Jews. This is a dubious proposition. In many segments of the Romanian and German populations (as well as in the populations of other European communities) both groups shared, and continue to share, the same ontological position as a hated population that was and is barely regarded as human. For example, both are seen as "race polluters," hence the hostility directed at the Rroma *Mischingle*. The hostility directed toward Rroma is more than a reflection of the hatred of the Rroma as a "social problem." Rejection of the Rroma was, and is, deeper. It was and continues to be a rejection of a population that, like the Jews, was and is seen as totally and radically *Other*. Third, if the Germans and the Romanians had achieved their goal of making Europe free of Jews, there is a high probability that the next group to which they would direct attention would have been the Rroma. Once the Jews had been liquidated, the death machines would have needed more bodies to justify their importance to the regimes and their claim on state resources, who better than the Rroma could have filled this need. Fourth, no other migratory population was targeted for liquidation in regions under the control of German forces, it was only migratory Rroma that were singled out for special processing. Fifth, Germans and Romanians naturally equated Rroma with crime, there is no evidence that other race-criminals classification was developed by the Germans and used as a criterion for extermination. What made Rroma "crimes" special were not the nature of the alleged "criminal" acts, themselves, but the fact that Rroma committed them. Sixth, "racial pollution" involving Rroma was seen as especially heinous by the Germans, much like it was for the Jews. The Nazis clearly regarded "race pollution" by the Rroma as a threat to the integrity of Germany's "Aryan" population. It was taken as a lesser threat than Jewish "race pollution" because of a difference in the relative size of the two populations. Seventh, and finally, Ioanid (2000) does find a clear chain of evidence implicating the Romanian head of state, General Antonescu, in the formulation and implementation of policies to transport the Rroma, as well as the Jews, to Transnistria. Given these considerations, one can state that the move to eliminate Rroma was something more than the action of fanatics who were concerned about addressing a local "social problem." The liquidation of Rroma was based on theories of race and would have been far more extensive had the Nazis and the Romanian fascists achieved their first priority, which, clearly, was the liquidation of Jews.

According to Mazower (2000: 172), the anti-Semitic behavior of the Romanians, and the Hungarians, "shocked the Germans." Attacks on the Jews often were far more extensive and intense than the Germans had anticipated or expected. In September 1941, Antonescu ordered the deportation of almost 120,000 Jews in Bessarabia and Northern Bucovina to camps in the area between the Dniester and Bug Rivers. This area came to be called the Trannsnistra region. Tens of thousands of Rroma were included in the deportation orders for Bessarabia and Northern Bucovina. German and Romanian soldiers preyed on the Jewish and Rroma populations as they prepared for departure.

The deportees were put in hastily prepared work camps. Sanitation and protection from the elements were minimal and their diets barely provided enough food for subsistence. During the winter of 1941-42, scores of thousands of Jews and Rroma died from typhus epidemics, starvation, overwork, abuse, and deliberate murder in the Trannsnistria's camps. High death rates continued in the camps as long as they operated.

Watts (1993) has argued that Antonescu had deported a large number of Jews into the camps less because of anti-Semitism than because of a fear that they compromised Romanian security. According to Watts (1993), Antonescu was concerned that a large number of Jews in these regions were sympathetic to the cause of the Soviet Union and, as a result, were a threat to the Romanian war effort. Even if there is some truth in Watts' claims, he still overlooks the fact that Antonescu was perfectly willing to engage in assigning collective blame to the Jews. Moreover, Watts' explanation certainly does not apply to the Rroma. It is unlikely that the Rroma were any more sympathetic to the Soviet Union than they were to Romania or that they were involved in radical left activities. It also is unlikely that the Rroma could, or would, have been able to sabotage Romanian military operations at the time.

While eliminationist ideology was common in Romania, it was not universal. There were a number of distinguished Romanians who attempted to defend the Jews, such as Iuliu Maniu, Constantin I. C. Bratianu, and the Queen Mother, as well as other Romanians of lesser social standing (Ioanid 2000). These people made up the minority of "righteous" Romanians who attempted to protect Jews, even Jews who they might not have known personally. There also were geographic areas that showed no signs of violence directed against Jews or against Rroma. There were also local communities in Romania that helped Jews escape detection and arrest by the fascist forces.

A more typical experience of Romanian Jews was that of Mr. Abraham P., who describes his own experiences as follows:

> I am from Transylvania, Romania. I come from a small town. The name of the town was Beclean. My family was father, mother, and six brothers. My older brother, his name was Isaac. After him I had a brother Menachem. He died in Auschwitz, and I am next. And then, I have a brother Yossi [who] is after me. He lives now in New York. He used to live in South America. After that is Schloima, who lives in Israel. And then I had a little kid brother. His name was Metzalah. He died in Auschwitz. My parents died in Auschwitz. Most of my aunts and uncles died – all of them died in Auschwitz. It was a large family, forty, fifty. Maybe twelve of us, fourteen of us have survived.
>
> The community had about five thousand people living there. There were two hundred fifty Jewish families. There were Hungarians living there, Romanians, German, Gypsies, and Jews. After the war, there were six or seven families who came home.
>
> Friday we used to get ready for the 'Shabes'. ...We used [to] clean up the house, scrub the floor, clean the windows. My mother,

may she rest in peace, was cooking and baking. We shined our shoes, we brushed our clothes. It was delightful. Oh God! We used to press our own shirts, then after that we went to the bathhouse because they didn't have showers or bathtubs like we have over here. As children we were forced to sleep in the afternoon on Fridays so we would be able to stay up for Friday night meal and to be able to go to the synagogue. It was happiness!

Except once in a while, some of the gentiles used to scream and yell from the other side. 'You dirty Jew!' Or something like that. There was always anti-Semitism. There hasn't been a week that went by when I wasn't told, 'You dirty Jew, go back to Palestine.' Our family was very religious; we all wore the side curls, 'peyes,' and we wore the dark clothes, the traditional clothes. It started to change around the late '30s. We were forced to go and do all the menial labor, work for the officials, clean the toilets, sweep the streets, and to top it all off, they blamed you for the start of the war. They blamed you for all the troubles that had been going on. One day we were walking down the street, and a priest, a Catholic priest, stopped and he said, 'Do you know these people are responsible for the war?' I'm fourteen or fifteen years old. I'm responsible for a war going on over there in Europe? We were always hoping it's not going to last very long.

In late 1943, one Friday afternoon, one soldier wanted to show off to his girlfriend, and the girl happens to be the daughter of the people who used to buy our milk. They used to come into our store to buy on credit, and we always trusted them. He says to me, 'Let me look at you.' He looked at me and he saw that I have 'peries.' So I remember he cut off this one over here, the left 'perie.' He cut it up and showed it off to his girlfriend, the very same girl, and she didn't say a word.

We just lived and we tried to stay away from the streets. On May the third in 1944, they put out an order that everybody has to shave off their beards, their hair, everything. My mother asked me, 'Did you see your father?' He was with his back to her. I said, 'He's right here!' And he turned around and she saw him. She's never seen my father without a beard. She broke down and she cried. I'll never forget it. She just – she looked so stunned – she couldn't believe it. (quoted in Greene and Kumar 2000: 19-21).

Mr. P. had attended a yeshiva for eighteen months in Sighet, a larger town near his home village. After Hungarians occupied Northern

Transylvania, he reported that there was a significant increase in anti-Semitism in the region. Hungarian forces, for example, drafted two of his bothers into a slave labor battalion. When the Germans occupied the region in 1944, he and his family were arrested. After three weeks, they were sent to Auschwitz/Birkenau. Mr. P. then was transferred to Buchenwald. From there, he was sent to Zeitz, then he was moved back to Buchenwald. He had several more transfers before he finally was liberated by Soviet military forces (Greene and Kumar: 2000).

After the defeat of the German and Romanian forces at the battle of Stalingrad (Summer 1942 – February 1943), Antonescu was convinced that Germany and Italy would lose the war. He began making secret overtures first to Britain and then to Britain and America to sign a separate peace agreement that would remove Romania from the war against the Western powers in return for recognition of certain Romanian territorial claims. The allies informed Romania that they would accept nothing short of unconditional surrender. Antonescu then offered to surrender unconditionally to the Western powers but indicated it would not surrender unconditionally to the Soviets. Romania also began secret negotiations with the USSR to end Romania's involvement in the war, hoping to avoid the loss of territory that was sure to come with military defeat and Soviet occupation. The Soviets laid out stringent conditions for accepting an armistice with Romania. Antonescu refused to accept the Soviet conditions.

On August 19, 1944, the Soviet army began moving into Romania. Romanian military resistance was collapsing rapidly in the face of withering Soviet infantry and tank attacks. Romania faced certain military defeat and Soviet occupation. On August 24, 1944, Antonescu was overthrown, arrested, and turned over to a communist militia group, led by Emil Bodnaras. Bodnaras later expanded the workers' militia in order to create the Guards of Patriotic Defense. Antonescu was transported to the Soviet Union. He was held in the USSR until his trial began in Bucharest.

King Michael I, having realized that the war was lost, began working with a coalition of leaders of the National Liberal Party, the National Peasant Party, the Social Democrats, and the communist party, to oust the Antonescu government. The communist who was directly involved in the negotiations with the king was Lucretiu Patrascanu, one of the party's founding members.

After Antonescu's arrest, Michael issued a decree law that proclaimed a general amnesty for persons imprisoned for political crimes. He also issued a royal order to close the fascist regime's prison camps. In a radio address to the country, the king also announced that Romania was ending its alliance with the Axis powers and would join the Soviet Union and its Western allies in fighting the Axis.

After switching sides in the war, Romania was subjected to intense bombing by the Luftwaffe. Bucharest was heavily damaged by the air raids. The Romanian army moved on Transylvania, where it fought German and Hungarian forces and suffered heavy casualties. In the meantime, Soviet forces were completing their occupation of Romanian territory.

In December 1944, the Iron Guard set up a government in exile in Vienna (Deletant 1999a). The Iron Guard government in exile sought to mobilize Romanians in Germany to serve in military units to fight the Russians. The Guard's efforts largely were unsuccessful. When Germany surrendered in May 1945, many of these former Guardists dispersed to other European countries and to North America, where they managed to escape trial and imprisonment for whatever involvement they had in various crimes against humanity, both before and during the war. Outside of Romania, former Guardists allied themselves with other Romanian émigrés as opponents of the communist regime.

After overthrowing Antonescu, Michael formed a provisional government headed by General Constantin Sanatescu. Patrascanu was offered an appointment as interim Minister of Justice. The Sanatescu government lasted for only a few months (August 23 to November 2, 1944). It fell after massive protests were launched over the government's delay in dismissing former fascists from state offices and prosecuting fascists who were guilty of atrocities. According to Deletant (1999a), Maniu was one of the major figures who had resisted a quick purge of fascists. Quinlan (1977), in examining American intelligence documents, found evidence supporting charges that Romania, in fact, was delaying a purge of fascists in the state bureaucracy. From the point of view of the historical parties, these former fascists were their "natural" allies in the coming struggle against the communists.

The protests were directed by the National Democratic Front (NDF). The NDF was an alliance of the communists and the social democrats. The alliance was agreed to in October 1944. This represented a major change in the policy of the social democrats, who had been strong opponents of the communists since the two political groupings had split in the early 1920s. It was also a major change in the policy of the communists, who regarded the social democrats as class traitors who wanted nothing more than to collaborate with the capitalist parties as junior partners in the exploitation of the peasants and the working classes. The NDF launched organizing drives in all of Romania's major industries and achieved remarkable success as the major force representing Romanian workers' interests. In no small part, the NDF's organizing successes were a result of the fact that the communists and the social democrats had gained moral stature from not having collaborated with the fascists, even though neither had formed resistance movements during the fascist period.

In November 1945, Romanian soldiers shot and killed two workers (Deletant 1999a). The murders led to protest by communists and Social Democrats and Sanatescu's government fell. The king asked General Nicolae Radescu to form a new government. Radescu's government included several communists. Teohari Georgescu was appointed deputy minister of interior, Patrascanu became Minister of Justice, and Gheorghiu-Dej was given the portfolios for communication and public works. Like Sanatescu's cabinet, Radescu's cabinet stayed in office for only a few months. It was installed on December 6, 1944 and it was removed in March 1945. During his brief tenure as Prime Minister, Radescu had continuing problems with the political left.

The left again accused the government of dragging its heels on purging fascists from state offices. The left also argued that the government needed to begin implementing a program of land reform. In February 1945, peasants, with the encouragement of leftist parties, had begun seizing land in the Prahova and Dambovita judets (counties). Radescu accused Deputy Prime Minister Petru Groza, who represented the Ploughmen's Front, of trying to start a civil war by urging peasants to seize land.

Social Democrats and communists organized protests across Romania against the Radescu government, demanding the government's resignation. In February 1945, soldiers, on Radescu's orders, fired over the heads of anti-government demonstrators who had gathered in front of the Royal Palace. During the demonstrations, gunshots killed several workers. It never was clear whether the shootings that killed demonstrators came from the military or from other sources. The Soviets, who had grown disenchanted with the Radescu government, used this incident against the king and the Radescu government. On February 28, the Soviet Union issued an ultimatum to Michael, either he would dismiss the government or face the chances that Romania might disappear as an independent state. Michael acceded to the Soviet demands. He asked Radescu to resign and Petru Groza was asked to form a new provisional government.

The Groza government was a key postwar turning point in Romania. Under Groza, who led the Ploughmen's Front, a radical left party based in Transylvania that represented the interests of Romania's landless peasants, communists were put in a position to conquer the Romanian state and society. For the communists, their goal of conquering state power and Romanian society was made easier by the past behavior of Romania's elites and the institutions they dominated between 1866 and 1944. A good example of this can be seen in the behavior of the boyars. While their place in the state was considerably reduced after 1918 and there no longer was a major political party that exclusively expressed their interests, the boyars continued to wield a great deal of indirect political and social power and remained the dominant economic force in Romania. Between the end of the 19th century and the start of World War II, the boyars had been highly successful in transforming themselves into agricultural capitalists. With their continuing economic interest in the countryside, the landed aristocrats had been able to block effective change in property relations in the countryside.

In the absence of meaningful land reform, the Romanian peasantry existed as a largely impoverished mass of propertyless farm workers or as owners of small plots of land that barely allowed them to attain subsistence levels of production. The continuing resistance of the historical parties to fundamental change in property ownership in the countryside in the years before World War II had eroded their support among the peasantry. This, in part, led significant sections of the peasantry to support the Legion, which had developed an economic ideology and, equally importantly, a social and political ideology that valorized the peasantry as one of the central embodiments of the essence of the Romanian nation. The Legion led the peasantry into organized anti-Semitic violence and, ultimately, a rejection of parliamentary democracy as a means for resolving the economic problems that were crushing them. The Romanian Orthodox Church also emerged from the war seriously compromised. The Church, which had been a pillar of the Romanian state and which had long been part of the traditional right, embraced fascism. The church long had been suspicious of democracy and other "alien" ideas and had been a strong supporter of authoritarian rule and the maintenance of the traditional hierarchical social order in Romania. In the 1930s, clerical fascism had become widespread in the church, both at the local level and in the hierarchy. The Iron Guard, from its earliest days, had concentrated on framing a message that would appeal to the rural clergy and other parts of the rural traditional intelligentsia. The higher clergy, under Patriarch Cristea, were strong supporters of the monarchical fascist dictatorship and they, later, backed the Antonescu regime and its general policies, even though the church's leadership was not entirely supportive of the regime's policies toward Jews (Ioanid 2000). The church's suspicion of democracy helped to seriously undermine the development of democracy in Romania. The church's close ties with the two fascist governments, as well as its strong support of the throne, raised serious questions about the church in the minds of many Romanians, especially those on the political left, following the war.

The throne also was discredited in the eyes of many Romanians before the war. Romanian nationalists and those who supported the radical right found Karol II's relationship with Madame Magda Lupescu, a Jewish woman, morally unacceptable. This relationship, coupled with Karol's general support for the economic agenda of the National Liberals, helped erode the legitimacy of the throne among those on the radical right (Fischer-Galati 1998). Karol II's seizure of power and his imposition of a monarcho-fascist dictatorship helped to destroy even the limited "guided" democracy characteristic of Romanian parliamentary government, and, as a result, compromised the position of the throne after World War II, even though Karol II no longer was king. The monarchy's legitimacy in the post-war period was seriously eroded by the support it had given to the Antonescu dictatorship until it became apparent that the war was lost and Romania was about to be invaded by the Soviet Union. Given its behavior before and during the war, it was difficult for the monarchy to present itself as a defender of democracy in the post-war period.

The historical Romanian political parties also had contributed to the destruction of democracy in the 1930s and thus helped prepare the way for the consolidation of fascist rule. Before the war, neither the National Peasant Party nor the National Liberal Party had been committed to building and sustaining an open, competitive democracy. Rather, at best, they both supported a limited, directed democracy that insured the perpetuation of their dominant position in the parliamentary system. After World War I, the two parties' behavior resulted in a continuing paralysis of the parliamentary system. In "normal" times this would have been problematic enough, however, with the onset of the Great Depression and the rise of a militant and increasingly organized fascism, it proved fatal to democracy. Moreover, the willingness of the political elites to reach compromises with and alliances with fascism, when it was convenient for them to do so, further eroded the possibility that democracy could survive the fascist challenge. Finally, the accommodation of the two parties to the king's and to Antonescu's dictatorship helped to undermine their post-war credibility, especially among Romania's left. The moral legitimacy of the parties after the war also was compromised by their public silence in the fact of their own formal liquidation and their failure to defend the civil liberties and property rights of Jews and others during the fascist period. It was difficult for them to posture as defenders of civil rights and property in the post-war period when they generally had ignored the abolition of these rights for minorities during the war and when they had been willing to crush the rights of political dissidents, especially on the left. Perhaps the greatest failure of the Romanian elites between 1866 and 1945 was that they created a state that was not based in the principle of rule of law. Civil liberties, civil rights, basic property rights, etc., which are taken to be fundamental to the formation of an autonomous civil society, were never recognized, in a practical sense, in the various constitutional systems put in place between 1866 and 1945. Individual rights always were seen to be contingent rights that could be suspended whenever the state deemed it necessary and appropriate to "defend" what it took to be the collective interests of the Romanian nation. Moreover, the right to not be a victim of state violence

The failure of the historical parties and the Romanian state was partly the legacy of the political forms that had been institutionalized by the boyars and carried forward even after they no longer controlled the state. The failure of the parties and the state also can be traced to the in-completeness of the bourgeois' "revolution." Romania's bourgeoisie had been unable to form themselves into a coherent, politically mature class that was capable of conquering the state and using state power to reshape Romania in its own image. Lacking effective economic domination of Romania and characterized by a split between the commercial-industrial bourgeoisie and the agrarian bourgeoisie presided over an increasingly chaotic state that undermined the legitimacy or parliamentary govern-ment and democratic values. Furthermore, the industrial-commercial bourgeoisie, while dominating Romanian politics for most of the inter-war period, never was able to develop inter-class alliances that would have advanced its political and economic interests. Relatively weak and divided, the Romanian bourgeoisie and its political parties were unable to devise a successful strategy to alleviate the economic misery the Great Depression brought to the social classes standing below them. Therefore, it was relatively easy for the fascists to mobilize the lower orders against the bourgeoisie and their directed democracy in favor of more authori-tarian "solutions" to Romania's economic and political crises. Given the demonstrated incapacity of the historical parties, their willingness to subordinate the general interest to their particular interests, and their direct and indirect complicity in bringing on fascism, when World War II ended, they were not in a strong position to reclaim leading roles in Romania's political life. Their past intentional exclusion of the lower classes from effective political participation (see Mouzelis 1986 and Mishkova 1994), and their reluctance to build deep and direct ties with the larger part of the Romanian population (Jowitt 1978), made it difficult for the historical parties to mount effective competition for general, popular support when they faced political challenges from the left after the war.

Romania's intellectuals also contributed to the collapse of democ-racy and the rise of fascism before World War II. A large number of Romania's leading intellectuals had always been skeptical of democracy as a political system, seeing it as an alien import from the West that did more to divide the Romanian nation that to unite it into an organic whole. Many of Romania's intellectuals became enamored with fascism as a philosophical position. Writers such as Eliade, among a large num-ber of others, valorized fascism and its authoritarian principles, seeing fascism as, among other things, a way to create a "new aristocracy" that would bring a new moral purpose to Romania. To many of Romania's most important thinkers, fascism was a third way between the "discredited" ideologies of bourgeois capitalism and Marxism, both of which were seen as materialistic belief systems that were incompatible with the spiritual character of the Romanian nation. Like intellectuals in other parts of Europe, fascism was seen as the "wave of the future" for a new commonwealth of European states under the leadership and hegemony of the Germans. Having rejected democracy and having embraced fascism and anti-Semitism and having taken strong stands against communism and the Soviet Union, Romanian intellectuals were complicit in the destruction of the old regime.

The throne's and the oligarchy's support of Antonescu and his military policy cost the Romanians dearly. The Romanian army ended up losing to wounds, injury, illness, and death in combat, almost 85% of the men it had mobilized for the war (Ferguson 2001). The national economy was destroyed, Romanian territory was occupied completely by Soviet military forces, and the country's international standing was sullied by its having been an active participant in the destruction of its own Jewish community and by its persecution and liquidation of large numbers of Rroma.

Gross (2001: 166) observes: "*If we have acted as instruments of violence, in the name of what principles can we oppose the use of violence turned against us by somebody else?*" This is precisely the situation in which the Romanian pre-War elites found themselves after 1945. Under these pre-war elites Romania had failed to achieve democracy, had failed to develop economically, had perpetuated an economy and state marked by horrendous levels of inequality, and had fostered the development of a political and cultural landscape that had produced a fascist state which stripped Romania's minorities, especially Jews and, to a lesser degree, Rroma of their basic human rights and, in some cases, their lives. The old elites also had waged war against the country's working class parties, imprisoning most of the key political leaders and intellectuals on the left.

Given all of this, when coupled with the total defeat of Romania's military forces and the destruction of a large part of the state's economic base, it is hard to imagine how the former elites could have believed that they would have been able to continue their rule in a post-World War II Romania. Other than among their own number, they had little support for claiming the mantle of leadership after the war. It also is hard to see how these elites could expect anything but harsh and, sometimes brutal, treatment at the hands of the former victims of their rule. These old elites and the classes in which they were based were doomed to destruction if the left consolidated its rule. When this happened, the united left of social democrats and communists, pushed the former political elites out of government, disbanded their political parties, imprisoned and/or drove into exile many of the key leaders of the old political and economic elites, and wiped out the economic arrangements that had been the basis of the old elites' power.

5
Romanian Communism:
The Dej Years (1945-1965)

Petru Groza's first cabinet included representatives of the National Liberal Party, the National Peasant Party, several members of the Ploughmen's Front, and three leading communists: Lecritiu Patrascanu, Gheorghe Gheorghiu-Dej, and Teohari Georgescu, all of whom had been in Radescu's cabinet. These communists, respectively, were given the ministries of communications, justice, and internal affairs. The representatives from the National Liberal and National Peasant Party included in the government were not from the senior leadership of either party. They were dissidents within these parties.

One of the Groza government's first acts was to draft legislation directed at punishing war criminals. In January 1945, Lecritiu Patrascanu wrote legislation providing for the trial and punishment of war criminals, which the king promptly signed. The first trials began almost immediately. Several score of persons were convicted of capital offenses, but later had their sentences reduced. Hundreds of persons were convicted of war crimes between 1945 and 1952. Most of these people were released from prison under various amnesties between 1958 and 1962 (Ioanid 2000). In 1946, General Antonescu, along with Mihai Antonescu, Gheorghe Alexianu, and C. Z. Vasilianu, was tried, convicted, and executed for war crimes, as were the three others. Antonescu, among other things, was charged with crimes against humanity and of having waged a war of aggression against the Soviet Union.

Antonescu has continued to be a controversial figure in Romanian history. The political right has been pressing for Antonescu's rehabilitation since the fall of the Bolshevik regime in 1989. For the right, rehabilitating Antonescu is about something more than exonerating a former leader. Changing history's judgment of Antonescu would rehabilitate the Romanian nation and its behavior during the Second World War. Romania would no longer have to be apologetic about having gone to war against Russia as an ally of Nazi Germany nor would the pre-war Romanian state have to be held accountable for its treatment of Jews and

Rroma during the War and for its crushing of civil liberties even before the start of the war.

The Groza government, in March 1945, launched a major land reform initiative. Groza's government secured passage of legislation limiting land holdings to fifty hectares or less. Without compensation, the state confiscated large estates, including those belonging to the various religious organizations in Romania, and distributed the largest part of the land to the peasantry. Aside from the large landowners and their political allies, there was little popular objection to the confiscation of the large estates.

The agricultural sector, despite several limited land reforms, still was badly in need of major reorganization. The major land redistribution that had taken place at the end of World War I had not solved agrarian land inequalities. In the early 1900s, Romania had the most unequal distribution of agricultural land holdings in the Balkans. Mazower (2000) notes that, at the turn of the century, one per cent of the population held fifty per cent of crop and grazing lands and that as much as eighty five per cent of the peasantry were producing at or below minimum household subsistence levels. These patterns of inequality produced strong tensions and conflicts in the countryside.

After the great peasant rebellion of 1907, the government made some minor changes in agricultural laws. But real agricultural reform had to wait until after World War I. In 1917 and 1918, King Ferdinand of Romania, in an attempt to maintain the loyalty of peasant soldiers, had promised that there would be significant land reforms. In 1918 some state lands, as well as lands in the hands of foreign and absentee owners, was redistributed. In addition, the government began a land expropriation directed at the large estates. Owners whose land was confiscated and redistributed were compensated by the state. The government, in 1921, continued its land reform efforts. As a result of these actions, the Romanian agrarian reforms were the largest in Europe outside of the U.S.S.R (Jelavich 1983).

The land reform at the end of World War I was not driven entirely by an economic rationale. The decision also was motivated by political considerations. As Jelavich (1983) notes, land reform did little to raise agricultural productivity, as tenants had farmed the great estates on an individual household basis. With land reform, peasants now owned their small plots and their farming methods did not change. Peasants lacked credit and the knowledge of how to apply modern farming methods to increase land productivity. But, the government had not redistributed the land merely in order to increase productivity. Land reform also was motivated by a fear of potential political radicalization among the peasantry. The National Liberal Party, under whom the reforms finally were adopted, shared the king's concern. In addition, the National Liberal Party saw land reform as a way to cement peasants, especially in the newly acquired territories, to their party, instead of to the National Peasant Party.

Because of Groza's land reform, approximately 900,000 peasant families received over 1,100,000 hectares of the almost 1,500,000 hectares expropriated. This left peasant households with plots that were too small to act as efficient production units, especially given the plans the communists would have for the country's overall economic development. Whatever had motivated the land reform, whether it was the result of a desire to wipe out large estate agricultural production, whether it reflected an attempt to lay the foundation for a mixed private/state production system in the countryside, or whether it represented pure political expediency (a wish to purchase the loyalty of the peasantry), the decision to redistribute land to the peasantry turned out to have been a serious political mistake. The first communist land redistribution produced economically inefficient farms and it created a sense of ownership among peasants that would prove hard to overcome when the state launched its drive to collectivize agriculture.

The Groza government passed legislation in July 1945 establishing *Sovroms*: joint Romanian-Soviet enterprises. The Soviet Union used these to extract surpluses from Romania, over and above the war reparations to which it was entitled under the terms that had ended the conflict between the Soviet Union and Romania. The *Sovroms* operated in the oil, natural gas, chemical, and timber sectors. The *Sovroms* and the war reparations put heavy burdens on Romania's already weakened economy. The Soviets sold most of the *Sovroms* to the Romanians in 1954. They kept control only of those in the oil and uranium sectors, which the Soviets saw as vital to their national defense interests. The Soviets also demanded that Romania send it workers to help rebuild its infrastructure. Romania used this as an opportunity to engage in the ethnic cleansing of German areas. Many of the workers sent to the Soviet Union were

Germans suspected of having supported the Nazis and the Hungarian Arrow Cross that operated in Northern Transylvania.

Meeting in Potsdam, in July and August 1945, the Western allies expressed serious concerns to the Soviets about developments in Romania. The United States delegation claimed that the Soviet Union was violating the terms of the Yalta accords in Romania. The Soviet Union called on the Western allies to recognize the Groza government, which they refused to do. The Western allies insisted the Romania hold free, democratic elections and that the winner of these elections would be recognized as Romania's legitimate government. The Russians claimed that demanding elections was inappropriate interference in Romania's internal affairs.

By August 1945, relations between the Groza government and the king had broken down almost completely. The king supported neither the land expropriation nor the *Sovroms*. The king used the fact that the Western allies refused to recognize the Groza government to go on a royal strike. The king went to his summer palace and refused to sign laws passed by the Groza government.

In an attempt to resolve the stalemate in Romania, the U.S. Secretary of State traveled to Moscow and met with the foreign ministers of Great Britain and the Soviet Union. In return for granting Groza's government recognition, the Soviet Union agreed that Romania's government would offer ministries to representatives of the National Peasant Party and National Liberal Party and that Romania would organize elections in the near future.

At the first annual meeting of the National Congress of the Romanian Communist Party (October 1945), Gheorgiu-Dej, with Stalin's backing, was elected General Secretary of the Communist Party. By mid-1946, under *Dej*'s leadership, the party enjoyed spectacular growth, reaching a membership total just over 700,000. By the end of 1947, membership in the party was just over 800,000. That the party had grown so rapidly is not altogether surprising. Some historians claim that the rapid growth in party membership was the result of pure opportunism. As evidence of this, they point out that before the war, the party, at best, had one or two thousand members on its rolls. This, however, overlooks the fact that the party during the pre-war period was illegal and was continually monitored by state security forces. To be a party member put one at considerable risk of harassment and imprisonment at the hands of the state. There is some indication that the party, despite its low membership, had the support of a not insignificant part of the Romanian electorate in the fact that during the 1920s it had elected five deputies to parliament, which was the same number that the Legion had elected in 1934. Had the party been free to compete openly for support in the 1920s and 1930s it might have become a significant political force in pre-war Romania, perhaps even rivaling the power of the radical right. Of course, this is conjecture, given that the communist deputies were not allowed to take their seats and the party faced continuing repression before between 1921 and 1944. However, having said this, one should not entirely dismiss opportunism as a motivating factor responsible for some of the growth in post-war communist party membership. It is quite possible that many Romanians who joined the party had realized that it was going to emerge as the dominant, if not the exclusive, political force in the country. Many may have wanted nothing more than to be part of the party in order to guarantee their own economic security and occupational success in a new communist regime.

There are a number of other possible reasons for why the communist party grew so quickly in Romania after the war. First, the communists and the social democrats were the only political forces in Romania that emerged from the war morally unscathed. While neither the social democrats nor the communists had formed organized resistance movements in Romania, in no small part because most of the communist leadership was in prison, the left, alone among Romanian political forces, had not cooperated with fascism. Therefore, the left, almost alone, was not implicated in the national catastrophe produced by the fascists and their supporters.

Second, one should not underestimate the degree to which the communists' economic program appealed to the material interests of large segments of the national population. It is easy to understand that the workers and peasants saw that they had little to gain from restoring the old elites to power, especially given that the communists were offering radical solutions to end the economic misery peasants and workers had endured under the former regime. There was nothing in the history of the old elites' behavior that would suggest to workers and peasants that restoring them to power would lead to new policies that would benefit the general population, rather than just the narrow socioeconomic base that the historical parties traditionally had served.

Third, communism, after the war, was attractive, as an ideology and a political and economic program, to at least a part of the Romanian intellectual elite. Across Europe, communism emerged from the war with a considerable amount of appeal to intellectuals, especially in France and Italy, two countries with which Romanian intellectuals strongly identified. Part of the party's prestige was based on the fact that, in both of these countries, the communists, including the parties' intellectuals, had made up the backbone of national resistance movements against fascism. For Romanian intellectuals and for European intellectuals, as a whole, the war had shown that fascism was not a plausible third way and that the struggle for the future would be fought between bourgeois capitalism and communism. A good number of intellectuals across Europe came to believe that in this battle communism provided the best hope for their nations' future, if for no other reason that capitalism had failed to prevent the Great Depression and the rise of fascist powers.

Fourth, communism seemed to provide a quick fix to many countries' economic development problems. It had provided Russia a means to lift itself out of its backwardness and to become a world power in a little more than a generation. Capitalism on the other hand seemed to only perpetuate the economic backwardness of many European countries. From the point of view of many Romanians, if communism had been able to achieve such rapid economic advancement for the Soviet Union there was no reason to expect that the same could not be achieved in Romania in just as short a time.

Whatever reasons people may have had for joining the party, the rapid growth in party membership was spectacular, especially in light of the ways in which previous regimes had tried to discredit the party and crush it, and the disastrous mistakes the party, itself, had made in formulating a political line before the war. For example, the party seriously damaged itself by having taken a stand, in the 1920s, supporting the return of Bessarabia to the U.S.S.R. and, in general, by aligning itself with the policies of the U.S.S.R.

In May 1946, in preparation for upcoming elections, the communist party, with Dej as its head, created the "Bloc of Democratic Parties." The communists held the leading position in the Bloc, which included a dissident wing of the Social Democrats; the Ploughmen's Front; and other small leftist parties.

The elections were held in November 1946. Amidst charges by the historical parties of fraud and voter intimidation, the Bloc won overwhelming support. It took almost 80% of the votes, winning 376 seats in the 414-member parliament. The National Peasant Party won 32 seats, making it the largest opposition party, and the National Liberal Party won 3 seats. If the communists had engaged in electoral fraud, they had followed a well-established Romanian political tradition. The National Peasant and National Liberal Parties long had engaged in voter manipulation, fraud, and the engineering of election results to achieve their parliamentary majorities and even before the formation of these parties, Romanian princes and kings normally manipulated elections to obtain whatever outcomes they wanted.

Once in power, the new government had to move quickly and decisively on the economic front. In 1946, Romania's industrial sector was producing less than half of what had been produced before the war. In addition, the agricultural sector still was not producing enough to feed the population. Consequently, for the first time in over a century, Moldova, traditionally one of the poorest regions of the country, began to experience a major famine. With the economy moving into a deepening crisis, immediate disaster was staved off by foreign assistance, but this could only be a short-term solution. In December 1946 the government took control of the Romanian National Bank and acted to dramatically increase the nation's money supply, which set off a round of high inflation, further compounding Romania's economic problems. One of the reasons why the government had to resort to debasing its money system was the need to offset the "strike" of Romanian capitalists. Capitalists, perhaps rightly so, as later events would demonstrate, were refusing to invest in the country, suspecting that if the communists managed to win the political battle for control of Romania all of their investments would be lost.

In February 1947, the government signed the Treaty of Paris, putting a formal end to World War II for the Romanians. The treaty was highly disadvantageous to Romania, as it was not treated as a co-belligerent in the way Italy was. Rather, Romania was treated as a defeated Axis power. Among other things, the treaty forced Romania to pay war reparations to the Soviet Union and forced Romania to officially recognize the loss of Bessarabia to the Soviet Union and Northern Bukovina to the Ukraine. In addition, southern Dobruja was given to

Bulgaria. Bessarabia and Bukovina had been taken by the Soviets in 1940, without Romanian resistance. The USSR's "right" to these regions was recognized in a provision of the secret Soviet-Nazi German pact of August 1939. From the Russian perspective, Bessarabia had been seized illegally from the Soviet Union at the end of World War I and Bukovina was a Ukrainian territory that had been inappropriately given to Romania at the same time.

With the government recognized by the West and the treaty ending the war signed, the communists began to move against those who were opposing their agenda for Romania. In July 1947, the government dissolved the National Peasant Party and the National Liberal Party. Later in the year (October, 1947), Iuliu Maniu, a three time Peasant Party Prime Minister before the war and a leading member of Antonescu's government, and Ion Mihalache, the second in command in the Peasant Party, were arrested and tried for treason. Both were convicted and given long sentences. Maniu died in prison in Sighet. By the end of 1947, all members of the National Peasant Party and the National Liberal Party had been removed from parliament. The communists must have taken special satisfaction in having imprisoned those who, just a few years before, had been responsible for imprisoning communist activists, including many of the people who now were in leading positions in Romania.

Having removed their parliamentary opposition, the communists and their allies next turned their attention to the throne. The Romanian communists saw the monarchy as a retrograde institution and the kings, themselves, as being part of the landowning class and as such, exploiters of peasants. In addition, Michael, to many in the party, could never be forgiven for having supported Romania's war of aggression against the USSR when he had replaced his father on the throne in 1940. To the communists and their social democratic allies, Michael, by supporting Antonescu, not only was complicit in the war of aggression against the Soviet Union, but he also was guilty of having tolerated the fascist regime's crimes against humanity. Moreover, since the end of the war, Michael clearly had sided with the forces of the traditional right in opposition to the social democratic and communist left and had protected fascists in leading positions in the state. Finally, the very idea of a monarchy was fundamentally incompatible with the development of a socialist state.

After considerable negotiation with Groza and the communists, Michael abdicated and left office on January 3, 1948. He was allowed to leave with a sizeable fortune. His abdication ended the Hohenzollern-Sigmaringen dynasty in Romania. Beginning with Karol I in 1866, the family had supplied Romania with four monarchs: Karol I, Ferdinand I, Karol II, and Michael I. Michael retired to Switzerland where he lived with his wife and two daughters.

Shortly after the 1989 revolution, Michael tried to return to Romania, but was rebuffed by the new authorities. He finally was given permission to return for his first visit since his resignation during the spring, 1992. Large crowds in Bucharest, some of whom had been agitating for a restoration of the monarchy, others of whom had come to see him out of curiosity, greeted him. Monarchist sympathizers felt that only a king could provide Romania with a figure that could provide a symbolic and, perhaps, material unity that they saw Romania lacking since the collapse of the old system. The king also was seen as a symbol of Romania's "historical continuity," despite the fact that the monarchy was a relatively new state institution, after the "abnormal rupture" of the Bolshevik period, which many argued was a regime "alien" to the historical trajectory of Romanian political, social, and cultural development.

With the former "bourgeois" parties liquidated and the monarchy abolished, in February 1948, the communist party merged with the social democrats who had been its ally in the Bloc. In 1946, the social democrats had split over the issue of whether or not the SDP (Social Democrat Party) should cooperate with the communists. A minority of the SDP seceded from their party to form an organization called the Independent Social Democrats, while the majority of social democrats supported cooperation with the communists and, later, the merger of the social democrats with the communists.

The fusion of the communists with the social democrats created a new party, the "Romanian Workers' Party" (*Partidul Muncitoresc Roman* or the PMR). The new party had a combined membership of over one million members, most of whom were members of the communist party who had joined the party after the war. The joining of the social democrats with the communists was less a merger of equals than it was a takeover of the social democratic movement in Romania by the communist party. The takeover of the social democrats was something more than a political "narcissism of small differences." It meant the political liquidation of a counter image of socialism, one that was identified with reformism within the context of the liberal bourgeois state. On another level, it also "demonstrated" that social democracy was an "historical error" that was superseded by Bolshevism, as institutionalized in the Soviet Union. From the viewpoint of Romania's communists, social democracy had been a failure as a revolutionary movement. Nowhere had it resulted in a peaceful "fundamental" transformation of social and economic relations. Only Bolshevism had demonstrated "true" revolutionary capacities.

With the disappearance of the social democrats, the communist dominated PMR was left as the sole voice of Romania's workers and peasants, although the Ploughmen's Front also remained politically active until 1953. The Ploughmen's Front continued as a staunch ally of the PMR, being the party's "voice" in a number of rural areas. The Romanian communists were not the only Eastern and Central European communist party that conquered and, then, liquidated social democratic parties. The same thing was happening across the region. In June 1948, the Hungarian communists merged with the Social Democrats and the same thing happened in Czechoslovakia in the same month. In August 1948, the Bulgarian communists merged with the Bulgarian Social Democrats and in December the communists and socialists merged in Poland. All of these mergers took place along the same lines as had been the case in Romania. Social democratic parties were incorporated into the communist parties and, as a result, were liquidated as an "alternative" to Bolshevism.

Now securely in control of the state, the communists, together with the Ploughmen's Front, held new elections to parliament in March 1948. Only candidates acceptable to the PMR and the Ploughmen's Front were allowed to stand for office. Needless to say, the new parliament and the new government, with Groza, again, at its head, were clearly under the control of the communists. By April 1948, a new constitution, modeled after that of the Soviet Union, was drafted and ratified. With the ratification of the 1948 Constitution, Romania, officially, became a "People's Republic."

The communists set about reconstructing Romania along the lines of the Soviet Union's model of socialism, which was to be expected, given that the Soviet Army was in Romania and that only the U.S.S.R. offered a successful model as how to organize a revolutionary socialist society, economy, and state. As was the case with the early Soviet Union, Romania faced the critical issue of capital formation. Shortly after the Bolshevik Revolution, one of the principal economic problems the Soviets had faced, once they had defeated the White armies and the invasion forces from the West, was modernization of the national economy. In the view of leading Soviet thinkers, as well as Western economists, economic modernization was equated with industrialization. But, industrialization required investment capital, which was in very short supply in the Soviet Union. Alternative would have been to import capital from the West or to earn it from trade with the West. However, given the West's economic isolation of the Soviet Union, neither of these strategies was possible. Evgeny Preobrazhensky (1965 [1926], a leading Soviet economist and an early ally of Lenin, proposed a solution to the problem of securing investment capital. He proposed that the Soviet Union needed to engage in "primitive socialist accumulation" in order to obtain investment capital. Under Stalin, this strategy entailed using surpluses extracted from agriculture to finance the rapid development of state owned heavy industry. The development of light industry especially that devoted to the production of individual consumer goods was to be kept at minimum levels. To the extent to which any investment in industrial production would be directed at meeting consumer needs, it primarily would be organized to meet the needs of collective consumption (housing, health care, education, etc.), rather than private consumption.

This system resulted in a "civil war" in which the state was pitted against the peasantry. Stalin launched a series of attacks on the countryside, often using force to extract grain and other surpluses from the peasantry. By 1928, Stalin had decided that small scale peasant production would never be able to generate the levels of agricultural surpluses that the regime required to meet its industrialization goals. Thus, in order to maximize the accumulation of agricultural surpluses, the Soviet Union, in 1929, launched a major drive to forcibly collectivize its agricultural infrastructure. Collectivization was successful, but it came at a tremendous cost to the peasantry. Hundreds of thousands of peasants were imprisoned, killed by security forces, or died of starvation. But Stalin achieved his goal of accumulating sufficient surpluses to support industrialization. As a result, during the years in which Western economies were contracting due to the Great Depression, the Soviet Union had

positive rates of growth and it achieved this without having been integrated into the Western, capitalist economic system.

During this time, Stalin completely eliminated markets as means
for establishing prices and for allocating goods. In place of the market,
he developed an elaborate state planning system that made decisions
about all prices in the economy, set wage rates for all jobs, and determined the allocation of raw materials. Such elaborate planning required
the development of an enormous bureaucracy that was empowered to
use various incentives, including force and coercion, to meet state planning goals. As its responsibilities increased, the regime frequently turned
to coercion to meet planned state economic goals.

The key elements in the Bolshevik system were: 1) one party rule;
2) democratic centralism as the organizational model for decision-
making within the party; 3) elimination of all other parties that could
serve as effective points of political opposition; 4) collectivization of
agriculture; 5) nationalization of a country's productive resources and its
financial, commercial, and industrial enterprises; 6) the institutionalization of a purge and repressive apparatus; 7) the substitution of central
planning for the market as the principal means of economic allocation
within a country; 8) the elimination of private organizations outside of
the direct control of the party-state apparati; and 9) integration into an
inter state Bolshevik network of states. This model of Bolshevism was
imported almost without change from the Soviet Union. This was
unfortunate for the regimes that imposed it on their societies. Importing
the Soviet model meant that structures that had emerged out of the interaction of Bolshevism and pre-Bolshevik elements in Russian society
would become "normative" for other states, even where these normative
structures raised the possibilities for manifold internal contradictions in
Bolshevism's development outside of the Soviet Union. For example,
Pipes (1993) has argued that as Bolshevism developed in the Soviet
Union it incorporated diverse aspects of Tsarist political structure and
culture into the political system it was building. Among the most important of such structures was Russian patrimonialism. In Pipes (1993)
view, patrimonialism was a uniquely Russian feudal structure that was
alien to feudal regimes both to the west and the south of Russia. The way
in which the Bolsheviks fused patrimonialism with the state and party
system they constructed meant that everywhere Bolshevism was introduced outside of Russia produced structural incompatibilities that

resulted in internal conflicts and contradictions. In addition, the over-arching structures of Bolshevism had to be constructed on top of the wreckage of the unique forms of feudalism found in the different Romanian provinces and on the remains of the neo-liberal capitalism that Romania had tired to put in place during the inter war period. The remains of these institutions and social practices brought over from older social formations had to be reworked by the Bolsheviks as they sought to incorporate them into the new institutional systems they were building.

In June, 1948, Groza's government set about nationalizing the country's major industries, its mines, its banks and other financial sectors, and transportation, thereby bringing almost all of the key sectors of the national economy, with the exception of agriculture, under state ownership. By 1951, the state had direct ownership of over 90% of Romania's industry. Nationalization did not generate much popular opposition in Romania. In fact, it was widely supported. In many of the nationalized sectors, the major firms and enterprises were in the hands of foreigners or national minorities, who the public did not trust to run their businesses in ways that met Romanian national interests. This first wave of nationalization eliminated, as a class, the urban bourgeoisie in Romania, as well as foreign investment in the country. The second wave of nationalization targeted petty producers so that, with only a few exceptions, most formal private economic activity was wiped out in the country eliminating the last potential base for urban bourgeois opposition to the communists.

In 1951, Romania launched its first Five Year Plan, covering the years 1951-1955. By this date, most of the other new socialist states already had introduced five year plans. Over the course of this plan, 57% of national investment went to industry. Eighty seven per cent of this was directed toward developing heavy industry. Consumer goods production and agriculture were relegated to secondary roles. This pattern persisted throughout the communist period in Romania, reflecting the party's adoption of Stalin's position that economic modernization equaled the development of heavy industry. Like elsewhere in Eastern and Central Europe, the Romanian planning process was patterned after the Soviet Union's. In Romania, the first plan put down a foundation for a major drive to industrialize and to urbanize the country. In both of these sectors, Romania significantly lagged behind most other European countries. The plan also was directed at meeting basic needs of the population, especially in the areas of education, health, and housing. At the same time, it provided very little in the way of economic resources for building an economic base for the production of personal consumer goods. With the implementation of its first five year plan, Romania had reached a point where virtually the entire state apparatus of Bolshevism was in place and the regime had synchronized its political and economic structures with those of the Soviet Union and of the other emerging Bolshevik states in Europe.

In May 1948, the new government moved against former members of the Iron Guard who had not been caught up in the first wave of war-crimes trials. Over 4500 people were arrested (Deletant 1997). Later in the same year, the state purged over 1,000 members of the security forces who had been appointed before the communists came to power and replaced them with communist loyalists. Also in 1948 (June), the government passed legislation that disbanded the old regime's political police, the *Siguranta*, and replaced it with the *Securitate* (the *Directia Generala a Securitati Poporului*). The *Securitate* absorbed the functions of the *Siguranta,* as well as some of the functions of the Special Services. The Special Services had emerged from the worker militias organized by Emil Bodnaras toward the end of World War II.

The *Securitate* was charged with protecting the new Romanian State from internal and external enemies. It was patterned after the security services of the Soviet Union and it worked closely with the Soviet security services, as well as the security services of other communist states. Many of the *Securitate's* agents, and almost all of its commanding officers, were sent to the Soviet Union for advanced training and professional development, where they met not only Soviet agents, but agents from across Eastern and Central Europe. Soviet advisors were assigned to all of the Romanian internal security services and the Soviet Union managed to insert a number of spies into the Romanian security forces.

The *Securitate* developed an effective foreign intelligence system that operated in Eastern Europe, as well as in Western Europe, Canada, and the United States. It ran continuing investigations of Romanian émigré communities, using an extensive network of informants and professional agents. A Romanian émigré in the United States told the author how he once had been approached by a man who wanted him to supply information on some of his Romanian friends. When the émigré refused, the man showed him potentially compromising photographs taken when he was with his male lover. The man told him that he would send them to his employer unless he cooperated. The émigré told the man to go ahead and send them because his employer knew he was gay. The émigré never heard from the man again. The *Securitate* also continually spied on the general Romanian population. *Securitate* agents tapped telephones, bugged offices and homes, monitored mail, and used an extensive network of informants (both voluntary and forced) to gather data on Romanian citizens. Reportedly, the Romanian security police had at least ten million microphones for its twenty three million inhabitants (Pacepa 1987). Even if Pacepa exaggerates, it was widely believed among Romanians that electronic eavesdropping was everywhere. There were stories that even the public parks were bugged. With widespread belief that the state was always watching them, paranoia was rampant among Romanians, especially under Ceausescu. People developed elaborate hand-signals to indicate to one another that their conversations were likely being monitored.

Informants were drawn from all walks-of-life. Orthodox clergy reported on members of their congregations and on each other, spouses were recruited to spy on each other, children were encouraged to report on their parents, friends were encouraged or forced to inform on each other, university faculty and teachers at all levels reported on colleagues and students, physicians reported on patients and colleagues, workers reported on co-workers and supervisors, supervisors reported on each other and their subordinates, and so forth. The security services needed very little evidence to act against a citizen. No sector of Romanian society was immune to *Securitate* scrutiny. Even senior leaders of the party were regularly subjected to continual monitoring (Deletant 1997).

The pervasive system of internal espionage seriously eroded social trust among Romania's citizenry and generated widespread paranoia. No one could be confident that even their family members and close friends were not reporting on them to the security services. Everywhere and at almost all times, people were reticent in talking about any subject that could bring them to the unwanted special attention of the security forces. Under this system, realms of personal privacy were abolished. One could never be sure that anything was private or personal. Every thought and every behavior had the possibility of being given an untoward political meaning and political significance.

Eventually, the security police grew to become one of the government's most powerful institutions. It became a virtual state within the state. Over the years, the *Securitate* acquired a domestic and international reputation as an especially effective, ruthless, and repressive force. It extended its presence into virtually every aspect of Romanian public and private life, creating a climate of suspicion and paranoia unequaled almost anywhere else in Eastern and Central Europe. As the *Securitate* expanded its scope of activities, it became a mainstay of state and party control, introducing continuing terror, with all of its consequences of confusion, fear, and suspicion, into the very fabric of social life in Romania. The *Securitate*, especially in the late stages of the Ceausescu government, shattered almost all possibilities for non-familial social relations that were predicated on even the most minimal levels of social trust between strangers or between and among social intimates. The secret police not only colonized most Romanian institutions, but also the hearts and minds of the Romanian people. The secret police were carried around in the heads of the Romanian people structuring what they thought, felt, and believed and this affected how people related to each other and to their own selves.

In March 1949, the Central Committee of the PMR adopted a program authorizing agricultural collectivization. The issue of agricultural collectivization generated considerable internal debate in the party. The debate dealt with strategy, rather than the ultimate outcome. Historians and commentators on agricultural collectivization have long accepted the idea that one faction of the party, led by Ana Pauker and others in the party's so-called Moscow wing, wanted to immediately nationalize all agricultural land and create state farms, much like the Soviet Union had done with its *kolkhozy*. The other faction, said to be led by Dej, was said to have wanted to create a dual system of collective agricultural property based on state farms and agricultural cooperatives (Associations or, in Romanian, *Intovarasiri*), which, eventually, would give way to state farms as the only form of agriculture (Brucan 1993).

Dej, in a meeting of the Central Committee held between November 30 and December 5, 1961, roundly condemning Pauker and what was alleged to have been her position on collectivization, stated that:

> Flagrantly violating the party line and the decisions of the party, and subverting the authority of the party leadership, Ana Pauker

organized an unprecedented adventurist and provocative action, which gravely undermined the alliance with the working peasantry. On the basis of directives she gave to [Interior Minister] Teohari Georgescu, mass arrests were simultaneously organized throughout the country of peasants accused of not respecting their obligations to the state. Many tens of thousands of peasants, the great majority of whom were working peasants provocatively labeled as kulaks, were arrested by the security organs, imprisoned and then tried in public trials (quoted in Levy 2001: 90-91).

Recently published research (Levy 2001) has built a compelling case that this interpretation of Pauker's role is incorrect. Rather than being on the left on the issue of agricultural collectivization, Levy builds a convincing case that Pauker, in fact, was on the "right." She favored a gradualist approach to collectivization built on peasant consent rather than compulsion. It also is evident, according to Levy (2001) that Pauker believed it was premature to collectivize agriculture, given Romania's lack of appropriate machine technology to support large-scale agricultural production. Levy (2001) shows that it was Dej who pushed forward the very policy for which he denounced Ana Pauker.

Pauker also had shown herself to be a defender of the peasants' economic interests during the 1947 currency reform (Levy 2001). Dej and his allies supported currency reform policies that would lead to higher prices for manufactured goods and lower prices for agricultural products (Levy 2001). This would result in a massive transfer of wealth away from the countryside toward the cities, where industry was concentrated. Pauker supported a policy that would have achieved a greater parity between prices for agricultural commodities and industrial products (Levy 2001). Pauker, and her ally, Vasile Luca, also supported the continuation of free agricultural markets, while the Dej wing of the party supported rigid state controls over rural markets. Dej and his supporters, following Stalin's policy in the Soviet Union, wanted to eliminate market relations as determinants of supply and prices for agricultural commodities. From Dej's perspective, to perpetuate free rural markets only would lead to national industrial development being held hostage to the economic interests of peasant households.

Aside from ideological considerations, for the communist leadership to realize its goals of developing Romania into a "modern" industrial state, agricultural collectivization was taken to be necessary on two grounds. First, Romania's system of small plot agricultural production did not generate sufficient surpluses to support an industrial, urban population, let alone generate sufficient surpluses that could be converted into investment capital. Peasant production yielded surpluses barely beyond subsistence levels. Furthermore Romania's peasants, historically, had shown little inclination to move beyond this level of production. Without increasing agricultural production and without confiscating agricultural surpluses, industrialization would have been impossible in Romania. What industry that did exist after the war simply did not generate sufficient surpluses that could be used to increase investment to the levels the country required.

Second, the party leadership, if it were to lead a successful drive to industrialize the country, was looking to the peasantry to meet the country's need for a larger industrial workforce. The party intended to use peasants, displaced by agricultural modernization, to staff new industries being planned.

Cooperatives were to be formed by "voluntary" donations of land to the cooperative. In return, households would be given land to construct a home and a small plot for private production. Families in the cooperatives did not receive salaries; instead, they were given a share of the dividends accruing to the cooperative. Payment of their share would be cash or in-kind agricultural returns. Families in cooperatives also were allowed to keep what they earned from their private plots. In return for their participation in the cooperatives, families would have access to various inputs to production, including machinery for planting and harvesting. Private plots could not be sold, but they could be inherited, provided the heir was capable of working the land. On the other hand, workers on state farms received wages. By the 1980s, wages for state farm workers closely approximated those of urban industrial workers, although the overall quality of rural life continued to lag considerably behind that available in the cities. Rural areas lacked many of the collective amenities found in a great number of larger towns and in almost all Romanian cities. The rural-urban gulf that marked pre-World War II Romania had diminished considerably as a result of state policy, but it continued to be quite substantial.

According to the laws governing agricultural collectivization, state farms were to be managed by directors appointed by the state and would be worked by paid labor, comparable to workers in a nationalized factory or other state enterprise. In other words, state farms were managed in the same way as any other type of socialized property. On the other hand, cooperatives were to be managed only by those who had contributed property to them. Supposedly, the state had no authority to dictate what happened within the cooperatives. At most, in theory, the state and the party could only recommend policies and practices to them. Over time, the practical differences in management between the two systems blurred in many parts of Romania, with the two systems blending together more along the lines of authority characteristic of the state farms rather than the cooperatives. Throughout the period of agricultural collectivization, which was reported completed in 1962, government investment favored state farms over the cooperatives. State farms received the best of the land that was nationalized in 1949. They also received better machinery, more fertilizers and pesticides, and better irrigation systems than did the cooperatives.

Collectivization did not proceed smoothly in Romania (Levy 2001). When agricultural collectivization was accelerated in 1950 and large numbers of peasants were compelled to form cooperatives, resistance, some of which was violent, broke out across the country (Levy 2001). Peasants fought against the heavy-handed methods that the regime was using, including the use of the *Securitate* and other police forces against the independent peasantry. During this time, Pauker was on leave from her job as administrator of the collectivization program. She had gone to Moscow to be treated for cancer. She returned to Bucharest in the late summer of 1950 to find that, in her absence, the regime had reversed her policies of non-coercion of peasants (Levy 2001).

Because of peasant resistance, collectivization slowed down considerably. In 1964 Dej gave Nicolae Ceausescu the job of completing the state's collectivization efforts. Ceausescu launched a reign of terror in the countryside and completed collectivization in 1965, three years ahead of schedule (Levy 2001). According to Levy (2001), throughout the period of forced collectivization, Dej continually denounced the use of terror against the peasants, but tacitly approved it, and, most likely, encouraged it. By using surrogates to carry out the policies of terror and coercion, Dej was able to distance himself from repression and maintain his legitimacy among the Romanian population.

Dej and his allies were convinced that the regime would never be able to anchor itself in Romania unless the party won its class war in the countryside. They were especially opposed to the prosperous peasant farmers, the *chiaburi*, who were seen to be Romania's version of the Russian *kulaks*. Between 1947 and 1952 the party struggled with how to define the *chiaburi* and what policies it ought to pursue toward them. One of the main issues was whether peasants would be defined as *chiaburi* on the basis of the size of their land holdings, on the basis of their incomes, or on the basis of whether or not they employed agricultural wage laborers. A subsidiary question was how much land did a peasant need to own in order to be regarded as a *chiaburi,* rather than as a member of the middle peasantry. The question also arose as to whether *chiaburi* should be allowed to donate their holdings to cooperatives and whether they should be allowed to become members of an agricultural cooperative.

Party hard-liners, which included Dej, eventually supported an expansive definition of who was a chiaburi and who was not. They also came to reject the idea of allowing the chiaburi to donate their land to a cooperative and become members of cooperatives. Instead, they decided that the land of the chiaburi was to be confiscated and that the chiaburi were to be arrested and expelled from their villages and from the cooperatives that had allowed them to become members. Dej, true to his Marxist ideology, had pursued such policies because he was convinced that the *chiaburi* (kulaks) never would have voluntarily relinquished their land. History was on Dej's side in the debate. Classes do not voluntarily liquidate themselves. They disappear only when they are conquered. If the *chiaburi* had not been defeated, they would have continued to reproduce themselves, as a class or as a class fraction, and they would have perpetuated capitalist agriculture in Romania's countryside. As a result, they would have been a continuing source of resistance to the state's plans to construct a socialist economy and society in Romania. The *chiaburi* (kulaks), had they not been defeated, would have not only frustrated the socialization of agriculture. They also would have made it difficult for Romania to build a socialized industrial base in Romania. The development of Romanian industry needed to be built around principles of unequal exchange between the agricultural sector and the industrial sector, with resources flowing from the former to the later. Without extracting surplus capital from the countryside and converting this to investment capital for industry, the Romanian authorities would have been unable to finance the expansion of the state's industrial base.

A large number of peasants not only struggled with the regime over agricultural collectivization, but also over production quotas established by central authorities in the Ministry of Agriculture. In 1950, peasants had supplied only 18,000 wagonloads of wheat. The quota for the year had been 40,000 wagonloads (Levy 2001). The party debated how to respond to the peasants' passive-aggressive resistance. Dej was furious that the peasants would hold back the larger part of their production from the state. When Stalin believed that the kulaks had done the same thing in the Soviet Union, he had brutally crushed them. Between 1928 and 1932, Stalin arrested and deported millions of peasants for much the same type resistance that Romania now was facing from its peasantry. A large number of the deported peasants were sent to labor camps from which they never returned (see Pipes 1993, among others, for a discussion of the mass arrests).

Pauker felt that rather than retaliating with mass arrests, as Stalin had done, the Romanian party should respond by making selective arrests and prosecutions of leading peasant resisters and, over the short run, reduce production quotas, which she felt were unrealistically high (Levy 2001). Pauker had several unusual supporters for her position, including Alexandru Moghioris, who had replaced her while she was being treated for cancer and who had been the author of the 1950 reign of terror that was designed to compel peasants to join cooperatives (Levy 2001).

The next year, 1951, Romania had a bumper agricultural crop. Pauker believed that under these conditions the peasants would respond positively to the state quotas and that there would not be a repeat of last year's withholding of crops. It turned out she was badly mistaken. The peasants again withheld a large part of their production from state collectors. By November 1951, peasants had turned over to the state only 30% of their quotas for all agricultural products (Levy 2001). Pauker was hesitant to use force against the peasants, as a result the state failed to meet its agricultural goals.

By 1980, the communist party had won its class war in the countryside, completely conquering the once independent, land-owning peasantry. By 1980 ninety one per cent of agricultural land had been collectivized (Turnock 1986). Sixty one per cent of the collectivized land was organized into cooperatives and thirty per cent was in state farms. Nine per cent remained in private hands. A large part of this private land was in regions where geography made collectivization almost impossible. Even private land holdings did not mean that owners were free. The state had almost completely obliterated private agricultural markets, although a shadow economy in agricultural commodities continued to survive and, later, would thrive in rural areas. Private farmers were given state production quotas and had to distribute much of their product through state distribution systems at prices set by the state. They also were controlled through the fact that most of their inputs to production came through the state.

Agricultural collectivization was more than merely an instance of economic aggression by the state against the peasantry. Collectivization produced a radical transformation of the space-time order in the Romanian countryside, as Verdery's (1996) work, in part, shows. The countryside, along with its embedded "structures of feeling" (Williams 1977) and of sense of belonging and sense of place (Harvey 1996), was drastically reshaped to meet the communist political and economic ends, which included the elimination of a land-holding peasantry. As the communists consolidated their power in the countryside, peasants were stripped of their sense of control over and their sense of agency within their local communities. With collectivization and, more importantly, with peasant migration to the cities, accelerated the peasantry's sense of time. The old rhythms of life increasingly were dissolved and replaced by communist rhythms of time and seasonal markers. The communists continually struggled with peasants to squash the traditional cycle of festivals, holidays, and feasts, especially those with religious associations. The communists, however, never were able to completely annihilate such practices among the peasants and supplant older forms of communal celebrations and rituals.

Under the terms of the 1948 law authorizing agricultural collectivization, private ownership of agricultural land was to be eliminated. Shortly after the law was passed, the security forces evicted over 17,000 families from their households and some 89,000 peasants were arrested between 1950 and 1952 for resisting collectivization (Brucan 1993; Levy 2001). Of this 89,000, 37,000 were "middle" peasants, 7,500 were poor peasants, and the remainder, 45,000, were so-called rich peasants, i.e. they held 10 hectares of land or more and/or employed non-family labor (Levy 2001).

In some cases, peasant resistance was violent, with some peasants joining guerilla movements that were operating in Romania's remote mountain regions. The guerilla movements had begun to form in 1944. They were made up of diverse groups: former members of the Iron Guard who remained loyal to the exiled Hora Sima and the memory of their "martyred" former leader Codreanu, supporters of the old "bourgeois" parties, and religious dissidents, as well as peasants. Guerilla activity continued until 1959, when the government proclaimed their final "defeat." Two of the larger resistance groups were the *Divizia Sumanelor Negre* (The Black Greatcoats' Division) and the *Haiducii lui Avram Iancu* (Avrum Iancu's Bandits). The latter had strong tied to the National Peasant Party in Transylvania (Deletant 1997). These resistance movements had scattered successes, but they never amounted to a substantial threat to the communist regime.

Many of the peasants who resisted collectivization, through violence or other means, joined other enemies of the state in Romania's growing system of political prisons. Political prisons, after 1948, became a growth industry in Romania, advancing beyond even that which had been put in place by Antonescu and the fascists, as more and more sectors of the population and a greater number of individuals came to be identified as "enemies of the state." Among the first to be moved into the penal system had been persons tied to the Iron Guard and to the Antonsecu regime, followed by leaders of the former "bourgeois" parties. With the creation of the *Securitate*, the numbers of prisoners increased dramatically and the social composition of the imprisoned shifted, peasants resisting collectivization, purged party members, dissident workers, religious believers and others came to be swept up and deposited in the growing networks of labor camps and prisons. While harsh everywhere, conditions in the political prisons varied to some degree. The worst camps seem to have been those put in place to build the Danube-Black Sea canal. Work on the canal had begun in 1949 and construction relied heavily on prison labor. Survival rates among the prisoners working at the camps were very low. Food rations were barely enough to keep the prisoners alive, let alone meet the high work norms imposed on them. The canal came to be known as the "Canal of Death" project.

While working in Romania, on several occasions, I had a chance to speak with a number of people whose family members or friends had survived these camps. Almost to a person, they related how they had barely recognized former friends and family members who returned from the prisons and the camps. Former inmates returned home as walking skeletons with broken bodies and broken spirits. Few of the returnees ever were able to reintegrate themselves into normal life. Most of the returnees lived out the remainder of their lives much as they were when they returned from prison, refugees from a land of the living dead.

Deletant (1997) and Bartosek (1999) report that the Romanians were among the first of the communist regimes to experiment with the techniques of political reeducation in their camps. Techniques of political reeducation came to be one of Romania's unique contributions to communist penology. Political reeducation was introduced into the camp system in Pitesti in 1949. It was initiated by a secret police officer named Alexandru Nikolski, who worked with a prisoner named Eugen Turcanu. Turcanu had been imprisoned in 1948 for his work as a student organizer with the Iron Guard between 1940-1941. At some point between his work with the Iron Guard and his time in prison, he had converted from being a true believer in fascism to being a true believer in communism, as was quite common with former fascists throughout Europe. For Turcanu and others like him, one closed ideological system was easily substitutable for another. It was not hard to find in any communist party, in states that had been conquered by fascism and then had turned communist, tens of thousands of people who, like Turcanu, had undergone some form of a conversion experience. Turcanu became one of the organizers and leaders of a group called the Organization of Prisoners with Communist Beliefs (OPCB). Relying on the study of communist literature and the continual application of rituals of degradation, humiliation, and torture, Turcanu and a core group of at least fifteen other prisoners in Pitesti, who worked closely with prison authorities, engaged in stripping away prisoners' former identities and beliefs. Seminarians and clergy were especially targeted. Given the apparent successes of political reeducation in Pitesti, in 1952 the same practices were extended to the camps on the Danube-Black Sea canal. However, when news of what was happening was leaked to the Western press, the Romanian authorities ended the experiment. In 1954 Turcanu and six other members of the OPCB were tried and sentenced to death for torturing prisoners. However, none of the prison authorities that had allowed the organization to form and to practice torture were tried, let alone charged, with any violations. To act against the prison authorities would have been to admit the regime's complicity in this especially inhumane treatment of prisoners. This was something the regime never would acknowledge at this time (Bartosek 1999).

The prison population expanded considerably after 1951, as Dej began a series of purges, partly in response to demands from Stalin and partly out of his own self-interest. According to Sylviu Brucan (1993), at a meeting between Stalin and Dej in Moscow, Stalin pointedly expressed his disappointment with Romania's unwillingness to act against agents of Titoism (see the discussion of the "Titoism" phenomenon below) and of Zionism. By 1951, if not even earlier, Stalin, had become increasingly anti-Semitic and increasingly hostile toward Zionism and the state of Israel. Stalin apparently demanded that Romania take immediate action against the "cosmopolitanist" Zionists and the Titoists in Romania, some of whom belonged to both of these categories of enemies of the state, the party, and the international communist movement.

When Dej returned to Romania, after carefully laying the foundation for a number of charges against the cosmopolitans and shoring up his support inside of the party, Dej launched an attack on the newly identified enemies of the regime. Coincidentally, among the first of those against which he moved where those who had been among his major rivals for control of the party and the state. Vasile Luca, a long time party activist, a member of the party's Moscow wing, and the minister of finance, was removed from his position in May 1952. He was later tried, convicted, and sentenced to death. His death sentence was later commuted to a life sentence. He died in prison. Teohari Georgescu, who was minister of interior and, as such, commanded the Romanian security and militia forces, and had been the first communist to hold a government position in post World War II Romania, also was removed from office in May 1952. He was assigned a job as manager of the 13 Decembrie (December) printing plant in Bucharest. (Deletant 1997). This was a minor position that afforded him a comfortable living in relative isolation from Romania's internal political affairs. For the rest of his work life, his only major concern was that he not publish something that had gotten by the censors or that would later get him in trouble if the party line were to shift.

Ana Pauker was removed from all positions of authority in the party in July 1952. She was arrested in February 1953 and was released in 1954. By the time of her arrest, she had few allies in the party's leadership. Following her release, Pauker retired to a comfortable private life in a villa in Cotroceni, a very fashionable pre-war neighborhood in Bucharest. She never again tried to regain power in the Romanian party or state. Counting herself lucky to have not received a long-term prison sentence or not to be executed, she was content spending her time reading and meeting with old friends going back to the days when she was a powerful figure not only in Romanian communism but in international communism as well.

Dej and his party faction also turned against Patrascanu, one of the party's earliest members and one of the candidates who had won a parliamentary seat in 1931. In part, Dej deeply distrusted Patrascanu because of his bourgeois origins and his continuing ties to bourgeois politicians and intellectuals in the years immediately after World War II. Patrascanu came from a family of distinguished Romanian intellectuals, while Dej, and most of those closest to him in the party, had proletarian origins. It is not clear that Dej ever had felt personally comfortable with intellectuals and with those who had bourgeois origins. To Dej, class origins were an important predictor of a person's character and political positions. Patrascanu carried with him all of the baggage of a high status, bourgeois family and bourgeois intellectual preparation. Dej saw these as the main reasons for Patrascanu's close relationships with the leaders of the historical parties and his apparent sympathies for the West. Dej never felt comfortable with intellectuals recruited into the party from the old elites. It is almost as if he had an ingrained suspicion of their motives for joining the communist movement. Throughout his tenure as head of the communist party, Dej kept Romanian intellectuals on a very short leash. Dej understood that the party needed intellectuals, produced under the old order, to staff key positions in the state and party. He, however, did not want intellectuals to become an autonomous force inside of society or inside of the party that would be capable of challenging the party's leading role in Romania. Intellectuals drawn from the old elites had to become more communist than Stalin, if they wanted to work in the new Romanian state. Any sign that their beliefs in the communist cause were less than totally enthusiastic could, and did, cost them dearly.

The Soviet Union also distrusted Patrascanu. There is strong evidence that Dej had received considerable pressure from Stalin to purge Patrascanu (Levy 2001). Patrascanu's problems with the party's leadership stemmed, in no small part, from the fact that he, unlike them, had never served a long prison sentence, despite having been arrested and convicted of political crimes a number of times. Moreover, when he was in prison, Patrascanu was segregated from the communists. He was put in an area reserved for prominent bourgeois politicians, writers, and others who had run afoul of the fascist state (Levy 2001). This aroused suspicions among some of Patrascanu's communist colleagues, who suspected that he might be working for the state's intelligence services.

In late February 1948, at the first congress of the newly constituted Romanian Workers' Party, Patrascanu was denounced for having "fallen under the influence of the bourgeoisie" and he lost his job as Foreign Minister (Levy 2001). The party suspected that he, Patrascanu, had been too close to the British and American diplomats at the peace conference that produced the treaties formalizing the end of the Second World War. Moreover, they distrusted the close personal relations that Patrascanu had with "bourgeois" politicians and with the monarchy. In June 1948, at a plenary of the Central Committee, Patrascanu was attacked as "the bearer of the ideology and interests of the bourgeoisie" and as someone who "supported national-chauvinist policies" and "counterrevolutionary theories inspired by...the class enemy" (Levy 2001: 140-141). Patrascanu had taken a hard line, at the wrong time, against the Hungarian minority in Romania. He was taking a "nationalist" stance at a time when the party was strongly supporting "socialist internationalism" and was trying to assure the Magyars in Romania that they would have a secure future under the communists.

It was not until April 1954 that the regime felt it had "sufficient" evidence, all of which it evidently had manufactured, to proceed with Patrascanu's trial. He was tried, convicted, and executed in April, along with Remus Koffler. Koffler, like Patrascanu, was charged with treason for alleged espionage activities. Koffler had been a member of the party's central committee during World War II and he had been in charge of party finance. Six others were tried and convicted at the same time and were given severe prison sentences. Patrascanu was executed forty-eight hours after the sentence was announced. He later was rehabilitated by Ceausescu and the party in 1968, three years after Dej's death.

Patrascanu's plight, in part, was an object lesson to Romanians about the "fragile" loyalties of communists who had bourgeois origins. If someone with Patrascanu's credentials and with his long-term involvement in the communist movement could have engaged in "treason" to the communist movement, what could Romanians expect of more recent bourgeois converts to communism. After Patrascanu's arrest and eventual trial and execution, it was easy for the average Romanian to see any member of the former bourgeoisie as someone who was likely to betray communism. The clear implication of the investigation, arrest, trial, and execution of Patrascanu was that it was extremely difficult, if not impossible, for someone, no matter how initially well intentioned the person was, to overcome his/her bourgeois or aristocratic origins and to maintain a consistent communist ideology.

Beginning in 1948 and lasting until 1950, Dej also launched a major party purge, removing roughly 400,000 names from the party rolls. Virtually every one who was purged had joined the party after it had taken power. In conducting the purge, Dej not only wanted to get rid of supporters of his internal enemies in the party, but he also wanted to remove persons with suspect backgrounds, careerists, and other opportunists who had joined the party for reasons other than a commitment to building a communist society.

Dej blamed Ana Pauker for having allowed these suspect elements to become party members. He accused her of having not been sufficiently vigilant in vetting applications for party membership. He was especially appalled by the fact that many former Legionnaires and Iron Guard activists had been allowed to join the party, with only cursory examination of what they had done for the fascists and only minimal demonstrations that they had abandoned their former allegiances and ideology. Later, party rolls were reopened and many of those who had been purged had their membership restored.

In June 1952, Petru Groza stepped down as Romania's prime minister, an office he had held since March 1945. Dej replaced him and remained as prime minister until 1955. Between 1952 and 1955, Dej also held the position of General Secretary of the PMR , marking the first time in the post war period when the same person formally held the highest offices in the government and the party. The consolidation of party and state rule in the person of Dej marked a turning point in the party's history, if for no other reason than that it was the beginning of the end of democratic practices in the party's highest circles. It set a precedent for personal rule within the party.

With the party cleansed of his main enemies, Dej implemented a new constitution, which went into effect in September 1952. The constitution, replacing that of 1948, strengthened the role of the state in the national economy and strengthened the position of the party as the country's leading political force. Groza became the President of the Grand National Assembly, a position he held until January 1958. The President of the Grand National Assembly was the head of state. It was largely an honorary role without any effective power. That, however, changed when Dej assumed the presidency in 1961. Dej remained president and continued as General Secretary of the *PRM* until his death in March 1965.

The Emergence of the Nomenklatura

As the party expanded its control and as the state expanded its role in Romanian society, both developed huge bureaucratic apparati, along the same lines as that in the Soviet Union. Those who held the leading positions in the state and, more importantly, the party bureaucracies came to form themselves into a privileged ruling elite grounded in the very organizational structures of the party and the state. The party/state elite formed itself into a "nomenklatura."

The nomenklatura was based on new principles of social stratification that were unique to European communist states. The nomenklatura was not merely a political directorate, but neither was it a "new social class," as the Yugoslavian writer Milovan Djilas (1982) called it. Rather, as it developed, the nomenklatura represented a synthesis of selected characteristics of medieval "Stande," along with characteristics of a social class, and of a political directorate. The distinguished German social theorist Max Weber saw "Stande" as being relatively closed corporate social groups whose boundaries were defined by a common style and level of living grounded in access to common privileges.

Being relatively closed, "Stande" were marked off vertically and horizontally from each other, which also was the case with the nomenklatura. Members of the nomenklature, as the Romanian communist regime matured, came to have quite different living conditions than did the rest of the nation's population. There also were significant variations in living conditions within the nomenklatura. At the top, the nomenklatura had access to villas and mansions in the best neighborhoods in Romanian cities. In some cases, these neighborhoods were sealed from general public access. Armed guards monitored who went into these very special neighborhoods and who went out. The nomenklatura also had access to consumer goods, especially foreign products, that were inaccessible to other Romanians. The nomenklatura also had access to more and better stocks of domestically produced foods and commodities. The nomenklatura also had their own health care system. They were treated by physicians specially assigned to care for them and they went to clinics and hospitals specially designated for their use. Children of the nomenklatura were virtually guaranteed access to the best schools and to university admissions to faculties of their choice. Nomenklatura families vacationed together at the same resorts set aside for their use in the Carpathian mountains, the Black Sea, and other Romanian resort areas. In addition, children of the nomenklatura often married each other, creating an even stronger sense of collective solidarity among the families making up this corporate body.

The nomenklatura took on the character of a distinctive, quasi-closed corporate group within Romanian society. Membership, initially, was relatively open to those with working class or peasant origins who had obtained appropriate credentials, sponsorship, and/or offices. Some persons were identified as potential members of the nomenklatura at an early age, as they moved through the Pioneers, the communist youth league, and various communist student organizations. For those who proved their mettle in such organizations, a coveted invitation to join the party awaited them when they finished their education, job training, or, for men, compulsory military service. With such an invitation, one was put on a fast-track for upward mobility in the various bureaucracies of the party-state system. With the passing of time, the nomenklatura in Romania became more closed, as children of the elite moved into party and state positions, monopolizing many of the better bureaucratic positions in the party-state system.

For some of the very best university graduates, an invitation to join the party frequently was accompanied by an offer of employment in one of the state's security services. Working for the security services was a choice job in communist Romania, especially if one was assigned to work abroad gathering intelligence against Western governments. However, working for the security services often came at a cost. In a society in which everyone's behavior was closely monitored, analyzed, and evaluated, the behavior of security workers was even more closely scrutinized, especially if they were working outside of Romania. The nomenklatura was replete with vertical and horizontal distinctions. There were several analytically distinct groups within the nomenklatura: a dominant bureaucratic fraction that was responsible for the political management of the party and the state; a technocratic fraction that was responsible for technical matters of administration, management, and governance, a cultural fraction that oversaw ideological and aesthetic work in the party and the state; and a security fraction composed of the military and the police forces, including the *Securitate*.

The types of resources over which they exercised control within the party-state system, as well as the offices people held, defined each of these major groupings. The bureaucratic fraction was defined by its control over the state and party apparati. They constituted themselves as a political directorate, defining regime policy and overseeing the general functioning of all institutions within the state. The technocrats generally were specialists whose goals were to make the communist system, in all of its aspects, work more efficiently and effectively. Generally, the technocrats were not as much interested in ideology as they were in enhancing the performance of the regime's basic institutions. The key resources over which they had a monopoly were specific forms of professional competencies acquired through long years of experience and/or education in universities or other specialized institutions of advanced education. The cultural nomenklatura controlled ideological production. They were the regime's intelligentsia. Their position was predicated on the monopoly positions they had in Romania's various institutions of cultural production and reproduction. They acquired their skills, both theoretical and practical, mainly from Romania's universities and from the advanced research institutes under the control of the Romanian academy.

Position within the party-state system was not only a function of the types of personal resources an individual brought to it. Position in the party-state system also was a function of one's membership (as well as the memberships held by one's family) in one or more of the personal networks that were threaded throughout the system. These networks cut across the functional distinctions mentioned above and the hierarchies within them. Horizontally, these networks were organized around personal relations of mutuality among network members. Sometimes the networks were outgrowths and expressions of extended kinship ties, of common geographical origin, of shared educational experiences, of shared military experiences, or the like. Vertically, they were built around ties similar to the horizontal axis. Vertical integration, however, also sometimes included patron-client relations that expressed obligations of personal dependency, fealty, and loyalty. In many respects, the personal networks that largely were based on relations of mutuality rather than on patron-client relations resembled both in their structure and their functioning the *blat* networks that arose in the Soviet Union (Ledeneva 1998). As in the Soviet Union (Ledeneva 1998: 2), in Romania these informal networks became embedded in various formal systems of power, be these systems based in economic, political, military, and/or security (such as, but not exclusively, the *Securitate*) organizations and relations.

Among other things, the networks functioned as a way for their members to manage scarcity, both in their work lives and in their personal lives. For example, the networks helped organizations and individuals achieve their formal goals by giving them access to supplies and other forms of resources necessary to the success of an individual in his/her work role and/or to the success of the organization in which a person was employed. On a purely personal level, these networks gave individuals access to goods and services or to more and higher quality goods and services than they otherwise would be able to access. The networks, also, were defensive/protective structures offering some degree of protection against the arbitrariness of the regime in areas such as jobs, housing, and the like.

Not all networks were of equal standing and significance. Just as in the Soviet Union (Ledeneva 1998), some networks were far more powerful and of far greater political significance than were others. The power and the significance of a network was dependent on the resources over which it had control or to which it had access (for example, food distribution or distribution of imported goods, especially from the West) and the ability of the network to reach into the inner leadership circles of the party and state.

The Romanian party-state system, as a whole, constituted itself as networks (systems) of networks that spanned and integrated both the state and party apparati into a functional whole. For any given individual, power and rewards flowing from power, including opportunities for career mobility, within the party-state system was a function of the position his/her network and/or his family's networks had in the overall system of networks. These systems of personalized networks represented a direct, albeit modified and reworked, continuation of the ways in which political and state elites had ruled and governed Romania during the boyar and bourgeois "epochs." In some cases, especially at the local level, the very networks that once had constituted the base of the old regimes were incorporated directly into the communist party-state system.

When the communists took power, they believed that wiping out private property and imposing collective property not only would eliminate the material base of the old systems of class and estate domination in Romania, but also would eliminate the class practices, social behaviors, attitudes, values, and ideology stemming from and built around private property ownership. The communists also believed that putting a system of collective property in place would lead to the development of a new socialist culture and a new socialist humanity in Romania. However, as matters turned out, the communists underestimated the "stickiness" of certain institutions, institutional behavior, class practices, and the like that pre-dated their coming to power. The communists had not foreseen the degree to which people, at all levels in Romanian society, could modify and adapt supposedly outmodes behaviors, cultural patterns, etc. to the new political reality and meld them into the new institutional order the communists were building.

The Romanian communists, or, for that matter communists elsewhere in Eastern and Central Europe, were unable to completely liquidate all traces of pre-communist classes, class fractions, or the remnants of the former boyar estate, despite having wiped out almost all forms of private property. For example, parts of the bourgeoisie, having lost their property, converted other resources they had at their disposal to maintain certain aspects of their old life and, even, to maintain positions of importance in the new regime. Members of the old bourgeoisie and of the old landed-aristocracy managed to sustain themselves during the communist period in Romania by adopting a number of different social strategies and by using a variety of resources at their disposal to secure some degree of continuing symbolic, if not material, privilege. Not the least important of these strategies involved using their intellectual and cultural "capital" (see Bourdieu {1983} 1986 for a discussion of the concept of variable forms of capital) on behalf of the communist regime.

Using their previous class advantages, which had given them a near monopoly over access to education, many former bourgeoisie and boyars managed to maintain privileged positions within the new communist state by moving into professional, intellectual, artistic, and managerial occupations. In the years immediately following their coming to power, the communists had no choice but to use certain remnants of the former bourgeoisie and educated members of the old landed aristocracy in certain key roles in state institutions. The regime had no one else with the skills and the occupational preparation to take these jobs. This also was the case in most of the other Eastern and Central European communist states, just as it had been in the Soviet Union after the Bolshevik revolution. Having to rely on parts of the old elites to administer the new regime created a number of significant problems for the communists, not the least of which was that they never could be sure about the loyalty of these people, nor could the communists ever be sure that members of the defeated classes weren't sabotaging the new state and its policies. But, in the early years of their rule, the communists had little choice but to rely on members of the old elites to staff the party-state bureaucracies. Former members of the boyar estate and the bourgeoisie also used their skills to enhance their incomes, over and above that earned from the state. To do this, they often became active in the informal, illegal, secondary economy as sellers of their services.

Often members of the former aristocracy and the bourgeoisie used the broad networks of informal connections at their disposal and at the disposal of their families to maintain some semblance of a corporate life, which allowed them to mark themselves off from other Romanians, especially from those who were achieving upward mobility through the new communist system. In this way, the remnants of the aristocracy and the bourgeoisie produced and reproduced distinctive ways of living that earned them some degree of deference from others. Deference was expressed through the status recognition they received for being members of "good families," usually referring to the former bourgeoisie, and "old families," indicating aristocratic or landed gentry family origins. It would be interesting to see the degree to which these families managed to reproduce themselves through a variety of means, including continuing class endogamous marriages. The former aristocrats and bourgeoisie submerged their class values and behaviors into the realm of the private, where it could be sheltered from the scrutiny of the communists.

Families' old class claims were kept alive in people's memories, in family stories, in art and book collections, in training in old forms of etiquette, in cultural interests and tastes, and in sundry pieces of furniture and personal objects – all of which, if properly read and understood, clearly marked a family's social origins. All of this could not help but maintain a continuing sense of Stande, estate, or class identity and identification among the old elites, even if it was identification with an estate or class or Stande that had suffered historical defeat at the hands of the communists.

Just as with members of the former bourgeoisie and boyar estate, the communists never were able to eliminate completely the corporate character of subordinate classes. For example, peasants continued to maintain a quite distinctive mode of existence in Romania. Peasant culture in Romania did not need private property as a base. Peasants had developed their own distinctive life styles without a base in private land holdings long before the communists came to power. Peasants proved adept at adapting and modifying their institutions and behaviors to the new communist reality. Therefore, despite agricultural collectivization and the development of state farms and despite industrialization in the countryside, the peasantry persisted as a distinctive group in Romanian society. They clung to many of their traditional values, customs, habits, and social practices, including loyalty to extended kinship networks, village social structures, and the Romanian Orthodox Church, despite considerable pressures by the communists to abandon these "outmoded" loyalties, beliefs, and social practices. Also, peasants like the old elites found ways to participate in the secondary, informal economy to supplement their incomes from the state.

The Party and Religious Organizations

While struggling to put into place its own social, economic, and political structures, the PMR set out to reconstruct not only Romania's class system. It also sought to reorganize almost all other aspects of Romanian society. One of the first institutions to which the PMR directed its attentions was religion. Romania, while predominantly an Orthodox country, had a number of other significant religious traditions, especially in Transylvania, where the Romanian Orthodox Church, while being the single, largest confession, was a "minority" church (see the Romanian Census of 1930). Significant religious diversity had been introduced into

Romania after World War I, when Transylvania was awarded to Romania and joined with the *Regat* (composed of Wallachia and Moldavia) to form the modern Romanian State. The *Regat* was overwhelmingly Romanian Orthodox. It had only a small proportion of other types of Western and Eastern Christians, Jews, and Muslims.

With the unification of Transylvania and the Regat, Romania absorbed large numbers of Roman Catholics, Romanian Uniates, and Protestant confessions, including Unitarians (not to be confused with the Romanian Uniates), the Reformed (Calvinist) Church, and Lutherans. The Lutherans mainly were based in German ethnic communities, although there also were a number of Hungarian Lutheran congregations in Transylvania. The Transylvania Lutherans emerged from the Saxon communities in Kronstadt (Brasov) in the sixteenth century. Kronstadt was the first Saxon community in Romania to join the Lutheran movement. Other Saxons soon followed them in the Siebenburgen region. Relations between Roman Catholics and the Lutherans varied across Transylvania. In some cities, such as Sibiu, they appear to have settled into relations of mutual accommodation, once the passions of the Reformation's early stages subsided, while elsewhere relations were marked by long term suspicion and hostility. The Unitarians were exclusively Hungarian. Protestant confessions had a very uneasy relationship with the Romanian state. In 1942, the Antonescu government had moved against Romania's Protestant congregations, especially the Baptists and the Unitarians. Protestant churches were closed and many Protestant pastors were imprisoned as threats to the state. There were pressures put on Protestants to convert to Romanian Orthodoxy as a way to avoid prison. Thus, the communist government was hardly setting a precedent when it waged war against "non-Romanian" churches.

Roman Catholicism was based in the Swabian, Saxon, and Hungarian villages and towns in Transylvania, although there also were a small number of Romanian Roman Catholic communities in the region and in the Banat, some of which still exist today. The Swabs' and Saxons' ancestors had come into Transylvania and the Banat almost 500 years earlier and had played an important role in developing Transylvania's and the Banat's commercial, manufacturing, and urban base. The cities the Germans created had enjoyed a high degree of autonomy in relation to the Transylvanian princes and the landed aristocracy, as discussed earlier. The cities functioned as self-governing communes that existed outside the normal requirements of medieval feudalism in Transylvania, as previously noted. The culture of these cities was overwhelmingly Hungarian and German, while the countryside was Romanian before 1918. The Roman Catholic Church was the oldest and largest of the minority Christian confessions. The Roman Catholics had two bishoprics in Transylvania that dated back to the eleventh century. One was in Alba Iulia/Gyulafehervar and the other was in Oradea/Nagyvarad. By the start of the Second World War it had about one and a quarter million adherents (Bucharest: Romanian Census, 1930) and a highly developed and relatively complete institutional structure, including over a hundred monasteries and convents and six theology schools.

As early as 1947, the new post-war government began moving against the Roman Catholic and the Uniate Churches. In 1947 and 1948, the government arrested almost 100 Roman Catholic priests and closed a number of Catholic church publications and newspapers. Priests were deported or imprisoned. All of this took place before Romania had become a "People'Republic." There were both national and international reasons for the government's attacks on the Catholics and the Uniates. On the international level, across Europe, the Catholic Church long had been engaged in a struggle against communist and social democratic movements, as well as against centrist, democratic, republican movements. For example, the Catholic Church had stood behind the anti-democratic forces in Spain, allying itself with Franco and his fascist allies. The Church also strongly supported the "authoritarian," right-wing dictatorship in Portugal. Moreover, the Catholic Church had not mounted public opposition to the Nazis and other fascist movements outside of the Iberian Peninsula. It had signed a concordat with Mussolini's fascist government, it had failed to denounce the fascist state in Slovakia, which was led by a Catholic prelate, and it had failed to publicly denounce Nazism and its genocidal policies. In addition, the Catholic Church, through its Christian Democratic movement, actively opposed social democrat and communist political parties, partly by sponsoring trade union movements to fight the communists for the loyalty of Europe's working classes.

In addition, the Church was vigorously opposing communist political forces in Poland, Hungary, Transylvania, Yugoslavia, particularly in the heavily Catholic regions of Croatia and Slovenia, Czechoslovakia, and in the Catholic and Uniate areas of the Ukraine. The Catholic Church also had mobilized its resources to fight growing communist electoral strength in Western Europe, especially in Italy and France, after World War II. In its war against communism, the Roman Catholic Church had taken the rather drastic step of excommunicating Catholics who supported communist political parties. Excommunication had not been applied to Catholics who had belonged to fascist parties in Germany, Italy, Hungary, Slovakia, Romania, Spain, Portugal, the Ukraine, or elsewhere in Europe.

On a local level, the Catholic Church and the Uniates were suppressed for specific historical reasons. The Uniate and Roman Catholic Churches had an especially strong presence in Transylvania and, to a lesser degree, in the Banat. The Uniate Church (the so-called "Greek Catholics") practiced an Orthodox liturgy, while acknowledging the primacy of the Roman papacy. Uniate congregations were almost entirely composed of Romanians, while the Roman Catholic congregations were made up of Germans and Hungarians. The Uniates had played a leading role in developing Romanian nationalism in Transylvania. Its clergy had helped form what came to be called the *Scoala Ardeleana* (Transylvania School). Despite the involvement of Uniate clergy and lay people in the nationalist movement, there were significant numbers of Romanians who saw the Uniates as something less than "complete" Romanians, because of their ties to the Vatican and their consequent rejection of the leadership of the Romanian Patriarch in Bucharest. This was especially the case among Orthodox clergy and prelates. Romanian Orthodox prelates saw the Uniates as a creeping outpost of Western Christianity that, by virtue of its liturgical forms, threatened to draw away adherents of the Orthodox Church.

Feelings of suspicion and hostility toward Uniates, however, were not confined to Orthodox clergy. There was a broad-based skepticism about the Uniates among the general Orthodox population, especially among Romanian intellectuals who had strong ties to the Orthodox Church and its religious traditions. The Uniates were seen as heretics who had gone over to Western Christianity as a way to maximize their economic and political positions during the time Transylvania was under Austro-Hungarian rule. Uniates also were perceived to be indigenous spokespersons for the West, helping to undermine some of the very traditions that many believed contributed to the core identity of Romanians, individually and collectively. For example, the distinguished Romanian philosopher, Nae Ionescu, claimed that Uniates could not be true Romanians. He stated: "...a Uniate can perhaps be a 'good Romanian,' because this quality can be earned, but he cannot, and never will be, a Romanian, because being a Romanian implies being born and baptized as an Orthodox Christian, and this religion implies a mentality, a state, and a Church fundamentally different from those in the West" (Mungiu-Pippidi 1998). Nae Ionescu, echoing the great Romanian poet Eminescu, argued that Romanians were not a European people and should not aspire to be and that Western institutions were nothing more than "failed implants" in Romania (Mungiu-Pippidi 1998). Ionescu claimed that traditional Romanian law originated in Thracian traditions, that the Romanian State essentially was patterned after Byzantine models, that the Romanian church was Eastern rather than Western, and that the mental structures of Romanians' were "contemplative" in nature (Mungiu-Pippidi 1998). Nae Ionescu was a strong supporter of Codreanu and the Legionnaires.

The Romanian Constitution of 1923, building on the Alba Iulia Resolutions of December 1918 and the Minorities Treaty of December 1919, had guaranteed the freedom of private and public religious belief and worship. The 1923 Constitution, while recognizing religious pluralism, defined the place of the Romanian Orthodox Church in a way that gave it a dominant position in the nation's life. In a way, the Uniate Church also was given a privileged place in Romania, but it was clear in the constitution that Uniates had a position of lesser privilege than did Orthodoxy. Together with Romanian Orthodoxy, the Uniates were said to make up the "national" church of Romania. The Uniates, almost, but not quite, were put on a par with the Orthodox. In this way, the 1923 Constitution tried to legally recognize the similarities between the two confessions while, at the same time, making it clear that Orthodoxy was more "Romanian" in its nature than was the Uniate Church. To Romanian nationalists and the Romanian political elites, the Uniate Church, while claiming to be a Romanian institution, subordinated itself to the power of the Vatican. Therefore, it could not be legally recognized as having the same legal and cultural status as Romanian Orthodoxy. This idea was reaffirmed when the Romanian government passed a law in May 1925 that made explicit the preeminent position of Orthodoxy in the spiritual life of Romania.

The Roman Catholic Church and the Romanian government had signed a Concordat in 1927. The Catholic hierarchy saw a need for this because of what it took to be an increasingly hostile political environment in Romania. The Orthodox hierarchy strenuously objected to the Concordat. The fact that the Uniates, as one might expect given their ties to Rome, did not oppose the Concordat only increased tensions between the Orthodox hierarchy and the Uniate bishops. To the Orthodox, Uniate support of the Concordat only re-enforced the idea that the Uniates were not really a part of the Orthodox spiritual world. The Vatican had begun negotiating for a concordat with the Romanian government not only as a result of the valorization of the position of Orthodoxy but also because of its concern about the material position of the Catholic Church. In 1921, Romania, as part of the general land reform, had confiscated a substantial amount of land from the Catholic Church, as well as from the Lutheran and Calvinist churches. This put the Roman Catholic Church, as well as the Protestant churches in a difficult financial position, as they relied on their land holdings to generate their income.

The Romanian government in 1928 had ratified a Concordat with the Vatican, following passage in April of the "Law on Cults" (*Legea cultelor*). This law expanded state control over minority religions in Romania, especially the Protestant denominations in Romania. For example, it gave the state administrative authority over all of the churches and the state gained control over religious education, among other things. The law also prohibited the cults from engaging in political activities and required state permission if the cults intended to establish new congregations. This seriously weakened their ability to proselytize, which had been one of the main goals of supporters of the Orthodox Church who has written and passed the legislation. Because of the Concordat, many of the provisions of the 1928 "Law on Cults" did not apply to the Roman Catholic Church. The Catholic Church was given more freedom to control its schools and to run its own extensive institutional network of social service organizations. In return for the exemption of the Roman Catholic Church from some of the more restrictive provisions of the "Law on Cults," the Vatican agreed to subsume the diocese and bishops in Transylvania to the Roman Catholic Archbishop of Bucharest. The Archbishop of Bucharest, at the time, presided over a relatively small number of Catholic communities, many of which were made up of ethnic minorities.

In 1930, the Romanian census showed that there were almost 1.25 million Catholics in Romania. The largest number of these, almost 950,000, lived in Transylvania. The Uniates, at the same time, numbered almost 1.5 million, with close to 1.4 million living in Transylvania. The remainder of the Catholics were scattered around the country.

The "Law on Cults" continued to be the major controlling legal statute on religion in Romania until passage of the Constitution of 1948. Before the new constitution was adopted, the Groza government had taken several measures to harness the Romanian Orthodox Church to the new regime. With government encouragement a "Union of Democratic Priests" was formed. It attracted some interest and support from among the younger clergy, but it was not as successful as the new authorities had hoped it would be in mobilizing significant Orthodox clerical support for the state's radical social, political, and economic agendas. The government also established a mandatory retirement age for priests, hoping in this way to flush out the older, more conservative members of the clergy. Many of these older priests, especially in Romania's communes, villages, and small towns had been clerical fascists, supporting, first, the royal dictatorship, then the National Legionary State, and, finally, Antonescu's regime.

The communists were especially concerned about the hostile attitudes of the Orthodox Church's higher clergy, who were among the communists' major ideological opponents. The higher-ranking Orthodox clergy were among the most vocal opposition to the communists. Like the lower clergy, the senior members of the church hierarchy had been among the strongest supporters of the pre-war Romanian regimes, including the fascist regimes. Most of the higher clergy were drawn from Romania's landed aristocracy and the higher reaches of the bourgeoisie. They, therefore, had little sympathy for the communists or for any political force bent on destroying the power of the landed aristocracy or of the bourgeoisie.

Using the new authority of the Constitution of 1948, the Grand National Assembly (the parliament) of the People's Republic, with the support of the Romanian Orthodox Church's leadership, ended the 1927 Concordat with the Roman Catholic Church. As a result of the Concordat's termination, the Roman Catholic Church lost its special legal privileges in Romania and was left in a highly ambiguous position, which the state would exploit in order to control and repress Roman Catholicism.

A new "Law on Cults" (*Legea cultelor*) was passed in August 1948. The new law repealed its 1928 counterpart. The 1948 "Law on Cults" differed from that of 1928 in that it extended and deepened state control over religious organizations, a precedent that had been set by the 1928 law. The only matters over which the churches continued to have some degree of autonomy were liturgy and pastoral work. All other aspects of church organization and operations passed to the state. More importantly, the very existence of the churches, other than the Orthodox Church, no longer was guaranteed. The state could force them to cease operation whenever it chose to do so. In a move mainly directed at the Catholic and Uniate Churches, religious organizations operating in Romania were no longer allowed to have direct contacts with any foreign organizations. All such contacts had to take place with the cooperation of the Ministry of Foreign Affairs and had to be approved by the Ministry of Religious Affairs. This meant that the Catholic and Uniate Churches no longer could work directly with the Vatican. To continue to do so would threaten the very existence of the two religious organizations in Romania. Only churches whose organizational ties were with religions in other communist countries, such as the Armenian Orthodox Church, were allowed to maintain foreign ties. Control over the Roman Catholic Church was assigned to the Catholic diocese in Bucharest.

In a move to further weaken religions in Romania, the government passed a decree law in 1948 that extended the controls over religion provided for in the "Law on Cults" and the educational reform law of August 1948. Under the decree law, all property left in the hands of churches after the land reform act of 1921 and all land and properties acquired since that date were expropriated by the state. This completed the process, set in motion by Cuza in the 1860s, to bring the church under state control. In 1947, even before the passage of the Law on Cults, the communists adopted legislation that gave the state a major role in the election of Orthodox bishops, insured that communists would control the largest number of votes in the Orthodox Church's governing Synod, and forced a centralization of church authority under the Patriarch. The communists also took over direct supervision of the training of Orthodox clergy and banned the celebration of Easter and Christmas as public, religious holidays. The Orthodox Church resigned itself to the demands of the regime and as a result, according to some commentators, seriously compromised its moral authority. This last point may have been an exaggeration, as the Orthodox Church emerged after 1989 as one of the country's most respected and trusted institutions, as any number of opinion polls showed.

The communists reserved the right to suspend the recognition of any religious organization and to stop paying the salaries of church priests or ministers if the church or the clergy expressed opposition to democratic rule, meaning, of course, communist rule. In principle, this was a reasonable position, given the wide prevalence of clerical fascism before and during the war and given the support the clergy, especially the Orthodox clergy, had given to the monarchy and to Antonescu. This law, however, was not meant to apply only to Orthodox prelates and clergy, it also was intended to apply to clergy in other denominations, many of whom, especially in the German and Hungarian areas, had provided ideological support, at the very least, for the Nazis, in the case of the Germans, and the Arrow Cross, in the case of the Hungarians.

In addition, the decree law eliminated the role of churches in running schools. All elementary and secondary education passed over to control by the state. A conference of Catholic bishops protested this action, but to no avail. The decree law exceeded the constraints on the churches that were put into effect in almost all of the other Bolshevik states at the time. The state's motivation in ending religiously controlled education was related not only to the hostility that the PMR had to organized religion but also to the problems it perceived itself to be having with national minority communities. The state wanted to insure that the Germans and Hungarians would be educated to speak, to read, and to write Romanian and that they would be taught literature, history, and related disciplines from a secular, communist oriented Romanian perspective. In this way, the state hoped to minimize the chances that irredentism, especially among the Hungarians, would be sustained by church based schools. Romanian communists knew the power that mobilized national minority churches could have in undermining not only a communist Romania, but also the very idea of a unitary Romanian State. Removing the church from education had the added benefit of giving the party and state control over thousands of jobs in the education sector, thus providing employment opportunities for graduates of Romanian teaching institutions who, presumably, would have more of an understanding of and commitment to Marxism, as the regime defined it, than did the former teachers, almost all of whom were clergy or, in the case of the Roman Catholics, members of religious teaching orders. At the same time that the party and state were attacking the Transylvanian churches, it tried to cement the loyalty of the Transylvanian Magyars to Romania by granting them limited forms of local autonomy, while not undermining the principle that Romania was a unitary state. Dej and his fellow leaders knew that the party could ill afford to make it appear as if the attacks on Roman Catholicism, as well as the Protestant churches, was driven by anti-Magyar sentiments.

The Romanian Constitution of 1952 provided for an Autonomous Hungarian District in Transylvania. Within the Autonomous District, Hungarians were granted considerable language rights in those places where they made up more than three fourths of the population. Hungarian rights were narrowed considerably after the Hungarian uprising in 1956, when Transylvanian Hungarians, especially students, demonstrated against the Warsaw Pact invasion, in which Romanian intelligence forces had played a supporting role. Also, key members of Hungary's political elite were confined in Romania until they were returned to Hungary for trial and eventual execution. The suppression of the students' demonstrators helped create the career of Ion Illiescu, who would become Romania's first post-Bolshevik president. Under Ceausescu, Hungarian autonomy was sharply circumscribed. Among other things, Ceausescu abolished the Hungarian Autonomous District.

By the end of 1948, using the constitutional and legal frameworks in place, the state had reduced the number of Catholic diocese from five to two, closing several Episcopal seats that were centuries old. Only the diocese of Bucharest and Alba Iulia were allowed to continue in existence. Having abrogated the Concordat, the regime asked the Catholic Church to draft new governing statutes for review and approval by the Ministry of Cults. Bishop Aron Marton of Alba Iulia drafted the statute. The communists rejected what he had written and placed him under arrest in June 1949, along with Bishop Alexandru Cisar, who was the former bishop of the Bucharest Diocese, his successor, Bishop Augustin Pacha, and Bishop Anton Durcovici, who had administered the Iasi diocese, which was composed largely of Csangos, an Hungarian people who were predominantly Catholic (Deletant 1999a). Bishop Ioanos Scheffler, who had administered the former Oradea-Satu Mare diocese, which largely had served Hungarians, had been arrested, earlier, in March 1949.

In 1949, the communists dissolved all Catholic monasteries and religious orders in Romania. The Catholic priests, monks, and nuns expelled from the monasteries and convents were put in prison or deported from the country. All totaled, the state imprisoned over a thousand Catholic priests, monks, and women religious. The state also closed all other organizations run by the Catholic Church, including Catholic newspapers and other publications.

The regime followed the initial arrests of Catholic bishops, clergy, and religious with the formation of a Catholic Committee for Action (Bossy 1955: 174). One of the purposes of this organization was to develop a base of support for a national Catholic Church that was autonomous from the Vatican. One of the leading activists in this movement was a Catholic priest, Andrei Agotha (Deletant 1999a). Because of his activities on behalf of the Committee, Agotha, first, had his clerical faculties suspended, and, later, was excommunicated by the Catholic hierarchy. The excommunication, again, showed the double standard the Catholic Church had toward fascism and communism. Few, if any, Catholic clergy in Europe had been excommunicated for their support of and involvement in various fascist movements or political organizations, while priests who showed any signs of supporting communist movements or governments were seriously punished.

Catholic priests who opposed Agotha or the Committee were arrested and imprisoned. Having cleared the ground of opponents of the Committee, the Ministry of Cults began to negotiate with the Committee for the purposes of developing a document that would define the position of the Roman Catholic Church in the Romanian People's Republic. The Committee's leadership agreed to develop support in the Catholic communities for a proposal called the "Statute for the Organization, Direction, and Functioning of the Roman Catholic Confession in the Romanian People's Republic" (Deletant 1999a: 94). Among the major points in the proposed Statute were, first, that the Roman Catholic Church in Romania would continue to recognize the supreme authority of the Papacy in matters of faith and morals, but that the governance of the Church would be in local hands. Second, the Vatican would retain its authority in appointing bishops and other senior church officials in Romania but they had to choose from a list of candidates recommended by the Romanian Roman Catholic Church and approved by the Ministry of Cults. Third, the Statute required that all communications between the local Catholic Church and the Vatican had to take place through the Ministry of Cults. The official local Church and the Vatican Papal Nuncio, an American Prelate appointed by the Vatican to be its "ambassador" to the People's Republic, rejected all of these proposals, apparently without attempting to negotiate with the Ministry of Cults. By taking such action, the Roman Catholic Church escalated its conflict with the regime and all but guaranteed that the Church would be exposed to even further persecution by the Romanian communists. The Vatican clearly should have recognized this fact, but, given its larger geopolitical interests, the papacy did not seem to care that it was virtually guaranteeing that the Romanian Catholic communities would be repressed. It almost seems as if the Vatican wanted the Romanian Catholic Church to be a community of martyrs. The Vatican, perhaps, also was guided in its decision by the fact that Catholics were a minority religious confession and that it, the Vatican, did not think it worth the expenditure of resources that could be more profitably used elsewhere in the Church's struggle against communism, especially in places, such as Poland, Italy, and France, where the Vatican had a stronger base and a greater likelihood of resisting the communists or, as in the case of Poland, achieving significant compromises with the regime.

While all of this was going on, the Papal Nuncio in Bucharest secretly appointed a large number of apostolic administrators for the Romanian Catholic Church, as well as alternatives, should the initial appointees be arrested (Deletant 1999a). The Nuncio also consecrated a number of bishops, including one for the Bucharest diocese. Some of these were consecrated clandestinely. In a move that was bound to antagonize the Romanian Orthodox Church, as well as the communist government, the Nuncio also secretly consecrated a number of Uniate bishops. By consecrating, secretly, a number of Roman Catholic and Uniate bishops, it became clear that the Vatican was preparing to operate an underground Catholic Church in opposition to the government and whatever Catholic Church it created.

As a result of his actions, the Papal Nuncio was ordered out of Romania. The government charged him with, among other things, being a spy for the American government. All of the apostolic administers and the alternates he appointed were arrested, along with the secretly conse-crated bishops. They were tried, convicted, and sentenced to long prison terms. The bishops who had been openly consecrated, such as the Bishop of Bucharest, were allowed to remain free, at least for the time being. Whether he and the other bishops who were not imprisoned consecrated additional clandestine bishops is not known. Nor is it known whether these bishops ordained an underground Uniate and Catholic clergy in Romania that remained independent of the "official" Catholic Church that eventually came into being.

Based entirely on circumstantial evidence, it is possible that the bishops may have done exactly this. The Vatican created a significant underground Catholic Church in other communist countries. In Czecho-slovakia, for example, it even went so far as to ordain married men who clandestinely served illegal Catholic communities. The principle reason one could suspect that relatively vital underground Uniate and Catholic Churches were formed in Romania and continued to operate during the entire communist period is the rapid emergence of Uniate and Romanian Catholic communities following the overthrow of Ceausescu in 1989.

With most of the opposition to the Catholic Committee for Action having been neutralized or imprisoned, Andrei Agotha, the suspended priest, called for an assembly of Catholic priests and laity to meet in Transylvania in September to 1950. It was attended by 120 priests and 150 laymen (Deletant 1999a: 96).The gathering approved the general principles outlined in the Statute. In order to gain wider support among Romanian Catholics, the assembly agreed to hold four additional regional assemblies in Timisoara, Brasov, Oradea, and Bucharest. In this way, they would reach the heavily German Catholic communities in Brasov and Timisoara, the Hungarian Catholics in Oradea, and the mixed Catholic communities in Bucharest.

The Catholic Committee for Action followed the regional meetings with a national assembly in Cluj in March 1951. At this meeting, the delegates approved a declaration "…to incorporate the Catholic Church within the legal order of the state…" (Bossy 1955: 177). Priests, prel-ates, and religious across Romania were asked to sign the general decla-ration. Those who refused to sign were arrested and imprisoned. Those who did sign were allowed to continue their ministry. Several clergy who already were in prison signed the document. For agreeing to support the declaration, the regime released them from prison.

In February 1951, the bishops of Bucharest and Timisoara, along with several of their clergy were arrested, tried, and imprisoned. Bishop Schubert of Bucharest was given a life sentence and Bishop Boros of Timisoara was sentenced to eighteen years in prison. Both were charged, among other things, with having been spies for the Vatican and the United States (Deletant 1999a: 97).

Among the clergy who had been released for signing the Catholic Committee's declaration was Father Train Iovanelli. The government named him Vicar of the Diocese of Bucharest (Deletant 1999a: 96). The Vatican, however, refused to recognize his appointment. The Vatican continued to insist that Bishop Schubert was the legitimate leader of the Diocese of Bucharest and it called on all of its clergy to follow Bishop Schubert's moral example, i.e., to resist the communists even if that meant prison. The Vatican never trusted those who cooperated with the communists in any way.

In 1954, Father Franz Augustin, who, like Father Iovanelli, had been released from prison after he agreed to sign the Catholic Committee's declaration, was elevated to Bishop of Bucharest, with the approval of the regime. The Vatican refused to recognize his appointment. In 1961, however, the Vatican agreed to recognize him as the temporary "ordinary," or administrator of the Diocese of Bucharest. He, however, never was fully accepted by the Papacy, who refused to admit him to the deliberations of Vatican II, which began in 1964. According to Deletant (1999a: 98), the Vatican would not seat him because Romania denied several other Catholic leaders permission to attend the conference.

The communists eventually forced the Uniates to merge with the Romanian Orthodox Church, which willingly took control of all Uniate financial assets and property. Priests were forced to renounce Catholic doctrine and accept the Orthodox Church's theology and ecclesiastical principles. The regime's hostility toward the Romanian Uniate Church was consistent with what was happening in other parts of Eastern and Central Europe, where the Uniate Church had an effective institutional presence. Stalin deeply distrusted the Uniate Church. It had a large following in the Ukraine, especially in those areas that were taken from Poland when its borders had been moved westward following World War II. Stalin saw the Uniates as a possible subversive force in that they did not share the longstanding Orthodox tradition of church subordination to the state. Rather, like other branches of Roman Catholicism, the

Uniates argued for autonomy from the state and, indeed, saw their position as expressing a power superior to that of the state, not derivative from it. The Romanian State and communist party developed an ambiguous relationship with the country's Jews. While the party officially condemned anti-Semitism and while it did not take the same actions against Jewish congregations that it did against other confessions, the party did little to counteract popular anti-Semitism in the country, especially in the rural areas. Jews also faced continuing discrimination inside of the party and the state. This became especially intense with the purge of Anna Pauker and the so-called "Moscow" faction inside of the party (Levy 2001). The move against Pauker had a strongly anti-Semitic coloring, much like the purges Stalin was planning with his infamous "doctor's plot" in the early 1950s and the increasing hostility shown toward "cosmopolitans" by many of East Europe's communist party.

At the end of the war, the vast majority of Romania's Jews were in a desperate economic situation. Those who had survived the camps had few economic resources. Most of what they had owned had been confiscated by the state. In the Regat, the larger part of the Jewish community had been pushed out of their jobs by the various anti-Semitic laws passed under Karol II and Antonescu. The initial post-war governments did little to help the Jews, economically. Instead, the Romanian governments devoted most of their resources to help ethnic Romanians, especially veterans returning from the front and being released from prisoner-of-war camps. The communists and the social democrats supported these policies. The economic problems of Romania's Jews were further worsened by the 1947 Currency Reform and the nationalization of commercial and industrial properties and by the government's reluctance to return Jewish properties and assets seized by the fascists. In addition, the Romanian state preferred to hire ethnic Romanians for critical positions, rather than Jews.

Because of their economic situation and their fears about what appeared to be a rise in anti-Semitism, a good number of Romanian Jews wanted to emigrate from the country. Israeli Zionists were especially interested in attracting Romania's Jews, a large number of whom, among the survivors, were scientists, engineers, technicians, skilled workers, and the like. Romania had the second largest Jewish population in Europe. Only the Soviet Union had more Jews who had survived the war.

By the beginning of 1945, over 100,000 Jews had applied to the Romanian government for permission to emigrate. Britain, who held a ruling mandate in Palestine, was attempting to restrict migration to Palestine. It had allocated to Romania only 3500 visas for Jewish emigration to Palestine (Levy 2001). Moreover, the British had instituted a naval blockade to prevent illegal immigration of Jews to Palestine. As a result, most of the Jews who left Romania in 1945 moved toward the west, moving across Hungary and Yugoslavia into Austria. Zionist organizations inside of Romania and in Western Europe helped organize and fund this immigration. In addition, the Romanian government gave the emigrants tacit support. Among other things, the Romanians left parts of the border unguarded in order to ease the departure of Romanian Jews.

As Levy (2001) notes, the Romanian's support of emigration of its Jewish population, especially to Palestine, was consistent with policies being pursued by the Soviet Union. At this time, the Soviet Union was strongly supporting Jewish efforts to create an independent Jewish state in Palestine. The Soviets saw the development of a Jewish state as a way of weakening British and Western influence in the Middle East.

Jewish emigration from Romania continued to grow as the country's economic situation deteriorated and as it became more clear what the contours of state policy was going to be with respect to private enterprise. In 1947, Romania, apparently in response to a Jewish "brain drain" from the country (Levy 2001), began taking steps to sharply restrict Jewish emigration, both legal and illegal. The state especially restricted emigration of persons employed as skilled workers, physicians, and engineers, unless there were medical reasons for wanting to emigrate.

In 1948, the state began repressing Zionist organizations and launching a propaganda campaign against them, labeling Zionism as a reactionary movement of the "Jewish bourgeoisie" (Levy 2001). In response to the closing down of emigration, the Israeli government offered the Romanians a large sum of money to give Jews a chance to emigrate. The Romanians refused the offer, saying to accept it would be tantamount to engaging in a form of "slave trade" (Levy 2001).

Zionist organizations in Romania responded to the emigration shutdown and the attacks on themselves by organizing three large demonstrations in Bucharest in February 1949. On February 18th, over 20,000 people participated in an illegal demonstration (Levy 2001). The government took immediate action to suppress all Zionist organizations and blocked virtually all Jewish immigration from the country.

By late summer 1949, the Romanian state began to rethink its policies on immigration. The party allowed persons in skilled occupations, physicians, and engineers to emigrate if they were at least sixty years old or at least age fifty if they had family in Israel (Levy 2001). These changes increased the number of Jews who were allowed to emigrate.

In March 1950, the state again changed its policies on Jewish emigration. All Jews now were to be permitted to leave, except for those who were having troubles with the Securitate and/or with the police. There were to be no more restrictions on emigration for Jews in certain "critical" occupational categories. Dej had supported these changes in the belief that removing restrictions would make more Jews feel comfortable about staying, while, at the same time, Romania would be able to get rid of committed Zionists and the Jewish bourgeoisie.

The party's leadership was not prepared for the huge number of applications to emigrate that were submitted by Romanian Jews. Across Romania, as much as 70% or more of established Jewish communities decided to emigrate. All totaled, more than 200,000 Jews applied to emigrate (Levy 2001). Dej promptly moved to reverse the new policy, but the Party Secretariat did not agree with him. Instead, it supported educating Romania's Jewish population about the problems of life in Israel and the prospects of a better life for Jews in the new Romania (Levy 2001). Dej then took his case to the Politburo, where he won support for his position to again impose restrictions on Jewish emigration. Persons employed in key heavy and light industries, in the state ministries, in certain professions (e.g. medicine, pharmacy), and in skilled occupations and technical fields were refused permission to emigrate, unless they were at least 65 years of age. Additional restrictions later were added. Persons who had knowledge of state secrets, who were in the third year or later of medical school, who were architects, and who were employed in other occupations that the state deemed important were prohibited from emigrating (Levy 2001). By the summer of 1952, almost all Jewish emigration from Romania ended and would stay closed until the late 1950s.

While Romania's policies on Jewish emigration did not move to the same rhythms as that which was taking place in other communist states, the conflict over the emigration of Romanian Jews took place against a backdrop of increasing state organized anti-Semitism in what was becoming the Soviet bloc. The signs of growing hostility toward Israel, Zionism, and "cosmopolitanism," often used as a code word to indicate Jewish intellectuals, and the restrictions placed on Jewish emigration could do nothing but raise the fears and anxieties of Romania's Jewish population. The virtual shut-down of emigration from Romania in 1952 coincided with anti-Semitism's reaching a fevered pitch. In January 1952, the Soviet Union, in but one example of Stalin's increasingly visible anti-Semitism, arrested and later tried and executed (with one exception) the leadership of the Jewish Anti-Fascist Committee, which had been organized to help the Soviet war effort against the Nazis.

Following hard on the Soviet executions, in November 1952, Czechoslovakia launched the trial of Rudolf Slansky and thirteen other people on charges of treason. The Slansky trial had direct effects on Romania's communist party politics. Slansky's allegedly treasonous behavior was linked to Ana Pauker and to the American banker Henry Morgenthau, giving "substance" to the idea of an international Jewish "conspiracy to overthrow communism in Eastern and Central Europe.

No sooner did the Slansky trial end than the Soviet Union began publicizing the so-called "Kiev Affair." A large number of Jews were arrested, tried, convicted, and sentences for a host of supposed economic "crimes" in the Ukraine (Levy 2001). This was followed by the exposure of the infamous "Doctors' Plot" in the Soviet Union. Jewish physicians were charged with attempting to assassinate a number of Soviet leaders, including Stalin, himself.

The upshot of this broad-based attack on Jews, Zionists, and "cosmopolitans" was to define Eastern and Central European Jews as inherently and essentially untrustworthy. The various states' anti-Semitic attacks were meant to show that Jews, no matter how committed to communism they might appear to be, they still were Jews and that meant that they would always put their "nation's" interest ahead of that of the interests of the world-wide communist movement. The trials, the other anti-Semitic attacks, and the anti-Jewish propaganda also were designed to show that Jews were involved not only in internal conspiracies but that they also were involved in international conspiracies with Jews both inside of the communist bloc and outside of it.

In 1952, Romania launched its own anti-Jewish, anti-Zionist campaign. This involved a lower grade of internal terror than was the case in the Soviet Union. Nonetheless, it had substantial negative consequences for Romania's Jewish population, including those Jews who no longer were practicing their religion. Beginning in July 1952, Romanian Jews were dismissed from key jobs in the state and in the party on the pretext that they did not have a sufficiently "proletarian" past (Levy 2001). Jews were purged from university faculties, along with non-Jewish colleagues who were regarded as suspect by the regime. Jews were dismissed on the basis of their alleged "bourgeois" backgrounds and sympathies, as well as their alleged support for Zionism. This broad, frontal assault on Jews, in no small part, was designed to help strengthen the party's legitimacy in Romania. Given popular suspicions about Jews, which included the idea that they were a dominant, if not *the* dominant, force in the party, it was important for the Romanian communists to create a distance between themselves and Romania's Jews.

By the end of 1952, with opportunities to emigrate almost completely ended and with dramatic increases in state sponsored and state organized anti-Semitism, Romania's Jews were left in a highly precarious situation. The Jews' situation was made even worse by the state's forced closing of many of their local community's institutions, especially those that were linked, in any way, with Zionism and by the close scrutiny that the state security apparati applied to Jews and Jewish organizations, including specifically religious organization. The communists actions worked to reinforce pre-war anti-Semitic attitudes and beliefs, especially the belief that the Jews could never be anything but an "outside" population, a fifth column, if you will, that was ever ready to betray Romania when it was in their self-interest to do so. Eventually, Romania "solved" its perceived problems with the Jews by once again opening opportunities to emigrate. Under Ceausescu, Jews were allowed to migrate, after compensating the state for the costs of having educated and having provided a variety of social services to them. Supposedly each Jew who was allowed to move to Israel brought the Ceausescu regime $10,000.

Nothing much has been written about the fate of other religious communities in Romania during the communist period. For example, there have been no systematic studies of what happened to the Turkish and Tatar Muslim religious communities, that were concentrated mainly along the Black Sea coast, or to the Armenian or Greek religious communities, or to the Russian Old Believers who lived in the Danube delta region.

The communists also deeply distrusted the Romanian Orthodox Church, as it was highly integrated into the country's old institutional system. The first Romanian Patriarch, Miron Cristea, who had taken office in 1925, when the Romanian Orthodox Church was recognized as autocephalous, had served as prime minister during Karol II's monarchical dictatorship, had been an anti-Semite and supported the suppression of leftist parties, including the communists. Nonetheless, the PMR, despite its hostility to the Romanian Orthodox Church, allowed the church to retain its organizational structure and its position as the country's leading religion. However, the church, and especially its hierarchy, was subordinated to the state and party, as it once had been to the boyars and to the prince. Under these conditions, the Romanian Orthodox Church became part of the state's ideological apparatus. Evidence just now emerging is showing that the church, especially its hierarchy, was seriously compromised by the party, with a good number of priests and higher ranking church officials both in Romania and in the Romanian Orthodox Church abroad, including the current Patriarch, having served as *Securitate* informants.

Despite the complicity of large parts of the Church with the regime, some of the clergy continued retained the support and trust of large parts of the population. This was especially the case among the rural peasantry. In the countryside, the Romanian Orthodox Church was part of the structures of living and feeling that under girded village life. Many rural priests, while appearing to actively support the state, resisted the regime and its policies. Whenever discovered they faced arrest and imprisonment, as well as loss of their clerical positions. Resistance took a variety of forms. For example, Orthodox priests would conduct private baptisms for couples who could not afford to let it be known that they were silent and secret believers. For people working in the party and/or the state, if it became known that they had their children baptized or that they were believers, their careers would be seriously compromised. Priests also conducted private marriage ceremonies for the same reasons. It would appear, then, that a large number of people, especially in the countryside, maintained some degree of loyalty to and contact with the church, despite the risks this entailed for their careers. Because of continuing, generally positive relations between the Romanian people and the lower clergy, after 1989 the Orthodox Church emerged as one of the two most trusted institutions in the country. The other institution with a high degree of trust was, and is, the Romanian army. While the Romanian Orthodox Church lost a large part of its landholdings to the communists and while some of its schools of theology and some of its monasteries were closed, the Church's willingness to accept the communists as legitimate rulers kept the church organizationally intact and allowed it some limited degree of autonomy in its actions. Thus, during the communist period, the church was able to function as something more than just a mere "transmission belt" for the regime's ideology and policies. Among other things, the Church helped keep alive an independent sense of Romanian identity.

The Party and Its Intellectuals

When the communists came to power, they faced the task of reconstructing Romania's intelligentsia. They not only needed to replace and/or reeducate the "traditional intellectuals" that populated Romania's institutions, but they also had to develop their own "organic intelligentsia." According to Gramsci (1971), the task of "traditional intellectuals" (e.g. teachers, clergy, and various types of functionaries and subaltern professions) is to contribute to preserving existing arrangements of domination and power in a society by legitimating and disseminating the various discourses that contribute to the reproduction of hegemonic cultural and social practices. "Organic intellectuals," on the other hand, are those parts of the intelligentsia who have direct connections with groups, organizations, and classes in a society and, by virtue of these connections, actively contribute to organizing the interests of those to whom they are tied. In other words, organic intellectuals play an important social mobilization role on behalf of specific social, political, and economic interests in a society.

At the end of World War II, Romania's traditional and organic intelligentsia represented and expressed the interests of the formerly dominant estates and classes. Few were tied to the working classes. The social democrats and the communists had only a handful of intellectuals with strong ties to the working class and its interests. Prior to World War

II, the organic intellectuals of the old regime, almost exclusively, were drawn from families who made up the country's landholding aristocracy and its urban bourgeoisie. The only notable exception to this were Jewish scholars. Few Jewish intellectuals were drawn from families that were part of Romania's various traditional elites.

Even the most cursory examination of intellectual work produced in Romania before the communist era will show few examples of topics, themes, representations, or whatever that can be seen as organically connected with Marxism. The intellectual left, to the extent that it had any presence in Romania, was more reformist than it was revolutionary. Most Romanian intellectuals stood on the traditional or radical right, culturally and politically. Thinkers such as A.C. Cuza, Mircea Eliade, Constantin Noica, and Emil Cioran are examples of prominent intellectuals identified with the radical right. Left-wing politics attracted few Romanian intellectuals, even among the artistic avant-garde.

The PMR faced a double task in reorganizing the country's intelligentsia. It, first, had to eliminate the ideologues of the old order and, second, it had to create its own organic and traditional intellectuals, who would be loyal to the Romanian state, organized as a People's Republic, to the party, and to the Romanian nation. The move against sectarian religious education (see above), in part, can be understood as one aspect of the PMR 's larger drive against the traditional intelligentsia. When it took control, the party's base among the intelligentsia was weak in both categories of intellectuals. In its early years in power, few of the country's traditional intellectuals supported the PMR and the number of intellectuals with an organic connection to the party was small. Moreover, among those intellectuals who identified with the party's agenda, the overwhelming majority had their social origins in the same classes against which the party was struggling. This fact led many of the PMR's leaders who had working class origins, such as Dej and Ceausescu, to be suspicious of the motives of intellectuals, such as Pauker and Patrascanu, who had attached themselves to the party.

The Bolshevik leadership clearly understood that in order for the party and the state to be anchored as legitimate structures in Romania they would have to create their own traditional and organic intellectuals. Without new intellectuals, the Bolshevik dream of creating the new "Socialist" man, who would be the foundation of the new society the party wanted to build, would be unattainable. In 1948 the government's education reform law, in part, designed to give the state the power to dismantle and to reorganize university faculties. Using its new authority, the state closed all universities' faculties of letters and philosophy. A large number of professors in these faculties, including some of Romania's most imminent national and international scholars, were dismissed from their posts and their work was removed from general circulation. Disciplines that were the hardest hit were the social sciences and humanities, especially history.

Intellectuals, whose work in the past, had "demonstrated" support for, or affinities with, the right not only were fired from their jobs, but some also were arrested and imprisoned. Some of those who were dismissed in the first round of purges of intellectuals in 1952 eventually were "rehabilitated" and restored to their positions. Those who were not restored to their former university posts ended their lives on the intellectual margins of the society. Many of the intellectuals purged were given jobs as minor functionaries in insignificant state bureaucracies. Former colleagues sometimes smuggled books and professional publications to them so that they could remain current in their fields and not a few of them would spend their spare time writing long essays that no one ever read, except their families and a few old friends. Many of them had their former work proscribed. Their books and other publications were removed from general circulation, so that almost all of them became intellectual non-entities.

In addition to closing faculties, research institutes, and cultural organizations, a number of academic publications ceased operating. The communist authorities opened new research institutes and cultural organizations, and started new publications that were under more firm party guidance and control. History faculties seem to have been especially singled out for repression, as history became an important terrain for political contention in Romania. Under the communists, historians were required to develop new interpretations and analyses of Romania's past based on Marxist models of historical change.

While large numbers of intellectuals ended up being purged from the universities, others managed to come to terms with the new regime, at the cost of recasting their work in ways that would make it suitable to the new regime. The intellectuals who accommodated themselves to communist rule went on to have good careers within the ideological and political contexts of the reconstructed Romanian universities, research institutes, and cultural organizations.

For many Romanian intellectuals who approached the new regime with open minds, the advent of communism offered a whole new range of opportunities for intellectual work. Marxist philosophy provided a new way for intellectuals to approach old problems. For example, one of the major challenges that faced the pre-war intelligentsia was the development of theoretical models that would serve to constitute the unity of the Romanian people. The theoretical models that the intellectuals developed, especially those developed by intellectuals on the radical right, had relied on organicist theoretical conceptions of national unity. These models proved to have lethal side effects insofar as they were picked up by fundamentalist nationalists and were used to justify the attempted liquidation of Jews, Rroma, and other outsiders living in Romania. The very nature of these theories precluded their being sufficiently inclusive so that national minorities could be seen to have a legitimate place in Romania. Moreover, these old theoretical approaches had not proved satisfactory for coping with the "devastating" effects that Romanian intellectuals saw coming from modernization and, more critically, from modernism.

As was discussed earlier, most major pre-war Romanian intellectuals saw cultural modernism as an inherent threat to the "spiritual" integrity and, thus, to the very "essence" of Romanian identity, Romanian culture, and Romanian society. Many, if not most, Romanian intellectuals saw modernism and modernism as leading to the breakup of the old organic social and cultural connections that they believed had characterized pre-modern Romania. With the failure of fascism to recover Romania's "lost" unity and to provide new ways of being modern, communism became an attractive alternative theoretical basis on which to overcome what Romanian intellectuals long had believed to be the destructive and alienating effects of bourgeois capitalism and its consequent "pathological" forms of bourgeois individualism. Marxism offered many Romanian intellectuals a new way to think about constituting the unity of the Romanian state and a new way of connecting Romania and its various peoples to an international project designed to establish human community on terms other than those of discredited feudal/aristocratic or capitalist social formations. In other words, Marxism provided Romanian intellectuals with a new and, seemingly, progressive totalizing vision of human community within and between states to replace the former fascist ideas of establishing what the Germans had called a *Volksgemeinschaft*. Marxism held out the promise of a regime without class rule, without exploitation, without alienation and estrangement, and without ethnic domination. It also offered the promise of bringing rapid economic development and an end to the uneven development of rural and urban areas. Many Romanian intellectuals found these ideas inherently exciting and attractive and were enchanted by the fact that communism seemingly offered them a critical role, in alliance with the working class and the party, in building this new society. For the first time in Romanian history, intellectuals were being expected to produce a culture that transcended the limits of class and ethnicity. What kind of intellectual would not be attracted to such an opportunity? Only a hard-core fascist could resist the excitement of participating in such a project of national and international reconstruction. The alternative, with fascism being totally discredited, was for Romania to build a crisis-prone, class divided, exploitative, alienating, bourgeois democracy. To choose this option would be to put Romanian intellectuals, once again, on what now looked to be the likely losing side in history. With the exception of those intellectuals who had been purged or imprisoned, hard-core fascists, bourgeois sympathizers, some Orthodox theologians and religious believers, some Zionists, various free-thinkers, and "contrarians" of various stripes, almost all of Romania's intellectuals moved en masse to support the new regime and communism's historical projects of building a new Romania and, with along with this, of creating new forms of socialist humanity.

By taking this stand, Romania's communist intellectuals, and intellectuals who were sympathetic to the communists even if they were not party members, attempted to accomplish what some of their intellectual predecessors, during the era of boyar and bourgeois hegemony, had sought. A large number of influential Romania intellectuals, since at least 1848, if not earlier (see Hitchins 1996 for a discussion of Romanian intellectuals stance on modernizing their state prior to the emergence of an independent Romania), had played the role of a *"Bidlungsburgertum"* (Eyal et al. 1998: 51 ff.).

Using Kocka's (1988) work, Eyal et al. (1998: 51) draw a distinction between the economic bourgeoisie (*Wirtschaftsburgertum*) and the cultural bourgeoisie (*Bidlungsburgertum*). Eyal et al. (1998: 51) note that in Western Europe capitalism was primarily the result of the activity of the a relatively well-developed and politically strong *Wirtschafts-burgertum*, with the *Bidlungsburgertum* playing, at best, a supportive secondary role as a "professional class" (Eyal et al. 1998: 51). In Eastern and Central Europe, on the other hand, the *Wirtschaftsburgertum* was poorly formed and politically weak, while the *Bidlungsburgertum* was relatively strong and politically effective, at least as compared to the *Wirtschaftsburgertum*. Under such conditions, the *Bidlungsburgertum* played the leading role, in alliance with the *Wirtschaftsburgertum,* in bringing capitalism and the beginnings of a bourgeois society and political order to Eastern and Central Europe.

As we have seen in previous chapters, this also was the case in Romania, where intellectuals led the drive to create a bourgeois liberal state and, then, used the bourgeois state they were creating in order to try to build a capitalist economy in the years between 1859 and the royal dictatorship of 1938. In Romania, however, the intellectuals never had been able to take complete control of the state from the boyars and, certainly, from the throne. Thus, the Romanian intellectuals' attempt to build capitalism from above was highly incomplete and largely unsuccessful. In part this was a result of the fact that in Romania the development of an effective *Wirtschaftsburgertum* was even more limited than it was in other parts of Eastern and Central Europe, such as Hungary and the Czech lands. The general failure of the Romanian *Bidlungs-burgertum's* project meant that Romania never developed a *Burgertum* (bourgeois) social order. The Romanian cultural bourgeoisie and the economic bourgeoisie were too weak to overcome the structural resistance and the structural obstacles put in place by the boyars and the throne in order to obstruct fundamental changed to Romania's social, political, and economic orders. For example, the throne, in alliance with the boyars, never allowed Romania's cities to develop the autonomy that cities had elsewhere in Europe, including large parts of Central and Eastern Europe. Therefore, both components of the bourgeoisie were effectively blocked from forming themselves into a well-defined class actor.

Communism offered Romania's intellectuals the possibility of once again launching a drive to modernize the economy and the society. This time, however, they could participate in a modernization effort without having the goal of developing a society modeled after the West and its bourgeois values and social structures, with which a large number of intellectuals, including even a large number of the modernizers, never felt comfortable. Instead of the bourgeoisie, the intellectuals now would be allied with the working class and its vanguard, the communist party. As the power of the state expanded, so-called "free" intellectuals, such as painters, musicians, poets, dramatists, film-makers, playwrights, novelists, and others, came under increasing party control, some voluntarily and others acceding to the state's control that was exercised mainly through newly established or recently reorganized professional associations, unions, and cultural organizations. A good number of free intellectuals harnessed themselves, some willingly and some reluctantly, to communism's new aesthetic criteria and cultural objectives. Free intellectuals, at the minimum, were encouraged to avoid presenting antisocialist and anti-Romanian themes in their work and they were rewarded for producing works that portrayed Romanian life in positive terms. As the regime's trust in Romanian intellectuals increased, there was a decreasing need to engage in direct censorship. The larger part of Romania's intelligentsia quickly internalized what the regime expected and engaged in sufficient self-censorship to obviate the need for the heavy hand of state censors. It is clear that Romanian intellectuals understood what the limits of the regime's boundaries of acceptability were and that they generally stayed within these limits. For conforming to the regime's expectations, writers, artists, and other free intellectuals were generously rewarded by the state with prizes, awards, cash, and a broad range of other privileges, not the least of which was the opportunity to travel and, even better, study abroad. Those intellectuals who, for whatever reason, could not, or did not, conform to the regime's cultural policies simply disappeared from the cultural scene, sometimes literally and sometimes figuratively. Nonconforming "free" intellectuals were not immune from arrest and imprisonment, especially during the communist regime's early years when the party leadership felt they could give little tolerance to intellectual faithlessness. For dissenting and/or nonconforming intellectuals who managed to stay out of prison, disappearance from intellectual and cultural life was insured by closing down their access to publishers or to other vendors of their work. Dissident and/or nonconforming painters, sculptors, and graphic artists found it hard to get gallery space to display their work. Their counterparts in theater, dance, and the like found it impossible to find companies to perform their work. Writers who fell out with the regime could not find publishers for their work. Without access to audiences, dissident free intellectuals became ever less relevant to Romanian cultural and intellectual life, except in ever smaller circles of like-minded people in and outside of Romania.

In order to build its own intelligentsia, the party expanded enrollment in universities and put into place university admission policies that were intended to alter the social composition of student populations. The communists also changed the pattern of investment in the kinds of programs offered within universities. From the mid-1950s to the mid-1960s, enrollment in Romanian universities more than doubled in size. Many of the new students were women, who had been markedly underrepresented in the universities before the communists took power. In 1945 women made up approximately 33% of the students enrolled in universities. By 1980 this had increased to forty four per cent. Under the communists, women continued to be over represented in the humanities and in the helping professions, while men continued to be over represented in the sciences and in technical fields.

Students were admitted to universities on the basis of an elaborate point system, which favored the children of workers and peasants and penalized the children of the classes that formerly dominated Romania. By putting a class criterion into place for university admissions, family background and academic competence, which was highly correlated with class position, came to play lesser roles in determining who was admitted to universities than they had before the war. Eventually, this policy was abandoned and coming from a working class or from a peasant family, while still playing a part in the admissions process, became far less important as a criterion in determining entry into the universities. University admission came to be a function of performance on competitive examinations, which favored the children of the more politically and socially advantaged whose parents lived in areas with better schools and who could afford to pay for their children to receive private tutoring to prepare them for the examinations.

The state invested heavily in expanding natural science, life science, and mathematics programs in the universities and engineering and various technology programs in the Polytechnic and Agronomy Universities. Faculties in these disciplines developed significant reputations for the quality of their work, moving Romania into a leading position in international science, mathematics, and engineering. The state investment that made possible Romania's growing scientific reputation often took place at the expense of the social sciences and the humanities. But, even in these fields, Romanian university faculty and researchers, most of whom were attached to the various institutes of the Romanian Academy, produced work of international significance. For example, Romanian sociologists were producing interesting and important work in the areas of social psychology, social theory, demography, and in what Westerners would call community studies, among other sub-areas of the discipline, before Ceausescu closed down the field in the mid-1970s. Ceausescu had decided that sociology was a "bourgeois" discipline and, as such, it had no role to play in Romania's intellectual life.

Other disciplines in the social sciences and the humanities had scholars with the same degree of international visibility as had the Romanian sociologists. For example, Romanian literary criticism, philology, and linguistics also were fields with distinguished scholars and Romanian philosophy continued to enjoy an excellent reputation in European circles. Romania also continued to produce outstanding artists, musicians, writers, filmmakers, poets, classical singers, classical dancers, musical conductors, playwrights, and composers whose work was widely appreciated in Europe.

Romania, under the communists, also launched programs aimed at wiping out national illiteracy, especially in the countryside. The literacy programs, targeting both peasants and workers, showed a remarkably high level of success. Illiteracy was virtually eliminated in the country. The communists also expanded elementary and secondary schools, opening opportunities for subaltern social strata and social classes, once excluded from schools, to have the chance to receive a basic education and, for the most talented, an education in the polytechnic or regular universities. Included in the expansion of lower levels of education was a system of trade schools that were attached to factories and other enterprises, giving graduates a seamless transition from school to work. A major aim of elementary and secondary education was inculcating socialist values and culture in Romanian children.

The changes in educational practices that Romania's communist regime introduced produced new intellectual cadres, who "owed" their positions entirely to the social reforms that the communists had introduced. These new intellectuals, drawn largely from social classes and social strata who would not have had an opportunity for an education under the old regime, staffed the growing state bureaucracies and, even, the universities and the ranks of creative intellectuals. By and large, they were committed loyalists to the communists and remained so almost to the end of the communist regime in Romania. The new intellectuals came to constitute the Bolshevik regime's traditional and organic intelligentsia, along with those intellectuals trained under the old regime who demonstrated subservience and loyalty to the new state power.

From 1948 until 1989, the educational system built by the communists worked as an engine of upward occupational and social mobility for the Romanian masses. Never before in Romanian history did so many people get the opportunity to leave behind their family's class origins and move upward in the economic and social hierarchy. Despite the later distortions introduced into open university admissions and, hence, to access to higher status jobs, by social, political, and economic privilege, countless Romanians, whose chances to obtain a university education before 1945 would have been miniscule, were able to attend universities and move into jobs far above what their grandparents and parents could have hoped for themselves or their descendents. The only price they paid was the expectation that they would be loyal to the regime that supplied them the opportunity to succeed and that they would meet its various demands and needs, including working where the state the state decided they were needed, for as long as the state deemed necessary.

The Task of Creating a Romanian Proletariat

Another major problem that faced the communists when they came to power was the need to create a proletariat, the class in whose name and for whose interests the party ruled. At the end of World War II, Romania's actually existing proletariat was small and poorly developed, as a class. It lacked many of the institutional structures that, under more "normal" circumstances would have given it some degree of objective and subjective identity and consciousness. While the small working class, before the war, had possessed virtually all of the objective characteristics of a social class, it had failed to develop a clear sense of class identity, class consciousness, and a mass-based class political mobilization.

As a result, the communists needed to expand the size of the Romanian working class and enhance its consciousness. In effect, this meant that the Romanian communists had to create the very class whose needs and interests defined the party's historical mission. The objective development of the proletariat would come about because of the party's focus on industrial development, especially the development of heavy industry. The communists had introduced one-year plans for the economy in 1949 and 1950. By 1950, there were signs that Romania's industrial production was beginning to grow. It had returned to its levels of 1938. The two one-year plans were followed by the first five-year plan for 1951-1955. The largest part of capital investment under the five-year plan went to heavy industry and to developing the national transportation infrastructure. The plan led to Romanian industrial production jumping to almost three times the level it had been in 1938 (Fischer-Galati 1998b). Consumer goods production increased at a slower rate but, nonetheless, it stood at almost twice its 1938 level (Fischer-Galati 1998b).

This rapid industrial growth led to a significant increase in the absolute and proportional size of the Romanian proletariat. From under twenty per cent of the work force after the war, the proletariat came to constitute almost sixty per cent of the work force by 1989. The new industrial work force largely was drawn from an increasingly redundant peasantry and from residents of small towns in the mostly underdeveloped Romanian countryside. Many of the industrial workers commuted from the countryside to jobs in the industrial centers, returning to villages and towns at the end of the workday. Most, however, became permanent city residents. Between 1948 and 1953, the number of people living in cities increased from about 3.7 million to over 4.4 million (Fisher-Galati 1998b). This created pressure on the state to house and to feed the new urban residents. Urbanization continued throughout the communist period. At the end of World War II, less than a quarter of Romania's population lived in cities, by 1990, over half of the population had become urban. Industrial jobs in the cities came to be in such demand that the communists were forced to close a number of cities to internal migration. The state could not afford to build and maintain an urban infrastructure to meet the needs of all of those who wanted to live in the cities. As a result, commuting from rural to urban areas to work in industry became a part of the life of large numbers of peasants.

Under the communists, the proletariat occupied a privileged position in the Romanian economy. After all, the party was the vanguard of the proletariat and ruled the state in its name. As the state accumulated larger surpluses, a good part of these surpluses were transferred to the working classes in the form of wage increases and a variety of other benefits, such as access to new apartments, vacations, medical care, and the like. The wage policies put in place by the Romanian regime, decreased the wage gap between the proletariat and other kinds of workers. In some cases, proletarian occupations, such as those in transportation, mining, and other selected areas, received wages and benefits far higher than most non-manual occupations. In this way, the state went a long way toward securing the mass loyalty of the Romanian working class. Worker loyalty to the regime was reflected in the fact that until the mid-1970s the Romanian working class did not show the rebellious tendencies that workers in the German Democratic Republic, Hungary, and Poland had shown in the early years of Bolshevik rule. In part this may have been due to repression, but a more important reason was the regime was keeping its implicit social contract with the proletariat. From the end of the war until the mid-1970s, workers, like a large proportion of other Romanians outside of the peasantry, saw continuing improvement in their personal and collective living conditions. As long as this continued, the workers maintained their loyalty to the Bolshevik system.

The state did not rely merely on material incentives to anchor worker loyalty. The RMP, through a variety of mechanisms, deeply penetrated into virtually all aspects of workers' lives, both on and off the job. The party's objective was to develop the proletariat's subjective class identification and class political and social capacities. Party committees were active in all enterprises and all workers were expected to take a role in party meetings and in party ideological work, including its myriad education activities.

One of the major instruments for anchoring worker loyalty was the trade union movement. Romania's trade unions, like unions in other Central and East European regimes, were brought into one central organization, the General Trade Union Confederation of Romania (the *Uniunea Generala Sindicatelor din Romania* or the UGSR). The UGSR had a membership of over 7 million workers in the mid-1980s. It was headed by a Central Council and it was made up of eleven different labor federations that, in turn, had over twelve thousand locals. The Central

Council had a chair, directly appointed by the party, eight vice-chairs, two party secretaries, and a forty-eight member executive committee. Romania's labor organization had almost no autonomy vis-à-vis the party-state bureaucracy The UGSR was a major pillar of the party-state system. The unions played a critical role in helping the party-state transform a work force that was overwhelmingly peasant in its social origins into a modern, skilled, industrial proletariat. The Romanian unions were the first-line guarantors of the socialist production regimes being put into place in new enterprises and recently nationalized enterprises.

Unions not only were designed to be a fundamental component in the disciplinary regimen of the shop floors that was intended to insure that workers would maintain levels of production and productivity consistent with the requirements of the state plan, but they also were assigned an important ideological role. They also were charged with the key responsibility of building the new "socialist citizen." Building the new citizen required that the unions be active agents in shaping individual and collective forms of consciousness in ways that were consistent with party ideology and practice. As part of the ideological apparatus of the communist system, the unions were but one of the many structural components being put into place in Romania that shared a goal of engineering and reproducing consent, not only to the new production regimens, but also to the entire communist institutional order that was being put into place.

The communist unions were organizations that had non-antagonistic relationships with the state and state appointed enterprise managers. Indeed, unions were expected to work closely with management, the state, and the party at all organizational levels in order to achieve the overall tactical and strategic objectives of the Bolshevik regime. They thus functioned as transmission belts of policies and objectives that emanated from central party and state organs to the shop floor. Working closely with management and the party, the unions had a variety of positive and negative incentives at their disposal to insure worker shop floor discipline and general political quiescence in the proletariat they were helping to build. Unions shared in the control of worker access to important parts of the social wage, such as housing, vacation privileges, job placements inside the enterprise, work transfers, and the like. In addition, the union, itself, constituted a career mobility path off the shop floor that intersected at several critical points with various career paths inside of the communist party and the state. The top leadership of unions was a part of Romania's "nomenklatura," or privileged section of the party. Unions also served as a means for disciplining workers. The unions supplemented the disciplinary mechanisms that were present on the shop floors. Labor discipline was highly problematic in the early days of industrialization. Workers coming from the peasantry often were unfamiliar with the expectations, routines, and demands of industrial work. The trade unions were expected to play a major part in socializing these former peasants into their new worlds of work. Union activism and party activism were ways for workers to achieve upward mobility in the communist system and many workers took advantage of these mobility tracks, gaining even more access to social and economic rewards than their counterparts had. At the highest levels, a leadership position in a union meant that a person was part of the nomenklatura. For ordinary rank-and-file workers, maintaining good standing with unions assured that one would have access to all of the benefits of the socialist regimes, including access to apartments (many of which were owned or controlled by enterprises), to internal career ladders in their enterprises, to safer jobs under better working condition, to inexpensive health care, to low cost vacations, and the like.

In 1971, Ceausescu had proclaimed that he planned to democratize Romania's unions. He pledged that the primary role of unions would be the protection of worker interests. He also promised that unions would have a role in appointing enterprise managers. Finally, he promised to give unions a major role in discussing and debating Romania's policies dealing with economic and social development. In 1972, however, the UGSR introduced new governing statutes that essentially blocked any reform, even in the areas of negotiating wages and negotiating working conditions.

At the same time that the proletariat was being built and was improving its position in the society, Romania's peasantry was being weakened. As industrialization expanded, requiring higher levels of investment in the national urban infrastructure, investment in the countryside lagged behind investment in the cities and in manufacturing, especially heavy manufacturing. Romania's rural areas continued to lack almost all of the amenities of life that were being developed in the cities. Many villages lacked adequate water and waste systems, they lacked paved roads, few villages had more than one or two telephones for public use, rural electrification was poorly developed, high proportions of housing were substandard, health care was inadequate, and schools were inferior to those in the cities. In addition, rural wages lagged significantly behind those of cities and the state exercised tight controls over peasant production on private agricultural plots, further limiting peasants' incomes.

As noted above, peasants responded to deteriorating rural conditions by moving to the cities permanently or by commuting to industrial jobs in cities and towns. In some Romanian provincial cities, commuters made up almost half of the industrial workforce. The ongoing peasant migration from rural to urban areas and peasant commuting had a significant effect on Romanian cities. Cities contained approximately twenty three per cent of Romania's population in 1948. By 1970 this had reached a little bit more than forty per cent and by 1992 a majority of Romania's population was urban. Not only did cities increase in size and the proportion of Romania's population living in cities increase, the massive influx of peasants led to a ruralization of a good number of Romanian cities, restricting the capacity of these cities to develop more "modern" forms of urban culture. Because of processes of chain migration from country to city, many Romanian urban areas were made up of a large number of people from the same rural villages. Many of these rural migrants imported their traditional social practices, values, and cultures into urban places, which gave Romanian cities a rather distinctive rural or semi-rural character, at least as compared to Western European cities. Some of Romania's smaller provincial cities took on the character of large-scale urban villages and even in the largest cities, one could find large areas that only were partially urban, in a cultural and behavioral sense. It was not unusual, for example, to find neighborhoods where recent migrants to the cities kept a variety of small animals to supplement their food supplies.

In order to cope with the rapid urbanization, the Romanian government nationalized a large number of housing units in the cities. Large villas and mansions were confiscated and subdivided into apartments. The government also launched a major program to build apartments in all of its cities. With the massive movement to the cities, the state also was required to extend the urban infrastructure. Roads were built, water and waste systems were modernized and extended into new urban neighborhoods, and heating and electrical grids were built to service the new populations. As in other Bolshevik countries, Romania used prefabricated construction techniques to build high rise apartments, done in an "international socialist" style, on the edges of its cities.

The Party and Women's Rights

The communists took significant steps to advance the position of women in Romania. Women moved into politics in larger numbers than was the case in Western Europe. For example, in 1970 women made up sixty-six of two hundred and seventy five legislators in Romania. As already noted, women also increased their enrollment in Romanian universities, although, many of the women students were concentrated in disciplines that traditionally had attracted women. Women also had increased opportunities for employment outside of the household, reaching levels much higher than were found in Western Europe. However, women's wages for comparable jobs lagged behind those of men. Infant mortality, a measure of well being for women, fell dramatically in the first two decades of communist rule in Romania, so, too, did maternal mortality rates. The drop in infant and maternal mortality was a direct result of Romania's having introduced free, universal health care.

Until the late 1960s, Romanian women had vastly increased access to contraception, including abortion, and divorces became much easier for women than they had been before the war. Ease of access to contraception and divorce would end during Ceausescu's rule, as will be discussed in more detail below.

But at the same time that the state was taking a progressive stance on the status of women, Romania was unable to break the patriarchal attitudes that were prevalent in the general population, especially in the countryside and among the rural migrants to the cities. In general, in Romanian households, men retained dominant positions. Women continued to carry the main responsibility for domestic tasks, even when they were employed outside of the household. Women thus had a "double burden" of responsibilities. In some cases, women had a "triple burden," by adding extra work in the shadow economy to what they already were doing. Educated women, for example, would have a regular job, would have domestic responsibilities, and, then, might work as private tutors during the evening and/or on weekends to help students prepare for university entrance exams. Working class women, on the other hand, often had their official jobs, their household responsibilities, and, then, be active in the informal economy, sewing clothes, watching children, and the like.

Male dominance was not exercised just in the household. It also was characteristic of most state institutions, despite communism's ideology and its rhetoric of gender equality in the years following World War II. The *PRM* created a number of organizations for women. As with trade unions, women's organizations served as transmission belts for the party and the state. While women were in charge of most of these organizations, the organizations and their leaders were not free to advocate policies or press demand for changes without prior party approval. The party, of course, was dominated by men. Few women were in leading positions in the party, with the notable exception of Ana Pauker, until she was purged, and, later, Elena Ceausescu.

Women also faced clear limits on their professional mobility. Almost all enterprises, state institutions, and party organizations restricted women's opportunities for movement into top leadership positions. Women working in factories tended to be segregated into less-skilled and lower paying jobs. Higher paying skilled positions tended to be reserved for men.

Romania and East-West Conflict

The changes the communists introduced in Romania did not take place in isolation from the international context of the time. The most important aspect of the international context that influenced internal developments in Romania was the growing estrangement between the Soviet Union and its former Western allies, especially the United States. At the end of the war, the Russian army underwent significant demobilization, dropping from twelve million to three million in three years (Mazower 1998). According to Mazower (1998), the evidence is not altogether clear that the Soviets intended to occupy Eastern and Central Europe and impose communist rule. During the war, the Department of International Information of the Soviet Communist Cenral Committee had identified the post war agenda of the Soviet Union to be cooperation with democratic parties and movements inside the countries conquered and occupied by the Red Army. Stalin and the party had felt that conditions inside of these countries were not ripe for the development of socialism. Given this, the Soviet Communist Party planned to work with united fronts in order to make the transition from war to peace in the countries it was occupying. Mazower (1998) notes that at the end of the war, it seems that the Soviets had no clear plans for Eastern and Central Europe, other than to work with progressive forces to create social and economic reforms that would produce broad-based support for reconstituted communist parties. Early Soviet post-war policy seemed focused on what was to be done with Germany, rather than what was to be done with Eastern and Central Europe, as a whole. The Soviet Union's only strategic interest in Eastern and Central Europe was to create a buffer zone between Germany and its own borders.

Nineteen forty-seven marked a turning point in the relations between the Soviet Union and its former Western allies. From this point on, relations between the Soviet Union and the West began a prolonged period of reciprocal deterioration. In 1947, the Soviet Union created the Cominform, it replaced the Comintern, which had ceased operations during the war because of Stalin's concerns about the ways that the Western allies looked at it. The formation of the Comintern gave the Soviet Union a tool for closely coordinating the changes in Eastern Europe that it had begun to introduce. With the creation of the Comintern, Stalin appears to have abandoned the idea of possibly different national roads to socialism in Eastern and Central Europe. Thus, as the PMC was consolidating its position within Romania and it was contending with various forms of internal opposition to what it was attempting to do, it also was acting within an international context that helped shape the direction the country would take. Like the other Communist states, Romania faced increasing hostility from the United States and its allies in Western Europe, who defined Romania as part of a Soviet "bloc" of states.

As noted above, the Western powers, at first, had refused to recognize Groza's government after the war. Increasingly the West began to define Romania as part of the Soviet camp and, as a result, treated it more and more like an enemy of Western interests. As a result, like other countries defined in this way, the West reduced its trade and other economic relations with Romania. Romania had no choice but to expand its trade ties with the Soviet Union and with other countries that were coming to be defined as part of an Eastern European Bloc of Soviet "satellites."

In 1947 the United States proposed a program for reconstructing post-war Europe, the Marshall Plan. At the same time, communist parties in Western Europe were coming under increasing pressure from hostile states, this was particularly the case in France and Italy, where commnist parties emerged from the war as among the strongest political parties, partly because of the roles they played in the anti-fascist resistance. In both France and Italy, communists were removed from national governments dominated by the left and American intelligence services funded movements, organizations and political parties opposed to communism.

The Soviet Union opposed the Marshall Plan, seeing it as a way to integrate the Eastern and Central European countries into a greater Europe dominated by the United States. The United States apparently expected such a response, as the Marshall Plan included a number of political conditions for participation that almost seemed designed to antagonize the Soviet Union (Longworth 1997). The Soviets, fearing Western intentions, walked out of the initial meetings held in Paris to discuss implementation of the Plan. Czechoslovakia and Poland, both of which had expressed an interest in participating in the reconstruction effort, following the lead of the Soviets, announced that they no longer wanted to be part of the Plan's reconstruction processes.

Recent research has shown that American diplomats saw the Marhall Plan not merely as a means to provide economic assistance to Europe and, therefore block perceived attempts by the Soviets to cxpand its influence into Western Europe, but also as a tool for weakening Soviet influence in Eastern and Central Europe by integrating states in these areas into the Western, capitalist economy (Parrish, n.d.). In other words, the Marshall Plan was intended to have both a defensive and an offensive component. Parrish (n.d.) reviews new evidence that shows that before the introduction of the Marshall Plan Stalin was hoping that the Soviet Union and the West could negotiate settlements in most of the areas that were producing conflict at the end of World War II. This changed after the U.S. introduced the Marshall Plan, which Stalin and the Soviet leadership gradually came to see not only as a simple mechanism for assisting European economic recovery, but also as a way for the United States and its European allies to undermine recent Soviet gains in Eastern and Central Europe and, eventually, to build a new *cordon sanitaire* around the Soviet Union.

Parrish (n.d.), using recently available evidence, also indicates that it was only *after* the Soviet Union perceived the Marshall Plan in this way that it began a policy of Sovietizing Poland, Czechoslovakia, Hungary, Bulgaria, East Germany, and Romania. Soviet tolerance of coalition governments in these states ended and the communist parties in these states were encouraged to impose a Stalinist party-state model of political control and economic development. At the same time, the Soviet Union forced the Italian and French communist parties to end their attempts to participate in coalition governments and go on a revolutionary offensive against the Italian and French governments.

As the Soviet Union's new policies became apparent to the Western allies, they responded by increasing their attempts to politically and economically isolate the Soviet Union and its allies in Eastern and Central Europe (Parrish, n.d.). In turn, the Soviet Union increased its integration of Eastern and Central Europe into a more coherent and centrally dominated block. As each side organized against the other, the foundation was laid for forty years of "cold war" antagonisms and conflicts "stabilized" within a context of mutually assured nuclear destruction.

Around the same time, the Western allies introduced a major currency reform for their zones of occupied Germany. They also wanted the new currency introduced for all of Berlin, which was under joint allied administration. Fearing that the new currency would wreck the increasingly socialized economy of their zone of occupation in Eastern Germany, the Soviets refused to agree to a new currency being used in Berlin and, in turn, demanded that the currency then in use in their Eastern zone of occupation be the only currency allowed in Berlin. The West refused and the Soviets proceeded to blockade the city. The blockade lasted from 1948 to 1949. The West, led by the United States, airlifted supplies to the Berlin zones under their direct administration, saving the city from falling under the complete control of the Soviet Union.

In 1949, the Western Allies created the North Atlantic Treaty Organization (NATO). The NATO alliance initially included the United States, Great Britain, France, Belgium, Norway, Denmark, Iceland, Luxembourg, Canada, Italy, and Portugal. In 1952 NATO expanded to include Greece and Turkey, which completed a process of Western encirclement of the Soviet Union. The alliance's explicit purpose was to check possible Soviet expansion into Western Europe. NATO was formed just as the civil war in Greece was drawing to a close. The Greek civil war had been going on since the end of the Second World War. The communists lost in Greece. Many of the communist combatants fled to Romania, where they lived as political exiles. The Soviet Union and its partners formed COMECON in 1949. This was a countermeasure to the Marshall Plan. It was designed to provide mutual economic assistance and economic coordination between and among the Soviet Union and its allies. Western Europe moved to enhance its own economic integration by establishing the European Economic Community (EEC) in 1957. The EEC was an extension of the post-war economic treaties between France and West Germany dealing with coal and steel production. The EEC eventually led to the current European Union (EU). The EU currently is negotiating with Romania and other former Communist states as to their terms of admission to the Union. COMECON was dissolved after the collapse of the Soviet Union. Nothing emerged to replace it.

The Soviets, while seeing NATO as a force that threatened its national security interests, did not build a counter military alliance until 1955, following the West's decision to admit the German *Bundesrepublik's* military forces into NATO. Seeing clear danger to itself and its allies from an expanded NATO that now included a rearmed Germany, the Soviet Union took the lead in forming the Warsaw Pact Alliance. Romania was one of the Pact's original members. At this time, Soviet military forces still were in Romania. The Pact further strengthened the integration of Eastern and Central Europe into a Soviet zone of influence. Soviet troops were withdrawn from Romanian soil in 1958, although they still had the right of transit through Romania and the Pact had the right to conduct joint training exercises in Romania.

Romania and Tensions Inside the Bolshevik Inter-State System

As tensions between the Western and Eastern blocs increased in the second half of the 1940s, the Eastern bloc experienced its first signs of internal conflict. In 1948 Yugoslavia, led by the former partisan leader Marshall Tito, and the Soviet Union broke diplomatic relations and Yugoslavia was expelled from the Cominform. At this time, Romania sided with the Soviet Union and, at Stalin's urging, purged a large number of alleged Tito sympathizers from the ranks of the PMR. In addition, Romania, like most of the other communist states in the region, broke economic and military relations with Yugoslavia. While initially costly to the Yugoslavs, their split with the Soviets and their allies gave the Yugoslavs the freedom to develop economic ties with the West and to take an independent path in developing its own form of socialism. Tito had taken power at the end of World War II without the direct involvement of the Red Army. Tito's partisans not only had contributed to the defeat of the Axis powers and their allies in Yugoslavia, but also managed to defeat partisan groups tied to the West. Once in power, Tito established a federal state in which the various interests of the major nationality groups were carefully balanced. His drive to develop and maintain an independent socialist state would have far reaching consequences for Romania in the 1960s and later.

Developments in Hungary in 1956 also had major effects on the Warsaw Pact countries. After the initial successes of the Hungarian uprising and the announcement that Hungary was planning to leave the Warsaw pact, Hungary was invaded by the Warsaw Pact powers. Despite its desire to supply troops for the invasion, the Soviets decided to keep Romanian military forces out of Hungary. Instead of supplying military forces, Romania ended up sending Hungarian-speaking intelligence officers into Hungary to assist the invaders. The Warsaw Pact invasion, violent suppression of the revolution, and the arrest of the revolutionary leadership, inspired a wave of Magyar protest inside of Romania. Magyar university students played a leading role in these protests, especially in the university centers in Transylvania. The protests were quickly suppressed under the direction of Ion Illiescu, a rising star in the PMR. Building on the reputation he established for his handling of student dissent in 1956, Iliescu would have a successful career, becoming a member of the party's central committee. He was removed from his major party posts when he ran afoul of Ceausescu in the 1970s, but would return to prominence in 1989, as the leader of the National Salvation Front (NSF).

After Stalin's death in 1953 and despite Krushchev's denunciation of Stalin at the 20th Party Congress in Moscow, Dej continued to maintain a rigid Stalinist structure inside of Romania. If anything, Krushchev's attack on Stalinism led to a greater degree of repression in Romania, rather than to internal political relaxation, as was beginning to take place in other communist states. Dej had been too strongly committed to Stalinist ideology and practice to change his style of rule. Any repudiation of Stalinism would have been a repudiation of his own tenure as Romania's leader. This was not something he willingly would do or allow others to do as long as he tightly held the reigns of power. While Dej clung to the old orthodoxy when dealing with internal matters, he began taking steps to distance Romania from control by the Soviet Union. As already noted, he negotiated the withdrawal of Soviet troops from Romanian territory in 1958. By acting in concert with the other Warsaw Pact armies in invading Hungary, Dej had demonstrated to the Soviets that he was a loyal ally who was willing to follow its lead in foreign affairs, giving the Soviets the confidence that they no longer needed military troops in Romania. The Soviets also were convinced that the Romanian military had sufficient skills and resources to defend the country from internal and external aggression, until such time as Soviet and Warsaw Pact troops could be deployed to assist the Romanians, if this should become necessary. The Soviets also were assured that Romania would make no claims on the territory it had seized in Bessarabia or Bukovina, even though Bessarabia's and Bukovina's occupation by the Soviet Union were serious problems for the Dej regime. Bessarabia was especially problematic in that Stalin was forcing a Russification of this former Romanian province. Stalin's efforts to Russify Bessarabia included extensive ethnic cleansing of Romanian speakers from the territory. Under Stalin, Bessarabia was being redefined as a historically Slavic region that had been conquered by the Romanians when the Tzars and, later the Soviets, had been too weak to resist Romanian incursions. While the Romanian communist leadership maintained a public silence about what was happening in these former Romanian territories, privately they were far less accepting of Soviet policy in Bukovina and, especially, in Bessarabia.

Dej also had suggested to the Soviets that the legitimacy of the Romanian communist regime would be enhanced considerably if it no longer appeared that it was being maintained in power by the Red Army. While, no doubt all of these points were true, Dej's desire to see Soviet forces out of Romania also reflected something more: his basic Romanian nationalism. Like other Romanians, he saw the Soviet Union's occupation as one more example of a long tradition, stretching back to the Tzars, of Russian interference and meddling in Romania's affairs. As previously discussed, Dej had long bristled at the role the "Muscovite" wing of the party leadership had in Romania's communist movement. It was Dej's belief that the presence of "Muscovites" and other national minorities in the life of the party and the state should be sharply limited. In his view, Romanian communists were the most able to define what Romanians needed and how their needs best should be met, not communists in other countries.

At its meetings in 1955, the RMP, for the first time, discussed the possibilities for developing communism on purely Romanian terms. Although Stalin was dead, this still was a dangerous idea, as later events in Hungary in 1956 and Czechoslovakia in 1968 would show, especially since Soviet troops were still in Romania. In 1958, the RMP's inner circle adopted policies that stressed the importance of expanding its drive to industrialize, to enhance efforts to collectivize agriculture, to begin improving national living standards, and to seek Western credits and trade assistance.

In 1955, Romania joined the United Nations and in 1956 it joined UNESCO. These two steps indicated that Romania was beginning to open itself to the West, even before Soviet troops withdrew from the country. Romania also began to develop and expand its trade relations with Western countries and Romania reached agreements with the West on compensation for assets that had been nationalized by the communists. Romania's trade with the West, especially with West Germany, France, Italy, and the United Kingdom grew dramatically after 1958. By 1960, trade with the West constituted 25% of all Romanian trade (Fischer-Galati 1998b)

During Krushchev's rule, the Soviet Union tried to reorganize COMECON. Soviet planners argued that the economic alliance could function more efficiently and effectively if there was a higher degree of national specialization of economic activity. The Soviet Union argued in COMECON meetings held in 1961 that the alliance could enhance the overall development of member countries if the Soviet Union, the German Democratic Republic (the GDR), and Czechoslovakia were to continue to move forward in their drive to industrialize, while Romania, Poland, Hungary, and Bulgaria specialized in agricultural production. Bulgaria joined with the Soviet Union, the GDR, and Czechoslovakia and supported these proposals. Romania took the lead in opposing it. Poland and Hungary supported Romania. Dej had resisted these proposals on the grounds that Romania's future was to be found in developing a modern industrial economy, not in supplying agricultural products to others. Poland, Hungary, and Romania prevailed and COMECON withdrew the idea of national economic specialization within the alliance.

Romania remained "neutral" in the growing tensions between the Soviet Union and China. It offered to mediate the dispute between these two countries, much to the annoyance of the Soviet Union. The Soviets were suspicious of Romania's motives. Key members of the Central Committee in the Soviet Union believed that Romania favored the Chinese and its arguments that communist states should be willing to accept the idea that there could be many different ways to build socialism and that the communist states needed to treat each other with mutual respect and should acknowledge the importance of national sovereignty in framing their policies toward each other.

In return for Romania's "neutrality" in the Sino-Soviet conflict, China greatly expanded its trade and its cultural relations with Romania. Romania and China signed a number of treaties that enhanced economic relations and cultural exchanges between the two countries. Romania also began developing better relations with Albania and Yugoslavia. Among other things, Dej went to Beograd in 1963 and signed an agreement with Tito to build a hydroelectric complex at the Iron Gates on the Danube. While important to Romania, this project was of far greater economic significance for Yugoslavia than it was for Romania. Even beyond its economic importance to Yugoslavia, the agreement had enormous symbolic significance to the Yugoslavs. It showed that they were no longer isolated from other Balkan Communist regimes. For the Romanians, it showed the Soviets that they no longer would follow the USSR's lead in defining how the various communist states would relate to each other. Dej also ordered that Romania's ambassador to Albania return to Tirana. Dej had withdrawn the ambassador when Albania, in support of the Chinese, had broken diplomatic relations with the USSR in 1960. This act to end Albania's isolation within the communist camp was a bold diplomatic move on Romania's part and drew extremely hostile criticism from the USSR, who feared the development of an independent communist bloc in the Balkans, which had been one of Tito's early aspirations that had brought him into conflict with Stalin in the first place.

Romania also began working to improve its relations with France and England, establishing full diplomatic relations with these two countries for the first time since the end of World War II. Both France and England were allowed to open embassies and to develop cultural exchanges and programs in Romania. Dej also made diplomatic overtures to the United States, with a view to improving relations between the two countries. Dej was especially interested in opening up economic relations between the United States and Romania. Dej had the full support of the RMP Central Committee for these efforts. In April 1964, the party adopted its "Statement on the Stand of the Romanian Workers' Party Concerning the Problem of the International Communist and Working-Class Movement," the so-called "April Declaration." The Declaration was a clear statement of Romania's support for the idea that there were multiple paths to socialism and that no communist state or party had the right to make claims of hegemony over any other based on what it took to be the only acceptable way to achieve socialism. The Declaration was an unequivocal demand that the USSR had to respect the principles of national sovereignty and party sovereignty within each communist state and it acknowledged that Russia had long meddled and interfered in Romania's internal affairs. In taking this position, Romania was arguing for national equality among communist states and for respect for the principle of non-interference in internal affairs within the Warsaw Pact and within COMECON. The Declaration became the foundation for Romania's national communism, which linked communism, in general, and the party, in particular, with the Romanian nation and its interests.

China, Albania, and Yugoslavia supported Romania's position. The USSR now the Declaration as a serious provocation and challenge. Cuba, which had recently become a part of the international communist movement, was sufficiently concerned about the state of Soviet-Romanian relations that it offered itself as a mediator to calm the situation between Romania and the Soviet Union. Both the Soviets and the Romanians rejected Cuba's offer.

By 1961 Dej had consolidated his position in Romania to such an extent that not only was he Secretary General of the PMR but he also was head of state, by virtue of his holding the office of President of the Grand National Assembly. As he moved to distance Romania from the USSR and to expand relations with the West, Dej also began to support limited internal "liberalization," which stood in sharp contrast to the Stalinist practices that had been characteristic of his rule in Romania from its earliest days. In 1962 Dej declared a broad amnesty for all political prisoners in Romania and began a gradual program that resulted in freeing over 12,000 political prisoners who had remained in confinement. He also allowed increased cultural contacts between Romania and the West, including the United States.

As part of this greater cultural openness, Romania allowed a far wider range of Western publications to be imported and paid for the translation of many works of American literature, as well as literature from other Western countries. Western films also began to be shown in Romania's major cities, and Western artists were invited to perform in the country. Romanian writers whose works had been politically out of favor began to reappear. Most noteworthy was the republication of Mihai Eminescu's writings. Eminescu had been one of the 19th century giants of Romanian literature. Eminescu's work had been suppressed by the communists because it was "anti-Russian" and it espoused a conservative philosophy that was anathema to Romania's communists. Dej also allowed the work of a number of historians, philosophers, and social scientists who had been purged from universities to reappear. Dej also began a process of "de-Russification," which included purging "Russified" elements from the Romanian language. Most important of all, Dej gave a speech at a party congress in which he blamed most of Romania's social, political, economic, and cultural problems that had arisen since 1948 on the undue influence that the Soviet Union had exerted on the country.

Dej, ever the practical politician, began loosening internal controls because he recognized that support for his form of Stalinism was weakening in key inner circles of the party elite. He also was concerned that if he continued engaging in surplus repression that Romania could face problems like those that had developed in the German Democratic Republic, Poland, and Hungary. Romanian party elites, while not wanting to abandon communism, were interested in various structural speculations as alternatives to the Stalinism Dej and his allied had put in place over the past twenty years.

Dej died politically intestate in 1965. Within weeks of his death, his photographs disappeared from public places, his writings were pulled from bookstores, and the national press no longer mentioned him. Dej never quite became a non-person, but for those who knew how to read political signals, it was clear that all of this suggested that a good part of his political philosophy and his political program were likely to be on their way out in Romania. For a time, with the exception of the principles of the April Declaration, this is exactly what happened.

Even before he died, key political actors were jockeying for position in the contest as to whom would be Dej's successor. The winner was Nicolae Ceausescu. Ceausescu, a relatively young man, had met Dej while both were in prison for their political activities on behalf of the then illegal communist party. From their earliest days together in prison, Ceausescu became Dej's acolyte. After the party took control of the state, Ceausescu's fortunes rose with Dej's ascent in the party leadership. The key party leaders of the time saw Ceausescu as a cipher and a sycophant, claiming that while he was in prison with Dej he was more Dej's man-servant than his confidant and that he continued to play this role after Dej had become the dominant leader of the party.

Ceausescu was regarded by his colleagues as someone who was, and who always would be, completely loyal to whomever was leading the party. His career had been built totally on a base of absolute subservience and loyalty to Dej. Shortly after the communists took power in Romania, Dej sent Ceausescu to Moscow where he took a short course in political and military theory. When he returned from Moscow, Ceausescu was given the rank of Major General in the Romanian Army and was put in charge of army political indoctrination, even though his mastery of Marxism extended little beyond the level of slogans, which could be expected given that he had never had an opportunity to acquire a formal education in philosophy and/or political economy. As what the Russians called the "chief political commissar" of the army, Ceausescu was in a powerful political position. At the time he held this post, the government was vetting all officers and non-commissioned officers in order to purge and replace all those military men who were believed to be sympathetic to the old regime and, thus, who were seen as possible threats to the new People's Republic.

Ceausescu was born in Oltenia in southwestern Romania in 1918. At the age of eleven (1929), he left his native village and moved to Bucharest, where he began an apprenticeship as a shoemaker. Three years later (1932), at the age of fourteen, the young Nicolae joined the Romanian Workers' Party, as the communists were called at the time. This put him among the earliest members of the Romanian Workers' Party. He immediately became involved in clandestine, illegal activities, for which he seemed to have a special talent.

In 1933, at the age of 15, he was arrested for the first time on charges of inciting a strike and of distributing literature that was deemed a threat to state order. In 1934 he was again arrested for circulating a petition in support of railroad workers who were being tried in Craiova for their participation in the Grisiva railroad strike. Ceausescu was arrested twice more in 1934 and in 1935 he was exiled from Bucharest. Scheduled for confinement in Scornicesti, Ceausescu secretly returned to Bucharest, where he continued his work on behalf of the party. In 1936 he was tried in Brasov, along with six others communists for political crimes. He was sentenced to six months in prison for having tried to disrupt the trial and was given a sentence of two years on the original charges.

In 1940, now age 22, Ceausescu again was imprisoned for political organizing on behalf of the communist party and was sent to the Jilava prison, just outside of Bucharest. In November 1940 a group of Iron Guard militants attacked the prison and killed sixty-four inmates who were their political enemies. The prison guards protected Ceausescu and the other communists, allegedly because Ceausescu had successfully engaged in politically educating the prison personnel. In 1943, Ceausescu was moved to a prison camp in Tirgu Ju, where he met Dej, Chivu Stoica, and Ion Maurer, all of whom would play a critically important role in his later career. Ceausescu was released from prison in August 1944, when Romania had withdrawn from the war against the Soviet Union and its allies and had begun fighting the Germans and Hungarians, its former allies.

On leaving his military post in 1946, Nicolae Ceausescu married Elena Petrescu, the daughter of a Wallachian peasant and failed small business owner. The party appointed him regional party secretary for Oltenia, his home province. In 1948 Ceausescu was elected to the Grand National Assembly and became a candidate member of the Central Committee. A year later, he was given the position of Deputy Minister of Agriculture. One of his chief responsibilities during this period was overseeing collectivization. He was one of the more enthusiastic and brutal leaders of the drive that resulted in 80,000 peasants being arrested for resisting agricultural collectivization.

In 1961, the party reorganized its leadership structure. Dej resigned as General Secretary of the party and that office was abolished. Dej continued to be President of the Council of Ministers. In this role, he was head of the government. Party leadership was put in the hands of a four person Party Secretariat, led by Gheorghe Apostol. Its other members were Mihai Delea, Janos Fazekas, and Nicolae Ceausescu. Ceausescu, along with the Interior Minister, Alexandra Draghici, was raised to candidate member of the party's politburo (Deltant 1997).

Coming from a peasant background, Ceausescu was regarded by many in the party elite as a buffoon. This was reinforced by his utter lack of any signs of social sophistication and social grace, by his atrocious grammar, and because of his tendency to stammer when he was under stress. His colleagues in the central committee saw him as crude, vulgar, and totally lacking in intellectual sophistication. He often was the butt of Dej's and others' jokes about his lack of social skills and his diminutive physical stature.

His wife was regarded as even more crude than he. Like many Romanians of the time who had peasant origins, she had never finished high school, spoke a poor Romanian, and lacked the social skills of wives of party leaders who had "higher" social origins or who paid careful attention to "overcoming" the signs of their lowly origins. Despite her past disadvantages, Elena later would attain a Ph.D. in chemistry from the University of Bucharest under questionable circumstances (Pacepa 1987).

If one had been able conduct a survey of Romanians in 1965, including even those in the inner most circles of the communist party, few would have identified Ceausescu as the person most likely to be Dej's successor. Of course, the average Romanian was not consulted, nor was the average party member. The Central Committee made the choice, not the people, or the rank-and-file delegates to the party Congress.

Dej, during the time he ruled in Romania, created a communist state modeled closely after Soviet Bolshevism. The regime was built on the application of organized state control, repression, and, at least in its early years, terror (Deletant 1997). But this is not the whole story. By the time Dej died, Romanian communism had secured mass legitimacy among the larger part of Romanian society. It had achieved mass legitimacy for a number of reasons. The communists had improved the overall living conditions for the majority of Romanians. Romanians enjoyed better health and lower levels of mortality under the communists than they had under the monarchy. Romanians had better opportunities for education and employment than they previously had. Illiteracy was virtually eliminated in Romania. The communists did a better job than had the monarchy in protecting minority rights, especially for Jews and

Rroma. Under the communists, women's rights were expanded. The communists also improved housing conditions for the average Romanian. The communists also reduced inequality. Their policies created a far more egalitarian society than what had existed before they came to power. The communists also invested heavily in democratizing and improving Romanian cultural institutions and in making "high culture" far more accessible to the average citizen.

Dej also kept Romania from being permanently occupied by the Soviet Union. He developed a foreign policy that gave Romania considerable latitude in its actions. Dej also resisted Soviet attempts to turn Romania into an agricultural dependency of the Soviet Union and its COMECON allies. Under Dej, Romania moved toward establishing itself as a state with a more balanced economy, mixing both agriculture and industry.

The overall improvement in Romanian material and cultural life came at a cost. Under Dej, Romania continued to be ruled by a small, relatively closed, and increasingly privileged oligarchy. It is a mistake, however, to characterize the new Romanian state as "totalitarian," much as it was a mistake to apply this concept to the Soviet Union or other Central and Eastern European regimes (Cohen 2000). It also is a mistake to see the regime as not resting on a popular base. By the time Dej died, the Romanian regime had established widespread popular legitimacy, especially in the working classes, in the new intelligentsia being created under party auspices, in the military, and in the party-state bureaucracy.

It also is a mistake to interpret communism as a complete "historical rupture" with Romania's past. Communism did not move into an institutional void that it filled with its own unique institutional system. Rather, Romanian communism was built within and on the institutional remains and ruins of the social formations that preceded it. We can find clear traces of the institutional structure of the old boyar dominated feudal system, of institutional structures formed within Romania's brief period of bourgeois capitalism, and, finally, of institutions and institutional practices that took shape within and on the remains of Romania's monarchical and Legionary fascism. All of these supplied raw materials for the creation of the new communist state and society. Thus, many, if not most, of Romania's key institutions and institutional practices did not disappear into the proverbial dustbin of history. Some institutions continued into the communist period with little alteration in their basic structure and functioning. Others, such as the old class system, were submerged almost entirely into the private sphere of family, household, and intimate friendship circles, where they were hidden from public scrutiny and possible public condemnation and legal repression. Other institutions were melded into the communist system and were reworked and adapted to the new political and economic context. For example, rural village life was reorganized to accommodate new ways of maintaining membership in rural communities for people who migrated to the cities to work in new industries. The idea of what it meant to be an urban worker also changed to a significant degree. A large number of urban workers, despite being employed full time in industry, also directly engaged in agricultural production, sometimes to earn more money but, more often, to supplement their food supplies. Other institutions underwent various forms of combination and recombination in adaptation to the new regime. All of this gave the new, communist Romania a strong continuity with the past.

Given such continuity, when the communists set about attempting to construct their own institutional "world" in Romania, the Romanian people responded in a number of creative ways to adjust to and accommodate the new demands placed on them. They were not merely passive victims of an "alien" system of values, rules, behaviors, and the like. They sometimes preserved what predated communism and in other cases they reworked and adapted their pre-communist institutions to help them manage their relations with a new type of regime.

Thus, in many respects, Romania was substantially the same *society* after communism as it was before the communists came to power. There were some significant social changes, such as the entry of women into the wage labor force, sharp declines in fertility, the rapid development of an industrial work force, massive migration from rural to urban areas, and the like, but these were absorbed into prevailing institutional frameworks.

In terms of state and party policies, we also can see a number of continuities between the communists and what had come before them in Romania. For example, the communists, before they banned independent opposition political parties, manipulated elections to guarantee that they and their allied parties would prevail. Such manipulation was nothing new to Romania. Virtually every Romanian election in the 19th and 20th centuries, with the possible exception of one or two contests, was characterized by various forms of fraud, coercion, and or manipulation, as Romanian political elites engaged in "directed" democracy. It is a stretch to accuse the communists of having destroyed Romanian democracy. Democracy was very limited in pre-communist Romania and it was the king, in his royal dictatorship, the fascist Legionary State, and the Antonescu dictatorship that killed even Romania's limited, "directed" democracy.

The communists used political repression to eliminate their enemies. This, too, was not new to Romania. Political repression was no stranger to the pre-communist Romanian state. It was used against a broad variety of political actors, including both the radical right and the communists. The communists did not invent the idea of a repressive secret police in Romania. The pre-communist regime had a large and highly active secret police force that it deployed against its real and its imagined opponents. The communists, like their predecessors, also imprisoned their opponents. Previous regimes, however, had never imprisoned quite as many of their enemies as did the communists.

Previous regimes, like the communists, also limited press freedom. There were only brief periods in Romanian history, before the communists came to power, when Romania's press operated without restrictions and various forms of state imposed censorship. What passed for press freedom was obliterated in 1938 by the king's royal dictatorship. The communists continued the practice of a controlled press when they finally consolidated their rule, eventually moving from a controlled press to one totally dependent and overseen by the state.

The communists, like their predecessors in Romania, launched an effort to build a highly centralized state, marked by direct rule from above. The center, under the communists, continued the long struggle of previous Romanian regimes to gain control over local areas and to reduce their autonomy. Under the communists, the Romanian party-state functioned as a closed system. It was only weakly and indirectly influenced by popular opinion, just as had been the case in former Romanian regimes, where state policies and practices were the result of decisions made by a small number of men from the boyar and bourgeois political oligarchy that dominated the state and the society.

The communists destroyed a large part of the stock of autonomous social groups in Romanian society, either by annihilating them or by bringing them under the direct control of the state. This did represent a degree of change from what went before, however, it perhaps is not as significant a change as one might first imagine. Before the communists came to power, a good number of private groups already were dominated, if not directly controlled by the state. For example, organizations such as the urban workers' and merchants' guilds were under the direct control of the throne. The Romanian Orthodox Church also was under state control. One can find a large number of other examples to make this point. Pre-communist Romania was not marked by a dense and rich system of private associations. The Romanian bourgeoisie was too weak and too ill-formed to have produced a wide variety of such associations, as were other classes and class fractions in Romania.

All in all, the major break that communism represented with the past was in the area of the economy. But, even in this area, the break was less than might appear at first glance. In the regimes between the two world wars, the state began to play an active role in the national economy, especially when the National Liberal Party controlled the government. State intervention was directed toward building a modern industrial economy and toward "rationalizing" the rural economy. The communists, like the National Liberals, were interested in economic modernization through industrialization. However, unlike the National Liberals, the communists were not interested in using the state to build and strengthen the bourgeoisie. However, the National Liberals were not adamant defenders of private property over the course of their history. For example, the National Liberals supported the confiscation of property from the boyars, when they believed it was in the interests of the state and of their party to do so. The National Liberals did not denounce the seizure of Jewish private property during the fascist period, nor did any of the other major political parties in Romania. This attitude set a precedent for confiscating property from enemies of the state that the communists could rely on when they confiscated the property of class enemies of the state.

6

Romanian Communism:
The Ceausescu Years (1965-1989)

Between July 19th and July 24th 1965, the PMR held its Ninth Congress. The "keynote" speaker was Nicolae Ceausescu. In a rambling, often semi-coherent, address, Ceausescu provided an over view of Romania's economic situation, stressing all of the positive things the party had achieved in moving Romania toward socialism and he spoke of the need for Romania to continue moving forward in developing its industrial base. Then, in what must have been shocking to those in the audience who were "not in the know," he proceeded to outline and to denounce a broad range of abuses that had been committed by Dej, ignoring the fact that many of those at the Congress, including himself, had been complicit in some of the worst of these abuses. His speech seemed to signal that the PER was ready to abandon what was left of Stalinism and intended to continue and expand the relatively more liberal practices that Dej was institutionalizing just before his death.

In what must have been the most surprising announcement to most of the party's delegates, it was reported that Nicolae Ceausescu would be the new Secretary General of the party. It also was announced that Chivu Stoica, who had succeeded Dej as President of the State Council, would continue in his position and Ion Gheorghe Maurer would continue as Prime Minister. Maurer had held the office President of the Grand National Assembly between 1958 and 1961. When that position was redefined as President of the State Council in 1961, he had been replaced by Dej and had become Prime Minister.

By naming Stoica President of the State Council, Maurer Prime Minister, and Ceausescu party Secretary General, the PER returned to the pre-1958 situation where party leadership and state leadership were in separate hands. The party's leaders had felt that many of Dej's "abuses" of power had resulted from his holding the top positions in both the state and the party. The Ninth Congress also authorized the establishment of a commission to investigate the possibility that there had been widespread illegalities carried out by the state and party during the years Dej had been in power. Ceausescu used this commission to rid the party of many of those who opposed his election as General Secretary. Among those purged because of the findings of this commission was Alexandru Draghici, who had been a member of the Politburo from 1961 to 1974, who had headed Romania's vast security apparatus, and who evidently had worked as an agent of the Soviet intelligence services. Among other things, Draghici was dismissed for having violated norms of "socialist legality" in the arrest, interrogation, trial, and execution of Patrascanu.

The Ninth Congress also changed the name of the party back to the Romanian Communist Party (*Partidul Communist Romania* or PCR), the party's name prior to its merger with the Social Democrats in 1948, recommended the adoption of a new constitution to the Grand National Assembly, and also recommended that the Assembly change Romania's name from the "People's Republic of Romania" to the "Socialist Republic of Romania" (*Republicii Socialiste Romania*). The change in the country's name was believed necessary in order to reflect Romania's having achieved a new and higher form of socialist progress and development.

Supposedly, the party passed over the man Dej would have preferred to be his successor, Gheorge Apostol. Apostol's power base was in Romania's trade unions. The larger faction of the party opposed Apostol in the belief that he was opposed to de-Stalinization. They also believed that he would consolidate all formal power in his own hands and would reproduce Dej's one-man rule. Having been rejected for the position of General Secretary, Apostol was given the symbolic position of First Secretary of the PCR as a consolation prize in the new leadership group.

Ceausescu's appointment as Secretary General was a result of serious divisions within the party. One faction, apparently centered on Maurer, was arguing that the party needed to adopt a strategy of limited, controlled reform, which included a wider dispersal of power within the party/state system and a greater degree of openness toward the West. The Maurer wing saw in Ceausescu a young leader who had a strong base of support among the party rank-and-file, a leader who apparently was committed to reform, a leader who was committed to collective rule, and a leader, who, because of his youth and relative inexperience, could easily be controlled, if not dominated, by older, more experienced party leaders.

Another faction, centered on party hard liners, did not want to completely abandon Stalinism and wanted to rebuild Romania's increasingly spoiled relations with the Soviet Union. Included in the second faction were several leading members of the military and the security services and some of Dej's closest personal friends and former allies, such as Apostol. Many of these people believed that Dej had made a serious mistake in flirting with liberalization in the last years of his life, even if he had done so less out of a change in ideology and more out of perceived "necessity."

Between his appointment in 1965 and 1971, Ceausescu generally acted as if he was fully in the camp of those party leaders who supported the ideas of a limited "reform" communism. At the same time, by maintaining a commitment to continued industrialization, to collectivized agriculture, to central planning, and to the party principles of democratic centralism, Ceausescu was able to secure the loyalty of a large part of the party bureaucracy, who remained deeply suspicious of any attempts at reforming the party-state system from within. Yet, they remained loyal to Ceausescu, in no small part because he, Ceausescu, had put many of the party-state bureaucrats into their jobs during the time he had served as the Central Committee's Secretary for Organizations and Cadres.

By the time of the Tenth Party Congress (August 1969), the commission had finished its work and only three members of the old Dej leadership group still were in power. These were Ccausescu, Maurer, and Emil Bodnaras, a former Army General, Minister of Defense, and a longstanding member of the Politburo. Ceausescu was appointed president of the State Council, which gave him control over the state, while he also was allowed to keep his role as the party's leader. Ceausescu also used the Tenth Party Congress to put his own supporters on the party's Central Committee, giving his backers a majority in this key party group.

In trying to demonstrate that he was a new kind of leader, in the fall of 1965 Ceausescu began setting up a series of meetings across Romania with groups of intellectuals, military personnel, peasants, students, and workers. In these early meetings, Ceausescu engaged in fairly open dialogue with those in attendance. One could not help but coming away from these meetings believing that the new General Secretary was interested in hearing people's problems and in finding ways to solve them.

When Ceausescu took office as General Secretary, he benefited from the slight openings to the West that Dej already had tentatively begun. Because of Dej's willingness to partially open Romania to the West, Romania was moving into an international position that would allow it to share in the general expansion of global prosperity led by the capitalist West. Dej had begun a process wherein Romania was able to gain access to Western markets for its export of selected commodities and goods in return for hard currency. For example, Dej had begun negotiations with the Bundesrepublik to expand economic relations between the West Germans and Romania.

The Romanian economy appeared to have started to boom in the early to mid-1960s. The economic expansion was driven by sharp increases both in agricultural and industrial production and by the end of reparation payments to the Soviet Union. In the late 1960s and early 1970s, Romanian economic growth was hovering around a more than respectable 10% annual rate. As production increased, the state was able to pass on a small proportion of the surplus to workers and peasants in the form of increased personal income and increased social expenditures, while still continuing to invest very heavily in building its urban and industrial infrastructure. Incomes rose and prices, because of state subsidies and controls, remained stable. As a result of economic prosperity, things began to look very good for Romanians. The urban population, at least, could begin to think that the hard times they had to endure because of the war and then because of the need to build a modern socialist economy were, if not over, at least showing signs of coming to an end.

Under the terms of the Five Year Plan adopted by the Ninth Party Congress, Ceausescu continued to invest heavily in industrial development. Over half of national investment was directed toward this sector over the course of the plan. At this time, Romania exported a good part of its manufacturing products to other bloc countries and to the so-called "Third World." Agriculture, while receiving less investment, roughly twenty per cent, achieved substantial increases in output, allowing Romania to significantly increase its agricultural exports.

In 1967, Ceausescu introduced several economic changes that were popular with Romanian citizens. Among other things, he relaxed controls on internal migration, allowed for the formation of small private shops and businesses, and legalized the construction of privately owned buildings and housing units. By permitting carefully controlled and highly regulated petty entrepreneurial production, Ceausescu provided Romanians a way to realize some of the consumer needs the state had neglected. It also created the illusion that it might be possible for petty producers to emancipate themselves from state employment and to become "free" economic agents, within the strictures laid down by the party and the state. While it was allowed, small scale, entrepreneurship appears to have been a very successful and popular economic innovation, especially in Romanian cities. Private shops, service providers, and restaurants effectively competed for customers with their state counterparts. The private economy also moved money out of circulation in secondary, informal circuits and into the official economic sectors, where it could be tracked and taxed. Ceausescu's introduction of limited private enterprise had many parallels with Hungary's introduction of "goulash" communism, although it was not nearly as large an economic experiment as was taking place in Hungary.

Ceausescu also took steps to relax cultural controls beyond even what Dej had begun to permit in the early 1960s. While Dej had allowed greater access to Western culture and expanded the creative boundaries of artists and intellectuals, he never abandoned his commitment to "Socialist Realism" as the most appropriate aesthetic for countries trying to build communist societies. It is deserving of note that even though Dej was a devotee of "Socialist Realism," this standard never became absolutized in Romania in the same way as it did in the Soviet Union. Rather, it was more of a general guideline than an absolute demand to which art had to conform.

Under Ceausescu, Romania continued to expand its investment in cultural production. Theaters, orchestras, dance companies, opera companies, art galleries, writers, composers, poets, visual artists, and museums received heavy subsidies. Accompanying the subsidies was a relaxation of controls on the creative intelligentsia. Intellectuals and artists were given considerable freedom to express themselves in experimental forms and to address issues that at an earlier time would have gotten them into a good deal of political trouble.

During Ceausescu's early years, the Writers' Union became far more permissive in its definitions of what was appropriate to write and to publish. Under Ceausescu, direct censorship appears to have relaxed considerably. As a result, Romanian literature experienced an eruption of creativity as novelists, playwrights, and poets were free to pursue themes and plots and styles that just a few years before were to be avoided. Romanian writers also were given access to a wider range of works by Westerners and were allowed to go abroad to attend conferences and read their own work. Western and Eastern Europeans began to take notice of the high quality of what Romanian intellectuals were producing. Much the same thing took place in the visual arts. Romanian painters, sculptures, filmmakers, and the like had been as constrained as writers had been during Dej's rule. Now, under Ceausescu they too were given a great deal more freedom to create than they had been given in the immediate past. Many young artists, especially in film, began to win respect from artists and audiences throughout Europe. If the regime had maintained its cultural openness there is a good chance that Romania's reputation in the visual arts, especially film, would have been the equal of any country in Europe. In the mid- to late-1960s, Romanian filmmakers already were showing that they could rival the creativity of Polish and Czechoslovak filmmakers. After the crack down on cultural production that began in the mid-1970s, many Romanian artists, especially film directors, migrated to Western Europe and had a significant continuing effect on Western European arts. France, Germany, and Israel were the principle beneficiaries of out-migration by Romanian artists, writers, and cultural figures.

The universities also benefited from the general relaxation of cultural control. Perhaps no field gained more from the relaxation of party controls than did history. For the first time since before World War II, history no longer was written with an eye toward the historical vision of those holding power. Historians were free to define their own research agenda and were free to reach whatever conclusions were supported by their data, rather than forcing their findings to fit with prevailing ideology. Historians had not been free to do this since Karol II established his monarchical dictatorship. Like artists, Romanian historians were given more opportunity to travel abroad to international conferences and to study and lecture abroad for short periods-of-time. Historians outside the orbit of communist states were given permission to come to Romania and study, conduct research, and teach.

The social sciences also were given a great deal of freedom in the late 1960s and early 1970s. As with the historians, the party cultural bosses no longer dictated subject matter to them and they were free to employ a variety of theoretical perspectives and methodological approaches in carrying out their work. No longer was it obligatory to relate all of one's research to Marxist dogma or to twist one's research strategies to make it appear as if they embodied a "dialectical" methodology. As if all at once, Romanian social scientists began appearing at international conferences and began contributing to international journals and conference proceedings. Western social scientists, including Americans, in turn, began to receive invitations to come to Romanian universities to work with faculty, students, and researchers at the various institutes of the Romanian Academy.

For Western Europeans and others, it is hard to imagine the change in "structure of feelings" in Romania during this brief period of cultural openness (see Williams 1977 for a discussion of the concept of "structures of feelings). Romanians who passed through adolescence or entered young adulthood during this time describe the era almost as a golden age of communism, especially in Bucharest, the country's political and cultural capital. They talk about how wonderful it was to walk down the capital's broad boulevards with their open air cafes and *taverna*, to enter a shop to buy *chocolat* or a *pasteria*, to drink coffee and sample fresh baked goods, or to simply walk through the city's parks. Romanians who lived through these times also talk about how lively cultural life was. Bucharest and other Romanian cities took on an air of cultural creativity and artistic experimentation.

With all of these promising developments taking place, Romanians could delight in what they seemingly had managed to achieve under the direction of the communist party. All of the sacrifices they had endured since 1948 now appeared to be paying off. The sufferings and distortions that had been introduced into Romanian life came to be seen (wrongly of course) as temporary aberrations that, ultimately, were the fault of the backward, semi-barbaric Russians and the undue influence they had exerted over Dej and the RMP.

At the same time that these promising changes were being introduced, three repressive measures were introduced into Romanian life at Ceausescu's direction. None of these measures seemed to have been upset Ceausescu's new Western admirers or his male supporters in Romania. The first two laws dealt with marriage and fertility. They were passed in 1966. The third, the now "infamous" Law 200, dealt with homosexuality and homosexual relationships.

The laws dealing with abortion, marriage and divorce, and homosexuality are an example of the state's intention to establish greater levels of command over human bodies, human interpersonal relationships, and the forms which human intimacy could take. By restricting divorce and banning homosexuality the state and party asserted their rights to organize the human feelings of Romania's population in the party's and in the state's interests.

Ceausescu's Views on Modern Romanian Family Life

The marriage law focused on divorce, which, for all intents and purposes, was banned. This was a sharp reversal of regime family policy. After the communists came to power, as part of their general ideal of emancipating women, they passed laws that made it much easier for women to get a divorce. More liberal divorce policies were especially beneficial for women. After divorce was virtually banned in 1967, the number of divorces dropped to almost zero and continued to stay at extremely low levels for several years, recovering only very slowly.

The Romanian communists, especially Ceausescu, were motivated to limit divorces by their belief that the building of a strong socialist society required intact "socialist families." Ceausescu saw the socialist family as the basic building block of the socialist state and society. In virtually all respects, Ceausescu's vision of what constituted a strong socialist family was built on a synthesis of traditional, patriarchal, Romanian Orthodox, and peasant values. In Ceausescu's view, women's primary value was as wives, mothers, caregivers, and keepers of the domestic household.

This view of the family was outlined in a party document, *Programul Partidului Comunist de Faurire a Societatii Socialiste Multilateral Dezvoltate si Iniantare a Romaniei spre Comunism,* published in 1975. The document stated that in order for Romania to build a "multilateral developed society," the party and the state needed to strengthen the socialist family, which it defined as the "nucleus" of the socialist society. All other social institutions were dependent on the strength and unity of the socialist family.

Romania, like other communist countries following World War II, underwent a socialist variant of the demographic transition (Cole and Nydon 1990). Under the impact of the efforts to recover from World War II, rapid industrialization and urbanization, and rural collectivization, Romanian fertility declined sharply from 1966 to 1965. In 1955 the birth rate stood at 25.6 per thousand. Ten years later it was 14.6 per thousand. Similar declines also took place in other Eastern European countries, which led many of the communist states to introduce a variety of pro-natalist policies, reversing laws that had liberalized access to contraceptives, including abortions. Declines in fertility throughout Eastern and Central Europe also were brought about by improvements in the conditions for women. Especially important in improving women's conditions were declines in illiteracy. Wolchik (1985) notes that female illiteracy in the Balkans dropped significantly after the communists came to power. Fertility also declined in Romania and elsewhere in Eastern and Central Europe because of the passage of liberal contraceptive policies, including the legalization of abortion.

On assuming power, the Romanian communists liberalized laws governing contraception, especially abortion. The widespread availability of contraception, coupled with the changing economic structure of Romania, contributed to the drop in Romanian fertility rates. Romanian women's fertility was rapidly coming to approximate that of Western women. Ceausescu and state planners saw declining fertility as a threat to Romania's long term well being. Adopting a physiocratic model of development, Ceausescu and Romanian planners believed that only a larger population could lead to national growth and national strength. A larger population, among other things, would reduce future labor shortages, would increase domestic markets, would offset the negative effects of an aging population, and would supply enough men to maintain and expand the nation's military strength. Such a pronatalist philosophy ran counter to what was happening in the West, where most population experts maintained that national development was enhanced by lowering fertility, not raising it.

On June 23, 1966, in his opening address to the National Conference of Romanian Women in Bucharest, Ceausescu warned his audience that Romania faced dire threats if it did not reverse the decline in its birth rate. In the report that was issued following the conference, it was reported that the liberal abortion laws introduced under Dej in 1957 would have to be modified. The conference report was quickly followed by a presidential legal decree that banned most abortions and discouraged contraception. The abortion ban stayed in place until Ceausescu's ouster in 1989. The decree law also encouraged families to have no fewer than three children.

Claiming that the fetus is the property of the state, Ceausescu adopted increasingly draconian policies to deny women access to abortions (see Kligman 1998; Keil and Andreescu 1999). Consequently, women needing abortions had to obtain them from underground sources. Under these conditions, what had been a safe, practical, and easily obtained medical procedure became increasingly dangerous, both medically and politically. It is estimated that over 10,000 women died because of having to turn to clandestine sources for abortions from 1967 through 1989 (Stephenson et al. 1992).

Ceausescu mobilized the schools, the police, and the country's medical establishment to monitor pregnant women and to identify women who had illegal abortions. Health professionals were turned into agents of police power during this period. They were given the authority to closely scrutinize the populations' sexual behavior, especially the sexual behavior of women.

Women who were found to have had an abortion after 1966 were subject to arrest and imprisonment, as were those who had assisted them. This led to a large number of women securing illegal and unsafe abortions at considerable risk to their health, safety, and life. When an illegal abortion generated medical problems, women who sought treatment were forced to identify who had performed the illegal procedure. If they refused, they were denied access to medical care. After 1966, contraceptives, with the exception of condoms, virtually disappeared from the Romanian market. The regime refused to import contraceptives, determining that it simply was not worth the loss of hard currency to import these goods. In 1966, Romania adopted legislation that taxed childless couples. The state's idea was that the tax would be a financial incentive to marry and to have children. Romanians referred to this tax, with a good deal of irony, as a "celibacy tax."

The regime did not rely only on negative sanctions to raise fertility. It also offered a number of positive incentives. Parents received increased subsidies from the state for each child they had. Couples with children were given advantages in securing apartments and they had better access to rationed goods than did single people or childless couples. The state also expanded child-care facilities and introduced maternal leave policies into places of unemployment.

In 1967, Romania's fertility rate increased dramatically and remained high in 1968. Gradually, fertility rates began to fall, only for the regime to crack down again in 1973. The state's renewed scrutiny of women's fertility behavior, again, had short-term effects. Fertility underwent another decline, forcing the regime to put pressure on women to increase their fertility in 1983.

The regime's post-1966 fertility policy had the effect of increasing the nation's fertility rates compared to 1955-1966. However, the government found that it had to remain vigilant in enforcing its policies. Otherwise, fertility would drop. However, each time the state applied pressure on women, there was a diminishing return. The magnitude of increase in fertility was smaller after 1973 than it was after 1966 and it was smaller after 1983 than it was after 1973. In response to the decline in fertility, Ceausescu, in a 1983 address to a conference of National Women's Councils in Bucharest, told women to "breed, comrade women, it is your patriotic duty" (Aspinall 1984). The diminished effectiveness of repeated state interventions in women's fertility behavior was a result of a number of circumstances, such as: a decline in the vigor of enforcement, a decline in the effectiveness of positive incentives, and a weakening of the basic control capacities of the state, and the development of a more efficient underground market in abortion services (Keil and Andreescu 1999).

The regime's coercion in the area of fertility behavior brought the regime into increasing conflict with the population. This especially was the case with the onset, in the 1980s of the *timpuri grele* (hard times). As the economy deteriorated throughout the decade of the 1980s, the cost of each additional child was not offset by the incentives the state was offering for increased fertility. Indeed, the costs of each additional child rose exponentially, while the "rewards" increased arithmetically or decreased in value.

The regime's fertility policies, which stayed in place until after Ceausescu's fall, had continuing deleterious effects on women and children. Large numbers of women were physically damaged as a result of unsafe, unsanitary, and, sometimes, botched abortions. Other women were killed while undergoing illegal abortions. Women who had no access to illegal abortions or to effective contraceptives often had repeated births with short intervals between pregnancies, which threatened the woman's emotional and physical health. It also left poorer Romanian families with a large number of children they could not support. As a result, large numbers of children were turned over to state orphanages to be raised or were sent out to live in the streets on their own. The remnants of this generation of "surplus" children can still be seen on the streets of Bucharest and other Romanian cities where they survive by begging, petty theft, prostitution, and other criminal activities. A significant number of these children suffer from a variety of physical and emotional illnesses, including chemical dependency. In the mid-1990s, it was easy to find large groups of street children who were addicted to various inhalants and bore clear signs of serious neurological damage from such behavior.

The damages to women from the regime's fertility policy were not only physical. The fertility policy also had serious social effects on women. The emphasis on the role of women-as-mothers reinforced the strong patriarchal values of Romanian society (see Kligman 1998). Thus, the fertility policy contributed to the continuing subordination of women to men in the household and in society in general.

The Romanian pronatalist policy ran counter to the regime's initiatives to attract women into the paid labor force. Communist political theory had long maintained that exploitation of women, one consequence of which was the exclusion of women from paid work, was grounded in the private ownership of property and that when private property was eliminated so, too, would the exploitation and subordination of women be ended. While the Romanian regime had promoted women's equality since it first came to power, it was not until the 1973 Plenum of the Central Committee that the party launched a major initiative designed to bring women into the paid labor force and to increase women's presence in management positions in enterprises, the state, and the party (Fischer 1995). It was no coincidence that the party's emphasis on gender equality emerged at precisely the moment when Elena Ceausescu was pressing to expand her role in the state and the party.

However, although women were encouraged to become more politically and economically active under Ceausescu, they did not advance as far and as fast as did men. Clearly, a glass ceiling restricted their access to the highest jobs and political roles in Romania. Romanian women had a higher rate of participation in the labor force than did their counterparts in Western Europe, as was the case in most countries in Eastern and Central Europe. However, women tended to be concentrated in low wage economic sectors and within any given sector in the lowest paid jobs. Fischer (1995) notes that the campaign to put women in higher level positions was short-lived. It gradually ended after 1974, when Ceausescu's wife, Elena, secured a seat on the party's Executive Committee.

Law 200: An Attack on Romania's Gay Population

In 1968 at Ceausescu's urging, the Grand National Assembly passed Law 200 directed at homosexuals and lesbians. Law 200 stated:

> Sexual relations between persons of the same sex, if committed in public or causing public scandal, are punished with imprisonment from one to five years.
>
> The adult who is having sexual relations with a minor of the same sex shall be punished with imprisonment from 2 to 7 years and interdiction of certain rights. Sexual relations with a person of the same sex who is not able to defend itself or to express its will or if they are undertaken by means of compulsion are punished with imprisonment from 3 to 10 years and interdiction of certain rights.
>
> If the act provided...is causing great harm to physical integrity or health, the punishment shall be imprisonment from 5 to 15 years and the interdiction of certain rights and if it causes the death or suicide of the victim, the punishment shall be imprisonment from 15 to 25 years and the interdiction of certain rights.
>
> Enticing or seducing of a person in order to determine sexual relations between persons of the same sex, as well as propaganda or associating or any other acts of proselytism committed with the same purpose are punished with imprisonment from 1 to 5 years, (Source: Romanian Penal Code – Article 200, Romanian Ministry of Justice, Bucharest, Romania, 1968).

The law gave the authorities a great deal of leeway in attacking gays and lesbians. It does not define what "in public" means or what it means to cause a "public scandal." Two persons of the same gender who might be having sex in a private apartment could, and were, charged under this law if a neighbor happened to complain about the situation or suspected that same-sex relations were taking place. The law also does not define what it means to cause "great harm to physical integrity or health." This was left to the police and the courts to decide. They often did this in the most general sense imaginable.

The last paragraph of the act was the most threatening to gays and lesbians. It amounted to outlawing being gay or being a lesbian. Anyone engaging in same sex contacts or who was known to have done so or was believed to have been doing so was susceptible to charges of enticement and seduction. It also was illegal under the provisions of the last paragraph for anyone to associate with a gay or a lesbian, even if the intent of the association was not to engage in sexual conduct. The paragraph also made it a crime to let people know if one was gay. This was construed as proselytizing by the police and the courts.

Because of Law 200, gays and lesbians were driven underground, where they led clandestine sex lives. Many gay men and lesbians, in order to deflect suspicions about their sexual orientations, married and had children. A number of gay men with whom I spoke reported that they were married and carried on secret sexual relations with men. There was no other way they that they felt they could manage their sexual needs. The wives of some of these men knew about their alternative sexual practices and helped protect them from detection. Several men had said that they had married in order to give their parents grandchildren. They told me that their parents would be "heart broken" if they, the men, had not had children.

Stratified "public" sexual markets for gays and, to a lesser degree, lesbians developed in most Romanian cities. These were organized in public parks and in public toilets in universities, schools, train and bus stations, as well as in selected bars, restaurants, and underground "clubs." These "clubs" sometimes offered very specialized sexual trade. For example, in Cluj, Transylvania, one club catered to gay cross-dressers and another to men who were interested in more "rough sex." The way these markets were organized led gay men into casual and anonymous sexual contacts with a large number of men. According to informants in the gay community in Romania, these sexual markets often were stratified by the social status and ethnic background of the partici-pants. It seems to have been the case that higher status gay men moved in much different circles for sex than did men of lower status, thus limiting the chances for cross-status sexual relations. There also appears to have been segregation of sexual markets by economic sector. For example, apparently gay artists and other professionals had their own relatively closed circles from which they drew partners.

From discussions with informants, it appears that ethnic discrimination was especially pronounced for Rroma gay men. Both Hungarians and Romanians excluded Rroma from their networks of even the most casual contacts. Both Hungarian and Romanian gay men seem to have regarded sexual contact with Rroma gays as less than desirable behavior, if not a bit "kinky" sexual behavior.

Lesbians organized and used such markets far less than did men. Romanian lesbians seem to have met their sexual needs through more private networks of acquaintances and friends. They also largely used private apartments for sex, rather than relatively public places.

Romanian police were highly proactive in searching out and arresting gay men. They used sophisticated electronic equipment, including infrared telescopes and binoculars and various listening devices, to monitor parks and other areas and places where gays were believed to congregate. Informants also reported that the police used microphones hidden in apartments of men suspected of being gay to monitor the men's sexual behavior. The police also used decoys to entrap gay men. They would send young police recruits into areas where they suspected gays were making contacts with each other and arrest men who "propositioned" the police decoys.

Being arrested for homosexuality was a personal disaster, especially for Romanian men. It was a cause for great scandal and humiliation. One was publicly marked as a sexual deviant, as someone who was something less than a "real" man. Several men told me how their arrest had destroyed their family lives. Parents and siblings disowned them, spouses divorced them, children avoided any contact with them, and they lost their jobs. The breakdown in interpersonal relations and the economic problems men experienced subsequent to arrest were not the only difficulties these men experienced. Almost everyone who was arrested for being gay or for engaging in homosexual activities reported that they had been severely beaten while in police custody.

Men who were arrested under Law 200 did not always face being "outed" by the police. The easiest way to avoid being publicly stigmatized was to cooperate with the police and become one of their informants. Men blackmailed in this way were expected not only to report on other homosexuals. It was expected that they would serve as general informants, reporting on anything or anyone that might be of interest to the police. If it became known that one had been picked up by the police, one's sex life was likely to become extremely complicated. Other men could not trust someone who had been questioned by the police to not report on them.

Men who did not cooperate with the police or who, for other reasons, were sentenced to prison for homosexuality faced miserable conditions. In prison, they were subjected to general harassment and, in some cases, torture by guards. They also were subjected to sexual abuse and assault from other inmates and they could not count on the guards to protect them from such attacks. Their daily existence was one of continuing degradation and brutalization. On their release, they were subjected to continual close monitoring by the police and rejection by their families and former friends, including former sexual partners. After release from prison, it was extremely difficult for these men to find sexual partners. Few men were willing to risk arrest for being sexually involved with those who had done time for violating one or more of the provisions of Law 200.

The three laws dealing with sexuality were a clear statement of the state's belief that it had the power and the right to exercise command over human bodies, human emotions, and human sexual relations. Nothing, not even forms and outcomes of human intimacy, was to be beyond the purview of the state. The state already had established its "right" to control and to command how human bodies and time could and would be used. It had done this by compelling people to attend public events, to participate in various festivals, to attend party meetings and ideological training sessions. It extended its command further by requiring people to stand in long queues to gain access to scarce commodities and by its ability to command citizens to contribute "voluntary" patriotic labor on their days off from work.

Under Ceausescu, the regime, more so than was the case during the Dej period, not only proved itself a master over human bodies, it also demonstrated its ability to control people's time. Private time and personal time were something that the state could, and did, mobilize whenever it saw the necessity for doing so. The regime also (re)defined the Romanian calendar. It established new holidays, reduced the importance of others, and, in some cases, obliterated traditional holidays, especially those associated with the liturgical calendars of the Romanian churches.

Personal time was not the only time over which the state exercised control. It also showed itself to be master of historical time. As Verdery (1991) has noted, the Romanian communist party, in collaboration with Romanian historians, established the content of historical time. The party also established the "official" dates when various historical events were said to have taken place. The regime also established its own memorials and monuments glorifying its history and its present achievements. Statues of various communist leaders were built around the country and a huge park with a perpetual flame was established in Bucharest as a memorial to communist heroes. Many older monuments representing Romania's triumphs and historical figures were left intact, even though the state whose glory they expressed no longer existed. The monuments to the pre-communist past stood as so many mocking grave-markers for a state system that had failed the Romanian people by having been unable to achieve a modern society and a modern economy that could guarantee a reasonable level of living and, instead, had ended its existence with a descent into the obscene depravity of a murderous, anti-liberal, anti-human fascism.

Ceausescu introduced structural changed in Romania's administrative system in 1967. The reform was passed by the Grand National Assembly in 1968. It allowed Ceausescu to appoint his own loyalists as Prefects of the judets. In the same year, Ceausescu also purged most of the highest-ranking military officers and replaced them with his own people. This gave Ceausescu almost complete control over the civilian and military authorities.

Structural Changes Introduced by Ceausescu

In the late 1960s, Ceausescu also began allowing Germans to emigrate to the *Bundesrepublik* and Jews to emigrate to Israel. However, Ceausescu demanded payments from both states for each person allowed to leave Romania (Pacepa 1987, Deletant 2000b). This was a reversal of an earlier party decision, which had rejected Israel's offer of cash payments to Romania for allowing Jews to emigrate. The cost varied with the age and education levels of the person immigrating. Almost 500,000 Germans and Jews left Romania between 1967 and 1989 under the provisions of the "ransom" policy. Germany paid the costs of ransoming its ethnic counterparts by granting Romania economic credits (Deletant 2000b), while Israel made cash payments (Pacepa 1987).

Under Ceausescu, Romania began to experience an increase in goods available for domestic consumption. The national automobile company began producing its *Dacia*. This was a functional automobile based on a former model of the French *Renault*. Automobile sales jumped from 9000 in 1965 to approximately 45,000 in 1975 (Deletant 2000b). Production also significantly increased for goods such as washing machines, refrigerators, and television sets (Deletant 2000b). Perhaps most importantly, the regime devoted considerable resources for housing. Between 1966-1970, 648,000 apartments and houses were built and this increased to 751,000 between 1971-1975. Romanians were allowed to own their apartments and houses, which was not always the case in other countries in the region. Because of this massive construction effort, the skylines of most Romanian cities underwent significant alteration. In Bucharest, there were miles after miles of newly built apartment houses, all looking alike and all constructed of the same inexpensive, sometimes defective, pre-fabricated materials. When the regime went into economic crisis in the 1980s, many of these buildings were in dire need of repair, but there was no money available for building maintenance. As a result, the quality of the housing stock rapidly began to deteriorate.

In this context of prosperity and cultural openness, party membership soared. In the early 1970s, around ten per cent of the adult population were party members. This was one of the highest proportions of national membership in any communist state. Party membership became respectable among large segments of the population who formerly had shunned formal affiliation with the party. The party really appeared to be doing something for the nation and membership became more honorable. As membership grew, the composition of the party changed. It no longer was so overwhelmingly proletarian, rather it was increasingly composed of people from a variety of class backgrounds. Membership growth was particularly strong among academicians, engineers, professors, teachers, and other parts of the intelligentsia. The party was becoming a model organization, where people from various classes and strata could come together to collaborate and to work toward solving the country's problems by engaging in non-antagonistic personal and class relationships.

However, once Ceausescu made his ideological (re)turn to Stalinism in the 1970s the composition of the party changed once again. Starr (1988: 196) presents data showing that between 1970 and 1980 workers increased their representation in the party from 43.4% to 55.1%, while the proportion of intellectuals decreased from 24.4% to 24.0%. The decrease in the proportion of the party who were intellectuals does not so much reflect a drop in the number of intellectuals who were in the party as it does the fact that worker membership grew dramatically, indicating a clear shift in Ceausescu's priorities in building the party membership. As the proportion of workers in the party increased, so did worker representation among party activists. In 1988, workers, foremen, and technicians made up almost 80% of the members of the party political apparatus, indicating the strength of the working class in the party's internal life and the generally weak position of intellectuals and technocrats in the governance of the party, itself.

The first major crisis Ceausescu faced occurred in 1968, when the Warsaw Pact forces invaded Czechoslovakia and overthrew its reform communist government. In 1968, Czechoslovakia also was liberalizing its regime. It was moving toward the creation of a communism "with a human face," as the expression went at the time. Alexander Dubcek, who had replaced the old Stalinist and neo-Stalinists in Czechoslovakia, was moving ahead on a number of fronts to open up his society. Change in Czechoslovakia was far more broad, rapid, and extensive than what was taking place in Romania. From all appearances, to those looking at what was happening from the outside, the party seemed about to lose control of the situation in Czechoslovakia by summer, 1968. The communist leadership in the German Democratic Republic (GDR), Hungary and Poland were especially disturbed by what was happening in Czechoslovakia. They all had their own individual dissidents and oppositional social movements with whom they had to contend from time to time and they were not about to let happen in their countries what was happening in Czechoslovakia. In August 1968 Warsaw Pact troops, under the Soviet Union's leadership, invaded Czechoslovakia. Dubcek and his colleagues were forced out of office and arrested. Unlike the Hungarian leadership in 1956, they avoided execution. Following the invasion, the Soviet Union promulgated the "Breshnev Doctrine," which gave the Soviet Union the right to intervene, with military force, if necessary, to protect socialism in any country where it was established.

Romania did not participate in the invasion of Czechoslovakia. Citing the principles of the April Declaration, Ceausescu delivered a moving speech from a balcony overlooking the National Square on

August 21, 1968. The speech, which was broadcast live over the national radio, denounced the Soviets and their allies for having invaded a sovereign state. During this crisis, the Romanian people were very nervous. They were afraid that Ceausescu had made a serious mistake and that Romania would be the next country to be invaded. As a precaution, the population began to stockpile food and other goods they thought they might need to survive in the event of a Soviet invasion. The Soviet Union did not invade Romania. Neither the Soviets nor their allies saw what was happening in Romania to be a threat to them, not least of all because the party still was in firm control of the state, despite the reforms that had taken place.

Denunciation of the invasion of Czechoslovakia was not Ceausescu's only deviation from Warsaw Pact foreign policy. For example, he recognized the German *Bundesrepublik*, making Romania the first communist state to do so. The Soviet Union and the GDR leadership were furious with him for having done this. However, there really was little that the USSR and the GDR could do to prevent him from recognizing the Bonn government.

He also refused to break diplomatic relations with Israel following its victory in the Six-Day War. All of the other Warsaw Pact countries had supported the Arabs and had broken ties with Israel because of the war. Ceausescu maintained a continuing interest in the Middle East throughout his time in office. Among other things, he continually tried to broker a peace between Israel and the Palestine Liberation Organization. He also established training bases for various Arab guerrilla forces

Ceausescu also met with Tito in Bucharest in 1966. This was the first of a number of meetings between the two communists who were resisting Soviet dominance. Ceausescu saw an alliance with Tito's Yugoslavia as essential to maintaining Romania's freedom of movement within the Warsaw Pact and on the world stage.

Given his increasingly independent foreign policy, Ceausescu became the darling of the West. He was every Western leader's "favorite" communist. He was young, was willing to defy the Soviets, and appeared to enjoy popular support in his own country. The leaders of the three most powerful Western countries, England, France, and the United States, visited Bucharest to pay their respects and to express their gratitude for what he was doing. The visits of these leaders further enhanced Ceausescu's popularity with large segments of the Romanian population. In return, he was invited to visit France, England, and the United States. Because of his willingness to assert Romanian independence from the Soviet Union, Romania was invited to become a member of the World Bank and the International Monetary Fund in 1972. It also was given "Most Favored Nation" (MFN) trading status by the United States in 1975. World Bank and IMF membership gave Romania considerable access to foreign credits and loans, which Romania used to help accelerate its industrialization and to help develop its consumer sectors in the national economy.

The U.S. Congress, in passing the 1974 Trade Act, had given the president the authority to extend MFN status to communist states for a period up to eighteen months. The Jackson-Vanik Amendment to this act required prohibited the extension of MFN status to any country that restricted its citizens' right to migrate. However, the president was given the authority to waive this restriction if he thought it would help promote emigration. The initial waiver could be granted for eighteen months and renewed for another twelve months. In 1975, President Ford granted MFN status to Romania. Ceausescu had given Ford assurances that he would "contribute to the solution of humanitarian problems on the basis of mutual confidence and good will" (Kirk and Raceanu 1994). As a result of acquiring MFN status, Romanian exports to the United States shot up dramatically. Ceausescu, in 1988, under increasing pressure from the U.S. Congress for human rights violation, renounced Romania's MFN status (Deletant 199b). This had serious adverse affects on Romania's trade relations with the U.S. at a time when it least could afford this.

Having lost its MFN status and having begun to experience political difficulties with other Western states, primarily because of its abysmal human rights record, Romania began taking steps to reincorporate itself into the COMECON trade network, reversing what had been taking place in the 1960s, 1970s, and early 1980s. Michael Shafir (1985: 49) presents data showing that, between 1960 and 1980, Romanian trade with COMECON countries decreased from 66.8% of all of its trade relations to 33.7%. At the same time, trade with advanced capitalist economies grew from 22.1% to 32.8%. Even more dramatic was Romania's increase in trade with developing countries, which increased from 4.6% in 1960 to 25.2% in 1980. This, in part, reflected Romania's having found a niche for exporting some of its manufactured products to countries whose quality standards were not quite so high as those of the Western markets. Romania's economic reintegration with COMECON is shown in the following data. Romanian trade with COMECON countries rose from 33.7% in 1980 to 57% in 1985. Trade with the Soviet Union grew from 17% in 1982 to 33% in 1986 (Georgescu 1988: 77). Even though Romania "returned" to the communist economic fold in the 1980s, it continued to maintain a maverick foreign and domestic policy within the trading block.

At the beginning of the 1970s, it appeared as if Ceausescu's domestic policies, except in the areas of family, fertility, and sexuality, and his policies in foreign affairs had secured an enhanced legitimacy for Romania's communist party both within the country and internationally. While there were some who continued to see communism as a foreign ideology alien to Romania's religious, political, social, and cultural traditions, increasingly this was becoming a minority position. Under Ceausescu's leadership, Romania appeared to have moved far down the road of building a humanistic communism, something that had failed in Hungary and Czechoslovakia. In 1971 Ceausescu further enhanced his standing with Western powers, by helping the Nixon administration establish contacts with the People's Republic of China, which led to Nixon's famous visit to China in 1972 and the consequent reestablishment of diplomatic relations between the US and the PRC. Ceausescu went to Cairo in 1972 and met with Egyptian President Anwar Sadat and Yasser Arafat, the leader of the Palestine Liberation Organization, in an attempt to mediate the dispute between the Arabs and the Israelis. In recognition of his efforts at attempting to bring peace to the Middle East, Israel's Prime Minister, Golda Meir went to Bucharest in May 1972 for discussions and consultation with Ceausescu, serving to increase his stature as a world statesman.

Ceausescu Begins a (Re)turn to Stalinization of the Romanian Communist Party

In 1971, a sharp reversal in Ceausescu's internal policies began. Ceausescu started moving to the hard left. Many analysts (see Brucan 1993 for an example) have interpreted this change in policy as if Ceausescu, during a visit to North Korea and China, had a "Damascus Road" experience, converting from a reformer to a hard liner in the process of seeing what he, Ceausescu, took to be a "purer" form of communism. There, however, are other ways of looking at what happened. For example, it could be that Ceausescu never had been a committed reformer, but postured as one in order to gain support from Maurer and his wing of the party in his drive to become party leader. There is some support for this idea in the fact that during his years working under Dej, there were no signs that Ceausescu had identified with or independently advocated reform in the party or the state. In fact, he appears to have been the direct opposite of a reformer. The positions he took and supported generally were highly Stalinist. If this is the case, then one might ask what was the basis of his reformist stance during the early period of his rule.

To answer this, one first must look at the internal dynamics within the party during the later stages of Dej's life. When Dej died, few inside or outside of the party could have expected that Ceausescu would emerge as the party leader. Ceausescu owned his position in the top echelon of the party leadership entirely to Dej. Within the inner circle of leaders, Ceausescu was a marginal figure. He does not appear to have belonged to any personal or social networks within the leading group. Because of his marginality, it was very likely that he would be demoted under a new leadership. Most of those surrounding Dej were committed Stalinists, just as Dej had been. The only place Ceausescu could turn for support in his bid to become Secretary General was to the moderate re-formers, i.e. to people like Maurer and his allies. Because the hard liners, themselves, were internally divided and could not coalesce behind any one candidate, Ceausescu was able to secure the votes he needed to take control of the party. He then used reform as a way to keep the support of those who had backed him and to remove those who had opposed him from key leadership positions. Once he had eliminated his Stalinist opponents, he was then able to turn on the reformers and begin moving against them in the early 1970s. In attacking the reformers, he returned to his old Stalinist positions, which he shared with almost all of those who he had elevated to leadership positions in the party and the state and with those few hard liners remaining who had been allies of Dej.

As Ceausescu replaced the old party leadership with his own people, Maurer and other reformers became increasingly isolated in the party and the state. By 1971 Ceausescu had enough support to turn on the reformers and to take the party back to a Stalinist political path, which he seemingly had left behind when he had assumed his leadership position.

Following his trip to the Far East, Ceausescu proclaimed his "Theses of July 1971". The Theses outlined a program of substantial change in Romanian cultural policies, with a view toward shaping the development of "socialist consciousness" in Romania. Among other things, the *Theses* indicated that there would be increased control over cultural production in Romania. Control would be exercised through the newly created Council on Socialist Culture and Education. In Ceausescu's view, cultural production had lost contact with Romania's proletariat and peasantry. As a remedy, he proposed that all publishing houses and theaters would be required to have representatives of workers' and peasants' organizations on their boards of directors. It was the task of the worker and peasant representatives to insure that writers, actors, theater directors, and theater producers created work that furthered the interests of workers and peasants. This virtually guaranteed that Romanian artists and writers would have little room to experiment with avant-garde techniques and/or themes. Ceausescu did not believe that any form of aesthetic experimentation was compatible with a society that was trying to implement scientific socialism as its main organizing principle. He had held these views even before his trip to the Far East. Ceausescu's aesthetic appreciation always had run toward popular, peasant culture. He enjoyed watching peasant dances and listening to *musica taranesc* (peasant music) and he relished folk tales, believing they expressed the essence of the Romanian soul. These were the types of artistic expression he had seen when he was an adolescent and his cultural tastes never developed beyond this point.

The Theses also demanded that Romanian cultural institutions produce more work with a national content and fewer works that reflected Western values and norms. He denounced "cosmopolitanism," in a not so subtle attack on Romania's Jews in the communist party, and demanded that more Romanian cultural works needed to become more ideologically pure by stressing, among other things, the values of "socialist patriotism. In order to accomplish the ideological purification Ceausescu wanted, his Theses indicated that the party needed to exert greater control over Romania's mass media and over its schools and universities where, during the period of liberalization, intellectuals had begun to abandon or ignore communist ideology. As a result of the publication of the Theses, intellectuals and artists lost many of the privileges they had begun to enjoy following the Ninth Party Congress. Ceausescu's proclamation led to intensified ideological education in all Romanian institutions. Party committees in enterprises across the country were required to increase their efforts to improve the ideological understandings of white-collar workers, the proletariat, and the peasantry.

Ideological work also was increased in the universities. Universities were especially hard hit by the return to Stalinist controls on intellectual activity. Whole faculties were closed. In 1975, for example, Ceausescu decided that sociology was a bourgeois science that was not needed in a socialist country. He ordered all faculties of sociology to close and universities to cease awarding sociology degrees. Students enrolled in the faculties of sociology, especially at the University of Bucharest, which had the country's strongest Sociology faculty, protested. The students wrote to Ceausescu asking him to reconsider his decision. He dismissed their request and sociology would not be reestablished until after 1989. Because of the shut down of the discipline, Romania lost an entire generation of sociologists. He also closed down Romania's nursing programs, seeing no need for this profession in Romania's health care system, and psychology programs.

Ceausescu also sharply reduced Romanian intellectuals' opportunities for having contacts with Western counterparts. Fewer Romanians were allowed to attend international conferences and to study abroad. The right to travel in the West was put under the control of Elena Ceausescu. She used her power to dole out permission to visit the West to her allies and supporters among Romania's intelligentsia. Romanian intellectuals came to be believe that the only way one could get permission to study abroad or attend Western conferences was if one was a member of one of the Romanian security forces or if one had agreed to be an informer for one or more of them. Ceausescu also cut back on the number of Western intellectuals who were allowed to teach and conduct research in Romania. The number of U.S. scholars teaching or studying in Romania on Fulbright and/or IREX (International Research Exchange) grants fell sharply.

Romanian intellectuals also began experiencing difficulties in obtaining access to Western scholarly publications. As a result, they had a hard time keeping abreast with the most current research in their fields and disciplines. This had a serious negative effect on the advancement of Romanian science, which began to lag behind the West in many areas of potential national importance, e.g. the information sciences, agronomy, nuclear power and technology, etc.

Venerable cultural and intellectual institutions that had been fairly autonomous, even under Dej, came under increasing state and party control. For example, the Romanian Academy was forced to abolish many of its research institutes and, in what many Academy members regarded as the ultimate humiliation, was forced to grant Elena Ceausescu membership in the Academy in recognition of her hundreds of publications as a chemist. In fact, Elena knew little or nothing about chemistry. Her doctorate was awarded on political grounds. All of her publications were based on the research of others and written by others, who then felt compelled to list her as first author. She had been appointed as head of the Institute of Chemistry in 1965, which she ruled over with an iron hand. She expected to be listed as an author on every publication. Everyone in the Academy knew the questionable character of her degree and of her limited involvement in the research for which she took credit. However, no one felt that they could refuse her membership in the Academy, even though her admission cheapened the life-time achievements of those who had earned membership in recognition of the sustained superior quality of their intellectual work. The Academy, however, managed to resist pressures to elect Elena as its president. This resistance came at great political cost to the Academy, as Elena created a number of new research centers under her direct control, resulting in reduced funding to the Academy's standing institutes.

Ceausescu's (re)turn to a Stalinist path, in part, also can be understood in the light of what was happening in the world-wide communist movement. In Hungary and, later, in Czechoslovakia, the communist party bureaucracies had lost control over their own intellectuals. In each case, the intellectuals, working with the support of key sectors of the party-state bureaucracy, had seized the political initiative in Hungary and Czechoslovakia. The intellectuals had played a leading role in challenging their parties' monopoly positions and their countries' positions in the European communist inter-state system. They had succeeded in mobilizing significant parts of the population, including workers and peasants, to oppose the regime and to take direct action to overthrow the old leadership. In both Hungary and Czechoslovakia, this had led to disastrous consequences. The local leadership was overthrown by Soviet led forces, new leaders were installed, and Soviet forces turned into an occupying power. Ceausescu was not about to let this happen in Romania. Ceausescu knew that the Soviets had not appreciated Dej's hesitant steps toward gaining some degree of independence for Romania and were even more upset with Ceausescu's international policies. Ceausescu knew quite well, given the experiences of Hungary and Czechoslovakia, that his new found friends in the West would do little to save him, his government, or Romania if the Soviets lost confidence in him and in his ability to maintain communism and, as a result, decided to invade Romania. To the West, Romania had less strategic and political value than either Hungary or Czechoslovakia and if they had stood aside and allowed the Soviets to lead invasions of these two countries, the West would not think twice about leaving Romania stand on its own to face Soviet forces should the Soviets decide to invade. To stave off a potential invasion, Ceausescu had to demonstrate to the Soviet Union and to other Warsaw Pact states that, despite his independent foreign policy, he was maintaining strong internal party control and that he was not allowing dissidents to emerge and threaten communist rule.

In order to demonstrate that the party still was the master in Romania, Ceausescu believed that he had to crack down on intellectuals who, from his and other hard liner's point of view, were becoming increasingly independent and increasingly outspoken about their needs to be even more free of state control in Romania. While Romania's intellectuals, by no means, were the strong force that their counterparts once had been in Hungary's and Czechoslovakia's communist parties, and while Romanian intellectuals were largely isolated from other groups in the society, Ceausescu seemed to believe that they constituted a potential threat to his rule, if for no other reason than that they could raise Soviet anxieties about the strength of the party's leading role in Romania.

Ceausescu, like Dej, had a deep distrust and dislike for intellectuals, many of whom had "suspect" class origins. He also believed that Romania's intellectuals had very little respect for him as a thinker and as a leader and he was correct in believing this. In private, the Romanian intelligentsia mocked his poor grammar and his ponderous writing that was filled with nothing but banal sloganeering. Intellectuals, especially those who had boyar or bourgeois origins, also ridiculed his and other members of the elite's social pretensions. As was the case elsewhere in communist Europe, Romania's communist leadership had taken to emulating what they understood to have been the lifestyles of the old boyar estate and the bourgeoisie. Not having been "to the manner born," as the saying goes, the communist leaders' attempts to behave in the manner of the old elites often came off looking forced and ridiculous, if not a bit absurd.

Knowing how Romania's intellectuals felt about him and fearing their potential for disrupting the party and, possibly, bringing Soviet intervention in Romania's affairs, Ceausescu made war against the intelligentsia as part of his general strategy of enhancing ideological rigor among the entire Romanian population. Following his trip to North Korea and to the People's Republic of China, Ceausescu came away having learned several important lessons. First, he learned that his version of national communism would succeed only if the party and the population were completely united behind him. Second, he learned that to gain such support no dissent in the population or the party could be tolerated. Third, as a result of his trip, he came to believe that support for the leading role of the communist party and its leadership required considerable ideological work among the general population. He understood that he needed Romania's workers and peasants as allies against other factions within the party, especially against the intellectuals. Fourth, he came away from North Korea and China believing that only a charismatic leader was capable of building a true communist society. Finally, he came to believe that reform communism was not the way to advance the building of a communist society. Communism would advance only if it returned to its Leninist-Stalinist foundational principles, modified by the successful leadership techniques and organizational practices introduced by Chairmen Mao and Kim. It was this body of lessons that were the basis for the 1971 April Theses.

It was not only the intellectuals who were forced to reduce their contacts with Westerners. Any Romanian who had even the most casual unauthorized contacts with a Westerner was expected to immediately report this to the police and to tell the police what the nature of the contact was. In addition, no Romanian was allowed to have a foreigner as a guest in his/her house or apartment. When foreigners came to Romania, they were given hotel rooms that were bugged by the security services and were assigned guides and/or translators that were expected to report on what the visitor wanted to see, who they met, and what they spoke about to the security police. The Tourist Ministry was dominated by the *Securitate*. If a foreign visitor did not need a guide or a translator, security personnel were assigned to follow the visitor wherever he or she went and to monitor all of their contacts with Romanians. Often the security personnel would do nothing to disguise their presence, adding to the anxiety of Westerners in the country and any Romanians with whom they dealt.

The few Westerners who stayed in Romania for any length of time and were living in housing supplied by the state could be sure that their phones and their apartments were wired by the security services. Their travels around Romania and their contacts with ordinary Romanians were constantly monitored. Under these conditions, it was as easy for a Westerner to become as paranoid about their every-day experiences as were a large number of Romanians.

Cultural repression in Romania went to extremes seen in few other European countries. Romanians were denied access to duplicating equipment such as photocopying machines or ditto copying machines. Typewriters had to be licensed when purchased and the owner had to supply a copy of the typeface to the police.

She and He's Dual Personality Cults

The 1970s also saw the emergence of a "personality cult" in Romania that rivaled that of Mao and Kim Il-Sung. Romanian court poets and intellectuals of all stripes turned out hundreds of pieces of work praising the leader, who came to be called, among other things, "the genius of the Carpathians." A whole industry developed within Romanian intellectual circles that had no other purpose than to extol Ceausescu's accomplishments and the glory to which he was raising the Romanian nation. Later, this industry would add the glorification of Elena to their tasks.

In recognition of his "genius," Ceausescu's writings on a vast range of topics became required reading in Romania's schools and universities and party circles. Among other things, all university theses were required to cite Ceausescu's work in building the theoretical foundations and in describing the conclusions of their work. Ceausescu's status as the country's leading intellectual was ratified when the Romanian Academy gave him an honorary membership. They simply could not refuse to keep an "intellectual giant," whom "everyone" recognized as the "genius of the Carpathians," out of the Academy. The "personality cult" was extended to include Ceausescu's immediate family. Elena not only was glorified as one of the world's leading researchers in advanced chemical theory and processes, but, she, too, was increasingly recognized as a political theoretician and political practitioner of great eminence. In recognition of her political value to the country, in 1974 she was appointed to the party's central committee. In January 1989, Elena was put in charge of the Central Committee's organization that oversaw party organizations and cadre. This is the same position that her husband had held earlier. Like her husband, she used this position to seed the party with people loyal to her and her husband and to purge those she suspected of disloyalty. According to Pacepa (1987), under Elena appointments and dismissals to party and state posts became increasingly arbitrary and whimsical and often had little to do with competence, expertise, or experience.

Beginning in 1979, by virtue of her chairmanship of the National Council of Science and Technology, Elena also was an ex officio member of the President's cabinet. In 1980 Elena was made First Deputy Prime Minister, thus holding a position of national power second only to that of her husband. She held these roles until the end of 1989.

She and *He* shared the accolades of the nation for as long as they held power. Their birthdays became important national holidays, especially *His*. On January 26, 1988, Nicolae Ceausescu's seventieth birthday, the central committee sent him a message which stated, in part, that this day was "...a most significant moment for the entire Romanian nation." He, the "greatest son of the Romanian nation," received awards on his seventieth birthday from across Eastern and Central Europe. Moscow awarded him with the Order of Lenin, from Prague he received the Order of the White Lion, and from the German Democratic Republic he was given the Order of Karl Marx. From his own country, Nicolae, for the fourth time, was named a "Hero of the Socialist Republic of Romania." Only he and Elena had been given this award. All other Romanian Communists had to be satisfied with lesser awards, such as "Hero of Socialist Labor" or "Hero of the New Agricultural Revolution." There was no end to the songs of praise that Romania's party and its court poets heaped on *Him* and *Her*. One could not but help to think of the great honor and blessing it was to have lived while *He* ruled and to have had the opportunity to serve *Him* and *His* state and to have been glorified by his wisdom and beneficence.

When Ceausescu assumed the role of President of the Socialist Republic of Romania, an office specially created for him in 1974, he became the country's *Conducator,* an appellation last associated with General Ion Antonescu. In Romanian, the term connotes something more than "leader of the state." The term implies a more exalted status, along the lines of Il *Duce,* or *El Caudillo,* or *Der Fuhrer.* A *Conducator* coordinates and commands the entire nation as its Supreme Leader. The personal views and policy positions of a *Conducator* are the final word for the nation, they are beyond dispute and are changed only when the *Conducator,* himself, decides they need to be changed. Because the *Conducator* understands the nation, as a whole, and can act for the nation, as a whole, uniting and transcending particular and special interests into an organic whole, the *Conducator* expresses the general will of the people and translates this into state policy and state action.

The couple had three children and they groomed their younger son, Nicu, to follow them as Romania's leader. Their oldest child was Valentin, who was born in 1949. The Ceausecus, as part of the party's campaign to find homes for war orphans and other children, had adopted him. Valentin was trained as a physicist and worked in a research enterprise, where he appears to have been well thought of by his colleagues. Valentin had little interest in or inclination toward a political career. Their middle child, Zoia, was born in 1950. She was trained as a mathematician. Like Valentin she showed no interest in politics. Nicu, the youngest child, was born in 1951. He was groomed from an early age to be his father's successor. His first government position was as Minister of Youth, a job he held from 1972 to 1982. During this time, he acquired a substantial reputation for his skills at drinking, partying, and womanizing. His favorite haunt was his private club in Bucharest. Following his appointment as Youth Minister, Nicu became party secretary in Sibiu, where he remained until 1989. While serving as party secretary in Sibiu he is credited with having saved the historic architecture of the city's center from the ravages of his father's plan to redesign the city.

After the 1989 uprising, all three children were arrested. Valentin and Zoia were released from custody after a short time with no charges filed against them. Valentin's colleagues at his research institute testified on his behalf, claiming that he had never abused his family ties to gain personal benefits nor had he engaged in activities that threatened his fellow researchers. If anything, his colleagues argued, Valentin had used his position to protect many of his colleagues from some of the more odious forms of bureaucratic harassment that were regular features of Romanian workplaces.

Nicu, on the other hand, was sentenced to prison for twenty years. He was released for health reasons in 1993 and died shortly afterwards. Nicu had been imprisoned for political crimes that allegedly were committed while he was party secretary in Sibiu. Among other things, Nicu was convicted of having sanctioned the use of force against those involved in the 1989 uprising in Sibiu, causing the deaths of at least ninety people. During his tenure in various party positions, Nicu had regularly demeaned, intimidated, and harassed a number of party officials (Pacepa 1987), some of whom ended up in key leadership positions under the National Salvation Front. Because of his past behavior, no one stepped forward to defend him once his family had fallen from power. He died at the age of 43. He was a broken and isolated man. His body was wracked with the devastating effects of an advanced case of cirrhosis of the liver. All of his old friends, who had found his company so valuable when his parents ruled Romania, had ignored him in his final days.

Nicu was not the only Ceausescu who went into the family business. It has been estimated that perhaps as many as fifty members of Nicolae's or Elena's family held influential positions in the state and/or party (Rupnik 1989). Nicolae Ceausescu appointed five of his brothers to important posts in the government. Nicolae Andruta Ceausescu was appointed a General in the *Securitate* in 1975 and was in charge of the agency's training center for its officers. Illie Ceausescu was a General in the Romanian Army and was appointed Deputy Minister of Defense in 1980. Ioan Ceausescu was Deputy Chairman of the state's national planning committee. Florea Ceausescu served as editor of the party newspaper, the Spark and Marin Ceausescu held a diplomatic assignment in Vienna. Elena's brother served as deputy chair of the Romanian trade unions (see Brucan 1993).

The Emergence of "Feudal Communism"

In 1971, Ceausescu had launched changes in party personnel practices. He required that party officials regularly be rotated through their assignments and he prohibited officials from being appointed in their home areas. Ceausescu, given his years in party personnel work, recognized that one of the principle problems that the communists had been unable to overcome was Romanian localism. The communists, like the regimes that preceded them, never had been able to gain complete control over local affairs. Romania always had been a state built on top of a system of well entrenched local networks. Many of the local networks that had existed when the communists came to power were immediately incorporated into the new regime, others, especially those that had close tied to the Legionnaires and the Iron Guard, were reworked and refurbished before being incorporated into the new system. In other areas, new networks emerged and took control over local areas. Ceausescu had hoped that by rotating party and state officials he would keep them from becoming incorporated into the local networks and that, as a result, they would be more willing and able to impose policies and programs from the center. In fact, this did not happen. Instead of weakening the power of localized networks, the rotation scheme actually strengthened them. An official moving from one place to another would extend the national interconnections of the network from whence he had come.

In many respects, the Romanian communist state, when it was moving into the economic crisis that began in the late 1970s, took on the characteristics of a "feudal communism" (Verdery 1991). Local power, that once had been based on land holdings and that now was based on office in the party and state and the resources over which these offices gave one control, was strengthened. Office holders, just as had landlords, used their positions to tie together family, extended kin networks, and relations of personal and collective dependency and fealty on the local level, just as had been the case in Romania's old regimes that had been dominated by the boyars and then by the cultural bourgeoisie.

Local party and state officials constructed personal fiefdoms. These personal fiefdoms engaged in ever more frantic accumulation as the regime slid into economic crisis. While they might vary with local conditions and circumstances, generally the local networks included the party secretary and the centrally appointed prefect, enterprise managers and directors of state farms and agricultural cooperatives, persons who held key positions in the state's ideological apparati, local militia commanders, ranking officers of military bases (if there were any in the area), *Securitate* commanders, and leaders of other key state institutions.

These networks functioned as patronage systems, using elaborate systems of clientage to extend their influence and power through the use of the old Romanian practice of *protectia*. This is a social practice wherein persons use informal relations with office holders to achieve their goals. The local networks had the power to bend and shape dictates emanating from the center. The central government never could be sure that the policies it ordered would be put in place in the way the center expected them to be. Verdery (1996) provides an interesting discussion of one aspect of this when she writes about current policies dealing with post-Communist privatization of agricultural land. Verdery (1996) notes that during the period of land collectivization in the early years of communist rule, peasants managed to "hide" significant amounts of land from the central authorities. Presumably, this land was held in escrow and/or was used for illegal private agricultural production. The hiding of this land could not have taken place without, at a minimum, the passive collusion of local agricultural officials. In most cases, the collusion was not passive but, rather, local officials cooperated in hiding the land in return for various returns, such as a share of the private production in cash or through in-kind tributes.

Seen in this way, we can understand that the local power networks functioned as something more than systems of mutual protection and mutual career assistance. They also were engines of illegal economic accumulation and distribution. In this respect, they had a partially parasitic relationship with the state economy. In many regions, the networks engaged in diverting resources and commodities from the state sector and appropriated them for their own use.

As has always been the case in Romania, office holders used their positions to trade official and unofficial favors for cash, goods, immediate reciprocal favors, and future considerations from those who benefited from official favors. This long had been standard practice in Romania. During the Ottoman period, government officials, up to and including ruling princes, obtained and held their offices through a system of reciprocal tribute. As the economy deteriorated, the "feudalization" of Romanian communism grew. Local networks retained increasingly larger portions of the surpluses they generated for their own use. They diverted a large part of the surpluses they held back into the secondary economy, changing the fundamental nature of the party. It increasingly became a corrupt system that enriched local leaders at the expense of the national interest. This transformation took place exactly at a time when the center was in ever greater need for local surpluses in order to finance its own activities and its activities on behalf of overall national goals. The policy of rotating local party and state leaders did little to end the corruption. Leaders and party activists who were transferred found it easy to slip into the informal networks in their new locations. In the face of these challenges from local networks, Ceausescu took drastic steps to increase the flow of resources to the center, including increasing the regime's reliance on coercion and repression to weaken local centers of power. However, the use of these techniques led to diminishing returns. Each increment in coercion yielded fewer results and proportionately smaller returns to the center.

The Rural Systematization Program

In 1974, Ceausescu launched his rural "systematization" program. When the communists came to power in Romania, they took over a wrecked economy that, among other things, was marked by high levels of uneven development. There were sharp differences in the levels of economic development between regions, between cities and countryside within and across regions, and within cities. During the Dej period, tentative steps were taken to rectify these economic imbalances. The most important of these steps was the attempt to diversify, by region, the country's industrial base. The regime began locating industrial enterprises in formerly rural, agrarian areas.

Ceausescu and his planners began realizing that if they were to develop a regionally balanced economy much more would have to be done in terms of decentralizing industrial development and in limiting growth in selected urban areas by closing certain cities, especially Bucharest, to in-migration. But, they also recognized that even this would not be sufficient to redress significant differences in the levels of economic and social development between cities and the countryside. In Ceausescu's view, what was needed was a countrywide program of systematization that completely would eliminate, the economic, social, and cultural developmental imbalances between the city and the countryside that were seen to be the remnants of pre-communist Romanian regimes. As we have seen, previous regimes, as far back as the *Regulations* period, had tried to rationalize the countryside's ecological order. But all such efforts had failed in the face of peasant resistance.

An attempt to "systematize" the countryside was entirely consistent with Marxist theory. In his 1853 essay on English rule in India, which had led to the destruction of traditional village life, Marx had written:

> Now, sickening as it must be to human feeling to witness those myriads of industrious patriarchal and inoffensive social organizations dissolved…, thrown into a sea of woes, and their individual members, losing at the same time their ancient form of civilization and their hereditary means of subsistence, we must not forget that these idyllic village communities, inoffensive as they might appear, had always been the solid foundation of Oriental despotism, that they restrained the human mind within the smallest possible compass, making it the unresisting tool of superstition, enslaving it beneath the traditional rules, depriving it of all grandeur and historical energies.(Marx quoted in Fernbach 1974).

Ceausescu defined rural systematization as essential to his goal of insuring that Romania would be characterized by "multilateral development." Multilateral development was an agenda that sought to iron out differences in levels of development across the country in order to eliminate gross disparities in the living conditions and cultural characteristics of rural and urban areas. In implementing the systematization program, several thousand rural villages were destroyed. Residents of the villages that were eliminated were moved into high rise apartment towers that were intended to have many of the same amenities as their urban counterparts. This massive program of rural reconstruction was harshly criticized by international opponents of the regime. Critics claimed that systematization was destroying historically valuable villages and that, in part, it was disproportionately affecting minority communities, especially rural Magyar villages. Neither of these charges was completely true. Many of the rural villages that were destroyed amounted to little more than a rural slum (a rural *mahala*). Their housing stocks were substandard, their sanitation infrastructures were in poor condition, roads often were unpaved, and they had only minimum telecommunications connections with the outside world. Their historical value was more in their longevity than in anything else. Also, there is little evidence that systematization was an excessive burden on the Magyar community, despite the claims that they were disproportionately burdened by the policy.

According to Deletant (1999b), Romanian Magyars believed that the multilateral development initiative, in general, and the systematization program, in particular, were meant to weaken them politically and socially. Magyar leaders saw multilateral development as nothing more than a means for the regime to diminish their demographic dominance in a number of the judets in which Magyars constituted a majority of the population. To the Magyars, this was but one further instance of Romania's suppression of their cultural and linguistic rights within the Romanian state.

The Magyars had grounds for being suspicious of Ceausescu's intentions in implementing systematization in their regions of Romania. Ceausescu was far from being a friend of Romania's Magyar minority. He had eliminated the Magyar's Autonomous District and he had taken a number of other actions which could not but help raise Magyar anxieties about his rule. In 1977, a Magyar *samzidat* literature appeared in some regions of Transylvania and several individuals publicly criticized the Romanian state for having stripped the Magyar minority of a right to be educated in their own language. Magyars also feared that overall state social, economic, and demographic policies being applied to areas with high Magyar concentrations were designed to lead to Magyar assimilation into Romanian society and their consequent elimination as a distinct corporate group in Romania.

Systematization, however, was more than merely a strategy to further multilateral development. It was an attempt to reconstruct the very essence of peasant life. Romanian villages were a spatial instantiation of layer upon layer of historical experiences, social practices, cultural patterns, and ways if life, including how people ought to properly relate to one another within the village and with people outside of it.

When the communists took power, they encountered a rural world of multiple sub-regions and provinces, each of which had its own distinctive character as well as its universal characteristics that it shared with other rural areas in Romania. Among the distinctive aspects of the local areas were different ways of relating to the center and to other rural areas, the way peasants related to the land and to those who owned or who controlled the land on which they worked, lived, and died. The village and the land surrounding it had embedded within them people's concepts of the natural and supernatural world and the very "structures of feelings" that helped define who they were and how they related to others and to the world around them (Williams 1997). All of this had undergone change as feudalism was dismantled, as land reform proceeded, and later as rural collectivization had proceeded. Rural space also was changed by the decentralization of industry under the communists, the commuting of rural workers to towns and cities to take industrial jobs, and by the mechanization of agriculture.

However, despite all of these changes, rural space, and all it entailed (see Harvey 1996, among others, for a detailed discussion of the social meaning of space) still lacked a significant degree of "socialist" standardization. It was Ceausescu's aim to bring this standardization about through his rural systematization program. If he had accomplished his goals, rural space would have been entirely changed in terms of its meaning and significance for rural residents. Residents of Romania's countryside would have become even greater strangers in a land already made strange enough.

The Construction of the "Casa Poporului"

In 1984, with the economy in shambles, Ceausescu began building his *Ansambul Bulevardul Victoria Socialismuli* (The Boulevard of the Victory of Socialism Complex). According to the plan for the complex, it was to be centered on the gigantic *Casa Poporului* (House of the People). The House of the People eventually came to stand at 84 meters high and has a surface area of 265,000 square meters, making it the second largest office building in the world. It is exceeded in size only by the Pentagon in Washington, D.C. The building was designed to serve as the center for most presidential functions and "agencies" and would have matching offices for Nicolae and Elena Ceausescu. The House of the People was to be surrounded by a House of Science and Technology, the Ministry of the Interior, a National Library, and the State Archives. It was intended to face a giant monument to the spirit of socialism that was to be constructed at the other end of the Boulevard. Exterior construction on The House of the People was substantially completed when the regime fell. *Casa Poporului* not only was a gargantuan building, it also was incredibly ornate. Among other things, it had hundreds of crystal chandeliers in each of its long corridors on the main floor, hand crafted Romanian marble was used throughout the building, and hand made draperies and carpets, which had been made through the "voluntary" labor of Romanian Orthodox nuns, were throughout the building.

The construction of the *Casa Poporului* created significant disloca-tions in the Romanian economy, when the country least could afford it. Not only were the materials used in the building extremely expensive, but construction required huge quantities of labor and scarce energy. Costs for the building were driven upward by Ceausescu's continuing modification of the building's design and construction materials. Work-ers, especially skilled craft workers, were brought in from all across Romania to contribute to its construction. Military construction teams supplemented civilian work teams assigned to the project.

To build this complex, Ceausescu ordered the destruction of some of Bucharest's oldest neighborhoods in the center of the city. The entire Uranus district and much of the Rahova and Antrim districts were wiped out. These districts contained lovely old villas that once had housed a good part of Romania's bourgeoisie. They also had a number of historic churches and monasteries. The areas also had high concentrations of what was left of Bucharest's Jewish population.

At the same time Ceausescu was redesigning central Bucharest, the same thing was happening in other Romanian cities. Ceausescu ordered that the centers of many of Romania's oldest cities be ripped out and re-designed in more "modern" and more "socialist" forms. One of the few places this did not take place was in Sibiu, where Nicu Ceausescu was the party secretary.

These efforts were just but one more instance of the communists' attempt to redefine the meaning and the significance of space, especially urban public space in Romania. The communists, like those who had ruled Romanian before them, constructed their own monuments to their history and leading figures. Until the *Casa Poporului,* the other major monuments to the glories of communism in Bucharest had been built by Dej. One was the government publishing house, which was a gift of Stalin to Romania. Another was the monument to "Communist Heroes" built in *Parcul Tineretului* (Youth Park) in southern Bucharest. There also was a giant statue of Lenin in Bucharest. It later was featured in the film *Ulysses Gaze.* Communists also renamed streets and entire towns after their leading historical figures and events. For example, Dej had re-named Brasov, for a time, after the Soviet leader Josef Stalin. All of this showed the communists' command over the Romanian landscape. It demonstrated their ability to alter the memorial landscape of the country and, hence, how people viewed the past and the new communist regime in the light of Romania's history.

Ceausescu also began work on completing the Danube Canal, which had been begun under Dej, at Stalin's behest. This also was a wasteful and expensive project that used civilian and military labor. The canal never generated the traffic that was necessary to make it economically worthwhile. Romanians joked that the only craft that ever used it was Ceausescu's personal yacht.

The Regime Draws to a Close

The dawn of the 1980s marked the beginning of the *timpuri grele* (hard times). For all practical purposes, it was during the hard times that communism, as an ideology and political practice, ended in Romania. When the communists took power, we know that there were only a handful of party members. The party members were the regime's inner-core, its true believers, if you will. There were tens of thousands of others who supported the party and its agenda but, because of state repression, they had not joined the party before the Second World War ended. This second group supported the party not because they feared the Red Army, which was occupying the country, or because they were opportunists. Rather, like party members, they believed that communism was the best means by which Romania could recover from the war and modernize itself. This group believed in the values and the ideology of the communist movement and they saw the former regimes and the political oligarchies that controlled them as having failed Romania and its population. Then there were the opportunists and careerists who had no commitment to the party's ideology or its political, economic, and social goals. They had joined the party in order to further their own, personal interests. During the hard times, ideology dissolved and faith in communism collapsed for virtually everyone.

The communist regime was transformed into a system of personal accumulation for the nomenklatura. Party activists and state officials acted as if they recognized that they were living in a world that was on the verge of extinction and that they had to get as much from it as they could before it collapsed around them and left them with nothing, not even a career. There was a certain degree of feverishness to the accumulation behavior of the party-state elites. They ruthlessly pillaged the economy and ostentatiously displayed their plunder to each other. It must have driven the average Romanian to despair when they walked through beautiful neighborhoods like Cotroceni and Primavera to think of what the lives of the privileged were like, compared to that of the average citizen.

If Pacepa (1987) is to be believed, no one in Romania exceeded the Ceausescus in living lives of luxury. While they received no salaries for their positions, they had palaces and presidential homes all over the country. They, and their children, also had a fleet of Western limousines at their disposal, large wardrobes, and Elena had a large collection of furs, gold jewelry, and diamonds. Elena was an inveterate collector. She especially relished collecting domestic and foreign academic awards (Pacepa 1987).

Part of Romania's growing economic problems was tied to its increasing national debt. Ceausescu continued and, indeed, accelerated Romania's drive to industrialize. In order to expand industrial development and, at the same time, increase goods available to consumers, Ceausescu borrowed heavily from the West. In 1977, Romania had only a modest foreign debt of roughly $3.6 billion. By 1981, foreign debt had risen to $10.2 billion. A good deal of the borrowed funds was squandered on developing inefficient industries and industries for which there was little demand for their products on international markets.

Ceausescu, resenting and fearing the effects of IMF demands, committed Romania to paying off the foreign debt by 1990. Ceausescu did not want to see happen in Romania what he believed had happened in Poland. The IMF and the World Bank had put Poland's economy in virtual receivership in return for rescheduling its considerable international debt. As the 1970s drew to a close, Romania was buffeted by a number of economic changes that did not auger well for its future.

In order to reduce its foreign debt, Romania had to reduce its imports, while, at the same time increasing its exports. While Ceausescu dramatically increased exports, especially to the "Third World," imports and domestic consumption was cut dramatically. While trade with the Third World helped advance some of Romania's international political objectives and enabled the regime to import some cheap goods for domestic consumption through various barter arrangements, it did little to solve Romania's debt crisis. To liquidate the debt, Romania needed hard currency and that meant it had to increase its trade with the West.

At first, the regime relied primarily in agricultural exports to pay its external debt. The increase in agricultural exports put a heavy burden on the rural work force. There were not a sufficient number of agricultural workers to meet the regime's continually increasing output norms. In order to help resolve the problems of rural labor shortages, the state commandeered military units and rural and urban students to help bring in the harvests. Every fall, university students from across the country would perform their "Patriotic Labor" by going into rural areas to work during the harvest. Peasants found it hilarious to see these urban sophisticates stumble through their daily work on the state farms and collectives, totally ignorant of what it was they were supposed to be doing and how it was to be done.

As more and more agricultural products entered the export stream, basic food commodities were rationed on internal markets. By early 1982, the regime introduced a system of rationing in some of the provincial towns and cities. By 1983, rationing was imposed on the entire country, with the exception of Bucharest. Between 1983 and 1989 rations were continually reduced. People in the cities took to growing their own food in gardens they planted on their apartment terraces or in their back yards. Gardens also were planted in public parks and in the public spaces around apartment buildings. Some urban residents also kept small animals like chickens and ducks and, more rarely pigs as food sources. Romanians living in the cities, who had relatives in the countryside, often worked out arrangements to exchange labor for food. On weekends, it was common to see urban families returning to the cities with their cars filled with various foodstuffs, which they pickled and canned to take them through the winters.

In 1983, Ceausescu also introduced a new wage policy for Romanian workers. Fixed wages were abolished in all sectors of the economy and workers' incomes became more closely tied to meeting the state's output plans for an enterprise. Before this, workers were guaranteed 80% of their nominal wage, with another 20% being given based on productivity. The new policy led to massive wage reductions across the economy. In 1988, partly in response to strikes and work stoppages that were occurring with ever greater frequency throughout Romania, Ceausescu gave the lowest wage workers sizeable pay increases. At the same time, he gave the highly paid workers a smaller increase. This narrowed the income gap among workers, while alienating those at the top of Romania's pay scales. Ceausescu also refused to reduce the work week. Most Romanians, as late as 1985, were working 48 hours per week at their jobs and many were expected to contribute additional "voluntary patriotic labor" to state and/or party projects and organizations. Food shortages led to considerable profiteering in informal markets largely dominated and controlled by state bureaucrats in the various ministries charged with administering food production and distribution. Large amounts of food were diverted out of normal distribution channels and put on the black market, where huge profits were to be made. People who had access to these markets and the money to spend in them seldom had to suffer the consequences of the national food shortages.

As the food situation deteriorated, the regime charged scientists with developing a minimum national diet. Scientists calculated how many calories each individual, depending on age, job, and the like, needed for minimum sustenance. They then attempted to calibrate how much food needed to be distributed on domestic markets to meet these standards. The rest was exported.

Countless hours of people's time were commandeered by the state because of people having to stand in long lines to get basic foods and other consumer goods. People often got in whatever line they happened to pass by, because a line signaled that something of possible value was available. Even if they did not need what was being sold, consumers often would buy the commodity because they might need it in the future or they might be able to find someone who did need it and they could sell it or barter it for something they might need. A job market developed in relation to the queues. Pensioners, in return for a small fee, would stand in lines as surrogates for people who did not have the time to waste waiting for goods.

Food was not the only commodity that was in short supply. So was energy. Gasoline was rationed. There were periods when private automobiles were banned on certain days of the week. When fuel was available, it was common to see lines of trucks and cars that stretched out over several kilometers waiting to get gasoline. As with food, large amounts of gasoline were diverted to the informal economy, where it was sold at premium prices to those who had access to these markets. The restrictions on private automobile usage put heavy demands on public transportation. Heavy demand, along with deferred maintenance of equipment, led to continual breakdowns in the public transit systems in urban areas, which included a modern subway system in Bucharest. Following Ceausescu's decision to increase industrial production, primarily for export purposes, major energy shortages erupted. This led to continuing disruptions in production, as factories were not given enough energy to run their machines at efficient levels. In some cases, factories had to suspend operations because they could not get the energy to run any operations. When there was no power, workers would show up at their enterprises and stand around all day with nothing to do, while being paid their full salary. An engineer at a major plant in Bucharest told me that once when Ceausescu had visited their factory he was told about how energy shortages were limiting production. Ceausescu's response was to run their turbines at a slower pace. The engineers knew this was ridiculous. Nonetheless, the enterprise manager followed the advice of the "genius of the Carpathians," only to have the enterprise's turbines destroyed, which forced the plant to close a good part of its operations.

In the face of the energy shortages, the state limited the hours during which electricity was available to apartments and houses, as well as to state enterprises. Even when power was available, families were limited as to the number and wattage of light bulbs they could have for their homes. The state also significantly reduced its allocations of heat and hot water to apartments. Days would go by when apartments would have no heat or hot water or would have heat and hot water for only an hour or two.

It is hard for Westerns to imagine what it was like to wake up on a winter morning in a freezing apartment and to have no hot water for bathing and dressing. To go to work in an office or factory with no heat and thus be forced to work while dressed in a hat, coat, and gloves. At the end of the day, people would leave work and walk through snow covered sidewalks to a market, hoping against hope that there might be something worth while to buy. They then would return to their apartments and walk up several stories (sometimes as many as twelve) only to enter dark and freezing rooms that sometimes did not have enough gas to cook a meal. To do this, day after day, through the long Romanian winters, was nothing short of maddening. Daily life was nothing more than a continuing exercise in misery and degradation. These routines of daily misery reinforced in everyone's mind how the dream that once was socialism had turned into a seemingly unending nightmare of deprivation that was inscribed into the reality if everyday life in Romania. I talked with several people about what these experiences were like. A younger woman who was an engineering faculty member at the Polytechnic University in Bucharest told how every September she would start crying uncontrollably and that she would remain disconsolate until spring arrived. This woman's feelings were common among Romanians.

With production being directed at exports, there was a serious decline in the quality of almost all consumer goods. Clothing apparel, shoes, and other goods produced for domestic consumption were poorly made from inferior materials. Manea (1992) describes this situation as one characterized by "substitution." He claims that "...in areas like food and clothing: genuine products were gradually replaced by substitutes, not just of incomparably lower quality but often simply by fakes" (Manea 1992: 66). Like food, significant amounts of apparel and shoes destined for foreign markets were diverted into the underground economy, where they commanded high prices, especially if they carried the labels of the foreign merchandisers for which they had been made.

Shortages of almost everything not only led to the diversion of Romanian products into clandestine markets, but it also led to considerable smuggling of Western goods into Romania. In some cases, the long distance smuggling from the West was organized and carried out by *Securitate* operatives stationed in Western countries. Smuggling, on a smaller scale, was carried out by virtually everyone whose occupation gave them access to the West, e.g. merchant mariners, airline flight personnel, railroad workers, long distance truckers, and the like. Smuggling also was common among longshoremen in Romania's ports on the Danube and the Black Sea.

Romania's health care system rapidly deteriorated, wiping out many of the gains the regime had made in health care during the period of Dej's rule. Medicines, especially imported pharmaceuticals, disappeared from retail and hospital pharmacies. Hospitals and other treatment facilities were understaffed and the staffs they did have were underpaid. If a person was admitted to a hospital, the only way the person could insure that s/he received proper medical attention was by giving appropriate gratuities to hospital personnel. Personnel treated those who gave gifts of appreciation much better than those who would not or could not present them with a gratuity. In order to insure that patients in medical facilities were adequately fed, friends and relatives provided them with food. The average patient could not depend on the facility to provide them with sufficient food. Overall, then, in the 1980s, on almost all indicators, the health situation deteriorated sharply in Romania. This was a reversal of what the communists had achieved during their first decades in power when improvements in health were a major national priority.

Hospitals and medical facilities were poorly maintained, as was most of their equipment. They also were affected by Romania's chronic energy shortages. Advanced diagnostic equipment was rare in medical facilities outside of Romania's larger cities. Even in the larger cities, this equipment often was not available because it had broken down and was in need of expensive repairs, which the medical facilities could not afford. A Romanian physician, trying to find some solace in the situation, told me, not without a hint of irony, that the lack of modern diagnostic equipment worked to physicians' advantage in that it forced them to develop their own skills, rather than relying on technology to make diagnoses. He went on to say that as a result Romanian physicians became much better diagnosticians than their Western counterparts.

Ceausescu incorporated Romanian health care personnel into the state's system of social control and repression. We already noted how physicians and other health workers were compelled to police women's reproductive behavior. But, in addition to this, health care personnel, especially those working in psychiatry and related fields, also were used to repress dissidents. Following the same practices as other communist regimes, the Romanian State often forcibly admitted dissidents to psychiatric facilities where they were subjected to treatments that amounted to nothing short of medical torture.

During this time of hardship, petty property crime increased, especially in Romania's cities. People who owned cars often would take their windshield wipers, external mirrors, and sometimes their vehicles' battery into their apartments in the evenings. People reinforced locks on their doors and windows. Persons also were more cautious when in the streets to avoid being victims of pickpockets or other types of thieves.

Economic shortages also resulted in illicit production. A worker in a sewing machine factory told me how he regularly smuggled parts out of his factory, assembled sewing machines in his apartment, and then sold them in the underground economy. Another worker reported how he did the same at a bicycle factory. Other workers, who had illegal private jobs as plumbers, electricians, or the like, regularly removed materials from the enterprises where they worked to support their private economic activity.

Workers also engaged in illegal barter behavior. I met dozens of workers who told me how they would get private medical and dental care for themselves and their families, clothing, food, and private tutoring for their children by performing work off the books for physicians, dentists, clerks and managers of retail enterprises, and teachers. Workers also bartered among themselves, exchanging their skills for services.

All of this illicit economic activity came to be regarded as normal economic behavior during the *timpuri grele*. Virtually everyone in the country was involved in illicit economic behavior as a producer, distributor, or consumer, thus undermining respect for the law and for the regime. One had to become an economic criminal, simply in order to survive.

In order to curb such behavior, the state policed consumer behavior. Investigative officers had the authority to enter a person's apartment and demand an explanation of how any given item found had been acquired. If one could not explain where it had come from and how it had come into one's possession, the item could be confiscated and the person could be charged with a criminal offense, subjecting him/her to a heavy fine and/or possible imprisonment.

While the general citizenry went through this daily torment, the nomenklatura were largely protected from the harshness of everyday existence. Their homes did not lack heat, hot water, or energy for cooking. Their children went to the best schools and they had the resources to afford tutors for their children. The nomenklatura had access to private stores selling food and imported Western clothing. They also had access to the underground economy, in which many of them participated not only as consumers, but also as distributors. This, of course, was illegal and those involved in it were subject to severe penalties if caught and prosecuted, but few ever were.

While all this was going on, Ceausescu seemed to be oblivious to the real suffering Romanians were being forced to endure. He refused to pay attention to the consequences of his policies for the everyday life of Romania's populations and his key aides did everything in their power to mask the truth from him. For example, when his motorcade moved through Bucharest all of the streets that intersected with his route were closed to keep potential protesters out of his sight. If his route was scheduled to pass a market, his aides were sure to have it well stocked with food and to have the window displays in all the stores filled with merchandise. As he drove by and looked at these Potemkin displays, he could convince himself that nothing was wrong and that Romania, indeed, was a land of abundance – such was his capacity for self-deception, if not his dementia.

During the hard times, political repression increased considerably. The *Securitate* ratcheted up its scrutiny of the population. According to Manea (1992), there was one police officer for every Romanian. The police developed a wide network of informants, some of whom were volunteers and others who were coerced into participating in domestic espionage. Even members of the clergy were recruited as informants for the state. This included the current Primate of the Romanian Orthodox Church, who has publicly acknowledged that he had been a *Securitate* informant. Manea (1992) estimates that there were fifteen informants for every police officer. This extensive system of surveillance that the regime put in place was meant to establish and maintain a high degree of order and social discipline. The high levels of social control seemingly had no particular purpose other than to instill fear in the population.

The belief that informants and security agents were everywhere created high levels of fear and paranoia in the Romanian population. Everyone believed that they were vulnerable to the scrutiny of the security police. To some extent, the threat was exaggerated. The *Securitate* never had the resources, the skills, or the personnel to monitor the entire society to the degree that people suspected it did, although Ceausescu certainly aspired to give the agency such capabilities (Pacepa 1987). The *Securitate*, however, did have the capacity to closely monitor the nomenklatura, especially its highest-ranking members, who it watched very closely. The homes, cars, and offices of even the most senior officials were wired for sound. According to Pacepa (1987), these tapes regularly were turned over to Elena Ceausescu for her review after she was put in charge of party organizations and cadres. *He* and *She* were the only two people in the country who could be sure that they were not vulnerable to domestic espionage. Everyone else always was a potential, if not actual, target. The *Securitate* also had the capacity to monitor a large part of the general population through its use of voluntary and involuntary informants.

The development of a state increasingly based on the security forces is an interesting example of the complex interplay between a leader and the social structure he helped create and stamped with his own personal characteristics. Ceausescu, by all reports, was a person with marked personal insecurities, suspicions that bordered on paranoia, feelings of insecurity, and a general megalomania. Ceausescu governed through manipulation, deceit, and blackmail. He was a man motivated by his strong hates and he had a powerful sadistic streak when dealing with his underlings and his perceived enemies.

As the overall economic situation in Romania deteriorated and as Romania's relations with the West began to break down in the face of Western criticism of the regime's human rights abuses, Ceausescu's worst personality characteristics were amplified. He became more personally isolated and cut off from the party's leadership and its base, increasingly relying only on Elena for advice. This was unfortunate because she shared many of his worst personality characteristics and she, too, was isolated from the party leadership and its base.

Both of the Ceausescus projected their own worst characteristics on others, believing that what they personally felt and what motivated them likewise organized the internal lives and the behavior of everyone around them. This belief was a self-fulfilling prophecy because the only one's who were able to survive in Romania's internal circles of power were those who, in fact, resembled the Ceausescus in most important respects. Thus, the Ceausescus came to be surrounded by people who confirmed their hypotheses about what motivated Romania's leading party cadres.

The Ceausescus came to be surrounded by party and state leaders who were guided more by self-interest than by the interests of the country. These leaders spied on each other, as the Ceausescus spied on them. They often withheld critical information from one another. They lied to each other. They debased their subordinates as the Ceausescus debased and degraded them. They continually undermined each other to weaken each others position in the eyes of Him and Her and in the eyes of other colleagues. As a result of all of this, the regime's leadership became more and more conspiratorial. In such an atmosphere, only the most ruthless and distorted personalities could survive and flourish.

In this way, the personalities of the Ceausescus penetrated and were imprinted on the social organization of the party and the state. The personalities of the Ceausescus attracted and maintained a tier of top leaders who were like polished mirrors of themselves. In turn, these leaders gathered around themselves subordinates who were mirror images of themselves, and so on. In this way paranoia became institutionalized in the party and was projected outward onto the society.

The overall effect of real and/or imagined *Securitate* activities was the erosion of social trust within Romanian society. Not only did people lose trust in Romania's institutions, trust in interpersonal relations also was diminished significantly. Romanians also lost trust of space. They lived in fear that their workplaces, homes, and public spaces were being monitored. In many cases, they were right. For example, cameras regularly recorded who was going in and out of the American Embassy's library and cultural center. People who visited "too often" could expect to be questioned about their reasons for having gone there. A pre-1989 dissident labor activist in Timisoara told me how he would never engage in confidential conversations, even on park benches or around light poles, because he feared that they contained microphones. Romanians developed a system of hand signals to indicate to one another that they suspected their conversation might be monitored. They also learned to speak to each other using various codes in the hope that they could avoid coming to the attention of various police forces.

In this type of atmosphere, no Romanian ever knew, with any degree of certainty, how much confidence one could place in colleagues, friends, or, even, family members. Most informers were ordinary people who lived ordinary lives. There was nothing special about them, so there was no way to identify who they might be. This fact contributed to the development of a culture of doubt and suspicion in interpersonal relationships among Romanians. This lack of generalized trust in interpersonal relations rendered social life unpredictable and unstable, resulting in the "...continuing emotional and behavioral anguish..." about which Giddens (1990: 97) has written.

Despite this generalized paranoia, with its consequent emotional and behavioral anguish, Romanians were not completely socially disabled. They proved themselves capable of constructing extensive, overlapping interpersonal social networks in order to survive during the times of generalized scarcity. Romanians, literally, could not have survived without being members of networks of mutual assistance. These networks were based on highly personalized relationships. Participants had deep and extensive knowledge about each other. It was this personal knowledge that enabled members of any given network to trust each other.

Internal paranoia and repression, however, were not the only glue that held the regime together as the economy spiraled downward and as living conditions seriously deteriorated.

Unlike in other Communist states, there were few examples of sustained, organized, popular resistance in Romania. Romania never saw the emergence of organized oppositional groups such as the Workers' Defense Committee (KDR), Solidarnosz (Solidarity), and other such organizations in Poland. Nor did Romania see the development of such self-organizing opposition groups such as Hungary's *Duna Kor* (the Danube Circle); *Dialogus* (Dialogue), a peace movement; and the Democratic Forum. Romania also failed to develop movements such as Czechoslovakia's Charter 77, a human rights group established to monitor the state's compliance with the Helsinki Accords or the closely allied group Committee for the Defense of the Unjustly Prosecuted (VONS) that was organized to protect those who had signed the Charter. Romania also had no parallel to Vlacel Havel's *Obkanske Forum* (Civic Forum) that was organized in 1989. When open, explicit dissent was expressed by Romanians, it invariably was a statement of a single individual who no longer could or would repress his/her conscience any longer. While many intellectuals might agree with the person speaking out, this agreement, too, was a quiet, individuated response, rather than a public or collective response.

Despite the presence of a powerful repressive apparatus that was built around the *Securitate* (the secret police), however, open dissent and sometimes protest could not be contained completely. For example, in 1977 over 30,000 miners in the coalfields of the Jiu Valley went on strike. The strike was an economic action, rather than a political revolt. The miners were protesting about their wages and pension system. They also expressed complaints over working and safety conditions. The strike ended only after Ceausescu went to the region to negotiate directly with the strike leaders and pledged to take care of their grievances. The regime either failed to implement most of the agreements or quickly broke those that it had put in place.

In 1979 an organization called the "Free Union of the Romanian Working People" was formed. With less than 2000 members in branches in the Banat, Transylvania and Wallachia, it offered a platform demanding the rights of workers to organize into free unions. The movement was short lived. Its leaders were arrested and imprisoned and the movement collapsed. This was one of the rare instances of public dissent, aside from work disturbances, in Ceausescu's Romania.

In 1983, in Maramuras, which is located in Northern Transylvania, workers in a number of metal mines struck. They were protesting wage cuts resulting from a new national law on wages. Armed security forces entered the region and broke the strike.

Both Magyar and Romanian workers, in an unusual display of unity, struck at two enterprises in Cluj and one in Turda in November 1986. The workers produced Hungarian and Romanian language leaflets in which they demanded "meat and bread" and "milk for our children" (Delatant 1999a: 134). The party, rather than using force to crush the workers, moved food into the region and agreed to meet with the workers to discuss their problems and grievances. Several workers who were charged with leading the strike eventually were forced to relocate to other parts of the country.

Protests erupted in Iasi, the old capital of Moldavia, in February 1987. About 1000 workers marched on the party headquarters in protest of wage cuts and the meager food supplies available in the city. Again, the regime agreed to meet the workers demands and did not use coercion to force the protesters to return to work. However, about 150 workers who were believed to have been the prime movers behind the march eventually lost their jobs (Delatant 1999a: 134).

The day following the workers' march, students from Iasi's University and from its Polytechnic University engaged in a large scale demonstration. The students were protesting their poor living conditions in their universities' housing facilities. The regime agreed to redress their grievances and the students returned to their classes without experiencing retribution from the authorities.

In 1987 there was a major strike in Brasov, an ancient city in Transylvania. Before World War II, Brasov was named Kronstadt. After the war, for a brief period, Dej changed its name to *Stalin*. Kronstadt was part of what German settlers in this region called "*Siebenburgen*" (Seven Cities). The strike began on November 15, as workers marched to vote.

The strike originated among workers at the Red Flag Truck Factory. This was more than an economic action or a protest over wage cuts, the lack of heat, or limited food supplies. It had a political component. As workers marched, they chanted anti-regime slogans and sang the old song *Desteapta-te romane* (Romanians Awake!), which had served as the anthem of the 1848 revolutionaries. As the march moved toward the center of the old city, they were joined by workers from the Brasov Tractor Factory and by a large number of the town's general citizenry. When they reached the center of the city, the marchers were confronted by a police patrol. At that point, several workers reportedly began throwing stone at the police patrol car. Workers seized the car, overturned it, and set it on fire. The crowd then marched on city hall, which held the offices of the county Communist Party. The workers broke into the building and sacked it. They smashed windows and threw documents and files into the plaza (*piata*). The paper became the raw material for a bon fire they later ignited. The situation had deteriorated to a point where the local militia could not control it. The army was mobilized and surrounded the central city and sealed it off. Security forces (mainly *Securitate*) were dispatched to the city and regained control of it. Reportedly over 200 workers were arrested and tortured (Brucan 1993). On December 3, the official press agency, *Agerpres*, reported on a meeting held at the *Red Flag* factory. The agency announced that: "The arbitrary and abusive cuts of wages were criticized, the manager was fired, and both the political leaders of the city and the organizers of the riot will be tried" (quoted in Brucan 1993: 137). According to Deletant (1999b), there were a number of other labor actions around this time, but they never received publicity in the West or in Romania.

Active dissent apparently was not confined to workers. In the 1970s, according to Silviu Brucan (1993), there had been a discussion between two generals about the need for action to overthrow Ceausescu. The "conspirators," General Ion Ionita, Minister of Defense, and General Ion Gheorge, the army chief of staff, decided not to proceed when they concluded that there would not be sufficient popular support for their actions or sufficient support from other institutional forces in the state. In 1983, another attempt to overthrow Ceausescu was discussed among a number of military leaders. By this time, General Ionita had retired. Nonetheless, he approached two former colleagues with whom he had once studied in Moscow, Generals Nicolae Militaru and Stefan Costyal.

Militaru and Costyal approached Ion Iliescu as a possible replacement for Ceausescu. Iliescu was the son of a communist activist from the period when the party was illegal. Illiescu declined to participate in a coup at this time.

Iliescu, in 1944, when he was 14, joined the Union of Communist Youth. After the party came to power, Iliescu was sent to Moscow to study, where he met and became a friend of Mikhail Gorbachev. He returned to Romania and became a high-ranking bureaucrat in the Union of Communist Youth. In 1965, Iliescu received an appointment as a candidate member of the party's Central Committee, where he ran party agitation and propaganda departments. With Ceausescu in power, Iliescu was promoted to full membership of the Central Committee and became a candidate member of the party's Political Committee. In 1971, Illiescu had gone with the Ceausescus on their tour of China and North Korea. When Iliescu returned from Asia, he was demoted. He was given a number of party posts in provincial areas. He had held the position of party secretary in Timisoara and in Iasi. In 1984, he was appointed to a position directing a technical publishing enterprise. At the time of the revolt of 1989, Iliescu directed the Ministry of Waters. During the time of his "exile" from inner party circles, Illiescu maintained contacts with key political actors and military officials with whom he had come in contact during the period when he was part of the party's inner circles. Even though he had been demoted, Iliescu maintained his reputation as a dedicated communist and an effective administrator who was loyal to his friends and political allies.

Dissent also was present in the party. Throughout Ceausescu's regime, there had been cases of individual party members protesting regime policy. Usually this would result in demotion and loss of privilege. None of these protests ever seemed to gain public and widespread support within the party. However, in March 1989 a group of six leading party members wrote an open letter to Ceausescu complaining about the devastating effects his policies were having on the party and on the country. The signers of the letter, which came to be known as the *Letter of Six,* included Gheorge Apostol, a former member of the Central Committee and the Politburo (the party's inner governance circle), as well as a former Minister of Trade Unions (some party insiders had claimed that he has been selected by Gheorgiu-Dej as his successor); Alexandru Barladeanu, a former member of the Central Committee and the Politburo and chairman of the Romanian Planning Committee; Corneliu Manescu, who once had been Minister of Foreign Affairs and was a past president of the United Nations' General Assembly; Constantin Parvulescu, one of the founders of the Romanian Communist Party and a long time activist, going back to the days when the party was illegal; Grigore Raceanu, another long time party activist; and Silviu Brucan, a former editor of the party paper, a former Ambassador to the United States, and a leading party ideologist. A number of the signers were subjected to repeated interrogations and some were placed under house arrest, but none were imprisoned.

There only was limited dissent from Romania's intellectuals. They earlier had been defeated by Dej and, later, by Ceausescu. Ceausescu continued Dej's policy of not allowing an independent faction of intellectuals to emerge in the party. Instead, they were kept under the thumb of the party's bureaucracy. This, however, did not mean that Romania's intellectuals were completely subordinate to party dictates. Within the general hegemony of party rule, intellectuals had wide latitude in developing their ideas. This can be seen in the ways in which intellectuals dealt with the issues of national identity and the nature of national culture during the communist period. Neither of these questions, which had dominated intellectual debate throughout the entire period of modern Romanian history had come to a successful resolution before the communists had come to power. During the communist period, they continued to have intellectual saliency among Romania's intelligentsia, who had to struggle with the questions in the entirely new context of communist internationalism. We saw earlier that issues touching on nationalism had become important during Dej's rule, especially when he asserted Romania's independence vis-à-vis COMECON demands that it develop a more highly specialized economy and when he began making moves to improve Romania's relationships with the West. Issues pertinent to nationalism also arose during Ceausescu's tenure in office. Again, many of these had to do with Romania's autonomy vis-à-vis its COMECON and Warsaw Pact allies. But, Ceausescu's interests in developing a specifically Romanian vision of communism went beyond merely using nationalism to define Romania's foreign policy positions. If Ceausescu made any contribution to the overall development of Marxist theory, it was the way in which he developed the idea of the nation, rather than the proletariat, as the historical agent that would move society toward its communist future.

Finding a way to use nationalism as a means of maintaining regime legitimacy was critical of critical importance to Ceausescu during the years following Romania's plunge into economic crisis. Unable to use material incentives to insure popular loyalty to the communist cause, Ceausescu attempted to use nationalism in order to provide a symbolic basis for tying the population to the regime. Ceausescu was able to make use of nationalist ideas circulating within the various circuits of Romanian intellectual discourse to help bolster his regime, until the economy had become so depressed and repression had become so intense that even nationalism no longer could sustain his regime.

Ceausescu and the party's ideologists connected with nationalist discourse in an example of a process that Max Weber has described as "elective affinity." In such a process, ideas have their own logic of development and have real consequences for their proponents. Intellectuals struggle to have their ideas accepted as "truth" in order to enhance their own prestige and the rewards that flow to them for their work. In this ongoing elaboration of, modification of, and struggle for intellectual dominance, certain ideas are picked up by social actors outside of intellectual circles and are used to advance the social actors interests. In this process, the ideas, themselves, are often modified in sometimes subtle, but important, ways. The modified ideas are fed back into intellectual discourse and are again reworked in an endless interaction between thought and material interests. This is precisely what happened to nationalist ideas in Ceausescu's Romania.

Romanian party ideologists picked through the intellectual debates taking place in Romanian intellectual circles and identified ideas that would help legitimate Ceausescu's rule (see Verdery 1991 for a discussion of the specific contending intellectual schools the party used for these purposes and which intellectual schools it rejected). The result was a party ideology in which the nation was moved to the forefront of discussions about historical transformation, replacing the proletariat as *the* historical agent of human emancipation and movement toward communism. As the party incorporated nationalism into a central place in its ideology, the persons who had developed the ideas that the party was using saw their careers advance substantially. They won the national prizes, they received subsidies for their research and the publication of their works, they received permission to travel and study abroad, and their students received the best jobs for newly produced intellectuals.

As party ideology unfolded during the time of economic crisis, it became increasingly anti-Magyar, anti-"cosmopolitan" (read anti-Zionist or, in its most extreme form, anti-Jewish), anti-Rroma, and generally anti-foreign. In the final analysis, The Romanian party used nationalism to try to stabilize party rule. But, in the end even nationalism could not save party rule from the bad economic and political decisions it had made and/or agreed to under Ceausescu and from the deteriorating position of the European inter-state communist system.

The regime's end came in December 1989, as a result of a confluence of events in Timisoara in Romania's Banat Region. Despite being a provincial city, Timisoara was a cosmopolitan place. It had a heterogeneous population, composed of Romanians, Germans, Hungarians, Serbs, and Rroma. In general, relations among the ethnic groups were quite relaxed. The city, for example, had far less tension between Hungarians and Romanians than did Cluj. Timisoara also had access to information from abroad. It was fairly easy to receive radio reports from Hungary and from Yugoslavia, as well as Voice of America and Radio Free Europe/Radio Liberty in all of the major languages represented in Timisoara. Timisoara also was situated along the clandestine trade routes between Romania and Yugoslavia.

Timisoara had undergone extensive growth and industrialization under the communists. A belt of relatively new large apartments ringed the old city, parts of which dated back to the middle ages. As in the case of almost all Romanian cities, the older, inner core was inhabited by the party and state elites and the economically prosperous. The countryside beyond the city limits also was ethnically mixed. Beyond the apartments was an agricultural zone of small villages, many of which were composed entirely of one ethnic group or another, giving even the rural areas a certain cosmopolitan character.

In 1981 and 1982, the Magyars in and around Oradea were publishing a *samzidat* journal that was identifying alleged human rights abuses against Magyars that were being carried out by the Romanian regime. It paid special attention to the rural systematization program. A pastor in the Hungarian Reformed Church in Transylvania, Laszlo Tokes, wrote several pieces for the journal. Laszlo was the son of Istvan Tokes, a prominent pastor who, at one time, had been an assistant bishop in the Hungarian Reformed Church.

Laszlo Tokes' work with Magyar dissidents eventually brought him the attention of the *Securitate*, whose agents began closely monitoring his behavior. Laszlo Tokes' bishop, under pressure from local security forces, removed him from his pastoral position. Rather than accepting a new assignment, Tokes returned home Cluj to live with his father. Having no church assignment, Lazlo, in the mid-1980s, became involved virtually full-time in various Magyar dissident activities in Cluj.

At this time, Cluj, which had been the historical center of Transylvania even before the region had been incorporated into Hungary, proper, was a center of Magyar nationalism in Romania. It once had been the home of an old Jesuit university that had served the Romanian Uniate, the Magyar and the German populations. The University became a state institution. Because of the presence of this university, Cluj had a well-developed Magyar intelligentsia who were becoming more and more embittered by their experiences in Romania.

Many of the Magyars in Cluj believed that Romania had never lived up to the obligations it had to national minorities under the terms of the post-World War I treaties that had ceded Transylvania to Romania. The Magyars also maintained that their culture was in danger of being liquidated through "forced" assimilation, which included, among other things, a limiting of their language rights. They also continued to protest the rural systematization program and the destruction of Magyar villages. All of this was compounded by the fact that Hungary had experienced a much more balanced and higher level of economic and social development than had Romania. As a result, their ethnic counterparts across the border were living lives far better than were the Magyars in Romania. Magyar antagonism toward Romania also was increased by propaganda and other forms of agitation that came from Hungary itself. Hungarian irredentism toward Transylvania had remained strong, even under the communists. Many of Hungary's communist leaders believed that Transylvania was Hungarian territory and should be restored to Hungary, even though Romania was a "fraternal" communist state.

In 1986, Laszlo's bishop decided he needed to be removed from Cluj in order to protect the position of the church in the city. Laszlo was assigned to a congregation in Timisoara, where he was to serve as an assistant pastor. He immediately plunged into Magyar dissident activity in Timisoara and, once again, he ran afoul of the *Securitate*.

In October 1989, Tokes helped organize a youth cultural festival in Timisoara. The festival was co-sponsored with the Catholic Church in Timisoara. To the regime this was an especially "dangerous" event, in that it threatened to unify the two major factions – Catholics and Protestants – in the Magyar community. Tokes' bishop, presumably under pressure from the security forces, denounced the festival and banned any further events of its kind. Undeterred, Tokes pressed ahead with plans for a cultural festival of Magyar Protestant youth and youth from the Orthodox Church, with the approval of the Orthodox Church's metropolitan bishop for Timisoara and the Banat.

At this point, Tokes' own bishop decided to suspend his pastoral duties in Timisoara and to reassign him to another congregation in a rural region of Transylvania. Tokes refused to accept reassignment. While receiving no public support from his fellow clergy in the city or in his diocese, members of his own Hungarian Reformed Congregation immediately mobilized to support him and his family.

Tokes' problems soon came to the attention of the Hungarian state media, which took up his cause and treated him as a hero of the Magyar "nation," and its Diaspora. The Hungarian media descended on Timisoara and in July 1989 interviewed Tokes for a broadcast on Hungarian national television, which was becoming ever more vocal in its public denunciation of the treatment of Magyars in Romania. All of this infuriated the Romanian communist authorities, who continued to be suspicious of Hungary's intentions in Transylvania, where it was rumored there had been a number of minor border skirmishes between Hungarian and Romanian armed forces. Hungarian publicity about Tokes' situation and of the general status of Magyars in Romania also antagonized Romanians who, while not normally sympathetic to the Ceausescu regime, did not trust Magyars' political objectives in Transylvania.

Following his interview on Hungarian television, in August 1989, Tokes was detained and questioned by the *Securitate*. This was followed by an attempt on the part of his bishop to strip him of his clerical status. By this time, Tokes had secured legal representation. Tokes' lawyer informed the bishop that, according to the Hungarian Reformed Church's canon law, Tokes could not be deprived of his clerical status by the bishop acting alone. The lawyer pointed out that the bishop could remove Tokes only with the concurrence of the Hungarian Reformed

Church Council. The bishop called a meeting of the Council in October 1989. Only eight of the twenty three Council members showed up for the meeting, apparently the rest were hiding from the bishop, not wanting to get involved in the bishop's drive to purge Tokes (Tupper-Carey 1990: 181). Meeting in a rump session, the Council voted to dismiss Tokes from the Hungarian Reformed Congregation's clergy. Tokes appealed the decision.

While formal pressures on Tokes were increasing, members of his congregation continued to support him. According to Deletant (1999b), his supporters brought food and other supplies to his family and to him. The security forces retaliated by arresting some of his more vocal supporters, as well as his father, Istvan, when he visited Timisoara to offer his son support. In November 1989 four attackers broke into Laszlo Tokes' apartment and in an ensuing struggle with Tokes and his supporters Tokes was cut on the head by one of the men who had invaded his home. Following the attack on Tokes, a large number of his supporters surrounded his apartment building to protect him from any further violence.

At the same time that all of this was occurring, workers in several of Timisoara's major enterprises had been meeting to plan a demonstration and a "general strike." The workers wanted to protest wage cuts, increases in production norms, increases in worker injuries as managers tried to speed up production to meet increased state output quotas, and the continuing deterioration in the quality of life. Like elsewhere in Romania, Timisoara's workers had to deal with rationing of almost all key commodities, shortages of other consumer goods, and cutbacks in heat, hot water, and electricity for illuminating their apartments. In what was a rare event in Romania, some of these early meetings were attended by a number of artists, writers, and other intellectuals who were friends of several of the workers' leaders. At these early meetings, according to interviews I conducted with a number of participants in the summer of 1991, no one expected that their actions would start a cascade of events that would bring down the regime. Rather, what they were planning had all of the characteristics of a rather traditional pre-political rebellion (Hobsbawm 1959). The workers merely wanted relief from their plight, in much the same way that workers in Brasov had seen their conditions improve following their protests in 1987. The Timisoara workers had planned to walk out of their plants in mid-December. The worker action was not directly a response to what was happening to Tokes and his supporters.

Meanwhile, however, the situation was deteriorating rapidly in Tokes' neighborhood. On December 16, 1989, his supporters held a large demonstration. On December 17, Tokes' supporters again began a second day of protest and demonstrations. They were joined by other residents of Timisoara, who came to express their anger at the regime. A large crowd moved into a large public square, *Piata Libertate,* not far from Tokes' neighborhood. It was a mixed crowd, composed of Hungarian Protestants, Hungarian Catholics, Serbs, Romanians, and Rroma. The army moved to seal the crowd in the square with tanks, armored personnel carriers, and troops.

As evening approached, a personnel carrier caught on fire, a kiosk selling newspapers was torched, and windows began to be broken in shops and offices surrounding the plaza. Later, leaders of the demonstration denied that anyone in the square had been involved in these acts. Instead, they blamed it on agent provocateurs from the *Securitate.* Shortly after the outbreak of violence, soldiers were given the order to fire on the crowd in the square, which the vast majority of them did. Almost all of the rank-and-file soldiers, with the exception of the non-commissioned officers, were draftees serving their compulsory service in the Romanian army. Shots rang out from the troops, from machine guns on tanks and personnel carriers, and from machine gun emplacements on roofs and balconies on buildings around the square. These machine guns were manned by *Securiatate* military units. Bullets rained down on the crowd and the square began to fill with bodies and blood. A man who was in the square told me how he had seen women, the elderly, and children killed by army soldiers. He described an incident in which a father was holding his child on his shoulders when the shooting started. The child was shot through the head and the father also was hit several times by gun shots.

Blood, bodies of the killed and wounded, and body parts were everywhere in the square. Panicked, the crowds rushed to escape, only to find their exit blocked by soldiers who fired on them as they approached the troops. In the meantime, the firing on the crowd in the main square continued, as some people refused to flee. The people who managed to break through the military cordon were chased down the adjacent streets and alleys and were shot at by the soldiers and the security forces.

One of the men who did manage to make it out of the square told me that he was seriously wounded. He lay in the street and feigned death. He watched security forces hunt down others and kill them close to where he was laying. He also described how he had seen several young soldiers lined up against a wall and shot by a firing squad. He later learned that these were soldiers who had not obeyed the order to fire on the crowd.

The man, who was trained in the health sciences, managed to tie off his wound once the soldiers left the neighborhood. He was picked up by an ambulance team and was brought to a city hospital for treatment. He said that he was left in a corridor to await treatment while medical personnel took care of what appeared to be more serious wounds. The corridor where he was put was filled with gurneys that held the dead and wounded. As he lay there, he saw a team of men, who he assumed to be from the *Securitate,* come into the corridor. Two men began going into rooms, while two others walked down the hall. He claims they started shooting all of the wounded. He was able to pull the sheet over his head and, for the second time in 24 hours, pretended he was dead. The gunmen left the area of the hospital where he was and moved on to another part of the hospital. He managed to escape from the hospital and get to his own office, where he and a friend patched his wounds, which left him with a very bad limp. He reported that he later learned that the security forces sent a crew into the hospital to remove the bodies which, he says, were burned and the remains were put in a mass grave. He said that security agents went to many of the families of people they had killed and threatened to kill them if they reported anyone from their family was missing. Trucks were sent to the square to collect and dispose of the bodies in hastily dug mass graves. Workers arrived and washed the blood from the square and the surrounding streets. There were other instances of guns being fired into the late evening, but apparently no one was reported killed during these exchanges.

News of the slaughter soon spread around the world. Reporters from the Soviet Union, Yugoslavia, Hungary, and other Warsaw Pact countries had been in Timisoara covering the protests. They reported that tens of thousands of people had been slaughtered in the city. This proved to be a gross over-estimate of the number of fatalities. One of Romania's leading newspapers later reported that only a hundred or so people had been killed (*Adevarul,* December 21, 1991, pp. 2-3). However, activists in Timisoara claimed that the figure was substantially higher, numbering perhaps 500 to 600, all totaled.

On December 18, workers, protesting the slaughter, walked off their jobs, but were unable to get off their factory grounds. Their earlier planning activities had been penetrated by the security services, who were aware that the workers had been organizing a mass strike. Security forces rushed to the factories and blocked exits from them. The security forces proceeded to arrest key leaders at a number of plants. Among other things, several leaders were stripped naked, tied to chairs, and doused with cold water in front of their assembled colleagues. Other leaders were beaten severely and left to lie on the ground outside of their factories.

While all this had been going on, Ceausescu had gone to Iran to make a state visit to the Ayatollah Khomeni. Romania had long enjoyed good relations with the Shah and Ceausescu was determined to build strong ties with the new Islamic government. The Shah had supplied Romania with large quantities of cheap oil and Ceausescu was hoping to regain access to this supply from the new Islamic Republic. Ceausescu had good ties with a variety of Arab governments, he had given diplomatic recognition to the Palestine Liberation Organization (PLO), and in the past he had opened and maintained training bases for guerillas, such as those from *Al Fatah,* and for military forces from a number of Arab countries. Ceausescu apparently wanted to assure the Ayatollahs that despite his past ties with the Shah he could be a strong ally of a "radical" Islamic state, even if it was being led by Shia Muslims, rather than his traditional Sunni Muslim allies in the Arab world. Ceausescu left Elena and the President of the Parliament behind in Bucharest to run national affairs in his absence.

On December 20, the workers again walked out of their plants at the sound of factory whistles across the city. The first enterprise to strike was the huge *Timisoara Electric* complex. Tens of thousands of workers began marching on the center of the city. On the way, they chanted anti-regime and anti-Ceausescu slogans and sang patriotic songs long banned by the communists, including *Desteapta-te romane* (Romanians Awake!). Army generals, once again, brought forces to confront the workers. This time, however, the army refused to fire on the marchers. Instead, they began defecting in large numbers to the side of the marchers. They also supplied the marchers with weapons from local armories.

At this point, the army garrisons in Timisoara basically had joined the side of the protestors who, by this time, had become a self-conscious revolutionary force. They no longer merely wanted their work-related and consumer-related grievances addressed. Instead, they wanted the regime brought down.

Between the massacre of the 17th and the march on the 20th, ad-hoc committees had been formed at almost all of Romania's factories and leaders of these committees kept in constant touch with one another. Gradually, according to people who participated in these meetings, you could see a clear shifting of opinions as discussions unfolded, with more and more workers becoming committed to revolutionary action, rather than mere protest. With the "surrender" of the army to the marchers on the 20th, an ad-hoc revolutionary committee was formed to take control of the city. It included many trade union leaders, as well as some of the city's leading intellectuals. The new leaders stood before a huge crowd in the center of the city and proclaimed Timisoara Romania's "First Free City." Volunteers poured into Timisoara from all over Romania to help defend the city and neighborhoods organized themselves to maintain order and protect themselves from the terrorists. Timisoara began to take on the character of a revolutionary commune.

According to several of the people who formed this committee, they realized that their proclamation was an act of sheer bravado. They all knew, even though the city's population may not have known, that whether their revolution succeeded or failed had less to do with what they had accomplished than what direction developments would take in other parts of the country, especially in Bucharest. The trade unions and the leaders of the ad-hoc ruling committee, not knowing whether news of what they had done had reached other Romanian cities, sent delegates around the country to make contact with people who they believed would support them and help these contacts mobilize their cities to over-throw communist power. What followed were rebellions in a number of other cities, including Cluj and Sibiu, where another, but smaller, attack on civilians took place. It is interesting that outside of the Banat and Transylvania, with the exception of Bucharest, there were no major signs of rebellion in most of Romania's other cities and towns. There also were no rebellions in Romania's rural areas. Peasants and residents of small towns simply decided that they were going to sit out the uprising and wait to see who emerged victorious and then seek an accommodation with whomever the final victor was. Thus, overall, the overthrow of the Ceausescus primarily, if not exclusively, was the result of selective urban rebellion.

When protesters gathered in the central square in Sibiu on December 21, 1989, they met *Securitate* forces, armed militia, and students from military academies located in the city (Deletant 1999b: 167). The first attack on the protesters came from the *Securitate* units, who began firing on the demonstrators around mid-day. The militia moved on the protesters and arrested a large number and confined them in the *Securitate* and militia headquarters, which were adjacent to each other. Protesters marched to these headquarters and demand that they release everyone who had been arrested. When their demands were refused, the demonstrators attacked the two buildings. In the violence, that day, four persons were killed and eleven were wounded (Deletant 1999b: 167). Violence ended when regular army troops entered the city and deployed a protective force around the militia and *Securitate* headquarters (Abrudan 1990: 24-27).

The protesters remained in place during the night of December 21. The next day they attacked the two buildings, but were rebuffed by firing from the *Securitate* and the militia. Forces inside of these two buildings, then began shooting at the military academy, from which fire was returned. The gun battles went on all day. Snipers joined in, shooting at the military cadets who had sided with the protesters and at citizens who were protesting or simply walking in the streets. By the time the fighting ended in Sibiu, another fifty people were killed (Deletant 1999b: 168). The dead included thirty civilians, the rest were militia, soldiers, and *Securitate*. In the aftermath of the violence against the population and the military cadets, among those held criminally responsible was Nicu Ceausescu, who was serving as party secretary of the city at the time.

The army and the newly armed revolutionary forces in Timisoara had to confront an unknown number of Ceausescu supporters, who they called the "terrorists," who regularly carried out sniper attacks on soldiers and citizens in Timisoara. Some of these terrorists had been stationed in Timisoara, while others came into the city from surrounding areas. Most of these attacks consisted of relatively brief barrages of gunfire, after which the terrorists melded back into the population and disappeared. During the time of the terrorist actions, no one felt safe anywhere in the city. The terrorists shot at people in the streets and in their apartments. It was becoming evident that the only goal of the shooters was to inflict absolute terror on Timisoara's population.

On the 20th of December, Ceausescu, having cut short his visit to Iran, returned to Bucharest to take command of the rapidly deteriorating situation. Reportedly he was in a rage when he returned to the capital. He charged his top generals with having engaged in "treasonous" behavior for not crushing the rebellion and demanded to know why the army had failed in its duty to control Timisoara's population. The members of the party central committee joined Ceausescu in condemning the senior military leadership for their "inaction" in Timisoara. Shortly after the meeting, the Central Committee was informed that Romania's senior general, Vasile Milea, who also served as Defense Minister, had committed suicide. It later was reported that Milea had been killed by the *Securitate,* on direct orders from Ceausescu.

Ceausescu ordered that all contact between Timisoara and other cities in Romania be cut. Timisoara radio was forced off the air, mail was suspended between Timisoara and other cities, and telephone links were severed. Meanwhile, the regime launched its own propaganda campaign, denouncing the insurrection in Timisoara as having been organized by Magyar nationalists, with the direct support secret agents of the Hungarian government, and various criminal and asocial elements in the population.

Scattered signs of support for the Timisoara rebels began to appear in Bucharest. Students met at the University and the Polytechnic to discuss what was happening and workers at enterprises across the city began to form their own ad-hoc committees to take control of their enterprises and to take to the street in support of any revolutionary action that might take place.

Ceausescu decided he needed to address Bucharest's population directly. He sent out orders to party activists to bring people to the *Piata Republicii* (Plaza of the Republic). The party brought hundreds of thousands of people to the plaza. Ceausescu went out on to the balcony of the party headquarters to deliver his speech, which was to be nationally televised and broadcast over national radio. Elena and other senior party leaders surrounded him on the balcony. His speech started well enough. However, as he began to denounce the rebels in Timisoara, a lone voice yelled out in protest against the denunciations of the Timisoara rebels. He was standing near microphones that had been placed in the crowd to pick up the cheers for Ceausescu's speech. There was instant panic among those who stood near to the man who had yelled out. They scrambled to get away from him, lest they be identified as the person having made the denunciation. Romanian television picked up the chaos that was bubbling up from the crowds moving away from the man. The broadcast briefly went off the air. It returned after a few minutes and continued its coverage of Ceausescu's speech.

Now, however, the crowd had become disorderly and a roar of protests and denunciations began to rise against Ceausescu. Romanian television, in what will stand forever as one of its greatest moments, caught Ceausescu freeze in mid-sentence as he realized that the sounds coming from the crowd were not praises for him but denunciations. His face totally collapsed and his body seemed to fold in on itself. Romanian television cut off the broadcast and shortly thereafter filled the air with patriotic music, as did the national radio.

The Ceausescus and their party stalwarts quickly recomposed themselves and fled inside of the party's headquarters building. This was the last live appearance that the Ceausescu's had on national television where, each night, they had appeared for two hours of broadcast to the Romanian people. During these two hours, they would receive delegations from all over the country who would bestow gifts and praise on them for the wonderful leadership they were providing Romania. They also subjected the population to regular spectacles of peasants, dressed in "traditional" costumes, performing "traditional" songs and dances.

During these nightly spectacles, Nicolae and Elena would harangue the Romanian population, in their frequently mangled version of Romanian, about the glories of the nation and of their wise and generous rule, which was completely responsible for the wonders Romanian society had achieved. You could not watch these performances without coming away believing that somehow you had become lost in Lucky's world and never would be able to escape. Broadcasts like these made even Bulgarian television, which was hardly scintillating viewing, popular in Bucharest and other areas in Romania where it could be received. Many Romanians had taken the trouble to learn colloquial Bulgarian so that they could watch its nightly programming.

Inside of the building, the Ceausescus and other leaders tried to plan on how to respond to the outrages committed against them in the square. In the meantime, some protesters remained in the square, where they organized speeches against the regime and planned for further protests. People who had seen what had happened on television or heard the radio broadcast of the speech began gathering spontaneously in various parts of the city. A large number of students and others gathered in *Piata Universitati* (University Square) in central Bucharest and took control of the area, setting up barricades around the square to protect it from the police and from military units.

During the early evening, military commanders, having heard of General Milea's suicide, which many of them believed was actually a murder, withdrew troops from the *Piata Republicii,* leaving the party headquarters building and other key government buildings open to attack. While troops were being withdrawn from the *Piata Republicii,* other army and *Securitate* forces prepared to attack the protesters holding up in the *Piata Universitati.* The forces began their attack on *Piata Universitati* during the night. They quickly overran the barricades and entered the square. They shot and killed a large number of the protesters, beat and arrested others, and forced the rest to flee to other parts of the city.

With troops having withdrawn from the *Piata Republicii,* the large crowd that had gathered there on the morning of December 22 began an attack on the building. Nicolae and Elena and a few other of their shrinking number of supporters, along with two bodyguards, boarded a helicopter that had landed on the roof of the party headquarters in order to extract them from the rioters who threatened to overrun the building.

On the evening of the 22nd of December, Iliescu, Roman, Brucan, Militaru, Alexander Barladeanu, General Nicolae Militaru, General Stefan Guse, and General Ion Vlad (Brucan 1993) met at the Central Committee offices. We already have seen who Iliescu was. Silviu Brucan had been a long-time party member and activist. As already noted, he had served as an editor of the party newspaper, had been a member of the Central Committee, had served as an ambassador to the United States, had been a vice-president responsible for national television, and has been one of the signers of the so-called "Letter of Six." Petru Roman was the son of a long-time communist activist and leader, Valter Roman, who had been a general in the communist forces that had fought against Franco's forces in Spain during the civil war (1935-1936) and who had been a member of the party's Central Committee since 1950. Petru Roman had received advanced degrees from the Sorbonne and was serving as a professor at the Polytechnic University in Bucharest. Alexander Barladeanu had been a member of the Politburo, had headed the state planning committee in the 1960s, and, more recently, he also had signed the "Letter of Six." General Nicolae Militaru had been a participant in the failed coup of 1984 and a close friend of Iliescu. General Guse was the chief of staff of the Romanian army. He had been sent to Timisoara to try to suppress the insurrection. General Vlad was the commanding general of the Securitate.

These men began discussing the formation of a new government, but nothing was decided at that time. They all later returned to the television station. Several of the men gathered at the studio and began constructing an organization that they called the National Salvation Front (FSN) and they began drafting a proclamation that they would deliver over national television to the Romanian nation (Brucan 1993). The FSN's original membership was a highly diverse group. It included a number of people who had held various leadership positions in the party, some rising technocrats, intellectuals, and military and security officers. From the start, it was clear that the FSN senior leaders were members who long had held leading positions within the party and that they had selected Ion Iliescu for the top position within their organization. As the leadership later discovered, one of its key people, General Vlad, the head of the Securitate, was a traitor to their cause (Brucan 1993: 178-181). Vlad later was arrested and sentenced to eleven years in prison.

Meanwhile, the helicopter carrying Nicolae and Elena flew to the Ceausescu's palace at Lake Snagov, the place where legend had it Count Dracula had been buried. At Lake Snagov, Nicolae and Elena picked up suitcases that they kept there for just such purposes as they now needed them. Nicolae tried to make contact with his unit of special bodyguard forces. But they did not respond to him. Leaving behind Manea and their other companion, Nicolae, Elena, and the two bodyguards returned to the helicopter and evacuated Lake Snagov. Initially, they appear to have been headed to the Otopeni international airport, which was still in the hands of forces loyal to the Ceausescus. During the flight, however, the pilot received a radio message informing him that if he attempted to land at Otopeni, the helicopter would be shot out of the sky. A few minutes later the pilot received a radio message informing him to land and discharge his passengers on the Bucharest-Pitesti highway near the small town of Boteni. He followed his instructions and landed where ordered.

The pilot told the Ceausescus and the bodyguards that he needed to refuel the helicopter. Everyone except the pilot got out of the helicopter. He took off, abandoning everyone on the side of the road. They flagged down a car that was passing buy. Nicolae and Elena got into the vehicle and ordered the driver to take them away. The two body guards were left behind. The driver took them toward the town of Tirgoviste. Just before he got to the town, he pulled over to ask another driver for gasoline. The Ceausescus got into the second car and ordered the owner to get in and drive them to Tirgoviste, which he did. At this point a number of versions of what happened next were reported. The most plausible of these narratives had the Ceausescu's recognized by local police officers in Tirgoviste. The Ceausescu's were held until a military unit took them into custody and brought them back to their base. Officers at the base reportedly contacted the vice-president of the FSN in Bucharest, Gelu Voicelescu-Voican, who had emerged as the number two person in the FSN leadership, and informed him that they had the Ceausescus in custody but that they did not know how long they could hold him. The officers were afraid that when loyalist units of the Securitate discovered where the Ceausescus were being held, they would attack the base, overrun its defenses, kill all of the defenders, and release the Ceausescus.

Voicelescu-Voican relayed the information to a number of the leaders of the FSN. It was not clear that everyone in the new leadership was told what was happening. The leaders decided that a tribunal needed to be assembled and sent to Tirgoviste to put the couple on trial, to convict them, and to execute them. The role of judge was given to Major Georgica Popa. Colonel Virgil Maureanu was appointed prosecutor. These two, along with three other members of the tribunal, a court reporter, a defense attorney, a cameraman, and General Victor Stancelescu were told to leave immediately for Tirgoviste to conduct a trial. Only a few of them knew who the accused were when they left Bucharest on December 24th.

Back at the party headquarters, protesters broke through the doors and went to Ceausescu's office, which was located just off the balcony from which he always had addressed the masses, sometimes for hours on end. They through open the doors and tossed Ceausescu's books, many of which he had "written," off the balcony and onto the square below to the loud cheers of those who had remained there.

In Bucharest, while the Ceausescu's were being detained, fighting expanded throughout the city. Helicopter gun ships flew into the air above *Piata Republicii* and opened fire on demonstrators and on buildings where regime opponents were thought to be hiding. During the conflict at the square, the major building of the University of Bucharest's library was hit by shells, caught fire, and burned to the ground. Hundreds, if not thousands, of ancient and very rare manuscripts were destroyed.

Fighting also broke out in Baneasa, where the Securiatate had a major training facility, offices, and barracks for troops and at the international airport in Otopeni. The Securitate base was under the command of Nicolae Ceausescu's brother, General Andruta Ceausescu. The situation was completely chaotic, as army forces did not know how to respond to what was happening. A young officer who was serving in the army during those days told me how his military unit was mobilized and was being sent to Bucharest to defend the government against the "traitors." About five kilometers from the city, their column was stopped on a highway by a roadblock composed of men from a different military unit. Their commander, who was a major, approached the commander of the blockade. After a brief discussion, their commander was taken into custody by several armed soldiers and was escorted into the back of a military truck parked on the side of the road. The commander of the blockade came over to them, along with several of his officers. He pointed to one of his men and told them that they were going to be given white armbands, which they were to wear at all times, and that they would be going to Bucharest to defend the revolution. He asked them if anyone objected to this change in mission. No one responded in the affirmative. The white armbands were passed out, they put them on, and they went into combat in Bucharest where they were joined by other army units wearing the same armbands. Their men ended up fighting at Baneasa, at the national airport located not far from there, and at the international airport at Otopeni.

One of the soldiers involved in this fighting reported that they were mostly battling against militia, Interior Ministry armed troops, and uniformed and non-uniformed Securitate forces, as well as special units from the Presidential Bodyguard. He also told me that at one point in the fighting one of his officers came to him and asked him to follow him back to a rear area. When he reached his destination, he found four Arab men being detained. His officer, who knew that he, the soldier, had been trained in Arabic at the University, told him he needed to translate for him. The young soldier told me that the Arabs, who had been captured while fighting the Romanian army forces who were supporting the rebellion, claimed they had been forced to join the Securitate combatants against the revolutionaries. They refused to tell what their nationality was or why they had been in Romania. After translating questions for more than an hour, the soldier was told to report back to his unit, which he did. He said he later tried to find the Arabs, when there was a break in the fighting, but no seemed to recall where they had been taken and many claimed they could not recall having seen any Arabs. Their appearance and subsequent disappearance was just one of many equally "odd" events the soldier says he witnessed during the fighting.

As was the case in Timisoara, "terrorists" began attacking citizens and rebellious soldiers from the shadows. They killed and wounded a large number of people, many of whom had no connection at all with the rebels. Like spirits, small groups of terrorists would materialize in various parts of the city and open fire on anyone who came within range of their guns. They used the vast network of tunnels the Securitate had constructed beneath Bucharest to connect government and party buildings to move about the city with impunity. The terrorists shut down their resistance on December 28, 1989. By that time, over eight hundred of them had been arrested (Deletant 1999b: 166), all of whom were released at various times during 1990.

While the battle in Bucharest raged on, the Ceausescu's remained sequestered in Tirgoviste. They were being held in custody by a heavily armed military detachment who had arrived in the city and sent the local police away. It has been reported that the couple seemed disoriented. They did not appear to comprehend what was happening to them. Nicolae kept walking to the window and checking his wrist watch, which contained a signaling device that let his bodyguards know where he was located. It was quite clear to his guards that he was expecting his personal guards to arrive and rescue him. The guards, however, knew this was not likely to happen, but they did not tell him that.

On the morning of December 25, 1989, Nicolae and Elena Ceausescu were told that they were about to be tried by a special military tribunal. They were to be charged, among other things, with having committed genocide against the Romanian nation; with having destroyed the national economy; and with having attempted to flee the country with money stolen from the state. The trial was convened, the charges were quickly read to the defendants, and they were given an opportunity to address each of the accusations. Neither Nicolae nor Elena responded directly to the accusations made against them. Instead they, especially Elena, replied by denouncing the tribunal. She accused them of being traitors to the nation, of being ingrates who did not appreciate the magnitude of what He and She had achieved for the country, of being dupes of foreign powers, and even worse. Both Nicolae and Elena denied the legitimacy of the court.

When the tribunal finished its reading of the charges and had given the Ceausescu's their opportunity to respond, it adjourned to private deliberations. It unanimously voted to convict both of them of all charges. In a separate deliberation, it decided the appropriate sentence was death. The Ceausescus were read the decision and the sentence. Nicolae and Elena were informed that they had been found guilty on all counts and that they had been sentenced to death. It later was reported that the entire trial had taken nine hours, but there had been no documentation of this claim.

The Ceausescus, upon being told of the verdict, immediately were brought to a small courtyard, had masks put over their faces, and were stood against a wall. While they were being prepared to receive their sentence, a firing squad assembled in the courtyard. Reportedly, all of the soldiers in the squad had been supplied with ammunition. The soldiers assumed their positions facing the Ceausescus and on command they sighted their weapons. They then heard the order to fire. They did just that and the couple fell to the ground. They died with their bodies riddled with bullets. The bodies were taken to Bucharest and buried without any ceremony in unmarked graves in an unidentified cemetery. Thus ended over twenty-four years of Ceausescu's rule and forty-two years of communist rule in Romania.

The trial and execution had been captured on film, a heavily edited version of which was shown repeatedly on Romanian television, as if the Romanian population needed to be convinced that *He* and *She* truly were dead. Watching these films one could not help but notice how frail and bewildered the couple looked during their trial. They looked like two shrunken old people who were confused about who they were, where they were, and why they were being treated so badly. All of the pretensions of grandeur with which they once had carried themselves in the past had disappeared from their presentations of self as they faced their judges and executioners.

Within days after the announcement of their deaths, resistance to the new provisional government quickly ended. The terrorists ceased their operations and disappeared back into the Romanian population to wait and see what the fall of the Ceausescus would bring for them and their political allies and supporters. The largest number of the terrorists had come from a number of special security units. They were drawn from forces headquartered at the *Securitate* military academy at Baneasa commanded by General Andruta Ceausescu; from among the USLA, which was a specially trained anti-terrorist unit under the command of Col. Gheorghe Ardeleanu; from among the presidential security forces commanded by General Neagoe; and, finally, from the Bucharest *Securitate* detachment that was commanded by Col. Ion Goran (Brucan 1993: 185). There also were a number of Arab fighters who had been trained at Baneasa who joined the "terrorists" (Brucan 1993: 185).

Looking back on how quickly the regime fell one still can not but be surprised at how events had transpired. Only a month before his execution, Ceausescu had appeared at the 19th Party Congress in Bucharest to accept his reelection as party leader and to see his policies and his commitment to continue them in the future overwhelmingly accepted. As at past congresses, Nicolae and Elena received overwhelming displays of adulation from their party colleagues. The cult of personality was in full operation. He could not help but to come away from the congress seeing himself as an invincible force within Romania. Never could he have imagined that by the end of the next month He and She would be overthrown, executed, and buried in unmarked graves and that their children would be arrested and interrogated by revolutionary forces. As they had turned the communist dream into a Romanian nightmare, the Ceausecus' worst nightmares finally were turned into the average Romanian's seemingly most impossible dream.

The final totals of those killed in the overthrow of the Ceausescu regime was put at around a thousand people, although no one can know for sure what the real count was (Deletant 1999b: 169). The death toll was just one of many questions that later emerged about the events of December 1989. One of the most important questions was why so many people in the old regime escaped punishment for their actions and/or for the orders they gave during the events of December. Only twenty-five members of the Central Committee and Politburo, one of whom was Nicu Ceausescu, and eleven generals in the militia and *Securitate* were put on trial (Deletant 1999b: 169). Twenty-nine people from the party, the militia, and the *Securitate* were tried for "incitement to murder" in Timisoara (Deletant 1999b: 169). However, all of the 800 people arrested on charges of "terrorism" were released without trial and several senior military and party officials who had been accused of various atrocities in Bucharest and other cities never have been charged with any crime, let alone been tried for what they allegedly did during the events of December 1989. Left unanswered in the trials that did take place was the ultimate responsibility of the army and other military forces for the deaths of civilians.

It has not been explained how the National Salvation Front had so rapidly organized itself that it could proclaim itself a provisional government within hours of the rebellion having started in Bucharest. Many Romanians came to believe that there had been a conspiracy within the party that was waiting for an opportunity to overthrow the Ceausescus and that the uprising provided an opportunity for the conspirators to act and seize power.

There also have been serious questions raised as to whether there was any foreign involvement in the planning and execution of the initial uprising in Timisoara. There had been speculation that the Hungarian security forces had worked with members of the Romanian Magyar community and had provided training in insurrectionary behavior. No evidence has emerged to support this idea.

Speculation that is more serious identified the Soviet Union as having played a part in stimulating the rebellion. There is some evidence for this. It later was discovered that in December 1989 there had been an unusually high number of Soviet tourists in Romania (Deletant 1999b: 171-172). Moreover, a number of high ranking officers in the Romanian military and security forces had strong ties with their Soviet counterparts. The question, however, arises as to why the Soviet Union would be interested in overthrowing the Ceausescu regime. It is known that Gorbachev and Ceausescu had a bad interpersonal relationship and had sharp differences in their ideas as to the direction in which communism should be moving. In May 1987, Gorbachev paid a state visit to Romania. While in Romania he delivered a significant speech that was broadcast live on national radio to party leaders and other Romanian notables.

A person who attended the speech reported to me on how uncomfortable Gorbachev appeared with the trappings of the cult of personality attached to the Ceausescus, especially when the audience attempted to express the same adulation to him and his wife, who was an urbane, well-spoken, fashionable, Ph.D. trained sociologist who had received her advanced degree at Moscow State University. During his speech, Gorbachev outlined his ideas on *perestroika* and *glasnost*. Ceausescu and his inner circle found both of these ideas appalling examples of the worst kind of revisionism, a point that would later be elaborated in a theoretical article written by General Illie Ceausescu, one of Nicolae's brothers, in 1989 and published in a leading military journal. Given Gorbachev's low regard for the Ceausescus and given that he saw Romanian communism as an obstacle to his vision of transforming European communism, Gorbachev certainly had reason to want to get rid of the Ceausescus and he had the means to do so. Whether he actually helped organize the overthrow of the regime by assisting in the events in Timisoara or by helping the party leaders who later formed the FSN remain unanswered questions.

The overthrow of the Ceausescus was less a revolution against socialism that it was an example of what Max Weber called a "traditionalist revolution," which involves a rebellion against a master because he, the master, has failed to observe the traditional limits of his power and has failed to meet his traditional responsibilities and obligations to his subjects. It is clear that the FSN had not come to power with an intention of restoring capitalism and the bourgeoisie. It also is clear that the people who fought in the streets, for the most part, did not expect to overthrow socialism. But that is what happened.

7
The Post-Communist Era

In almost all of the communist states in East Central Europe, there had been a number of "round table" talks between the party and various opposition groups. These talks had helped define the ways that the societies in question would extricate themselves from communism and provided a basis for developing a general "consensus" as to what type of political economy would replace the old communist order.

Romania did not have the benefit of such conversations. Ceausescuism had not permitted organized opposition groups to form in Romania and, even if they had formed, Ceausescu's absolutist rule within the party would have meant that they had no one with whom they could negotiate. Thus, Romania was especially ill-prepared for dealing with the fall of the old regime.

A already noted, following what only can be described, using Weber's (1978) terminology, as a "traditionalist revolution," i.e. a revolution not directed against the system, per se, but, rather, against the ruler, personally, for not having respected the "traditional" limits to his power, a group of former or currently high ranking members of the nomenklatura took control of the state, calling themselves the National Salvation Front (FSN). It is preferable to see the events of 1989 as an example of a hybrid event involving a "traditionalist revolution" coupled with the taking of power by an established elite within the party structure.

At the point they took power, the FSN core leadership did not have a clear idea of where they wanted to take Romania, either politically or economically. Because of Ceausescu's style of rule, which was more like that of an Ottoman Sultan than a "typical" communist leader, an opposition, either outside of or inside of the party, that had a general idea of what type of country they wanted to see develop, had not emerged.

While they may not have known what type of political economy they did want, it is clear, however, that the core leadership of the FSN, initially, did not entertain notions of building a neo-liberal capitalist order with completely free markets and a watchman state. Nor did they appear to want to build a society that was organized around the principles of bourgeois individualism. They were too committed to socialism as an ideal to want such complete transformations. Quickly upon seizing power, the FSN proclaimed itself a provisional government and set about ruling by decree. While it unhesitatingly committed itself to instituting a system of parliamentary democracy, its ideas about what type of an economy it wanted to see developed were largely undefined. There appears to have been a great deal of contention within the FSN during those first months as to how far Romania should move, and how quickly it should move, in dismantling the socialist economic system and implanting neo-liberal capitalism. The majority of the FSN's leadership seems to have been reluctant, at this time, to take quick and decisive steps to abolish socialism and replace it with capitalism. Instead, they appear to have wanted to devise a political economy that would balance popular demands for social and economic security with internal and international pressures to begin institutionalizing a capitalist economy.

Within the group of people who made up the FSN, real power seems to have been concentrated in the Executive Bureau, which was chaired by Ion Iliescu. At the time, Iliescu was an advocate for developing a political democracy, but he was not an advocate for developing an unrestrained capitalist economy. It appointed Petre Roman the Prime Minister of the provisional government. Among the first things the provisional government did, was outlaw capital punishment and restore women's rights to seek and obtain abortions. It also tried to win public support for its rule by increasing supplies of electricity and gas to Romanian households, by suspending the export of agricultural commodities and putting these commodities on domestic markets, and by raiding the food reserves that had been set aside for the nomenclature. These actions provided immediate short-term relief to Romania's population. However, everyone involved in these decisions knew that these actions were nothing but a temporary "fix" and that something more would have to be done to improve the country's long term economic prospects.

When the FSN took power, there were no individuals or factions within its leading circles who were committed to transforming Romania in any particular direction. Unlike in several other communist countries, such as Poland and Hungary, where powerful networks had developed both within the party and outside of it to change the fundamental nature of economic and political life in their countries (Eyal et al. 1998, see especially pp. 82-85) in Romania this was not the case. In Romania there had been very little activity directed at formulating an alternative economic order or, even, at formulating experiments designed to reform the system while preserving its overall socialist agenda. Instead, Romania remained committed to its traditional economic system of Stalinist accumulation.

But, despite the lack of a clear economic agenda, the FSN launched Romania on an economic path that very quickly proved disruptive for most of the country's citizens. But it was not only the economy that would change. Romanians would find that the demise of communism would bring significant other changes to their personal lives and their collective life. The average Romanian could not help but to come to believe that the last 45 years of the country's history had been nothing more than a monumental waste of their time. It was becoming ever clearer that all of the sacrifices the Romanian people had endured in trying to build a socialist society had come to naught. In effect, Romanians were being told that, once again, they would be called upon to endure major personal and collective sacrifices to build another new economy and society, without much consideration as to how personal and collective life would be disrupted.

To a significant number of Romanians, the overthrow of communism, in general, and the Ceausescu regime, in particular, provided Romania with an opportunity to "rejoin" the West and to begin creating a "normal" country, with a "normal political system," by which they meant a parliamentary democracy, and a "normal economy," which they translated as liberal capitalism. However, for many others, their immediate post-revolutionary euphoria began to give way to a feeling that their society had lost its bearings. They began to believe that the society's basic social structure, its values, its principles of order, and its laws all were falling apart. Many Romanians began to perceive an increased personal risk of being victims of crime, came to believe that the state was inherently corrupt and self-serving, saw rising unemployment, rapidly escalating price increases, a seemingly never ending stream of protests, demonstrations, and strikes (see Keil and Keil 2002 for a discussion of post-revolutionary labor conflict in Romania), and began to notice subtle changes in their rhythms of life as Romania began to shift toward capitalist economic relations. All of which seriously frightened them and they slipped into believing that Romania had degenerated into a chaos from which there might not be any easy and quick exits.

In the midst of this perceived chaos, the FSN struggled to be accepted as the legitimate state authority. This, however, was no easy matter, if for no other reason that the FSN had no real basis for taking control of the state. There is little evidence that it had initiated or guided the insurrection that had overthrown the Ceausescus and their kleptocratic networks in the party and the state. Rather, in the view of many, the FSN was nothing more than a collection of opportunists, who once had played central roles in the kleptocracy, who had mounted a coup within the context of a popular rebellion. Moreover, once it seized control of the state it did very little to reach out to the people who actually had led the December 1989 uprising and bring them into leading positions in the FSN.

Rather than being made up of revolutionary activists who had taken to the streets against Ceausescu and his supporters, the core leadership of the FSN was made up of relatively high-ranking members of the old nomenklatura, coupled with a handful of dissidents and others who were outside of the old party-state elite circles. The FSN's leadership was made up of men who had stood at the pinnacle of several interconnected party-state networks that quickly pledged their loyalty to the new provisional government. Among the more important of these networks were the military and key parts of the security services.

The key actors in the inner circles of the FSN felt comfortable selecting Iliescu as the leader of the provisional government and the public face of the FSN. In their circle, Iliescu was seen as someone on whom the party-state elites could count to keep control of the pace and direction of change in post-Ceausescu Romania. The last thing the elite wanted was dramatic, rapid, and thorough changes that threatened their immediate and long-term interests. Iliescu also was seen to be a competent administrator and a first-rate politician who understood what it would take to balance the various interests that were represented in the FSN's upper echelons.

Nothing showed Iliescu's decisiveness in the early days of the revolution more than the arrest, trial, and execution of the Ceausescus. Evidently, there was considerable debate in the FSN's inner circle as to what should be done with the dictator and his wife. The hard liners did not want the couple brought back to Bucharest, where their supporters could mount a movement to put him back in office. Therefore, it was decided that the couple needed to be tried, convicted, and executed. The decision to do away with the Ceausescu's proved to be a wise move. Within days of the Ceausescus' executions, "terrorist" activity ended throughout the country. Had the Ceausescus not been killed, it is likely that the "terrorists" would have continued their activity, in the hope that they could free the couple and restore their power. With their death, the terrorists saw that they could gain nothing from continuing to resist the new authority and decided it was best to try to come to terms with the new government.

In the first weeks after December 1989, Iliescu also presided over the formal liquidation of the communist party. However, he was not able to prevent the disappearance of the party's considerable financial assets. Hundreds of millions of dollars disappeared without a trace from the party's treasury and, despite considerable efforts by various Romanian authorities, none of this money has been recovered. Romania has sent teams of forensic accountants around the world to try to track what had happened to the money, but they have had no success. Whether the money was stolen and later invested in Romania or whether it was smuggled out of the country and put in secret bank accounts abroad remain open questions.

The provisional government proceeded with a great deal of caution in dealing with communists charged with crimes against the people during the 1989 uprising. The new government ordered the arrest and trial of several hundred people for criminal acts allegedly committed during the December 1989 uprising. However, the new regime did not attempt to put on trial the large number of men who had been arrested as "terrorists" nor did it try to track down "terrorists" who had avoided arrest. The Romanian public assumed that the government's failure to act against the "terrorists," most of whom they suspected were drawn from various bureaus of the Securitate, showed that the FSN was not strong enough to take on the power of the old regime's security forces or was not willing to challenge these forces. The exoneration of the terrorists seriously compromised the legitimacy of the provisional government in the eyes of many Romanians.

The FSN also resisted calls to establish a "lustration" program in Romania. Unlike the post-communist governments of the GDR,

Hungary, and Czechoslovakia, the Romanian government refused to establish any organization that would look at the political crimes alleged to have taken place during communist rule. The FSN provisional government argued that it was a time for national healing and that lustration would do more to divide the population than unite it. The FSN also refused to open *Securitate* files for public examination and action against the former secret police forces and their collaborators. It was only later that the files that survived what undoubtedly was a careful selective purging of records were opened to Romanians. The opposition suspected that the FSN leadership was motivated more by a desire to protect its membership and its allies than by a desire to unite the country when it refused to open security files for public examination and when it refused to consider establishing a lustration program. In taking such a stand, the former communists who now were leading the FSN behaved in much the same way as had the communist leadership who took power after World War II. Then, there were executions of the principal leaders of the fascist state and a handful of trials, but there was no full-scale attempt to look at the question of who had supported and who had participated in the fascist movements and the fascist state and who had been involved in its racist and genocidal practices. Instead, rank-and-file fascists and a good part of the lower leadership in the fascist movements, if not exonerated, were pretty much left alone by the state, as long as they did not oppose the communist regime.

In hindsight, it appears that Romania might have benefited by having adopted, after the fall of communism, some form of a national reconciliation council, akin to what was established in South Africa after the fall of its racially fascist state. Such a council would have helped heal the deep wounds left by the communists and it would have helped reduce suspicions about the backgrounds of the FSN leaders, as well as the backgrounds of other political actors who began to emerge out of the wreckage of the old system.

While the FSN was able to secure almost total support from the former nomenklatura, it had a harder time gaining and holding legitimacy among key sectors of the Romanian public. This was especially the case with Romanian intellectuals. Almost immediately on taking power, the FSN faced considerable opposition from people who believed it had illegitimately usurped power. Many of the people who had been active participants in the 1989 insurrections, and who regarded the FSN as usurpers, feared that the FSN was nothing more than a reconstituted communist party. They believed that the FSN that would try to maintain a centrally planned economy and that it would attempt to define itself not only as Romania's leading party, but as its only political party, just as the communists had done.

Within months after the overthrow and killing of the Ceausescus, opposition to the FSN began crystallizing into formal political parties. The old "historical parties," mainly the National Liberal Party, the National Peasant Party, and the Social Democratic Party, quickly moved to re-establish themselves. The three historical parties, along with approximately sixty other newly formed parties, prepared themselves to contend for votes in the elections the FSN promised would soon take place.

As the new and historical political parties were struggling to re-establish themselves as viable political forces in Romania, a mass rally was held in Timisoara in March 1990. The rally was organized by workers, students, and other activists who had taken part in the city's uprising. The rally led to the drafting of the "Timisoara Proclamation." The proclamation, among other things, was written to lay out an alternative vision of the December 1989 rebellion from that being articulated by the FSN and its leading ideologist, Silviu Brucan. The Proclamation's authors, who were forming themselves into a quasi-political organization they called Civic Alliance, tried to delegitimate the FSN's claims to leadership of the provisional government. The Proclamation made thirteen points, including a statement to the effect that the Romanian revolution had been a revolt not just against the Ceausescus but against the entire ruling elite of the communist party. This assertion was a direct challenge to the FSN and its supporters. The proclamation went on to demand that former members of the nomenklatura be banned from standing for any seats for parliament for three consecutive parliamentary elections. Moreover, in a direct challenge to Iliescu, the Proclamation demanded that no member of the party's old leadership, of which Iliescu was one, should be eligible for election as president of the new Romanian state. The FSN provisional government rejected the political limitations on its key leaders and members that the Proclamation proposed.

In addition to growing opposition from within the ethnic Romanian population, the FSN also began to face rising opposition from Romania's Magyars. The FSN, along with a good part of Romania's majority population, were suspicious of the long range intentions of the Magyars, as well as the intentions of Hungary's new government toward Transylvania. In the aftermath of the revolution, the Romanian Magyars began articulating a host of demands, including increased language rights and increased political autonomy in those *judets*, towns, and villages where they were a majority of the population. Few of Romania's Magyars had grounds for complaining about economic discrimination against them. Under communism, the Magyars had not been formed into an ethnically scheduled work force or an ethnically defined underclass. Mostly what the Magyars complained about was Romania's unwillingness to recognize Magyars as an ethno-political category deserving of special attention.

In the 19th century, both Romanians and Magyars had built their identities around Herderian ideas of *Sprachtnationalismus* that stressed the principles of unity of territory, a presumed (often mythical) common descent, common traditions, and common language. Thus, both Romanians and Magyars held to a principle of *ius sanguinis* to define who "truly" was a member of the national community. After 1989, this principle, in an apparent regression into an archaic self-image and into archaic practices of social closure was resurrected by the radical right both in Hungary and Romania.

In addition to demands by Romania's Magyars, irredentism seemingly was on the rise in Hungary. Several right-wing, nationalist politicians were making noises that, to some Romanians, sounded as if they were demanding that the Romanian-Hungarian boundary be redrawn in Hungary's favor. Romanians were disturbed that the Hungarian government was not taking actions to distance itself from the more radical nationalist elements in the country. Romanians were especially upset when the first non-communist Prime Minister of Hungary asserted that he was the "Prime Minister of fifteen million Hungarians" (Eyal et al. 1998: 94), which meant that he was claiming leadership not only of Hungarians living in Hungary but also of the Hungarian Diaspora. This could be regarded as a direct political challenge to Romania, Slovakia, and Serbia, each of which had sizeable Magyar minority communities.

In March 1990, a violent conflict erupted between Romanians and Magyars in Tirgu Mures. Tensions between Romanians and Magyars had been building for several years and had become even more sharp in the months immediately after December 1989. Magyars had been active in overthrowing the Ceausescu regime, especially in Timisoara, Cluj-Napoca, and Sibiu. As a reward for the role they played in overthrowing the Ceausescu regime, Magyars were given representation in the FSN.

A large number of Magyar community activists, despite Magyar representation in the FSN, were not willing to take a "wait and see" stance as to what special rights Romania was going to grant them. The more "radical" elements among the Magyars were pressing for a clear and immediate response to their demands. They expected to be rewarded immediately for the role they had played in bringing about the Ceausescus' downfall.

With the government seemingly hesitant about meeting their demands, the Magyars began taking matters into their own hands. In several areas where Magyars were the majority population they began firing Romanian teachers and began to require that all classes be held in the Magyar language, forcing Romanian students to leave school. They also insisted that Magyar be used as an official language for all government business in areas where they, the Magyars, were a majority of the population. The Hungarians also formed their own ethnic political party, the Hungarian Democratic Union, later renamed the Hungarian Democratic Union of Romania (the HDUR). In turn, radical right nationalist parties began forming in Transylvania, especially in Cluj-Napoca.

Magyars and Romanians engaged in a series of demonstrations and counter-demonstrations against each other. The Romanians living in areas of Transylvania, where inter-ethnic conflict was especially tense or where Magyars were in a majority organized themselves into a movement called *Vatra Romaneasca* (Romanian Fatherland). The leadership of this organization was strongly nationalistic and became even more so with the passing of time. Vatra Romaneasca's leadership wanted to give the Magyars no quarter. They believed that the only long-term solution to the "Magyar problem" was total assimilation of the Magyars into the Romanian population. As long as the Magyars insisted on maintaining a distinct cultural identity, distinct communities, and their native language, from the point of view of Vatra Romaneasca, they posed a continuing challenge to Romania's control over Transylvania.

The FSN was not about to take any drastic steps. All of the Romanians in the Front had reached their political maturity during Ceausescu's era of "national communism." Moreover, they had a real fear that the Magyar's language demands and demands for control over the education of Magyar children and young adults easily could be come a stepping stone to demands for real autonomy in the Magyar regions, demands which Magyar radical right nationalists were voicing, and, even to secession. On the other hand, Magyar political activists with ties to the FSN were concerned that the Romanians were unwilling to grant them any concessions that they could take back to their people as examples of the good faith efforts the FSN would make on their behalf once it was able to fully consolidate power and establish its legitimacy as the governing force in the county. As a result, tensions between the two communities rose dramatically in the years right after the revolution and the Magyar politicians moved into the coalition of forces that were opposed to the FSN and its successor parties.

In looking at the situation at the time, there were good reasons for the new Romanian government to try to reach an accommodation with the Magyars by recognizing the validity of the Magyars' demands for limited special rights in Romania. The Magyars, based on their experiences under communism and, even, their experiences under Romanian political rule following World War I, did have a distinctive political perspective in Romania. A strong case could be made that the FSN government and, indeed, any subsequent governments formed by other political parties, would not take Magyar interests, concerns, and perspectives into account. This had been the case between the two World Wars and during most of the communist era. Given what they took to be the suppression of their national rights for most of the post-1918 history of Romania, the Magyars, not without cause, believed that without special language rights and special education rights, their culture would be seriously threatened with annihilation. To prevent this they demanded special statutory/constitutional protection in a new post-communist Romanian state.

Magyar leaders claimed that the vast majority of Magyars did not want to continue in a political situation that threatened to ultimately detach them or their children from their communal identity, which they believed was the Romanian state's ultimate goal. In conversations with me, a number of Magyar intellectuals claimed that they could not understand how Romania could be so "short-sighted" in its policies toward their community. They believed that if Romanian leaders were to grant Magyars cultural rights, they, the Romanians, would be developing a valuable internal asset in the new Europe, where, they believed, Hungary would have a prominent place.

The Romanian political elite refused to see any national or international benefits in granting the Magyars what they were demanding. Even those FSN leaders, and others, who understood why the Magyars would want such protection were not about to publicly support making concessions to the Magyars. Politicians realized that taking any action which would appear to be a "surrender" to Magyar demands would threaten their own political positions. In the months after the revolution, any politician or party who appeared to be sympathetic to the Magyars' cause was bound to lose potential votes. This was especially true in the areas of Transylvania, where the political rhetoric and the intercommunal conflict between Magyars and Romanians was threatening to escalate into something very serious. Thus, most Romanian politicians as well as leading intellectual figures adopted what Ben-Rafael 1996:139), dealing with another context, calls a "Unifying Syndrome" as opposed to a "Pluralist Syndrome." In the former, states adopt policies and practices that define the political system as "embodying a unified cultural personality," accord full acceptance to "…members who are 'different' on the condition that they conform to general models," accept those "who are ready to fully integrate into society," and do not provide for "special institutions" that "give expression to cultural particularities" (Ben-Rafael: 1996:139). The Pluralist Syndrome, on the other hand, is exhibited in a society that adopts a "Self-definition which leaves room for social and political differences." Where there is "No a-priori assessment of undiscriminated participation by…members in any sphere." It also involves the state adopting a "Partially exclusionist attitude which may even be plainly segregative" and where the state facilitates an "Institutionalization of cultural differences in the social order" (Ben-Rafael: 1996: 139).

Just as the new government and its successors proved reluctant to institutionalize special rights for Magyars, they also have resisted implementing special rights for Rroma who, unlike the Magyars, are an ethnically scheduled work force that have been organized into an ethnically based sub-proletariat in the Romanian economy. Unlike the Magyars, who formed a political movement behind a hegemonic party within their community, the Rroma have remained politically fragmented, divided between a half-dozen or so political parties, none of whom can claim to speak for the entire "community" of Rroma in Romania. Instead of developing a cohesive ethnic party, the Rroma have "chosen" to have their interests represented through Rroma and non-Rroma politicians in the major political parties. There are some advantages to the option the Rroma have followed and clear disadvantages to the practice of representation the Magyars have followed. According to Heller (1998: 341-354), to opt for a form of auto-representation or to reject any form of hetero-representation in favor of a single party, which has been the Magyars' strategy in Romania, is to seriously compromise a key principle of liberal democracy, i.e. citizens acting in their capacity as individuals, instead of acting exclusively in terms of their ethnic identity. Moreover, when representation is constructed entirely on the basis of ethnicity, the representatives, themselves, find it difficult, if not impossible, to act in terms of the common good of the entire population. Instead, they pursue political strategies aimed at maximizing their own group's interests, instead of some general society-wide interest (Heller 1998: 341-354).

A politics of exclusive ethnic representation, moreover, contributes to, reproduces, and strengthens fundamentalist politics, among other things, by promoting extreme rhetoric on all sides (Heller 1998: 341-354). In the rhetoric that various groups develop within such a context, the give and take characteristic of politics in liberal states is set aside. Politics becomes a matter of staking out an extreme position and discrediting opponents not on the basis of the logic of their arguments, but, instead are discredited because it comes for people who are "not us" and that, alone, is enough to discredit them (Heller 1998: 341-354). A system of ethnic, only, representation, thus, places limits on compromise, on the give and take of "normal" politics in states trying to become (or trying to remain) liberal democracies. Groups become closed off from one another and politics tends to become a zero-sum conflict between the ethnic sub-groups in a state.

Also, politics formally organized along ethnic lines, according to Heller (1998: 341-354), denies the plurality and, indeed, heterogeneity of interests within the various ethnic communities. Interests, other than those tied to one's ethnic identity, are suppressed in favor of the all-encompassing agenda of advancing the presumed collective interests of the group.

Finally, exclusively ethnic representation, creates the very real danger of installing in power within the ethnic community persons whose own, personal interests are served by creating and sustaining an over-arching "ethnocracy" (Heller 1998: 341-354) whose goal becomes maintaining themselves in positions of power for as long as they are able. Once an ethnocracy is institutionalized within a given community, it is difficult to break its power, any dissent from the policies and goals it pursues is seen as tantamount to treason against one's own "people" and to aiding and abetting the enemy of one's people.

Ben-Rafael (1996: 139) points out that that a given dominant culture very well might be more tolerant of some minority cultures than it is of others, which certainly has been the case in Romania. Between 1918 and 1945, the Sache and Swabs, the Lipovinians, Turks, Greeks, and other smaller minority communities did not face the hostility of the Romanian state in the same way that Magyars did. And, even, the Magyars never faced the genocidal practices of Romanian fascism, as did Romanian Jews and Romanian Rroma.

In the midst of all of this internal turmoil, the FSN announced that Romania's first post-communist national elections for parliament and president would be held in April 1990. It angered many of its opponents when it also declared that it would organize itself as a political party and offer candidates for election. The new parliament and the president would have responsibility for overseeing the drafting of a new constitution, which would define Romania's post-communist political system.

Politics became complicated even further in Romania when the former king, Michael of Romania, announced that he planned to make a visit to Romania. The king claimed that he had no political agenda for his visit. He said that his only purpose was to visit the graves of his ancestors. Initially, the FSN gave him a temporary visa to make a short-term. However, it quickly changed its mind and withdrew the visa in April 1990. The FSN feared that the king's return would raise support for making Romania into a constitutional monarchy. There were a number of political leaders, especially among the top leaders in the historical parties, who supported the idea of turning Romania into a constitutional monarchy. These politicians and their supporters saw the king as a symbol of national unity and national continuity and as a figure they could use in their political struggle against the FSN and its allies.

The king did nothing to discourage Romania's monarchists. He had not given up the idea that he could be restored to Romania's throne, where he would preside over a new parliamentary-monarchical system. The king was not about to passively accede to the FSN's ban on his return. The king hastened a minor political crisis over the issue of monarchism, when he attempted to make an unauthorized visit to Romania in December 1990. When the king and his traveling companions arrived at the Otopeni Airport, just outside of Bucharest, they were denied visas to enter the country and were detained in the airport for a brief time until the government could arrange passage back to Switzerland for them. The FSN hoped that their refusal to allow the king to visit Romania would put an end to whatever illusions the king, and Romanian monarchists, might have had about the possibilities of restoring the monarchy.

The former king finally was allowed to return to Romania during the Easter season in 1992. Wherever he went, he was greeted by large crowds, many of whom had come for no other reason than to see this historical curiosity. Eventually, the former king was given permission to take up residence in Romania and was accorded all of the privileges of a former head of state. However, controversy continued to swirl around the former king and his claims to the Romanian throne, should it ever be restored.

Mihai, was Karol II's second son. In 1918, Karol had married Madame Zizi Lambrino, a flamboyant Bucharest socialite whose family were commoners. They had a son, Carol Mircea, born in 1920 (Simpson 2002: A4). Karol II's marriage to Zizi was short-lived. He caved into pressures from his family and his court and allowed the marriage to be dissolved. Soon after, he married Princess Helen of Greece, a lineal descendant of Britain's former ruler Queen Victoria. Through this marriage, the Romanian king became connected to most of the important royal families in Europe of the time. Recall, because Romania had sided with the *Allies* during World War I, rather than with Germany and the Austro-Hungarian Empire, the Romanian branch of the Hohenzollern family were denied the privilege of using the family name, so, winning ties to other royalty through marriage was important to the Romanian Hohenzollerns' legitimacy claims in Europe. Mihai (b. 1921) was the first son born to Karol II and Princess Helen and he was designated as the official heir to the throne. Eventually he was crowned king, only to abdicate under pressure from the communists.

In 1948, Mihai married Anne of Bourbon-Parma, whose family was tied to former French, Spanish, and Italian royalty and nobility. Mihai and Anne did not produce a male heir, instead they had five daughters born between 1949 and 1958. Karol Mircea, Mihai's older half-brother, had married and produced a male heir in 1948. The heir calls himself Prince Paul Phillip of Hohenzollern of Romania. When Mihai abdicated, Karol Mircea won recognition of his claims to the Romanian throne in courts in Spain and France. These decisions, however, had no import in Romania, where the monarchy had been abolished.

In 1996, a provincial Romanian court recognized Karol Mircea as Karol II's legitimate heir. From exile in Switzerland, Mihai immediately challenged the provincial court's decision. The decision of the local court was convenient for the Romanian government at the time, because it helped undermine any legal claims that Mihai had to any status in Romania. Romanian monarchists have refused to support Carol Mircea's claims to the throne. They continue to only recognize as the legitimate former king of Romania. In the meantime, "Prince Paul Phillip of Hohenzollern of Romania," along with his American born wife, has taken up residence in Bucharest where he has pressed his father's royal claim, much to the continuing anger and embarrassment of Romanian monarchists. However, with Mihai now recognized as a former head of state, it appears that "Prince" Paul Phillip no longer has a chance of winning much government sympathy or support for his father's cause. No longer useful to the government, he is now more of an annoyance than a possibly valuable political asset to be used against the royalists.

As the government prepared for the May elections, which initially were scheduled for April, but which were postponed for a month because of technical reasons, it also began facing increasing public demonstrations against its rule, especially in the capital. A large public protest held in Bucharest quickly turned into an occupation of *Piata Universitati* (University Square), which the demonstrators proclaimed to be Romania's "first communist free zone." The demonstrators were an odd collection of dissident workers, students, some persons claiming to represent various minorities, activists in the historical parties, and a small number of intellectuals.

At the most general level, what united the demonstrators was their common support for the Timisoara Proclamation, especially its demand that former leaders of the communist party and/or its various front organizations not be allowed to stand for office in the coming elections. Beyond this general point of agreement, and the view that the FSN were nothing more than a party of neo-communists, there was little else to political unity demonstrators, as there were a wide range of political views represented among those occupying the square.

Some of those who gathered in the square were supporters of the National Liberals, some backed the National Peasant Party, some were monarchists, some were workers who leaned toward the Social Democrats, and still others were from Romania's extreme right wing. The occupiers, generally, were peaceful. They did not attempt to disrupt the life of the city. Nonetheless, the police continually harassed them, but were unable to drive them out of the square.

In the May elections, which observers declared were open and free, the FSN won an overwhelming vote of confidence from the Romanian electorate. Ion Iliescu received 85.1% of the votes cast for president. Radu Campeanu, who stood as the candidate for the National Peasant Party, won 10.6% of the vote, and Ioan Ratiu, of the National Liberal Party, took 4.3% of the vote (Socor 1990: 24-32). Both Campeanu and Ratiu had been in exile for a good number of years and had returned to Romania to run for the presidency in the hope that they would be able to capitalize on what they perceived was their moral stature as long-time émigré opponents of communism. Their hopes were sadly misplaced. The Romanian electorate had no desire to see them, or the political positions they articulated, restored to positions of political power.

In the May parliamentary elections, seventy-five parties offered candidates. The FSN won 263 of the 296 seats in the "lower-house," the Chamber of Deputies, and 92 of 119 seats in the Senate, the parliament's upper-house. The HUDR (the Magyar party) won the second largest number of seats when they took slightly more than 7% of the parliamentary vote (Sucor 1990). The Liberal Party came in third, ecological parties finished fourth, and the National Peasant/Christian Democrat Party came in fifth.

The elections put the FSN firmly in control of the new Romanian government. Iliescu asked Petre Roman to serve as prime minister and to form a cabinet to run the government, which he did. Roman set out a number of economic goals for his government. These included price "liberalization," giving state owned enterprises more autonomy from the central government, encouraging the formation of new private enterprises, changing state laws to allow for private land ownership, developing new monetary and fiscal policies modeled after those of Western states, modernization of the Romanian banking system, opening the Romanian economy to increased foreign investment, and changing the Romanian system of social benefits and social services (Institut fur Hohere Studien 1994).

The losers in the May voting immediately charged the FSN with having won the election through fraud, voter intimidation, and generalized corruption. While there undoubtedly were instances of irregularities in the voting process, international observers did not find enough examples to support the accusations that the FSN had "stolen" the elections. The findings of the international observers, however, did not deter the opposition, who continued to insist that the FSN was a corrupt, neo-communist political organization, a charge that they have repeatedly made against the FSN and its successor political organizations.

The FSN won the election not because it cheated but it won because it was better organized and better prepared to compete in an open election than the other parties had been. It also won because it adroitly used the considerable resources it had at its disposal as the governing party, including control of the national media, to its advantage. The principle organizational advantage the FSN had was that it had inherited the overall structure of the former communists, so it had representatives in all geographical regions and in all social sectors of Romania. It did not have to build party organizations from scratch, as the National Liberal and National Peasant parties had to do. The FSN also had a better understanding of the fears and aspirations of the Romanian people than did the two other major parties, many of whose key leaders had not lived in Romania for a number of years.

The FSN also was helped by the fact that the national elections were held less than a year after the old regime had fallen, which really did not give other political forces time to develop effective party organizations. The National Liberal Party and the National Peasant/ Christian Democrat Party organized themselves in much the same manner as they had before the communists had come to power. Just as they had done when they first were formed, the two parties attempted to organize themselves around the leadership of a "great man" and had not paid much attention to effectively organizing the grass-roots electorate. In this sense, they merely had reproduced the principles of political organization that had characterized both parties before World War II. Neither party seemed to understand that the old networks on which they once could count for loyalty on the basis of personalistic ties no longer existed or, in fact, might not even be able to be rebuilt, particularly in a short time. In building their parties from above and by informally limiting participation in them to institutional elites, the leaders of the National Peasant-Christian Democrats and the National Liberals showed that, *exactly like* their prewar predecessors, they were blinded by their old ideologies, organizational principles, and organizational practices. Neither party could, nor did, trust the Romanian masses. This lack of trust blocked their ability to develop grass-roots organizations that could rival the FSN.

In addition, neither of the historical parties, at this time, had developed a clear agenda for change that matched the aspirations of the Romanian people. The National Peasant/Christian Democrat Party was vague about its program for change in Romania. While it made it clear to the voters that it favored the development of capitalism and the institutionalization of parliamentary democracy, except in the area of agriculture it did not go much further in developing a specific economic agenda. With respect to agriculture, the National Peasant/Christian Democrat Party ran a campaign that argued strongly for privatization of agriculture and for support for the development of a class of free, small-scale agricultural entrepreneurs. What the party seemed to not understand was that this was not a message with a broad initial appeal in all rural areas in Romania. The party leadership had thought that a call for agricultural privatization would resonate strongly among the peasantry. What they, however, failed to appreciate, was that there was not a great deal of support for private farming among the peasantry, especially among those who worked on state farms. By 1990, few of the state sector agricultural workers had ever worked their own farms and few had any idea as to how they might be able to run a private farm if the land was turned over to them. In addition, many of the state farm workers realized that any land redistribution would result in their acquiring very small parcels from which they would have a difficult time generating enough produce to meet their own household's subsistence needs, let alone a surplus that they could bring to emerging agricultural markets. Given their ambiguities about agricultural privatization, many of the state farm workers ended up voting for the FSN, rather than the National Peasant/Christian Democrat Party.

The National Peasant Party, defining itself as a center right political party affiliated itself with the Christian Democrat International in Brussels. When the Christian Democrat International accepted the National Peasant Party's bid for membership, the National Peasant Party became the only member of the International that that was based in the Orthodox religious tradition. All of the other Christian Democrat parties were tied to Western European Christianity. After the election, given its especially disappointing performance among rural voters, the National Peasant/ Christian Democrat leadership charged that the peasants had been manipulated and coerced by local farm managers to support the FSN, rather than them. External observers found no evidence to support these charges. The NP/CD had not lost the election because of voter fraud and/or voter intimidation, it had lost because its message was rejected and because it had a woefully inadequate political organization in the Romanian countryside.

The National Liberal Party, like the National Peasant/Christian Democrat Party, ran on a platform of economic neo-liberalism. Among other things, it advocated a rapid privatization of all state enterprises, the development of a free market economy, the opening of Romania to foreign investment, the ending of government subsidies to producers and consumers, and the like. It also argued for the development of a dynamic "civil society" in Romania and a rapid political, as well as economic, opening of Romania to the West. The Liberal Party, along with the NP/CD, continually denounced the FSN, defining the FSN as a neo-communist party with authoritarian tendencies or worse. The Liberal Party's s message also was rejected by the Romanian electorate and it, too, lacked an effective grass-roots political organization.

The National Salvation Front (FSN), better than any of the other organized political forces of the time understood what Romanians wanted. The FSN knew that the general electorate wanted an effective democratic state that would end the long history of repression in Romania and that no longer would engage in arbitrary rule. In short, the Romanians wanted a state controlled by the "rule of law." The FSN also understood that Romanians wanted economic security within a generally capitalist economy. What this meant was that Romanians while Romanians supported the development of new private enterprises in their country, they did not necessarily want to see a massive sell-off of state enterprises and they did not want to see an end to the broad social welfare programs built by the communists. Finally, the FSN, better than any of the other parties, understood that Romanians were suspicious of, if not fearful of, the possibilities that economic change would lead to the emergence of a powerful class of capitalists who would push to dismantle the Romanian welfare state and would crush its powerful labor unions.

Better than other political parties, the FSN understood that while various polls showed that Romanians wanted economic change, they wanted to go about this gradually. Romanians were almost unanimous in rejecting any economic agenda that smacked of "shock therapy." The general population was well aware of what shock therapy was doing to the Poles and the Russians and they wanted no part of it.

In response to its understandings of what the electorate was feeling at the time, the FSN cast itself as a center-left social democrat party. It endorsed an agenda of gradual economic change, it promised that it would preserve the social welfare system put in place by the communists, it pledged to not break up the state farms, it endorsed a gradual privatization program that would insure that Romanians shared in the disposal of the national patrimony, it claimed that it would maintain wage rates even in the face of inflation, and it pledged that it would be a democratic party that respected the rights of the opposition.

Overall, the FSN's message was that it, alone among the country's parties, understood the aspirations of the Romanian people and understood how to realize these aspirations. The FSN was able to convince the electorate that a vote for them was not a vote to return to communism. Nor was it was not a vote for a party that would not allow Romania to degenerate into the anarchy of a capitalist economy, where the strong prayed on the weak and the weak were left to fend for themselves. Its political message, coupled with its superior political organization, allowed the FSN to win the election handily. It received most of its electoral support from workers employed in the larger state manufacturing enterprises, from miners, from functionaries employed by the state, from pensioners, from state farm workers, from the military, and from voters in the most underdeveloped parts of the country. With this electoral base, the FSN easily overwhelmed the opposition.

After the elections, some of the groups that that had been part of the occupation of *Piata Universitati* withdrew from active participation in the protests. A hard core of demonstrators, however, remained committed to staying in the square, believing demonstrations against the FSN now were more important than ever. Those who remained in the square, many of whom were members of the University of Bucharest Students' League, became increasingly isolated politically. On June 13, 1990, the police moved on the occupiers and forcefully removed them from the square. On the night of the 13th, some of the protesters and their supporters responded to the police violence with violence of their own, attacking a number of government buildings in central Bucharest. At this point, the police appeared to be in danger of losing control of the situation. Police commanders did not really know how to respond to the protesters' attacks. Seemingly, the police would have to use massive force to get control of the situation and they were reluctant to do this for several reasons. First, police commanders were not sure that if they demanded that their men use overwhelming force that they would be obeyed. A large part of the police force was made up of young draftees who might be reluctant to attack the students. Second, remembering what had happened to military commanders who had used excessive force during the events of 1989, the police commanders feared that if there were casualties among the protesters that they might later be brought up on charges that they had overreacted. So, the police reacted in a relatively passive manner. They merely tried to protect state property, hoping that once the protesters vented their anger, they would disperse.

The FSN leadership had been bristling for some time about the occupation of the square and about the charges that protesters and their supporters were leveling against the party, especially the charges that the FSN were neo-communists who had stolen the election. The FSN feared that if the occupation of the square and the ongoing protests were allowed to continue that there was a real danger that things could get out of control and that there would be a repeat of December 1989, when street demonstrations and protests in Timisoara had escalated into a revolution. Yet, the FSN leadership also believed that if the state appeared to be excessively repressive, it could lose its legitimacy.

On the 14th of June 1990, the problem for the FSN seemingly was resolved when a large number of miners from the Jiu Valley "invaded"

Bucharest. The miners claimed that they were coming to Bucharest to "to protect" the Romanian revolution. Shortly after they arrived in the capital, the miners proceeded to attack and drive out the demonstrators in University Square.

The protesters were not the miners' only targets. As the miners marched through the capital, they also attacked private shops and kiosks, showing the miners' disdain for the petty merchant capitalists who had set up shop since December 1989.

The miners also attacked persons who appeared to them to be "intellectuals." People wearing eye glasses, carrying brief cases, carrying books, or who were too well dressed all were suspected of being intellectuals and, hence, opponents of the revolution. The miners also attacked the offices of opposition parties. There were reports that the miners also assaulted Rroma who they encountered on the streets. In some cases miners reportedly went to Rroma neighborhoods where they beat people on the street and attacked newly established Rroma small businesses.

The police did very little to restrain the miners while they were on their rampage. After two days of violence, the miners withdrew from the capital and returned to the Jiu Valley. They had accomplished what they had set out to do. The protesters had been driven from the University Square.

Iliescu was denounced by the domestic opposition and by international media for supposedly having called in the miners to do the regime's dirty work. To the FSN's critics, it appeared that once again Romania was being ruled by a party that had little tolerance for dissent and overt opposition. This was the second *minerada* (miners' invasion) since the fall of the Ceausescus. The first had take place in February 1990 when some 4000 miners from the Jiu Valley had marched into Bucharest to show their support for the FSN after several hundred anti-FSN forces had attacked and damaged the government's headquarters and offices.

If the FSN had hoped it could crush the opposition to its rule by calling on the miners from the Jiu Valley to attack the protesters, it was mistaken. In fact, it helped mobilize many opposition groups and strengthen the ties among them. One of the leading groups that had opposed the FSN was an organization called the Group for Social Dialogue (GSD), which published its own newspaper, *22,* which was named for

December 22, the key day in the Romanian revolution. GSD had a multiethnic membership that was composed largely, but not exclusively, of some of Romania's leading intellectuals, almost all of whom at one time or another, themselves, had been members of the communist party. Many of the leading members of the GSD, at one time or another, had fallen out of favor with the regime for personal and/or ideological reasons. The GSD's leadership was deeply distrustful of the FSN. On more than one occasion they had charged that the FSN with being nothing more than a reconstituted Romanian communist party, whose commitment to democracy and the rule of law was weak, at its very best, and absent, at its worst. The GSD also criticized the FSN with having betrayed its implicit pledge to not organize itself as a party and offer candidates for office in the first elections following the Ceausescus fall.

Another major opposition group was *Alianta Civica* (Civic Alliance). It was formed in November 1990. The Group for Social Dialogue was one of the most important organization behind the formation of the Civic Alliance. Civic Alliance intended to operate as an opposition political movement rather than as a political party. However, in July, 1991, it reorganized itself into a formal political party. Civic Alliance, while well intentioned, was largely ineffective as both as a political movement and, later, as a political party. Its membership overwhelmingly was composed of intellectuals and professionals who, while they might express an interest in working with other strata in Romanian society, had little ability to reach out to other strata in order to build a multi-class political party capable of challenging the FSN. Moreover, intellectuals and professionals made up a very small portion of the Romanian electorate. Because of its inability to attract a mass base, it remained a party primarily for Romanian intellectuals and professionals who could not find a political home in any of the other Romanian parties. Civic Alliance defined itself as a political party of the center, in the European sense of "center."

A third major oppositional grouping was the Democratic Anti-totalitarian Forum (DAF). It was formed in Cluj-Napoca in June 1990 and represented an "alliance" of the National Peasant Party, the National Liberal Party, the Hungarian Democratic Union of Romania, the Social Democratic Party, and a number of smaller parties and groups. Participants at the meeting committed their organizations to work to oppose the "totalitarian" tendencies of the FSN and to work to expand democracy in Romania. Relations between the Civic Alliance and the DAF, at first, were marked by mutual suspicions. However, as parties prepared for the first local elections to be held in 1992, Civic Alliance joined the DAF coalition to oppose FSN candidates for local office. The campaign for local offices pointed up a fundamental weakness of the Romanian political opposition. The opposing parties proved unable to articulate a unifying political vision or political agenda that could put them on the offensive. Instead, their unity was based only on a shared opposition to the FSN.

The cause of the opposition was taken up by the independent newspaper *Romania Libera* (Free Romania). This newspaper had a national circulation and received strong support from the Group for Social Dialogue and from Western sources that wanted to see an independent, free press take root in Romania. In the days immediately following the revolution, Romania Libera would never have been able to survive on revenues from its paid circulation or on advertising, which was virtually absent in Romania. Western funds and Western expertise not only kept the newspaper alive, but such aid also helped its reporters and its editorial staff learn the craft of journalism, as it was understood in the West. Romania Libera was not the only media outlet that opposed the FSN. There were a number of smaller scale publications, for example, 22, that catered almost exclusively to Romanian intellectuals, that also struggled to become independent political voices in Romania

The Group for Social Dialogue and Civic Alliance, saw the creation of a viable "civil society' in Romania as one of their most important goals. They wanted to create open and democratic political spaces at the local and national level. This was a daunting challenge, as Romania never had been richly endowed with networks of private organizations that were autonomous from the state and could serve as the basis for a civil society. After the fall of communism, the situation with respect to private groups was even worse. The Romanian communists had suppressed all attempts to organize independent of the state. So, there were few groups or institutions to which GSD or the Civic Alliance could turn for assistance in their project of building a civil society.

GSD's and Civic Alliance's task of building a viable civil society also was made more difficult by the fact that Romania also lacked a tradition, in the modern era, of relatively autonomous local government.

Local control had been destroyed by the princes and, later, by the king and the bourgeois political parties in favor of a highly centralized national state. Romania, outside of Transylvania, had not even developed independent cities that could help foster the development and institutionalization of a political culture and of political factors favorable to the emergence of civil society.

The development of a civil society in post-communist Romania also had to contend with the fact Romania never had been a democratic state with an open political system in which mass parties contended for power. Between World War I and World War II, Romanian politics was dominated by bourgeois political parties that worked with the throne to preserve the country's system of "directed democracy." This system, as we already have seen, was meant to preserve bourgeois and royal rule and it was designed to insure that workers and peasants would be organized out of the political system, except through participation in the bourgeois parties. Within the system of directed democracy, political parties floated above the general population, they were not anchored in a firm base of grass-roots political organizations. The parties were controlled by the bourgeoisie's political elite and were designed to serve the interests of this elite, the class from which they came, and the throne.

The Romanian state did not have a history of being controlled by the rule of law, which further complicated process of creating a civil society after the fall of the communists. Citizens, at best, had limited and contingent rights that could be wiped out by the state at any time it chose to do so. The Romanian press always had been subject to censorship and government repression, dissident political organizations could be and were banned whenever the state thought it was necessary to do so, and national minorities could be and were subjected to onerous restrictions at the whim of the state. Moreover, even before the fascists had come to power Romania's population was subjected to scrutiny and monitoring by a powerful secret police force whose actions seldom were restricted by the courts. Nor could Romanian citizens be assured of fair and equitable treatment at the hands of the courts, in either criminal or civil matters and Romanian courts had no real rights to review and reverse decisions of the parliament or the throne.

In striving to create a viable civil society, the Group for Social Dialogue and Civic Alliance have helped nurture and protect a wide variety of organizations and social movements and to have worked to promote the cause of building an open society committed to Western liberal values. These two organizations have continued to pursue such goals despite the fact that even in Western societies, where civil societies first had taken root, the basic preconditions for civil society were being eroded or already had eroded (Habermas 1989). If Habermas and others are correct in arguing that the structural preconditions of civil society have been seriously undermined, if not obliterated in the West, one can only wonder what the possibilities are for building a civil society in Romania, where the preconditions for constructing such a social order either were absent or only present in embryonic forms over the course of its history.

The Group for Social Dialogue and Civic Alliance had serious doubts that the FSN had the capability or the interest in creating a state based on the rule of law, especially after the way in which the FSN had used extra-legal force to suppress legitimate dissent and protest, to attack private businesses, to attack opposition political parties, and to assault minorities. These groups also found it troubling that the FSN was unwilling to hold the "terrorists" legally accountable for their behavior during the uprising and for the FSN's unwillingness to open a full-scale examination of who might be held responsible for a wide variety of political crimes committed during the communist period. Romania has not engaged in the practice of lustration (Eyal et al. 1998: 119) to vet politicians and state officials following the overthrow of communism. Nor was it willing, until very recently, to open the files of the *Securitate* so that people could see what information that state had collected about them and who had helped supply the state with it.

There was a certain naiveté in the Group for Social Dialogue's and Civic Alliance's position on the importance of the "rule of law" to the development and maintenance of a democratic state and society. While certainly necessary for democracy, the "rule of law" is not sufficient for its development and continuation. After all, Hitler had come to power under the rule of law and had made sure that the German parliament provided him with a legal basis for most, if not all, of his regime's policies and practices.

Arrayed against the small opposition press was the power of state television and radio and a number of major newspapers, including the FSN's national daily newspaper *Azi* (Today), which had ample resources and expertise at its disposal. The right-wing weekly magazine *Romania*

Mare (Greater Romania) also generally supported the FSN. *Romania Mare* was a highly nationalistic publication that regularly denounced the threat to Romania of the Magyars, the Jews, and the Rroma, who, among other things, were continually defined as an inherently criminal population that threatened public safety and law and order in the new Romania. The communist party's paper, *The Spark,* changed its name to *Adevarul* (The Truth) and generally supported the FSN. In the months immediately following the revolution there was no independent television or radio that amounted to much.

Romania Struggles to Establish an Independent Media

Like other major institutions, in the aftermath of the revolution the Romanian media struggled to establish itself as an independent voice in the new social and political landscape. This has been an especially difficult task in Romania, although it is not alone among formerly communist countries in this regard (Freedom House, n.d.).

At the time of the Freedom House reports, there were 15 national dailies and several score local daily newspapers. There were 50 private television stations and over 100 private radio stations. These radio and television stations serve local markets, the only electronic media that serviced the entire country were Romanian National Television and Romanian National Radio, both of which were state owned and managed, with senior management being appointed by whichever party had control of the government. National television and radio continued to serve more as government organs than as independent media. The state also had maintained considerable indirect control over a large part of the print media, principally through state control over the allocation of newsprint and state ownership of the principal printing plant on which most papers are forced to rely. The government also had exercised considerable control over the distribution channels for the daily newspapers. Because of its control over the allocation of newsprint, the main printing plant in the country, and most channels of print media distribution, the government had been able to apply both subtle and not so subtle pressures against newspapers and magazines that aroused its wrath.

In the case of the broadcast media, the state exercises control over the allocation of broadcast licenses and the assignment of frequencies. There was a supposedly independent Audio-Visual Council that held responsibility for assigning frequencies and awarding broadcast licenses, but how independently it operated is open to debate. Some owners of private radio stations have complained that the Council has shown favoritism in the assignment of broadcast frequencies and licenses, giving licenses and preferred frequencies to those who had the best political connections.

Media that were autonomous from the FSN and the state faced a number of serious problems. In Romania, journalists often were finding it difficult to gain access to even the most simple, straightforward information from the government, even though the 1991 Constitution guarantees access to information and the freedom of expression. State bureaucrats, however, resisted disseminating information that was routinely released to the press in Western countries. State bureaucrats were especially reticent about providing the press with general economic statistics, detailed budgetary information, information on public procurement, data on privatization, data on tax revenues, and the like. As a result, journalists were and are forced to rely on back-channel communications, unnamed sources, innuendo, and rumor for their reporting, making news accounts of various government actions (or inactions) open to questions of validity and reliability. Such a situation is not unique to present-day Romania. Even before the fascists and, later, the communists came to power, the Romanian state functioned as a semi-secret organization. Thus, there is no tradition to which the Romanian state can return in order to learn how to operate a relatively transparent state system.

Romanian journalists work is also made difficult by draconian, punitive laws pertaining to libel and slander. These laws contain provisions not only for high civil judgments, but some of them also have criminal penalties. The libel laws make it a criminal offense to insult public officials or to publish anything that may harm the interests of the Romanian state. These laws have a chilling effect on many journalists and produce high-levels of journalistic self-censorship (Freedom House n.d.).

The independent Committee to Protect Journalists reported that over one three-year period there were 19 separate cases of harassment of journalists, including threats of violence and legal action. This total, if anything, is a serious underestimate of the number of actual threats made against journalists.

Attacks on journalists continued even after the PDSR was removed from power in the 1996 elections and was replaced by the supposedly more Western-oriented parties that made up the Democratic Convention of Romania. The Associated Press (September 30, 1999) ran a release that reported that attacks on journalists who were investigating allegations of corruption had increased significantly in recent months. The Agency for Media Monitoring, according to the Associated Press, had been physically attacked before they had published stories dealing with "illicit business deals" (Associated Press September 30, 1999). One of the reporters, identified as Marian Tudor, age 22, was beaten and thrown from a moving train as he was going to Bucharest with manuscripts that were scheduled to be set in print. The manuscripts, which were said to deal with illegal business activities in the Black Sea port of Constanta, were stolen and never found. None of the money Tudor was carrying was taken. The thieves only wanted the news copy he was transporting.

In another incident, two female reporters, Lorena Boros and Dorina Tataran, who worked for the daily newspaper *Gazeta de Nord-Vest,* were attacked by a number of workers while they were conducting an investigation of a large construction project in Satu Mare, a city located about 500 km. northwest of Bucharest. Ms. Boros was knocked to the ground and her digital camera was taken from her, according to the Agency for Media Monitoring, the workers told the police that they "were forced to beat Boros as she attacked 12 of them" (Associated Press September 30, 1999). Hearing the workers accusations the Satu Mare police officers were taken into custody by the police, according to a story about the incident that ran in the *Gazeta de Nord-Vest.* Following the appearance of the story in the *Gazeta de Nord-Vest*, the Interior Ministry pressured the head of the national police in Satu Mare to issue a public apology for the way in which the police officers had handled the incident, which he did.

Political and police harassment is not the only problem journalists faced in Romania in creating accurate and reliable accounts of what was happening in Romanian society. Even before the fascists and then the communists seized power, the established Romanian press only had limited freedoms and the dissident press, especially on the left, had even less freedom. The press was continually monitored by the secret police in all of the regimes. Under the fascists and the communists, the press functioned as a transmission press for party and government ideology, policies, and practices. When the communist regime fell there was a burst of new publications. Many of the new papers and magazines were, and continue to be, directly tied to political parties and see one of their most important journalistic roles to be the presentation of information that justifies and demonstrates the validity of their party's analysis of events and its political programs.

"Professional" standards of "fact-based" reporting was not a journalistic standard that had taken root in the Romanian press and it still struggles to establish itself as the norm for working journalists and for Romania's newspaper and magazine editors and publishers, for that matter. While there has been noticeable progress in the Romanian press toward realizing a standard of fact-based journalism, especially for papers that circulate outside of the country. A large number of domestic Romanian newspapers are characterized, more often than not, by a mixture of fact, opinion, and speculation.

In the view of many Romanian journalists, their role is not simply to record what is happening, but to provide their readers with an interpretation of the meaning and significance of events. Romanian journalists tend to define themselves as "public intellectuals," that is, they see themselves as part of the intelligentsia, whose right and responsibility it is to be more than mere observers, recorders, and reporters of what transpires in their society. Instead, they struggle to provide their readers with their own analyses of the "facts" of any given story.

The Romanian press also has struggled to separate the various professional roles on a newspaper and a magazine. For example, reporters write articles that are more appropriate to an editorial page, editors often exert undue influence on the content of stories and on what it is appropriate or not appropriate to cover, and publishers/owners frequently write articles and actively intervene in the news side of their publications, shaping editorials and articles to reflect their political views rather than the objective situation.

Western critics of the Romanian press, not only comment negatively on the relative absence of fact-based journalism and the intrusion of owners into the news content of their media outlets, but they also have criticized Romanian journalists for what they, the Westerners, see as ethical lapses. Romanian reporters, according to their critics, have been known to slip into their paper stories favorable to someone or to some organization or to attack others in exchange for a gratuity. Given the meager pay journalists receive, it is hard for them to resist marketing their skills and services to whomever is willing to compensate them for their services, even if this means engaging in actions that are serious conflicts of interest or amount to little more than the outright acceptance of bribes.

Some Romanian journalists also have been faulted for actively serving in political campaigns on behalf of various candidates and, at the same time, writing supposedly objective, neutral news stories about these candidates. Such practices, of course, were not unknown in U.S. journalism.

Western governments, including the United States, and private foundations, such as Freedom House and Freedom Forum, have devoted considerable resources to try to upgrade reporters' "professionalism" and ethics and to educate Romanian editors and owner/publishers as to what their responsibilities ought to be, from the point of view of Western journalism. Special attention has been given to working with universities to establish schools of journalism modeled after Western academic programs. These programs have turned out a number of extremely well-trained, reform-oriented students. These university-educated journalists, often filled with a strong sense of idealism, however, have become frustrated when they have tried to apply the practices and the standards they learned in their degree programs. They quickly find that the reality of journalistic practice in Romania is far different from the ideal that they learned about in their university programs. As a result, many of the young journalists quickly adopt a cynical attitude toward their profession.

Romania Experiences the Building of Militant Free Trade Unions

By the summer of 1991, opposition to the FSN began to emerge among Romania's new trade unions. Free unions had emerged out of the wreckage of the old communist trade union movement. Under the communists, Romania's trade unions, like unions in other Central and East European regimes, were brought into one central organization, the General Trade Union Confederation of Romania (UGSR). The UGSR functioned as a major pillar of the party-state system. Unions had very little autonomy vis-à-vis the party-state. The unions played a critical role in helping the party-state transform a work force that was overwhelmingly peasant in its social origins into a modern, skilled, industrial proletariat. The Romanian unions were the first-line guarantors of the socialist production regimes being put into place in new enterprises and recently nationalized enterprises.

Unions were designed to be a fundamental component in the disciplinary regimen of the shop floors. They insured workers would maintain levels of productivity consistent with the requirements of the state plan. They also were assigned an important ideological role. They were charged with the responsibility of building the new "socialist citizen." Building the new citizen required the unions to be active agents in shaping individual and collective forms of consciousness in ways that were consistent with party ideology and practice. As part of the ideological apparatus of the state system, the unions were one of many structural components being put into place in Romania with the goal of engineering and reproducing consent to the emerging communist institutional order.

The communist unions had non-antagonistic relationships with the state and enterprise managers. Indeed, unions were expected to work closely with management, the state, and the party at all organizational levels in order to achieve the overall tactical and strategic objectives of the communist regime. They thus functioned as transmission belts of policies and objectives that emanated from central party and state organs to the shop floor. Working closely with management and the party, the unions had a variety of positive and negative incentives at their disposal to insure worker shop floor discipline and general political quiescence in the proletariat they were helping to build. Unions shared in the control of worker access to important parts of the social wage, such as housing, vacation privileges, job placements inside the enterprise, work transfers, and the like. In addition, the union, itself, constituted a career mobility path from the shop floor that intersected, at several critical points, with various career paths inside of the communist party and the state. The top leadership of unions was part of Romania's nomenklatura.

By the time of the 1989 overthrow of the Ceausescu wing of the Romanian Communist Party, the country's trade unions had been highly successful in working in tandem with the party, the state, and with enterprise management to maintain communist domination of the labor process and of workers in Romania. The country had very few strikes and little in the way of organized political opposition among the working classes. During the Ceausescu years, there had been only a few instances of major worker rebellion, as noted earlier. Until the mid-1970s, Romania did not experience the major conflicts with workers that the communist regimes in the German Democratic Republic, Hungary, and Poland had experienced, nor did it develop an organized worker led opposition movement that spanned the entire country. Even as worker restlessness increased in the 1970s and 1980s, the Romanian working class did not come together as a unified social movement that challenged the regime. The integration of the official trade unions with the party and their role as major supports of the regime were put to an ultimate test in December 1989 in the insurrection that eventually brought down the regime. The rebellion that broke out in Timisoara showed that the unions, at least at the level of the rank-and-file, had been so extensively hollowed out that they no longer could function as pillars of the regime. Indeed, in Timisoara and, later in Sibiu, Cluj-Napoca, Brasov, and Bucharest, dissident workers were at the forefront of the demonstrations and the fighting in the streets.

Shortly after the overthrow of Ceausescu's regime, workers in several industries took control of their unions and their enterprises, throwing out of office the former communist leaders and factory managers and replacing them with their own representatives. The FSN lacked the power and authority to keep workers from acting on their own in taking over the means of production. Subsequent to taking power, the FSN began dismantling what was left of the Ceausescu regime. One of the first casualties from the old order was the UGSR. It was formally disbanded and a "Provisional Committee" of workers was formed to take its place. The Provisional Committee's leadership largely was drawn from the second and third tiers of the old communist labor confederation. The top leadership of the old USGR did not survive the revolution, they all were purged and went into retirement. The FSN leadership had hoped that the majority of the proletariat would accept the Provisional Committee as the main union to represent its interests. This, however, was not to be.

In June 1990, the Provisional Committee organized itself into the National Confederation of Free Trade Unions in Romania (*Confederatia Nationala a Sindicatelor din Romania*, or CNSLR). CNSLR became one of the largest labor confederations in Romania. In its early days. it closely identified itself with the FSN, but by the mid-1990s CNSLR began distancing itself from the party and its program, becoming a leading voice in the opposition to the government's economic programs. When the FSN, as part of its initiative to restructure Romania's economy, granted workers the right to organize free trade unions, to bargain collectively, and to strike, it opened the door for workers to form organizations that would be alternatives to what the Provisional Committee was putting into place. The FSN's early labor legislation tried to get a semblance of control over relations of production in state enterprises, which had become a hotly contested terrain after the fall of the communists. In late January 1990, the first free trade union confederation with no direct ties to the UGSR was formed. It was called *Fratia* (Brotherhood). Fratia defined itself as a free and independent trade union confederation. Its organizational base was the Driver's Union, however, it was willing to take members from other occupations as well. Initially, its philosophy and program was modeled after American style "contract unionism." which enabled it to get support from the International Labor Organization (ILO) in Geneva. Aronowitz (1983) defines "contract unionism," sometimes referred to as "business unionism" in other works, as an orientation that "...renounces ideological politics" and, instead, focuses on "The business of gaining higher wages, better working conditions, and social benefits for union members through contract bargaining..."(p.65).

In the fall 1990, a second confederation, *Alfa Cartel,* was formed. Alfa Cartel consisted of unions representing workers in heavy industries, such as mining (outside of the Jiu Valley, where the miners elected to keep their union independent of any confederations), steel, heavy equipment manufacturing, electrical equipment, and the like. Alfa Cartel is a self-described Christian Democratic union, which politically aligns itself with the National Peasant-Christian Democrat party. From its first days, it rejected the philosophy of "contract unionism," preferring to construct a politically active trade union movement that was guided by an explicit political philosophy and political practice. Its early political tendencies were strongly anti-communist and strongly anti-FSN. It saw as its major political enemies not only the state and management, but also the former communists in CNSLR. As Alfa Cartel began organizing, its members often had direct and, sometimes, violent conflict with CNSLR organizers. Alfa Cartel's leadership, as well as most of its members, feared that CNSLR, given its ties to the FSN, wanted to integrate trade unions into the state apparatus in the same way that the UGSR had integrated trade unions into the communist state apparatus. Alfa Cartel was determined to resist the subordination of its members to the FSN, which it saw as a neo-communist political party that would turn workers into simple pawns of the state. Among the political demands that Alfa

Cartel advanced was an accounting for the assets of the party's trade union. These assets had disappeared after 1989. Alfa Cartel's stronghold is in and around Timisoara. Many of its earliest leaders and activists had been actively involved in the demonstrations and fighting in Timisoara in December 1989.

In late 1993, Fratia and CNSLR merged, creating a labor confederation with over three and a half million members. The merged union, along with Alfa Cartel and other unions, represented almost eighty five per cent of Romania's organized workers. In addition to Alfa Cartel, Fratia, and CNSLR, a number of smaller confederations had emerged in the months following the overthrow of the Ceausescu regime. Among these were BNS (*Blocul National Sindical* – National Union Bloc), which came into being in early 1991, COSIN (*Confederatia Sindicatelor Independente Neafiliate* – the Confederation of Non-Affiliated Independent Trade Unions), and Hercules. Originally, most of BNS affiliates were in the *Regies Autonomes*. These are organizations and enterprises that the state intended to maintain as public owned entities, including such things as the water works, gas works, and electrical utilities. COSIN is made up of a mix of small unions that banded together into a confederation in order to achieve national scope for their joint activities.

The labor confederations were formed from union federations that had decided to affiliate with one another. Labor union federations are formed from affiliations of local unions. Federations and confederations appear to have developed as a result of grassroots decisions within individual unions. Union consolidation, then, came about as a result of a bottom-up-movement. The local unions involved in federations and confederations have retained a great deal of autonomy. In addition, the largest part of union dues (one per cent of a member's income) remains at the local level. Given the relatively loose organizational ties that bind unions to a federation and confederation, the national level organizations have few resources at their disposal to exert control over or to discipline the local unions. In addition, there has been a good deal of switching of affiliations by the local unions.

Romanian labor law and labor confederation constitutions provide little in the way of centralized control. Under the law and the terms of the confederations' constitutions, it is relatively easy for local unions to disaffiliate from their federations and confederations. A number of unions have remained outside of labor confederations. Among the more important of these is the union representing the Jiu Valley coal miners. It has played a political role in post-Ceausescu Romania far out of proportion to the size of its membership, mainly due to the willingness of the miners to engage in militant and often violent actions, such as it displayed in its multiple Bucharest *minerada*. As will be discussed later, the miners' militancy repeatedly has blocked attempts to restructure their industry since the fall of the Ceausescus, whether these restructuring initiatives have come from governments of the right or of the left.

While the miners were among the most militant workers in the period immediately following the revolution, they were not the only part of the work force to engage in strikes and protests. Strikes had broken out in almost all sectors of the Romanian economy, with the noteworthy exception of the state farms and co-operatives. Workers in the agricultural sector generally remained passive, as they had during the 1989 rebellion. In the early post-rebellion period, a significant proportion of the strikes involved issues of "worker control" and "politics," as well as economics. L.S. Bush (1993) observed that a good number of worker demands at this time included the removal of managers appointed by the communists.

When, following the May elections, Petre Roman took office in June 1990 as Romania's Prime Minister, he had requested a moratorium on strikes until restructuring could be put in place and the economy had begun taking a turn for the better. This was not to be. Strikes continued in virtually all sectors of the Romanian economy. Strikes occurred over a number of issues, some of which had little to do directly with wages and benefits. L. S. Bush (1993) identified several major early strikes that had worker control issues as one of their foci. On January 10, 1990, there was a walkout by public transportation workers. In the same month, there also was a multi-plant strike in Braila, and a strike occurred at a wood processing plant in Bucharest. In March 1990, there was a short "warning strike" at the Ministry of Petroleum. Teachers struck, as well, in the same month. May 1990 saw a major demonstration by pharmacists, who were protesting the promotion of former party activists as health inspectors. All of these strikes had a control issue as one of their foci. The workers were trying to establish rights to participate in the management of their enterprises free of the influence of the state.

An additional indication that the trade union movement was taking a political turn can be seen in the response of some of the unions to the so-called "Timisoara Proclamation," that was promulgated in 1990. The proclamation, put together by leading intellectuals, academics, journalists, and artists, laid out a set of principles for restructuring the Romanian economy, polity, and society along Western lines. On March 11,1990, trade unions in Iasi and Timisoara participated in nation-wide demonstrations that had been called in support of the Proclamation. Trade unions in Bucharest distanced themselves from these demonstrations. A month later, however, Fratia organized national demonstrations among its members on behalf of the Proclamation.

In addition to strikes over issues dealing with control of the processes of production and political issues, workers also engaged in walkouts and protests because of the rapidly deteriorating economic situation that was reflected in falling production, increased unemployment, wage stagnation, and high levels of inflation. Miners struck in Maramures in February 1990 and later they struck in Baia Mare. Also in February, merchant marine seamen struck for improved pay and working conditions. Around the same time, the Jiu Valley miners went on strike, as did air traffic controllers at Otopeni International Airport, just outside of Bucharest, and Bucharest's subway workers. In May 1990, merchant seamen struck in Galati. In each of these cases, appropriate union bodies had sanctioned the strikes.

There were times when workers struck in defiance of union officers' requests that they stay on the job. This was the case in February 1991, when three railway workers' local unions struck, even though the national union had requested that they stay on the job because the government had met most of the national organization's demands. In August 1990, there was a major strike at the Red Flag tractor plant in Brasov, where the 1987 uprising had taken place. Strikers returned to work after a few days when they were promised that the prime minister would meet with them to discuss their grievances and demands. In September 1990, workers struck at the shipyard complex in Constanta. In addition to striking for increased wage levels, the Constanta workers demanded the removal of managers who were not supportive of economic reform and they wanted "...changes in the fundamental nature of the business operation of the shipyard" (Bush 1993: 395).

By the end of 1990, the political demands of the unions were becoming clear and explicit. Many of the trade unions were demanding that the FSN government be replaced. On December 10, 1990, the powerful Drivers' Union called a nationwide strike. The union demanded that the government resign and that a government of national reconciliation be appointed by the president. The government did not fall. It, however, agreed to examine the problem of food shortages, against which the workers were protesting, and to look at the effects economic change was having on the drivers' wage levels. In addition, the government agreed to consider some of the changes that the union was demanding in basic provisions of pending labor legislation.

The local unions and the confederations that formed after the 1989 rebellion did so in a legal vacuum. There was no labor legislation defining trade unions and what they could and could not do. In early February 1991, the FSN-controlled parliament passed two pieces of labor legislation that President Iliescu promptly signed into law. These two bills, together with the Law on Trade Unions that had been passed and put into effect in August 1991, formed the basic legislation governing labor relations. The laws were designed to incorporate labor into an emerging political economy in ways that would minimize its potential for disrupting the political process and that would not discourage potential investors for the state enterprises that had been targeted for privatization. The underlying objective of the three laws was to provide a legal framework that would force the new unions to develop a more cooperative approach toward participation in the transformation process and, should they resist being more cooperative, to provide means for seriously disciplining them. Worker subordination to management was re-established, rights to union political activism were seriously restricted, and curbs were placed on the ability of unions to carry out legal strikes (Bush 1993).

Contrary to what the framers of these laws had intended and what academic experts expected, workers sometimes showed that they were willing to ignore the new labor legislation and to strike when they saw this to be in their interests. Workers also showed that they were unwilling to eschew political strikes and strikes over labor process/worker control issues, despite specific prohibitions against such actions in the newly adopted labor legislation. In their earliest days, most of Romania's fledgling unions saw active political engagement of their members and of their organizations as central, if not essential, to a union's success.

On an economic level, the early strikes attempted to force the government to deal with the rapid price inflation, the continuing shortages of key consumer goods, and the dramatic drop in industrial production that were taking place in the months immediately following the overthrow of the Ceausescu regime. In the months after it took power, the FSN did not have a clear economic program as to how Romania would rebuild its economy. Within the FSN's inner circles, there was a great deal of reluctance to launch a radical, shock therapy agenda of economic reform. Indeed, there was a great deal of internal opposition to any attempt, whatsoever, to begin reinstituting capitalism in any way, shape, or form. Some of the most powerful figures in the FSN wanted to develop an economic program in which the state would continue to own and manage most of the country's major enterprises, while making limited concessions to capitalism by experimenting with highly restricted market relations in certain sectors of the consumer economy. Others within the FSN leadership believed that Romania had no choice but to move in the direction of building a capitalist economy, but they felt that this needed to be a very gradual process consisting of small, incremental changes being made over a long period-of-time. This seems to have been the position advocated by Iliescu and his allies within the FSN leadership, as well as by the larger part of the FSN's voting base. Iliescu was a strong advocate of maintaining state ownership of Romania's largest enterprise for as long as possible and for keeping intact virtually all parts of the social safety net that had been put in place by the communists.

While the FSN was debating its long-term economic program, the Romanian population was experiencing severe dislocations in its economic life. For the first time, large numbers of workers were being dismissed from their jobs. This had been unthinkable under communism, when part of the general social contract between citizens and the state was a guaranteed job for everyone. Even if one's job involved little real work, one still was guaranteed employment.

The economic changes that Romania began introducing brought about a dramatic increase in unemployment. Between 1989, when unemployment was non-existent, and 1993, unemployment rose to 10.4% of the workforce. Between 1993 and 1999, unemployment increased to 11.5% of the workforce. Most of the unemployment burden fell on the working classes, especially on workers who had less than a high school education. Women also were especially hard-hit. The rate of female unemployment between 1993 and 1999 consistently has been higher for women than it has been for men. One of the complaints that Western experts have had about the Romanian unemployment situation was that it has not been *high enough,* especially in comparison to the unemployment rates in former communist countries that were going through "shock therapy."

Petty Merchant Capitalism Emerges

During the first months after the revolution, it was interesting to see the spontaneous creation of small-scale capitalist enterprises in the retail sector. Merchants began appearing in hastily built kiosks or simply set up tables on the street where they peddled a wide variety of goods, some legally acquired and some not. Pirated music tapes from the West were especially popular items being sold on these tables, along with pirated VCR tapes of Western movies and television programs. Other popular items sold on the streets were Western, especially French and American, cigarettes and Western whiskeys.

As grass-roots capitalist activity began to spread and take hold, there was little product specialization. Merchants sold whatever they could get their hands on and what they were selling one week might completely change by the next week. For example, on one of Bucharest's main streets a merchant who was selling a variety of household products out of space that once had been a state store had an engine for a *Dacia* displayed in his window, along with a sign advertising its price. People set up cases of soft drinks and sold them on street corners. One man in central Bucharest sold fresh Turkish coffee directly from large bags in an alley just off *Piata Universitati.* At first he had just his bag of coffee and a set of scales. Later he added a hand grinder and for a small charge he would grind the beans for his customers. Within a year, he was renting space in a building to sell his coffee beans and other goods, such as pastries and individual cups of coffee. In the early days of street capitalism, sellers made no attempt to differentiate themselves from competitors, so that you could walk down the street and find table after table or kiosk after kiosk selling exactly the same products. In almost all markets, prices were negotiable. It seemed that no one, except possibly foreigners (*strainii*) paid the asking price for goods that were on sale. The entrepreneurial spirit even penetrated into state shops. One Friday evening, I needed to buy bread to take to some friends' home for a dinner. The bread store had nothing on the shelf. I asked the store's manager if there was any bread left in the back of the store. The manager shrugged his shoulders. I told the manager I needed two loaves and put an American dollar on the counter. Bread at this point was selling for less than the equivalent of five cents a loaf. The manager just looked at the dollar and didn't respond. A second dollar was put on the counter. The manager still did not respond. As I reached to take back the two dollars, the manager put his hands on them, scooped them up, went to the back of the store, and returned with the two loaves of bread.

Sometimes the markets contained products that were very puzzling. In a "smugglers' market" on the Romanian side of the Ukrainian border, I encountered one Ukrainian man who was selling shoes. Along with about a dozen complete pairs of shoes, he had five or six different single shoes, some of which were the right foot and some for the left foot. When he was asked about the single shoes, the seller said he had bought them at a good price from some Soviet soldiers who had lost a leg or a foot in Afghanistan and he thought there might be some Romanians with one leg who would be interested in buying the shoes. In the same market, another Ukrainian man was selling a partially filled package of birth control pills. I asked him where the rest of the pills were. The man replied that his wife had been using them but that she got pregnant and didn't need the rest so he thought he would bring them along to the market, where he normally sold used clothing.

The immaturity of Romania's retail sector was a temporary phenomenon. It did not take long for stable and viable commercial establishments, modeled after Western European commercial businesses, to emerge in all sectors of the retail economy. The veritable explosion in retail trade for all levels of the market took place soon after the FSN removed restrictions on such activity and abandoned its attempts to control retailers' profits. By the end of the third year after the overthrow of the old regime, the Romanian retail sector had been almost completely revolutionized and the old state retail sector was all but dead. The state retail and service enterprises were a sad sight compared to their private competitors. The state retail shops often had few products for sale. What they did have was locally made, was often poorly designed, was poorly packaged and poorly displayed, and sometimes was clearly defective. The sales staff in the state enterprises often were completely indifferent toward, if not disdainful of, their customers. It was as if the staff saw their customers as bearing some kind of stigma that caused them to be reduced to shopping for goods in the state sector. The contrast between state enterprises and private enterprises was even greater in the service sector. One noticed the biggest difference in the experiences one would have in state restaurants compared to private restaurants. State restaurants had limited menus and it was rare when they had all the items listed on the menus. The quality of the food and its preparation were vastly superior in the private restaurants, as was the quality of the beverages sold. There also was a world of difference in the quality of the service. In the state restaurants, the service personnel seem to have the same attitude toward customers as did the staff of state retail stores. It was not hard for a customer of these establishments to come away feeling that the staff wondered what was wrong with you that you had to eat in their restaurant. The staff looked at you as someone who either was totally without resources or as someone who suffered from terminally bad taste.

The speed with which a capitalist retail and service sector emerged demonstrated how totally the communists had failed in their project to instill a new socialist consciousness in Romania's citizens. Liquidating private property and replacing it with socialist property and subjecting the population to years of ideological education and training had not eliminated entirely capitalist impulses from the Romanian population. The rapid development of this grass-roots retail capitalism also was surprising to Western experts who had flooded into Romania after 1989 to teach the principles of capitalism to a population (wrongly) thought to be totally ignorant of the basic principles of capitalist economic exchange. Rare was the Romanian who did not understand how small markets worked and who had not participated in them even during the Ceausescu era, despite the risks involved in such participation. There were few Romanians who had not been active in the as buyers and sellers of goods and services in the secondary economy.

Not all Romanians were pleased to see the rapid growth of private commercial activity in their country and not all of those who were displeased were former hard-line communists. Among many sectors of Romania's intelligentsia, commerce had been regarded as a morally suspect activity even before the advent of communism and those who were involved in it were not accorded a great deal of social respect. It was not an activity in which any self-respecting person from a "good family," an "old family," or a person who aspired to status parity with them would engage. To pursue a career in business resulted in far less social esteem than one could garner from being employed in the liberal professions or the creative arts. Merchants, in the popular mind, were seen as people who made their money without producing anything of value. In a sense, they were regarded as little better than parasites. It did not help the merchants that they were functioning as a comprador bourgeoisie, i.e. as a bourgeoisie that merely served to channel Western goods into Romanian markets at the expense of locally produced commodities. Merchants also were looked upon as predators, especially when prices for many basic goods, as well as "luxury" items soared in the new private retail establishments that were springing up around the country. The government tried to control the prices in the private retail structure by limiting the amounts of profits that merchants could realize. This, however, proved to be an unworkable and short-lived "solution" to rising prices. The cap on profits simply meant that there were less goods being sold in legal markets. Merchants moved their goods into the underground economy, where prices were even higher than they had been in the legal markets and where the state had no possibility of collecting tax revenues on sales.

One of the most vibrant markets that appeared shortly after the revolution was the buying and selling of currencies. Licensed private shops that bought and sold currency sprouted all over the city. Licenses were awarded to those who had good political connections. In addition, to the licensed shops, there also were a number of other places that engaged in currency trade, without the benefit of a government license. It was always possible for registered guests to get hotel personnel to buy and sell currency for them. Many merchants would do the same for their regular customers or they would allow their customers to pay their bills in hard currency, preferably dollars or marks.

There also was a large and lively street trade in foreign and domestic currencies. The street trade in currency was a risk filled market for the customers. Many of the street dealers were highly skilled at cheating their customers. An American acquaintance of mine used to take $5.00 at least two or three time a month and would go into the street to change it into Romanian currency. His goal was to see if he could figure out how he was being cheated. He never was able to catch the money-changers in the act of defrauding him. Despite watching the exchanges very carefully, he never was able to find the exact moment when he was being cheated. But when he counted his money afterwards, he was invariably short of what he was supposed to get. Street money-changers aggressively pursued foreigners, offering spectacular exchange rates. For someone new to the country, these deals seemed too good to resist, but, unfortunately for the foreigners who used street money-changers, they ended up losing far more money than it would have cost them if they had used legitimate dealers.

When the government began to let allow the lei to float, within a broad range, the costs of hard-currency on the legal markets and the illegal markets began to converge. However, this did not wipe out the black-market. Illegal trade in hard-currencies continued to flourish. The market was kept alive by government regulations that allowed Romanian nationals to convert only the equivalent of $500 worth of lei into hard-currency in any given year, that allowed Romanians to take only the equivalent of $1000 abroad for the purposes of tourism, and which forbade Romanians from holding foreign bank accounts or owning foreign stocks. The restrictions on the amount of hard-currency a Romanian could acquire by converting lei and the limits on the amount that could be taken out of the country for tourist purposes were kept in place until 1997.

The state officials condemned the illegal money markets and the selling of other illegally produced or acquired contraband and, from time to time, aggressively tried to stamp out this type of trade. But it never could eliminate the underground markets. Merchants and buyers devised a wide variety of strategies to avoid detection, including paying bribes for protection from arrest and prosecution.

The Development of Secondary Illegal Markets

Other far more lucrative illegal markets sprouted up after the fall of communism. Soon after the revolution, thriving sex markets began to appear in most Romanian cities. During the communist era, prostitution existed, but it was hidden away and the market was difficult to access for almost all Romanians and for a lot of foreigners, as well. During the post-communist period, prostitution is controlled by local *mafiyas* that function under the protection of local officials. A large number of the street-level members of these *mafiyas* were drawn from Romania's criminal classes, others were former police officers, former military personnel, former officers in the security services, and former members of the communist state's extensive network of athletic associations, teams, and sports clubs. These people were not hard to spot in and around any

Romanian city. They dressed alike, used the same speech idioms, and behaved alike. Their clothing seemed to emulate the stereotypes depicted in bad American movies about the mob. They liked to wear track-suits or leather jackets and coats and they usually wore large rings and gold necklaces. Some of these men were heavily tattooed, which was a good sign that they had served some time in prison.

After the revolution, the prostitution markets became more open and accessible both to Romanians and to foreign visitors. While street-walkers continued to be a rarity in almost all of Romania's cities, prostitutes easily could be found in hotel lobbies, in bars, and in certain restaurants. They also could be accessed through taxi cab drivers, who frequently would inquire of foreigners if they had any special interests or needs that the driver could help them with. This type of solicitation was particularly common on taxi trips from airports to city hotels. Prostitutes' services also could be purchased through hotel employees and from other service workers who had extensive contacts with the general public and with tourists.

Romania also developed a flourishing trade in homosexual prostitution. Romania became a popular destination for gay sex tourists from Northern and Western Europe. Many of these tourists came in the belief that Romania's gay men would be relatively free of AIDS, given that the country had been sealed off during the Ceausescu years. Romania also was attractive as a stop for gay tourists because the prices charged by Romanian male prostitutes were substantially lower than what was being charged in most other parts of Europe. Several homosexual tourists told me that the only place better than Romania for finding inexpensive gay male prostitutes was Poland. According to these men, Poland's prices for male prostitutes not only were far cheaper than what one found in Romania but Poland's male prostitutes were far less inhibited, far more adventurous, and had far more "extreme" sexual interests than the typical Romanian male prostitute who was serving the gay trade.

Romania also began to see the emergence of a thriving illegal drug market. Even more than was the case with prostitution, access to illegal drugs markets was highly limited during the Ceausescu period. It was difficult even to acquire marijuana. Buying, selling, and using illegal drugs carried heavy jail penalties. One had to be a very well connected member of the nomenklatura or the relative of such a person to get access to most of the country's illicit drug markets when Ceausescu was in power.

This changed dramatically after the revolution, when Romania became an increasingly important transit country for drugs coming out of the Middle East, Central Asia, Turkey, and even more distant places. Romania is located on what has come to be called the "northern Balkan route." Romania's importance to international drug smuggling networks increased partly because traditional smuggling routes through Yugoslavia were disrupted by the wars being waged there. Smugglers bring drugs into Romania by air, by land, and by sea. Romanian drug enforcement authorities estimate that only about 10% of what enters the country remains there for local use. The remaining 90% is moved into Europe, either immediately or after having been warehoused for a brief time in Romania.

Romania does not appear to be a significant drug producer country, either for domestic or international markets. According to Romanian law enforcement authorities, there is a limited amount of local cannabis production and there are "a few" producers of methamphetamines for local markets. Romania does not have a large problem with cocaine or heroin abuse.

One of the country's biggest public drug problem involves the widespread use of inhalants by homeless young people who live on the streets in most Romanian cities. It has been estimated that there are as many as 3000 young children living on the streets of Bucharest, with another 10, 000 working the streets but who return to their families at night.

One can see the same phenomenon in other Romanian cities, but, in other cities, the homeless children are not as prevalent as they are in Bucharest. These young people, some of whom do not appear to be much older than 7 or 8, survive through petty crime, begging, and prostitution. Many of these children had been abandoned or driven from their homes by parents who could not afford to provide for them. Some of them had been sent to orphanages from which they eventually escaped, while others had run away from abusive family environments. A large number of these children had drifted into Romania's largest cities from rural areas and from small towns where their chances of surviving on their own were minimal. Many of the street children are physically or mentally impaired and seem to have been so before they became homeless. There is anecdotal evidence indicating that some of these children have turned to heroin use.

After 1989, Romania became a center for automobile smuggling in Southeastern Europe. Cars stolen in the United States and in Northern and Western Europe found there way into Romanian markets, where some stayed and some were sent on to other markets in the Balkans and places even farther afield. The Transylvanian city of Cluj-Napoca became one of Romania's most important markets for stolen cars. At one point, and still perhaps, one could walk around the city and see cars being driven by Romanians with license plates from Western European countries and from American states still on them. Cars that could not be sold to Romanians are wholesaled to other regions in Southeastern Europe.

The smuggling of human cargo also became a lucrative market in Romania. Romanian smugglers, working with smuggling networks in other countries, became involved in bringing illegal immigrants, largely from Asia, Africa, and the Middle East, into Romania, which the illegal immigrants then used as a jumping off point for movement into Western Europe. Romanian smugglers also became involved in illegally "exporting" young women to Israel and other parts of the Middle East, Western Europe, North America, Turkey, and Cyprus, to name just a few of the more important destinations, where they were forced to work in the sex trades. Along the way, the women's money, passports, and other documents are confiscated. When they arrived at one of their destinations, the women are told that they are in debt to the people who had brought them out of Romania. They then are forced to work in various sex businesses, including prostitution, the production of pornographic videos and films, and the like in order to pay off what they owed to the smugglers and the person or persons who had bought them from the smugglers.

When women no longer were useful to their owners, they often are sold to someone else and moved along to a new destination, where they again are put to work in the sex trades. If, and when, women try to escape their situations, they are severely beaten and sometimes killed.

Romanian smugglers also became heavily involved in the illegal baby trade. After the Ceausescus' fall, the international media focused on the human interest story about thousands of Romanian children and babies who were reported to be living in under-funded and under-staffed orphanages. Many of these children had been sent there because their families could not afford to keep them. They had been born because of the regime's ban on abortions and because of the difficulty the average Romanian had in buying safe and effective contraceptives. These stories, which saturated Western newspapers and television reports, especially in the United States, led to an enormous number of Western families wanting to adopt these children, a significant number of whom had serious health and/or emotional problems. American lawyers opened offices in a number of Romanian cities and sought local partners who could help them understand and apply Romanian adoption laws, which, as one could imagine, were extremely complex, especially when the prospective adoptive parents were foreigners. It took months and sometimes years for a legal adoption to work its way through the Romanian courts. The courts gave the birth parent(s) a number of chances to reclaim their parental rights, so the process was fraught with risks for the foreigners. It soon became clear to anyone involved in the adoption market that demand far outstripped supply. Very quickly, smugglers entered the market. They bought children directly from parents or paid pregnant women to sell them their prospective infant and made arrangements with Romanian lawyers to put these children on the adoption market. So blatant did the smuggling become that the Romanian government suspended all adoptions until it could reassert control over the market.

Petroleum products also became an important commodity for Romanian smugglers, especially during the Yugoslav wars, when an oil embargo was placed on Serbia. Despite widespread, popular support for Serbia in Romania, a succession of Romanian governments agreed to side with the Western powers in their ongoing attempts to undermine the Milosevic regime, one of they key weapons of which was the oil embargo. After the oil embargo was imposed on Yugoslavia, an unusual number of gasoline stations sprang up along the Romanian-Serbian border. Far more were built than local traffic or tourist traffic seemingly could support. It was suspected that Serbia was sending gasoline tank trucks and other vehicles to a number of these stations to get fuel. There also were cases where large Romanian airliners, carrying no passengers, would land at airstrips along the Serbian-Romanian border and would offload jet fuel, sometimes into on-site tanks and sometimes into tank trucks. A large amount of this fuel, if not all of it, made its way into

Serbia. Smugglers also regularly ran the blockades that Romania had set up on the Danube to prevent trade with Serbia.

These large-scale criminal activities were, and are, carried out by fairly sophisticated and often violent criminal networks that are the heart of the Romanian *mafiya*. The Romanian *mafiya* is not integrated into a nation-wide overarching hierarchical structure. Instead, it is made up of a number of localized networks, perhaps as many as two dozen, that have some marginal ties with one another but, which, for the most part, act an independent criminal enterprises. These networks operate in local areas where they have taken control of illegal activities or, in more rare cases, they operate nationally by virtue of a monopoly that they exercise over certain domains of criminal activity and/or illegal commodities.

There is a good deal of competition and conflict among these networks, especially where more than one network is operating on the same territory or when there is more than one network involved in the same domain of criminal activity. In the Transylvanian city of Brasov, two criminal networks once engaged in an open fight in the city's streets over control of part of the city's illegal economy. Internally, the criminal networks are bound together by strong ties of reciprocal dependencies, long-term friendships, inter-marriage, kinship, and/or common ethnicity in the case of the criminal networks in the Magyar and Rroma communities.

Immediately after the revolution, the Rroma long-distance trading networks proved especially adept at using their contacts with Rroma communities throughout Europe to expand their trading activities. Under the communists, there was a good deal of "tolerance" of Rroma trading activities. It was one of the few ways that Western products could get into the country after Ceausescu suspended almost all imports from the West. After the revolution, there was an explosion in the smuggling of Western, especially American and French cigarettes, into Romania. Rroma smugglers found ways to ship these cigarettes to places like Berlin, where they traded them for goods still scarce in Romanian markets, such as various medicines and pharmaceutical products acquired by their trading partners from the German national health service at very low costs. They then brought these back to Romania and sold them to pharmacies or directly to individuals who might be in need of them. When these pharmaceuticals became more readily available on Romania's domestic markets, the Rroma trade networks proved highly flexible in identifying new goods for which there was a demand in Romania. Even more dangerous has been the smuggling of arms and explosives out of Romania. There even have been arrests for the smuggling of various nuclear materials.

The Romanian national police and security networks have proven unable to successfully combat international smuggling operations. The police forces have been woefully under funded, under staffed, and under trained. In addition, after the revolution they lost a large number of their more experiences police commanders, who chose to retire rather than work in the uncertain post-revolutionary climate. Police effectiveness in fighting against the smugglers and against organized criminal networks, in general, also has been limited by the police's lack of experience in dealing with this type of crime and by the virtual absence, especially right after the revolution, of good working contacts and relationships with Western European police forces. The Romanian police have had a difficult time fighting the organized crime networks because many of these criminal networks often have more resources at their disposal to resist police penetration than the police have to fight them.

The various Romanian *mafiya* networks have proven themselves very adept at building extensive trading relationships with their counterparts across Europe and even further. For example, there have been claims that Romania's criminal networks have established relationships with the Sicilian Mafia, with other Italian criminal organizations, with Serb and Albanian crime groups, with Turkish racketeers, and with various criminal syndicates in the Middle East. The importance of the Romanian criminal networks to international crime in Europe increased dramatically when the transportation routes through Yugoslavia broke down because of the various wars being fought there. Because of the wars, Romania replaced Yugoslavia as a major smuggling route. The Romanian criminal syndicates also have been reported to be involved in the smuggling of weapons and, even, nuclear materials. Romanian criminal networks also have been active in Western Europe, for example Germany, where they operate as independent groups or in conjunction with criminal gangs in these countries.

The Romanian *mafiya* networks have used their enormous profits to finance even larger scale criminal activity and to invest in legitimate businesses in Romania. In the process, they appear to be becoming a significant component in Romania's emerging bourgeoisie. They also have exported capital abroad sequestering money in secret bank accounts in Switzerland, Cyprus, and other places were hot money can be hidden or investing in Western European businesses.

There have been a number of allegations that the various *mafiyas* also have used their money to penetrate the state and corrupt state offices as well as individual office holders. Such allegations especially have been made against the criminal networks that supposedly have been built by former members of the *Securitate* and other police services that once had worked in the Ceausescu regime.

Undoubtedly it is true that some former members of the *Securitate* turned to organize crime after December 1989 and have used their contacts with former colleagues still working for the state to obtain protection or at least tolerance for their criminal activities. However, there is a tendency among Romanians to exaggerate the role of former and present *Securitate* agents in organized crime. In present-day Romania, the old *Securitate* has taken on the character of a *chimera,* to which all types of fantastic malevolent powers and influence have been attributed. There is a tendency among Romanian commentators to blame the former *Securitate* and its successor organization, the Romanian Information Service, for virtually everything that has gone wrong in Romania since the end of the Ceausescu regime. It, the former *Securitate,* often is presented, in the media and in popular opinion, as the heart of a vast conspiracy that is keeping Romania from making a successful transformation from communism to capitalism and from dictatorship to democracy by thoroughly corrupting the Romanian state and Romanian culture and society.

The rapid growth of large-scale criminal enterprises has taken place at the same time that there has been a growth in "petty" crimes against persons and property, especially in Romania's larger cities. Before the revolution, street crimes, burglaries, car thefts, robberies, and breaking and entering crimes were negligible, as were assaults, rapes, and murders. This changed after the revolution, when almost all types of such crime showed sharp increases, although their levels remain far below those of Western European and, especially, American cities. Calin Mateescu, the director the police unit responsible for battling organized crime, in an interview with the daily newspaper *Meridian,* that part of the reason for Romania's increase in crime was its geographical location at the boundary of the former Yugoslavia and its proximity to the former Soviet Union (British Broadcasting Corporation July 29, 1993).

Mateescu said that there were substantial increases in murders, especially murders-for-hire, banditry, blackmail, rape, weapons and explosives trafficking, and drug smuggling. He also observed that organized crime, some of which had an international dimension, was beginning to take hold in Romania. In September 1993, Major General Ion Pitelescu, chief of the General Police Inspectorate of Romania, released figures showing that crime was increasing dramatically in the country (British Broadcasting Corporation September 16, 1993). Pitelescu reported that the police had registered 139,104 criminal offenses in the past eight months, which was an increase of 35,930 offenses compared to the same period of the preceding year (British Broadcasting Corporation September 16, 1993). The general stated that property crimes had increased over the past year by 30% and that various kinds of what, in the United States, are called "white collar crimes," e.g. fraud, influence peddling, corruption, and the like, had increased by 51% (British Broadcasting Corporation September 16, 1993). The general claimed that the most troubling criminal development over the past year was the growth or organized criminal gangs that were trafficking in drugs, smuggling humans in and out of Romania, engaging in currency forgery, and car theft, among other things (British Broadcasting Corporation September 16, 1993). The chief reported that over 1000 Indians, Sri Lankans, Somalians, and Nigerians who had entered Romania illegally had been detained by the police and that the police had succeeded in breaking up a gang of street toughs who had been preying on foreign tourists (British Broadcasting Corporation September 16, 1993).

As crimes against persons increased or were perceived to be increasing, Romanians began to feel less safe on their urban streets, in their neighborhoods, and in their homes. Crimes against retail establishments and other enterprises also increased. Romania also saw an increase in truck hijackings and robberies of passengers on trains. People who had the resources to do so, began installing a number of security protections for their homes and their properties. These often included the installation of alarm systems, reinforced doors, and windows, and the like. Many businesses have hired private security forces to protect themselves and their customers. Perceptions that crime is increasing and that it is in danger of getting out of control (which is far from the reality of the situation) has led to demands from some quarters of Romanian society, especially the radical right, for reinstituting harsh criminal penalties, including restoring the death penalty (Keil, Vito, and Andreescu, 1998), and for targeting national minorities for special police attention. As in their struggles against organized crime, the Romanian police have had to try to wage a war against street crimes, robberies, assaults, burglaries, rapes, and the like without the resources necessary to do so. Romanian police commanders often feel that they are being overwhelmed by increases in these types of crimes and that they are being blamed, unfairly by the government and by popular opinion for seemingly having failed to keep such crime under control. However, when one looks at police staffing, their lack of adequate equipment, and the poor state of the forensic infrastructure within police departments it is easy to understand police frustrations over the limited success they have had it combating increasing crime rates. Romanian police effectiveness also was limited because for many of the newly promoted commanders nothing in their past training and their past experience had prepared them to deal with the increases in crimes that they were facing. Police commanders did not know how to deploy their limited resources in the most effective ways possible and they did not know how to evaluate the success or the failure of what they were doing. Police commanders also had to deal with a confused and often demoralized corps of rank-and-file officers. After the revolution, many of Romania's police officers had no clear understanding of what was expected of them. They knew that the old rules of the game no longer were valid, but new rules about how to do their job had not been developed and communicated to them. As a result, they often avoided taking actions against alleged criminals in order to avoid getting themselves in trouble with their superiors, with the courts, or with the public. Police commanders also had to deal with low morale among the rank-and-file because of their very low pay. Commanders found it hard to ask officers to put themselves in harm's way to enforce the law when they knew how little the officers were being paid. Low pay also complicated law enforcement efforts in Romania because it increased the likelihood that individual police officers would fall prey to various forms of corruption.

Police work also was made more complicated in Romania after 1989 because the police had to make a considerable effort to win the respect and the trust of the public, which was no easy matter. The average Romanian did not have a great deal of trust in the police prior to 1989. The police were seen as part of the repressive apparatus of the

Ceausescu dictatorship. So it was relatively rare for the average Romanian to willingly cooperate with the police. In addition, most interactions between the average Romanian and the police were filled with tension and not an inconsiderable amount of mutual hostility and mutual mistrust. Building the general public's trust and respect has been one of the most important and critical challenges the police have faced at all levels of rank, from commanders to street patrol officers.

The Plight of the Rroma in Post-Ceausescu Romania

Building relations of respect and trust have been very difficult for the Romanian police working in minority communities, especially in the Rroma communities. It has been estimated that there may be as many as three million Rroma living in Romania (Kinzer 1992). Rroma community activists repeatedly have charged that the Romanian police have singled them out for selective law enforcement practices. The activists argue that they are far more likely to be arrested for various offenses than are non-Rroma and are more likely to be tried and convicted of crimes than are other citizens. Rroma community leaders also charge the police with being less willing to protect individual Rroma from crime than they are of protecting individuals from other communities.

I once witnessed an example of this in a subway stop near *Parcul Tineretului* (Youth Park). One evening, a young Rroma man ran down the steps of the subway. Two Romanian men were at his heels. The Romanian men caught the Rroma teenager at the foot of the stairs and began beating him. A policeman, in uniform, was standing at the platform but did nothing to stop the assault. An older Rroma woman, who usually sold flowers at the subway stop, started screaming at the policeman to help the boy. The policeman just turned his back on her. Three Rroma men who had been watching from about 30 feet away, seeing that the policeman was not going to help the boy, rushed to his assistance and broke up the fight. It was obvious that the two Romanian men had been drinking heavily, which, as it turned out, had been partly responsible for their behavior. One of the Romanian men explained to the crowd, who had gathered around, that he and his friend had been trying to put money in the subway turn still. His friend finally had managed to put his token in the slot, but had fallen down before he went through the gate. The Rroma boy, evidently having seen what was happening, rushed through the gate, in effect "stealing" an admission to the subway. The men, outraged at this, chased the boy.

As the men were telling their story, the subway bound for the center of the city arrived. Everyone got on the train. The old Rroma woman kept shouting at the policeman for not having helped the boy. The policeman told the woman to leave him alone. He said he was off-duty and had no responsibility to get involved in the fight.

Later, relating what had happened to about half a dozen Rroma acquaintances, I was told that events like this were common. They all had a similar story to tell. They went on to say had the situation been reversed, that is, if two Rroma men had been beating a Romanian man, the policemen would immediately have intervened and arrested the Rroma men. Several human rights experts working in Bucharest confirmed the Rroma's opinions. They said that they had received a large number of complaints from Rroma about the police's lack of willingness to protect them and their property while, at the same time, being more willing to arrest Rroma for alleged offenses than members of other national communities. Many of the human rights activists pointed to the attacks by the miners on the Rroma, for which no one was arrested, as an example of "typical' police behavior.

Shortly after the incident described above, a more serious example of what the Rroma took to be police "favoritism" took place in a Bucharest neighborhood. Two off-duty Romanian soldiers, from a military installation not far from the neighborhood, were drinking in a tavern, most of whose patrons were Rroma. The Romanian soldiers were dressed in civilian clothes. During the course of the evening, the soldiers got in an argument with several of the Rroma patrons. Soon, the exchange of words turned into an exchange of blows. The soldiers were severely beaten. How many Rroma were involved in the fight was not known.

The soldiers returned to their base and told their friends and colleagues what had happened. The next night, a large number of soldiers, were brought close to the neighborhood in military vehicles. Dressed in civilian clothes and armed with clubs and other such weapons, they attacked the neighborhood and the bar, injuring several patrons and a number of people on the street. Several Rroma later claimed they had contacted the police, but none had come to protect the neighborhood. When the police came, they took statements from witnesses, but, according to neighborhood residents, none of the soldiers who had attacked them were arrested or charged with any crime.

In the aftermath of the event, Rroma activists brought a number of complaints to European human rights groups that had offices in Bucharest. The Group for Social Dialogue offered its good services to mediate the dispute between the Rroma and the police and the army. The Group for Social Dialogue set up a meeting at its Bucharest headquarters, inviting representatives from the Rroma community, the police, the military, and human rights organizations, as well as representatives from the United States Embassy.

The meeting was interesting in several respects, not the least of which was because of the tensions inside of the Rroma community's leadership the meeting inadvertently exposed. The first to speak were a number of older Rroma men who represented the traditional leaders of the various Rroma communities in the city. For the most part, the traditional leaders took a conciliatory stand, stressing the need for Rroma-police and Rroma-government cooperation to avoid a repeat of such events in the future. The next to speak were a group of much younger men, many of whom had been involved in starting community organizations in Rroma areas after 1989. The younger men used strong language to attack the military commanders at the local base from which the soldiers had come, the police for not intervening in a timely manner, and the government for allowing all of these events to take place without any apparent attempt to hold people responsible for violating Rroma rights. They made it clear to the government officials, the police, and the military that the Rroma community could not be expected to tolerate such behavior in the future. It was clear that to these young men the traditional leaders' approach to the situation was not adequate. The traditional leaders had not wanted to embarrass government, military, and police officials. It was evident that the traditional leaders would have preferred to not be at the meeting, they had wanted to rely on informal networks to manage the situation, rather than create a public conflict.

The government officials, the police, and the spokesperson for the military laid out their views of the situation. They tried to convince the Rroma that there had been no intent to violate Rroma rights and that all elements of the Romanian state were committed to protecting Rroma and advancing their rights. None of the officials admitted that their organizations had made mistakes in the handling of the situation, nor did anyone apologize for what had happened. The officials, however, did promise to look into the events surrounding the attack on the neighborhood to try to insure that there would be no further incidents like it.

While the presentation of officials and the subsequent discussions seemed to have satisfied the Rroma traditional leaders, it was very apparent that the younger men were less than pleased with what they heard. After the meeting had adjourned, the young men made it clear that in their view if the government continued to fail to protect Rroma communities, then the communities would need to take steps to protect themselves and that they were willing to help organize the communities to do so. The organizations from which most of these younger men were drawn represented an interesting and important development that apparently was taking place in Bucharest's Rroma communities: the emergence of pan-Rroma organizations. As anyone familiar with Rroma society is aware, historically Rroma have organized themselves along tribal lines. The tribe has been the basis for one's personal and collective identity and it has defined one's occupational specialization. Under the communists, who pushed to settle the Rroma in fixed locations and to incorporate them into modern educational and economic institutions, it was hoped that traditional tribal identities would be weakened. Under the communists, a significant cadre of Rroma intellectuals developed in Romania, who became advocates for the Rroma cause. One of the major projects of these intellectuals was to develop a pan-Rroma consciousness within the Rroma population. Their efforts included attempts to standardize *Romaney,* the Rroma's traditional, non-written language, and to develop a written form for the language. The intellectuals, working with traditional leaders, also tried to help Rroma communities develop economically, within the parameters of what was allowed by the communist state.

Largely as a result of communist policies, the Rroma in Romania are predominantly a settled people. The Romanian communist regime, like other communist states, had pursued policies, which sometimes were highly coercive, that were designed to force the Rroma into a settled existence. In Romania, the authorities had tried to confiscate all of the Rroma's horses so that they would not have the means to remain mobile. There, however, continue to be a small number of Rroma who live a traditional, nomad life. The nomads are propertyless wanderers in a land where relative fixity, defined in terms of ties to land, localized job markets, and community were, and continue to be, valued as symbols of personal trustworthiness and respectability. The nomadic Rroma, living under the "open skies," as they put it, have high levels of fertility; high infant and child morbidity and mortality rates; high levels of maternal mortality; low levels of literacy and educational achievement; relatively large proportions who speak only Romany; and generally lack occupational skills that would allow them to be integrated into modern sectors of the Romanian economy. The nomads' social structure is based on traditional craft groupings, of which there are nine in Romania. Within the craft groupings, which have strong parallels with tribal social organization in other societies, the extended family is a vital part of Rroma life. The nomads' family structure is rigidly patriarchal. Women marry young, are expected to bear a large number of children, and are expected to be active in the cash economy. Nomads, usually, have high levels of poverty.

A second grouping among the Romanian Rroma are the partially settled. These Rroma are only marginally better off than the nomads. The partially settled Rroma differ from the nomads in that they have fixed residences in a village, town, or city, but live as nomads for part of the year. They usually speak both Romany and Romanian and they possess some skills that allow them to work in modern economic sectors, even if their participation only is in peripheral activities. They are concentrated disproportionately in jobs that offer irregular employment, low wages, high physical risk, and almost no opportunities for promotion. Like the nomads, the partially settled Rroma have high fertility rates; high infant and child morbidity and mortality rates; high levels of maternal mortality; low levels of educational attainment; and high levels of illiteracy. Identity as a member of a particular craft grouping among the partially settled is highly attenuated, compared to the nomads. Instead, they are more likely to identify themselves in terms of an emerging collective consciousness of being a Rroma.

A third grouping is the assimilated Rroma. While they retain some identification with their ethnic heritage, for all intents and purposes, these Rroma have become almost fully incorporated into Romanian society. While they may participate in selected aspects of traditional Rroma life, such participation is elective, rather than a matter of communal obligation. The assimilated Rroma are more likely to live in larger towns and cities in Romania than are the nomads and the partially settled Rroma and they also are more likely than these groups to live in ethnically mixed neighborhoods in the towns and cities. The assimilated Rroma are more likely than other Rroma to have achieved higher degrees of occupational stability in modern economic sectors; have higher levels of educational attainment; and have higher levels of functional literacy than do the nomadic and partially settled Rroma. Their fertility rates; child and infant morbidity and mortality rates; their maternal mortality rates; and their overall life expectancy are closer to the Romanian average than is the case with the nomads and the partially settled Rroma. The assimilated Rroma participate in non-Rroma social institutions at much the same level as does the dominant population, they are willing to enter into informal relations with non-Rroma, and they are more willing than are the nomads and the partially settled to marry outside of the group. For the nomads and the partially settled, to marry a Gadja (a non-Rroma) is to break a taboo that leads to complete expulsion from one's family and one's community.

The last category of Rroma in Romania are the Passed Over. This group is made up of an unknown number of Rroma who have lost virtually all contact with their cultural heritage and their people. They no longer think of themselves as Rroma, nor are they perceived to be such by the Rroma or by the larger Romanian population. Their levels of social attainment and their behavior differs little from that of other Romanians. They have no involvement in Rroma communal institutions and all of their social activities are in the formal and informal institutional relations of Romanian society, in general.

Under the communists, state policies led to a number of important gains for the Rroma populations in Romania. Communist policies led to the raising of educational levels in Rroma communities, expanded their access to public health services, provided Rroma with a number of social supports, improved Rroma housing, provided the Rroma with jobs in modern sectors of the economy, and, overall, raised Rroma standards of living. However, despite all of these improvements, the Rroma continued to lag behind other Romanian national communities in just about all measures of personal and community well-being. In return for these "benefits," the Rroma find that they were surrendering significant parts of their traditional way of life in order to live as settled peoples. Among the most important "risks" Rroma faced was that their increased interactions with *gadje* (outsiders), including living with them in mixed neighborhoods, apartment buildings, and in other group quarters, increased Rroma exposure to *mahrimi* (pollution).

These four categories should not be thought of as expressing developmental stages in a general process of inexorable assimilation. Some Rroma individuals and groups may remain fixed in one grouping indefinitely, while others may move back and forth across the categories depending on personal circumstances and/or on collective social, political, and/or economic exigencies. The general proportions of Rroma found in any of these categories in Romania, in part, depend on the historical opportunities the Rroma are afforded to maintain their traditional life ways and the opportunities they have to assimilate and relative attractiveness and opportunity costs and benefits of these various options.

In Romania, just as is the case in every other European country (see for example Helsinki Watch 1991a, 1991b, and 1991c), as well as in North America, the Rroma are cast as a radically and fundamentally *Other* population. To be a Rroma is not merely to occupy a statistical category, it is to be defined as being part of a population that falls short of being culturally competent and, even, of being completely human. A Rroma is someone who is seen to be literally outside of the cultural Pale of normality. Being a Rroma does not mean one is merely politically, socially, or economically marginal and inferior. It also means that one stands in a generally antagonistic, conflictual relationship with the dominant population groups in the larger society. A survey carried out in the early 1990s by researchers at the Center for Urban and Regional Sociology in Bucharest showed that the majority of Romania's population had unfavorable attitudes toward the Rroma. The researchers found that 100% of the ethnic Germans in the sample, 77% of the ethnic Romanians, 50% of ethnic Magyars, and 69% of others (mainly Jews, Ukrainians, and Russian Lipovinians) viewed Rroma unfavorably (Badescu and Abraham 1995: 103). The authors reject the idea that these views are a reflection of "racism" directed toward the Rroma. Rather, they see it as the response of the Romanian populations to the Rroma as a "social problem," meaning that the Rroma's behavior and cultural is responsible for the ways in which others view them. The implication they draw from their work is that if the Rroma were to assimilate or, at the very least, to model their behavior after that of Romanians and other "acceptable" minorities then they, too, would be accepted and many of their difficulties with others would disappear.

The Romanian mass media have played a continuing role in reinforcing popular prejudices against the Rroma. A conference recently (1997) was held and a report released by the Project on Ethnic Relations dealing with the Romanian media and the way it reported on the Rroma (Tanaka 1997). Reporting on the results of several studies, conference participants found that there was a strong tendency in the Romanian press to equate the Rroma with criminality. Participants also noted that in the coverage of anti-Rroma riots there had been a noticeable shift in the nature of the coverage. Early coverage of attacks on Rroma settlements tended to place the blame on the inability of society to absorb the members of the Rroma minority. In later stories, society was no longer held to be at fault; rather, it was the Roma themselves who were considered responsible for their lack of integration into Romanian society. This approach could be described as a kind of 'interpretive scheme,' in which the behavior of the majority was treated with understanding and compassion, in contrast to the shameless and incorrigible conduct of the Roma" (Tanaka 1997). An example of this can be seen in a Romanian Press Agency Release in 1995 dealing with crime in the country. Writing about the number of criminal arrests in 1994, the press release noted that among those arrested were "2,282 gypsies, which proves the existence of the crime potential within the ranks of this latter ethnic group" (BBC Summary of World Broadcasts, January 18 1995). Nothing was said about the ethnicity of the other 7,011 who had been in police custody. It was clear that the author of the press release did not understand the meaning of arrests statistics and the difference between them and the real universe of crime. What the author wanted to do was to justify his/her position, shared by many Romanians, that the Rroma were the principal criminal population in Romania.

The radical nationalist press has been even more harsh in its treatment of the Rroma, with one publication going so far as to claim that the Rroma are engaged in a "war" against Romanian society and that they needed to be segregated on reservations from the rest of the population (*Noua Dreapta* [The New Right] 1993). In February 2000, *Romania Mare* ran a front-page piece in which the Rroma were cast as *Mafiya* criminals, thieves, drug dealers, pimps, murderers, and rapists who were "...spreading like a plague all over Romania" (*Romania Mare*, February 25 2000). These are but two examples of the harsh treatment Rroma generally receive in the radical nationalist press.

Being an identifiable Rroma is to occupy a thoroughly devalued "master status" (see Becker 1963 for an extended discussion of the concept of "master status") that colors all aspects of a Rroma's life. To be a Rroma, in Romania and in Europe, in general, is to encounter a significant limit-condition for the type of life one may have, the forms of life one may create and live, the range of private and public identities one will be allowed to claim legitimately, and the nature of the social contacts one may have with non-Rroma.

In Romania and in other places where they live, the antagonistic and conflictual relations Rroma have with the rest of society is grounded in and expressed in and through an interpersonal system of "spoiled social relations" that characterizes their cross-group contacts with others (see Goffman 1963 for an extended discussion of the concept of "spoiled social relations"). Social relations between the Rroma and the non-Rroma are spoiled because the Rroma, themselves, are defined as having spoiled individual identities and a spoiled collective identity. Having such an identity, the Rroma, personally and collectively, occupy a degrading and disabling moral position in the eyes of dominant groups. Therefore, all social relations between identifiable Rroma and non-Rroma are marked by mistrust, suspicion, a sense of threat, and a sense of dread.

The only way that Rroma can successfully "manage" the bad feelings toward them and "successfully" interact with non-Rroma is by engaging in culturally prescribed displays of "appropriate" deference toward their "superiors." Such deferential behavior allows the non-Rroma to exercise a level of demeanor "appropriate" to their standing as social and cultural superiors of the Rroma. The elaborate system of "deference/demeanor" relations the Rroma are expected to express in Romania *are* the ethnic hierarchy, as experienced and expressed on a personal and interpersonal level (see Goffman 1956a, 1956b). Through deference/demeanor relations a member of a rejected ethnic group experiences the whole weight of ethnic superordination/subordination. Even the most casual observations walking around the streets of Romanian villages, towns, and cities (or any other European city for that matter) show very quickly examples of such deference/demeanor relations between Roma and non-Rroma.

On various trips to Romania, I have seen older Romanians spit and cross-themselves after having had contact with a Rroma, has seen people on subways and trams hold handkerchiefs over their noses to "protect" themselves from the "bad smell" Rroma were giving off, have seen police hassle Rroma youth for "loitering" on street corners while non-Rroma youth are not bothered for engaging in the same behavior, and have listened to conversations in which prosperous Rroma with high standing in their communities were forced to address Romanians of far lower social standing, and who were much younger than they, with the formal "you" (*dumneovoastra*), while the Romanians addressed the Rroma with the informal "you" (*tu*). This social distancing that non-Rroma demand be imposed in all social relations reflects the general social definition of the Rroma as a polluted, dirty, untrustworthy, crimogenic people.

After the 1989 revolution, the Romanian Rroma intellectuals became active in a number of activities designed to protect and expand Rroma rights. Romanian Rroma intellectuals made common cause with Rroma intellectuals throughout Europe and North America. Rroma intellectuals have been unable to develop a consensus on a number of critical issues. Among these issues is development of a common understanding and definition of the nature of Rroma identity that would be useful within the various national contexts in which Rroma are found.

In 1970, a trans-national Rroma organization emerged. It called itself the International Romani Congress. The Congress held its first meeting in 1971 in London. The Congress eventually created an executive arm, the International Romani Union, which took responsibility for advancing Rroma interests in various international organizations and arenas. A faction of the union pressed the claim that the Rroma constituted a "nation," and went so far as to create a "national" flag and a "national" anthem. However, when one looks at the actual situation of various Rroma populations it is readily apparent that after more than twenty years since the first Congress was held the Rroma "nation" is more a symbolic entity than an empirical reality. The Union also tried to create a written form of Romany. The efforts to create a standardized written form of the language had met with only limited success. In trying to refine this notion of the Rroma nation, Rroma intellectuals have tried to qualify the idea of nationhood by defining the Rroma as a "stateless nation," a "nonterritorial nation," a "transnational people," or a "truly European people" (Gheorghe and Mirga 1997). The idea of Rroma nationhood largely has been embraced by the more militant Rroma leadership circles. Traditional Rroma leaders have not been as quick as the militants to embrace the ideas of a pan-state, pan-community Rroma nation.

Rroma intellectuals also have pressed for recognition of the Rroma as a "minority" (Gheorghe and Mirga 1997: 14). However, Rroma intellectuals differ among themselves as to what it means for Rroma to be a "minority" and some Rroma intellectuals reject the very idea that the Rroma should be defined as a "minority." Opponents of defining Rroma as a minority, claim that the best political prospects for Rroma is in having them defined as citizens of a civil state who are entitled to all of the rights and privileges of any state citizen. This dispute among Rroma intellectuals and political activists reflects the difficulties of finding a common way to assert a social definition of Rroma identity and a legal-political definition of Rroma peoplehood. Such definitions are extremely difficult, given the widely divergent circumstances within which Rroma live and differences in how they live within these varying circumstances. As Gheorghe and Mirga note, these variations in the lives of Rroma populations are the result of being part of different waves of migration, different cultural heritages and histories, various levels of adaptation or acculturation, and different degrees of attachment to 'their' territory." It is clear, given the internal differences within Rroma populations, that developing a universally acceptable "identity" is going to be a very difficult task for Rroma intellectuals, especially if they hope to develop an identity that is more "accommodating" to the modern world than have been the traditional highly localized identities characteristic of Rroma populations.

In addition to finding a way to resolve the legal standing of Rroma and an acceptable definition of their identity, a major need of the Rroma populations, according to Gheorghe and Mirga (1997: 20), is developing new leadership elites that have the skills necessary to build modern organizational structures that are better able to relate to the new types of state authorities that are developing in Eastern and Central Europe and the states of Western Europe, as well. Gheorghe and Mirga (1997: 20) basically argue for Rroma intellectuals assuming a vanguard role in Rroma nation-building activities. At present, there is a good deal of tension between a large part of the traditional leaderships in Rroma communities and Rroma intellectuals. Traditional leaders are deeply suspicious of the Rroma intellectuals, who they see as representing no one but themselves and who they suspect are trying to displace them as the leaders of their communities. The Rroma intellectuals, on the other hand, see the traditional leaders as being unreasonably suspicious of their intentions. Intellectuals interpret the suspicions of the traditional leaders as a hyper-defensiveness that is doing more harm than good to Rroma communities. However, among Rroma intellectuals there is a very real belief on the part of Rroma intellectuals that the traditional leaders are not competent to deal with the changed political environment, especially in Eastern and Central Europe, within which the Rroma find themselves. From the viewpoint of the Rroma intellectuals, traditional community leaders lack the kinds of cosmopolitan orientations that are necessary if the Rroma communities ever are to overcome their fragmentation and localisms to build an internally coherent "nation," that is more a social reality than a symbolic reality.

The Rroma intellectuals also believe that the traditional leaders lack the political, economic, and social skills necessary to deal with the newly emerging democracies and market economies of Eastern and Central Europe. The Rroma intellectuals see themselves, only, as having the leadership skills and orientations that will allow the Rroma to effectively access the world outside their local communities and to frame Rroma issues in ways that the outside world can understand and to which they can respond effectively.

In addition to finding a way to resolve the legal standing of Rroma, a major need of the Rroma populations, according to Gheorghe and Mirga (1997: 20), is developing new leadership elites, who are more attuned to contemporary realities than is the traditional community leadership. As one might expect, given their own status, Gheorghe and Mirga (1997: 20) propose that this leadership be drawn from among the Rroma intellectual elites, who would (should) come to constitute what Gramsci (1971) calls an "organic intelligentsia" for the Rroma. For this to happen, however, the Rroma intelligentsia will have to be recognized by Rroma communities as their legitimate spokespersons. This is unlikely to happen in the near future. Gheorghe and Mirga recognize that Rroma intellectuals will have considerable difficulties being accepted by traditional Rroma communities, in which intellectuals now are viewed with suspicion as "hyphenated" Rroma. Traditional Rroma communities and their leaders see Rroma intellectuals as people who, because of their education, have been partially, if not totally, assimilated into the dominant societies in which they live. The Rroma intellectuals are not seen as having the full and complete social connections with other Rroma that would warrant these communities accepting them as leaders. One of the major reasons why Gheorghe and Mirga propose that intellectuals assume a mantle of leadership within Rroma communities is that they, more so than the traditional leadership, have the skills necessary for dealing with the "new" circumstances in which Rroma communities, especially in Eastern and Central Europe, now find themselves. Gheorghe and Mirga (1997: 20) propose that it is time for Rroma to develop new institutions and organizations to represent and to express their interests. They see traditional organizations and institutions as no longer functional in the "modern" world. It is clear from Gheorghe and Mirga's (1997:20) arguments that these institutions will have to be led by Rroma intellectuals.

Gheorghe and Mirga (1997: 22) also suggest that Rroma intellectuals are uniquely prepared to contribute to a fundamental redefinition of Rroma social and cultural identity that will bring Rroma identity more into line with the demands of modernity. They note that the key to transforming identity is education, but that many traditional sectors Rroma populations fear education, because they see it as undermining community solidarity insofar as it gives the young an opportunity to move into the dominant society, leaving their old worlds behind.

A number of grass-roots Rroma organizations have emerged in recent years that have, as one of their goals, transcending traditional Rroma particularities in order to develop a more generalized consciousness that ties together the various Rroma tribal worlds into a more coherent, larger scale ethnic community. The very idea of integrating Rroma tribal groups into a larger ethnic group made sense, in the first place, only because of the structural changes that the communists introduced into Rroma life. By pursuing policies of moving Rroma into settled communities in both urban and rural areas and opening employment to them on state farms, agricultural cooperatives, and state industrial enterprises the communists brought together Rroma from different tribal groups and thus made it possible for these Rroma to gain an expanded sense of common identity and common problems.

These, and related, changes created the structural preconditions for creating a growing, more general, ethnic collective consciousness among Rroma in Romania (see Keil 1989; Yancey, Erikson, and Juliani 1976;

Oppenheimer 1974; and Cox 1948, among others, for a discussion of the factors that have been involved in bringing about the rise of "ethnic" consciousness among populations in the United States, some of which are relevant for discussing the rise of Rroma consciousness in Romania and, perhaps, elsewhere in Europe). Since 1989, all evidence points to the presence of a continuing, ongoing emergence of more global forms of ethnic consciousness among Romania's Rroma.

The rising ethnic consciousness among Romania's Rroma has not yet supplanted tribal consciousness among the Rroma. Rather, the more generalized ethnic consciousness has developed alongside of traditional forms of tribal consciousness. The more global consciousness of Rroma identity appears to be strongest in Romanian cities, where different groups of Rroma share space and common living conditions, and among Rroma who, wholly or in part, have undergone structural and/or cultural detribalization. A generalized consciousness of themselves as Rroma also has been stimulated by the attacks on Rroma from the outside by various individuals, groups, and organizations in Romania. By being defined as "Rroma," by outside groups, without distinction as to tribal affiliation, the Rroma have been helped to begin thinking of themselves in more "universal" terms, which has been of tremendous benefit to Rroma intellectuals and community organizers who have been working to bring about a larger collective consciousness among Rroma.

While there have been strong signs of a growing communal consciousness among the Rroma, its development has been uneven within and across the various Rroma communal groupings. Rroma community organizers have had to contend with a number of obstacles in attempting to build a generalized Rroma collective consciousness and a Rroma social movement that is capable of identifying, defending, and advancing generalized Rroma interests. First, organizing the Rroma is made difficult by the presence within the community of nomadic and semi-nomadic populations. Second, organizers have to contend with a complex linguistic situation in which there are a number of Romany dialects and in which there is no standardized written form of the language. The linguistic variety makes it difficult to develop effective communication systems across space and time. Third, the historical divisions and traditional hierarchy among the craft groupings have served as a limiting condition in forming the Rroma into a coherent ethnic community and movement. I was at a meeting where members of some of the newer community organizations were discussing their strategies for expanding their activities. During the course of the meeting, it became apparent that a large Rroma neighborhood to the south of Bucharest was being ignored in the discussions. When the activists were asked why no one was working with this neighborhood, the question was ignored. After the meeting broke up, one of the young men agreed to talk about this. He said that the neighborhood in question predominantly was made up of "Gypsies with bears." When he was asked what difference that made, he went on to report that these people were *necivilizat* (uncivilized). He claimed that the "Gypsies with bears" were very clannish and that few other Rroma trusted them and that they, the "Gypsies with bears," trusted no one outside of their own community. He said that they "liked to get drunk" and "fight," so it could be very dangerous dealing with them. He believed that given their general lack of respectability, if they were included in Rroma organizations, they would undermine these organizations' attempt to show that the Rroma, in general were a *popor civilizat* (civilized people). Fourth, organizers have to contend with the strong identification that Rroma have with their extended kinship groups. Among Rroma, a sense of collective obligation weakens as one moves from the household to the extended kin group to the craft grouping and, finally, to the Rroma population, as a whole. The farther one moves away from the household, the more abstract and remote a sense of collective identification and obligation becomes. Fifth, the Rroma lack a centralized and over-arching political structure that could contribute to their internal unification. Rroma political structures are highly, if not exclusively, local and particularistic. What political unification that does exist beyond the local area and the craft group is very amorphous and very weak.

Having had their traditional collective institutions, including those that helped defend their communities from external power and influence, pulverized and having had only limited resources with which to build new institutions, the Rroma have been forced to rely on highly personalized forms of resistance and escape from the consequences of being an internal colony. They flee when attacked, retreat deeper into their families in the face of external pressures and threats, or they engage in personal forms of rebellion, or they attempt to escape their misery with alcohol or other personalized forms of deviant behavior. All of these modes of individual adaptation to their circumstances further contribute to the collective quiescence Rroma have displayed in the face of discrimination, repression, or direct assaults on them and their communities.

It is not only the above factors that have limited Rroma political organization and social mobilization. In order to understand why the Rroma are more a dispersed rather than a highly organized ethnic group, one also must take into account the socioeconomic and political opportunity structures that they face in the larger society. Rroma organization and mobilization have been limited by the fact that in Romania, as in most other European societies, the Rroma have been constituted as an "internal colony" (see Clark 1965 Carmichael and Hamilton 1967; Blauner 1969, 1972; Hechter 1975; and Zureik 1979 for discussions of and applications of the concept of "internal colonialism"). Like many other populations organized into internal colonies in other parts of the world, Rroma did not enter Romania voluntarily. They were brought to Romania as slaves and a large part of the Rroma population remained slaves until the middle of the 19th century.

As with other groups that are organized into internal colonies, the Rroma must deal with a racist ideology that is used by dominant groups to justify their continued exploitation and suppression of the Rroma. This ideology defines Rroma as an inferior people who are "uncivilized" and in need of "cultural" and "moral" development before they can expect to be trusted and accepted as equal by others. Rroma are defined as a dirty and polluted people who are a repository of a special kind of moral evil that makes every contact with them problematic, if not dangerous. The Rroma are not only seen as marked by evil, but they are defined as carriers of it. They are seen an a people who can infect other people and communities with their moral "corruption." This way of viewing the Rroma is an example of an archaic conception of evil (Ricoeur 1969) that exposes Rroma to widespread popular hatred and physical aggression from others.

During the early to mid-1990s, Romania experienced a wave of inter-communal violence directed at Rroma in a number of rural areas (Human Rights Watch 1991a). In this violence, Romanian and Magyar villagers, separately, and, in some cases, mixed groups of Romanian and Magyar villagers attacked their Rroma neighbors, beating some of the Rroma and, in what resembled ancient acts of "purification" designed to purge the community of "evil," burning Rroma houses. The villagers' goal was to drive Rroma villagers from the villages and from the land. Typically, the attacks on Rroma were preceded by weeks or, sometimes, months of a build-up of tensions between the Rroma and others. The actual attacks came following an alleged crime committed by a Rroma against a non-Rroma. In one village, the precipitating circumstance had involved the supposed theft of a chicken from a Romanian household. What generally seemed to have happened in all of the communities where there were anti-Rroma riots was that following an alleged Rroma crime, rumors would begin circulating, often exaggerating the nature of the alleged crime and magnifying its threat to the non-Rroma populations. People would gather, in one case they were summoned by an Orthodox priest who rang his church bell to summon a crowd, and then they would proceed to march on the Rroma neighborhoods, attacking the residents and burning buildings and Rroma caravans. The Romanians and Magyars who participated in these attacks did not direct their violence only against the alleged perpetrators of the crime, instead, they engaged in widespread collective punishment of Rroma communities.

In the summer of 1991, sixty Rroma families were burned out of their homes in a mining village close to Valea Pietrelor (Valley of the Stones), which is situated in Northern Romania, not far from the Ukrainian-Romanian border. According to Ingram (1992a), this was the fifth such attack that had been directed at Rroma settlements since December 1989. The attack was precipitated by the alleged rape of a pregnant Romanian woman by a Rroma. The attack followed after a crowd was summoned to the center of the village by the ringing of a church bell.

Earlier, in 1990, in the town of Mihail Kogalniceanu, a crowd estimated to number over a thousand people attacked the Rroma section of the town, burning down over 30 houses (Ingram 1992b). The attack was carried out in retaliation for the alleged beating of Romanian worker by a Rroma.

In none of the cases of attacks on Rroma villagers did the police intervene. The Romanian government was seriously criticized by Western governments and human rights organizations for its failure to have prevented the attacks and for its failure, afterwards, to find and arrest those who had perpetrated the violence. A major Western human rights organization brought a group composed of American police and academics who had done research and training on police-minority relations in the United States to Romania to meet with police commanders and with Rroma leaders to discuss the Romanian police's reaction to the attacks on the Rroma villagers. Over the course of these meetings, which led to a federal grant being given to a U.S. university to train Romanian police commanders in police-minority relations, it became clear that, while some of Romania's police commanders shared popular attitudes toward the Rroma, the commanders' failure to intervene in these riots, in a timely manner, in order to protect Rroma, was more a result of a lack of appropriate resources to do so than it was of police racial attitudes. This, however, is not to say that there have not been additional examples of police abuse of Rroma. These abuses, however, do not stem from official government policy. Rather, they stem from decisions made by individual police officers and individual police commanders, acting out of their own biases against Rroma.

Romania has not been the only place in Europe where Rroma communities have come under direct attack. There have been attacks on Rroma villages and individuals in Germany, Hungary, Czechoslovakia, and Spain, to name just a few places. In Spain, Rroma houses were burned in several cities (Riding 1991). In addition, Spaniards have blocked Rroma migration into their neighborhoods and have boycotted schools that enrolled Rroma children. Helsinki Watch (1991b; 1991c) has documented acts of discrimination against Rroma in Bulgaria and acts of violence against them in Czechoslovakia.

After the split between the Czech Republic and the Slovak Republic, the former refused to grant citizenship to Rroma who had been born in Slovakia, despite the fact that the treaty of separation required them to do so. One town in the Czech Republic had built a high wall between the Rroma and non-Rroma neighborhoods, which later was dismantled because of international pressures related to the Czech Republic's petition to become part of the European Union. The Czechs also send Rroma in disproportionate numbers to special schools designed for children with mental impairments. The attitudes toward Rroma in the Czech Republic is interesting because it often is reported to be among the most democratically oriented of all of the former communist states.

On September 24, 1992, Germany signed an agreement with Romania to repatriate almost 100,000 Romanians who had sought political asylum in Germany. Over 80% of these people were Rroma. Germany agreed to pay Romania to take these people back. Rroma were rounded up by German police, put on buses, and were sent to detention camps where they were held until they could be transported back to Romania. I interviewed a Rroma woman whose son had been caught up in the German dragnet and who was being held in an abandoned Soviet military barracks in the former GDR. She said that what the Germans had done reminded her of the stories her mother had told her about how the Romanians had arrested and shipped "our people" to the "death camps" during the last war. She was terrified about what would happen to her son.

In the popular press, the attacks on Rroma in Romania, as well as in other parts of Europe, are often depicted as having grown out of economic crisis. Such an explanation would have more plausibility if the Rroma were directly competing with dominant populations for scarce jobs. This, however, is not the case. The Rroma, as noted above, when they have regular occupations, usually are employed in jobs that members of the dominant population don't want. The Rroma largely remain concentrated in the pre-industrial sectors of the Romanian economy. It is more the case that the attacks on the Rroma are an expression of the cultural structures and processes that define the Rroma as a repository of evil, that is, as a not quite civilized and not quite human population. To the extent to which this is the case, the perpetrators of such attacks can be seen as an attempt to purify and to restore order and harmony to their own moral universes by driving the offending people (the Rroma) from their midst.

The Rroma have been especially hard hit in the economic aftermath of the collapse of communism. While the communists provided jobs in modern economic sectors to Rroma, most of these jobs involved unskilled or, at best, semi-skilled work and the Rroma were given few opportunities for moving upward on enterprises' internal career mobility ladders. Often among the last hired in many enterprises, the Rroma have been among the first to be dismissed by privatized firms or by state enterprises that have been compelled to shed "redundant" workers.

The Rroma in rural areas have been seriously affected by the Romanian privatization of the land that had been part of collective farms. Few, if any Rroma, had owned land that had been "voluntarily" contributed to form the collectives, therefore, they received no land when the collectives liquidate themselves. With the breakup of the collectives, Rroma who have worked on collective farms have lost their jobs.

It is hard to imagine the degree to which some of the rural Rroma populations have been economically marginalized and impoverished. I went with a group of medical aid workers to several impoverished Rroma villages around the Transylvanian city of Cluj-Napoca. One Rroma community had set up its living quarters next to a large municipal refuse dump. Their houses were nothing more than make-shift shacks, pieced together out of whatever scrap materials they could find. Many of these dwellings were overcrowded, with four or more people living in fewer than 50 square feet of space and some were home to two or more generations of the same family. The young children did not go to school. Instead, they worked alongside the adults to harvest anything of value that they could from the deliveries of trash and garbage to the dump. Several of the children bore the mark of serious birth defects. Many of the children and almost all of the adults bore signs of the adverse health effects of this type of work. Skin diseases were prevalent, there were obvious signs of dietary deficiencies among children and adults, many of the people had a variety of respiratory problems, and there were signs everywhere of work injuries that people acquired picking through the garbage. While this village was at the extreme end of Rroma poverty, other Rroma villages visited in the same general region around Cluj-Napoca showed signs of significant economic problems and the effects of such conditions.

Rapid Economic Decline in Post-Revolutionary Romania

As crime increased and as ethnic conflict intensified, the FSN government had to struggle with the rapid economic decline Romania was experiencing. In 1990, the Romanian GDP dropped 7.4%, it fell another 13.7% in 1991, and 15.4% in 1992 (Institut fur Hohere Studien 1994: 9). By the end of 1992, Romanian industrial production stood at 46% of what it had been in 1989, when the communist centrally planned economy still was functioning. In 1990, industrial production, alone, declined by 16.6%, while agricultural production actually had increased by 10.4%. In 1991, industrial production fell another 20.2% and in 1992 it declined by a further 21.8%. In 1991, agricultural production declined by 5.2% and it dropped another 9.2% in 1992 (Institut fur Hohere

Studien 1994: 9). There were at least two factors that were responsible for the immediate declines in industrial output. First, there were shortages of key raw materials and other inputs, such as energy. Second, there was a major decline in labor productivity. Declines in labor productivity were partly the result of the large number of strikes that were spreading throughout the economy. Agricultural production declined between 1991 and 1992 principally the result of severe conditions of drought, coupled with a breakdown of agricultural irrigation systems in key agricultural areas and shortages of key inputs such as fertilizers and pesticides.

In order to increase levels of agricultural production, the government introduced new legislation, Law 18, in February 1991. This law governed the privatization of Romania's collective farms (*cooperative agricole de productie*). These collective farms had been formed by the "voluntary" contribution of land by peasant households during the communists' drives to collectivize agriculture. Law 18 did not change the status of property owned by state farms and state farms were not scheduled to be privatized under its terms. Law 18 did place a number of strong restrictions on those who acquired property formerly held by the agricultural collectives (Verdery 1999: 57). Land owners were not allowed to let the land lie fallow. If they failed to cultivate the land, they were subject to heavy fines. Land could not be changed from production of one set of general commodities to another, without the written permission of the Minister of Agriculture. People who failed to file land claims within a thirty-day period, starting from a date established by law, lost rights to their property. Ownership of the property would revert to the state. The law also limited the amount of property that could be acquired. No individual family could file a claim for more than 10 hectares, after which they could not acquire more than a total of 100 hectares. Restrictions on the amount of land that could be owned were meant to block the re-emergence of large agricultural estates or, even, of large-scale agribusiness production in the countryside and to help insure that inequality in the countryside would be held at some minimal levels. Sale of land privatized from the collectives could not occur unless it was authorized by the Agency for Rural Planning and Development, however, the state was slow to establish this agency (Verdery 1999) delaying the establishment of free markets in agricultural land in rural areas.

The downside to the decision to limit the size land holdings acquired from privatization of the collectives was that, initially, Romanian private farms were much smaller than private farms in the European Union (Institut fur Hohere Studien 1994: 12). The small size of private farms has seriously limited the efficiency of Romanian agricultural production. The only way that the private farmers would be able to achieve high levels of efficiency would be to form agricultural associations (*associati*), which would enable them to pool their resources to purchase production inputs and to buy or lease agricultural machinery. The former collectives did not own farm machinery. Most machinery was owned by the state and kept at large agricultural stations. This continued to be the case after 1989. However, private farmers faced considerable increases in the costs of accessing these machines. The state also maintained ownership of the enterprises that sold virtually all inputs to agricultural production and it retained ownership of all of the channels for buying and distributing agricultural commodities in Romania. The state also retained a monopoly on all sources of credit for private farmers. While pertinent laws guaranteed farmers access to relatively cheap credit, the reality was far different. Farmers were forced to obtain loans at extremely high rates of interest, which limited their profit opportunities. By maintaining the controls it did over agriculture, the state hoped it could keep food prices from spiraling out of control and thereby prevents more strikes and, perhaps, more violent forms of opposition to it. The policies adopted by the FSN were a more modern form of the primitive accumulation in which the communists had engaged. Agricultural policies of the FSN were intended to continue the unequal exchange between the countryside and the cities, to the detriment of rural areas, that had marked communist economic policy.

In introducing agricultural privatization in the form it did, the FSN was adopting a model of "land reform" that Romania had tried to put in place between World War I and World War II. Those changes, which also had produced a large class of free peasants working very small farms, had done little to relieve the economic plight of the peasantry and did little to improve economic efficiency. And it is unlikely that the changes the FSN introduced would accomplish more than had the "reforms" introduced by the bourgeois regimes between 1918 and 1941. However, the land restitution scheme that the FSN put in place did seem to insure that there private, large-scale agricultural production would not be re-established in Romania. The FSN seems to have been determined to not permit the restoration of the system of agricultural production that had been controlled by the boyars. For this reason, the FSN also wanted to limit not only the amount of agricultural land restored to private owners, but also the amount of forest lands that would be returned to private hands. Blocking an extensive privatization of forest had both an economic and symbolic value to the FSN. Economically, forest and wood products was a fairly healthy economic sector and was an economic sector that readily could be developed as a source of significant exports. Symbolically, the struggle over the use of forests and the game that lived in them had been a significant political, social, and economic battle between peasants and boyars, once the boyars converted their estates into modern forms of private property. The boyars' limitations on peasant access to forest lands had been responsible for widespread discontent in the Romanian countryside. Turning the clock back to allow private exploitation of national forest reserves was something the FSN simply was not prepared to accept.

The farms given to the peasantry are too small to take advantage of any economies of scale. They almost guarantee that most peasant households will not be able to produce much beyond the subsistence needs of the family working it. It is not only the size of farm-plots that will impede agricultural production in post-communist Romania. Land was given to households that lacked the economic skills to run a modern small-farm and little attention has been given to building these skills among the peasantry It is as if the government assumed that because peasants were being given land that they would be able to work it without any training in modern farming techniques, including modern farm management. Without having had the opportunity to acquire such skills, the peasant landowners have had a hard time running their farms as viable economic enterprises, especially given the virtual absence of modern machinery; access to irrigation systems, fertilizers, and herbicides; the lack of agricultural credits at low interest rates; the state monopoly of agricultural inputs; state monopoly over transportation networks to markets; the absence of open, wholesale markets for agricultural products; and the small size of most of these farms.

The agricultural land reforms adopted by the FSN appear to have emerged more from internal political considerations rather than from a desire to introduce economic rationality into the rural economy. The FSN knew that it had won the 1990 elections because of votes in the rural areas, where farmers saw, rightly or wrongly, their economic opportunities to be greater with an FSN government than it would be with an opposition government, even one run by the National Peasant/ Christian Democrats. If they were to have any hope of winning the 1992 elections, the FSN leadership knew that it would have to find a way to anchor not only workers on state farms to their cause, but also to win the support of peasants in cooperatives and peasants who had managed to remain formally independent during the communist period. The FSN's land reform was meant to do this. It also was meant to secure the support of urban residents whose ancestors lands had been confiscated by the communists during the drive collectivize agriculture. At the same time, by not breaking up the state farms, the FSN continued to serve the interests of several of its major internal constituencies, such as state farm workers, state farm managers, and managers and workers in the old food-industrial complex. The food industrial complex had been a powerful system of networks, if not the strongest, aside from the military and the security forces, in communist Romania. The elites within these networks wanted to make sure that they would continue to play an important role in the new economic order. This only could be accomplished if they could preserve the production and distribution systems they controlled during the communist period, while, at the same time, insuring that their competition in the new private agricultural sector would be weak and would continue to be dependent on them. By controlling the inputs to agricultural production and by controlling the wholesale markets and the food distribution networks, they could make sure that the state farms remained a dominating force in the Romanian agricultural sector. The FSN agricultural policy encouraged the independent farmers to form production associations. The FSN saw this not only as a way of increasing the efficiency of small farmers, but it also was seen as one more way for farm managers to extend control over the independent producers. The peasants receiving land were reluctant, however, to join co-operatives, if for no other reason than that they remembered that this had been one of the first steps the communists had taken to collectivize Romanian agriculture.

As economic output declined, inflation increased. Between December 1989 and the end of September 1990, the government continued to maintain control over most prices in the Romanian economy. However, it was apparent to most Romanian economists that the government was not going to be able to avoid freeing prices. In October 1990, the government made a move to introduce free prices into the Romanian economy. Prices began increasing sharply for all goods and services. In 1991, the *monthly* average rate of inflation was 10.3%. It fell to 9.6% in 1992 and shot-up to 12.1% in 1993 (Institut fur Hohere Studien 1994: 18). In 1991, the greatest increase in prices was taking place for food products, which were increasing, on the average, of 12% per month. Non-food products, in 1991, increased at 8.9% per month and services, in the same year, increased 8.6% per month. In 1992, monthly average price increases for food, while remaining high, decreased, somewhat, compared to 1991. The average monthly increase for food in 1992 was 10.2%. Non-food products' monthly average price increases in 1992 were slightly higher than they were in 1991. In 1992, they stood at a monthly average increase of 9.3%. Services in 1992 increased at a monthly average of 8.6%. In 1993, food products had a monthly average price increase of 11.6%, non-food products' average monthly increase was 12.9%, and services increased at a monthly average of 11.8%. Overall, then, from the beginning of 1991 to the end of 1993, food prices increased by 348.9%, non-food products increased by 369%, and services increased by 340.3% (Institut fur Hohere Studien 1994: 18). At these rates of inflation, the monetary overhang that existed at the end of 1989 quickly disappeared.

By 1992, prices in the overall economy were almost 13 times higher than they had been in October 1990, when the state ended its subsidies to consumer goods and allowed prices, throughout the economy, to reflect prevailing market conditions (Institut fur Hohere Studien 1994: 17). By April 1993, prices were about 20 times greater than they had been in 1990. Wage increases lagged far behind general price increases. As a result of wages not keeping pace with price increases, in April 1993 the purchasing power of the average Romanian was only 43% of what has been in October 1990 (Institut fur Hohere Studien 1994: 17). The cost of food, as a proportion of the family budget, increased by almost 1% between 1992 and 1993. Another indicator of how bad matters had become for the average family was the change in the ratio of the average net earnings index to the consumer price index. For persons working, the 1993 level was only 85.1% and for retired persons it was 87.8%.

The rapid increases in prices upset average Romanians not only because of the economic difficulties inflation introduced into their lives, but also because the inflationary spiral violated one of the basic principles of the moral economy under which they had lived for the past half-century. Under communism, the economy was more of a moral order than a "pure" economic order. Economic relations were embedded within a system of values and customs that contributed to the definitions of prices, wages, levels of employment, the supply of housing, and the like. The rapid increases in prices and the increasing unemployment were a clear sign that this basic moral arrangement was being dismantled and that the market was coming to dominate political, social, and economic arrangements.

As the economic situation deteriorated and the FSN struggled to develop a coherent economic program, Petre Roman asked workers and unions to show patience and restraint. Few heeded his words. One of the most important labor actions directed against the government at this time involved miners from the Jiu Valley. The Jiu Valley miners launched a third *minerada* (miners' invasion) between September 24 and 28, 1991. The miners came to Bucharest, after rioting at the rail station in Craiova as they passed through that city, to protest the Roman government's program for restructuring the Romanian economy. The miners had a number of perceived grievances. The miners claimed that the ending of price controls was eroding their wages, that the government was not supplying enough food stuffs and other goods for the stores in the region, that the government was not giving them sufficient supplies and adequate equipment to do their jobs, and that the government was ignoring their demands to improve working conditions and safety conditions in the pits.

When the miners entered Bucharest on September 24, a good part of the city was near a state of panic. Shopkeepers, remembering the last time the miners came to the city, closed their businesses and brought down protective metal coverings over doors and windows. Some hired private security guards to protect their merchandise should the miners or their supporters try to loot their shops.

Average citizens hastened to get off the streets, fearing that the miners would engage in random acts of violence against the general population. Fear was especially high among Bucharest's Rroma population, which had been attacked by groups of miners in 1990, and among intellectuals, who also had been singled out for attacks by the miners in 1990.

Entering the city late on the 24th, several thousand miners, armed with axe handles, wooden clubs, and various mining tools they had converted into weapons and wearing their mining hats equipped with head lamps, marched through central Bucharest. It was an intimidating sight, even for those who had not seen what the miners had done the last time they had come to Bucharest. The largest part of the miners who arrived on September 24th were young men, some barely out of their teens and some still teenagers. Sprinkled through their ranks were older miners who seemed to be functioning as group "commanders." Most of the Jiu Valley's older miners had remained behind to defend their home area against a possible government counter-attack. As the miners marched, they shouted "*Jos Iliescu!*" (Down with Iliescu) and other anti-government slogans. This surprised almost everyone who watched them arrive. Onlookers were startled to discover that the miners had come in opposition to Iliescu and the FSN government.

The miners began attacking government buildings in central Bucharest. A combined force of local police officers and the *militia*, after several hours of fighting, were able to drive the miners away from the buildings without using deadly force. At the end of the fighting, the miners moved en masse to *Parcul Tineretului* (Youth Park) in the south central part of Bucharest, where they set up their base camp. By the time the fighting had ended on the first day, word had begun to spread throughout Bucharest that the miners had come to attack the government not in support of it. Hearing this news, a number of physicians and other persons with medical training went to *Parcul Tineretului* to help tend to the miners who had been injured during the fighting. Other people from surrounding neighborhoods brought food and drinks to the camp. Many sat with the miners and talked to them about their grievances and why they had come to Bucharest.

On the morning of the 23rd the miners paraded back from *Parcul Tineretului* toward the center of the city. Along their route a large crowd had gathered and began cheering the miners. Overnight they had been changed from devils into heroes in popular opinion. Here and there, people waved the old communist flags with holes in the center that had become the symbol of revolutionary Romania. Young children ran alongside the miners and cheered them on and some people stepped forward to offer them gifts of food, beverages, and, even, flowers. The miners' march had all the flavor of a community celebration. As the miners entered *Piata Universitati* some of them began banging their axe handles and clubs on the ground creating an eerie sound effect to accompany the noise from their heavy boots hitting the pavement.

The miners again launched attacks on government buildings and on the headquarters of the national television, which had come to symbolize the FSN's "seizure of power" following the overthrow of the Ceausescus. They met even heavier resistance from the police and the militia, who again engaged them with night-sticks and truncheons, protective shields, and heavy barrages of tear gas, for which the miners were totally unprepared. All day the two sides battled each other in the streets of Bucharest. As the day wore on, it became clear that the police and the militia were gaining the upper-hand. The miners were taking heavy casualties and a large number of them were arrested and jailed. In the event that the miners threatened to overwhelm the police and the militia, the government had stationed armed troops and armored personnel carriers in areas close to the fighting. These military units were prepared to attack the miners with lethal force if it appeared that they were about to defeat the police and the militia.

At the end of the day, the miners began marching back toward *Piata Universitati.* As they came into the square, people heard the sound of their weapons being dragged across the ground, rather than being defiantly hammered against the street.

On the night of September 23rd, rather than returning to their encampment in *Parcul Tineretului,* the miners concentrated what was left of their depleted forces in and around *Piata Universitati.* By this time there only were a few hundred of them left who appeared able to fight. The miners immediately set up a defensive perimeter a few blocks away in each direction from the square. They overturned trams, buses, and other vehicles to build barricades to seal themselves off from the police and the militia. They deployed guards up and down the streets that they controlled. People passing through had to approach the guards for permission to continue. If they received approval, the guard would use the lamp on his miner's hard-hat to signal the next guard that someone was coming.

The air in the square, in the areas surrounding it, and in the subway beneath it, was filled with the remains of the tear gas the government forces had used against the miners. The tear gas continued to have lingering effects on the miners, their eyes watered heavily and most of them had trouble breathing. Only a few hearty souls came to the square to tend to the miners who had been wounded and to offer them food and drinks.

The miners understood that they would be making their last stand in the square within a few hours. They were right. Their move was very somber that night. Very early on the morning of September 24th, the police and the militia began firing a heavy barrage of tear gas canisters into the square and advanced from all directions on the blockades the miners had built. The police first breached the miners' defenses at *Piata Roseti*. The miners rushed reinforcements from the square toward *Piata Roseti* but they were unable to stop the attack. Using tear gas, clubs, and truncheons, the police moved quickly to *Piata Universitati* and began fighting the miners who still were there. Miners rushed from the other barricades to save their colleagues and the police quickly overran the men who remained behind to defend the remaining barricades. Within a few hours, all of the miners were rounded up by the police. They were brought to a railroad station where a heavily guarded special train was waiting for them. They were put on the train and shipped back to the Jiu Valley in defeat. The crowds that had cheered their arrival did not reassemble to watch their humiliating march to the train station.

The Jiu Valley mine workers have been able to quickly respond to what they see as threats to their personal and communal interests because they, like miners almost everywhere in Europe and North America, have a very high "mobilization potential" (see Tilly 1978, Jenkins 1983, and Keil 1989 for a discussion of this concept). Given the relatively isolated nature of mining communities, which is the case in the Jiu Valley, workers in mining regions, including those not directly employed in the mines, themselves, typically develop higher levels of collective solidarity where their very communities and the institutions within them become part and parcel of a generalized "platform of collective action" (Wardell and Johnston 1983) designed to resist encroachments on what the miners perceive to be their "rights." Mobilization of the entire community as an integral part of mine workers' platform of collective action usually is an essential component of mining regions' overall "repertoire of contention" (Tilly 1978). In mining communities, generally, and this certainly is the case in the Jiu Valley, collective solidarity is generated not only from immediate relations at the point of production, but also from mutually reinforcing social relations within all popular institutions in the mining community.

Because of the nature of their work and because of the nature of their communities and the way in which they are integrated into and complement the miners' work experiences, miners and mining communities develop a different kind of "interpretive horizon" (Gadamer 1982: 269) than do other workers and other working class communities. Miners' interpretive horizon, i.e. the "shared, collective vantage point from which they define, comprehend, and evaluate their life world" (Keil 1989: 40) invests ideas of solidarity, collective militancy, and collective resistance with a more or less universal moral meaning for all members of the mining community and, indeed, for all workers. This gives whatever stance they take significance, to them, beyond their own immediate self-interest. For this reason, when the miners have stood up to fight against economic restructuring they presented their actions as being taken on behalf of all workers in Romania. When they marched through Bucharest in the third *minerada* the miners viewed their actions as being taken on behalf of Romania's entire working class, miners or not.

The *minerada* of September 1991 produced the first major split in the FSN. Prior to September 1991, there had been a number of prominent members of the FSN who had left the FSN after disputes over policy and administrative practices. For example the distinguished Romanian poet and dissident intellectual, Anna Blandiana, had broken with the FSN because of deep disagreements over a range of policies and because of the unwillingness of the leadership to take her views and recommendations into account. Silviu Brucan also had split with the FSN leadership, partly because of personality conflicts with other leaders and partly because of serious ideological differences with the FSN's top leadership. These and other defections, while harming the image of the FSN, had little effect on the overall solidarity of the movement. However, because of the miners' invasion, President Iliescu decided to dismiss his Prime Minister, Petre Roman. He blamed Roman for the governments' failed economic policies and he also blamed him for not having been better prepared to deal with the miners when they invaded the city. Following his dismissal, Roman denounced Iliescu and announced he was leaving the FSN to form a new political party. When he left the FSN, he brought a large number of his key supporters with him to help organize his new political party.

Union strikes and political mobilization seriously constrained the Romanian government's ability to adopt even a semblance of an economic program of "shock therapy," such as had been adopted by Poland. The unions were strong enough to force a gradualist policy on the FSN, even after it had won the first elections under the new Romanian constitution in September 1992. The new constitution had been overwhelmingly approved in a national referendum in December 1991. In the run-up to the first national elections under the new constitution, Western governments, especially the United States, provided considerable support to the opposition parties. The United States and its Western allies contributed substantial formal and informal support for the formation of the Democratic Convention, which was meant to replace the Democratic Antitotalitarian Forum. The Democratic Convention was intended to serve as a tool for uniting the opposition parties into a coherent political movement capable of challenging the FSN for control of the government.

Under pressures from Western financial institutions, mainly the IMF and the World Bank, the Romanian state began reducing its subsidies to large, supposedly inefficient industries. The state also initiated a program to restructure the economy and it struggled to control wage increases, even in the face of increasing strike activity and protests by organized and unorganized workers. In May 1992, workers at the national radio and television struck, demanding wage increases, the removal of "unreformed" communists from management positions, and a freeing of the broadcast systems from political influence and ideological content. In August 1992, miners' unions and other trade unions began a series of protests against government economic policies. Physicians and nurses went on strike in November 1992. The medical personnel demanded wage increases and more investment in the rapidly deteriorating health care sector. Printers at the government owned printing house also went on strike in late 1992, shutting down Bucharest's major daily newspapers.

The 1992 Elections

In the elections held in September 1992, the Iliescu wing of the former FSN, now calling itself the Party of Social Democracy of

Romania (PDSR), received 27.7% of the votes for the Assembly of Deputies, giving it 117 seats, making it the largest bloc in the lower house of parliament. The parties united into the Democratic Convention, mainly the Liberals and the Peasant/Christian Democrats, won 20% of the vote, or 82 seats. Petre Roman's new party, the Democratic Party (FSN), received 10.2% of the vote, giving it 43 seats. The Democratic Party (FSN) ran as a center-left social democratic party. A right-wing party, the Party of Romanian National Unity (PUNR) won the fourth highest vote total, receiving 7.7% of the vote, giving it 30 seats. The party representing Magyar interests in Romania, the Hungarian Democratic Union of Romania (UDMR), obtained 27 seats, based on having secured 7.5% of the votes. UDMR more often than not voted with the parties making up the Democratic Convention. *Romania Mare* (Great Romania (PRM)), a second right-wing nationalist party, received 16 seats for its 3.9% of the vote. The Socialist Party of Labor (PSM), which defined itself as the successor to the former communist party, was awarded 13 seats for having won 3% of the vote. All of the remaining parties won 20% of the vote and got 13 seats in the lower-house of parliament. The distribution of the 143 seats in the Senate, paralleled that in the Assembly of Deputies.

PDSR, while winning the greatest number of seats in the Assembly of Deputies, had not received enough support to form a government on its own. It turned to PUNR and PRM, and the PSM, as well as to other parties that were not part of the Democratic Convention, to form a coalition government, with Nicolae Vocaroiu, an economic technocrat, given the job as prime minister. The two right-wing parties, PUNR and PRM, agreed to vote with PDSR, even though they were not given cabinet level positions in the new government. PDSR gave its right-wing allies a number of second and third tier ministerial posts and a number of administrative positions. To the opposition, it did not matter that the radical right was excluded from the cabinet. The mere fact that the radical right parties pledged to vote with the PDSR in return for relatively minor posts and a share of the state's patronage was enough to define the new government, in the opposition's view, as a "red-brown" coalition.

PUNR was founded shortly after the overthrow of the Ceausescu regime. It ran several successful candidates for parliament in the 1990 elections. PUNR has been especially strong in and around the city of Cluj-Napoca, where one of its leading figures, Gheorge Funar, has been repeatedly elected as mayor. The party is highly nationalistic. It is strongly anti-Magyar and anti-Rroma. Funar and his party have resisted extending Magyar language rights and Magyar political autonomy. The party has been able to maintain its strength by playing on popular fears among Romanians that Hungary has designs on bringing Transylvania back under its direct rule.

Romania Mare party was founded by Eugen Barbu and Corneliu Vadim Tudor in November 1990. Both Babu and Tudor were ultra-nationalist Romanian intellectuals. Tudor had been a close friend and ally of the Ceausescus. Following Barbu's death in 1993, Tudor became its sole leader. The party's ideology is an odd mixture of right wing, nationalist social theory and left-wing economic theory. Through its various publications, the party has continually waged an attack on Jews, Rroma, and Hungarians. It also has denounced the increasing influence of the West on Romania's economic and social policies and it had argued for retaining state ownership of Romania's key industries. Romania Mare's initial base of support appears to have been drawn from lower level technical workers and professionals who had come from relatively low social origins and who had experienced significant upward economic and social mobility under the communists (Veiga 1997:60-61). Since it was founded, it has considerably expanded its electoral base beyond the strata which initially had been drawn to it.

The Socialist Party of Labor (PSM) was established in November 1990 by Ilie Verdet, who had been a primo minister under Ceausescu. It achieved formal recognition by the state in January 1992, which allowed it to compete in that year's elections. Following the 1992 elections, the PSM and *Romania Mare* formed a parliamentary alliance called the National Bloc. Adrian Paunescu, another close ally of Ceausescu, had been the intellectual leader of the PSM, until he severed relations with the party in 1998. Paunescu owns two influential nationalist publications, the weekly paper *Totusi Iubirea* and the daily paper *Vrema*. Paunescu is an active owner, regularly writing signed articles for both publications. Like the party *Romania Mare,* PSM combines an ultranationalist, right-wing social ideology with a left-wing economic agenda. Paunescu has endorsed a return to a centrally planned economy and continuing state ownership of most means of production in Romania. PSM also was strongly anti-Western, claiming that the goal of Western economic institutions was to turn Romania into a colony of Western capitalism.

In the first round balloting for president in 1992, Ion Iliescu, running as a candidate backed by the PDSR, won 46.4% of the votes and Professor Emil Constantinescu, rector of the University of Bucharest and a distinguished geologist, obtained 31.3% of the vote. Professor Constantinescu ran as the candidate of the Democratic Convention. He, himself, had close ties to the National Peasant-Christian Democrat Party, a party that defined itself as representing the "liberal" right. The remaining votes were distributed across a large number of candidates. With no presidential candidate having received a majority of the vote, a run-off between the two candidates with the highest number of votes was required. In the second round, Iliescu won an overwhelming victory, getting 64% of the vote. Constantinescu received 31.3% of the vote.

The new Romanian government set an ambitious economic agenda for itself. Among its major goals was stabilizing the state budget, adopting a value-added tax, ending subsidies for state enterprises, ending state price subsidies for all consumer goods, and moving ahead with privatizing state owned enterprises (Institut fur Hohere Studien 1994). This agenda, in part, was a response to intense pressures from the International Monetary Fund (the IMF) and the World Bank to develop and to implement a neo-liberal program of economic "reform."

Adopting a neo-liberal economic agenda created serious political problems for the PDSR. Neo-liberalism ran counter to the interests of its constituency, which continued to be composed of managers of state enterprises, functionaries employed by the state, workers in large state enterprises, the retired, workers on state farms, and voters from the most economically distressed sections of the country. Neo-liberalism also conflicted with the economic and political interests of voters who supported the right-wing parties that were allied with the government. In addition to seeing neo-liberalism as a threat to their economic interests, right-wing voters also saw neo-liberalism an example of Western attempts to reduce Romania to an economic colony of western capitalism.

The neo-liberal agenda, sometimes called the "Washington Consensus" (see Unger 1998 and Eyal et al. 1998 for non-technical discussions of neo-liberal economics and Pieper and Taylor 1998 for a more technical discussion of the same ideas) has been the main economic program the IMF and the World Bank have sought to impose on Eastern and Central Europe, Romania, Russia, and Central Asia, among other places. Unger (1998: 53) notes that in its most general form neo-liberalism is directed at "macroeconomic stabilization." Such stabilization is to be realized through achieving a "fiscal balance" (Unger 1998: 53). In order to achieve fiscal balance, neo-liberalism advocates: 1) keeping strict controls over government spending, rather than relying on increased levels of taxation to balance budgets; 2) expanding a given state's integration into the international trading system; 3) increasing the level and scope of privatization in a national economy both in terms of adopting standards of Western private property laws and by withdrawing the government from direct involvement in the ownership of the means of production; and 4) developing an appropriate social safety net to counteract the more extreme negative effects of an economy operating according to neo-liberal economic policies (Unger 1998: 53).

One of the most fundamental assumptions of neo-liberalism is that there is a "class" of actors who have the resources, interests, and abilities to act as capitalists before the fact. This has not been the case in most of the former communist states of Eastern, Central, and Southeastern Europe, including Romania. Therefore, in attempting to implement neo-liberalism, all of these former communist states were faced, and continue to face, the fundamental problem of constructing a neo-liberal capitalist economy without a significant presence of indigenous capitalists. In Hungary, Poland, and Czechoslovakia, the process of creating a capitalist economic order and a capitalist class had begun developing even before the communists lost power. According to Eyal et al. (1998), such projects were led by the intellectual elites (both inside and outside of the party) within these countries. These intellectual elites, along with technocratic allies, constituted themselves as a second *Bildungsburgertum* that would lead their societies away from socialism toward bourgeois capitalism (Eyal et al. 1998: pp. 46 ff).

In Romania, the process of building a capitalist society has been far more difficult and complicated than it has been in Central and Eastern Europe. During the communist period, as we have shown in a previous chapter, Romanian intellectuals and the Romanian technocratic intelligentsia were unable to establish a degree of independence from and autonomy from the party bureaucracy that would have allowed them to engage in a similar project. As we have noted, the Romanian communist party kept its intellectuals under tight political control, not so much in terms of dictating what they could or could not write, but in terms of allowing them to develop an independent organizational base within the party or within society. In the absence of such intellectual developments, Romania had to start virtually from scratch in building a new set of economic institutions and in building a class of capitalists to preside over them and a capitalist social system. In many respects, this was the same challenge that the intellectual bourgeoisie faced from the time it took effective control over the Romanian state in the late 19th century until the end of World War II. During that time, as we noted previously, the Romanian intellectual bourgeoisie, having taken control of the state, tried to organize a capitalist revolution from above. They never really succeeded in this project before the communists took power. Before World War II, the Romanian economic bourgeoisie was very poorly developed.

Since 1989, the Romanian political elite, which did not have its origins in the bourgeoisie but, rather, had its origins in the communist bureaucracy, once again was being asked to build capitalism along neoliberal lines and at the same time provide the opportunities for a capitalist class to emerge and assume a leading role in Romanian society and politics. Neo-liberal economists hope that an emerging Romanian capitalist class will accept its historical "responsibility" of building a strong civil society, without which a capitalist economic order will have a difficult time stabilizing itself.

When the Romanian revolution took place, there was no class of capitalists who could step forward to take control over the economy, nor, as noted above, were the intellectuals and/or the technocrats prepared to step forward and act as a second Bildungsburgertum. Therefore, the management of the post-revolutionary economy was left in the hands of the former nomenklatura networks. In Romania the nomenklatura networks have acted, and continue to act, as structural speculators. As such, they looked for the "best" ways to redefine political and economic institutions so as to maximize their short-term and long-term positions in Romania.

As structural speculators, they looked for ways to accommodate structural change to their private economic and political interests, as was reflected in their agricultural privatization program and in the ways they dealt with industrial privatization, as well. It is not clear, when one looks at the behavior of these networks in the political arena, that they were or that they are interested in creating a powerful capitalist class that would challenge their own dominance of post-communist Romania. Indeed, exactly the opposite appears to be the case. The former nomenklatura have resisted making any changes in the economy until they could figure out how they could best take advantage of the proposed changes or could modify the proposed changes for their own benefit. They resisted any changes being proposed, unless they believed that they would dominate the change process and its outcomes.

The Romanian Constitution of 1991 contained a provision that guaranteed a right to the ownership of private property, which the FSN had pledged to support even before the constitution had been adopted. FSN support for private property had allowed retail trade to flourish, which, in turn, had permitted the rapid development of a state of petty bourgeoisie shopkeepers and service providers, including providers of professional services in law, medicine, dentistry, and the like. Existing state enterprises in this sector eventually were liquidated through direct offers of purchase and through a series of auctions. Many of these former state enterprises were bought by their managers and/or by their employers. They were sold at very cheap, below possible market value, giving rise to suspicions among the general public that the FSN was allowing the state "patrimony" to be looted by insiders.

One spectacular case involving the sale of a major Bucharest hotel seemed to confirm many of these suspicions. The government had received a number of bids for the property, including some from abroad. The highest bid, which had come from a Western firm, and the sale was awarded to a Romanian who had close political ties to the inner-most circles of the new government and the people who were overseeing the bidding and sale process.

Similar complaints were raised in the media sector. Following the revolution, a number of private radio stations emerged, some of which had heavy investments from foreign capital. When the state finally got around to passing legislation dealing with access to radio frequencies and set up an administrative process for assigning frequencies, there were complaints that people with ties to the old nomenklatura were treated more favorably than were others who lacked such connections.

Planning for Privatization

In order to privatize major state enterprises, the Romanian state began by converting all state enterprises into two categories: commercial companies and *Regies Autonomes*. The commercial companies were corporatized with the passage of Law 15/1990, which dealt with the restructuring of state-owned enterprises. The *Regies Autonomes*, which included mining and natural gas enterprises, rail and urban transportation systems, state radio and television, the weapons industry, and most public utilities, were to stay under state ownership for an indefinite period of time. The decision to keep these as publicly owned enterprises secured the position of their managers as part of the general state apparatus.

The Romanian law on privatization (Law 58/1991) required the Romanian state to distribute coupons representing 30% of all state assets to Romanian over age 18. The coupons represented a broad spectrum of the state owned companies that were not designated as *Regies Autonomes*. The state retained ownership of the 70% of the nation's corporate assets in a privatization account that it, the state, owned and managed (Frydman and Rapaczynski 1994). The plan was to sell 10% of these assets over the next several years, until such time as the fund was liquidated of its holdings.

The law on privatization established the National Agency for Privatization (NAP). The NAP was charged with the responsibility of overseeing the general privatization process. The law also authorized the creation of five "Private Ownership Funds" (POFs) and a "State Ownership Fund" (SOF). The National Agency for Privatization was charged with managing the privatization of Romania's smaller enterprises and the POFs were assigned the responsibility for managing intermediate sized enterprises and for working with the NAP to privatize the enterprises within the various funds. POF 1 was composed of enterprises in the wood processing and non-ferrous metals sector. POF 2 managed textile and clothing enterprises. POF 3 handled naval transportation enterprises (except in the defense sector), fishing firms, and enterprises in the tourism sector. POF 4 handled industries in the glass and ceramics sector, enterprises that dealt with construction materials, the cosmetic industries, and pharmaceuticals. Finally, POF 5 oversaw the electronic sector, enterprises dealing with leather products, and the footwear industry (Institut fur Hohere Studien 1994). The SOF was given control over the management of the largest state enterprises. The portfolio of enterprises managed by the SOF was disproportionately made up the proverbial "white elephants" of communist industrialization. Their physical plants were run-down, their technology was outdated, they were inefficient in that they consumed huge amounts of energy, and they employed large numbers of workers who soon would be declared redundant." These enterprises, generally, were over-valued, making them difficult to sell on domestic or on international markets.

As a result of the passage of Law 58/1991, by the end of the 1992 30% of the shares of over 6300 Romanian companies were distributed to the adult population, giving equity in the national economy to about 16.5 million people. The state began distributing these shares in June 1992 and by August 1992, the Romanian Foreign Trade Bank had set up a brokerage operation to facilitate the buying and selling of the equity shares. In 1993, a stock market was established with a view toward developing a general market for trading in the ownership shares that had been distributed to the adult population. Also in 1993, the government began selling shares in the SOF.

Along with designing and beginning to implement a privatization program, the Romanian government launched a number of fiscal reforms, including a "reform" of the tax system. One of the first tax "reforms" introduced was designed to reduce taxes on enterprises, which were seen to be carrying a disproportionate share of the society's tax burden. It was hoped that a reduction of taxes on businesses would lead to an expansion of entrepreneurship and an expansion of existing business enterprises.

In order to offset losses due to a reduction in business taxes, in July 1993 Romania introduced a value-added tax (VAT). The rate for most goods falling under the tax was 18%. Goods sold to universities, hospitals, and the public sector were taxed at the lower rate of 9%. Basic food commodities, household energy, pharmaceutical, and public transportation were exempted from the VAT.

During the communist period, the wage fund of all enterprises was taxed. This tax was abolished and a tax on personal income from wages was introduced. Individuals were required to pay taxes on a number of income benefits that had previously been exempt from taxation.

As it struggled to stabilize the sources of state revenues, the government also introduced a program designed to reduce government subsidies to consumption. In May 1992, it cut all subsidies by 25%. In September 1992, the government reduced subsidies another 25%. Shortly after forming a new government following the 1992 elections, the Prime Minister, Nicolae Vacaroiu, in an interview he gave to

Romanian National Radio on December 30, 1992, outlined his agenda. He announced that there would be further liberalizations of prices, but that these would be accompanied by an improved system of income indexation. He also assured listeners that the government had taken appropriate measures to insure that there would be sufficient energy for heating and lighting for the remainder of the winter (British Broadcasting Corporation, January 1, 1993). He said that his government would implement programs to improve worker productivity, to improve the management of state enterprises, and to accelerate privatization (British Broadcasting Corporation January 1, 1993).

As prices increased, workers responded with protests demonstrations and strikes. For example, on February 22, 1993, the Siderurgistul Independent Trade Union of Hunedoara organized a protest demonstration that was attended by over 2000 iron and steel workers and other residents of Hunedoara (British Broadcasting Corporation, February 25, 1993). The protesters demanded that wages in the iron and steel production sector be raised to the levels prevailing in other branches of industry, that the government provide investment credits at low interest rates to attract new capital to the iron and steel sector, that the government pledge money for technological upgrading of the industry, to provide for wage levels that would give workers in the iron and steel industry an "equitable price-salary ratio," and for the government to take steps to combat profiteering and corruption. The union leadership announced that they and their members would take part in a proposed national labor demonstration to be held in Bucharest on February 24, 1993.

In order to try to quell growing worker discontent, Prime Minister Vacaroiu made visits to a number of key areas outside of Bucharest, where there was considerable discontent over Romania's economic situation. On March 26, 1993, Vacaroiu toured the Jiu Valley coal fields. He then went to Hunedoara and Sibiu. During the trip, the prime minister struggled to get his message across about the need to reform the price system in Romania so as to accelerate the country's economic transformation.

The government planned to end all subsidies to consumer products in May 1993. In order to minimize Romanian concerns about the ending of price subsidies, Prime Minister Nicolae Vacaroiu went on national radio to answer listeners' questions about the proposed "reform." There had been massive labor demonstrations conducted across Romania on

April 12, 1993 protesting government economic policies, including the freeing of prices and the ending of subsidies, and the broadcast's monitor asked Vacariou to keep these protests in mind as he answered listeners questions (British Broadcasting Corporation: April 15, 1993). During the radio broadcast, Vacaroiu stated that "...the transition to a market economy is a painful process at least until we get out of the current crisis, meaning that...[sic] ...economy will work well enough to be able to offer sufficient resources to be used for social purposes and we want to achieve that before the end of this year. Until then all of us, practically the whole population, had to put up with such difficulty." The Prime Minister went on to acknowledge that the reductions in state subsidies would worsen the situation of many families, especially those with a large number of children. However, he claimed that cuts in subsidies was required in order to "do away with corruption and the black market, because we are subsidizing goods that never reach the population directly, but rather via the black market where prices are as high as if subsidies already had been cut."

Vacaroiu answered several more questions dealing with economic problems that were facing young couples, national housing problems, economic problems of pensioners and the elderly, and the general difficulties of handicapped persons in Romania. At one point in the broadcast, Vacaroiu claimed that the government was examining different ways in could provide economic assistance to handicapped persons, but that before anything could be done the government had to identify the large number of persons who had obtained fraudulent certifications that they had a handicap. He next addressed a complaint from a listener about the "doubling" of princes for certain goods in Bucharest's markets over the past week. Vacaroiu again blamed the black market and economic "corruption" for the price increases. He then went on to say that Romania could not freeze prices in domestic markets because it would endanger the nation's transition to a market economy, but he claimed that the government was conducting "thousands" of active investigations to see who were responsible for the "abhorrent" increase in prices.

On April 23, Vararoiu made a major address to his party, the PDSR. Many of the party's major figures, including a large number of its parliamentary representatives, were very uncomfortable about the ending of subsidies and the massive worker protests this action already had produced. Vacaroiu used the party meeting to try to allay their fears and set aside their objections to his policies on prices. With respect to the end of price subsidies, Vacaroiu informed the party that the average amount of worker compensation, plus the salary indexation program the government was following, would reach 13,000 lei per worker per month and 7,860 lei per retired person per month (British Broadcasting Corporation, April 27, 1993). According to Vacaroiu (British Broadcasting Corporation, April 27, 1993), these amounts would totally cover the expected price increases in electricity, heating, bread, milk, and butter. He added that wage increases plus indexation would average 30%, while prices were expected to increase by 29% with the end of subsidies. The Prime Minister also informed party members that there would be significant increases in family subsidies for children, that pensioners would receive income increases, and that the government planned to increase subsistence allowances for agricultural workers. Vocaroiu argued that the end of consumer subsidies was absolutely essential to the Romanian economic reform program and that the plan his government was putting into place was superior to that agreed upon after three weeks of negotiations with twelve of Romania's trade union confederations, pensioners' groups, and employers. Six of Romania's trade union confederations had refused to participate in these negotiations. Instead, they had appealed to the president, Ion Iliescu, to participate directly in the talks and mediate the disputes between the unions and the government, which, until that point, he had wisely refused to do (British Broadcasting Corporation, April 27, 1993). As it turned out, however, the government did not have the funds to meet the promises it was making about raising wages and other contributions to household incomes, which drove a deeper wedge between the PDSR and the organized labor movement.

The Romanian National Council of Free Trade Unions which, at the time, was headed by Victor Ciorbea, was planning a nation-wide strike for early May. Ciorbea postponed his group's participation in the scheduled May 5 action, while the National Trade Union Bloc and *Fratia* went ahead with the strike. The subway workers in Bucharest had gone on strike earlier in May. Worker resistance continued throughout 1993, partly in response to price increases in consumer goods, which eroded the overall level of living in the general population. From early November 1990, when Romania began to institute a policy of price liberalization, to the end of 1992, prices had increased fifteen-fold, while wages had increased only by a factor of nine. Over this period real wages had declined by fifteen per cent and unemployment had reached almost one million, or ten percent of the work force, and high inflation was ravaging the average Romanian households' budget.

As controversy swirled around the government's program ending consumer price subsidies, Rompres (the Romanian National Press Agency) released the results of a national poll that had been conducted for the press agency by a national research organization, SRL-IRSOP. The poll had been conducted between the 5th and 10th of April. Surveying 1,056 respondents over the age of 18, SRL-IRSOP asked people what they had liked most about life in pre-1989 Romania: 20% reported peace and social order; 18% identified lower costs of living; 16% job security; 10% a secure future; 9% the quality of their professional life; 8% the quality of their family life; 6% personal safety; 5% hobbies; 4% nothing; and 4% responded with "don't know" (British Broadcasting Corporation April 24, 1993). Asked about they liked most about life in present day Romania, 42% of respondents stated freedom; 23% plenty of goods in the market; 9% the standard of living; 7% land resettlement; 9% democracy; and 5% family life (British Broadcasting Corporation April 24, 1993). When they were asked what they liked least about life at the present time, persons answered as follows: 33%, the high cost of living; 17% corruption; 12% politics; and 10% unemployment, the degradation of human relations, uncertainty about the future, and crime and violence (British Broadcasting Corporation April 24, 1993).

In response to a question about overall life satisfaction, 6% said that they were very satisfied with the general quality of life; 51% were satisfied, and the rest (43%) were either dissatisfied or very dissatisfied (British Broadcasting Corporation April 24, 1993). These levels of dissatisfaction were considerably higher than what such surveys typically find in most Western countries. Forty nine per cent of the respondents thought Romania was moving in a good or very good direction and 44% thought Romania was moving in the wrong direction. Fifty two per cent of the Romanian respondents approved of the government's program of economic reforms, while 48% did not (British Broadcasting Corporation April 24, 1993). Finally, when asked about what was the best way to improve Romania's overall standard of living, 40% said it was more work; 23% identified better government economic policies; 18% said economic privatization and the development of private enterprise; and

9% an increase in foreign investments (British Broadcasting Corporation April 24, 1993). The results of this survey were interesting in several respects. First, there appears to have been quite a large amount of support for what the PDSR led coalition government was doing at this time, despite the large number of people who were concerned about inflation. Fewer people seem to have been opposed to government policy than what one would think was the case if one focused on the street demonstrations and on what was being reported in the opposition press. Second, Romanians were less satisfied with the quality of life than is typically the case in Western countries. While reports on the survey did not identify specific reasons for this, it most likely was the result of the poor economic conditions prevailing in the country. Third, Romanians were more likely to blame themselves for the nation's economic problems than they were the state. Hence, they believed that by working harder that they would be able to improve the country's economic life. Fourth, given the overall pattern of results it appears that the government had a political base on which it could have pressed ahead with a broad program of economic change, even if it caused personal dislocations to most of the population.

By May 1993, all consumer subsidies were ended, despite the opposition of the trade unions. The ending of subsidies contributed to the sharp increases in prices that Romania was experiencing during this time. Prices also increased when the government introduced a Value Added Tax on July 1, 1993 and ended the 30% limit on retail mark-ups by merchants. The economic dislocations Romania was experiencing brought about a significant devaluation of the Romanian currency, the leu (pl. lei). In 1989, the leu stood at 18.98 lei to the dollar. One year later it was 49.38. In 1991, the dollar was worth 260.4 lei. In 1992 the dollar bought 632.5 lei at official exchange markets. The dollar was worth 1275 lei in 1993.

With the new government in power less than a year, it came under an increasingly vitriolic attack by the opposition political parties. Shortly following the government's implementation of the VAT in July 1993, the Democratic Convention of Romania (DCR) accused the Vacaroiu government of tolerating and, indeed, fostering widespread corruption and of total incompetence and the DCR offered itself as a willing candidate to form a new government that would be better able to handle the growing economic dislocations the country was experiencing.

The DCR mobilized its allies in the Romanian press to declare a boycott of government news (British Broadcasting Corporation, July 17, 1993; Jackson, July 19, 1993: 18). The Romanian dailies *Romania Libera, Adevarul, Evenimental Zile,* and *Tineretul Liber,* along with the news agencies AR Press and AM Press, announced that, given the government's "lack of credibility" (British Broadcasting Corporation, July 17, 1993), they would suspend their coverage of government activities for a period of at least two weeks. Petre Bacanu, editor of *Romania Libera,* stated: "We decided to sanction the government for its constant refusal to react to the parliamentary report which says that government officials have been involved in serious corruption" (Jackson July 19, 1993: 18). He continued: "We expect the national television and radio to join us. If this happens, the government is in big trouble" (Jackson July 19, 1993: 18).

The decision received the support of the steering committee of the Romanian Journalists' Association. As a reason for supporting the boycott, the steering committee released a document stating that: "The present Romanian government is an agonizing body which seems to have been especially designed to bar the way to democracy. The government's manner of approaching the grave corruption cases, the way it pronounces on the guilt of highly-placed officials, are in defy [sic] of the public opinion. The government does not seem willing to rid itself of the corrupt, disgraced persons and tries to dodge the corruption scandal" (British Broadcasting Corporation, July 17, 1993).

The parliamentary report to which Jackson (July 19, 1993: 19) refers had suggested that corruption was widespread in the highest reaches of the Romanian government, including the prime minister, himself. The prime minister and the transport minister were accused of avoiding an explanation of their involvement in the sale of *Petromin,* one of the country's leading fishing enterprises, to a Greek businessman, Stelian Katounis. Katounis paid $355 million for 92 ships, which supposedly were worth twice the amount. It was alleged that the prime minister and the transportation minister, Paul Teadoru, had engaged in exercising improper influence to ensure that Koutinis' bid was accepted over others.

In addition to accusations levied against the prime minister and the transport minister, Emilian Idjelea, former head of the Romanian Development Agency (ARD), accused the Tourist Minister, Dan Matei, and the state secretary of Strategic Affairs, Viorel Hrebengiuc, of improperly intervening in agency affairs to secure a contract that would be favorable to their private interests (Mutler August 31, 1993).

Corruption charges had become a major weapon in the opposition's struggle against the PDSR led government. The opposition had hoped that charging the government with pandemic corruption would sufficiently undermine its legitimacy that it would be forced to resign. Toward this end, the opposition made it seem as if corruption was so rampant in Romania as to threaten the very existence of Romania's infant democracy. The PDSR responded in kind, charging leading figures of the opposition, such as the former prime minister Petre Roman, of being engaged or of having been engaged in corrupt activities. Roman was accused of having illegally acquired an 11 room house from the Ministry of National Economy while he had been prime minister and of having rented his apartment to foreigners in exchange for hard currency (Rodina October 13, 1993). Despite the rhetoric and the charges and counter-charges of corruption by the government and the opposition, most corruption was of a petty nature and it certainly was not purely a legacy of the communist period, as some commentators claimed it was. While communist officials and functionaries began accepting money in exchange for services as the system began to decay, they were not the first to use state office for personal gain, as we previously we have shown. The monetarization of state services for private gain had been institutionalized as far back as the boyar state system and had been part and parcel of the way office holders earned their incomes during the bourgeois and fascist periods. The second major form of corruption was tax evasion, which, like accepting gratuities for services rendered, had a long history in Romania, going back to the earliest days of Ottoman rule. To claim, as the opposition did, that the PDSR government was corrupt because it was filled with former communists was disingenuous, to say the least. It ignored the way in which the state had operated long before the fascists and, later, the communists had come to power. Much of what now was being labeled as corrupt behavior had long been accepted in Romania, as well as in Western Europe, as "normal" and acceptable behavior. Before the communists had taken control of Romania, many of the country's richest families had acquired a good deal of their wealth through control over state offices, as we have previously shown. The escalating accusations of corruption coming from all political quarters was but one sign of a general deterioration of political discourse in

Romania. Politics became less concerned with differences of political philosophy and policies and became more and more a war directed at the total personal destruction of one's opponents.

The opposition's denunciations of corruption were a bit disingenuous, if not economically naïve. Unregulated, free-market capitalism generates corruption. In that sense, it is a crimogenic economic system. One only has to look at the experiences of the United States, supposedly the most transparent economy in the world. As neo-liberal ideology triumphed in the United States and as corporate interests penetrated the political process through campaign contributions to both political parties, state regulation of the economy weakened, beginning, first, with the Carter administration and continuing under Reagan, Bush, Clinton, and the younger Bush. Deregulation and a cut back in policing corporate behavior, in part, was justified by the claim that American corporations need to be made "more competitive." This produced a spate of spectacular economic scandals, near-crimes, and outright crimes that cost investors billions of dollars and workers scores of thousands of jobs. Among the corporations whose behavior has come to be questioned are some of the giants of the United States' economy: Enron, WorldCom, Global Crossing, Tyco, Halliburton (whose one time CEO was the U.S. Vice-President Richard Cheney), the accounting firm Arthur Anderson, Adelphia, Xerox, Quest Communications etc. Of course, from America's point of view, its problems with its own corporations is described as a result of the "greed and gluttony" of a few bad apples, while in the case of other countries, Americans see similar behavior to be a product of cultures that generate and tolerate corruption. There also have been significant financial scandals in France and in Germany, to name just two additional capitalist countries. Given that it is difficult to control capitalist "excess" in the most advanced countries, where there are laws and policing mechanisms in place, it should not have been surprising to find economic irregularities in an emerging market economy like Romania, where few institutions were in place to control the new business class.

To add to its problems, in late July 1993, the government failed to reach a new agreement on a standby arrangement with the International Monetary Fund (Marsh and Corzine July 27, 1993: 3). The failure blocked loan credits from the European Community and the G24 developed countries that totaled around $3 billion. The talks had stalled over the IMF's concerns about the slow pace of restructuring and privatizing of medium sized and large state enterprises and the perceived lack of financial discipline which the IMF saw as the basis for Romania's high rate of inflation

At this time, state-owned enterprises accounted for almost 90% of Romania's industrial production. The vast majority of these state-owned enterprises were heavily in debt. The government had written off inter-enterprise debts in 1992, however, by mid-1993 inter-enterprise debts had risen to about $2.4 billion, about 20% of national GDP (Marsh and Corzine July 27, 1993: 3). State enterprises also had taken advantage of negative real interest rates during this period and, as a result, accumulated huge debts to Romania's banks. The top 100 most indebted state enterprises had bank debts equivalent to almost $300 million (Marsh and Corzine July 27, 1993: 3).

The IMF also maintained that the government had failed to hold the line on wage increases. It felt that the government had caved into "excessive" worker wage demands in the face of massive demonstrations against the rapid increases in prices, thus contributing to high levels of inflation. The government continually caved in to demands for higher wages in order to offset the anger that was building in the country over the continuing rapid increases in prices. During the communist period, as was the case in almost all other European communist states, prices were not a function of relations of supply and demand, this was especially true of prices of essential commodities. This also was the case with wages. Wage rates bore little, if any relation, to worker productivity or to the profitability of an enterprise. While wages were low compared to Western Europe, prices were heavily subsidized, including the prince of housing. The introduction of market relations as the determinant of prices and wages threatened the whole basis of the moral economy that had been the foundation of Romanian life under the communists. The clear erosion of the moral economy was perceived as more of a long range threat to overall well-being by Romania's rank-and-file population than was the immediate rise in prices for most goods and services.

In early September 1993, the government sent a delegation to Washington in what was called a "last ditch effort" to win a standby agreement with the IMF (Marsh September 4, 1993). Between July and September, there had been no significant improvement in Romania's political or economic situation. Indeed, in many respects, the political and economic situations had deteriorated further. The nationalist parties on which the PDSR depended to stay in power had been agitating for one or more cabinet posts in the government. They were threatening to withdraw their support of the government if they did not get at least one cabinet position. In addition, Gheorghe Funar, a leader of the PUNR (one of the nationalist parties supporting the PDSR government) and the mayor of Cluj, had announced that he would try to secure the impeachment of President Iliescu if the president continued to support the idea that there should be bilingual signs in ethnically mixed territories in Romania (Marsh September 4, 1993).

To add to its problems, the government had faced two significant strikes in August 1993 and was likely to have to deal with more strikes in the near future. The August strikes had involved train-drivers and miners in the highly volatile Jiu Valley. Both groups wanted significant pay increases to match the increases in prices that had taken place. Initially, the government had tried to stop the train-drivers' strike by declaring it an illegal labor action. When this did not force the drivers back to work, telephone lines to the union's headquarters were cut and Romanian radio and television began broadcasting news bulletins to the effect that workers at most of the nation's train depots had returned to work, which witnesses subsequently claimed had not been true. The strike collapsed when, hearing this new, many of the drivers gave up their strike and returned to their jobs (Marsh September 4, 1993).

The strike in the Jiu Valley ended on more favorable terms for the striking workers. The state owned Jiu Valley Coal Co. gave in to the miners' demands for substantial pay increases. When the minister of industry heard the size of the pay increase given to the miners, he immediately cancelled the agreement. Miron Cosma, the rebellious head of the Jiu Valley mine workers' union, responded to the minister's actions by threatening another strike and by beginning legal actions to have the minister of industry's decision overturned (Marsh September 4, 1993). The minister had no choice but to reject the Jiu Valley Coal Co.'s wage offer. If he had not, other unions would have pressed for equal raises and this would have ended any hope that Romania could secure an IMF standby agreement.

At the same time that the government was trying to win assistance from the IMF, it also was seeking membership in the Council of Europe, as one of its first significant steps toward integrating itself with Western Europe. Membership in the Council of Europe also had appeared to be a goal of the major parties in the opposition. However, when a Romanian delegation met with representatives of the Council, the leaders of the Democratic Union of Hungarians in Romania (HDUR), which was one of the major parties in the Democratic Convention, gave the secretary general of the Council a lengthy memorandum on the current state of Romania's Magyar population. The memorandum was highly critical of the Romanian state's treatment of its Magyar minority. The president of the HDUR, Bela Marko, had turned over the memorandum to the Council without having notified the Democratic Convention that he intended to take such an action and without having informed his allies in the Democratic Convention of the memorandum's content. Corneliu Coposu, the president of the National Peasant Party-Christian Democrat (PNT-CD) was sharply critical of the HDUR's action and of the content of the memorandum. He was quoted as saying, among other things, that his party did not agree "with the Hungarian minority's claim to privileges at the expense of the other minorities of Romania" and that the PNT-CD also objected to some of the memorandum's points that it considered "inappropriate, subjective, and unrealistic" (Marsh September 4, 1993).

In the face of all of these problems, the PDSR government had to deal with a large demonstration in mid-September. According to police estimates, a crowd of 3000 people had heeded the request of the Civic Alliance, which supported the Democratic Convention, to gather in protest against corruption in the government (Agence France Presse September 14, 1993). The crowd held signs that read "Down with Iliescu," "Down with the Thieves," and "Long Live King Michael" (Agence France Presse September 14, 1993).

Charges of corruption were not confined to government officials or to opposition politicians. In October 1993, the Romanian dissident poet, Mircea Dinescu resigned as head of Romania's Writers' Union after having been accused of corruption (Agence France Presse October 8, 1993). Dinescu had been the person who had announced to Romania on national television that Bucharest had risen up against the Ceausescus. He had been elected president of the Writers' Union shortly after that event.

Earlier in the same week that Dinescu resigned as leader of the Writers' Union, two other writers, one of whom was the much acclaimed dissident poet Ana Blandiana, had resigned from the Writers' Union management committee. They had resigned in protest, alleging that

Dinescu had insulted them at a meeting the committee held to deal with the accusations against him (Agence France Presse October 8, 1993).

Dinescu was charged with having diverted printing equipment, given to the Union by Germany, to a foundation devoted to the promotion of German literature, which he also headed, and of using Union funds to construct a facility in which to put the new equipment. Dinescu denied the charges, claiming that the donated equipment had been a gift to both organizations. Nonetheless, he claimed he had resigned in order to "appease the accusers" (Agence France Presse October 8, 1993).

As the various charges and countercharges of corruption circulated in Romanian society, a financial scandal of major proportions was developing in Cluj-Napoca. In April 1992, an investment scheme called *Caritas* was formed (the investment fund had no relationship to the charity of the same name) by Ioan Stoica. Initially it was defined as a "mutual aid game" (*joc de intrajutorare*). However, after such schemes were declared illegal in September 1992 by the Romanian Supreme Court (Decision 150), Stoica claimed that Caritas was not a "mutual aid game," but, rather, was a "financial circuit" (*circuit financiar*). Irrespective of what Stoica called it, Caritas operated as a classic pyramid investment operation, where initial investors earned large returns on the backs of later investors. Over three million people are reported to have invested in the scheme. Branson (Sunday Times (of London) November 1, 1993) reports that at one point the total amount of money invested was 700 million pounds, which was about half of the national budget. During the summer of 1993, investors were receiving as much as a 700% return on their capital. For managing the fund, Stoica reportedly earned 66 million pounds in commissions. Investors initially were limited residents of Cluj-Napoca, but the fund soon proved so popular that it came to include all residents of Romania. Investors were drawn from all strata of the Romanian population. Included among the investors were members of parliament and several major figures in the national government. It is not surprising that Caritas was a popular investment instrument. In 1993, inflation was running at over 300 per cent a year; interest rates paid on savings accounts were in the negative range, meaning that persons with money in normal bank accounts were seeing their savings being wiped out; average income had fallen by 40% between 1989 and 1993; and many petty producers, in desperate need of capital, could not secure credit from the Romanian banking system and Caritas provided a means to get around the credit bottlenecks (Verdery 1996: 172). Romanian banks preferred to lend money to state enterprises and to joint ventures in which foreigners partnered with Romanian investors, than to individual Romanian entrepreneurs.

By the fall 1993, reports began to appear in Western newspapers about Caritas and the precariousness of its existence (Le Bor 1993; Maass 1993; Perlez 1993). Critical articles also appeared in the Romanian newspapers *Evenimentul Zilei, Romania Libera,* and *Cotidianul.* The Romanian president, Ion Iliescu, in a press conference in September 1993, predicted that Caritas soon would collapse.

The parliamentary opposition denounced the scheme as a "scam," but the government did nothing to restrain it, as the mayor of Cluj, who also was the leader of the PUNR, was a strong Caritas supporter and the PDSR government needed his party's support in order to stay in power. By the beginning of November 1993, Caritas was clearly in trouble. It had failed to make pay outs-to its investors for a second time in a month and it was attracting few new investors, which was its life-blood. The investment scheme was near to collapse. Stoica finally closed the scheme in May, 1994, setting off a round of protests and demonstrations by those who felt that they had not received what they had been promised by the investment fund. In August 1994, Stoica was arrested and charged with fraud, false representation, and fraudulent bankruptcy (Verdery 1996: 174). In his first trial he was convicted of fraud and received a six year prison sentence.

On November 8, 1993, roughly 40,000 Romanian union members and their sympathizers conducted a march in Bucharest. The march was organized by the CNSLR-*Fratia* confederation. The confederation issues an eleven point statement that, among other things, demanded that the government accelerate the privatization process, that it move more rapidly in restructuring state enterprises, that it increase its investments in public works projects and in projects designed to improve the country's infrastructure, that it take actions to end corruption, that it improve the system of social welfare, and that it increase the minimum wage to 60 per cent of the national average wage (Marsh November 9, 1993).

This demonstration was followed by another large demonstration on November 18, 1993, in which an estimated 50,000 protesters paraded through Bucharest and thousands of others marched on the streets of other cities. Victor Ciorbea, a leading figure in the labor movement, said, about the demonstrations, "We do not want words instead of heating, warm water, lodging, food" (British Broadcasting Corporation November 20, 1993).

Two weeks after the November 18th demonstration, two trade unions, the *National Trade Union Bloc* (BNS) and *Alpha Cartel,* again organized massive protests against the government across Romania. It was estimated that 30,000 people turned out in Bucharest, with thousands of others having marched in at least a dozen other Romanian cities (Agence France Presse, November 29, 1993). Alpha Cartel, which identified itself as a Christian-Democratic union and which enjoyed close ties to the National Peasant – Christian Democrat Party, and *BNS* both demanded the resignation of the national government and its replacement by a "cabinet of national unity" (Agence France Presse, November 29, 1993).

Constantinescu and his allies in the Democratic Convention of Romania used the mounting protests to intensify their parliamentary attacks on the government. By December 1993 it was clear that the DCR, rather than trying to seek some form of compromise with the government, was more bent on overthrowing it and replacing it with a government of its own choosing. On December 7, 1993, the executive committee of the DCR met. The leaders of all of the parties making up the DCR met. They also invited representatives of the Democratic Party – National Salvation Front (DP-FSN), which was led by Petre Roman. Although not a formal part of the DCR, Roman's party was a strong opponent of the PDSR, in general, and of President Iliescu, in particular. The various parties, claiming that they wanted to halt Romania's decline into a "national disaster," (British Broadcasting Corporation, December 7, 1993), agreed to submit to both houses of parliament a motion of censure against the government. In a press release to *ROMPRES,* the parties claimed that that they had taken such action because "...one year after the installation of the Vacaroiu government, the promised reform has not started. There is no political will for economic recovery. The results of the present governing are anarchy, unprecedented corruption, and uncertainty for tomorrow" (British Broadcasting Corporation, December 7, 1993).

In effect, by taking this action the DCR was hoping that it, in alliance with the DP-FSN, could overturn the results of the fully democratic elections, that had taken place a year earlier, and install itself in power, even though it had been soundly defeated at the polls. Failing that, at the very least, the opposition hoped that they could further weaken the credibility and, hence, the legitimacy of the government in the eyes of the general population, especially among those who had voted for the PDSR. Furthermore, the opposition hoped that a vote of censure against the government would place blame for Romania's continuing economic problems on Vocaroiu and Iliescu and not on the opposition parties, themselves, for having refused to cooperate in any meaningful way with the governing party.

The DCR and its trade union allies staged a huge protest against the government in mid-December, 1993 (Rodina: December 16, 1993). The demonstrators, made up mostly of workers and members of various student organizations from Romania's universities, numbering some 90,000 people, marched to bring pressure on parliament to vote out the Vacaroiu government. The largest protests were held in Timisoara, where it was estimated that 70,000 people marched. All of the major unions representing workers in the Banat, of which Timisoara is the capital, participated in the rally, as did trade union delegations from Brasov, Ploesti, Bacau, Lugoj, and Arad, as well as workers from smaller industrial towns and cities. Representatives of *HDUR* (Hungarian Democratic Union of Romania), the party representing Romania's Magyars, also played a prominent role in the protests in Timisoara (British Broadcasting Corporation, December 18, 1993). In Timisoara, the crowds chanted anti-government and anti-president slogans and demanded that immediate and drastic steps be taken to redress Romania's economic problems.

In Bucharest, the crowd was estimated to number 20,000. Student organizations had joined the workers as part of a nationwide strike of university students that had begun three days prior to the demonstrations. Among the student demands was cheaper public transportation and an increase in the amount of scholarship assistance from the government (Rodina: December 16, 1993).

At this point, the government was in a precarious position. The Romanian Party of National Unity (PUNR), a party of the radical right which normally voted with the government, was threatening to vote against the government. The PUNR leadership was using the threat of voting to remove the government in the hope that it would get one or more ministerial posts in return for supporting Vacaroiu and his cabinet, which, until this point, had kept the right out of the government.

Romania's Growing Health Crisis

Barber (December 22, 1993) noted that at the time that Vacaroiu was defending his government's policies and programs, Romania's tuberculosis rate, its rate of Hepatitis B infection, and its infant mortality rates were among the highest in all of Europe. In November 1993, the national Health Ministry announced that infant mortality had begun to increase, after having declined since 1989. The Health Ministry's data show that the infant mortality rate rose by 3 per cent, to 23.4 per 1000 live births in 1992. The European average, including former communists countries, was just slightly more than 10 per 1000 live births (Perlez November 24, 1993). Only Albania had a higher infant mortality rate in Europe than did Romania. During the Ceausescu period, after several decades of improving health statistics, virtually all indicators of public health reversed themselves and death rates began to rise precipitously, with the single exception of deaths from respiratory diseases, which was quite surprising, given the high levels of air pollution that prevailed in most industrial and urban regions of the country. After 1989, the overall health situation showed little signs of improvement, as the death rate per 100,000 people increased from 1068.2 in 1989 to 1197.8 in 1995. Deaths from cancer, tuberculosis, diseases of the circulatory system, and diseases of the respiratory system all increased markedly after 1989 (Cockerham 1999: 203). Part of the reason for the increasing death rate is related to the collapse of the former communist health-care system and the failure of post-communist governments to make significant investments in this social sector. Under Ceausescu, the public health sector had been starved for resources, on the average receiving only about 2.2% of the national budget between 1985 and 1989 (Valceanu 1992). In 1990, health care received only 2.9% of the national budget and by 1999 this had fallen to 2.5% (Cockerham 1999: 205). Most of these expenditures went to Romania's more affluent, urban areas and this continues to be the case, as a result public health institutions have continued to deteriorate even more dramatically in Romania's countryside (Valceanu 1992). Because of the low level of state funding of the health sector, in order to obtain services from physicians and hospital services, patients were expected to pay for their health care through an elaborate system of informal gratuities to physicians and to hospital staffs. When in a hospital, patients, and their families, often supplied their own linens, did their own laundry, and, even, supplied their own meals. In some cases patients and their families even supplied medications that were needed. This often was necessary case when the required medication was of foreign manufacture. The patients and their families, in these cases, often would have to secure the medication in the underground economy at considerably inflated prices. After 1989, with state investment in the health sector still at low levels, these practices have continued, although, many, if not most, foreign medications, are available on private, open markets.

During Ceausescu's rule, Romania experienced a significant outbreak of AIDS. The epidemic largely was concentrated in Romania's seriously over-crowded and under-funded orphanages. It was introduced into the country by a tainted blood supply that the government had purchased for medical use in the orphanages. Outside of the population of orphans, AIDS was not a significant health problem in Romania during the communist era. There are signs, however, that now, with its more open orders, with an increasing number of IV drug users, with the growth of prostitution along newly developed long-distance truck routes created to bypass the former Yugoslavia, and the emerging sex-tourism trade in Romania, that AIDS may become a significant health problem in the not too distant future.

Men have been especially affected by the decline in public health standards, particularly middle-aged men in working class occupations (Cockerham 1999). Male life-expectancy, as is the case in other former communist countries, has been dropping since 1989, while female life-expectancy has been increasing since 1989 in Romania. Female life expectancy, however, still lags behind levels in Western Europe. It has been middle-aged, working class men who have suffered the most in the post-communist era. They have experienced higher levels of unemployment, a sharper drop in real wages, and they have fewer reasons to be optimistic about the future than do most other sectors of the Romanian population, with the possible exception of retirees. Undoubtedly this has increased the levels of stress that they have to endure on a daily basis, which, in turn, has contributed to the general decline in their health, especially when coupled with "lifestyles" and behaviors, such as high levels of tobacco use, heavy alcohol consumption, poor diets, and the like, that contribute to the onset of a variety of diseases. Middle aged, working class men also have been a stratum of the population that has been exposed to heavy levels of pollution in many of Romania's factories, few of which ever exhibited much concern for worker health and safety.

In 1997, the Romanian parliament, then controlled by the parties making up the Democratic Convention of Romania, finally passed national health insurance legislation. This was the first major change in funding of the nation's health system since 1947 (Cockerham 1999: 206), although there had been minor changes introduced between 1947 and 1989. Under the terms of the new legislation, employees contribute 5% of their wages/salaries to a newly formed insurance company, *Casa de Asigurari pentru Sanatate* (which translates, literally, as Insurance House for Health), and employers match this contribution. Retirees are expected to contribute 4% from their pensions, with the government paying the rest. The disabled and the unemployed have their entire share picked up by the state. The new company is charged with using the money collected to purchase health care services from the state. The insurance system does not cover private health care services, which are available in most major cities at a considerably higher cost than state health care services. It remains to be seen whether the new insurance system has any significant effect on the provision of medical care to Romania's population and whether the care financed by the insurance system has a significant effect on the overall level of national health.

The obvious deterioration in national health statistics only added to the increasingly generalized sense of despair being felt by the average Romanian. The opposition parties hoped that they could capitalize on this despair to bring down the new PDSR government.

Crisis in the Educational Sector

Health care was not the only social sector that was in deep crisis, so, too, was education. During the later years of the Ceausescu regime, education was seriously under funded. The physical plants in many of the nation's schools and universities had deteriorated badly. University classes, for example, were conducted in poorly lighted and badly heated rooms. During the winter, faculty and students had to wear coats and gloves to classes in a vain attempt to keep warm. There were severe shortages of textbooks and other critical supplies for classes from kindergarten through the university. Although higher education was "free," only 6% to 7% of the population attended the national universities. Faculty salaries, as well as student stipends, were very low. The Romanian Academy's various research institutes also were seriously under funded, except in areas related to national defense.

After 1989, the new government had little money to commit to upgrading the Romanian educational system and to bring the Romanian Academy's institutes back to the levels of excellence they once enjoyed. The government not only faced the challenge of rebuilding the educational system's physical infrastructure, but also of changing the fundamental curricula of Romania's schools and universities in order to bring Romania's educational system into alignment with European and North American standards. Especially hard hit after 1989 were Romania's system of vocational high schools. These schools had been partnered with industrial enterprises. It was intended that students attending the vocational high schools would move into jobs in their partner enterprises. With the economic downturn that followed the 1989 rebellion, many, if not most, of the enterprises could not absorb the new workers the vocational schools were producing.

The European Union gave Romania substantial financial assistance to modernize all facets of its educational system and the United States provided significant assistance, as well. Western assistance consisted of supplying schools and universities with computers and soft-ware, training in Western languages, and assistance in redesigning curricula. The United States greatly expanded the number of grants it awarded to Romanian academics to study at its universities. The United States was especially interested in distributing fellowships and grants to people in the humanities and the social sciences, where academic exchanges between the United States and Romania had been minimal under the Ceausescu regime. While highly valued by those who received them and by those who sponsored them, the grants and fellowships to study in the West were not seen as beneficial by all university faculty. Academic on the far left and on the far right, viewed these awards, as well as those who received them, with a great deal of suspicion, believing that the West wanted to create a corps of intellectuals who would be nothing more than intellectual "Janissaries." These new Janissaries, it was feared, would be more interested in implanting Western ideas, ideologies, research traditions, and methodologies into Romania than in developing indigenous Romanian intellectual traditions, some of which had been suppressed during the communist era.

In addition to all of the problems they faced in their universities, graduates of Romania's institutions of higher learning had to contend with the problem of finding jobs once they graduated. Nothing in their education had prepared them for this task. Previous generations of graduates did not have this worry. Under the communists, university graduates were hired by the state and given a job assignment. While any given graduate, unless s/he were politically connected, might get a job s/he did not like or be assigned to a region in which they would rather not live, at least the graduate had guaranteed employment. After 1989, such a guarantee no longer was available. University graduates were expected to find their own jobs. Few of the students knew how to go about doing this. Romanian students had little understanding of how job markets were organized and operated and how they, the students, could connect with them. To make matters worse, private job markets had yet to emerge in many sectors of the economy. Potential employers, both in the state sector and in the nascent private sector, often did not know how to go about securing employees. They had little experience in bidding in "open" markets for labor. The lack of clearly defined labor markets made for a great deal of confusion and anxiety among new university graduates and students about to graduate.

Romania and the IMF

Feeling confident of its strength, the opposition went ahead with its vote of no-confidence despite the fact that the Vacaroiu government had reached a tentative agreement with the International Monetary Fund after months of negotiations. Under the terms of the proposed agreement, in return for promising to put into effect a package of market-oriented "reforms," the IMF promised to lend Romania $700 million over an eighteen month period. Many of the key opposition figures believed that the government did not have the political interest, will, or strength to implement the IMF reforms and that, as a result, Romania would never see the entire $700 million.

One of the chief IMF reform priorities was price stabilization. The IMF believed that one of the key reasons for the recent explosion of prices in Romania had been the government's unwillingness/inability to impose fiscal discipline on the highly indebted state enterprises (Marsh, December 31, 1993).

However, this was not the sole reason for the inflation that had become a structural feature of Romanian economic life. When the old regime collapsed, there was a considerable monetary overhang that began to be cleared as supplies of goods became more available. But the increases in supply were not equal to the increased demand, setting off price escalation. As prices increased in a seemingly uncontrolled manner, an inflationary psychology gripped the population and people began buying things at a feverish pitch rather than saving. It really made no economic sense to save under these circumstances. Banks were paying rates of interest far below the rate of inflation, so that people found the value of their savings accounts wiped out in a matter of a few months with a rate of inflation of 300% or more and with increases in wages and salaries lagging far behind, as we previously noted.

In an attempt to control the prices merchants were setting, the FSN parliament passed legislation that set a maximum profit of 30% of costs. This made little economic sense. It only managed to create bottle-necks in newly developing private supply chains, produced widespread tax evasion, and resulted in the diversion of large quantities of goods into illegal, parallel markets in the underground economy.

The attempt to limit merchants' profits had a good deal of public support. Most Romanians believed that merchants were economic parasites. This was an attitude that predated communism. Romanian intellectuals and the general population had long believed that merchants produced nothing of value, rather, they lived off the value produced by others. Moreover, before the advent of fascism in the 1930s, merchant capitalists suffered from the stigma of being identified with despised national minorities, especially Jews. These negative attitudes made the legitimation of commercial market relations an especially tricky task in Romania, where many people still saw *buzinizat* as morally suspect.

Matters were not helped by the fact that after 1989 Romania witnessed a dramatic increase in income inequality. Under the communists, Romania had achieved levels of economic equality that were among the highest in Europe. Except at the highest reaches of the nomenklatura, most Romanians in the countries largest cities had very similar income levels. In addition, while there were large discrepancies in income levels between urban areas and rural areas, within the rural areas there also was a high level of income equality. On the whole, among Romanians there was no widespread resentment of the egalitarian distribution of income that communist policies had produced. Rather, popular disgruntlement usually was expressed whenever there were signs that the government was tolerating a growth in inequality. After 1989, as signs of growing inequality became more apparent, criticism of the FSN grew for allowing this to happen, especially given the fact that the FSN had postured itself as a social democratic party that claimed that it would protect the population from excessive economic dislocations.

Post-revolution economic policies in Romania also increased geographical income inequality. The economic changes that began to be put in place after 1989 laid the foundation for the emergence of an archipelago of economic development in selected Romanian cities and widened the income gap between regions and between rural and urban areas, threatening to reverse the gains the communists had made in shrinking the phenomenon of uneven development in Romania. One of the communists' real achievements in Romania had been to reduce the differences in levels of living between rural and urban areas in Romania. While under communist rule rural areas continued to lag behind the level of living in urban areas, the gap between cities and the countryside was far less than it had been before the communists came to power, when peasants lived in an abject economic misery inflicted on them by the boyars and non-feudal private farmers.

Another goal of the IMF agreement was to allow the leu to float beginning early in 1994 (Marsh: December 31, 1993). IMF experts believed that the government's unwillingness to let the market determine the value of the national currency had led to the situation where the "black market" rate had risen from 600 to the dollar at the beginning of 1993 to 1700 to the dollar at the end of the year and where, according to Romanian central bank officials, over 80% of hard currency transactions were taking place in illegal markets (Marsh: December 31, 1993). Such a discrepancy between the official currency rate and the black market rate placed an especially heavy burden on Romanian exporters, as is typically the case in such circumstances (Easterly 2002: 222).

The IMF also demanded that Romania accelerate its privatization activities. The government had set a target of privatizing somewhere between 800 and a 1000 enterprises in 1993. However, it had managed to privatize only 220 small enterprise and not a single medium sized or large enterprise was privatized or closed because of bankruptcy (Marsh: December 31, 1993).

Amidst all of this economic and institutional turmoil, Vacaroiu's government survived the no-confidence motion by a vote of 236 to 223 on December 17, 1993. In responding to the vote and the charges that he and his government had been guilty of gross mismanagement of the national economy, Vacaroiu claimed that he was "proud" of the fact that he had been able to keep living standards at between 60% and 65% of what they had been in October, 1990 (Barber: December 22, 1993). To a large number of Romanians this offered little solace, given that under the Ceausescus Romania's living standards were the lowest in Europe, with the possible exception of Enver Hoxha's Albania

Having managed to defeat the vote of no-confidence by a rather small margin, Vacaroiu moved to strengthen the PDSR's parliamentary position by bringing various communist and extreme right nationalist parties into the governing coalition. Among the four parties with which the PDSR was negotiating were *Romania Mare* (*Greater Romania*) and the Socialist Labor Party. The latter was the self-professed successor to the former communist party and was led by Ilie Verdet, a former prime minister during the communist era. In an attempt to reach out to the labor movement, Vacaroiu offered the portfolio of the Ministry of Labor and Social Protection to CNSLR-*Fratia* labor alliance. The labor group turned down the offer, claiming it would not enter any government which included extreme nationalist or communist parties.

In order to strengthen its internal discipline, the government put pressure on political independents in the cabinet to join PDSR. In December, 1993, the formerly independent finance minister, Florin Georgescu, joined the party. He was followed in later January, 1994 by Mircea Cosea, a deputy prime minister whose responsibility was economic reform. Both ministers claimed that they had made their decision to join the governing party so that their influence within the government would be enhanced by their having joined the PDSR.

Amidst all of this political turmoil, the government postponed parliamentary debate on the proposed agreement that it had negotiated in December, 1993 with the International Monetary Fund. This threatened to delay the initial disbursements of the $700 million loan, which the government had hoped would be available no later than early March, 1994. By postponing the debate until it could consolidate its political position, the government was threatened with a significant delay in receiving IMF funds, at a time when the foreign hard-currency reserves had shrunk to $41 million at the end of December, 1993.

The CNSLR-*Fratia* labor alliance was determined to keep up its pressures on the government. It announced that it would call a one-day warning strike in early February, which it would follow with a general strike of its members unless the government quickly moved to begin a real program of privatization, restructured state enterprises, established a minimum wage that stood at 60% of the average national wage, increased pension payments to retirees, increased unemployment payments, reformed the tax system, and took immediate steps to fight corruption.

The labor coalition followed through on its threat to call a national strike in late February 1994. Once again, it reiterated its list of demands, which the government denounced as being unrealistic and irresponsible. On February 28, 1994, CNSLR-*Fratia* called its national strike. The strike coincided with a walkout by Romania's lignite miners, which had begun on January 26 and was continuing into late February.

By this point it had become clear that Romania's labor movement had become committed to neo-liberal liberal capitalism as *the* solution to the nation's various economic problems. The major labor unions had opted for an economy that would be dominated by a private bourgeoisie, rather than by an economy dominated by the state sector. If truth be told, it appears that the unions wanted to see the creation of a new bourgeoisie whose members did not have their roots in the former nomenklatura or people connected with them. The labor unions' elite, and a good number of union members, had managed to delude themselves into believing that bourgeois capitalism would deliver to them the glories of Western consumer culture, which they thought might be worth the trade off for the equality, full-employment, and social safety net that they had enjoyed under the communists. Of course, such might be expected in a society where consumption had been so problematic for so many years.

Of course, one of the key problems the trade unions faced was that such a bourgeoisie did not exist and, furthermore, the prospects of its forming as a class independent of the state were very slim in the short-run and not very bright for the long-run. Little has changed in this respect in Romania since the mid-1990s, a bourgeoisie independent of the former nomenklatura still has not taken shape, even as a proto-class. Instead, the national bourgeoisie that had begun to organize itself is based in the old party and state social networks.

The four small nationalist and communist parties that had been voting with the PDSR, especially PUNR, used the strikes to again demand more significant posts in the government. The PDSR continued to resist these pressures for extremist participation. In the meantime, the parties making up the Democratic Convention of Romania (DCR), which controlled 47% of the parliamentary seats, offered to join PDSR in a power-sharing government. PDSR turned down DCR's offer, believing that the opposition's demands were too excessive.

Continuing Political Conflict in Post-Revolutionary Romania

President Iliescu, in response to the growing political crisis, called on all of the major political parties and groupings to negotiate an agreement that would set aside partisan interests in order to deal with the country's economic and social problems. His call for political unity was futile. The major parties and their leaders proved unable to set aside their personal, policy, and ideological disputes in order to find some common ground on which they could begin moving toward solving Romania's problems.

Romania's radical right and its extreme left became increasingly disenchanted with the PDSR, in general, and with President Iliescu, in particular. Even though Iliescu had campaigned on a promise of supporting only gradual change to capitalism and remained faithful to his promises, the left felt that even the slow pace of change that was being implemented was taking place too quickly and that the change that was planned was too sweeping. The left did not want to see the Romanian state divest itself of ownership of the major means of industrial and agricultural production in any way shape or form. The left, in general, also objected to the growing reductions in allocations for social welfare benefits, fearing that the entire social safety net soon would be abolished or reduced some minimal level that barely provided a subsistence level of living for the neediest parts of the society. The extreme right shared these views. In addition, the radical right feared that Iliescu and the PDSR were too eager to seek integration with the West. The extreme right resented the idea that Romania was being compelled (even if only through the application of informal pressures) to make economic and political changes demanded by the IMF, the World Bank, and the European Union. The extreme right also believed that Iliescu and the government had not taken a sufficiently nationalist stand vis-à-vis the demands of Romania's minorities, especially its Magyar population. The PDSR government was able to maintain its alliance with the right only by giving PUNR a role in the government.

As evidence of the alleged growing subservience to the West, the extreme right pointed to the appointment of civilians to head the Ministry of Defense and the Ministry of Interior in March 1994 (British Broadcasting Corporation, March 19, 1994). The right charged that the government had introduced these changes as a response to pressures from, among others, the Council of Europe. The government denied these charges, claiming that while the Council of Europe had recommended that civilians be put in these posts it had not demanded it. The government claimed that it had appointed civilians to head the two ministries in order to adopt policies consistent with what one found in the "old democracies" (British Broadcasting Corporation, March 19, 1994).

As part of the its response to IMF demands on Romania to adopt its recommended macroeconomic stabilization policies, the National Bank of Romania (NBR) changed the country's foreign exchange auction system in 1994. The NBR abandoned its administered currency rate and replaced it with a market based rate that would be set by the actions of licensed commercial banks/currency brokers. By adopting such a policy, the official exchange rate was brought into a closer relationship with the exchange rates being offered in the legally licensed foreign exchange houses. However, there continued to be a gap between the new rates and the black market rates, although the difference shrunk appreciably. The leu appeared to have achieved stability as a result of these changes. In August 1994, the government introduced a full interbank market. In part, this move was designed to preserve the country's dwindling supply of hard currency assets, as the NBR (National Bank of Romania) no longer was committed to defending the leu's value by drawing down on its hard currency reserves.

In the winter of 1994-1995, there was a sharp increase in global energy prices, which caught the Romanian government off-guard. The government saw the rapid increase in energy prices as a threat to price stability throughout the entire Romanian economy. There was a strong possibility that there would be another wave of sharp price increases for virtually all goods and services in Romania. The Romanian National Bank began intervening in domestic currency markets, in the hope that it could maintain the leu at an exchange rate of approximately 1800 to the dollar.

The NBR's intervention contributed to serious disruptions in the domestic currency market and increased downward pressures on the leu.

The NBR did not have sufficient hard-currency reserves to keep the leu at its target level and had to abandon its defensive policy in February 1995. The official rate of the leu began dropping dramatically. Between the beginning of October 1995 and the end of November 1955, the leu fell from 2100 per dollar to 2550 per dollar. In the private, legal markets it was selling for 3000 lei per dollar.

The Romanian National Bank tried to defend the leu by tightening commercial banks ability to extend credit. Interest rates were raised from 42% to 52% in an attempt to get control over the monetary situation. In addition, the government limited citizens' rights to hold foreign currencies and it outlawed the holding of foreign bank accounts. Retail businesses were forbidden to accept hard currencies for customers' purchases.

The Democratic Convention of Romania (DCR) tried to use the continuing economic crisis to its own advantage. However, before it could do this, the DCR first had to achieve more internal unity than it had shown in the past among the various parties that composed it (British Broadcasting Corporation, August 27, 1994). In discussing the program and the problems of the DCR, its president, Emil Constantinescu, noted that Romanian political party formation had taken place differently that what had been the case in the Western democracies. Constantinescu pointed out that political parties in the West had emerged from the bottom up and expressed well-defined interests. In Romania, on the other hand, according to Constantinescu, the process of party formation was reversed. Parties were formed by "leaders and prominent figures," rather than the other way around (British Broadcasting Corporation, August 27, 1994). Constantinescu went on to observe that this led to political instability in that when these leaders and prominent figures left one party to form another some parties disappeared and others emerged. He expressed a belief that this was "normal" in a period of political "transition." However, Constantinescu went on to state his belief that this instability in Romania's system of parties was temporary and that "things are bound to change" (British Broadcasting Corporation, August 27, 1994).

What Constantinescu ignored in his diagnosis of the process of party formation in Romania was that what was happening was not unique to the period of "transition" from communism that Romania was experiencing. The top-down organization of political parties had been a stable feature of Romanian political life from the middle of the nineteenth century onward. In addition, parties continually split because of personal rivalries and jealousies within leadership circles. More often than not, these splits had little or nothing to do with political ideology or disputes over concrete policy differences. As we have shown, from the very beginning of political parties in Romania in the 19th century, parties were organized from above around dominant individuals and were prone to instability because of this. None of Romania's major political parties had been organized as movements from below.

In the years following the overthrow of Ceausescu, Romania reinstitutionalized its pre-communist practices of party-building. A large number of parties were formed from above and a number of these eventually joined the Democratic Convention of Romania or allied themselves with it, while avoiding "formal" affiliations. As a result, the DCR contained within itself a broad range of personal and/or organized political interests. The DCR had a great deal of difficulty organizing these disparate interests into an effective opposition parliamentary bloc following the PDSR victory in the 1992 elections. The DCR was proving itself unable to synthesize this diversity into a larger, coherent political organization. There was little interest in or will to achieve such a unity among the various constituent elements of the DCR. Most party leaders who supposedly were working through the DCR appeared to prefer being heads of small, relatively autonomous parties than to be part of a highly integrated, disciplined organization. Within the chaotic state of Romanian politics, by remaining largely independent, the heads of these parties believed that they could leverage their positions for the benefit of their members and of themselves in ways they could not if they allowed themselves to be absorbed into a larger political grouping. The tendency of Romanian parties to splinter is shown most clearly in the division of the FSN between the faction loyal to President Iliescu and the faction loyal to the former Prime Minister Petre Roman that took place in 1991 after Iliescu dismissed Roman following the miners' invasion of Bucharest in September of that year and in the continuing splintering of the Liberal Party.

The Liberal Party had re-formed itself after 1989 with the hope that it could reestablish the pre-eminent position it had enjoyed in Romanian politics prior to the fascist and, later, the communist period. After its poor showing in the 1990 and 1992 elections, the Liberal Party began breaking apart. Two factions joined the DCR: the Liberal Party – 1993 and the National Liberal Party – Democratic Convention. The other two liberal party factions were the National Liberal Party – Quintus, whose president was Mircea Ionescu-Quintus, and the National Liberal Party – Campeanu, named for Radu Campeanu, the former president of the National Liberal Party. These various factions found it difficult to come together on a common agenda because of personal differences among their leaderships, despite the fact that at a very general level they all had a common commitment to certain principles about how Romania ought to organize its social, political, and economic life. Americans who had come to Romania to assist in the building of new political parties, many of whom were ignorant of Romania's history of political fracturing, continually expressed frustration over the inability of political organizations to keep from falling apart over seemingly petty disagreements among key leaders.

In his national radio interview (British Broadcasting Corporation, August 27, 1994), Constantinescu sharply criticized the PDSR. In response to a question by the interviewer that asked if the PDSR was a social democratic party, Constantinescu tried to paint the PDSR as a successor to the old communist party in terms of its ultimate objectives. He observed: "The SPDR's evolution removes it still farther from the principles of social democracy. The explosive way in which the SPDR has been trying of late to subordinate almost all sectors of society – the administration, the economy, finance, and culture – to turn agricultural, trade union, youth, and revolutionary organizations into conveyor belts of its policy and to devour its former and present allies demonstrates the SPDR's ambition to completely dominate Romanian society." This was an exercise in political hyperbole. The PDSR, in fact, had no ambitions to reestablish a communist-like dominance over Romania, as its policies clearly were showing. It certainly gave no indication that it wanted to dismantle political pluralism or block the emergence and institutionalization of capitalism – too many of its key figures were earning handsome incomes and acquiring substantial wealth for them or for the party to want to return to the old forms of state ownership.

In 1994, the economy began to show some signs that it was improving. However, the Romanian economy continued to lag behind not only Western Europe but also was lagging seriously behind most of the other former communist states in Europe, except for Russia, Moldova,

Belarus, and the Ukraine in the development of a private sector, despite having passed privatization legislation. By 1995, the private sector accounted for about 40% of the GDP and an estimated 52% of the country's work force. There was a marked imbalance in private enterprise by economic sector. Private activity accounted for about 70% of retail activity and agricultural output. However, it accounted for only about 14% of industrial output. Most of Romania's industrial sector still was in state hands and was controlled by a powerful managerial strata that resisted privatization.

Romania also was having trouble attracting foreign capital that was interested either in purchasing state enterprises or starting new businesses, despite the fact that there are few barriers to foreign investment in Romania. The foreign investment law allows up to 100% foreign investment and there are no restrictions on investors' repatriation of profits to their countries of origin. Foreigners are permitted to enter long term lease arrangements for real estate, however, they are not allowed to own real estate. Yet, despite these liberal laws, foreign investors showed far less interest in putting money into Romania than they did in investing in other countries in the region.

In 1993, foreign investment in Romania totaled a paltry $390 million. There were increases in foreign investment in 1994 and 1995. But, while Romania was able to generate more interest among foreign investors in 1994, the amount of foreign investment constituted 1% of the national GDP. In the Visegrad (Poland Hungary, the Czech Republic and Slovakia) countries, foreign investment was a substantially greater proportion of national GDPs than was the case in Romania.

Between 1990 and 1995, Romania had registered more than 48,000 companies that had foreign capital participation. The value of this investment in 1995 was roughly $1.6 billion. The largest part of this investment was on a very small scale. Approximately 99% of the foreign investors accounted for only 30% of the total foreign investment. United States' investment accounted for around 10% of the total, with the major U.S. investors being concentrated in the production of consumer products.

A number of factors reduced the international investors' interest in Romania. The constantly changing legal and regulatory environment made potential foreign investors very uneasy about investing any significant amount of capital in the country. Potential foreign investors also frightened away by the lack of a pool of legal talent who were qualified to interpret and apply Romanian commercial law. In addition, there were few Romanian lawyers who understood Western contract law and how it might be applied in Romania. Foreign investment also was limited by the fact that investors could not get title insurance for property that they might purchase in Romania. This meant that foreign investors were exposed to potential losses that might result from legal challenges to their ownership by former owners or by state managers and/or workers.

While Romania had passed bankruptcy legislation, the fact that no companies had filed for bankruptcy and that there was no case law in this area also was an impediment to foreign investment. So, too, was the fact that there was no law that allowed enterprises to take legal action against debtors. This was especially problematic for persons investing in enterprises that would need to do business with state owned firms. The vast majority of these enterprises already were heavily in debt and there was little prospect that they would experience profitability in the immediate future. Thus, any private enterprise doing business with the state sector faced the very real danger that they would never be paid what the state enterprises might owe them as a result of any economic transactions between the private business and the state enterprise.

The costs of business operations in Romania were and continue to be relatively high. Businesses are expected to contribute gratuities to government officials and private persons with whom one does business. In addition, office space is expensive and the cost of establishing a telecommunications network is very costly. In the early 1990s, it was both expensive and technically difficult to develop high speed communications networks within the country and to connect to such networks outside of the country. While phone service and other telecommunications services were improving, they still were erratic. Businesses also had a hard time securing business supplies. In the early 1990s, almost all business supplies had to be bought in Western Europe and shipped to Romania. In the years right after the revolution, it was hard to get telephone directories that listed business and home phone numbers and it was nearly impossible to get accurate maps of streets for most Romanian cities.

Basic business services also were and are poorly developed. For example, for a long period after 1989 there was no efficient and effective means for making payments for goods and services or for receiving payments for them. Most business had to be carried out on a cash basis, with funds being delivered by couriers and it was a cumbersome to process to get the leu converted to hard-currency. There also was a dearth of translators who had in-depth knowledge of Western business terminology or who could translate Romanian economic concepts into English, which discouraged American, Canadian, and British investors. Far more Romanians could work with German and French than could work with English and there were even fewer English speakers who were fluent in Romanian, let alone commercial Romanian.

Business was also complicated by the poor state of Romania's transportation networks. Aside from the highways connecting the major cities, Romania's roads were not up to Western standards. Romania's rail network had been allowed to deteriorate under Ceausescu. Track beds were in need of major improvements and the rolling stock, including passenger cars, were old and run down. The airport terminal for domestic flights was small and was poorly maintained. The domestic air fleet consisted of a large number of propeller driven planes, many of which were of Russian manufacture and did not meet Western standards of comfort and service. Westerners also were put off by the fact that they had to pay far more for tickets on domestic flights than did Romanians. The international airport also was small and run down. The national airline, *Tarom*, had a more modern fleet of planes and its standards of comfort and service were equal to those of Western airlines. However, Westerners who began arriving in Romania in the first years after the revolution had a hard time dealing with the way they were received on disembarking from their flights. To many, it was a shocking and intimidating experience to walk off a plane and encounter an armored personnel carrier and armed troops lining one's path from the plane to the entrance of the airport or to a bus that carried them to the terminal. Recently, with Western financial assistance, especially from *Lufthansa*, the international airport has undergone substantial renovation and modernization.

Ground transportation, leaving aside the poor conditions of roads and many urban streets, was problematic in most Romanian cities. Buses, trams, and, in the case of Bucharest, subways were overcrowded and had problems maintaining regular schedules of service. Taxi service also was a problem in many cities. One could take five different cabs over the same route five different times and never pay the same price for the service. Foreigners were likely to be charged far more for taxi service than were Romanians.

Westerners also were discouraged from investing in Romania by what they took to be a lack of basic amenities and services. Westerners felt that the quality of Romanian health care was substandard. They also believed that except in the largest cities, there were few high quality hotels and even among the best hotels, few were seen to provide a sufficiently broad range of business services. As with the domestic airlines, hotels charged Westerners more for rooms than it charged Romanians. There also were only a handful of restaurants in the major cities that had menus that catered to Western, especially American, tastes, or met Western standards of service, food preparation, and food presentation. In the first few years after the revolution, it still was common to go to a restaurant and find that many of the items it listed on its menu were unavailable, to receive poor service, and to be overcharged, especially if one was a foreigner.

Westerners also found it difficult to find foods with which they were familiar in the early post-revolution's market places. It was also difficult to purchase clothes that were comparable in style and workmanship to those in the West. Conditions for Westerners have improved significantly in both of these areas since the mid-1990s.

The rapid drop in the value of the national currency and the high rate of inflation resulted in prices on Romanian markets converging toward international averages for various commodities and goods. The upward movement of prices was, and continues to be, a disaster for the average Romanian consumer, whose salaries were far below the average of other European consumers and still remain so. As a result, an ironic reversal in the relation of Romanians to the market took place. During the communist period, Romanians had money but nothing to buy with it. After the revolution, goods, many of them foreign, flooded into Romanian markets. Now, however, the Romanians had no money with which to buy many of the goods available to them.

In December 1994, the Romanian parliament again prepared to conduct a vote of no-confidence in the Vacaroiu government. The vote had been called for by Petre Roman, who charged the government with incompetence in its attempts to deal with the slow rate of economic change and the continuing decline in living standards (*The Ottawa Citi-*

zen, December 18, 1994). Once again, the government was able to fight off the opposition's attempt to bring it down.

In March 1995, Prime Minister Vacaroiu met with the prefects of all of Romania's *judets.* The prefects are the government's appointed representatives in the local areas. He pledged that his government would take steps to consolidate macro-economic stability, to accelerate the process of privatization, to expand the rate of economic growth, to increase real income, and to fight corruption (British Broadcasting Corporation, March 4, 1995).

Throughout 1995 and 1996, the government continued to come under relentless attack from internal opposition forces. These attacks increased as the run-up to the national elections that took place. In local elections that preceded the vote for a new parliament and president, the PDSR and its allies took heavy losses in almost all of Romania's major cities. Support for the PDSR even declined in rural areas, where historically it had its strongest support.

If one looks at the objective indicators of what was accomplished during Vacaroiu's government, it is hard to understand why it was so vilified as an economic failure. One of the major themes of the PDSR's philosophy, which it had clearly articulated during the 1992 election campaign, was that the party was committed to a gradual change from a centrally planned economy toward something it called a "market socialism." It aspired to create a market economy to define supplies of various commodities and their prices, while retaining state ownership of the means of production and state control over the ultimate direction and operation of the economy. The PDSR rejected the idea of introducing an unbridled capitalism into Romania. The party's leadership was committed to the idea that an economy is supposed to serve the people, rather than that the people were to serve the economy. PDSR also was committed to bringing about the changes to a market socialism in a gradual manner. It wanted to avoid significant dislocations to the nation's institutions and its people. The party also wanted to introduce economic change while maintaining a broad economic and social safety net for those Romanians who would be most negatively affected by the introduction of the new economic order.

In accordance with its philosophy, the PDSR government moved very slowly on the privatization front. Both domestic and foreign critics charged the government with resisting privatization, but this was only partially true. The first interim PDSR government, in 1991, had taken a significant step toward privatizing agricultural cooperatives by passing legislation that enabled the state to return rural property to its former owners or their heirs. The Vacaroiu government left this legislation in place and, slowly, tried to implement it. The Vacaroiu government also established a voucher mechanism that allowed the average Romanian to share in the proceeds yielded by the sale of state property. The voucher mechanism was very similar to what had been established in the Czech Republic. Between 1993 and 1996, the Vacaroiu government oversaw the privatization of roughly 2900 state enterprises, raising approximately 3570 billion lei for the state treasury. The vast majority of these enterprises were small and medium sized operations, a good number of which were turned over to workers in the enterprises and their managers, some of whom had been appointed by the state and some of whom had been elected by workers after 1989 in the struggles for control that took place in many state enterprises. Opponents of the government were sharply critical of the ways in which these small and medium enterprises had been turned over to insiders, rather than having been distributed on "open" markets through a competitive bidding process.

The opposition also was demanding that the government move more quickly to privatize the largest state enterprises and to do so in a transparent, competitive manner, rather than distributing the property on the basis of "crony" relationships or other "illicit" criteria. The government, given its philosophy, was very reluctant to begin privatizing the largest Romanian enterprises, which the PDSR firmly believed ought to be in state hands in order to try to protect the country from the most negative aspects of a bourgeois capitalist economy. The PDSR also was reluctant to privatize the largest enterprises because a good part of its core membership was made up of the managers of these enterprises and the functionaries employed in them, who were concerned that privatization would result in the loss of many of their jobs. Many of these managers and functionaries had achieved their positions through the state system and were terrified that they would not be able to maintain their occupational status and their overall social status in a world of private business. The managers and the functionaries were part of the powerful networks that had been the skeleton of the former communist system and were struggling to have the same role in the post-communist Romanian economy

The PDSR government also moved very slowly, when it moved at all, to restructure the state enterprises with the goal of turning them into efficient and effective profit centers. The government did not impose "hard" budget constraints on these operations and it did not force them into bankruptcy if they were incurring significant losses, which many of them were. The state also did not compel these enterprises to produce in response to market criteria, so that they would be competitive with the foreign goods that were pouring into Romania.

The PDSR also resisted privatizing the state financial sector. It maintained state ownership of Romania's banks and it used the ownership of the banks to provide relatively cheap credits to the largest state enterprises. As a result, the banks accumulated an enormous number of non-performing loans that kept the sector of state enterprises afloat. The allocation of loans to the state enterprises limited the amount of credit that could be given to the emerging private sector, which raised the ire of aspiring entrepreneurs. The PDSR government used its banking monopoly and its resulting control over hard-currency to try to maintain the value of the leu in the face of strong market pressures to reduce its value. The PDSR leadership and its economic advisors were fearful that a free-floating national currency would be a political disaster for the party in that it would substantially reduce the levels of living of key parts of its voting constituency. The opposition parties took the position that the value of the Romanian currency should be determined by market forces and that while this would be painful in the short-run, over the long-term Romanians would benefit more than they would lose. When the government relented in 1994 and allowed the currency's value to be defined by market forces, the opposition criticized it for the rapid fall in its value.

Because the PDSR struggled to maintain the largest state enterprises, it kept Romania from experiencing the massive unemployment that other economies in the region were seeing. In 1991 Romania had a 3% unemployment rate, which rose to 8% in 1992. At the end of Vacaroiu's first year in office (1993) unemployment was at 10%. It rose to 11% in 1994, then fell to 10% in 1995, and 7% in 1996. Even at its highest point of 11%, the unemployment level was quite respectable by European standards, as a whole. However, the opposition, including Romania's trade unions, did not give the government credit for keeping unemployment at reasonably low levels, given the circumstances the country was experiencing.

The Vacaroiu government's policies not only kept unemployment low, they also stimulated economic growth, much to the chagrin of the opposition and to Western financial institutions who were pushing the government to adopt more of the "Washington model." In 1990, the Romanian economy contracted by 5.6%, in 1991 by 12.9%, and, in 1992, it contracted by another 8.8%. In its first year in power, the Vacaroiu government produced a 1.5% growth rate. In 1994, the growth rate increased to 3.9%, in 1995, in one of the best years for the economy in quite some time, the growth rate rose to 6.9%. Growth slowed in 1996 to 4.1%, but this still was a good showing compared to what had been taking place under Ceausescu and the interim governments formed between 1990 and 1992. Economic growth, in part, was a result of the government's use of deficit financing, its promotion of production for export, and because of selective subsidies to various industries. As with the unemployment situation, the Vacaroiu government never received the credit it deserved for reversing Romania's many years of economic decline.

The opposition parties and their supporters, instead of attempting to work with the government to sustain growth, chose to focus on the two issues where the government's performance was supposedly the weakest: controlling inflation and the perceived growth of corruption. In 1990, inflation stood at 5%. At this time, Romania was continuing to subsidize a large number of basic commodities and maintained a tight control over prices, including prices in the private sector, as we noted above. As the government relaxed price controls, in large part because of pressures from international organizations, prices exploded. Inflation reached 175% in 1991 and 211% in 1992. During Vacaroiu's first full year in office, the rate of inflation stood at 256%, which was one of the highest levels in Europe. In 1997, the government brought the inflation rate down to 137% and in 1995 to 32%. In its last year in office, inflation increased slightly to 39%. Objectively, it is hard to hold the PDSR government entirely responsible for the explosion of prices that took place in 1993. It is even hard to hold the interim governments in place before 1993 responsible for the rapid escalation of prices in 1991 and 1992. Under the communist regime, Romania had one of the highest levels of price subsidy among the socialist states, although though there were signs that there was a "hidden" inflation in the later years of Ceausescu's rule. Heavy subsidies had been one of the elements of the social contract the state had with the Romanian citizenry. Once communism ended, it was impossible for the state to keep the extensive subsidies in place. Prices had to increase and they would have risen no matter what party was in power. Matters were complicated in Romania by the huge monetary overhang that had built up in Romania during the last years of Ceausescu's regime. This monetary overhang was generated out of the generalized scarcity of goods available to Romanian consumers. When goods became more widely available, this monetary overhang helped to drive up prices. The Romanian opposition chose to ignore these two basic facts and, instead, blamed the PDSR's policies for all of the inflation in prices, knowing full-well that much of the increase in prices was beyond the control of the state, unless it chose to maintain the elaborate system of subsidies that had been sustained by the communists. One area in which PDSR policies were a "failure" with respect to prices was the government's attempt to raise wages to keep state workers from experiencing too steep of a drop in their levels of living. The opposition parties attacked this policy, but not because it contributed to inflation. Rather, the opposition claimed that the government was not doing *enough* to raise wages in the light of the high rates of inflation. This was one of the more successful political tacks the opposition took. It was a message that struck a responsive chord with Romanian workers and their families. Romania's workers were confused and were angry over the rapid escalation of prices, the absence of wage increases that kept pace with the rate of inflation, and the resultant decline in the real value of workers' wages. Workers could not understand why prices, especially food prices, were skyrocketing and why an ever increasing proportion of their income had to be devoted to meeting basic subsistence needs, especially food, when the turn to capitalism once had held out the implied promise that they would be able to enjoy the same "benefits" of consumerism that marked Western capitalist economies. When coupled with the continuing fall of the leu's value, which raised the prices of foreign goods, and the economic fears being engendered in the population, the oppositions' message about the incompetence of the PDSR became ever more believable, especially given the workers' inexperience with and limited understanding of the ways in which capitalist markets work.

Also resonating with the workers was the oppositions' charges of growing "corruption" in the Romanian government and society. The opposition parties framed the corruption issue as if it were unique to the

PDSR and its supporters, rather than a generalized social phenomenon. While it is true that it was common practice for many Romanian officials and functionaries to engage in what in the West would be regarded as "petty graft," involving nothing more than trading small favors in return for a "gratuity," such practices certainly were not something that the PDSR or the communists had created. As we already have seen, the idea that state offices were to be used for profit can be traced back to the boyar regimes or even earlier. While many Romanians probably resented paying these gratuities, they generally accepted it as part of the "normal" process of doing business with the state. One might even be able to build an argument that the system of petty graft helped the state function more smoothly, if for no other reason than that the system of gratuities introduced a "price mechanism" that helped provide for a more "rational" means of allocating scarce services.

While annoying to the persons forced to provide the gratuities, it was not this type of "corruption" that angered the average Romanian. What generated the most popular anger toward the PDSR government, was the appearance that there was large-scale corruption in the disposal of state assets and in the appearance of favoritism in the ways in which the state structured the opportunities for new enterprise development. Romania's post-communist constitution, partly in reaction to what the country had endured under the communists, had created a "soft state," easily penetrable by private interests, thus allowing for a great deal of collusion between state actors and private entrepreneurs. Much of this collusion was perfectly legal, even though it was defined as "corruption" by much of the media and the political opposition to the PDSR.

Opposition forces continually charged the PDSR with allowing former members of the nomenklatura and the former members of the various state security services, especially the *Securitate*, to have an upper hand in gaining control over former state enterprises and in securing opportunities to develop new businesses. The idea that former *Securitate* officers were being allowed to emerge as private entrepreneurs was especially galling to the average Romanian, who had lived in terror of being caught in the web of the security forces.

Under Ceausescu, the *Securitate* had acquired a formidable reputation as an instrument of repression. Romanians attributed all types of fantastic powers to the *Securitate*. Rare was the Romanian who did not fear the *Securitate* before 1989. The 1989 rebellion did nothing to end these fears. Few Romanians believed that the rebellion had broken the power of the *Securitate*. Rather, Romanians believed that the reorganized secret police, now being called the Romanian Information Service, had taken up where the *Securitate* had left off. Fanned by rumors, innuendo, myth, and media speculation, the secret police came to be seen as one of, if not the only, real powers, within and behind the PDSR, dominating and manipulating the government for its own institutional ends and for the personal political and financial ends of its current and former senior cadres.

Such rumors and innuendo were given some degree of plausibility by the rapid economic success of many former senior *Securitate* officers, especially in Romania's emerging import-export sector. Many of the former *Securitate* officers turned importers-exporters had been involved in foreign intelligence operations. They were able to make use of the contacts they had developed in the course of their work both inside and outside of Romania, as well as their knowledge about foreign countries, to establish quite successful foreign trade businesses. With former *Securitate* officers also emerging as leading entrepreneurs in a number of other sectors, such as banking and finance, people's beliefs and suspicions about the supposed power of the secret services only grew. With all of the propaganda coming from the opposition, it was not hard for the average Romanian to see the PDSR as nothing more than the public face of the real holders of power, i e, the secret police forces and the former elites of the communist party.

Human Rights Conflicts in Post-Communist Romania

The Vacaroiu government not only had to deal with pressures from international organizations to change the national economy, but it also faced demands to improve its human rights record. International organizations focused on alleged violations of the rights of four groups: Rroma, whose problems we already have discussed, gays, Magyars, and women.

In the spring of 1992, shortly before International AIDS day, a group of Romanian gays met in a small apartment in a working class neighborhood in Bucharest, together with a gay activist from the U.S., a gay American who was the lover of one of the Romanian men, an American journalist, a Romanian journalism student who wrote for the University of Bucharest student newspaper and who had been invited in order to write a story about gays in Romania, and the senior author. According to Romanian law at this time, this gathering was an illegal meeting and everyone in attendance was subject to arrest. In the story the student later wrote for the University newspaper, the only persons named as attending the meeting were the American journalist and me, much to our chagrin. Among the Romanian men present at the gathering, a handful had "come out" and would not have objected if their names had appeared in the story, the rest had not. If their names had been used it would have created serious problems for them.

A candlelight ceremony was held in memory of the women, men, and children who had died of AIDS. Following the ceremony, the Romanian men began discussing their plight in Romania, including not only their problems with the police, but also their problems with their families, co-workers, friends, lovers, and their own struggles with their sexual orientation. A number of the Romanian men present previously had been involved in unsuccessful attempts to found gay organizations and felt it was necessary to launch another effort in this area. They went on to create the Bucharest Acceptance Group (Accept), a Romanian gay and lesbian rights group.

In 1991, the Romanian Independent Society for Human Rights (SIDRO) had added gay/lesbian rights to its human rights agenda. It was the first independent NGO (Non Government Organization) to have done so. SIDRO's efforts to add the cause of human rights protection for Romanian gays and lesbians was also picked up by a number of international human rights organizations, such as Human Rights Watch, Amnesty International, the International Human Rights Group, the International Gay and Lesbian Human Rights Commission, and the ILGA.

Following on the actions of SIDRO, in February 1992, the first Romanian gay/lesbian group was formed. It was called Total Relations. It lasted for less than a year. It apparently functioned more as a gay/lesbian self-help group that focused on gay/lesbian community building. After Total Relations fell apart, it was replaced, in February 1993, by *Group 200.* Apparently, Group 200 had a more specific political purpose that had Total Relations. It wanted to press the case of gay/ lesbian human rights in Romania. Both of these groups had sought to get international help for Romanian gays and lesbians. They had sent delegates to International Lesbian Gay/Lesbian Alliance (ILGA) conferences held in Western Europe. Group 200, like Total Relations, lasted for less than a year.

Both of these organizations had fallen apart because of internal political tensions and personal rivalries among persons who wanted to lead them. But, it was not only because of internal factors that both organizations fell apart. Perhaps more important for their demise was external factors. Gay/lesbian organizations were closely monitored by the police and their members were subject to possible arrest, if they were found to run afoul of Law 200. Moreover, given the social climate in Romania, it was difficult for homosexual men and women to "come out" and join an advocacy organization in the early 1990s. Socially, Romania was (and continues) to be a conservative, family-based, patriarchal society in which one of the principal obligations of young men and women is to get married and supply their parents with grandchildren. Because of such a moral imperative, there are quite a large number of gay men and women who married and had children while carrying on a clandestine existence as a homosexual. They did this because they could not bear to see their parents never experience the "joys" of being grand-parents, as more than one gay man told me.

The cause of gay and lesbian human rights was pushed to the fore-front in Romania by two events. The first was Romania's application to join the Council of Europe, which the Romanian state saw as its first step in integrating itself into the general community of Western Euro-pean nations. In the "hearings" that led up to Romania's admission to the Council of Europe in October 1993, Romania was told that the Council expected Romania to bring its laws on homosexuality into line with those of Western Europe, which meant that Romania would be expected to decriminalize homosexual behavior. The Council understood that Romania had agreed to do this. However, it did not conform to the Council's expectations. Between 1993 and 1994, according to human rights experts, there were 57 men in prison who had been charged with sexual offenses under Law 200 and police were continuing to aggres-sively enforce the anti-homosexual law, despite Romanian denials that anyone actually was in prison under provisions of Law 200 (see Ngatchou 1994). It later was reported that many of these men had been singled out for brutal treatment by the police while they had been in custody, by their fellow prison inmates, and by prison guards, merely because they had been identified as homosexuals.

The second event resulted from the arrest of five men in the Tran-sylvanian city of Sibiu in January and February 1993. All five men had been arrested under the provisions of Law 200, Paragraph 1 (see the earlier discussion of Law 200 passed during the Ceausescu regime). While in police custody, one, or all, of these men claimed that they once had sexual relations with a controversial and prominent newspaper publisher in Sibiu. According to local sources in Sibiu, the newspaper publisher, who had antagonized local elites in Sibiu on a number of occasions, had been the real target of the police investigation. Based on the incarcerated men's testimony, the publisher was arrested by the Sibiu police.

The publisher's lawyer appealed the arrest to the Romanian Constitutional Court, which was charged with hearing appeals on constitutional matters. The Constitutional Court agreed to accept the case and, in July 1993, it ruled that Paragraph 1, Law 200 was unconstitutional. Basically, the Court ruled that Law 200, Paragraph 1 could not be applied to same sex relations between consenting adults when the relations did not occur in public and/or did not create a "public scandal." The Court said its ruling would go into effect on January 1, 1994, giving the Romanian parliament time to amend Law 200 or repeal the Law before the decision was put into effect.

In February 1994, after the Constitutional Court decision had gone into effect, the Romanian Senate (the upper-house of the Romanian parliament) passed an amended version of Law 200, which it believed met the courts requirements. The Senate bill stated that same gender sexual relations were illegal and punishable by 1 to 5 years in prison if they occurred in public or if they caused a "public scandal," as the court had ruled. The Senate bill defined the age of consent for same gender sexual relations at a higher level than for heterosexual relations. The bill also established higher levels of punishment for homosexual sex crimes than it did for comparable heterosexual sex crimes.

Critics of the Senate's amended Law 200, felt that it many ways the new Senate bill was worse than the original. Critics were especially disturbed about the language referring to "public scandal," which was not defined in the Senate bill. The fact that what constituted a "public scandal" was left undefined gave the police and the courts wide discretion in enforcing the revised law. Critics pointed out that a "public scandal" could be claimed to have taken place on little more than rumor or vague innuendo.

Critics of the Senate proposals also denounced new provisions that stated that anyone could be sentenced to prison for 1 to 5 years for "encouragement of allurement of individuals, with a view to perpetration of such deeds described in the above paragraphs, as well as propaganda actions, associations, or any other proselytizing actions, carried out in view of the same purpose" (quoted in Ngatchou 1994). These new provisions, which had not been in the original Law 200 passed during Ceausescu's rule, in effect would have outlawed any gay/lesbian advocacy groups, gay publications, and gay clubs, taverns, and the like. Individuals who advocated gay and lesbian rights likewise would have been made subject to arrest.

The Senate, under the control of PDSR, had passed its amended version of Law 200 with the support of all of the major political parties. The only party that officially spoke in opposition to the amended law came from the Magyar party (the UMDR). It had two major reasons for opposing the proposed bill. First, UMDR argued that Law 200, in principle, infringed on the basic rights to privacy enshrined in the Romanian Constitution of 1991. Second, UMDR objected to the fact that defenders of Law 200 based a good part of their justification for the legislation on the moral values of Romanian Orthodoxy and UMDR legislators argued that this was inappropriate and set a dangerous precedent in a supposedly secular state.

The Senate version of the amended bill was sent to the Chamber of Deputies (the lower house of the Romanian parliament) for action. The Chamber of Deputies' leadership sent the Senate version to its Judicial Committee for review and recommendation. The Chamber of Deputies' Judicial Committee made a number of important recommendations that ran counter to the Senate version of the legislation. Among other things, the Judicial Committee recommended deletion of the phrase "... causing a public scandal" and substituted the phrase "... perpetrated in public." The Judicial Committee also eliminated the Senate provisions dealing with the criminalization of "propaganda," "proselytizing," and "associations." They also reduced the proposed prison terms for a number of offenses outlined in the Senate version (Ngatchou 1994).

The Judicial Committee's version of the bill was not immediately considered by the Chamber of Deputies. The Chamber of Deputies' leadership, made up of members of the PDSR, deferred consideration of any revisions of Law 200. Instead, the leadership held that the status of Law 200 would be reviewed as part of a general evaluation and modification of Romania's entire Penal Code. The proposed comprehensive revisions of the Penal Code were rejected in 1994 and, again, in 1995, so action on revising Law 200 also was defeated. In forming Accept, Romanian gay and lesbian activists wanted to create a multipurpose organization to serve Romania's homosexual population. Like the Rroma, Romania's gays and lesbians had dispersed social relations. But unlike the Rroma, gay and lesbian social relations were more serial than communal. The gay population was highly fragmented. It was organized into small intimate circles of friends and lovers with few, if any, extensive ties to other intimate circles ("intimate circles" does not refer to groups organized only on the basis of sexual ties among the members). Membership in any one of these circles expanded and contracted over time. Some men belonged to more than one circle at a time and some circulated in an out of various circles. Under the conditions of repression they faced on a daily basis, creating relatively isolated, and relatively closed intimate groups was one of the few ways that gays could help insure their own safety.

Romania's gays and lesbians wanted to create a multi-purpose, multi-function organization that could serve to unite and mobilize Romania's homosexual populations. They had hoped that this organization would function as a support group for men and women struggling with their sexual orientation. They also wanted to create an organization that would work to educate Romanians, in general, about homosexuality and that, ideally, would contribute to fundamental changes in Romanian attitudes toward homosexuality. Gays and lesbians also wanted an organization that would help individuals make a healthy adjustment to their sexual orientation. Many of the Romanian gays and lesbians who were racked with guilt and with feelings of low self-esteem because they were gay had nowhere to which they could turn for social, psychological, and emotional support. Accept's immediate political goal was the repeal of Law 200.

Accept's leaders and activist members knew that they had difficult tasks ahead of them on all fronts. They were well aware that it would be no easy task to educate Romanians about homosexuality and to change their basic attitudes toward it. The average Romanian looked upon homosexuality as a perversion that threatened the core values of the society. Even educated and progressive Romanians who saw the importance of building a liberal society were unlikely to become advocates of gay and lesbian rights. At the very best, liberal reformers tended to see homosexuality as a personal pathology, i.e. as a basic personality disorder or as a psychological problem that needed "treatment." Holding such views, generally, does not lead one to support gay/lesbian social and political liberation. Accept leaders and activists also were aware that it would not be an easy task to convince Romania's gays and lesbians of the need to "come out" and help the movement achieve its goals, given the personal and legal costs "coming out" entailed.

Not all of Romania's gays and lesbians supported Accept. They found the group's militancy and the "in-your-face" presentation of sexual orientation that many of Accept's younger members and leaders practiced to be deeply offensive, scandalous, and potentially threatening. Many older gays and lesbians did not accept the representation of what it means to be a gay that Accept activists seemingly were promoting. Accept activists had adopted models of gay culture and gay expression that had emerged in Western Europe and, to a lesser degree, the United States.

Older gay men and lesbians, as well as men and women who have yet to "come out," are somewhat leery about the development of an above ground, openly visible gay community. They fear that such a community is likely to generate a backlash from the general Romanian public and they also fear that it will put pressure for them to come out if they wish to have relationships with men and women who are actively involved in a "queer community." Among those gays and lesbians who have concerns about the emergence of a visible "queer community" there are some who believe that this type of community is not (and cant not be) a valid expression of what it means to be gay, especially in socially conservative, traditional societies like Romania. Many of those who are wary about the emergence of a "queer community" believe that such an expression of homosexuality distorts the "reality" of what it means to be a homosexual. They tend to downplay the distinctiveness of homosexuals in favor of a view that homosexuals did not constitute a distinct cultural or social group and that they differed from heterosexuals in no important respects, except for the nature of their erotic attachments.

On May 31, 1995, the Bucharest Acceptance Group, in conjunction with international human rights groups, held a symposium on homosexuality and human rights. The goal of the symposium was to initiate a dialogue between supporters and opponents of the decriminalization of homosexuality. In April 1995, the Senate had passed a bill that removed penalties for homosexual relations, per se, but contained provisions that criminalized homosexual relations in public and/or homosexual relations that caused a public scandal. The Senate bill, like previous revisions it had passed, also criminalized proselytizing, propagandizing, and engaging in associations that promoted homosexuality. The Chamber of Deputies had not yet acted on its proposed revisions of Law 200.

The symposium's moderator was Father Christopher Newlands, an Anglican priest who served Anglican parishes in Bucharest and Sophia, Bulgaria. The speakers were Ms. Cairn Berg, a native of Sweden who was serving as Director of the European UNESCO Center for Higher Education in Bucharest; Counselor Octavian Cojocaru, who was representing the Romanian Ministry of Justice; Andre Krouwel, a lecturer in Political Science in the Netherlands who was representing the Dacia Foundation (Bucharest Acceptance Group – the Netherlands); Father Dumitru Radu, a Professor of Theology at the University of Bucharest and a spokesmen for the Romanian Orthodox Church; Scott Long, a former American Fulbright Professor in Romania and the East Central European representative of the International Gay and Lesbian Human Rights Commission in San Francisco; and Deputy Nicu Vintila, a member of the Chamber of Deputies' Juridical Commission (Tanaka 1995). Each of these participants spoke for ten minutes, after which there was a discussion and question and answer period. Noticeable by their absence from the symposium were representatives from the Senate and representatives from some of Romania's leading political parties that were opposing decriminalization of homosexuality.

Following a general introduction by Father Newlands, in which he mentioned that 1995 was the International Year of Tolerance and that the symposium was consistent with this theme, the first speaker was Counselor Octavian Cojocaru from the Ministry of Justice (Tanaka 1995). Mr. Cojocaru denied that homosexuals were being denied their basic human rights in Romania and he stated that he believed that Law 200 did nothing to infringe on these rights, so Romania would not be out of compliance with the Declaration of Human Rights by passing the revisions of Law 200 that the Senate had adopted. He observed that the Romanian public and the Romanian Orthodox Church were experiencing significant anxiety about the possibility that homosexuality would be decriminalized (Tanaka 1995). Mr. Cojocaru went on to say that human nature is "...inclined to the romantic," and the "beauty of the Romanian woman allows us to be biblical and evoke God, who told Adam and Eve to go and spread the kin around the world. It is a matter of Christian morality and the laws of the bible" (Tanaka 1995). Apparently, Mr. Cojocaru was making three basic points: the Senate bill would not constitute a violation of homosexual's human rights, that the beauty of Romanian women helped Romanian men fulfill the biblical injunction to multiply, and that since gay sex did not involve procreation it did not conform to God's law. One can only wonder why he did not think that the presence of gays in Romania was not a testimony to the beauty of Romanian men rather than a denigration of the beauty of Romanian women.

After a talk by Ms. Krouwel, in he which denounced the standard of "public scandal" as one of the factors that made homosexual activity illegal, in which he laid out the history of the gay and lesbian rights movement in Western Europe, and in which he reviewed recent research showing that homosexuality was neither a social disease nor an aberration, Father Radu spoke (Tanaka 1995). Father Radu denounced homosexuality as a "plague" that should not be considered a human right. He went on to say that it homosexuality was "not natural," he and the Church saw homosexuality as "violation of nature" (Tanaka 1995). Father Radu went on to maintain that homosexuality was a profound "sin" and God does not forgive sinners unless they repent of their bad behavior. Father Radu also said that homosexuals can attract young people and produce a "sick youth" (Tanaka 1995).

Following Father Radu, Mr. Scott Long reported on a few of the police abuses of homosexuals with which he was familiar, abuses made possible because of the very existence of Law 200. Mr. Long also criticized the idea prevalent among a number of Romanians that homosexuality was something foreign to Romania that was being imported from abroad. Mr. Long made the further point that basing laws on religious morality and so-called laws of nature would impede Romania's ability to build a viable civil society. He also noted that Bulgaria, an Orthodox country, had decriminalized homosexuality over 30 years ago and that Russia, likewise, had decriminalized homosexuality in 1993 (Tanaka 1995).

The last speaker was parliamentary deputy Mr. Nicu Vintila. Mr. Vintila defended the right of the Orthodox Church to have a say in the formulation of laws touching on the moral order of the society. He presented the symposium a copy of a letter that had been signed by high Church officials opposing the decriminalization of homosexuality. He concluded by observing that he felt that Romania could not accept the decriminalization of homosexuality (Tanaka 1995).

The presentations at the symposium gave a good idea of what the major contours of opposition to decriminalization of homosexuality were in Romania in the mid-1990s. The only positions missing were those of the far-right political parties and the opinions of traditional psychiatrists, psychologists, and social scientists who continued to view homosexuality in terms of concepts of pathology that most of their Western counterparts no longer regarded as valid.

The parties on the far-right embraced the ideas that homosexuality was a moral abomination and a psycho-sexual pathology. To these ideas they added the notion that homosexuality was an alien, decadent behavior that was being imported into Romania from the West. In conversations about homosexuality with politicians on the far right, one can not help but to come away with the impression that they really believe that "average, healthy" Romanians, by their very nature, could not be homosexuals and that, left on its own, Romanian society would not produce homosexuals. To right wing politicians, homosexuality is not and never can be part of Romania's national character, except via of foreign corruption. The radical right sees homosexuality as an import from the West that is intentionally designed to undermine Romanian culture, identity, and virtue.

In 1996, the Romanian Parliament, again, took up the issue of Law 200 shortly before the national elections for parliament and for president. In August 1966, the Romanian Senate again passed a bill that declared that homosexual acts "committed in public or which cause a public scandal" were to be punished with prison sentences ranging from one to five years. The new Senate bill also included the provision criminalizing organizing, associating, or proselytizing for homosexuality. Such acts also were punishable with prison terms ranging from one to five years.

The Chamber of Deputies also passed a new version of Law 200. The bill passed by the Chamber was even more draconian than that passed by the Senate. The Chamber's bill outlawed all sexual acts between persons of the same gender, even in the acts were committed in private and were not a source of public scandal. Such acts were punishable by prison terms of six months to three years. When the acts were committed in public and/or caused a public scandal they were punishable with prison terms from one to five years. The Chamber version, like the Senate's, also criminalized proselytizing and organizing or associating for the purposes of promoting homosexuality. It made such actions punishable with prison sentences of one to five years.

One hundred and sixty five Deputies voted for the bill, twenty voted against it, and there were eleven abstentions. Most of the PDSR deputies voted for the bill, as well as almost all of the opposition deputies, with the exception of the Magyar party deputies. During debate on the proposed legislation, when it was brought out that international human rights organizations were likely to condemn Romania for the stand it was taking on homosexual behavior, one deputy is alleged to have referred to these human rights groups as "organizations of degenerates" and another was claimed to have said that Romania should not be swayed by the view of the European Parliament because "35%" of its members were homosexuals (ILGA Euroletter 44, 1996).

According to Long (1996), the general debate on Law 200 had degenerated into pure demagoguery. For example, at one point a deputy introduced legislation that would have attached a criminal penalty to any sexual act that was not intended to result in procreation. Fortunately, the deputies had the good sense to reject that motion.

It was especially disconcerting to gay and lesbian activists that the "reform-minded" parties, such as the National Liberal Party and the National Peasant-Christian Democrat Party, had opposed this legislation. Gay and lesbian activists could explain the opposition from the PDSR, which, to the activists, was mostly made up of very socially conservative former communists, but the opposition of the so-called "reform" parties was a completely different matter. These parties had postured as strong advocates of freedom, personal liberty, and the reduction of government's power to penetrate into the private lives of Romanians. Yet, when it came to gays and lesbians, this rhetoric was set aside and the "reform" parties supported state repression of homosexuality to the same degree that the PDSR did. The gay and lesbian activists also were disappointed in the unwillingness of the U.S. Embassy to take a stand on their behalf. The U.S. Embassy previously had taken a strong stance on human rights when the issues involved women, ethnic minorities, and the like, but when it came to issues of concern to gays and lesbians, the embassy and its staff remained silent; small wonder, given the ambiguous legal status of homosexuals in the United States. After all, in Texas, two men, were recently arrested and convicted for having consensual sex inside of the privacy of their own home and Texas is not alone in keeping "sodomy" laws on its books.

Finally, Law 200 was repealed in 2001, ending Romania's status as the only member state of the Council of Europe that criminalized homosexual behavior. Between 1996 and 2001, gays and lesbians had few things to cheer about in Romania, other than an amnesty that the newly elected president, Emil Constantinescu, whose political base was in the National Peasant-Christian Democrat Party, granted to persons arrested under provisions of Law 200 in 1998. When President Constantinescu announced his attention to pardon those convicted under Law 200, Paragraphs 1 and 5, he added that he hoped his action would send a message to all Romanians and he went on to say that "... homosexuality is the last remaining human rights problem we have in Romania, and we will address it" (ILGA Euroletter 57, 1998). This was a stunning announcement by the president, whose own party, the National Peasant-Christian Democrat Party, had been among the major opponents of decriminalizing homosexuality by the Romanian parliament.

In some Romanian cities, the police continued to aggressively pursue homosexuals, especially those who were cruising parks and other public places for sex. For example, in Bucharest the police regularly used infrared cameras and hidden listening devices in parks where homosexuals tended to gather and used police decoys to entrap gays. In other cities, the police and Romanian gays had reached an accommodation of sorts. The police had backed off aggressive law enforcement practices directed at gays, instead, they would take actions against them only if they found men engaging in sex in public or had received specific complaints about such behavior.

Romanian gays also continued to face considerable hostility from the general public and were constantly at risk of harassment and, sometimes, violence. For example, in the late 1990s a group of gay friends had gotten together to eat at a restaurant in a public park in Bucharest. While they were eating, they began to be insulted and taunted by a group of men at a nearby table. The tensions between the two groups rapidly escalated and one of the men who had been taunting the gays pulled a gun and began threatening to shoot them. One of the gay men ran to get a policemen, who refused to intervene in the situation. The tension between the two groups managed to be defused without anyone being injured.

While being threatened with weapons is an exceptionally rare event, other threats of physical violence directed against gays are not so rare. Almost all gay men report that they, themselves, have been physically threatened or personally know someone who has been threatened or, even, has been actually attacked. The hostility directed toward gays and the need for gays to be continually vigilant about their safety was brought home to me one evening while having dinner with two gay friends at a fashionable restaurant in Bucharest. Just as dinner was being finished, the restaurant's manager came to the table with the bill and told us that we needed to pay and leave immediately. This was a very unusual demand in a Romanian restaurant, where patrons often linger for hours after a meal talking and drinking. When the manager was asked why we were being requested to leave, without any hesitation, he said that some of the customers had complained about our presence and that he did not want his restaurant to become known as the type of place where "your kind" came. We loudly protested his request, but it was clear that he was not going to relent. Matters became very tense when two very large bouncers took positions close to our table. Sitting at a table not far from us was a table of people who worked in various jobs at the U.S. Embassy. Several of these people dealt with "human rights" issues in Romania. None of the American Embassy employees said anything to the manager about his behavior being inappropriate, nor did they make any attempt to ask us about what had happened, although it was clear that they had heard our argument with the manager and knew why we were being ejected.

After we left the restaurant, we walked toward central Bucharest to see if we could meet some other friends at a bar. On our way to the bar, we passed a group of young men standing on a corner close to the Hotel Bucharest. As we passed them, we were treated to a host of insults and slurs. We kept walking, two of the men followed us for a few meters, continuing their verbal assault. When we did not respond, they gave up on following us and returned to their companions. My friends handled this encounter with a great deal of aplomb. They said they were used to this type of public humiliation, as it was a frequent occurrence on the streets of Bucharest.

Now that Law 200 has been repealed, Romania's gays' fight for acceptance, or, if not acceptance, then at least for a modicum of accommodation to their presence really has just begun. Romanian gays need to be prepared for a long hard struggle if they are to have any hope of achieving levels of acceptance and tolerance that gays have been able to attain in most of Western Europe and in *selected* parts of North America. Romania continues to be a country with very traditional attitudes about homosexuality and these traditional attitudes are not confined just to religious conservatives, one also can see such attitudes among Romanian health and mental health professionals. When repeal of Law 200 was being debated, many of these professionals and many social scientists testified to the disastrous effects the repeal would have on Romania, in general, and on gays, in particular. To a large number of Romania's health professionals, if homosexuality were legalized, gays and lesbians would not be given the "therapy" they needed to "solve" their "psychopathology."

But even more important than the continuing opposition to homosexuality by Romanian religious organizations, mental health professionals, politicians, and the police, is the fear of and ignorance about the phenomenon in the general population. A large number of Romanian gays and lesbians continue to feel the sting of this ignorance and fear in their own families of origin. Many of Romania's gays and lesbians have faced, or expect to face, total rejection by their families of origin if their sexual orientation is discovered. As with Rroma, gays and lesbians are not seen as just being different from "normal' Romanians. Instead, gays and lesbians occupy a master status as a total and radical "other" that is completely alien to Romanian society. Repeal of Law 200 will do little to change this in the short run. It is going to take decades of work on the part of gay organizations and lesbian organizations, individual gays and lesbians, and liberally oriented human rights organizations to change the climate of opinion so that Romania's gays and lesbians no longer will be compelled to live a furtive sexual existence.

Women are another group that has faced an increasingly problematic existence since the 1989 revolution. Under the communists, women were guaranteed political representation in the Romanian parliament, were guaranteed employment outside the household, and benefited from the extensive economic and social supports that the communist state provided to families. However, the communists never had been able to change the traditional, informal status of women within the Romanian household. Under communism, as we have noted above, it is claimed that women bore a "triple burden" of spouse/mother, wage worker in the formal economy, and worker in the informal economy. In most Romanian families, patriarchy is the dominant principle and practice. Because of its relative isolation from social and cultural trends in Western Europe and North America and because of the way in which the communists had valorized the role of women as wife/mother, in Romania gender roles remained very traditional. Nonetheless, despite the archaic definitions of women's roles, women did experience significant gains during Romania's communist regime. Illiteracy among Romanian women was virtually wiped out, except in the case of minorities such as the Rroma. Levels of educational attainment among women increased dramatically. The proportion of women with college degrees also rose under the communists and so, too, did the proportion of women employed in professional and managerial occupations, although top management positions generally were closed to them. There also was a significant increase in women's health care and in the health care of families, in general, compared to what existed before the communists came to power.

After 1989, women became especially vulnerable to the changes that were being introduced into the country. For example, women's unemployment rates rose faster than did men's. The political representation of women in the parliament and their representation in cabinet level positions decreased sharply. Women, especially single mothers, were hard hit by the cut backs in social services, especially the relative declines in educational expenditures, subsidies for families with children, and the collapse of the Romanian public health care system. Women also were faced with the burden of meeting families' basic consumption needs in the face of high levels of inflation for basic goods and for declining levels of family income. Elderly women have been especially hard hit by the changes in the post-1989 period. They have had to subsist on pensions, the value of which have declined dramatically and continue to do so. In Romania's cities, it is now common to see old women begging on street corners and at subway entrances. This was something that one never saw during the communist period. But it is not only older women who are having problems in Romania, life is proving difficult for both elderly men and elderly women.

Romanian women also appear to be subjected to high levels of dis-crimination in the hiring processes of Romanian enterprises. In talking to women's organizations in the country, they recount instance after instance in which women are turned down for jobs in favor of make applicants and instances in which women are paid lower salaries than men for exactly the same work as a man in the same enterprise. They also report a large number of cases where women are given lower status jobs in an enterprise. Women's organizations also claim that sexual har-assment is rampant in Romanian enterprises.

Women's organizations also have struggled to deal with the issue of violence against women. While there are no hard statistics on a national basis to document the prevalence of domestic violence in Romania, women's organizations have enough anecdotal evidence to indicate that the problem of violence against women is widespread in all regions of the country and at all levels of the socioeconomic spectrum. In addition, in a survey carried out for me in 1996 by the Center for Urban and Regional Sociology, Bucharest, Romania. Data were collected from a probability sample of 400 adults (persons age 18 and older) living in Bucharest. I found that Romanian women in Bucharest, compared to a national sample of American women (Gelles and Straus 1988), were 2.28 times more likely than American women to be "pushed, grabbed, or shoved" by their male partner, 4.87 times more likely than American women to be "kicked, bit, or scratched" by their male partners, and, finally, were 13.25 times more likely than their U.S. counterparts to report being "beaten up" by their male partners. These data indicate that intimate relations are very dangerous for women in Bucuresti and, perhaps, for Romania as a whole, which is consistent with what women's organizations report.

In part, such violence is a product of the deteriorating economic situation in which most Romanian households find themselves and the traditional patriarchy of Romanian families – a patriarchy in which women are defined as legitimate targets for make physical aggression. Romanian women's organizations have complained that it is hard to convince the Romanian police and courts to take seriously charges of domestic abuse, especially accusations of spousal rape. There, however, is a growing recognition that domestic violence is a serious issue in the society. Recently, the Romanian Orthodox Church has begun to partly address the issue by setting up shelters for abused women under church protection.

Despite the problems experienced by Romanian women, women's organizations have had a difficult time developing an effective presence in Romania, just as has been the case elsewhere in Eastern and Central Europe. In part, this is because of the disrepute into which Romanian women's organizations had fallen during the communist era. Under communism, women's organizations, like labor unions, did not have an autonomous voice. Instead, they largely functioned as transmission belts for party ideology and policies. In addition, ordinary women now have very little time or other resources to devote to voluntary organizations, given all of the pressures put on them since 1989. The nascent Romanian women's movement has been kept alive by its ties to international women's organizations that have supplied Romanian groups with resources, expertise, and political support and by bringing women's issues in Romania into international arenas.

The Romanian authorities have not looked upon women's issues with a great deal of sympathy, nor have they seemed to take them seriously and most of Romania's political elite seem to think that women's issues are secondary to other concerns that affect the society as a whole and, further, that most problems women face will be resolved as part of a more general solution of problems associated with the transitions to a new society so there is no real reason to devote special attention to them at the present time. As a result, no major party has brought women's issues to the forefront of their political agenda.

In looking at what was happening in the years between 1989 and 1996, the question emerges as to why the opposition forces in Romania refused to acknowledge the successes the Vacaroiu government was achieving and the opposition continued to relentlessly attack the PDSR. On one level, the bitter struggle between the PDSR and the opposition was a result of disputes over specific policy trajectories. The opposition forces, along with personnel from international financial institutions, found it intolerable that the government was achieving economic success by adopting policies that stood in direct contradiction to what international institutions were recommending and which the opposition, itself, believed supplied the only way to achieve a successful reconstruction of the Romanian economy.

The specific disputes over economic policy and alleged corruption masked a deeper struggle between the PDSR and the opposition during the mid-1990s in Romania. The opposition forces were guided by a belief that they, alone, were the legitimate heirs of Romania's democratic and capitalist traditions and of political traditions that were Western oriented. The opposition deeply resented the fact that the former communists were trying to usurp their claims by posturing as supporters of parliamentary democracy, capitalism, and the West, when just a few years before they had championed dictatorship, communism, and were themselves more oriented to the East than to the West. Because of the history of PDSR's leadership, the opposition felt that the party's elite and their allies could never bring about the development of a mature capitalist democracy in Romania and, moreover, they did not deserve even the opportunity to achieve these goals. The opposition believed that whatever type of political system the opposition was creating, whatever type of capitalism it was creating, and the bourgeoisie it was building would be inherently and permanently flawed.

From the point of view of the opposition, only they had the *moral* right to become the new Romanian bourgeoisie that would lead the country's economic and political transformation. The opposition leadership, especially in the National Peasant/Christian Democrat Party, believed they (and only they) had *the* right to take up the task of modernizing society. After all, they believed that this had been their parties' mission before they were defeated first by the onset of fascism and, later, of communism. They were claiming the mantle of successor to the former political class, the Bildungsburgertum, that had taken control of the Romanian state following the political defeat of the boyar class and that had tried to modernize the Romanian economy, state, and society. In viewing themselves in these terms, the opposition defined themselves as the only political actors capable of shedding Romania's ties to the "Orient" and bringing Romania into alignment with the "West" as a liberal, capitalist democracy. The opposition understood itself as the only force in Romania that was capable of building a dense civil society, grounded in a capitalist class structure. The opposition parties felt that only a civil society patterned after the West would be capable of exercising a control over the state and, thereby, would be able to prevent the state from degenerating into "totalitarianism" or into some other form of dictatorship.

The opposition parties also felt that they alone had the *cultural* right, as well, to become Romania's leading political class and to preside over the formation of the country's bourgeoisie. They saw the former communist nomenklatura that dominated the FSN, and its successor, the PDSR, as lacking the education, values, aesthetic sensibilities, and cultural orientations necessary for creating the idealized "enlightened" and "humanitarian" bourgeoisie modeled after what the Romanian opposition thought existed in the West. The opposition felt that the former nomenklatura, if it had free reign over the Romanian economy and state, would develop a distorted, if not degenerate, bourgeoisie that would act only in terms of its crass material interests, rather than in terms of the interests of Romanian society as a whole. It almost seems that the opposition political elites and their intellectual allies felt that the former communists never would be able to embrace the values of humanism and liberalism that were intrinsic to a truly European bourgeoisie, let alone the principles of free-market capitalism and competitive parliamentary democracy.

The opposition parties truly believed that if the PDSR were allowed to consolidate a bourgeoisie in its own "distorted" image out of the raw materials of the former nomenklatura any hope that Romania had for creating a more "proper" and "fitting" Romanian bourgeoisie would be lost forever. Because they perceived the economic and social stakes to be so high, the opposition parties gave the FSN/PDSR and its governments no quarter. The opposition attacked the government relentlessly, refusing to acknowledge any of its successes and continually challenging its legitimacy.

Skillfully feeding on the anxieties and insecurities of the Romanian population, by the time of the 1996 elections, the opposition had convinced Romania's voters that the country's problems were beyond the capacities of the PDSR to remedy them. Having used charges of corruption, incompetence, and economic mismanagement effectively against the PDSR, the opposition parties, united under the banner of the Democratic Convention of Romania (DCR), dealt the PDSR and President Iliescu serious defeats at the polls. One of the major reasons for the electoral defeat of the PDSR was the turn to the center-right of Romania's trade unions. The largest part of Romania's trade union movement leadership, as well as significant proportions of its membership, had become convinced that the PDSR's brand of social democracy was not working, and would not work, to fix Romania's seemingly intractable economic problems. Leading circles of organized labor had become convinced that only a liberal, capitalist economy would lead Romania to greater prosperity. Workers had given overwhelming electoral support to the FSN in 1992. Along with peasants working on state farms, Romanian workers, especially in the smaller industrial cities, had been the backbone of the FSN's voting block in Romania's early elections. By 1996, this had changed. The unions' leadership and a good part of their rank-and-file membership had come to the conclusion that the government's version of social democracy was an economic failure and, thus, began mobilizing in support of the center-right opposition led by Emil Constantinescu. One of the key labor leaders who had joined this coalition was Victor Ciorbea. Ciorbea, who would become prime minister in the first opposition government formed after the 1996 elections, had been an activist and second tier leader in the communist trade union movement and had ascended to a top leadership position in the reconstituted communist labor organization, CNSLR, after 1989. Under Ciorbea's leadership, CNSLR had moved to the political center and it had embraced the economic philosophy of "contract unionism" at the work-site. As part of the political center, the trade union movement leadership and leading activists supported a more rapid process of industrial and agricultural privatization, demanded the end of the emerging system of "crony capitalism" that gave economic advantages to the former nomenklatura and to economic actors connected to their networks, demanded substantial wage and pension increases, and higher levels of funding for public services, such as health and education. Naively, the unions believed that all of this would be accomplished by a DCR government that modeled its economic policies after those of the United States and Western Europe's capitalist states.

This, after all, was what their Western, especially American advisors, were telling them. Advisors, who ostensibly, had come to Romania to help build free, democratic unions repeatedly told Romania's trade unionists that the only hope for Romania's workers to become part of the Western world of high level consumption was to back the opposition, because only the opposition stood for developing a Western style capitalism. The opposition parties and the Western advisors managed to convince the trade unions' leaders and activists that they would have to accept short term suffering during an "effective" transition in order to obtain long-term gains. These labor advisors, like their IMF and World Bank compatriots, truly believed that Romania, like other former communist states, had to endure an appropriate level of suffering in order to overcome the "excesses" of the communist period, when the state allowed people to live far beyond the national means. The Westerners believed that the greater the suffering, the stronger Romania's recovery eventually would be.

Not all major unions in Romania actively supported the liberally oriented opposition coalition. For example, the Jiu Valley miners union leader, Miron Cosma, joined Romania Mare, which, in 1996, was advancing an ideology that blended a "brown" philosophy of extreme nationalism with a "red" economic agenda that, among other things, stressed the need for Romania to maintain state ownership over large industries and to resist the demands of the IMF and World Bank for major structural "reforms" in the Romanian economy. Cosma, however, left the party before the 1996 elections and asked his union members to support the DCR.

It was not only Romania's trade unions that came to accept the opposition as offering the only realistic solution to Romania's problems. The opposition also secured the support of a large part of Romania's professional classes and petty entrepreneurs, as well as a large number of its intellectuals. Like the largest part of the trade union movement, these groups all saw their personal and collective interests better served by the opposition than by the PDSR. These groups shared the opposition's vision that the PDSR was unlikely to lay down the foundation for the development of a Western style society, economy, and polity. Resenting the apparent rapid economic success of the old nomenklatura and the "threat" that they would become Romania's new bourgeoisie, a large number of intellectuals and artists, petty producers, and professionals overwhelmingly gave their support to the opposition parties. In many cases, especially among the professionals and the intelligentsia, support for the opposition parties was a "return" to parties their ancestors may have supported before the communists had dismantled them. These strata also believed that only the opposition understood what was necessary to "modernize" the Romanian economy and the Romanian state. They feared that the PDSR's old communists had no real interest in economic, political, social, or cultural liberalization. Instead, they feared that the FSN/PDSR intended to revert to a highly controlled society, especially in the area of arts and culture, and to limit opportunities for Romanians to have contact with the West.

When Iliescu had run for the presidency in 1992, he had promised Romanians that if he won and if the PDSR controlled the government, the "transition" to capitalism would take place gradually and that no one would suffer serious negative effects in shifting from communism to capitalism. The PDSR, during the campaign, appears to have been intentionally vague about its intentions with respect to state property. It was not clear what, if anything, it wanted to privatize and what method of privatization, if any, it would adopt. After taking office, Iliescu and the PDSR faced enormous pressures from international financial institutions (the IMF and the World Bank), as well as the EU, to adopt a "transition" model favored by the Western powers. Iliescu and his party quickly found out that they had little flexibility in adopting policies favored by the West. Romania was in desperate financial straits and its economy was on the verge of collapse. Industrial production and agricultural production threatened to grind to a halt and the value of the national currency was crumbling. Given the internal economic situation, the foreign pressures, and the powerful internal opposition that was organizing against the government, the FSN/PDSR did not have the flexibility to pursue a social democratic economic agenda. Instead, the party and the government really forced to abandon their socialist agenda and, instead, were impelled to wage war against its natural constituencies, especially the Romanian working class. Seemingly, the government could do nothing other than to take steps that ultimately would lead to a decomposition of the Romanian agricultural and industrial proletariat and replace them both with a class of economically free wage laborers who would be compelled to sell their labor power on unregulated, relatively open labor markets. Everyone understood that the emergence of technically free labor markets would drive Romanian wages down, would lead to increased unemployment, and would increase economic misery in the working classes.

The most that the government felt it could do to resist Western pressures was to delay adopting radical reform policies before caving into the seemingly inevitable demands of the international financial institutions. As a result of their seeming lack of freedom to take a flexible approach to transition that would protect the interests of Romanian workers, the PDSR, to the general public, was perceived to be totally ineffective in preserving the real social achievements the communists had attained in building a socialist economy in Romania and of protecting Romanians from the ravages of "transition" to a new economic system. Given all of this, it is small wonder that voters abandoned the party in droves in 1996. PDSR simply had not achieved what it had promised. While this was not entirely the fault of the party, Romanian voters held the PDSR accountable for the economic chaos the country had experienced since 1989 and punished the party for its perceived failure at the polls in the 1996 elections.

If the PDSR had the right kind of economic expertise at its disposal and had it not faced a determined opposition that had bought the message of international financial institutions lock-stock-and-barrel and that had managed to convince a significant portion of the Romanian electorate that this was the only way out of Romania's economic mess, the PDSR could have taken a dramatic and, perhaps, even effective stance in defense of maintaining socialist gains and of advancing an economic policy that might have been less disastrous for the country than the one that was being forced on Romania by the West. But, instead of pursuing in a conscious and deliberate manner a social democratic economic program, the government, in fact, neither fully committed itself to social democracy nor to liberal capitalism, giving it the appearance of indecisiveness and incompetence.

Even the apparent improvement in the national economic picture as the 1996 elections approached was not enough to save the PDSR from the voters' wrath. The opposition parties took advantage of the increasing deterioration in public support for the PDSR's policies to secure the backing of the broad sector of the electorate who had become convinced that the opposition's claims that the government was inept and that the government and the PDSR were inherently corrupt were true. During the period between 1992 and 1996, the opposition parties, with outside advice and support, also had managed to put aside their differences and achieved a high degree of electoral unity, under the leadership of the center-right National Peasant/Christian Democrat Party and its most prominent spokesman, Emil Constantinescu. Constantinescu was a scholar with an international reputation and had been voted rector of the University of Bucharest after 1989. Constantinescu had a reputation as a man of high personal integrity who was committed to the values of classical European liberalism. He also stood close to the values and to the existing leadership of the Romanian Orthodox Church, one of the country's most trusted post-revolutionary institutions, as any number of surveys consistently have shown.

While the opposition portrayed itself as being dedicated to dismantling everything left over from the communist period and introducing a truly liberal capitalist economy, this was not the entirety of its message. The opposition promised more than just an economic reorganization of the country. It was clear that they also intended to lead Romania in a moral rejuvenation so as to "restore" Romania to the international stature it had during the "glory years" of the inter-war period, before the rise of fascism and communism sullied Romania's international reputation and standing. The opposition wanted to create a "new" Romania and a "new" type of Romanian built on all that had been historically in Romanian culture and its national character, before communism had distorted and deformed the society's culture, character, and people. Among other things, this entailed restoring the Romanian Orthodox Church to a position of prestige and respect in the society. However, the emphasis on rebuilding Romania's moral order did not mean that the opposition supported shutting off Romania from the West. Rather, the opposition saw increased integration with the West as important not only to rebuilding the Romanian economy but also as critical to Romania's overall cultural and social reconstruction.

As part of its emphasis on the moral reconstruction of Romania, they opposition also pledged to end all corruption and to introduce integrity into government decision-making. It promised a government that would not serve narrow party interests or the interests of powerful groups in the society but, rather, would serve the interests of all of the country's citizens, including its national minorities. As an indicator of its good intentions toward minorities, the Democratic Convention included the Magyar party in its electoral alliance and made overtures to the Rroma's traditional and intellectual leaders, pledging to reduce discrimination against Rroma and pledging to assist Rroma economic development.

In a crowded field of candidates, no one received a majority of the votes in the first round of the presidential elections in 1996. Iliescu, who was seeking his second term under the new constitution, was forced into a runoff with Constantinescu. At the same time, the opposition inflicted a stunning defeat on the PDSR's parliamentary candidates. The opposition captured enough seats to block any chance that PDSR and its allies could form another government.

The 1996 Elections and the Victory of the Democratic Convention

In the first round of the 1996 elections, President Iliescu, who was running for a second full-term under the new constitution, received the largest number of votes in a very crowded field. President Iliescu won 32.25% of the 12,652,900 valid votes. The runner-up was Emil Constantinescu who had the backing of the Democratic Convention of Romania (DCR). Mr. Constantinescu obtained 28.21% of the votes. The third place finisher, running as the candidate of the Uniunea Social Democrata (The Social Democrat Union), was Petre Roman. Mr. Roman received 20.54% of the vote. With no one receiving a majority of the votes in the first round of the presidential elections, President Iliescu and Mr. Constantinescu were forced into a second-round run-off.

In the second round, there were 12,972,883 valid ballots cast. Mr. Constantinescu received 7,057,906 votes, which was 54.41% of the total. President Iliescu won 5,914,579 votes (45.59%). Constantinescu won by putting together a voting coalition that carried almost all of Transylvania, the Banat (where Timisoara is located), Constanta, and Bucharest. These were (and continue to be) Romania's more prosperous regions. They also have large proportions of minorities, especially Transylvania, where there are significant numbers of Magyars and Rroma. Both of these populations had serious political conflicts with the PDSR and its policies toward minorities. Further support for the idea that Constantinescu did better in prosperous areas is shown by the fact that in the four *judets* with the lowest unemployment levels since 1989 (Bucharest, Satu Mare, Bihor, and Vrancea), Constantinescu carried three of the four, only Vrancea supported Iliescu. On the other hand, among the *judets* with the highest levels of unemployment (Hunedoara, Botosani, Neamt, Braila, and Vaslui), the President carried all five. Ethnicity and relative prosperity, then, seem to predict what *judets* voted for whom.

In the parliamentary elections, which were held in conjunction with the first round of the presidential elections, the DCR received the highest proportion of the vote for seats in the lower house, the Chamber of Deputies. It won 30.17% of the total votes cast, which gave it 122 (35.37%) of seats in the Chamber of Deputies. PDSR finished second in the voting, winning 21.52% of the votes cast. This vote total gave the

PDSR 91 seats, or 26.53% of the total. Uniunea Social Democrata finished third with 12.93% of the votes, which translated into 53 seats, or 15.45% of the total seats. The Magyar party Uniunea Democrata Maghiara din Romania (The Magyar Democratic Union of Romania) came in fourth in the voting, winning 6.64% of the ballots cast. The party received 25 seats, which was 7.29% of the total. The last two parties to secure enough support to win seats were the two larger right-wing parties, Partidul Romania Mare (The Great Romania Party) and Partidul Unitatii Nationale Romane (The Romanian National Union Party). Parttidul Romania Mare's presidential candidate was Corneliu Vadim Tudor, who had won 4.72% of the vote. Partidul Unitatii Nationale Romane's presidential candidate was Gheorghe Funar, the highly nationalistic Mayor of Cluj-Napoca. Mayor Funar won 3.22% of the vote. Fifteen seats in the Chamber were accorded to representatives of officially recognized national minorities. The geographic distribution of support for the various parties in the lower house elections followed a pattern very similar to what took place in the presidential election.

PDSR's old coalition, which had included the two rightist parties, if put together again would have 128 seats, which would make them the largest voting bloc, had not the Democratic Convention been able to forge an alliance with the Magyar party and with Petre Roman's Social Democrats. Neither of these parties was willing to make an alliance with the PDSR. The Magyar party resented the ties that PDSR had with the two right wing parties after the last election and Petre Roman still was hostile toward President Iliescu, who had forced him to resign as Prime Minister after the miners' invasion of Bucharest in September 1991.

In the vote for the Romanian Senate, the results paralleled those for the lower house almost exactly. The major parties finished in the same order in the Senate vote as they had for the Chamber of Deputies. DCR was given 53 seats, PDSR won 41 seats, the Social Democrats took 23 seats, the Magyar party was awarded 11 seats, Great Romania took 8 seats, and the Romanian National Union Party was accorded 7 seats in the Senate.

Overall, the results of the elections for parliament and, eventually for the president, was a repudiation of the role that President Iliescu and his party had played since 1989. They indicated the degree to which the Romanian electorate had come to believe that the center-right CDR and its allies was the only political force that could deliver Romania from its economic misery. Support for the opposition also indicated a faith that the economic agenda pushed by international financial institutions was *the* way for Romania to move toward developing a modern economy.

The assumption of power by the former opposition was heralded in the West as a major political breakthrough in Romania. Little comment was made about how the election belied opposition propaganda that had accused the PDSR of being an anti-democratic party. Having lost the election, the party accepted the results and moved into the role of the "loyal" opposition, as one would expect of any party committed to democracy. In the West, it was believed that the new parliamentary majority, the new prime minister, and the new president would move rapidly to introduce the structural reforms that Western financial institutions had been pressuring Romania to adopt, would increase the efficiency of the national government, would bring an end to "corruption," and would end various alleged human rights abuses that seemingly had been tolerated by the former governments.

As would become clear soon enough, however, Western hopes and the hopes of liberal elements within Romanian society were quickly dashed. As things turned out, those who had expected rapid "reform" had seriously over-estimated the unity of the Democratic Convention of Romania and the competence of the new president and prime minister, while seriously under-estimating the strength of the entrenched interests that had formed between 1989 and 1996. Reformers also seriously under-estimated the growing strength of the radical right or, at least, the radical right's capacity to position itself as a focal point for opposing change, especially change that seriously damaged rank-and-file urban and rural workers' interests (especially those employed in the state agricultural sector), as well as the interests of various strata of functionaries, whose economic and social mobility were predicated on the maintenance of pre-1989 economic and bureaucratic organizations.

Constantinescu began his presidency with much pomp and circumstance. He went to Alba Iulia, where he held a ceremony marking the beginning of his term in which the Patriarch of Romania was given a prominent role. To those with a long enough memory, this event could not help but to signify Constantinescu's hope that Romania had "returned" to the economic and political paths that it had been on before the "interruptions" of fascism and communism. In many respects, Constantinescu's hopes were realized, but not in the ways he might have wished or intended.

The new prime minister, Victor Ciorbea, and his government, immediately on taking office, began to implement a crash program of economic "shock therapy" that was more draconian than anything that had been tried in other Eastern and Central European countries. The new government believed that only the harshest measures could make up for the time Romania had "lost" in forging an effective transition program during the previous years, when the government had been in the hands of the "neo-communists," as the PDSR was described. In an interview with *Wall Street Journal Europe* reporter Anastasia M. Warpinski (August 25, 1995, pp. 4-5), Daniel Daianu, Chief Economist of the Romanian National Bank, pointed out that since the new government took power it had liberalized energy prices by reducing government subsidies and it had began to implement a plan for macroeconomic "reform." As part of its economic "reform" program, the new government, according to Daianu, had "jump started" the privatization program that had "stalled" under the former government and that it was speeding up efforts to join the European Union and NATO, both of which had rejected Romania's initial applications for membership.

Daianu also pointed out that the new government's programs had dramatically reduced inflation. In July 1997, the inflation rate stood at 0.7%, which was down from the 30% rate of March 1997. The drop in inflation was attributed to the new government's introduction of strong austerity measures and a drastic reduction in the monetary supply, the later being a policy strongly recommended by the IMF and World Bank, a fact the chief economist did not mention. The IMF was pressing the Ciorbea government to reduce government expenditures and the state's money supply in order to reduce inflation and, in turn, reduce bank interest rates, which stood at roughly 500% at the start of 1997. Daianu also noted that inflation had dropped because of a sharp reduction in domestic demand. Despite these promising signs, Daianu noted that inflation would remain high for some time, predicting an annual inflation rate of around 25% by the end of the year.

Daianu's predictions were shown to be far too optimistic only a month after he had given his interview. In August 1997 the inflation rate had jumped to 3.5% and experts were predicting it would total 130% at the end of the year, which would be a substantial increase from the previous year's 56.9% (*The Wall Street Journal Europe*, September 24, 1997, p. 4).

As evidence of the effectiveness of the "shock therapy" policies the new government was putting into place, Daianu mentioned that Romania's foreign reserves had increased dramatically between January and July 1997. In January, foreign reserves stood at $600 million. By July foreign reserves reached $1.8 billion in currency and another $1 billion in gold. Daianu attributed some of these gains to a sharp reduction in imports resulting from Romania's drop in economic activity brought about by the newly introduced austerity measures and the enhanced fiscal responsibility of the Ciorbea government.

Daianu also noted that the government finally had freed the exchange rate of the leu, allowing its value to be determined by market conditions, rather than by administrative fiat. He noted that this led to a large "initial" drop in the leu's value. At the time he was being interviewed, the leu stood around 7500 to the dollar. This was substantially lower than the 3000 per dollar value it had in November 1995. Currency traders, at this time, were predicting that by the end of 1997, the leu would fall to somewhere between 8000 to 8500 to the dollar. The decline, according to currency traders was expected to be gradual because the government was pursuing a policy of daily dollar purchases so at to keep the currency from a precipitous drop in value. This intervention in currency markets contradicted the government's stated policy of allowing the leu's value to be determined completely by the market. The decline in the leu's value had a negative effect on the average Romanian's consumption of imports. As the leu continually fell, Romanians were finding it more and more difficult to purchase Western imports, so they turned to domestic products or to goods imported from Turkey and from low cost Asian and Middle Eastern economies.

At the time Daianu was giving his interview, Romania's central bank had just announced that it had adopted new regulations that would permit foreign investors to repatriate profits made in Romania in hard currency (*The Wall Street Journal Europe*, August 25, 1997, p. 26). To do so, they only had to pay a small tax. This was offered as an incentive to raise levels of direct foreign investment (DFI) and reduce DFI gap between Romania and other Eastern and Central European countries. Romania also opened up its market in Treasury Bills to foreign investors for the first time (Brown, September 3, 1997, p.20). The government gave the monopoly on sales of this public debt to stock brokers in an example of its own tendencies to respond to important constituencies. The PDSR, guided by principles of economic nationalism, had not allowed an open repatriation of profits. Instead, it wanted to see profits earned in Romania to be invested in the country, rather than circulate out to international centers of capital in the West. The PDSR also had resisted opening sale of its debt to foreigners, believing that this would give foreign debt holders an opportunity to exercise undo influence on government policies. In both of these cases, the PDSR had rejected the recommendations of the IMF to allow for profit repatriation and to allow foreigners to purchase part of the national debt.

As part of its reforms, the new government also announced that it was going to adopt regulations of currency convertibility that had been put in place by the IMF. By adopting IMF "current-account convertibility" policies, the Ciorbea government was providing a further opening of the Romanian economy to foreign influence, penetration, and, even, foreign hegemony over it, which potentially had the effect of substantially diminishing the country's ability to effectively manage its own economic life.

As part of its macroeconomic structural reforms, the Ciorbea government also took steps to close down industries deemed too "inefficient" to salvage and/or to privatize. In the first six months, the new government closed seventeen plants and was reviewing the status of 212 more. Unemployment quickly increased from under 7% to over 10% as a result of the government's new policies. The government also forced other state enterprises, which it deemed could be saved, to substantially reduce their work forces, which added to the number of unemployed. Because of the state's new policies, unemployment quickly increased from under 7% to over 10%. In part, because of its industrial policies, industrial output plunged by 12.5% in the first half of 1997, service sector sales dropped by 21% compared to the previous year, and domestic investment declined by 23% in the first six months of 1997 (*The Wall Street Journal Europe*, September 2, 1997, p.16).

One of the first industries that Ciorbea "attacked" was the mines in the Jiu Valley. His government offered miners $2000 each if they would accept elimination of their jobs. The government claimed that it would help miners find alternative employment. When the workers who had taken the money realized that the government could not follow through on its pledge to find them other jobs, miners' resistance to the government's attempt to close mines strengthened.

Ciorbea's government also took a harder line on wages than had the previous PDSR government. The Ciorbea government's unwillingness to grant national unions wage increases indexed to inflation meant that Romanian workers experienced a significant decline in real wages, which, coupled with price increases due to a declining leu and the ending of energy subsidies, meant that the Romanian working class experienced a significant decline in its level of living.

Despite the adoption of a large number of austerity measures and the implementation of tight fiscal policies, the Ciorbea government was unable to meet its goal of reducing the state's budget deficit from 5.7% in 1996 to 4.5% in 1997 (*The Wall Street Journal Europe*, September 2, 1997, p.16). In response, the Ciorbea government decided to turn the screw even tighter on the Romanian population. It adopted even more stringent fiscal and monetary policies, which had the effect of only increasing the economic misery of the average Romanian. An IMF official, Mr. John Hill, announced that his employer was "pleased" with the "progress of reform to date" (*The Wall Street Journal Europe*, September 2, 1997, p. 16). But, Mr. Hill went on to note that much more still needed to be done in the second half of the year. Mr. Hill and others argued that given all of the changes that were being introduced, economic activity was sure to revive in 1998.

This did not prove to be the case, however. In 1998, agriculture production dropped by 8.8%, manufacturing declined by 6.4%, and services fell by 0.1% (*Social and Economic Indicators*, World Bank Office Romania, 2000, p.2). Also falling were gross domestic investments (-3.7%), private consumption (-6.8%), and the gross national product (-3.0%) (*Social and Economic Indicators,* World Bank Office Romania, 2000, p. 2). The terms of trade stood at 82, compared to a 1995 base of 100, showing a deteriorating position in the export/import ratio in Romania (*Social and Economic Indicators,* World Bank Office Romania, 2000, p.3). About the only thing that increased was the level of government consumption. It rose by 0.4% (*Social and Economic Indicators,* World Bank Office Romania, 2000, p. 2). The annual inflation rate stood at 55.0% in 1998 and the government deficit stood at 5% of the GDP (*Social and Economic Indicators,* World Bank Office Romania, 2000, p.3). None of these figures indicate that the DCR government's policies were a smashing success on the economic front. Its hard-line policies simply were not delivering in the way the government and its external allies in the European Union and in Washington had hoped and had predicted.

The next year (1999), in most respects, was just as bad on the economic front. Industrial production fell by 3.1%, services output declined by 8.4%, private consumption dropped by 6.8%, gross domestic investment was reduced by 3.7%, and the gross national product was down another 3.0%, according to World Bank estimates. There were a few bright spots. Agricultural production rose by 4.7%. The budget deficit fell to 3.5% of GDP and annual inflation dropped to 46.4%, which, while high, was 8.6% lower in the previous year, and the terms of trade index did not change compared to the previous year (*Social and Economic Indicators,* World Bank Office, 2000, p, 2 and 3).

Real wages continued to decline for what was left of the urban and rural proletariat, as the government refused to index incomes to the rate of inflation. In order to try to keep labor peace and stave off the strikes and protests that had helped turn public opinion against the PDSR. The new government was especially concerned about keeping the support of the unions that had backed them in the 1996 elections. To this end, Ciorbea's government, with the support of the U.S. Department of Labor, explored the possibility of constructing a system of labor-management-state corporatism that would develop labor policies and help establish wage levels for the economy (for an excellent discussion of the various forms of corporatism in the labor field and the consequences of corporatism see Kenworthy 2002: 367-388). Ciorbea had envisioned a national council composed of representatives from labor, management, and the government. He wanted a national council and a council for each of Romania's *judets.* Ciorbea's efforts did not produce much in the way of results. The trade unions were highly suspicious of the idea and of the processes that would be used to implement them. Moreover, they did not want managers of state enterprises included in any of the councils that would be established, believing this would give the state a disproportionate representation.

As economic crisis dragged on, the governing coalition's internal strains, contradictions, and personal and ideological rivalries and conflicts came to the forefront. In the context of these tensions, what might have been petty squabbles among the coalition's partners were magnified and turned into significant political conflicts. These conflicts cost Ciorbea his position on March 30, 1998, when one of the coalition partners threatened to withdraw its support of the government. This was the second major threat to coalition unity. In September 1997, the Magyar party had said it was considering withdrawing from the governing coalition. The Magyar's were protesting the government's refusal to support the establishment of a Hungarian language university in Cluj. The minister responsible for higher education had strongly opposed opening a Hungarian language university in Transylvania. The minister was former rector of the state university in Cluj, which offered a number of academic degrees both in Romanian and Hungarian and he believed it was a waste of state resources to open another public university that would duplicate what his university was doing. He also felt that a Hungarian language university would be a setback to his attempts to increase contact between Magyars and Romanians at the university level. The Magyar party agreed to stay in the government when it was agreed that the state would develop a university in Transylvania that offered instruction in Romanian, Hungarian, and German. While a compromise was reached, the government felt that it had been blackmailed by the Magyars and the Magyars felt that the new university really did not meet their needs. The government's decision to partially accommodate Magyar demands provoked widespread hostility from the parties of the far right and from a large number of Romanians in Transylvania who, while not necessarily supporters of the far right, always had been hostile to any government policy that seemingly singled out the Magyars for special treatment.

In April 1998 Ciorbea was replaced by Radu Vasile, the secretary general of the National Peasant Party. Vasile, in an effort to placate the IMF, the World Bank, and the EU, made it clear that he and his government were not going to back off the "shock therapy" program started by Ciorbea. Indeed, he indicated that he would push this agenda even harder than had his predecessor. One of his first pronouncements was that he intended to close at least 38 inefficient mines, two of which were in the Jiu Valley.

Cosma demanded that the miners be allowed to negotiate with Mr. Berceanu, the Minister of Industry, about mine closings. Cosma was especially interested in protecting the 2000 workers at the Barbateni mine, which had been modernized a few years before at a cost to the government of roughly $3 million. Cosma claimed that the Barbateni mine was not unprofitable and should not be slated for closing. Berceanu refused to meet with Cosma, claiming that he did not want to talk with a criminal.

Given the government's intransigence, the miners struck on January 4, 1999. The workers demanded that the government send a delegation to the Jiu Valley to negotiate with them. The government refused to do so. The miners responded by saying this left them with no alternative but to go to Bucharest. As the exchange between the miners and the government were going on, media allies of the new government attacked the miners and their union leadership, claiming that the inefficient mines had been draining money from the state budget that could (and should) be better used elsewhere in the economy. The miners engaged in massive protests in the city of Petrosani.

In order to prevent the striking miners from moving from there to Bucharest, the transport minister ordered that all trains running between Petrosani and Bucharest be cancelled. In the meantime, government security forces attempted to seal off the city where the miners were encamped.

On January 18, with no trains or trucks coming into Petrosani, the miners began to march toward Bucharest. They first encountered government forces at the town of Bumbesti, which is about 18 miles (roughly 30 km.) from where they had started. Rather than choosing to confront the government forces and push through their ranks toward Bucharest, the miners decided to camp in Bumbesti. Members of the local community brought supplies to the miners and offered them other forms of support.

On the 19th, the miners advanced on the government forces, which used tear gas to try to stop them. With the assistance of some of the town's residents, the miners broke through the police line. By the evening of the 19th, the miners had reached the capital of Gorg Judet, Targu Jiu. The miners claimed that on their march they had received expressions of support from peasants and villagers, just as they had when they arrived in Bucharest in 1991. On the 20th the miners reached Horezu in Valcea Judet. On the 21st of January the miners, whose ranks had swelled with workers who supported them and with miners from other regions, bringing their forces to about 15000 people, engaged in a pitched battle with the government forces. The miners and their allies overwhelmed the police, who broke ranks and retreated. Neither tear gas nor police dogs had been able to stop the marchers. In the afternoon of the 21st, the marchers moved into Ramnicu Valcea, the capital of Valcea Judet, and occupied government offices. Once again, the local population expressed support for the miners and their allies. All of the *judets* through which they marched and which expressed support for them overwhelmingly had voted for Mr. Iliescu in the presidential elections, so one might have expected that they would see the miners as heroes and as defenders of their interests.

The miners now were poised to mount their assault on the capital. The continuing defeats of government security forces created a panic in Bucharest. The general population and the government did not want to see a repeat of 1991. As a result of repeated defeats of government forces, President Constantinescu declared a state of emergency and Prime Minister Vasile agreed to meet with the miners, provided the meeting place was outside of Bucharest. Vasile and the miners reportedly reached an agreement that (from the miners' perspective) provided the Jiu Valley miners with a pay raise and a promise that mines that had been ordered closed in late December 1998 would be re-opened. In exchange for these concessions from the government, the miners pledged that they would return to their home base in the Jiu Valley and engage in no further violence. It was clear to the miners, at this time, that they had been victorious.

Immediately following the government's decision to accommodate the miners, the Vasile government came under attack from Romania's "liberally" oriented press and from foreign newspapers. The Romanian press damned the government for having given into violence and for having set a dangerous precedent that would come back to haunt it when it tried to restructure other industries. Much the same point was made by foreign financial experts and financial newspapers. The liberal, humanitarian organization, Group for Social Dialogue, joined in the chorus denouncing the miners and the government's decision to negotiate with them. Constantinescu could not help but to realize that the miners "victory" would not please the IMF, the World Bank, and the EU, as the agreement called into question the government's willingness to defend and proceed with its "shock therapy" program. The government now appeared weak and ineffective when confronted with the organized power of a militant segment of the working class and its supporters in areas loyal to PDSR.

Attacks from such domestic quarters and fear of foreign reaction unnerved President Constantinescu, who denied that Vasile had been authorized to conduct negotiations with the miners, thus calling the legitimacy of the agreement between the miners and the government into question. At the same time, government negotiators denied that they had promised the miners a raise. This was followed by an announcement by the Ministry of Industry that it would proceed with its restructuring of the mining industry in the Jiu Valley if the miners failed to bring forward an acceptable alternative. Cosma was taken into custody by the police, tried, convicted, and sentenced to 18 years in prison for having led the miners, once again, on a march to Bucharest. By all appearances, the government had managed to outmaneuver the miners, which it hoped would restore the confidence of international financial institutions and the government's key supporters in Romania.

However, if the government had hoped that its "defeat" of the miners and their allies was a clear example of its seriousness of purpose in pursuing a "shock therapy" agenda and its willingness to confront workers who demanded more than the state was willing to pay in order to meet the conditions for international loans, it was seriously mistaken. Worker dissent, protests, and strikes would continue throughout the period of DCR government as the economy continued to deteriorate and showed no signs of significant recovery, despite repeated promises that a growing economy was only a year or two away, at best. Teachers and transportation workers carried out major strikes over pay and working conditions. In addition, the teachers were protesting the deteriorating state of Romanian primary and secondary education. Schools did not have sufficient supplies, buildings were deteriorating, and the government was refusing to hire a sufficient number of new teachers.

The rapid decline of the state's system of public education was but one example of the negative effects state disinvestment was having on Romania's public institutions and on the everyday lives of large parts of the Romanian population. Retirees were finding it ever more difficult to meet their basic expenses on the money they received as pensions from the state, forcing many to beg to supplement their incomes. Parents who had lost their jobs or who experienced real wage losses as a result of the government's austerity program sometimes were forced to turn their children over to orphanages to raise, to give up their newborns or their infants to adoption, or to simply turn their older children out on the street so as to reduce their expenses. Young couples often were forced to delay marriage or cohabitation because they could not afford to obtain their own apartment or house. People who once had enjoyed free or heavily subsidized vacations at Romanian Black Sea coastal resorts or in the mountains no longer could afford vacations now that vacation costs were determined by the market. Large numbers of people could not afford to eat at the newly private restaurants. All of this generated increasing popular resentment of the DCR its government, and the president.

Disenchantment with Vasile's government also began to appear among some of the DCR's strongest pre-election supporters. A number of the coalition's strongest former supporters in the human rights community were especially upset by the government's apparent retreat from the coalitions once apparent support for various human rights causes. We already have seen how the government refused to change Law 200, which outlawed homosexuality, much to the disappointment of gays who had thought that once the "neo-communists" had been defeated they would be liberated from the legal burdens with which they had to contend. Women's groups began complaining that the new government did not take their needs seriously, especially in areas such as child care, education, and domestic violence. Ethnic minorities began charging that the DCR and its coalition partners were continuing to tolerate ethnic discrimination and the violation of the rights of minorities, especially Rroma and Magyars. So upset was the Magyar community that they petitioned the EU committee charged with overseeing the accession of new members demanding that Romania not be given membership until it addressed the question of Magyar human rights and their alleged violation in Romania. Minority communities and other human rights groups also charged that the DCR guilty of tolerating police violence against ethnic and sexual minorities and other criminal offenders. The Rroma communities were especially upset by what they believed was continued police harassment and law enforcement practices built on what, in the United States, is called "ethnic profiling." The old practice of solving a crime by finding "the closet Rroma who seemed to fit the description of the offender," as one activist put it in a discussion with me, continued unabated under the DCR. Despite the fact that under the new government many of the country's top law enforcement officials, including the director of the police in Bucharest, had been retired from their positions. Complaints about the behavior of the SRI, the successor organization of the Securitate, also continued, despite the fact that its former director had resigned when Constantinescu had won the presidential election. The government also managed to alienate the independent press, which had been one of the pillars of its support during the period when the PDSR governed. As was noted earlier, the independent press had been relentless in its opposition to the PDSR, going so far as to declare a strike against the government which entailed a refusal to carry its news reports. The independent press also, seemingly without question, supported the opposition's definition of the PDSR and its government as anti-democratic, inherently corrupt and inept neo-communists who could not possibly solve Romania's economic problems. In addition, the independent press had done everything possible to give a positive spin to the actions of the opposition parties. It continually portrayed the DCR, its leaders, and its allies, as high-minded, incorruptible democratic reformers committed to human rights who had a monopoly on the wisdom necessary to achieve meaningful economic development and integration of Romania into the West. By having served the DCR cause so well during what one journalist used to describe as "the dark days" of neo-communism, the independent press expected to be treated far better than they were by Constantinescu and the government that came to power with him. They were seriously disappointed when they found that the CDR government, under Prime Minister Vasile, was more than willing to use existing laws, that had been passed by the PDSR in an attempt to curb media criticism of the government and its officials, against the press. In 1998 the government refused to amend the provision in the criminal code that prohibited "defamation of the nation and/or state authorities" (Human Rights Watch 1999, p. 2). The independent media had lobbied heavily to have this provision eliminated from the penal code, with no success. According to Human Rights Watch (1999:2), the government used these provisions of the penal code to attack and to punish journalists who were investigating allegations of government corruption. The CDR government was especially sensitive about allegations of corruption in its ranks, it, after all, had managed to define itself as a party that was "more pure" than Caesar's wife and it did not appreciate challenges to its claim of moral purity and political/governmental integrity. On March 13, 1988, according to Human Rights Watch (1999: 2), three reporters working for the newspaper *Opinia* (Opinion), which was published in Buzau, were given sentences of one year each for having written a story that claimed a former government prosecutor's mother had once rented her house to people who had been involved in what was alleged to be an illegal pyramid scheme. In Bistrita, in May 1998, Cornel Sabou, the editor in chief of the press agency Trans-Press, was convicted and sentenced to ten months in prison for having dared to publish protests about a local judicial official. With cases like these resulting in stiff sentences, it became clear to the independent press that the DCR government and its coalition allies were far less sympathetic to issues pertaining to freedom of the press than they had portrayed themselves to be, when they had needed press support to discredit the PDSR.

It was not only the independent press that chafed under the press policies of the DCR and its coalition partners. There was significant hostility toward the government among journalists at the national radio and the national television. Many of the most "progressive" journalists at these media outlets had been closet supporters of the opposition when the PDSR had governed. These "progressive" journalists deeply resented the tight editorial control the PDSR government appointed managers exercised over the topics they covered and the way they were required to cover the news. The journalists believed that the government appointed managers did not respect their professional judgment and skills and wanted to use journalists as nothing more than another government voice. The less cynical (or, perhaps, the less realistic) journalists at the national radio and the national television had managed to convince themselves that things would be different if the opposition held power. It did not take them long to realize that they had been mistaken, as management continued to require them to hew closely to the new party line.

Voters interested in ecological issues had believed that PDSR lacked any commitment whatsoever to ending the environmental degradation practiced by the communists and to rehabilitating the Romanian environment, which, in many areas, had passed beyond being ecological disaster zones to become pure and unadulterated ecological wastelands. These wastelands were doing significant damage to the health and well-being of their residents, contributing to a wide variety of illnesses, especially respiratory problems.

When the communists ran the country, they, like their counterparts in other Eastern and Central European states had a Promethean attitude toward the environment. The communists, given their peculiar understandings of Marx, understood the environment as nothing more than one more input to production to be exploited in the name of expanding industrial and agricultural outputs. Pursuing economic "modernization" at any cost, the environment was subjected to extensive pressures. Romanians seemed to accept the environmental degradation all around them as one more cost of expanding economic outputs. Unlike in some of the other Bolshevik states, such as Bulgaria and the German Democratic Republic, Romania did not generate an ecological movement that was prepared to or that was capable of challenging the state's lack of attention toward protecting the environment.

In 1990, the provisional FSN government, recognizing the serious condition of the natural environment, established the Ministry of Environment, which, in 1992, was renamed the Ministry of Water Resources, Forests, and Environmental Protection (MWFEP). It was not the only state agency charged with environmental management and oversight. The Romanian Water Authority (Apele Romana), which was autonomous from MWFEP, shared responsibility for managing and protecting the quality of Romania's water supply with MWFEP, while the equally autonomous Forest Authority (ROMSILVA) shared responsibility with MWFEP for forest management, an important sector of the Romanian economy. While both the Water Authority and the Forest Authority had legal autonomy from MWFEP, they reported to it. The government also created a number of research institutes that were funded to address issues of environmental quality. There also were other ministries, such as the Ministry of Health and the Ministry of Agriculture and Food, were given charges relating to environmental issues. The wide dispersal of authority over environmental questions made coordination difficult. Despite the creation of research institutes and an entire new ministry that focused on the environment, under the FSN and, later, the PDSR, never provided sufficient funding to the research institutes and the environmental ministry. Funding never approached even 1% of GDP under the PDSR (Ministry of Water, Forests, and Environmental Protection 1996, 1997). The PDSR government, in 1995, passed the Environmental Protection Law (Law 137/1995) in December. This was a general framework law that, to become operationally effective, required additional enabling laws, regulations, and the like, which were very slow in forthcoming.

When the CDR took power, it indicated that, as part of its austerity program, it planned to reduce spending on the environment. It believed that the best way to improve the environment was to carry through on its "shock therapy" program and to allow the market to effect necessary changes in the current environment and to provide future environmental productions. CDR continued to under fund environmental programs and environmental research, to not demand strict enforcement of environmental laws and regulations, to not invest in new production technologies that were environmentally friendly, and to not offer incentives either to state or private enterprises to adopt practices that would lead to improvements in their environmental records.

One of the major factors behind the lack of serious attention to environmental problems in Romania is the virtual absence of direct, organized public pressure. Environmental activism tends to be a confined to Romanian intellectual elites. The "Green" cause has not caught on among the general public. There have been a number of attempts to organize ecological political parties, but little success has been achieved. For example, in the 1996 elections the *Partidul Conventia Ecologista din Romania* (The Ecologist Convention Party of Romania) entered the contest for seats in the Chamber of Deputies and the Romanian Senate. Nationally, in the election for the Chamber, the ecology party received on 27,544 votes, too few to gain representation in the lower house of the parliament. It did slightly better in the vote for the Senate, winning the support of 33,888 voters. Again, this was an insufficient tally to gain a place in the parliament's upper house. It is an open question as to whether the low levels of electoral support given to the ecological party is a result of apathy toward the issue on the part of voters, or whether it represents a belief that the existing major parties are better equipped to deal with environmental issues, or whether it represents a feeling that the country has more immediate and pressing problems in other areas that deserve attention more than do environmental issues.

Despite the absence of a strong ecological movement and/or the lack of interest in environmentalism among the Romanian political and ecological elites, the Romanian government, regardless of whom holds power, is going to be compelled to deal with its environmental problems in the near future. The pressure to become more active in improving the environment and preventing further environmental degradation will come from the EU as Romania comes closer to being accepted as a member of that community of states.

In the meantime, Romanians will have to endure continuing problems with the quality of its drinking water supply. In a large number of Romanian cities and towns, water treatment facilities are woefully inadequate and the supply of drinking water is further complicated by the compromised integrity of the cities' water pipe lines. This is especially a problem in Bucharest, where Westerners have been advised by their embassies to boil their water and to treat it with chlorine tablets before consuming it. In rural communes and villages, wells and cisterns are heavily polluted with residuals from pesticides and chemical fertilizers that the communist government generously applied in an effort to raise agricultural output. These pollutants also have entered streams and rivers, have damaged the Danube Delta, and have entered the Black Sea, threatening its viability as an ecosystem. Rivers, streams, the Delta, and the Black Sea also are threatened by the runoff from pollutants that are the by-product of various manufacturing enterprises located close to them and by accidental spills of pollutants into streams and rivers. A serious threat to Romania's rivers recently occurred as a result of an accidental river spill of cyanide by a foreign owned enterprise.

Romania has major problems with air pollution. There are many days when even healthy people have problems with breathing and with their eyes in almost all of the country's major industrial centers, towns, and cities. Because of the number of pollutants in the air, many of Romania's older buildings have had their stone facing heavily damaged. There are a number of reasons for the poor air quality. Romania heavily relies on the burning of cheap high sulfur coal to generate energy for plants and for heating office buildings and homes. Romanian produced automobiles also lack anti-pollution controls that can meet Western standards. Romanian industrial plants through off tons of unfiltered, polluting emissions. To see an example of how bad the environment was abused under the communists, one only has to go to the small city Copsa Mica, an old center of Romania's rubber and tire industry. When these industries were flourishing, in villages around the city farmers would send their white sheep into the feels in the morning when they returned to the barn in the evening they would be black. Virtually the entire water supply, in and around Copsa Mica, was/is undrinkable. Health experts report that the city and its surroundings have atypically high levels of respiratory illness, heart disease, and high incidence of various rashes and other skin disorders. While there are few other places in Romania as bad-off as Copsa Mica, there are many places that come close to it in terms of environmental damage.

Romania also has serious problems with waste management and waste disposal. In cities, sewage pipes, like pipes delivering drinking water, have been seriously compromised. Raw sewage leaches into the soil, percolates to the ground surface, and empties into the water system. In some localities untreated industrial and household waste water directly into streams and rivers. Romania also has serious problems with the way local governments dispose of solid waste and with the location of some of the major landfills.

Even before the new government took power in 1996, the PDSR had started to pass environmental legislation that met minimum EU standards and, in some cases, exceeded them. However, the legislation they passed, as well as the legislation passed by the DCR governments, have had only marginal effects on the overall quality of the Romanian environment. The state never provided sufficient funds to implement many of the laws that were adopted nor did it provide sufficient funding for enforcement agencies. Moreover, for what they are worth, marker incentives have not been developed that would encourage Romanian enterprises, both state owned and privately owned, to take effective action that would limit damage to the environment. Also, there has been little public demand for improvement in the environment, so that there has not been effective pressure applied to the political and economic elites.

With the economy in shambles, protests growing, charges of corruption increasing, strikes becoming routine, and the coalition unable to hold itself together, as the 2000 elections approached, Romania had descended into political chaos, which only was made worse when President Constantinescu announced he would not seek a second term. Constantinescu's decision was the death knell for the unity of the parties making up the CDR and its allies. Constantinescu was the glue that gave the coalition even its limited solidarity, without him there was little hope that the center of the political grouping would hold. Constantinescu claimed that the reason he would not seek another term was because of the intractable corruption that had come to dominate the economy and the state. In effect, he was admitting defeat, as one of his campaign promises was that he would root out corruption so that Romania could be a normal society.

The 2000 Elections

Nine major candidates stood for office in the November 2000 presidential elections. They were as follows: Ion Iliescu, *Partidul Democratiei Sociale din Romania* (Social Democratic Party of Romania); Corneliu Vadim Tudor, *Partidu Romania Mare* (Great Romania Party), Theodor Dumitru Stolojan, P*artidul National Liberal* (National Liberal Party), Constantin Mugur Isarescu, *Partidul National Taranesc Crestin Democrat* (National Peasant-Christian Democrat Party), Gyorgy Frunda, *Uniunea Democratica Maghiara din Romania* (Union of Democratic Hungarians of Romania), Petre Roman, *Partidul Democrat* (Democrat Party – this is the same party whose candidate he was in 1996, it had changed its name by dropping Social Democrat), Teodor Vorel Melescanu, *Alianta Pentru Romania* (Alliance for Romania), and two independent candidates, Eduard Gheorge Manole and Graziela-Elena Baria, the first women to run for president of Romania.

In the weeks leading up to the election, polls showed that the top two candidates were likely to be the former president, Ion Iliescu, and the candidate of the radical right, Corneliu Vadim Tudor. Political experts were shocked by Tudor's showing in the polls. Many of them believed when it was time to vote the Romanian electorate would come to its senses and vote for one of the more mainstream candidates. However, this was not the case. Former president Iliescu ended up with 36.4% of the vote and Tudor, as the polls predicted, finished second, with 28.3% of the vote. Stolojan, the National Liberal Party candidate finished third, with 11.8% of the vote. The top three were followed by Isarescu, with 9.5%, Frunda, with 6.2%, Roman, with 3.0%, Melescanu, with 1.9%, Manole, with 1.2%, and Barla, with 0.5%.

The distribution of these votes reflected the almost equal political divisions in Romania. Iliescu stood as the candidate of the left, Tudor was the candidate of the right, and the other candidates were centrists, some slightly to the left and some slightly to the right. The centrists had won roughly 35% of the vote, compared to the 36% for the left, and the 28% for the radical right. The question immediately arose as to what would happen in the second round, would the centrist voters move to the radical right or would they support the left. When he was president, the opposition had portrayed Iliescu as being as far to the left as Tudor was to the right, so, voters in the center, to the extent to which they had believed CDR propaganda, seemingly faced a very hard choice. In the election for the Chamber of Deputies the *Polul Democrat-Social din Romania* (Social-Democrat Pole of Romania) won 36.6% of the votes. The *Polul Democrat-Social din Romania* was composed of three parties: *Partidul Democratiei Sociale din Romania* (Democratic Social Party of Romania or PDSR), *Partidul Social Democrat Roman* (Romanian Social Democrat Party or PSDR), and *Partidul umanist din Romania* (Humanist Party of Romania or PUR). PDSR and PSDR merged and named the new party *Partidul Social Democrat* (Social Democrat Party or PSD). Together, the three parties won 155 of the house's 327 memberships. PDSR received 142, PSDR took 7, and PUR 6 seats. The voting bloc held 47.4% of all of the seats in the Chamber of Deputies. While not a majority, it was highly likely that this social democratic coalition would be asked to form a government by the new president, especially if Iliescu won the second round of the presidential election.

The second largest number of seats went to *Partidul Romania Mare* (PRM), the nationalist, radical right party headed by Corneliu Vadim Tudor. It won 19.5% of the vote, which gave it 84 seats or 25.7% of the total number of seats. From seemingly out of nowhere, PRM, which had only a handful of seats in the 1996 parliament, had become the country's second largest parliamentary party.

Petre Roman's *Partidul Democrat* (Democratic Party) took 7% of the vote, giving it 31 seats. It now was the third largest parliamentary party. The *Partidul National Liberal* (National Liberal Party) won 30 seats with 6.9% of the vote. The two Magyar parties, *Uniunea Democratica Maghiara din Romania* (Magyar Democratic Union of Romania)/*Romaniai Magyar Demokrata Szovesteg* (Hungarian Democratic Alliance of Romania) received 27 seats for the 6.8% of the votes it won. Together, these three groupings held 88 seats, or 26.9%. The remaining 19 seats went to "recognized" ethnic parties: Roma (*Partidul Romilor* – Party of the Roma), Germans (*Forumul Democrat al Germanilor din Romania* – German Democratic Forum of Romania), Armenians (*Uniunea Armenilor din Romania* – Armenian Union of Romania), Italians (*Comunitatea Italiana din Romania* – Italian Community of Romania), Bulgarians (*Uniunea Bulgaria dub Banat–Romania*

– The Bulgarian Union of the Banat – Romania), Greeks (*Uniunea Elena din Romania* – Greek Union of Romania), Jews (*Federatia Comunitatilor Evreiesti din Romania* – Federation of the Jewish Community of Romania), Lipovenian Russians (*Comunutatea Rusilor Lipoveni din Romania* – Lipovenian Russian Community of Romania), Croats (*Uniunea Croatilor din Romania* – Croat Union of Romania), Albanians (*Liga Albanezilor din Romania* – Albanian League of Romania), Muslim Tatars and Turks (*Uniunea Demcrata a Tatarilor Turko-Musulmni din Romania* – Democratic Union of Tatar Turkish Muslims of Romania), Ukrainians (*Uniunea Ucrainienilor din Romania* – Ukrainian Union of Romania), Macedonians (*Asociatia Macedonenilor Slavi din Romania* – Association of Slavic Macedonians of Romania), Serbs (*Uniunea Sarbilor din Romania* – Serbian Union of Romania), Ruthenians (*Uniunea Culturala a Rutenilor din Romania* – Cultural Union of Ruthenians of Romania), Turks (*Uniunea Democrata Turca din Romania* – Turkish Democratic Union of Romania), Slovaks and Czechs (*Uniunea Democratia a Slovacilor si Chehilor din Romania* – Democratic Union of Slovaks and Czechs in Romania), Poles (*Uniunea Polonezilor din Romania* – Polish Union of Romania), and a general ethnic organization (*Uniunea General a Asociatiilor Etniel Hutule din Romania* – General Union of Ethnic Associations of Romania).

The *Conventia Democrata Romana 2000* (Democratic Convention of Romania), composed of *Partidul National Taranesc Crestin Democrat* (National Peasant/Christian Democrat Party), *Uniunea Fortilor de Dreapta* (Union of Right Wing Forces), *Alianta Nationala Crestin Democrata* (Christian Democrat National Alliance), *Federatia Ecologista din Romania* (Ecologist Federation of Romania), *Partidul Moldovenilor* (Moldova Party) won only 5.0% of the vote, which was not enough to give them any parliamentary representation. Support for the coalition had completely collapsed between 1996 and 2000. The rapid disappearance of the CDR as an effective, organized political force in four years can be contrasted with what had happened to the PDSR in the previous election. After a difficult four years, PDSR managed to win a significant number of parliamentary seats and to retain its organizational cohesion during the years it was out of power. In contrast, CDR's support withered away and it has disappeared as an organized political movement in Romania.

The composition of the parliamentary blocs meant that the only possible coalition that could have blocked PDSR from taking power would have been an alliance between the far right and the liberal centrist parties. While not inconceivable, such a union for parliamentary purposes would have destroyed whatever credibility either had among their supporters. Therefore, there was no way to block Iliescu's party from taking power.

In the two weeks between the election, a Bucharest polling organization, IMAS (*Institutul De Marketing si Sondaje*), conducted a survey of possible voters to obtain information on their preference between the two candidates. The polling was carried out on December 6th and 7th, only three to four days before the election.

Among those polled who had "valid responses" (*Raspunsuri valide*), IMAS found that 72% supported Iliescu, while 28% claimed that they supported Tudor. Pollsters asked respondents for whom they had voted in the first round of the presidential elections, this was followed by a question asking them for whom they would vote in the second round. In the poll, Iliescu retained 97% of his first round supporters, with 1% claiming that they were switching to Tudor, and 2% reporting that they were not going to cast a vote (*nu votez*) or they did not know (*nu stiu*) for whom they were going to vote. On the other hand, 28% of the valid respondents claimed that they were going to vote for Tudor. Of those who had voted for Tudor in the first round, 83% reported that they would vote for him, again, in the second round, while 12% said that they would vote for Iliescu, and 5% said that they would not vote or that they did not know for whom they would vote.

The poll showed that Iliescu was going to pick up the majority of the voters who had supported all of the other candidates who had stood for election for president in the first round. The third place finisher in the first round of balloting had been Theodor Dumitru Stolojan. He had run as a candidate of the National Liberal Party. Of those who had reported that they initially had voted for Stolojan, 79% reported that they were going to vote for Iliescu and 6% reported that they were going to vote for Tudor, with 15% claiming they would not vote or they did not know for whom they would vote.

Constantin Mugur Isarescu, the candidate of the National Peasant-Christian Democrat Party, finished fourth. In the poll, 64% of Isarescu's supporters said they were going to vote for Iliescu, 9% said they were going to vote for Tudor, and 27% said they either were not going to vote or did not know for whom they would vote.

Supporters of Gyorgy Frunda, the Magyar candidate who had finished fifth in the first round, exhibited the largest shift of any group of voters toward Iliescu. Eighty seven per cent of Frunda's supporters avowed they were going to vote for Iliescu, 3% said they would vote for Tudor, and 10% either did not know for whom they would vote or reported that they would not be voting.

Petru Roman's supporters reported the lowest level of intended support for Iliescu of any of the major candidates. From the survey it appeared that 59% of Roman's voters were going to support Iliescu, 16% intended to vote for Tudor, and 26% said they did not know for whom they would vote or did not plan to vote.

Among those who voted for a candidate other than those listed above, 67% said they were backing Iliescu, 15% were going to support Tudor, and 18% did not know for whom they would vote or did not intend to vote. For those who had not voted in the first round, 53% said they would vote for Iliescu, 15% were going to support Tudor, and 31% did not know for whom they would vote or did not intend to vote.

When we look at the above numbers, it is clear that the vast majority of respondents who had not voted for Iliescu in the first round were going to support him in the second, rather than Tudor. Only among Isarescu's and Roman's supporters did there appear to be a relatively high per cent of first round voters who planned to not support Iliescu. However, rather than shifting to Tudor it appears from the poll results that they planned to sit out the second round of the presidential elections. It is relatively easy to explain why this was occurring. Isarescu was the candidate of the National Peasant-Christian Democrat Party, which had been the implacable foe of Iliescu, personally, and of his party. There was such deep animosity toward Iliescu and his allies among supporters of this party that many of them simply could not bring themselves to vote for Iliescu as the "lesser" of the two "evils." A large proportion of Petre Roman's party, evidently, were reaching the same conclusion. They could not forgive Iliescu and his party for forcing Roman and themselves out of the FSN in 1992. So, almost a third of Roman's voters were not will willing to commit themselves to anyone in the second round.

Among likely voters, the poll showed that Iliescu was likely to secure the support of a majority of both male and female voters. However, his support was substantially higher among women than it was among men. A large number of women found Tudor's rhetoric too caustic and too dangerous to vote for him. As a result, 65% of women said they intended to vote for Iliescu and only 18% indicated that they planned to vote for Tudor. Among men, 54% said they were supporting Iliescu and 29% reported that they planned to vote for Tudor. Among both men and women, 17% said they did not plan to vote or they did not know which candidate they preferred.

There was a clear difference in the age distribution of support for Iliescu and Tudor. While a majority of voters in all age categories (18-29 years; 20-44 years; 40-59 years; and 60+ years) indicated that they were going to vote for Iliescu, there was variation in his support across age groups. The poll indicated that Iliescu was going to win 58% of the vote in the youngest age group and 57% in the second youngest group. Tudor received support from 26% of the youngest voters and 27% from the second youngest group. In both age categories, 16% were undecided or were not going to vote. For voters 45 years old and above, Iliescu clearly was the preferred candidate among those surveyed. He secured support from 62% of those who were age 45-59 and 63% of persons 60 and older. Tudor only obtained the expressed support of 26% of voters 45-59 and 15% of voters 60 and older. Only 12% of the 45-59 year olds were undecided or did not plan to vote. However, 22% of persons 60 and older were undecided or did not intend to vote.

There was a clear split between persons intending to vote for Iliescu and those intending to vote for Tudor by level/type of education. Persons with higher levels of education (*Studii superioare* and *Liceu*) were the most likely to support Iliescu. Seventy three per cent of persons who fell into the *Studii superioare* (i.e. persons who had an education beyond the university level) category expressed an intention to vote for Iliescu and only 12% intended to vote for Tudor, with 16% being undecided or not planning to vote. Persons who fell into the category *Liceu* (persons with a college level education) also had relatively high levels of support for Iliescu, with 66% claiming they intended to vote for him and 21% reporting they would vote for Tudor. Thirteen per cent were undecided or did not plan on voting. Of those reporting that they had less than a university level education (*Scoala generala*), 57% responded that they planned to vote for Iliescu, 21% for Tudor, and 22% said that they would not vote or were undecided. Persons who had a vocational education (*Scoala profesionala*) gave the highest level of support to Tudor (34%) and the lowest level to Iliescu (50%). Thirteen per cent of this group was undecided or claimed they were not going to vote. The persons who fell into this category made up the elite of the old communist industrial and agricultural proletariat and, among all workers, they faced the greatest threat from the relentless expansion of market relations in the Romanian industrial sector and the dismantling of the state sector production system. Thus, Tudor's populist economic agenda could be expected to have a strong appeal to them.

There also were substantial differences in the division of support between Tudor and Iliescu based on residence of the voter. Tudor's appeal was strongest for voters living in rural areas. In rural areas, while Iliescu received the support of a majority of those polled (54%), Tudor was receiving the support of 30% of the voters, with 16% of rural voters saying that they did not know for whom they would vote or did not intend to vote. In small cities (*Orase mici*), Iliescu's support increased to 60% and Tudor's fell to 21%. However, 20% of the voters in small cities were undecided or did not intend to vote. In middle size cities (*Orase mijocii*), Ceausescu's support was about the same (61%) as it was in smaller cities, as was Tudor's (23%), with 16% of the respondents indicating that they did not know for whom they would vote or did not plan to vote. Iliescu received overwhelming support among respondents living in large cities (*Orase mari*). Sixty eight per cent of residents of large cities indicated that they would vote for Iliescu, while only 16% indicated that they planned to vote for Tudor, and 16% were undecided or were not going to vote.

The survey also revealed the presence of regional differences in support for the two candidates. Bucuresti respondents gave Iliescu the highest level of support of any of the regions. Seventy-five per cent of Bucuresti respondents indicated that they would vote for Iliescu and only 14% expressed support for Tudor. Only 11% of the Bucuresti respondents were undecided or did not plan to vote. Iliescu's support was weakest in Transylvania, where 54% of the respondents indicated that they intended to vote for him. However, only 23% of the Transylvanians indicated that they would vote for Tudor. A strikingly large per cent

(23%) of the Transylvania respondents indicated that they were undecided or did not plan to vote.

Tudor drew his highest levels of support from Moldova (26%) and Muntenia (25%), two of the region's most hard hit by the changes being introduced into Romania's economy. Muntenia was an area of mining and heavy industry, while Moldova was industrialized and the site of large state farms, both of which were being threatened by the emergence of a neo-liberal economic order.

Results of the survey were also reported by ethnicity. Iliescu captured virtually all of the votes of people who claimed they were Magyars (*Maghiara*). Eighty three per cent of Magyars indicated that they would vote for Iliescu, while only 3% of the Magyars indicated that they preferred Tudor. Fifteen per cent of the Magyars were undecided or claimed that they were not going to vote. Persons who claimed that they were Romanians (*Romana*) supported Iliescu over Tudor by 58% to 25%, with 17% undecided or reporting they were not going to vote. Among persons with an ethnic identity other than Magyar or Romanian (*Altele*), also gave Iliescu 58% support. However, 34% indicated that they would vote for Tudor. Only 9% were undecided or did not intend to vote.

Summarizing these results, the "typical" Tudor voter was drawn from a rural area, tended to be relatively young, was a male, was from Muntenia or Moldova, had a vocational education, and was from an ethnic minority (but not a Magyar). The "typical" Iliescu voter was older, was more likely to be a woman, was a Magyar, was from Bucuresti, and was highly educated.

These patterns suggest that Tudor's political success had been based on pulling away a substantial proportion of voters who had supported Iliescu and the PDSR in the 1996 election, especially voters in rural areas and voters who were drawn from the core of the old communist proletariat's skilled workers. One can only speculate as to why these two sectors of the population, coupled with younger voters, indicated that they were willing to support the radical right in such high percentages, compared to other Romanian voters.

First, it may have been the case that these voters were responding to the extreme positions that Tudor had taken on ethnic and social issues. He and his party had continually denounced Hungarians, Jews, and Rroma with a rhetoric that verged on outright racism. Tudor also had demanded that Romania take a harder line of law and order, going so far as to push for the reintroduction of the death penalty. Tudor also had taken a hard line on social issues, especially regarding gays and lesbians, who he saw as nothing more than degenerates who were engaging in alien behavior imported from the West and, thus, deserved no rights in Romanian society.

Second, and what we believe is the more likely explanation, Tudor may have drawn the support of the voters that he did based on his populist economic agenda and the past "failures" of the PDSR to meet these voters needs. While it had been in office, the PDSR had lost the support of a large number of workers, especially workers in unions. In part, the PDSR had lost worker support to the CDR in1996 because the PDSR had not been able to meet its commitments to preserve the old socialist system of production, at least until such a time that a transition could be made to privatized industry in which workers deemed redundant could be provided jobs at adequate wage levels. The fact that the PDSR had been more or less compelled by the IMF, the World Bank, and the EU to pursue economic and social policies it would have preferred not to adopt did not matter to the voters who deserted it in favor of Tudor and the far-right. It also did not matter to these voters that all across Europe the social democrats had been forced to move far to the center in order to comply with similar external demands and, as a result, also had lost votes to the center-right and the far-right, in some cases.

However, despite the defections of significant numbers of workers, young people, people in rural areas, and those who were less well educated, the PDSR was able to marshal enough support to elect Iliescu and win a substantial plurality of seats in both houses of parliament. The "good sense" of the majority of the Romanian electorate held and they rejected electing a far-right president and a far-right parliament and they had given the PDSR enough votes to form a minority government without having to enter into a coalition with right-wing parties, as it had been required to do it 1992. The much chastened opposition, while feeling no more positive toward the PDSR than they had in the past, was not about to threaten to bring down this government and face the danger that it would solicit an alliance with a much stronger far-right or, even, force new elections in which the far-right might become the dominant force in the parliament.

The elections of 2000 struck terror into the hearts of Romania's main stream politicians. The radical right's candidate for president made it into the final round of the presidential elections. He, however, lost in the general elections and Iliescu was returned to office as president, once again. Constantinescu earlier had indicated that he would not seek a second term as president, which, for him, was probably a good thing because, in all likelihood, he would have suffered an overwhelming defeat of the center-right coalition governments that had been formed while he was president were an unmitigated disaster. Their economic policies did little to improve substantially the performance of the national economy. Unemployment remained high by recent historical standards in Romanian, the country had alienated one of its long time allies, the former Yugoslavia, by siding with NATO forces in the Kosovo conflict. Inflation continued at very high levels and the various governments were not able to overcome the political chaos that marked Romanian parliamentary politics. In addition, there were a number of serious financial scandals in the banking sector that seriously threatened the country's financial stability. Romania continued to remain outside of the European community of states. It had failed in its bid to win membership in NATO and it was told it would have to make a variety of reforms before it could be considered a viable candidate for membership in the European Unions. The DCR also was riven with internal conflicts. The coalition members were unable to develop a comprehensive set of policies to which they all could agree, resulting in an increasingly ineffective series of governments.

Romania's radical right, despite its strong showing in the 2000 elections, really is not the country's most serious threat to its ability to maintain a liberal, bourgeois democracy. There is little danger that Romania will return to fascism. Nor does the radical left constitute a major threat to Romania's democratic experiment. Few in Romania would support the return to communism. The real threat to democracy in Romania, in our view, will come from the traditional right. In intellectual circles that are linked to Romania's traditional right, there is growing interest in and discussion of finding a "third way" that is more consistent with Romanian's sense of their own history and their own identity than are fascism, liberal democracy, or communism. The traditional right sees liberal democracy as a decadent, chaotic system imported from the West. Echoing Eminescu's views, the traditional right sees the implementation of liberal democratic political processes as an importation of and an attempt to institutionalize forms without substance. Its only real consequences are the production of excessive individualism in the Romanian population and political chaos, as each party is oriented only toward maximizing its own political interests rather than the interests of the nation, as a whole. In the view of Romania's traditional right this threatens to reproduce the political disaster of the 1930s, when people lost confidence in government's ability to solve their problems. Communism and socialism are just as alien as liberal democracy to Romania's history and identity from the viewpoint of the traditional right. Given these views, intellectuals and politicians from the traditional right have begun to explore the possibilities of building a "reform" movement in Romania that would lead the country in the direction of institutionalizing a social, economic, and political corporatism, that would take advantage of, strengthen, and realize the true "organic" nature of Romanian society. Corporatism also would allow Romania, in the view of its proponents, to develop a "moral" state and a "moral" economy more consistent with the demands of the nation's identity. In the 1930s, corporatism had been toyed with by a number of Romanian intellectuals and a number of members of the political elite. But before it could be put into place, the king had seized power and built his monarchical fascist state, cutting off any further development of a specifically Romanian corporatist philosophy and political economy. Should liberal democracy continue to seemingly produce nothing but a politically ineffective state and should liberal capitalism continue to produce dramatic increases in inequality and generalized economic misery for all, except for those at the top of the economy, corporatism will begin to appear as more and more attractive to ever larger segments of the Romanian population, provided that a corporate philosophy and a corporatist social, economic, and political agenda is adopted by an effective political party that knows how to spread such a message to the Romanian population.

The 2004 Elections

With Iliescu no longer eligible to run for another term, his party, now called *Partidul Social Democrat* (Social Democrat Party) supported Adrian Nastase as its candidate for president in the first round of the presidential elections held in November 2004. Nastase was a long time party stalwart, being a supporter of Iliescu since 1989. He also had held several important cabinet positions in various governments his party dominated. He ran against the popular mayor of Bucharest, Trian Basescu, who was a member of the *Partidul Democratic* (Democratic Party). Other candidates in the first round of the presidential election were Corneliu Vadim Tudor, who leads the radical right wing *Partidul Romania Mare* (Greater Romania Party); Marko Bela of the *Uniunea Democratica Maghiara din Romania,* George Coriolan Ciuhandu of the *Partidul National Taranesc Crestin Democrat* (National Peasant Christian Democratic Party), George Becali of the *Partidul Noua Generatic* (Party of the New Generation), Petre Roman from the Democratic Force Party, and Gheorge Dinu who had no party affiliation. No candidate won a majority, so there was a run off between the two top vote-getters, Nastase, with 40.9% of the vote and Basescu with 33.9%.

In the second round of the presidential election, held in December 2004, there was a dramatic turn around in the vote. Nastase increased his percentage to 48.8%, while Basescu raised his percentage to 51.2%, winning the presidency in the process.

In the meantime, in the parliamentary elections that were held in November the National Union PSD+PUR (made up of the Social Democrat Party and the Humanist Party) won 36.8% of the votes, making them the largest parliamentary bloc. The Social Democrats had won 113 seats and the Humanists had won 19, giving the coalition a total of 132 seats in the Chamber of Deputies. They also won 37.2% of the votes for the Senate, giving them 47 seats, 36 from the Social Democrats and 11 from the Humanists. The next largest bloc of votes was received by the Justice and Truth Alliance, which was composed of the National Liberal Party and the Democratic Party. Together they won 31.5% of the votes for the Chamber of Deputies. This gave them 112 seats, 64 for the National Liberals and 48 for the Democratic Party. In the Senate they won 31.8% of the votes, giving them 46 seats, with 25 coming from the Liberals and 21 from the Democrats.

The Greater Romania Party placed third in the parliamentary elections, winning 13.0% of the votes for 48 seats in the Chamber of Deputies and 13.6 % of the vote in the Senate. This gave them 21 seats. The Hungarian Democratic Union received 6.2% of the votes for the Chamber of Deputies. For this they received 22 seats. They had 6.2% of the Senate vote, which allowed them to take 10 seats. Neither the New Generation Party or the National Peasant Party Christian Democrat received a sufficient percentage of the votes for parliamentary representation. In addition, Petre Roman's party did not achieve representation in the new parliament.

8

Discussion and Conclusions

I have discussed the movement of Romania from feudalism under Ottoman hegemony to modernity by focusing on several key issues. In this closing section, I address where Romania stands with respect to these issues now that more than a decade has passed since the end of state socialism. In writing this book, my intent has been to show that many of the problems and issues that contemporary Romania is facing have a long history, longer in fact than is commonly thought to be the case. Most treatments of contemporary Romania focus on the difficulties that Romania is facing in rebuilding its society, the economy, and the state as if the problems Romania was encountering had emerged solely or mainly from the communist period. Instead, I have tried to show that Romania's contemporary problems are an extension of certain fundamental contradictions that have marked Romanian history for centuries, as the Romanian lands have come under intensive and extensive internal and external pressures to achieve "modernity," as that concept has been defined in any given historical epoch. "Modernity" is a complex concept that differs from historical period to historical period.

With the vanquishing of state socialism, if not of the Marxist experiment, in general, modernity, in the late 20th and early 21st centuries, has come to be seen as having two major components: first, a relatively open democratic society, organized as a parliamentary democracy, and second, a market economy that affords some degree of protection to the weakest members of a society. When considering how a society, such as Romania, for example, institutionalizes modernity, it is important to take into account the phenomenon of "mixed development." In other words, the institutionalization of modernity occurs within a specific historical context that conditions the ways in which modernity is formed and expressed in any given society. As previously noted, the concept of "mixed development" is extremely useful in approaching the issues surrounding change in any given society. Mixed development alerts us to the fact that whenever new institutions are introduced into a society or whenever there is an attempt to modify a society's existing institutions the results are likely to be far different from what the ideal type (in Weber's meaning of the term "ideal type") would have us believe is being created in the society in question. Except in extreme circumstances, change seldom can entirely obliterate old institutional routines and practices. Instead, old institutions and their social practices become the substratum and frameworks around which new social structures and institutions are built. As such the older social forms condition the nature of the new and the ways in which changes are expressed in the older institutions. Thus, the nature of the socialism that Romania built, in part, was a function of the nature of the pre-socialist economic and social institutions. Romanian socialism expressed the fact that it emerged from an essentially feudal, agrarian economy and society that had not yet developed into anything resembling a democratic, capitalist society and/or state. In the same vein, I should expect that what is emerging in post-state socialist Romania will and is being conditioned by the form that state socialism took in Romania as it developed from the end of World War II until the end of 1989. For this reason, I should not be disappointed that the form of capitalism and the form of parliamentary democracy Romania institutionalizes may not exactly reproduce the ideal types that theorists have in mind when they discuss such institutional systems and the social practices associated with them.

Before discussing each of the specific issues that have framed our discussion in the various sections of this book, a few general comments are in order. Since 1989, even to the most sympathetic observer, Romania's record in achieving the "promises" of its "revolution" has been less than what many had hoped it would be. But, it should be noted, what Romania has accomplished, in many spheres, has been far more extensive and positive than many of Romania's internal and external critics had believed would be possible, especially given the nature of the political class that emerged as the leading political force following the 1989 "revolution." In its earliest phases, especially in Timisoara, Romania's "revolution" was a popular, mass rebellion. Key political actors drawn from relatively high levels in the communist nomenklatura quickly seized control of the revolution and of post-revolutionary political structures. To many knowledgeable observers of the Romanian scene, this did not seem to auger ill for the country's future, as no one was certain that the new powers that be had any interest in building a democratic, capitalist Romania that was committed to becoming an integral part of a more broadly unified Europe. Much to the chagrin of Romania's harshest critics, this is exactly what happened. The process of transformation of Romania has been slow, occurring in fits and starts, and it has not been smooth. Nonetheless, even the strongest skeptic about Romania and the direction it would take after 1989 has to admit that Romania's post-state socialist leaders, especially those allied with Ion Iliescu and the PDSR, have achieved far more than most would have thought they would.

Geopolitical Position

I began this work by pointing out that one cannot understand much about Romanian history or about current events in Romania without taking into account Romania's geopolitical location. I have seen how Romania's geopolitical location shaped its past. Romanian lands always have been sandwiched between larger and more powerful political entities and have been profoundly affected by the interplay among these political entities as they have contended for hegemony in what they regarded as a highly strategic area. Historically, Romanian lands have stood on the "edge" of Europe, forming part of Europe's "frontier" with Islamic lands. In another sense, however, Romanian lands stood "outside" of the Europe that was forming in the early modern era. The Romanian lands stood as "other" to Europe in two senses. First, the Romanian principalities were vassals of the Ottomans and, second, the Romanian principalities were part of the world of Eastern Christianity. Because of these two facts, the Romanian principalities were seen as part of a larger zone of "backwardness" and "primitiveness" that existed on the fringes of Europe. Romanian lands were seen as places that were geographically of Europe but were not quite fully European in a cultural, political, social, or economic sense. At best, the Romanian lands were seen as a semi-European zone, with strong Oriental characteristics derived from old Byzantium and its Islamic successor Empire. As part of Europe's fringe, the Romanian principalities were seen, rightly or wrongly, as having been left unmarked, to any great extent, by the "great" events and processes that had contributed to the emergence of modern Europe – the Renaissance, the Reformation, the Enlightenment, and the emergence of capitalism and parliamentary democracy. Thus, the lands of the Romanians were not only perceived to be a geographical periphery, but also a political, cultural, social, and economic periphery, the primary importance of which to Eastern Europe was its strategic location and its natural resources, especially its oil deposits. Yet, despite the perception of Romania's relative strategic importance, the Eastern powers did not fight to keep it out of the Soviet sphere of influence that the USSR was building in the wake of World War II.

As World War II was drawing to a close, it was clear to the Eastern powers that the Soviet Union was going to demand that Romania be a part of the Soviet sphere of influence. In October 1944, Churchill and Stalin had agreed to respect each others spheres of influence in the Balkans. Churchill conceded Romania and Bulgaria to Soviet influence in return for Stalin's respecting Britain's preeminent position in Greece. Churchill recognized that Stalin was adamant about the Soviet Union having a dominant position in Bulgaria and Romania. Stalin defined Romania as an "aggressor" state, Romania having joined with the Nazis in invading the USSR in June 1941 and having occupied Soviet territory. Churchill also recognized the strategic concerns and interests the USSR had in the Balkans and he was willing to concede the Soviet's a leading, hegemonic role in Romania and Bulgaria.

President Roosevelt and, later, President Truman were not willing to give the Soviet Union a blank check to dominate Romania. In the Fall 1945, the US Secretary of State, James Byrnes, in advance of a meeting of the victorious Eastern allies, scheduled for Moscow in December 1945, appointed Mark Ethridge, a strong supporter of Roosevelt's New Deal and editor of the Louisville, Kentucky *Courier-Journal*, to head a fact finding commission that would go to Bulgaria and Romania to ascertain what the situations were in both of these countries. The fact-finding commission produced what came to be called the "Ethridge Report." According to the *Ethridge Report,* the USSR had established "front" governments in Bulgaria and Romania. In both cases, these so-called "front" governments were said to be ruling on behalf of the interests of the USSR. Ethridge's commission was concerned that Soviet domination of Romania and Bulgaria would permit the USSR eventually to put military pressure on Greece and Turkey, as well as on other Mediterranean states. Ethridge, and his commission, urged the US to force the Soviet Union to adhere to the Yalta Agreements, which, among other things, required occupying powers to hold free elections to representative bodies, something which Ethridge did not believe would be happening any time soon in Romania and Bulgaria. Ethridge's report fed into Truman's belief that the Soviet's were creating a "prison state" in Romania that was dominated by the Soviet communist party and its allies in Romania (Offner 2002:118).

Byrnes raised the US' objections to what was happening in Romania at the December Moscow meetings. Byrnes tried to pressure the Soviet Foreign Minister, Molotov, to allow for free elections and for broader representation of all political forces in a new post-war Romanian government. Eventually Stalin agreed to allow a "Big Three" delegation to visit Romania and meet with the new government in order to encourage more non-communist representation in the government and to gain a pledge to hold new elections. Those elections were held and the communists and socialists won handily. The West eventually acceded to Soviet hegemony over Romania because the Western powers recognized that they really had no choice in the matter. The Western powers recognized that it would be extremely difficult to try to use military force to keep Romania out of the Soviet sphere of influence, especially in the face of a substantial Soviet military presence in Bulgaria and the rise of a communist government in Yugoslavia. The years from the end of World War II until 1989 served to provide an additional distance between Romania and Western Europe, which the post-state socialist leaders have had to try to overcome, but not with much success. Romania has renounced all territorial claims against its neighbors in the hopes this would end tensions with Russia and the West simultaneously.

One of the most important challenges the post-state socialist governments in Romania have faced is to move Romania from being a peripheral European state into the European core. As I have shown, they have done this by trying to become a part of NATO and of the European Union. They have been more successful in the case of the former than in the case of the later. Romania has helped its case with respect to NATO membership by casting its lot with the United States and by consistently aligning itself with America's geopolitical military agenda. Romania supported the US in the 1991 Gulf War, it joined in the economic boycott of Serbia, supported the US war in Kosovo, became part of the coalition of forces arrayed against the Taliban government and al Qa'eda in Afghanistan, along with Israel was among the first countries to sign an agreement with the United States to exempt its military forces from the international court being set up in the Hague to deal with war crimes, and Romania backed the US war effort in Iraq in 2003. By aligning itself so closely with the United States, Romania was able to secure candidacy for membership in NATO in 2003 and it became a full member in May 2004. However, it is an open question as to how such support of American policies will affect Romania's future access to the EU. Romania's support for exempting the US military from the jurisdiction of the international war crimes court and its endorsement of the US' 2003 invasion of Iraq has not sat Ill with Germany and France, which may complicate Romania' eventual entry into the EU.

Immediately after 1989, Romania was viewed as a poor candidate for membership either in NATO or in the EU. It was among the poorest countries in Europe and the commitment of its military to making the changes necessary for membership in the Eastern military alliance was an unanswered question. Suddenly, however, because of the US' drive to establish hegemony in Central Asia and in the Middle East, Romania has become extremely valuable to the United States. Its value was demonstrated in the 2003 attack on Iraq by the United States and Great Britain. When Turkey opted to not participate in the Iraqi war, Romania became a crucial site for refueling US war planes bombing Iraq. Romania. Romanian officials hope that the US will open military bases in their country, especially an air force base at Mihail Kogălniceanu Airport, just to the north of Black Sea port city of Constanta. The opening of US bases in Romania, so Romanians believe, would be a catalyst for economic development in the regions where they may be located. To further ingratiate itself with the US, Romania pledged to send a military contingent to Iraq to work with forces from Bulgaria, Macedonia FYR, Albania, and the Czech Republic under Polish command. Like Romania all of these countries, with the exception of the Czech Republic that has EU and NATO membership, are hoping to become members of NATO and the EU in the near future. Bulgaria and Romania are expected to achieve EU membership in 2007.

According to an article on July 16th in *The New York Times* (Fisher 2003: A1, A3), even though the leaders of many of the former communist states of Eastern and Central Europe are aligning themselves with the US, they share a common fear:

The fear, which their leaders rarely state in public, is that their deepening military friendship with the United States could jeopardize their economic integration in Europe. Already the war in Iraq and the International Criminal Court, which President Bush opposes joining, have been areas where the United States has pressed its new allies for support against a strong...European position (Fisher 2003: A3).

Fisher writes that Charles A. Kupchan, who worked as a national security advisor in the Clinton administration, believes that Romania and other smaller Eastern and Central European states may be making a mistake by tying their fortunes so tightly to the United States and to NATO. Mr. Kupchan believes that NATO's days are numbered and that the "real gains" for the former communist states in Eastern and Central Europe will come from economic and political integration with the EU and that the leaders of these states should do everything possible to avoid compromising the chances for such integration.

Even before signing the agreement to exempt US troops and government personnel from the international court and before it decided to support US policy in Iraq, Romania already had a number of factors working against EU membership. It's economy is weak, it has high levels of poverty and a low per capita income, it is believed to have levels of corruption that are higher than most other European states, its economy and state are seen to be dominated by the former nomenklatura, and it continues to have a poor reputation for dealing with national minorities inside of its borders. The later is especially important to the EU. One can not help but to believe that Eastern European nations fear that if Romania is given membership in the EU scores of thousands of its Rroma population will migrate West in search of better economic opportunities. This fear, however, is seldom discussed openly in Eastern European deliberations on Romania's status as a candidate for EU membership. Nor is Romania's status as a largely Orthodox country openly discussed. At present, Greece is the only Orthodox state that is part of the EU and the EU has shown little enthusiasm for including additional Orthodox countries in its membership. Historically Eastern Europeans have not been altogether certain that the Orthodox nations are "really" a part of Europe, at least as Western Europeans conceive of Europe. This last point raises the question of Romania's identity in Europe and how Romanians, themselves, conceive of their post-communist identity.

Romanian National Identity

A second major challenge faced by the Romanian post-state socialist governments has been to construct and to maintain a "new" national identity that is "congruent" with Romania's generalized aspiration to become part of an enlarged European political, economic, and cultural community. When the state-socialist regime fell, many external observers of Romanian politics feared for what might come next. They were particularly worried about the danger of a resurgence of "fundamentalist nationalism" that would facilitate the rise, if not the political dominance, of a radical right movement that expressed some form of nationalistic red-brown synthesis. Some credence was given to these fears with the (significantly unsuccessful) attempt to resurrect the Legion of the Archangel St. Michael and with the formation of other nationalist, right-wing parties, two of which were part of the first post-constitutional coalition government put together by the FSN and with the early electoral success of the nationalist right in local elections in and around Cluj-Napoca.

The radical right had its greatest electoral opportunity and its greatest electoral success, as I have shown, in the 2000 national elections for parliament and the president. It did quite well in these elections, capturing a number of seats in both houses of parliament and forcing Ion Iliescu into a second-round of presidential voting against Vadim Tudor, the candidate of the radical right. Iliescu won the run-off handily. Once again observers of and commentators on Romanian politics felt that the votes given to the right-wing signaled a possible return to a form of fundamentalist nationalism that had proven so disastrous to Romania in the past. Throughout earlier sections of this book, I have shown how fundamentalist nationalism has continually bedeviled Romanian politics and how it has contributed to spoiled relations between Romania and several of its immediate neighbors, especially Hungary and the former Soviet Union, and how it culminated in the homicidal maltreatment of minorities, particularly Jews and Rroma, during the fascist period. I also have discussed how Ceausescu used nationalism to garner support for his increasingly repressive and dysfunctional regime. So, there have been good grounds to fear that fundamentalist nationalism continued to exist as an ongoing threat to the emergence of a democratic Romania that adhered to current European standards of human and political rights, particularly the rights of minorities. It also was thought by some commentators that the new national electoral strength of the right might be an indicator of a rejection of Romania's recent attempts to become part of an enlarged European community.

However, while I believe that there are some grounds for concern about the growth of electoral support for the right-wing in recent years in Romania, I also believe that there is a danger in exaggerating what this support might mean for Romania's political future. The radical right was successful in Romania in 2000 because of the confluence of a number of particular events, rather than because of long-term trends that have been unfolding in the country. First, the country had gone through four years of increasingly ineffective government at the hands of the Democratic Convention. So total was the popular rejection of the Democratic Convention that President Emil Constantinescu did not seek a second term and Convention candidates did not receive enough votes to achieve representation in either house of parliament. For all intents and purposes, the failures at governing by the Convention meant the demise of the center-right as a viable political option, leaving only the extreme right or one of the center-left or left parties as a viable electoral option. A vote for the far right under such conditions, essentially, was a vote of no confidence in the center-right and in the center-left and left, none of which had "shown" themselves, at least to a large number of voters, as being particularly effective in governing Romania and introducing the types of political change that large segments of the electorate wanted after the collapse of state socialism. What was especially upsetting to a large number of voters was their perception that the Romanian political elites had created a special type of "soft state," that is a state that was easily penetrated by powerful economic interests usually dominated by members of the former nomenklatura, while, at the same time, creating a "hard state" vis-à-vis the general citizenry. A large number of Romanians felt that the state was not accessible to them and did not represent and/or express their interests, neither when it was under the control of the center-left or the center-right. The Democratic-Convention seemingly was no different from the former governments in reversing this state of affairs where the privileged were able to use their power and influence on their own behalf, rather than on behalf of some more "general" collective good. The far-right was able to capitalize on these perceptions and the political vacuum created by the demise of the center-right to win the support of a large number of voters discontented with the political agendas of both the PDSR and the Democratic Convention.

Second, during the four years of rule by the Democratic Convention, economic conditions for the average Romanian deteriorated substantially. As I have shown, in many respects the Convention's economic policies proved more disastrous to the average Romanian than had those of the PDSR, and its precursor, the FSN. The Convention's presidential candidate, Emil Constantinescu, and its parliamentary candidates had won the 1996 election, in part, by running on an economic platform that promised to end hard times by embracing a neo-liberal economic agenda. In the 1996 elections, the Convention had received the support of a large number of unions and organized workers, who saw the PDSR's economic program as nothing but a pale imitation of what had been in place under the communists and that promised nothing more than many more years of economic decline. Trade unions and their members, as well as workers in general, soon learned that neo-liberalism was making matters even worse for them than they had been under the PDSR. Among the severest economic consequences were increased inflation, enterprises were shut down and unemployment rose, poverty increased, and real wages declined. It did not take workers and their unions long to turn against the neo-liberal economic agenda. Having seen the economic failures of the two major political forces, many workers, especially those under the most threat, were willing to support the left populism of the radical right.

Third, the radical right was popular with certain segments of the electorate because of the radical rights' anti-Eastern, nationalistic, anti-minority rhetoric. Leading up to the 2000 elections, and even before, the two major radical nationalist parties, especially Vadim Tudor's party, had engaged in a harsh anti-Western rhetoric. These parties tried to portray Romania's problems as the fault of Western cultural, economic, and political imperialism and its supporters and advocates inside of Romania. Western culture was portrayed as materialist, decadent, and immoral, and, as such, it was defined as a clear threat to "traditional" Romanian morality and values and to traditional Romanian religion. The radical right valorized the traditional culture of the Romanian peasant and the Romanian village. It was in the peasant village that one could find "authentic" Romanian culture. To the right, the peasant and the village constituted "authentic" Romania, as opposed to the middle classes and the city. The radical right in Romania has been arguing that the real objective of the West is to impose not only an economic subordination on Romania, but, also, to remake Romania culturally, fashioning it into a consumer of Western mass culture and cheap Western consumer goods. By refashioning Romanian culture along Eastern lines, Romanian identity will be destroyed. Romania, culturally, will be reduced to a point of very limited and particularized cultural production while, at the same time, it will function as a node of generalized consumption of Eastern cultural products. While this type of rhetoric did not appeal to the larger mass of cultural consumers in Romania, it did have an attraction to certain strata of Romanian intellectuals and artists, especially to those whose work had only limited circulation in and limited appeal in cultural and intellectual markets outside of Romania either before 1989 or after. Many of such artists and intellectuals had flourished in Romania behind the wall of cultural protectionism that the communists, especially under Ceausescu, had put in place. Opening Romania as a cultural and intellectual market, thus, constituted a possible direct threat to their material well-being and to their symbolic status as successful academics, artists, and/or intellectuals.

That the radical right's anti-Westernism has had little mass appeal is shown in the degree of popular support in Romania for integration into Eastern institutional structures. Surveys have shown that Romanians, to a higher degree than is the case in a number of other Central and East European states, are highly supportive of Romanian integration into European-wide institutional structures (see for example, The European Commission 2001). Eighty per cent of Romanians, the highest per cent of any country identified for possible accession to the EU, support their nation's membership in the EU, while only two per cent oppose such membership (The European Commission 2001: 56). Romanians also have the highest degree of trust in European institutions among the accession countries, with 74% claiming they trust EU institutions (The European Commission 2001: 52). Also, it should be noted, 90% of Romanians felt proud of their European identity, which was the highest level of such sentiment in Europe (The European Commission 2001: 34).

One cannot overestimate the significance of the above findings. A good part of Romania's history has involved an internal struggle over the issue of Romania's national identity and the relation of this identity to Europe, as a whole. In the 19th century, Romanian intellectuals were split over the nature of the nation they were building. One faction, linked to the Generation of 1848, and to those who led the unification and emancipation of Romania from Ottoman suzerainty, saw Romania as a European sate and society. They identified with the values of the Renaissance and the Enlightenment and, within certain limits, such as rejecting mass democracy and the emancipation of the country's Jews, sought to build a state more or less based on these principles. Standing against them were those intellectuals such as Eminescu who saw Romania as standing outside of the sphere of Western culture and its institutional base and as being more a part of the ancient commonwealth of Greek civilization than a part of the West. Until the fascists conquered the state in Romania, the Westernizers had dominated the Romanian state and economy. The Westernizing political and economic elites had made considerable progress over the course of the late 19th century and the early 20th century in expanding political democracy to include peasants and workers as part of the electorate, had begun to lay down a capitalist economic infrastructure, and, in general, raising the standard of living in Romania's cities and towns.

However, their principal failure, which proved to be their undoing, was their inability/unwillingness to modernize – economically, culturally, and politically – the countryside. The Romanian countryside, both in the rural villages and the small towns and cities, proved to be a fertile ground for the growth of Romanian fascism. This is not to say that fascism was exclusively a rural social movement in Romania, because it was not. Fascism, as I have discussed earlier, also had a strong urban component where it was especially appealing to specific strata of conservative Romanian intellectuals and students. Romanian fascism, in part, was built around a rejection of the "West" and for all that it was believed to stand. Fascist ideologues, drawing on a long running stream of Romanian intellectual conservatism, as well as introducing new and more radical elements, portrayed Eastern values and institutions as totally and fundamentally "other" to Romanian history and to the then contemporary Romanian culture. Western values and institutions were blamed for Romania's economic collapse during the Great Depression and for Romanian political and social fragmentation, conflict, and general social and political paralysis.

In many respects, the communists, especially under Ceausescu, continued Romania's turn away from the West, albeit in far different terms than that of the fascists. The communists integrated Romania into a Bolshevik interstate system that stood opposed to the institutions of the West. Under the communists, the "West" continued to be the "other" over and against which Romanian national identity was built and sustained from the end of World War II until 1989. Romania, after all, was part of *the* Balkans, a region Western and, even, Eastern and Central Europeans looked down on as mysterious, violent, chaotic, and somewhat depraved.

The generalized political support that Romanians now are giving to integration into the West indicates that Romanians no longer are seeing themselves and their national destiny as standing apart from the West's. There is very little popular support for Romania trying to make a go of it economically, socially, culturally, or politically on its own or to return to close ties with Russia and its allies in the Commonwealth of Independent States.

Romanians have returned to the dream of the founders of the Romanian state in the 19th century, who saw Romania's future as inextricably tied to Europe. The builders of the post-communist state realize this and have supported those who have tried to build a new way of understanding Romanian national identity – an understanding that rejects a retreat into neo-Romantic and fascist excesses and that sees Romania's "essence" as lying in the country's integration into pan-European institutional structures. While Romanians may strongly support integration into the institutional structures of a united Europe, it is not altogether clear that the elites of Eastern Europe unambiguously support the same objective for Romania. There are a number of factors, from the perspective of Western Europeans that work against Romania in its drive to become part of an enlarged European community. While Europeans clearly recognize that Romania has a geopolitical, strategic value for Europe as a whole, they are less certain of Romania's value to Europe on a number of other fronts. Nor have Europeans been convinced that Romania's transformation after 1989 has been extensive and intensive enough to warrant membership in a united Europe. Romania's entry into the EU has been delayed until 2007 when it will join Europe, along with Bulgaria.

Europeans have been ambivalent about Romania's identity as a European country. Romania always has had to contend with the fact that, for many Europeans, Romania generally has not been perceived to be a part of the "essential" Europe. Instead, Romania has been seen as an indeterminate entity, a place that is *in* Europe but not really *of* Europe. As such, its historical role has been to be a boundary and a buffer zone between Europe and the "Orient." As such, many Eastern Europeans see Romania as "incompletely" European or as a semi-formed European zone: a place that has not been strongly influenced by the great cultural shifts such as the Reformation and the Enlightenment that have defined modern "European civilization." Because of its perceived semi-Oriental character many Europeans do not trust the extent and depth of change Romania has undergone since 1989. A good example of this is found in an article written for *The Guardian* in 1993 by Bryan Jones. Jones, in commenting on Romania's political transformation, echoed Eminescu and subsequent generations of Romanian nationalists, when he, Jones, wrote:

> Ceausescu's shadows, real or imagined, are still in evidence. There are those indeed who say that many of the trappings and para-phernalia of parliamentary democracy, so painfully adopted by Romania since the overthrow of Ceausescu, are themselves mere phantoms or shapes 'mimicking' Eastern-style democracy without real conviction or substance (Jones June 7, 1993: 18).

This quote pretty much summarizes Europe's view of what has been happening in Romania. Europeans perceive that change in Romania has been change in institutional forms without changes in institutional substance. Underlying this quote is the idea that Romania, because of its history and its "culture," somehow, is unable to be a truly European society but, at best, merely can ape "European" institutional forms. Europeans see Romania to be "condemned" by its Ottoman legacy and, later, by its attachment to the Bolshevik interstate system to the social periphery of Europe. Romania is perceived as part of a "captured" part of Europe that is incapable of "reform" on its own. Its capture by the Ottomans and, later, the communists, is seen to have led to economic backwardness and its people are viewed as violent and licentious, its institutions inherently corrupt, and its politics are viewed as fractionalized, uncivil, and marked by conspiratorial intrigues. Only with Western assistance and control, it is thought, can Romania be "brought back" into the European fold, but this, according to Western, cannot take place immediately. Indeed, from the European point of view, it may take a generation, or more, before Romania "truly" can be considered "European" and not a peripheral buffer region between Europe and the Orient, whose importance to Europe is its strategic location, its natural resources, and its large supply of skilled and very cheap labor. Thus, it might be said that while Romanians in the post-state socialist period have opted for a European identity, Europe has not opted for a complete inclusion of Romania into its institutional system. The core states of the European Union simply do not trust the extent and the depth of the commitment Romania has made to redefine its national identity and its aspirations to become a full and equal participant in a united Europe. They worry about perceived corruption and the continuing dominant role the nomenklatura and its various remnants play in the state and in the economy.

Economic and Political Transformation

As I have noted in previous sections of the book, another significant problem Romania has faced is that it has been slow to institutionalize a capitalist economic system prior to the communist conquest of the Romanian state after World War II. Its economy remained heavily feudal and heavily agrarian until the communists took power and launched a program of rapid industrialization and defeudalization. When the communists took power following World War II, capitalism existed as a thin veneer covering only a limited surface of Romania's economic life. Capitalism in Romania was not a deeply entrenched system of economic relations and economic practices. The Romanian bourgeoisie, such as it was, had never succeeded in turning Romania into a fully developed capitalist state over which they exercised the role of a ruling class. Feudal agrarian economic relations remained strong in the countryside and the boyars remained a powerful force in Romanian politics, even if their political role was substantially reduced from what it had been in the

19th and early 20th centuries when they had exercised direct class rule in Romania.

The segments of the boyar class, who rose to power in the late 19th and early 20th century were faced with enormous challenges. Like elsewhere in Eastern and Central Europe they saw themselves as a *Bildungsburgertum*. In other words they saw their main functions as involving the creation of a "democratic" Romanian parliamentary political system and state, a capitalist economy in which the state would play a key role not only in capital accumulation and investment but also in forming and maintaining a bourgeois capitalist class, and the social and cultural modernization of the nation along Eastern European lines.

While, by the end of World War II, modern forms of capitalism dominated the production and accumulation of value in Romania's larger cities, elsewhere in Romania this form of capitalism was marginal to economic life and the Romanian bourgeoisie was virtually absent except in the largest cities and it had lost its direct political power to an alliance of the monarchy, the fascists, and the generals. Between the wars, at least to the Romanian masses, the bourgeoisie had failed in leading the Romanian state and nation. To the Romanian masses, the bourgeoisie had brought political fragmentation and stagnation. The bourgeoisie's attempt to develop capitalism had been an abysmal failure. Moreover, to many Romanians the bourgeoisie had failed the nation by importing corrupt forms of modernity that threatened traditional Romanian culture, values, and social practices. In essence, by the end of World War II, a substantial segment of Romania's population had concluded that their national bourgeoisie had failed to function as an effective *Bildungsburgertum*.

The monarchical, fascist, military alliance's political defeat of the bourgeoisie in the 1930s proved to be fatal. It left the bourgeoisie unable to defend itself when, after the Second World War, the socialists and the communists, with the assistance of the Soviet Union and the passive acquiescence of the Eastern powers, made their move to seize power in Romania. The communists and socialists found it relatively easy to deal crushing blows to the Romanian bourgeoisie, blows from which the bourgeoisie never recovered.

When the communists and their socialist allies took power in Romania, they faced the immediate tasks of building a state socialist economy, polity, and society, while, at the same time, building a modern industrial and agricultural proletariat in whose name and interests they, the socialists and communists would rule. The communists and the socialists had a relatively free hand to implement their various agendas. While they did face some armed resistance from peasants in selected rural areas who resisted agricultural collectivization and from some stalwarts and members of the old regime, the new authorities proved effective at keeping the resistance isolated and under control until, eventually, it could be defeated. Capitalism crumbled quickly and without much direct resistance in the cities.

With the relatively quick and easy defeat of the already weakened bourgeoisie the communists, having absorbed and subordinated the socialists to the communist political agenda, had a relatively free hand to implement their program for modernizing Romania. They would not find many Romanians who were willing to fight to defend the capitalists. Romanian popular opinion had a long history of suspicion towards and distrust of capitalist economic activity. Among other things, Romanians, even before the advent of state socialism, stigmatized capitalism, especially merchant capitalism, as inherently exploitative, parasitic, and divisive. Despite what one might think about the repressive aspects of state socialism in Romania, especially under Ceausescu, one must admit that the communists brought a number of undeniable economic and social benefits to the Romanian people. Under the communists, the Romanian educational system expanded dramatically. The communists created educational opportunities for all social strata, including the poorest peasants and workers. In turn the expansion of educational opportunities created pathways for occupational mobility for thousands of children of the peasantry and the working classes. The communists also raised the quality and amount of housing both in Romanian cities and the countryside. They also improved health care for women and children, especially in the villages. Under the communists women made significant educational and occupational advances and, until outlawed by Ceausescu, were granted abortion rights they hitherto had not had. Divorce laws also were liberalized, which benefited women until Ceausescu imposed stricter laws governing divorces. The elderly were guaranteed adequate pensions under the communists. The communists expanded adult literacy and provided extensive support for the arts. They also attempted to equalize development throughout the country, although their success in this endeavor was limited. Finally, the communists achieved a society with a high degree of job security and income equality. However, what they could not do in Romania was sustain a level of economic growth to match that of the West and they could not manage to build an economy marked by a superabundance of consumer goods. These failures proved to be two of the major internal economic causes of the Romanian state socialist regime's defeat.

The capitalism that has been in the process of being built in Romania since 1989, in some respects, represents an historical economic reversal on several fronts. For the first time in more than a generation, large numbers of Romanians have become truly impoverished as a result of the dismantling of socialism and the attempt to implant capitalism. And economic and social inequality has increased dramatically.

With the collapse of state socialism, Romania's political elites, once again, faced the challenge of building a capitalist economy in the absence of an effective national bourgeoisie. Thus, after 1989, the Romanian political elites had to function, once again, as a *Bildungsburgertum*. The political elites were forced to redesign the Romanian state, lay the foundation for a parliamentary democracy, and create the legal and institutional conditions for the emergence of a Western form of capitalism. So, once again, capitalism was being constructed by the state in the absence of an economically effective and/or politically effective bourgeoisie.

This was/is an extremely difficult challenge to Romanian governments and to the Romanian state. First of all Romania lacked anything resembling a classical bourgeoisie. With the collapse of state socialism and the decision of the provisional government had to develop a capitalist economy, the new state and those who controlled it needed to provide the functional and institutional conditions for the emergence of a new bourgeoisie. This new bourgeoisie had to be built out of the wreckage of the former nomenklatura. Romania had no alternative but to rely on what was left of the nomenklatura and enterprise managers to take control of the economy and move it in the direction of establishing a capitalist, market economy.

In the aftermath of the collapse of state socialism, at least two major social groupings, mainly drawn from the former nomenklatura, were trying to position themselves to take on the roles and functions of a national bourgeoisie. These groupings were drawn from different strata and different sectors of the nomenklatura. The first of these groups emerged from the networks of local and national alliances among party-state officials, functionaries, and economic and political managers. Arrayed against them was a fraction of the nomenklatura that had its base in the liberal professions, the arts, and in intellectual occupations, including some technical occupations. Each of these groupings had their own, relatively distinct ideas about the nature and the form of the capitalism that they wanted to see built in Romania.

The first grouping, politically organized in and around the FSN and, later its successor, the PDSR, initially had the upper hand. In the anarchy following the collapse of the Ceausescu regime, the members of this first group were ill positioned to simply seize managerial control (but not necessarily ownership) of most major economic assets. Their ties to major state institutions and political actors have enabled them to benefit from the various privatization initiatives put in place and have allowed them to maintain those structural conditions favorable to their emergence and perpetuation as the dominant owning and/or managerial class in Romania.

This dominant ownership group has come to form itself into a relatively small national-level economic elite that lives, dies, and is buried in opulence. In looking at their social, political, and economic characteristics, it should be noted that few of them have any direct connections with the pre-communist economic elites that ruled Romania, so that their presence in Romanian life does not constitute a restoration of the scions of the old families that once had dominated virtually all aspects of Romanian life. This new elite has been drawn from a wide variety of backgrounds. Even those who were members of the old nomenklatura have widely different social origins, with some having come from peasant and worker families and having benefited from the mobility policies of the communist regime. The lack of common social origins seriously impedes the economic elite's ability to form itself into a national bourgeoisie.

This group is largely composed of former members of the nomenklatura who were able to profit from the ways in which privatization took place after 1989 or who were able to take advantage of the linkages their former positions in the party-state structure to build profitable businesses, a small number of persons who had access to foreign capital to start new enterprises, a small number of entrepreneurs and professionals who managed to develop businesses that became highly profitable in Romania's new economic climate, an unknown number of people who built fortunes out of illegal activities of various sorts, and the top echelons of the national political directorate. The elite, as seen above, are a disparate lot and can not really be described as a bourgeoisie in the Western sense of that term. Even more so than their counterparts in the late 19th and early 20th centuries, they seem to be more of a proto-bourgeoisie than an actual bourgeoisie. Not only do their disparate origins impede their class formation, but so, too, does their lack of a common mode of existence, a common culture, and a common associational network that brings them together on a regular basis. However, what they do have in common, and that which eventually will provide the foundation for constituting themselves as a bourgeoisie, is a economic interest in constructing and sustaining a society that recognizes the sanctity of private property and the right to profits from ownership of property. Politically, the proto-bourgeoisie, as of yet, has not constructed its own party to pursue its own, distinctive economic and political interests. It continues to be "represented" in the state by the PDSR. In the long run, however, this is untenable, as the PDSR also claims to represent Romanian workers and peasants. At some point these claims on the PDSR are going to clash in fundamental ways and the proto-bourgeoisie will be faced with finding or building a new party to represent their emerging class interests and to present these interests as the universal interests of all Romanians or the workers and peasants will have to leave the PDSR as it abandons its identity as a party of social democracy.

At present, however, PDSR still manages to claim the mantle of representing the interests of private capital, state capital, and workers and peasants in a grand synthesis expressing the general interest and general will of all Romanians. But, one wonders how long it will be able to do so? PDSR's self portrayal as the most general representation of Romanians' interests was successfully challenged by the DCR in 2000 and if the Democratic Convention had not been so internally fractured and beset with conflicts and had it not bee so inept it might have been able to consolidate itself as a viable political alternative to the PDSR. As capital consolidates itself and as the proto-bourgeoisie becomes more and more a "true" and "proper" bourgeoisie, it is doubtful that PDSR will be able to continue to present itself as the party of the bourgeoisie and of workers and peasants.

It also is doubtful that any party will be able to anchor capitalism in Romania in the near term. Establishing capitalism and transforming social relations to be consistent with and supportive of a capitalist economy has been no easy matter for Romania. Romania, like all of Central and Eastern Europe, has faced the task of building a capitalist state and a capitalist economy from what amounts to a post-capitalist political and economic regime. European history, until 1989, had involved the emergence of capitalist social formations from decomposing feudal systems. So, in a sense, what I are seeing is an historical reversal for those who have long seen socialism, even in its statist form, as a system of reform that curtailed some of the worst economic and social abuses of unbridled capitalism. In none of the areas that have been dismantling state socialism and especially in countries like Romania, has bourgeois capitalism been a part of the taken for granted reality of economic life, except in the most developed urban areas.

In the United States, until at least the Great Depression and the "New Deal" put in place by the administration of Franklin D. Roosevelt, capitalism and the social relations, including capitalist individualism, that sustained it was produced and reproduced by the work routines and by the systems of exchange in and on factories and farms and modes of commodity circulation (Gramsci 1971). Until the economic crisis of the 1930s, there is every reason to believe that capitalism had the character of another "nature." Only with the crisis of the Great Depression did capitalism and the social relations and forms of individualism that sustained it lose their self-evident natural character and require massive state intervention to stabilize them. In Europe, as a whole, and in Eastern and Central Europe, capitalism had never acquired such a "natural" quality. It never was a second nature that was seen to be a structural inevitability that functioned at its "best" when it was only minimally regulated and/or controlled by the state.

Romanian Agriculture and the Romanian Countryside
The boyars never had been interested in reforming the relations of production in the Romanian countryside. They saw the peasantry as a class to be plundered for the well-being of the boyar class. The same

held true for the large-scale capitalist farmers. The communists followed the same path, using various strategies of primitive communist accumulation, the peasantry was brutally exploited in order to fund the urban and industrial development as well as projects that fed the leaders megalomania. Thus, Romania existed and continues to exist in a state of highly uneven development. Its major cities were emerging as centers of capitalism in the late 19th to mid-20th century, while Romania's small cities, towns, and rural areas lagged substantially behind the major cities. Especially problematic for Romania was the inability to resolve the problem of the countryside. The vast majority of the rural peasantry was landless and impoverished from the formation of the Romanian state until the communist seizure of power. Neither under the rule of the boyars nor under those who replaced them was the situation of the peasantry resolved. The problem of the peasantry and the countryside also proved intractable to the communists. While communist rule certainly had positive effects on the peasantry, the communists raised rural income, education, and health levels in the countryside; they were not able to eliminate rural-urban and regional differences in the overall quality of life.

Uneven development between urban and rural areas and between regions continues to be a problem in contemporary post-state socialist Romania. Poverty continues to be substantially higher in rural areas than it is in urban areas in Romania (United Nations Development Report 2003: 112). Rural areas lag behind urban areas in life expectancy, in infant mortality, in health care, and in living space, among other things (United Nations Development Report 2003: 117). There have been sharp differences between regions in Romania that have persisted, if not increased, as well, since the fall of state socialism. For example, The United Nations has reported that the Romanian 1999 Gross Domestic Product (GDP) per inhabitant at purchase power parity (USD) stood at $5,441 and its average Human Development Index score is .759 (United Nations Human Development Report 2003, 121). The North-East region, made up of the following *judets*: Bacau, Botosani, Iasi, Neamt, Suceava, and Vaslui, has a per capita GDP of $3,891 (United Nations Development Report 2003: 121), which is the lowest of any of the regions. This region also had the lowest Human Development Index score (.738) if any of Romania's regions. The next lowest region, in terms of per capita GDP, is the South, which is made up of the *judets* of Arges, Calarasi, Dambovita, Giurgu, Iolomita, Prahova, and Teleorman. The South's per capita GDP is $4,717. Its Human Development Index score is .740, which also is the second lowest of any of Romania's regions. The North-West has the third lowest GDP per capita in Romania, standing at $4,750 and the North-West has the third lowest Human Development Index score (.747). The *judets* making up the North-West are Bihor, Bistrita-Nasaud, Cluj, Maramures, Satu Mare, and Salad. The next lowest per capita GDP is in the South-West, which is made up of the following *judets*: Dolj, Gorj, Mehedinti, Olt, and Valcea. The South-West's per capita GDP is $4,957 and its Human Development Index score is .748. The final region that falls below the Romanian national GDP per capita average is the South-East, consisting of Brailia, Buzau, Constanta, Galati, Tulcea, and Vrancea *judets*. The per capita GDP in the South-East is $5,299 and its Human Development Index score is .752. Three of Romania's eight regions have higher per capita GDP scores and Human Development Index scores. These are the Center, made up of the following *judets*: Alba, Brasov, Covasna, Harghita, Mures, and Sibiu; the West, which consists of the *judets* of Arad, Caras-Severin, Hunedoara, and Timis; and Bucharest. The Center has a per capita GDP of $5,497 and a Human Development Index score of .762; the West's per capita GDP is $5,621 and its Human Development Index score is .763; and Bucharest's per capita GDP is the largest in Romania, standing at $10,452, and its Human Development Index score is .831 (United Nations Development Report 2003: 121). From these data one can see marked differences in regional economic and human development. All of the Romanian regions with low income also are characterized by high levels of unemployment, reflecting the withdrawal of capital from the regions as state sector industries are being shut down and private investment is not being made to replace former state investments in economic development.

By and large, the policies pursued by successive Romanian governments in the post-socialist period have done very little to diminish these regional differences and may, instead, have acted to increase them, to the long range detriment of the country. Certainly much needs to be done in the way of developing more balanced policies that will make for greater regional equality. Given the great disparity between Bucharest and the rest of the country, Romania seems to have returned to a pattern of regional inequality that prevailed from the 18th through the mid-20th century. All of the Romanian regions with low income also are characterized by high levels of unemployment, reflecting the withdrawal of capital from the regions as state sector industries are being shut down and private investment is not being made to replace former state investments in economic development.

In addition to regional and to rural-urban differences in economic well-being, the economic policies pursued by successive governments, including those claiming to be social democratic governments, there has been sharp increases in economic and social inequality in Romania, which have not been effectively addressed by the state, regardless of the government in power. A number of factors have contributed to the increase in poverty. One factor, certainly, is increased unemployment. However, with the generalized collapse of Romanian wage rates there has emerged a large stratum of working poor, made up of households, and individuals, in which adults are employed full-time but whose total incomes are not enough to raise them out of poverty. When the communist regime fell, it has been estimated that only 7% of the Romanian population was in poverty (United Nations Human Development Report 2003: 63). By 1994 the proportion of the Romanian population living in poverty increased to somewhere between 22% and 39% (United Nations Human Development Report 2003: 63). Poverty increased further between 1997 and 2000, partly as a result of the draconian neo-liberal economic policies of the Democratic Convention. By 2000, it was estimated that 42% of the population was in poverty and extreme poverty had doubled in size (United Nations Human Development Report 2003: 63). Large proportions of the Romanian population were unable to afford foods necessary for a healthy, balanced diet.

The implanting of capitalism in Romania has produced a dramatic increase in economic inequality that is reflected almost everywhere you look, especially in urban areas. It is not difficult to spot expensive Western European and American cars, new villas being constructed, men and women dressed in fashionable Western designer clothes, and children especially well turned out in the latest and most expensive fashions. The new wealthy seem to especially enjoy the most crass forms of conspicuous consumption. They have even begun to bury their own kind in elaborate mausoleums in formerly (pre-war) fashionable cemeteries as if to declare there is no equality even in death.

Beneath the national economic elite and closely resembling it in its origins are the networks of localized elites who dominate the extraction of value from a *judet* or a combination of *judets*. As the national economic elite do not constitute a national bourgeoisie, these local elites do not constitute local bourgeoisies. Instead what exists are serialized relations among networks of entrepreneurs and political officials, some drawn from the more unsavory characters of the old regime, who function as structural entrepreneurs whose aim is to create conditions of plunder for themselves, with the long range belief that matters will be straightened out when Romania eventually joins Europe. In the meantime, they are trying to accumulate as much as they can before becoming subject to European regulation and legislation and experiencing even more pressures to embrace political, social, and economic modernity.

References

Abrudan, P. 1990. *Sibiul si revolutia din deciembre 1989.* Sibiu: Casa Armatei.

Adeverul, December 21, 1999, pp. 2-3. Cited in Dennis Deletant (1999b), *Romania under Communist Rule.* Iasi: The Center for Romanian Studies and the Civic Academy Foundation, p. 163.

Agence France Presse. 1993. *Demonstration Against Corruption in Bucharest.* September 14, 1993.

_____. 1993. *Corruption Row Splits Writers' Union.* October 8, 1993.

_____. 1993, *Trade Unions Organize Demonstrations in Romania.* November 29, 1993.

Aronowitz, Stanley. 1983. *Working Class Hero: A New Strategy for Labor.* New York: Adama Books.

Ascherson, Neal. 1995. *Black Sea.* Hill and Wang.

Aspinall, D. 1984. "Romania: Queues and Personality Cults." *Soviet Analyst* (May 16), p. 4. Quoted in Dennis Deletant (1999b), *Romania under Communist Rule.* Iasi: The Center for Romanian Studies and the Civic Academy Foundation, p. 145.

Associated Press. 1999. *Media Watchdog: Romanian Attacks Up.* September 30, 1999.

Bar-Avi, Israel. 1966. *O istorie a evreilor romani,* v. 3. Jerusalem. Cited in Robert Levy (2001), *Ana Pauker: The Rise and Fall of a Jewish Communist.* Berkeley, CA: University of California Press.

Barber, Toni. 1993. "Poverty Sours Romanian Anniversary." *The Independent* (London), Section: European News, p. 8 (December 22, 1993).

Barbu, D. 1958. "Destinul colectiv, servitutea involuntara, nefericia totalitara: tres mitui ale comunismului romanesc." *Miturile Comunismal Romanesc.* Ed. L. Boia. Bucharest: Nemira, 175-197.

Badescu, Ile. 1997. "Frontiera kominernului: Dizedenta si rezistenta." *Noua Revista Romana,* no. 5-6 (May June), 28-34.

Badescu, Ile; Abraham, Dorel. 1993. "Empirical Ethnomorphology: The Ethnic Groups Cohabitating Territory in Romania." *Interethnic Relations in Romania: Sociological Diagnoses and Evaluation of Tendencies.* Ed. Dorel Abraham, Septimu Chelcea, and Ile Badescu. Cluj-Napoca: Editure Carpatica.

Bartosek, Karel. 1999. "Central and Eastern Europe." *The Black Book of Communism.* Ed. Stephania Courtois et al. Trans: Jonathan Murphy and Mark Kramer. Cambridge, MA: Harvard University Press, pp. 394-456.

Becker, Howard. 1963. *Outsiders.* Glencoe, IL: Free Press.

Ben-Rafael. 1996. "Multiculturalism in Sociological Perspective." *The Challenge of Diversity: Integration and Pluralism in Societies of Immigration.* Ed. Rainer Baubock, Agnes Heller, and Aristide R. Zolberg. Vienna: European Center, 133-154.

Blaga, Lucian. 1980 [1937]. "Elogiul satalui roamanesc." *Discursuri de receptie in Academia Romana,* pp. 250-262. Bucharest: Ed. Albatros. Cited in Katherine Verdery (1991), *National Ideology Under Socialism: Identity and Cultural Politics in Ceausescu's Romania.* Berkeley: University of California Press.

Blauner, Robert. 1969. "Internal Colonialism and Ghetto Revolt." *Social Problems* 16: 398-408.

_____. 1972. *Racial Oppression in America.* New York: Harper and Row.

Bourdieu, Pierre. {1983} 1986. "The Forms of Capital." *Handbook of Theory and Research for the Sociology of Education.* Ed. John G. Richardson. New York: Greenwood Press, pp. 241-258.

Bossy, Raoul. 1955. "Religious Persecution in Captive Romania." *Journal of Central European Affairs,* 15: 2 (July), pp. 161-181.

Branson, Louise. 1993. "Romania Faces a Hard Reality." *Sunday Times* (London), Section: Overseas News, November 7, 1993.

Braudel, Fernand. 1979. *Civilization and Capitalism, 15th-18th Century.* Volume III: *The Perspective of the World.* Trans: Sian Reynold. New York: Harper and Row.

Brucan, Silviu. 1993. *The Wasted Generation: Memoirs of the Romanian Journey from Capitalism to Socialism and Back.* Boulder, CO: Westview Press.

British Broadcasting Corporation. 1993. "Vocaroiu Outlines Immediate Priorities for First Few Months of 1993." *BBC Summary of World Broadcasts*: Romania: EE/1557/B (January 1, 1993). Source: Rompres (Romanian Press Agency, December 30, 1992).

_____. 1993. "Hunedoara Steelworkers Rally to Demand "Equitable Price-Salary Ratio." *BBC Summary of World Broadcasts*: Romania: EE/1622/B (February 25, 1993). Source: Rompres (Romanian Press Agency, February 23, 1993).

_____. 1993. "Vacaroiu Defends Cuts in Subsidies as "Absolutely Necessary" to Defeat Corruption." *BBC Summary of World Broadcasts*: Romania: EE/1663/B (April 15 1993). Source: Rompres (Romanian Press Agency, April 13, 1993).

_____. 1993. "Poll Finds Half of Romanians Satisfied With Life After 1989 Revolution." *BBC Summary of World Broadcasts*: Romania: EE/1671/B (April 24 1993). Source: Rompres (Romanian Press Agency, April 20, 1993).

_____. 1993. "Press Stops Coverage of Government Activities as "No-Confidence Vote." *BBC Summary of World Broadcasts*: Romania: EE/1743/B (July 17, 1993). Source: Rompres (Romanian Press Agency, July 14, 1993).

_____. 1993. "Police Chief Blames Events Abroad for Rising Crime." *BBC Summary of World Broadcasts*: Romania: EE/1753/B (July 29, 1993). Source: Rompres (Romanian Press Agency, July 27, 1993).

_____. 1993. "Trade Union March in Bucharest an "Ultimatum for Government." *BBC Summary of World Broadcasts:* Romania: EE/1851/B (November 20, 1993). Source: Rompres (Romanian Press Agency, November 18, 1993).

_____. 1993. "Constantinescu Explains Reasons for DCR's Censure Motion." *BBC Summary of World Broadcasts:* Romania: EE/B (December 9, 1993). Source: Rompres (Romanian Press Agency, December 7, 1993).

_____. 1993. "Trade Union and HDUR Rally in Timisoara Calls for New Government." *BBC Summary of World Broadcasts:* Romania: EE/1875/B (December 18, 1993). Source: Rompres (Romanian Press Agency, December 16, 1993).

_____. 1993. "Police Chief Gives Details of "Spectacular Rise" in Crime Rates." *BBC Summary of World Broadcasts:* Romania: EE/1795/B (September 16, 1993). Source: Rompres (Romanian Press Agency, September 13, 1993).

_____. 1994. "Premier on Appointment of New Defense and Interior Ministers." *BBC Summary of World Broadcasts:* Romania: EE/1950/B (March 19, 1993). Source: Rompres (Romanian Press Agency, March 17, 1993).

_____. 1994. "DCR President Views Democratic Convention Priorities." *BBC Summary of World Broadcasts:* Romania: EE/2085/B (August 27, 1994). Source: "The Old Structures Have Not Yet Been Dismantled," interview of Constantinescu by Ileana Lucaciu. *Expres Magazine* (Bucharest), August 24, 1994.

British Broadcasting Corporation. 1995. "Official Says Crime Rate was Relatively Stable in Romania Last Year." *BBC Summary of World Broadcasts:* Romania: EE/2204/B (January 18, 1995). Source: Rompres (Romanian Press Agency, January 16, 1995).

_____. 1995. "Premier Presents Economic Goals at Prefects' Meetings." *BBC Summary of World Broadcasts.* Romania: EE/2243/B (March 4, 1995). Source: Rompres (Romanian Press Agency, March 2, 1995).

Brown, Adam, 1997. "Asian-Pacific and Emerging Markets – Romanian Brokers Corner Rights to Some Debt Sales." *The Wall Street Journal Europe.* Brussels, September 3, 1997, p. 20.

Bugajski, Janusz. 1995. *Ethnic Politics in Eastern Europe: A Guide to Nationality Policies, Organizations and Parties.* 2nd edition. London: M.E. Sharpe.

Bush, L. S. 1993. "Collective Labor Disputes in post-Ceausescu Romania." *Cornell International Law Journal* 26:2 (spring): 373-420.

Butmaru, I. 1992. *The Silent Holocaust: Romania and Its Jews.* New York: Greenwood Press.

Carmichael, Stokely; Hamilton, C. V. 1976. *Black Power: The Politics of Liberation in America.* New York: Vintage.

Carroll, James. 2001. *Constantine's Sword: The Church and the Jews.* Boston, MA: Houghton-Mifflin.

Catanus, D.; Neascu, G. 1989. "Componenta P.C.R. in perioda 1945-1970: Evaluari statistice." *Archivele Totalitarismului,* no. 4, pp. 25-44.

Clark, Kenneth H. 1965. *Dark Ghetto.* New York: Harper and Row.

Cockerham, William C. 1999. *Health and Social Change in Russia and Eastern Europe.* London: Routledge.

Codreanu, Corneliu Zelea. 1937. *Pentru Legionuri.* Bucharest: Totul Pentru Tara, pp. 385-387, 396-398. Translated and reprinted in Stephen Fischer-Galati, ed. (1970), *Man, State, and Society in East European History.* New York: Praeger.

Cohen, Stephen F. 2000. *Failed Crusade: America and the Tragedy of Post-Communist Russia.* New York: W.W. Norton and Company.

Cox, Oliver Cromwell. 1948. *Caste, Class, and Race.* New York: Doubleday.

Craniac, Nichifor. 1929. "Sensul traditiei." *Gandirea* 9: 1-11.

_____. 1936. *Puncte cardinale in haos.* Bucharest: Ed. Cugeterea.

Crowther, William. 1998. "Romania." *Eastern Europe: Politics, Culture, and Society Since 1939.* Ed. Sabrina P. Ramet. Indianapolis: Indiana University Press, pp. 190-223.

Deletant, Dennis. 1999a. *Communist Terror in Romania: Gheoghiu-Dej and the Police State, 1948-1965.* New York: St. Martin's Press.

_____. 1999b. *Romania under Communist Rule.* Iasi: The Center for Romanian Studies and the Civic Academy Foundation.

Djilas, Milovan. 1982. *The New Class: An Analysis of the Communist System.* New York: Harvest Books.

Durkheim, Emile. 1947. *The Division of Labor in Society.* New York: The Free Press

Eliade, Mircea. 1934. "Citeva cuvinte mari." *Vremea* (Bucharest), June 10, 1934. Cited in Norman Manea (1992), *On Clowns: The Dictator and the Artist.* New York: Grove Weidenfeld, p. 109.

_____. 1937. "Democratia si problema Romaniei." *Vremea* (Bucharest), December 18, 1937. Cited in Norman Manea (1992), *On Clowns: The Dictator and the Artist.* New York: Grove Weidenfeld, p. 109.

Eliade, Mircea. 1938. "Noua aristocratie legionara." *Vremea* (Bucharest), January 23, 1938. Cited in Norman Manea (1992), *On Clowns: The Dictator and the Artist.* New York: Grove Weidenfeld, p. 109.

EU Business. 1994. "Millionaire businessman Calin Tariceanu – Romania's new prime minister." London: EU Business Ltd.

European Commission, The. 2001. "Candidate Countries Eurobarometer 2001." Brussels: The European Commission.

Eyal, Gil; Szelenyi, Ivan; Townsley, Eleanor. 1998. *Making Capitalism Without Capitalists: The New Ruling Elites in Eastern Europe.* London: Verso.

Ferguson, Niall. 2001. *The Cash Nexus: Money and Power in the Modern World, 1700-2000.* New York: Basic Books.

Fernbach, David, ed. 1974. *Karl Marx: Surveys from Exile, Political Writings*, Volume II, first American edition. New York: Random House.

Filotti, Eugen. 1924. "Gandul nostru." *Cuvantul liber* (ser. II) 1: 2-4. Cited in Katherine Verdery (1991), *National Ideology Under Socialism: Identity and Cultural Politics in Ceausescu's Romania.* Berkeley, CA: University of California Press.

Fischer, Mary Ellen. 1995. "Women in Romanian Politics." *Women, State, and Party in Eastern Europe.* Ed. Sharon L. Wolchik and Alfred G. Meyer. Durham, NC: University of North Carolina Press.

Fischer-Galati, Stephen. 1998a. *"The Interwar Period: Greater Romania." Romania: A Historic Perspective.* Ed. Dinu C. Giurescu and Stephen Fisher-Galati. Boulder: East European Monographs.

_____. 1998b. "Romania under Communism: From People's Republic to Socialist Republic (1948-1965)." *Romania: A Historic Perspective.* Ed. Dinu C. Giurescu and Stephen Fisher-Galati. Boulder: East European Monographs.

_____. 1998c. "Romania under Communism: The Golden Age of Ceausescu." *Romania: A Historic Perspective.* Ed. Dinu C. Giurescu and Stephen Fisher-Galati. Boulder: East European Monographs.

Fisher, Ian. 2003. "U.S. Eyes a Willing Romania As a New Comrade in Arms." *The New York Times*, July 16: Section A, p. 1, 3.

Fletcher, Richard. 1997. *The Barbarian Conversion: From Paganism to Christianity.* New York: Henry Holt and Company.

Freedom House. n.d. *Media Responses to Corruption in the Emerging Democracies: Bulgaria, Hungary, Romania, Ukraine.* Washington, D.C.: Freedom House.

Frydman, Roman; Rapaczynski, Andrzej. 1994. *Privatization in Eastern Europe: Is the State Withering Away?* Budapest: Central European University Press.

Gadamer, Hans-Georg. 1982. *Truth and Method.* London: Sheed and Ward.

Georgescu, Vlad. 1988. "Romania in the 1980s: The Legacy of Dynastic Socialism." *Eastern European Politics and Societies* 2 (1): 70-93.

Gheorghe, N.; Mirga, A. 1997. *The Roma in the 21st Century – A Policy Paper.* New York: Project on Ethnic Relations.

Giddens, Anthony. 1990. *The Consequences of Modernity.* Stanford, CA: Stanford University Press.

Giurescu, D. C. 1997. "Evreii romani – 1939-1944." *Realitatea Everiasca,* no. 51, May, 16-31.

_____. 1998. "Transylvania and the History of the Romanian People." *Romania: A Historic Perspective.* Ed. Dinu C. Giurescu and Stephen Fisher-Galati. Boulder: East European Monographs.

Goffman, Erving. 1956a. *The Presentation of Self in Everyday Life.* Edinburgh: The University of Edinburgh.

_____. 1956b. "The Nature of Deference and Demeanor." *American Anthropologist* 58: 473-502.

_____. 1963. *Stigma: Notes on the Management of Spoiled Identity.* Englewood Cliffs, NJ: Prentice-Hall.

Goldhagen, Daniel Jonah. 1996. *Hitler's Willing Executioners: Ordinary Germans and the Holocaust.* New York: Alfred A. Knopf.

_____. 2002. *A Moral Reckoning: The Role of the Catholic Church in the Holocaust and Its Unfulfilled Duty of Repair.* New York: Alfred A. Knopf.

Goldstone, Jack A. 2000. "The Rise of the West – or Not?: A Revision to Socio-economic History." *American Sociological Review* 18 (2): pp. 175-19.

Gramsci, Antonio. 1971. *The Prison Notebooks: Selections.* Trans. Quintin Hoare and Geoffrey Nowell-Smith. New York: International Publishers.

_____. 2000. *The Antonio Gramsci Reader: Selected Writings, 1916-1935.* Ed. David Forgacs. New York: New York University Press.

Greene, Joshua M.; Kumar, Shiva, eds. 2000. *Witness: Voices from the Holocaust.* New York: The Free Press.

Griffin, Keith. 1999. *Alternative Strategies for Economic Development.* 2nd edition. New York: St. Martin's Press, Inc.

Gross, Jan T. *Neighbors: The Destruction of the Jewish Community in Jedwabne Poland.* Princeton: Princeton University Press.

Habermas, Jurgen. 1989. *The Transformation of the Public Sphere: An Inquiry into a Category of Bourgeois Society.* Trans: Thomas Burger, with the assistance of Frederick Lawrence. Cambridge, MA: The MIT Press.

Hancock, Ian. 1996. "Responses to the Parrajmos: The Romani Holocaust." *Is the Holocaust Unique?* Ed. A. Rosenbaum. Boulder, CO: Westview Press.

_____. 1997. "Roma Slavery." *The Patrin Web Journal,* March 1.

Harvey, David. 1996. *Justice, Nature, and the Geography of Difference.* Oxford: Blackwell Publishers Ltd.

Hechter, Michael. 1975, *Internal Colonialism: The Celtic Fringe in British National Development, 1536-1966.* Berkeley, CA: University of California Press.

Heinen, A. 1986. *Die Legion "Erzengel Michael" in Rumanien: Soziale Bewegung und politische Organization.* Munich: Oldenbourg.

Heller, Agnes. 1998. "Self-Representation and the Representation of the Other." *Blurred Boundaries: Migration, Ethnicity, Citizenship.* Ed. Rainer Baubock and John Rundell. Vienna: European Centre, pp. 341-54.

Helsinki Watch. 1991a. *Destroying Ethnic Identity: The Persecution of Gypsies in Romania.* New York: Human Rights Watch.

_____. 1991b. *Destroying Ethnic Identity: The Persecution of Gypsies in Bulgaria.* New York: Human Rights Watch.

_____. 1991c. *Destroying Ethnic Identity: The Persecution of Gypsies in Czechoslovakia.* New York: Human Rights Watch.

Hitchins, K. 1996. *The Romanians, 1774-1866.* Oxford: Oxford University Press.

Hobsbawm, E. J. 1987. *The Age of Empires, 1875-1914.* London: Weidenfeld and Nicolson.

_____. 1990. *Nations and Nationalism Since 1780: Programme, Myth, Reality.* Cambridge: Cambridge University Press.

Hobsbawm, E. J. 1994. *The Age of Extremes: A History of the World, 1914-1991.* New York: Pantheon Books.

Ibraileanu, Garabet. 1909. *Spiritul critic in cultura romaneasca.* Iasi: Ed. Viata Romaneasca. Quoted in Katherine Verdery (1991), *National Ideology Under Socialism: Identity and Cultural Politics in Ceausescu's Romania.* Berkeley: University of California Press.

Ingram, Judith. 1991a. "Valea Pietrelor Journal. Gypsies Plight: Mobs, Torches, and Land Disputes." *The New York Times,* September 24: Section A, p.4.

_____. 1991b. "For Gypsies of Romania, Help at Last." *New York Times,* October 18: Section 1, p. 15.

Institute fur Hohere Studien. 1994. *Country Report: Romania.* Vienna: Bank of Austria.

Institut de Studii Sociale, Sondaje, Marketing și Comunicare. 1998. "Barometrul de Opinie Publică, Româna." Soros Open Network (Romania), November, p. 4.

Ioanid, Radu. 2000. *The Holocaust in Romania: The Destruction of Jews and Gypsies Under the Antonescu Regime, 1940-1944.* Chicago: Ivan R. Dee.

Jackson, Dominique. 1993. "News is Called Off." *The Guardian,* The Guardian Euro Page (July 19), pg. 18.

Jelavich, Barbara. 1983. *The History of the Balkans: Twentieth Century.* Volume 2. Cambridge: Cambridge University Press.

Jenkins, J. Craig. 1983. "Resource Mobilization Theory and the Study of Social Movements." *Annual Review of Sociology.* Ed. Ralph Turner and James F. Short. Palo Alto, CA: Annual Reviews, Inc., pp. 527-53.

Jones, Bryan. 1993. "The Power of Babel." *The Guardian,* The Guardian Euro Page (June 7), p.18.

Jowitt, Kenneth. 1978. *"The Sociocultural Bases of National Dependency in Peasant Countries." Social Change in Romania, 1860-1940.* Ed. Daniel Chirot. Berkeley: Institute of International Studies, pp. 1-30.

Juergensmeyer, Mark. 2000. *Terror in the Mind of God: The Global Rise of Religious Violence.* Berkeley: University of California Press.

Keil, Thomas J. 1988. *On Strike! Capital Cities and the Wilkes-Barre Newspaper Unions.* Tuscaloosa: University of Alabama Press.

Keil, Thomas J.; Andreescu, V. 1999. "Fertility Policy in Ceausescu's Romania." *Journal of Family History* 24(4): 478-492.

Keil, Thomas J.; Keil, Jacqueline. 2002. "The State and Labor Conflict in Post-Revolutionary Romania." *Radical History Review* 82 (Winter): 9-36.

Keil, Thomas J.; Vito, G. F.; Andreescu, V. 1998. "Perceptions of Neighborhood Safety and Support for the Reintroduction of Capital Punishment in Romania: Results from a Bucharest Survey." *International Journal of Offender Therapy and Comparative Criminology* 43(4): 513-34.

Kenrick, Donald; Puxson, Grattan. 1972. *The Destiny of Europe's Gypsies.* New York: Basic Books.

_____. 1995. *Gypsies under the Swastika.* Hatfield, U.K.: University of Hertfordshire Press. Cited in Guenter Lewy (2000), *The Nazi Persecution of the Gypsies.* Oxford: Oxford University Press.

Kenrick, Donald. 1989. Letter to the Editor. *Holocaust and Genocide Studies* 4: 251-54.

Kenworthy, Lane. 2002. "Corporatism and Unemployment in the 1980s and 1990s." *American Sociological Review* 67(3): 367-388.

Kerzer, David I. 2001. *The Popes Against the Jews: The Vatican's Role in the Rise of Modern Anti-Semitism.* New York: Alfred A. Knopf.

King, Charles. 2000. *Moldovans: Romania, Russia, and the Politics of Culture*. Stanford: Hoover Institution Press, Stanford University.

Kinzer, Stephen. 1992. "Germany Cracks Down: Gypsies Come First." *The New York Times,* September 12: Section 4: p.5.

Kirk, R.; Raceanu, M. 1992. *Romania versus the United States: Diplomacy of the Absurd, 1985-1989.* New York: St. Martin's Press, p.5. Quoted in Norman Manea (1992), *On Clowns: The Dictator and the Artist.* New York: Grove Weidenfeld, p. 109.

Kligman, Gail. 1998. *The Politics of Duplicity: Controlling Reproduction in Ceausescu's Romania.* Berkeley: University of California Press.

Kocka, Jurgen. 1988. "Burgertum im 19. Jahrhundert Europaische Entwicklung und Deutsche Eingarten." *Burgertum im 19. Jahrhundert,* vol. I. Ed. Jurgen Kocka. Munich: Deutsche Taschenbuch Verlag, pp. 11-78. Cited in Gil Eyal, Ivan Szelenyi, and Eleanor Townsley (1998), *Making Capitalism Without Capitalists: The New Ruling Elites in Eastern Europe.* London: Verso.

Le Bor, Adam. 1993. "Pyramid Game Grips Romania." *London Times,* November 19, p. 11.

Ledeneva, Alena V. 1998. *Russia's Economy of Favors: Blat, Networking, and Informal Exchange.* Cambridge: Cambridge University Press.

Levy, Robert. 2001. *Ana Pauker: The Rise and Fall of a Jewish Communist.* Berkeley: University of California Press.

Lewis, Bernard. 2002. *What Went Wrong? Western Impact and Middle Eastern Response.* Oxford: Oxford University Press.

Lewy, Guenter. 2000. *The Nazi Persecution of the Gypsies.* Oxford: Oxford University Press.

Lieven, Dominic. 2000. *Empire: The Russian Empire and its Rivals.* New Haven, CT: Yale University Press.

Livezeanu, Irina. 1995. *Cultural Politics in Greater Romania: Regionalism, Nation Building, and Ethnic Struggle, 1918-1930.* Ithaca, NY: Cornell University Press.

Long, Scott. 1996. "The Romanian Chamber of Deputies Voted No to Decriminalize Consensual Homosexual Acts Between Consenting Adults." *International Lesbian Gay Alliance Euroletter 44.* Helsinki, Finland.

Longworth, Phillip. 1997. *The Making of Eastern Europe: From Prehistory to Postcommunism.* 2nd edition. New York: St. Martin's Press.

Maass, Peter. 1993. "Romanians Grasp at a Straw." *Washington Post,* October 17, p. A25.

Manea, Norman. 1992. *On Clowns: The Dictator and the Artist.* New York: Grove Weidenfeld.

Marsh, Virginia. 1993. "Romania Struggles to Secure IMF Standby Agreement." *Financial Times,* September 4, pg. 2.

_____. 1993. "Romanian Demo Demands Reform." *Financial Times,* November 9, pg. 3.

_____. 1993. "Chorus of Discontent Grows in Romania." *Financial Times,* December 31.

Marsh, Virginia; Corzine, Robert, 1993. "Feet Drag on Road to Market: Change Goes Against Grain for Many in Government." *Financial Times,* July 27, p. 3.

Marx, Karl. 1853. "The British Rule in India." *Karl Marx: Surveys from Exile, Political Writings Volume II* (first American edition). Ed. David Fernbach. New York: Random House, pp. 301-307.

Maxim, Mihai. 1998. "The Romanian Principalities and the Ottoman Empire (1400-1878)." *Romania: A Historic Perspective.* Ed. Dinu C. Giurescu and Stephen Fisher-Galati. Boulder: East European Monographs.

Mazower, Mark. 1998. *Dark Continent: Europe's Twentieth Century.* New York: Random House, Inc.

_____. 2000. *The Balkans: A Short History.* New York: Random House, Inc.

McCarthy, Justin. 1997. *The Ottoman Turks.* London and New York: Longman.

Menocal, Maria Rosa. 2002. *The Ornament of the World: How Muslims, Jews, and Christians Created a Culture of Tolerance in Medieval Spain.* New York: Little Brown.

Mishkova, Diana. 1994. "Modernization and Political Elites in the Balkans Before World War I." Working Paper 94-1, Center for Austrian Studies.

Mosse, George L. 1999. *The Fascist Revolution: Toward a General Theory of Fascism.* New York: Howard Fertig.

Mouzelis, Nicos. 1986. *Politics in the Semi-Periphery.* London: Macmillan.

Mungiu-Pippidi, Alina. 1998. "The Ruler and the Patriarch: The Romanian Eastern Orthodox Church in Transition." *East European Constitutional Review* 7:2 (Spring).

Nagler, Thomas. 1998. *"Germans in Romania: Historical Perspective." Romania: A Historic Perspective.* Ed. Dinu C. Giurescu and Stephen Fisher-Galati. Boulder: East European Monographs.

New York Times. 2002 (May 26). "Alexandru Todea, 89, Romanian Cardinal." Section 1, p. 27. Source: Associated Press. Dateline: Bucharest, Romania, May 25, 2002.

Ngatchou, Yves Nya. 1994. "ILGA Euroletter 30." Prepared for the ILGA European Regional Conference, Helsinki, Finland.

Noua Dreapta. 1993. Vol. 1. Bucharest.

Oldson, William. 1973. *The Historical and Nationalistic Thought of Nicolae Iorga.* Boulder, CO: East European Monographs.

_____. 1991. *A Providential Anti-Semitism: Nationalism and Polity in Nineteenth-Century Romania.* Philadelphia, PA: American Philosophical Society.

Omi, Michael; Winant, Howard. 1986. *Racial Formation in the United States.* London: Routledge.

_____. 1994. *Racial Formation in the United States.* 2nd edition. London: Routledge.

Oppenheimer, Martin. 1974. "The Sub-Proletariat: Dark Skins and Dirty Work." *Insurgent Sociologist* 4 (Winter): 6-20.

O'Rourke, Breffni. 2000. "Central Europe: EU Warns Candidates Against Links With 'Nomenklatura'." *RFE/RL.* Brussels: July.

Ottawa Citizen, The. 1994. "Romania Five Years Later: What Happened?" Pg. C9, December 18.

Pacepa, Ion Mihai. 1987. *Red Horizons: The True Story of Nicolae and Elena Ceausescus' Crimes, Lifestyle, and Corruption.* Washington, DC: Regnery Gateway.

Palmer, Alan W. 1970. *The Lands Between: A History of East Central Europe Since the Congress of Vienna.* London: Weidenfeld and Nicolson.

Parrish, Scott D. n.d. "New Evidence on the Soviet Rejection of the Marshall Plan, 1947." Washington, DC: Working Paper #9, Cold War International History Project, Woodrow Wilson International Center for Scholars.

Perez-Diaz, V. 1993. *The Return of Civil Society.* Cambridge, MA: Harvard University Press.

Perlez, Jane. 1993. "Pyramid Scheme a Trap for Many Romanians." *New York Times,* November 13, pp. 1, 47.

_____. 1993. "Bleak Romanian Economy Growing Even Bleaker." *New York Times,* November 24, p. 3.

Pieper, Ute; Taylor, Lance. 1989. "The Revival of the Liberal Creed: The IMF, the World Bank, and Inequality in a Globalized Economy." *Globalization and Progressive Economic Policy.* Ed. Dean Baker, Gerald Epstein, and Robert Pollin. Cambridge: Cambridge University Press, pp. 37-63.

Pipes, Richard. 1993. *Russia Under the Bolshevik Regime.* New York: Alfred A. Knopf.

Preobrazenky, Evgeny. 1965 [1926]. *The New Economics.* London: Oxford University Press.

Quinlan, Paul D. 1977. *Clash over Romania: British, and American Policies Towards Romania, 1938-1947.* Los Angeles: American Romanian Academy.

Riceour, Paul. 1969. *The Symbolism of Evil.* Boston: Beacon Press.

Ricketts, M. L. 1988. *Mircea Eliade: The Romanian Roots, 1907-1945.* Boulder, CO: East European Monographs. Cited in Norman Manea (1992), *On Clowns: The Dictator and the Artist.* New York: Grove Weidenfeld.

Riding, Alan. 1991. "Madrid Journal: War on Drugs Becomes War on Gypsies." *The New York Times,* October 13, Section A, p. 4.

Roberts, Henry L. 1951. *Rumania: Political Problems of an Agrarian State.* New Haven, CT: Yale University Press.

Romanian Ministry of Justice. 1968. *Article 200, Romanian Penal Code.* Bucharest.

Roth, Andrei. 2000. "Who "Brought" Communism to Romania and Who "Destroyed" It?" *RFE/RL East European Perspectives,* vol. 2, no. 22 (7 December).

Said, Edward W. 1977. *Orientalism.* New York: Vintage Books Edition.

———. 1994. *Representations of the Intellectual: The 1993 Reith Lectures.* New York: Random House, Inc.

Sachar, Howard M. 2002. *Dreamland: Europeans and Jews in the Aftermath of the Great War.* New York: Alfred A. Knopf.

Schopflin, George. 1990. "The Political Traditions of Eastern Europe, Central Europe, Europe." Special issue *Daedalus,* Eastern Europe, Central Europe, Europe (Winter).

Seton-Watson, R. W. 1934. *A History of the Roumanians.* Cambridge: Cambridge University Press.

Seligman, Adam. 1992. *The Idea of Civil Society.* New York: The Free Press.

Shafir, Michael. 1985. *Romania: Politics, Economy, and Society.* Boulder, CO: Lynne Rienner.

Socor, Vladimir. 1990. "National Salvation Front Produces Electoral Landslide." *Report on Eastern Europe* (July 6): 24-32.

Starr, Richard F. 1988. *Communist Regimes in Eastern Europe.* Stanford: Stanford University Press.

Stephenson, P.; Wagner, M.; Badea, M.; Serbanescu, F. 1992. "The Public Health Consequences of Restricted Induced Abortion – Lessons from Romania." *American Journal of Public Health* (October), 1328-1331.

Stokes, Gale. 1998. "Eastern Europe's Defining Fault Lines." *Eastern Europe: Politics, Culture, and Society Since 1939.* Ed. Sabrina P. Ramet. Bloomington: Indiana University Press, pp. 15-31.

Sugar, Peter F. 1977. *Southeastern Europe under Ottoman Rule, 1354-1804.* Seattle: University of Washington Press. Quoted in Mihai Maxim (1998), "The Romanian Principalities and the Ottoman Empire (1400-1878)." *Romania: A Historic Perspective.* Ed. Dinu C. Giurescu and Stephen Fisher-Galati. Boulder, CO: East European Monographs.

Synovitz, Ron. 2000. "Romania: Land Restitution Law A Step Toward Farm Reforms." *RFE/RL* (Prague, January 13).

Synovitz, Ron. 2000. "World Bank Reports on Corruption, Names Worst Offenders." *RFE/RL* (Prague, September 27).

Tagliabue, John. 1991. "Right-wing Attacks Worry Prague." *The New York Times,* October 14, Section A, p. 3.

Tanaka, Jennifer. 1995. "Report on the Symposium Homosexuality: A Human Right?" Bucharest: Bucharest Acceptance Group.

_____. 1997. *Images and Issues: Coverage of the Roma in the Mass Media in Romania.* Princeton: Project on Ethnic Relations.

Taylor, A. J. P. 1948. *The Habsburg Monarchy, 1809-1918: A History of the Austrian Empire and Austria-Hungary.* Chicago: University of Chicago Press.

Tilly, Charles. 1978. *From Mobilization to Revolution.* Reading, MA: Addison-Wesley.

Trotsky, Leon. 1932. *History of the Russian Revolution.* Trans. Max Eastman. Ann Arbor: University of Michigan Press.

Tupper-Carey, F. 1990. "Romania." *Religion in Communist Lands* 18(2): p.181. Cited in Stephen Deletant (1999b), *Romania under Communist Rule.* Iasi: The Center for Romanian Studies and the Civic Academy Foundation, p. 260.

Turnock, David. 1974. *An Economic Geography of Romania.* London: G. Bell.

Tyranauer, Gabriel. 1986. "Scholars, Gypsies, and the Holocaust." *Papers from the Sixth and Seventh Annual Meetings, Gypsy Lore Society, North American Chapter.* Ed. Joanne Grumet. New York: Gypsy Lore Society.

United Nations Development Report Romania 2001-2002. 2003. "A Decade Later: Understanding the Transition Process in Romania." New York: The United Nations.

Unger, Roberto Mangabeira. 1998. *Democracy Realized: The Progressive Alternative.* London and New York: Verso.

Valceanu, Daniela. 1992. "Inequities in the Health Care System in Romania." Paper presented at meetings of the European Society for Health and Medical Sociology, Vienna (September). Cited in William C. Cockerham (1999), *Health and Social Change in Russia and Eastern Europe.* London: Routledge, pp. 199-200.

Veiga, F. 1989. *La Mistica del Ultranacionalismo.* Barcelona: Univesitat Autonomia de Barcelona.

Verdery, Katherine. 1991. *National Ideology Under Socialism: Identity and Cultural Politics in Ceausescu's Romania.* Berkeley: University of California Press.

_____. 1996. *What Was Socialism, and What Comes Next?* Princeton: Princeton University Press.

_____. 1999. "Fuzzy Property: Rights, Power, and Identity in Transylvania's Decollectivization." *Uncertain Transition: Ethnographies of Change in the Postsocialist World.* Ed. Michael Burawoy and Katherine Verdery. New York: Rowman and Littlefield Publishers, pp. 53-82.

Vucinich, Wayne S. 1965. *The Ottoman Empire: Its Record and Legacy.* Princeton, NJ. Quoted in Mihai Maxim (1998), "The Romanian Principalities and the Ottoman Empire (1400-1878)." *Romania: A Historic Perspective.* Ed. Dinu C. Giurescu and Stephen Fisher-Galati. Boulder, CO: East European Monographs.

The Wall Street Journal Europe (Brussels). August 25, 1997; September 2, 1997; September 24, 1997.

Wardell, Mark; Johnston, Robert L. 1983. "Intra-Class Conflict and Platforms of Collective Action." Paper presented at Annual Meetings, Southern Sociological Society, Atlanta, April 6-9.

Watts, Larry L. 1993. *Romanian Cassandra: Ion Antonescu and the Struggle for Reform, 1916-1941.* Boulder, CO: East European Monographs.

Weber, Max. 1968. *Economy and Society: An Outline of an Interpretive Sociology.* Ed. Gunter Roth and Claus Wittich. Berkeley, CA.

_____. 1947. *The Theory of Social and Economic Organization* Trans. A. M. Henderson and Talcott Parsons. New York: Oxford University Press.

Williams, Raymond. 1977. *Marxism and Literature.* Oxford: Oxford University Press.

Wolchik, Sharon L. 1998. "Women and the Politics of Gender in Communist and Post-Communist Central and Eastern Europe." *Eastern Europe: Politics, Culture, and Society Since 1939.* Ed. Sabrina P. Ramet. Bloomington: Indiana University Press, pp. 285-303.

World Bank. 2003. *Development Data.* Washington, D.C.

World Bank Office Romania. 2000. *Economic and Social Indicators.* Bucharest.

Wright, Eric Olin. 1978. *Class, Crisis, and the State.* London: NLB.

Wright, Vincent. 1978. *The Government and Politics of France.* New York: Holmes and Meier.

Yancey, William L.; Erikson, Eugene P.; Julliani, Richard N. 1976. "Emergent Ethnicity: A Review and Reformulation." *American Sociological Review* 41 (June): 391-403.

Zureik, Elia T. 1979. *The Palestinians in Israel: A Study in Internal Colonialism.* London: Routledge and Kegan Paul.